Red Hat™ Linux

Second Edition

David Pitts, et al.

SAMS PUBLISHING

201 West 103rd Street
Indianapolis, IN 46290

UNLEASHED

This book is dedicated to TM3 and Associates. Thanks, guys (non-gender)!!

—David Pitts

Copyright © 1998 by Sams Publishing

SECOND EDITION

International Standard Book Number: 0-672-31173-9

Library of Congress Catalog Card Number: 97-68008

01 00 99 98 4 3 2

Interpretation of the printing code: The rightmost double-digit number is the year of the book's printing; the rightmost single digit, the number of the book's printing. For example, a printing code of 98-1 shows that the first printing of the book occurred in 1998.

Composed in AGaramond and MCPdigital by Macmillan Computer Publishing

Printed in the United States of America

Trademarks

Publisher *Dean Miller*

Executive Editor *Jeff Koch*

Managing Editor *Sarah Kearns*

Senior Indexer *Ginny Bess*

Director of Software and User Services *Cheryl Willoughby*

Brand Director *Alan Bower*

Acquisitions Editor
Cari Skaggs

Development Editors
Mark Cierzniak
Richard Alvey

Software Development Specialist
Jack Belbot

Project Editor
Dana Rhodes Lesh

Copy Editors
Carolyn Linn, Kate Talbot, Michael Brumitt, Chuck Hutchinson, Nancy Albright

Indexer
Cheryl Jackson

Technical Reviewers
Bill Ball, Sriranga R. Veeraraghavan, Robin Burk

Editorial Coordinators
Mandie Rowell
Katie Wise

Technical Edit Coordinator
Lynette Quinn

Resource Coordinators
Charlotte Clapp
Deborah Frisby

Editorial Assistants
Carol Ackerman, Andi Richter, Rhonda Tinch-Mize, Karen Williams

Cover Designer
Jason Grisham

Cover Production
Aren Howell

Book Designer
Gary Adair

Copy Writer
David Reichwein

Production Team Supervisor
Beth Lewis

Production
Bryan Flores, Julie Geeting, Kay Hoskin, Christy M. Lemasters, Darlena Murray, Julie Searls, Sossity Smith

Overview

Contents

Part VI Automation, Programming, and Modifying Source Code

22 Automating Tasks 437

23 C and C++ Programming 455

Acknowledgments

I would like to thank Vaughn Blumenthal and the RS Admin Group at Boeing in Everett for allowing me to work an alternative schedule, providing the necessary time needed to work on my book. In addition, I would like to thank my wife for "living without me" for months as I worked on this book and for prodding me on when I did not feel like writing.

—David Pitts

About the Authors

David Pitts, Lead Author

David Pitts is a senior consultant with BEST Consulting, one of the premier consulting companies west of the Mississippi with over 1,400 highly trained consultants. Currently on assignment with The Boeing Company, David is a system administrator, programmer, Webmaster, and author. David can be reached at `dpitts@mk.net` or `dpitts@bestnet.com`. David lives in Everett, Washington, with his wonderful wife Dana. Everett, he explains, is like living on a postcard, with the Puget Sound ten minutes to the west and the year-around snow-capped Cascade Mountains to the east. David's favorite quote comes from Saint Francis of Assisi, "Preach the Gospel, and, if necessary, use words."

David B. Horvath

David B. Horvath, CCP, is a senior consultant in the Philadelphia area. He has been a consultant for over twelve years and is also a part-time adjunct professor at local colleges, teaching courses that include C Programming, UNIX, and Database Techniques. He is currently pursuing an M.S. degree in Dynamics of Organization at the University of Pennsylvania. He has provided seminars and workshops to professional societies and corporations on an international basis. David is the author of *UNIX for the Mainframer* (Prentice-Hall/PTR), contributing author to *UNIX Unleashed, Second Edition* (with cover credit), and numerous magazine articles.

When not at the keyboard, he can be found working in the garden or soaking in the hot tub. He has been married for over ten years and has several dogs and cats.

David can be reached at `rhu2@cobs.com` for questions related to this book. No Spam please!

Bill Ball, a retired U.S. Coast Guard photojournalist, has been playing with and writing about computers since 1984.

Rich Bowen is a CGI programmer working for DataBeam Corporation in Lexington, Kentucky. In his spare time (ha!), he enjoys hiking and reading, and he maintains Web sites at `www.rcbowen.com` and `www.wgm.org`, among other places. Rich lives in the heart of the Bluegrass with his border collie, Java, and his lovely wife, Carol, and there is a little Bowen on the way. Mungu asifiwe!

Eric Goebelbecker has been working with market data and trading room systems in the New York City area for the past six years. He is currently the director for systems development with MXNet, Inc., a subsidiary of the Sherwood Group in Jersey City, New Jersey, where he is responsible for developing new market data and transaction distribution systems.

Sanjiv Guha has 14 years of experience in managing and developing financial and other application systems. He specializes in C, UNIX, C++, Windows, and COBOL. Sanjiv holds a master of technology degree from Indian Institute of Technology, New Delhi, India.

Kamran Husain is a software consultant with experience in Windows UNIX system programming. He has dabbled in all sorts of software for real-time systems, applications, telecommunications, seismic data acquistion and navigation, X Window/Motif applications, and Microsoft Windows applications. He refuses to divulge any more of his qualifications. Kamran offers consulting services, and he is an alumnus of the University of Texas at Austin.

Cameron Laird manages his own consultancy, Network Engineered Solutions, just outside Houston. With over two decades of full-time experience in information technology, he has consistently found challenges during his career in bridging system heterogeneities with high reliability, high precision, or high performance knowledge bases. Most recently, that has meant engineering applications that combine components written in a range of languages to solve needs in process control. His bias that the most important communications requirements are those between humans has persistently led him back to sidelines in writing. Hypertext is his favorite medium. Check out `http://starbase.neosoft.com/~claird/` for examples of his work.

Steve Shah is a system administrator for the Center of Environmental Research and Technology at the University of California, Riverside. He received his B.S. in Computer Science with a minor in Creative Writing from UCR and is currently working on his M.S. there as well. In his copious spare time, he enjoys writing fiction, DJing, and spending time with his friends, family, and sweet, Heidi.

Sriranga Veeraraghavan is currently earning his B.E. from UC Berkeley. He is a GUI designer on UNIX and uses Java for multiple Web-based applications. He is currently working at Cisco Systems. Sriranga amuses himself with Perl, Marathon, and MacsBugs.

James Youngman is a graduate of the University of Manchester, still lives in Manchester, England, and is a software engineer specializing in embedded systems. James's first installation of Linux was MCC 1.0+ (thanks, Owen!). In his spare time, James writes and maintains GNU software and even sometimes does non–computer-related things.

Tell Us What You Think!

As a reader, you are the most important critic and commentator of our books. We value your opinion and want to know what we're doing right, what we could do better, what areas you'd like to see us publish in, and any other words of wisdom you're willing to pass our way. You can help us make strong books that meet your needs and give you the computer guidance you require.

Do you have access to the World Wide Web? Then check out our site at `http://www.mcp.com`.

> **NOTE**
>
> If you have a technical question about this book, call the technical support line at 317-581-3833 or send e-mail to `support@mcp.com`.

As the team leader of the group that created this book, I welcome your comments. You can fax, e-mail, or write me directly to let me know what you did or didn't like about this book—as well as what we can do to make our books stronger. Here's the information:

Fax: 317-581-4669

E-mail: `jkoch@mcp.com`

Mail: Jeff Koch
Comments Department
Sams Publishing
201 W. 103rd Street
Indianapolis, IN 46290

Introduction

I don't know how many times I have been asked what Red Hat is. When I say that it is a distribution of Linux, people tend to know what I am talking about. (At least the people I hang around with do!) The follow-up question is usually something like, "Okay, if it is a distribution of Linux, why should I use it, and not Linux itself?" This introduction should start to answer that question. Red Hat also answers the question on its Web page (`http://www.redhat.com`), which is summarized in this introduction.

Linux is a full-fledged operating system. It provides full multitasking in a multiuser environment. It gives a high quality of software for a cost far lower than other commercial versions of UNIX. Red Hat has opted to take Linux a step further.

Red Hat Software is a computer software development company that sells products and provides services related to Linux. Red Hat's mission is to "provide professional tools to computing professionals." Red Hat provides these professional tools by doing the following:

- Building tools, which Red Hat releases as freely redistributable software available for unrestricted download off of thousands of sites on the Internet
- Publishing books and software applications
- Manufacturing shrink-wrapped software, versions of the Linux OS, making Linux accessible to the broadest possible range of computer users
- Providing technical support

Red Hat's customer-oriented business focus forces it to recognize that the primary benefits of the Linux OS are not any of the particular advanced and reliable features for which it is famous. The primary benefit is the availability of complete source code and its "freely distributable" GPL license. This gives any user the ability to modify the technology to his or her needs and to contribute to the on-going development of the technology to the benefit of all the users, providing benefits such as security and reliability that commercially restricted, binary-only operating systems simply cannot match.

Linux, like UNIX itself, is a very modular operating system. The skills required to select, compile, link, and install the various components that are needed for a complete Linux OS are beyond the experience of most people who might want to use Linux. The various Linux distributions go a long way towards solving this for the average Linux user, but most don't address the problem of how to upgrade your Linux system once you get it successfully installed. Most users found it easier to delete their whole Linux system and reinstall from scratch when they needed to upgrade.

The Red Hat distribution makes Linux easier to install and maintain by providing the user with advanced package management, graphical (point and click!) system installation and control, and system administration tools.

Probably the best feature of Linux, the GNU utilities in general, and Red Hat Linux in particular is that they are distributable under the terms of the GNU Public License (GPL). This feature has allowed research institutions, universities, commercial enterprises, and hackers to develop and use Red Hat Linux and related technologies cooperatively without fear that their work would someday be controlled and restricted by a commercial vendor.

The huge development effort and wide distribution of the Linux OS will ensure that it takes its place as a real, viable, and significant alternative to commercially restricted operating systems. The open development model, availability of source, and lack of license restrictions are features of the Linux OS that commercial OS developers simply cannot offer. Software development groups that need this model include groups from government-affiliated research organizations, to academic research and teaching projects, to commercial software application developers.

The recent rapid increase in new applications becoming available for Linux and the rapidly growing user base of these technologies are causing even the largest computer industry organizations to take Linux seriously. Even Datapro (a McGraw-Hill Company) in its recent 1996 survey of the UNIX industry concluded that, "Programmers are taking a hard look at the viability of Linux on production platforms now that Linux costs less than Microsoft and has the added benefits of UNIX, such as great performance, inherent power tool sets, and communication capabilities."

It was said once that over half of the Web servers used around the world are run on Red Hat Linux. Although I cannot deny or substantiate this claim, it does show how rapidly Red Hat is taking on the commercial operating systems and succeeding. With the purchase of this book, you are taking the first step necessary to take back control of your computing system from the corporate giants. There is an exciting future for Linux, and we are glad that you are now a part of it!

Conventions Used in This Book

The following conventions are used in this book:

- Code lines, commands, statements, variables, and any text you type or see on the screen appears in a `computer` typeface.
- Placeholders in syntax descriptions appear in an *`italic computer`* typeface. Replace the placeholder with the actual filename, parameter, or whatever element it represents.
- Italics highlight technical terms when they first appear in the text and are being defined.

- A special icon ➥ is used before a line of code that is really a continuation of the preceding line. Sometimes a line of code is too long to fit as a single line in the book, given the book's limited width. If you see ➥ before a line of code, remember that you should interpret that "line" as part of the line immediately before it.

Part I

Introduction and Installation of Linux

IN THIS PART

CHAPTER

1

Introduction to Red Hat Linux and UNIX

by David Pitts

IN THIS CHAPTER

UNIX, not to be confused, as Dilbert's boss once did, with a eunuch, is one of the most popular operating systems in the world. It is a trademark of The Open Group, but was originally developed by AT&T. UNIX is a *real* operating system. A real operating system has, as a minimum, two qualifications: more than one person can access the computer at the same time and, while doing so, each person can run multiple applications. This is called being a *multiuser* and *multitasking* operating system. UNIX was originally designed to be such a multitasking system back in the 1970s, running on mainframes and minicomputers.

With UNIX, each user logs in using a login name. Optionally (and highly recommended), the user must also supply a password. The password ensures that the person logging on with the user login name is really who he or she claims to be. Users don't just log in to any no-name computer, either. Each computer has a "personality," if you will, which, at a minimum, is a hostname (mine is Lolly). If the computer is attached to a network, it will have several other identifying items, including, but not limited to, a domain name and an IP address.

UNIX will run on just about every platform made. Many vendors purchased the source code and have developed their own versions. The various vendors (IBM, Hewlett-Packard, Sun, and so on) have added their own special touches over the years. But they are not the only ones to further modify UNIX. When UNIX was first developed, the source code was given out freely to colleges and universities. Two schools, University of California at Berkeley and Massachusetts Institute of Technology, have been on the front edge of development since the beginning.

As you can imagine, the UNIX development went haywire. People all over the globe began to develop tools for UNIX. Unfortunately, there was no coordination to guide all the development. This caused a lot of differentiation between the different versions of UNIX. Finally, standards started to appear. For UNIX, many of the standards fall under the IEEE POSIX.1 standard.

The downside of UNIX is that it is big. It is also expensive, especially for a PC version. This is where Linux comes in. Linux, as explained in a little more detail later in this chapter, was designed to be small, fast, and inexpensive. So far, the designers have succeeded.

Linux was originally created by Linus Torvalds of the University of Helsinki in Finland. Linus based Linux on a small PC-based implementation of UNIX called *minix*. Near the end of 1991, Linux was first made public. In November of that same year version 0.10 was released. A month later, in December, version 0.11 was released. Linus made the source code freely available and encouraged others to develop it further. They did. Linux continues to be developed today by a world-wide team, led by Linus, over the Internet.

The current stable version of Linux is version 2.0. Linux uses no code from AT&T or any other proprietary source. Much of the software developed for Linux is developed by the Free Software Foundation's GNU project. Linux, therefore, is very inexpensive; as a matter of fact, it is free (but not cheap).

Advantages of Linux

So, why would you choose Linux over UNIX? As already mentioned, Linux is free. Like UNIX, it is very powerful and is a "real" operating system. Also, it is fairly small compared to other UNIX operating systems. Many UNIX operating systems require 500MB or more, whereas Linux can be run on as little as 150MB of space, and it can run on as little as 2MB of RAM. Realistically, though, you will want to have room for development tools, data, and so on, which can take up 250MB or more, and your RAM should be 12–16MB (although the more, the merrier!). Here's what you get in exchange for that valuable space:

- Full multitasking—Multiple tasks can be accomplished and multiple devices can be accessed at the same time.
- Virtual memory—Linux can use a portion of your hard drive as virtual memory, which increases the efficiency of your system by keeping active processes in RAM and placing less frequently used or inactive portions of memory on disk. Virtual memory also utilizes all your system's memory and doesn't allow memory segmentation to occur.
- The X Window System—The X Window System is a graphics system for UNIX machines. This powerful interface supports many applications and is the standard interface for the industry.
- Built-in networking support—Linux uses standard TCP/IP protocols, including Network File System (NFS) and Network Information Service (NIS, formerly known as YP). By connecting your system with an Ethernet card or over a modem to another system, you can access the Internet.
- Shared libraries—Each application, instead of keeping its own copy of software, shares a common library of subroutines that it can call at runtime. This saves a lot of hard drive space on your system.
- Compatibility with the IEEE POSIX.1 standard—Because of this compatibility, Linux supports many of the standards set forth for all UNIX systems.
- Nonproprietary source code—The Linux kernel uses no code from AT&T, nor any other proprietary source. Other organizations, such as commercial companies, the GNU project, hackers, and programmers from all over the world have developed software for Linux.
- Lower cost than most other UNIX systems and UNIX clones—If you have the patience and the time, you can freely download Linux off the Internet. Many books also come with a free copy. (This book includes it on CD-ROM.)
- GNU software support—Linux can run a wide range of free software available through the GNU project. This software includes everything from application development (GNU C and GNU C++) to system administration (`gawk`, `groff`, and so on), to games (for example, GNU Chess, GnuGo, NetHack).

At this point, the question is usually asked, "Okay, if Linux is so great, what is this Red Hat version, and why should I get it?" Well, I am glad you asked. There are several reasons to use Red Hat Linux:

- It is based on Linux 2.0*x*—The current version of Red Hat (4.2) is based upon version 2.0*x* of the Linux kernel. This means that it is at the same low cost as Linux—free! Anyone can use FTP to download Red Hat from the Internet and install it on their system. (This also means that the entire list of Linux's attributes applies to the Red Hat version.)
- Red Hat Package Manager is included—For the same low cost (free), Red Hat Package Manager (RPM) is included. This means that after you load Red Hat, you'll never have to load it again. The RPM is a sophisticated tool that includes intelligent file handling across package upgrades, shared file handling, documentation searching support, and package installation via FTP. You can install, uninstall, query, verify, and upgrade individual RPM packages.
- Good, clean copies—Red Hat has a commitment to providing, as the company puts it, "pristine sources." The RPM source packages include pristine, untouched sources, as well as patches and a control file, which define the building and packaging process. This enables you to work with other members of the Linux development community easily and effectively by clearly separating and documenting the code that comes from the Linux development community from any modifications that are required by Red Hat.
- Security—Red Hat leads the industry in providing the most up-to-date security features. In addition, the company strives, and succeeds, at providing the latest versions of software.
- Documentation—Red Hat provides more than 250 pages of installation and configuration information that can be downloaded via FTP or viewed from the Red Hat site. Complete coverage of the Control Panel tools, including the network, user/group, and printer tools, is included.
- Standards—Red Hat tracks both UNIX and Linux standards. Red Hat conforms to the Linux filesystem standard (FSSTND).
- Testing—Red Hat depends upon the open development model that Linus started with. Today, there are thousands of people working around the world testing applications and providing solutions for today's business and personal needs.

As you can see, Red Hat goes beyond the normal Linux system by providing tools, documentation, and standardization.

Copyright and Warranty

Red Hat Linux is copyrighted under the GNU General Public License. This section doesn't include the entire license, but it does highlight a few items. Basically, the license provides three things:

1. The original author retains the copyright.
2. Others can do with the software what they wish, including modifying it, basing other programs on it, and redistributing or reselling it. The software can even be sold for a profit. The source code must accompany the program as well.
3. The copyright cannot be restricted down the line. This means that if you sell a product for one dollar, the person you sold it to could change it in any way (or not even change it at all) and sell it to a second person for $10—or give it away at no charge to a thousand people.

Why have such a unique licensing? The original authors of Linux software didn't intend to make money from the software. It was intended to be freely available to everyone, without warranty. That is correct; there is no warranty. Does this mean you are left out in the cold when you have problems? Of course it doesn't. There are numerous resources, including this book, newsgroups, and the Web to assist you. What it does do, though, is provide the programmers the ability to release software at no cost without the fear of liability. Granted, this lack of liability is a two-edged sword, but it is the simplest method for providing freely available software.

Where to Get Red Hat Linux

Try looking on the CD-ROM that came with this book. Red Hat Linux is there. You can also get Red Hat from the Internet by pointing your browser to `http://www.redhat.com/products/software.html`. Here you will not only find Red Hat for each of the three supported platforms (Intel, Alpha, and SPARC), but also upgrades, updates, answers to frequently asked questions, mailing lists, and much, much more. You can call Red Hat at (888) RED-HAT1 and order products as well.

System Requirements

Red Hat keeps a listing of the system requirements and supported hardware for the three platforms—Intel, SPARC, and Alpha—that Linux will run on. Those lists are presented in this section. As with anything, these lists will change. If the particular hardware that you have is not listed, check Red Hat's Web page (`http://www.redhat.com/support/docs/hardware.html`) and see if it has been listed there.

System Requirements—Intel

According to Red Hat, these are the system requirements for running Red Hat Linux on an Intel platform:

- Intel 386 or greater, through Pentium Pro
- 40MB of hard drive space in character mode, or 100MB with X Window
- 5MB of memory (although 8 to 16 is recommended)
- Most video cards supported
- CD-ROM drive
- 3.5-inch disk drive

Plug and Play hardware is not, at the time of this writing, wholly supported. (There is some level of PnP support with the `isapnp` software.) Most Plug and Play hardware has jumpers or BIOS settings that will turn off the Plug and Play support. By turning off this support, the equipment should work with Red Hat Linux. Some Plug and Play support equipment doesn't have a way of physically turning off the Plug and Play option (such as the SoundBlaster 16 PnP). For these pieces of hardware to work with Linux, some sort of workaround must be performed.

System Requirements—SPARC

Red Hat Linux/SPARC is known to function on the following hardware:

- sun4c architecture machines (IPC, SS1, and so on)
- sun4m architecture machines (Classic, SS5, SS10, and so on)
- bwtwo, cg3, cg6, TCX frame buffers (24 bit on the TCX)
- cg14 frame buffer (in cg3 mode)
- SCSI and Ethernet on all of the preceding
- Type 4 and type 5 keyboards and mice
- External SCSI drives
- CD-ROM drives (external and internal)
- SCSI/Ether SBUS expansion cards
- Any original equipment Sun monitor for the listed frame buffers

System Requirements—Alpha

Red Hat Linux/Alpha supports a variety of hardware based on the Alpha processor and the PCI bus. Platforms on which this release is known to work include the following:

- AlphaPC64 (Cabriolet, Aspen Telluride)
- AxpPCI33 (No name)

- EB64+ (Aspen Alpine)
- EB66 (NekoTech Mach 1)
- EB66+
- Jensen (DEC PC 150, 2000 model 300, Cullean)
- Universal Desktop Box (UDB, sometimes called Multia)
- AlphaStation 200, 250, 255, 400 (Avanti machines)
- EB164 (Aspen Avalanche, Timberline, Summit; Microway Screamer)
- Platform 2000 machines from Kinetics
- PC164 machines (Durango)
- Alcor type machines (AlphaStation 500, 600; Maverick, Brett)
- Alpha-XL
- Alpha-XLT (XL 300, XL 366)
- Mikasa-type machines (neither AlphaServer 1000 nor 1000A is supported)

All the preceding platforms except the Jensen include an NCR 810 SCSI controller, though BusLogic PCI SCSI controllers (other than the FlashPoint), the Adaptec AHA-2940 SCSI controller, and Qlogic 1020 ISP controllers are also supported. The Jensen design uses an AHA-1740 SCSI controller and is supported.

NE2000, DE422, and DE4x5 (PCI) Ethernet cards are supported. This includes the UDB's internal Ethernet hardware. Token Ring support is also included in the kernels.

The X Window System should work on any machine with an S3-based video card except the Jensen machines. There is a server available from `ftp://ftp.azstarnet.com/pub/linux/axp/jensen` for S3 cards. TGA servers (which work on the UDB, for example) are available on your Red Hat Linux/Alpha CD in the X11 directory. Most of the cards from Orchid and Number 9 will work. Most Diamond Stealth cards are also supported. Digital TGA cards (based on the DC21030 chip) are supported in 8-bit mode, and an X server for Mach64 cards is also provided.

Summary

UNIX, as a real operating system, is a viable solution to many of the business needs today. It has been estimated that more than half of the Web servers on the Internet today are actually Red Hat Linux systems running Apache. Although I cannot confirm or deny that number, I do know that Red Hat Linux, with its support infrastructure, its multiplatform usability, and its reliability, is the choice of many system administrators trying to work real-world problems and coming up with real-world solutions. To quote Mike Kropinack of MK Computer Associates (`http://www.mk.net`), "Linux is an awesome system, be it Red Hat, Slackware, or whatever. I'd choose it over Microsoft or Novell any day because in over two years of using it, I've never seen it crash in any of our production servers."

CHAPTER

Installation of Your Red Hat System

by Jay Austad

IN THIS CHAPTER

One of the obvious differences between Red Hat Linux and other versions of Linux is the ease in which Red Hat can be installed. The process is quite straightforward and automated by the Red Hat installation program. The installation program can handle many different system configurations and problems nicely; so most problems are taken care of for you.

Before looking at the different methods used to install the operating system, you should understand the hardware system on which the operating system will be installed. After examining the hardware, the rest of this chapter guides you, step-by-step, through the installation process. This process is broken down, showing some of the differences between the four basic methods of installation. This chapter briefly presents the installation of LILO (Linux Loader), but leaves many of the details to Chapter 3, "LILO."

Be Prepared, Be Very Prepared!

Understanding the hardware is essential for a successful installation of Red Hat Linux. Therefore, you should take a moment now and familiarize yourself with your hardware. Be prepared to answer the following questions:

1. How many hard drives do you have?
2. What size is each hard drive (2.2GB)?
3. If you have more than one hard drive, which is the primary one?
4. How much RAM do you have?
5. If you have a CD-ROM, what type of interface do you have? If it is not a SCSI or an IDE CD-ROM, who made it and what model is it?
6. Do you have a SCSI adapter? If so, who made it and what model is it?
7. What type of mouse do you have?
8. How many buttons?
9. If you have a serial mouse, what COM port is it connected to?
10. What is the make and model of your video card? How much video RAM do you have?
11. What kind of monitor do you have (make and model)?
12. What is the allowable range of horizontal and vertical refresh rates for your monitor?
13. Will you be connecting to a network? If so, what will be the following:
    a. Your IP address?
    b. Your netmask?
    c. Your gateway address?
    d. Your Domain Name Server's IP address?
    e. Your domain name?

f. Your hostname? (I would suggest a hostname even if you were not connected to a network, because it helps give your computer some personality.)

g. Your type of network card?

14. Will you be running other operating systems on the same machine?
15. If so, which ones? OS/2? Windows 95? Windows NT?

NOTE

If you are running OS/2, you must create your disk partitions with the OS/2 partitioning software; otherwise, OS/2 might not recognize the disk partitions. During the installation, do not create any new partitions, but do set the proper partition types for your Linux partitions by using the Linux `fdisk`.

16. Will you be using LILO?

After you have answered these questions, the rest of the installation is fairly easy. The entire process is menu-driven, which means you don't have to remember all the configuration information you have to remember for other Linuxes you might want to install.

Installing Red Hat Linux

The installation or upgrade of Red Hat Linux can be done through any of several methods. Depending on which method you use, you need either one or two formatted high-density (1.44MB) 3.5-inch disks.

Installing from CD-ROM or via NFS requires only a boot disk. Installing from a hard drive, via FTP, from an SMB volume, or from a PCM-CIA device (which includes PCM-CIA CD-ROMs) requires both a boot disk and a supplemental disk.

Creating the Boot and Supplemental Disks

Before you make the boot and supplemental disks, label the disks so that you will know which is which. The process for making the disks is the same, except for one difference. When the program asks for the filename, you enter `boot.img` for the boot disk, and `supp.img` for the supplemental disk. To make the floppies under MS-DOS, you need to use these commands (assuming your CD-ROM is drive D):

```
d:
cd \images
\dosutils\rawrite.exe
```

`rawrite` asks for the filename of the disk image. Enter `boot.img`. Insert a floppy into drive A. It will then ask for a disk to write to. Enter `a:`. Label the disk `Red Hat boot disk`. Run `rawrite` again, enter `supp.img`, insert another disk, and type `a:`. Label the disk `Red Hat supplemental disk`.

To create the disks under Linux, you can use the `dd` utility. Mount the Red Hat Linux CD-ROM, insert a floppy in the drive (do not mount it), and change directories (`cd`) to the images directory on the CD-ROM. Use this command to create the boot disk:

```
dd if=boot.img of=/dev/fd0 bs=1440k
```

To make the supplemental disk, use the following command:

```
dd if=supp.img of=/dev/fd0 bs=1440k
```

Installing Without Using a Boot Floppy

If you have MS-DOS on your computer, you can install without using a boot floppy. The Red Hat installation program can be started by using these commands:

```
d:
cd \dosutils
autoboot.bat
```

Virtual Consoles

Red Hat's installation goes beyond just a simple sequence of dialog boxes. In fact, while installing, you can look at different diagnostic messages during the installation process. There are actually five different virtual consoles that you can switch between, which can be helpful if problems are encountered during installation. Table 2.1 shows the five consoles, the key sequence to switch to each console, and the purpose of that particular console.

Table 2.1. Virtual console information.

Console	*Keystroke*	*Purpose*
1	Alt+F1	Installation dialog box
2	Alt+F2	Shell prompt
3	Alt+F3	Install log (messages from the install program)
4	Alt+F4	System log (messages from the kernel and other system programs)
5	Alt+F5	Other messages

Most of the installation time will be spent in console 1 working through the dialog boxes.

Dialog Boxes

The dialog boxes consist of a simple question or statement. From this information, you choose one or more responses. To choose these responses, it is necessary to navigate the boxes. In most dialog boxes, there is a cursor or highlight that can be moved using the arrow keys. In addition to the arrow keys, you can use the Tab key to go to the next section and the Alt+Tab key combination to back up to the previous section. The bottom of each dialog box indicates which movement keys are valid for that particular box.

In addition to moving the cursor, you will need to make selections. There are two things that are selected: a button, such as an OK button, and an item from a list. If a button is being selected, the space bar is used to "push" the button. Of course, a second push of the button resets it to its original setting. When selecting a single item, you can press the Enter key to select that item. To select one or more items from a list of items, use the space bar. Again, a second push of the space bar deselects a selected item.

Pressing the F12 button accepts the current values and proceeds to the next dialog box. In most cases, this is the same as pressing the OK button.

CAUTION

Do not press random keys during installation. Unpredictable results might occur if you do!

Step-by-Step Installation

This section takes a step-by-step look at the installation process.

Booting

If you do not choose to use the autoboot program and start the installation directly off the CD-ROM, you have to boot with the boot disk.

Insert the boot disk you created into the A drive. Reboot the computer. At the `boot:` prompt, press Enter to continue booting. Watch the boot information to ensure that the kernel detects your hardware. If it doesn't properly detect your hardware, you might need to reboot and add some options at the `boot:` prompt. The following is an example:

```
boot: linux hdc=cdrom
```

If you need to enter any extra parameters here, write them down—you will need them later in the installation.

The Installation Program

After the installation program starts, it asks whether you have a color monitor (see Figure 2.1). If you do not have a color monitor, the cursor will not be visible, so you have to press Tab once and then press Enter.

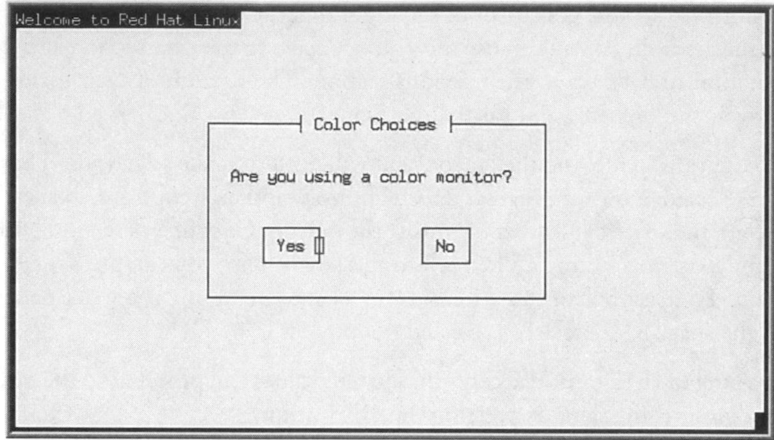

FIGURE 2.1.
Beginning the installation—Color Choices.

The next dialog box asks which keyboard configuration you have (see Figure 2.2). Use the Tab key to select the correct one and then press Enter.

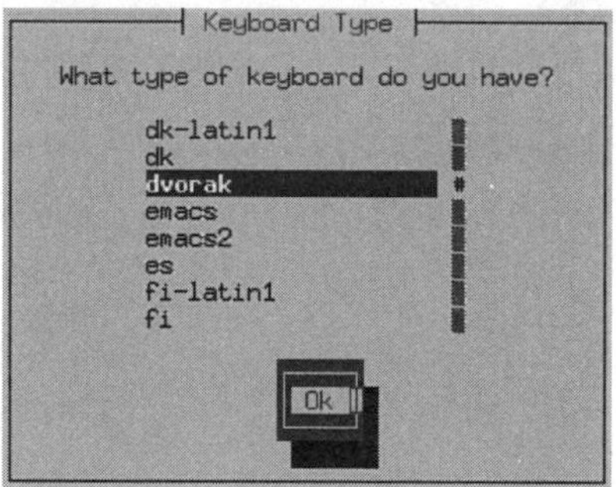

FIGURE 2.2.
The Keyboard Type dialog box.

The installation program then asks whether you need PCMCIA support. If you are using a CD-ROM connected through your PCMCIA port or an Ethernet card, choose Yes. If you choose Yes, you are prompted to insert the supplemental disk you made earlier.

The next dialog box asks which type of installation you want to use, as shown in Figure 2.3.

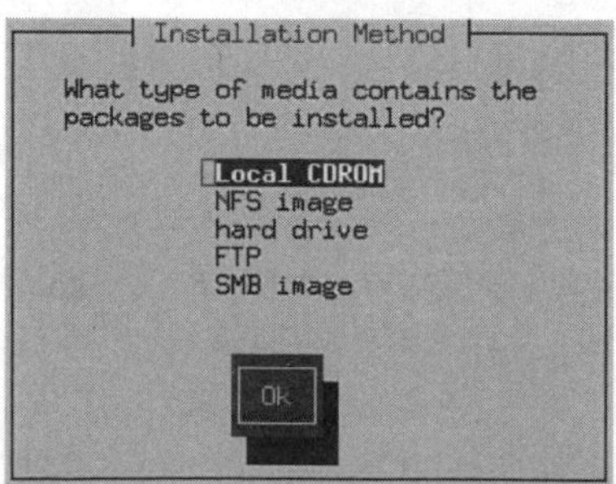

FIGURE 2.3.
The Installation Method dialog box.

Most likely you will choose CD-ROM because that is what is included with this book. Before you look at the installation process for a CD-ROM, let's look at the other ways of installing Red Hat.

Selecting an Installation Method

There are four basic methods of installing Red Hat Linux. The following is a summary of the methods:

- CD-ROM—If you have a supported CD-ROM drive and a Red Hat Linux CD and a boot disk, you can install Red Hat Linux with your CD-ROM drive.
- FTP—For an FTP install, you must have a boot disk and supplemental disk. You need to have a valid nameserver configured or the IP address of the FTP server you will be using. You also need the path to the root of the Red Hat Linux directory on the FTP site.
- Hard drive—To install Red Hat Linux from a hard drive, you need the same boot and supplemental disks used by the FTP install. You must first create a Red Hat directory called `RedHat` at the top level of your directory tree. Everything you install should be placed in that directory. First, copy the base subdirectory; then copy the packages you want to install to another subdirectory called `RPMS`. You can use available space on an existing DOS partition or a Linux partition that is not required in the install procedure (for example, a partition that would be used for data storage on the installed system).

  If you are using a DOS filesystem, you might not be able to use the full Linux filenames for the RPM (Red Hat Package Manager) packages. The installation process does not care what the filesystem looks like, but it is a good idea to keep track of them so you will know what you are installing.
- NFS—If you want to install over a network, you need to mount the Red Hat Linux CD-ROM on a machine that supports ISO-9660 filesystems with Rock Ridge extensions. The machine must also support NFS. Export the CD-ROM filesystem via NFS. You should either have nameservices configured or know the NFS server's IP address and the path to the exported CD-ROM.

The rest of the installation procedures presented here are for CD-ROM installation. As you can tell from the previous descriptions, using other methods is not that different. As a matter of fact, the installation is the same; it is just a matter of the origin of the installation. For example, if you are installing from a shared volume on a Windows 95 or a Windows NT Server, you will have to supply the name of the server, the name of the shared volume, and the account name and password for the volume.

CD-ROM Installation

The installation program asks what type of CD-ROM you have. Most CD-ROM drives for home PCs are IDE/ATAPI drives. If you have a SCSI CD-ROM drive, the installation program then asks you to select the type of SCSI adapter you have and possibly some parameters for it; however, most of the time, the installation program can automatically detect the parameters. If you do not have either an IDE/ATAPI or SCSI CD-ROM drive, choose other and select the driver for your CD-ROM.

If you are installing via NFS, choose NFS image. The program asks which network card you have; you must have one on the list. It then asks for the IP address you will use for installation, your netmask, the default gateway, and the primary nameserver. See Figure 2.4 for an example.

FIGURE 2.4.
TCP/IP configuration.

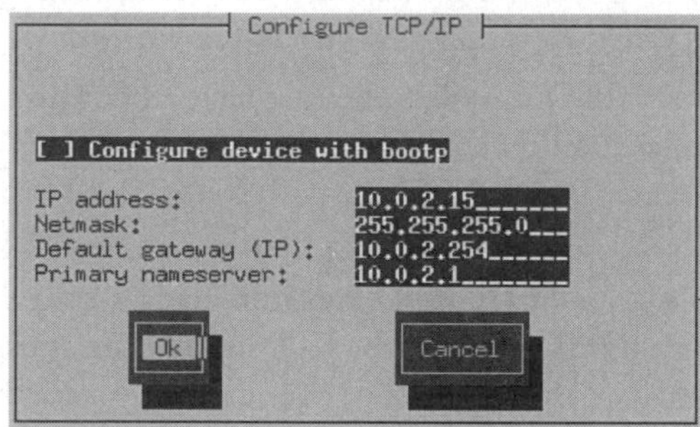

Next, as shown in Figure 2.5, the program asks for the domain name of your system, your hostname (the name of your computer), and a secondary and tertiary nameserver (you don't need these if you don't have them).

FIGURE 2.5.
Network configuration.

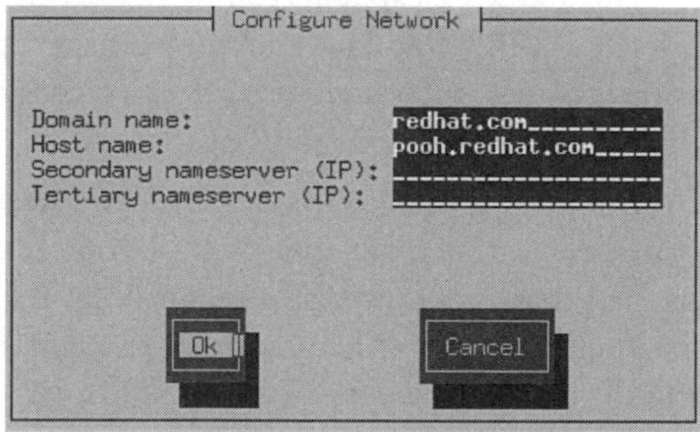

Then the program asks about your NFS server. Enter the address of the server and the directory that contains the Red Hat directory in the NFS Setup dialog box, as shown in Figure 2.6.

If you are installing Red Hat Linux using either FTP or SMB, you must have a supported network card. The installation program asks what card you have, just as in an NFS install.

The installation program presents you with the network configuration dialog box, just as in the NFS installation (refer to Figure 2.5). The installation program then asks for information for the FTP server (see Figure 2.7) or the SMB server (see Figure 2.8).

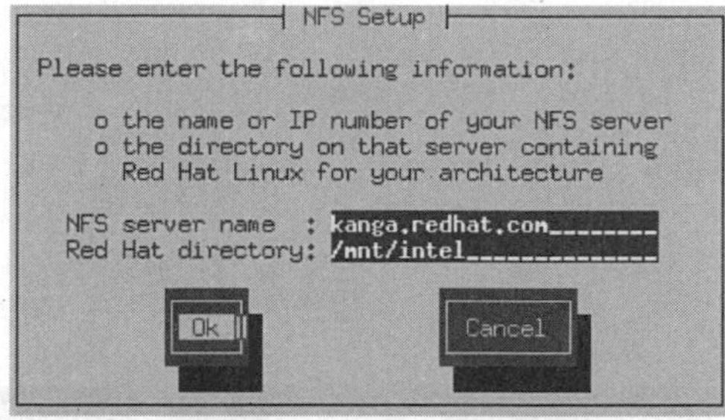

FIGURE 2.6.
NFS information.

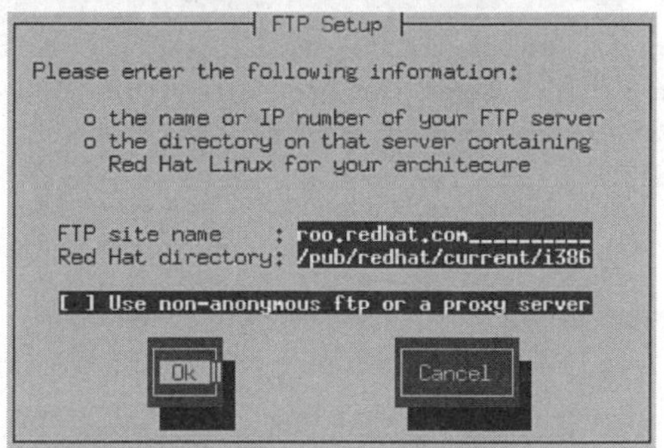

FIGURE 2.7.
The FTP Setup dialog box.

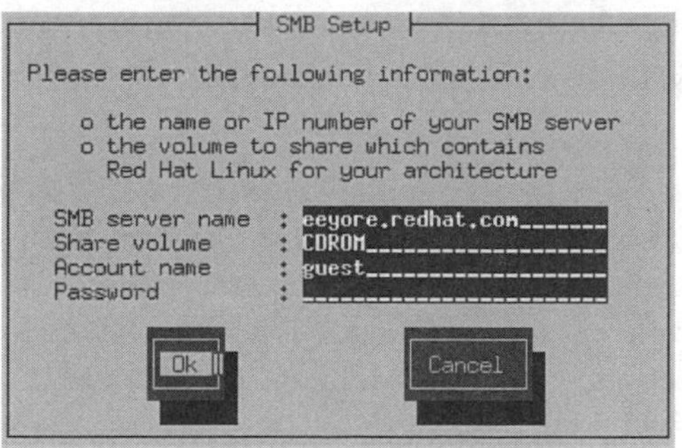

FIGURE 2.8.
The SMB Setup dialog box.

After you finish selecting which method to use and completing the appropriate information for the method, the installation program asks whether you want to install or upgrade in the Installation Path dialog box, as shown in Figure 2.9. You should choose Upgrade only if you currently have a previous version of Red Hat Linux, which is based on RPM technology, installed on your system. Otherwise, choose Install.

Disk Partitioning

If you choose Install, the installation program automatically starts the Linux `fdisk` utility, which sets up the partitions on your hard drive.

FIGURE 2.9.
Choose Install or Upgrade.

WARNING

This is the most volatile step of the entire procedure. If you mess up here, you could delete your entire hard drive. I highly recommend, therefore, that you make a backup of your current system before proceeding with the disk partitioning.

Here are some commands and a walkthrough of using `fdisk`:

- `m` provides a listing of the available commands.
- `p` provides a listing of the current partition information.
- `n` adds a new partition.
- `t` sets or changes the partition type.
- `l` provides a listing of the different partition types and their ID numbers.
- `w` saves your information and quits `fdisk`.

The first thing you will want to do is use `p` to check the current partition information. You need to first add your root partition. Use `n` to create a new partition and then select either `e` or `p` for extended or primary partition. Most likely you will want to create a primary partition. You are asked what partition number should be assigned to it, at which cylinder the partition should start (you will be given a range—just choose the lowest number), and the size of the partition. For example, for a 500MB partition, you would enter `+500M` for the size when asked.

You will now want to create your swap partition. Some thought must be given to the size of this partition. The swap partition is used for swapping the unused information in your RAM to disk to make room for more information. You should have at least 16MB total between your RAM and swap space. If you are running X Window, you should have at least 32MB between them.

The problem with using the generic formula mentioned previously is that it doesn't take into consideration what the user may be doing. A better estimate of the amount of swapping you need is given below. Note that if you run out of swap space, your system will thrash about trying to move memory pages into and out of the swap space, which will take your system to its knees.

A better estimate of how much RAM you need is to figure out the size of all the programs you would run at one time. Add this total to 8MB (to cover the OS). If this number is less than 32MB, then use 32MB; otherwise, use the actual value.

You should always configure some swapping space regardless of how much RAM you have. Even a small amount of swapping space will have good results on a system with a lot of RAM. For example, on my system I have 64MB of RAM, which is more than enough for all of the programs I run. I still have 32MB of swap space for those programs that I have running but am not actively using.

To create your swap partition, you need to use `n` for a new partition. Choose either primary or extended; you will most likely need primary. Give the partition a number and tell it where the first cylinder should be. Lastly, tell `fdisk` how big you want your swap partition. You then need to change the partition type to Linux swap. Enter `t` to change the type and enter the partition number of your swap partition. Enter `82` for the hex code for the Linux swap partition.

Now that you have created your Linux and Linux swap partitions, it is time to add any additional partitions you might need (for example, Windows 95). Use `n` again to create a new partition, and enter all the information just as before. After you enter the size of the partition, you need to change the partition type. Enter `l` to get a listing of the hex codes for the different partition types. Find the type of partition you need and use `t` to change the partition type. Keep repeating this procedure until all your partitions are created. You can create up to four primary partitions; then you must start putting extended partitions into each primary partition.

After your partitions are created, the installation program will look for Linux swap partitions and ask to initialize them. Choose the swap partitions you want to initialize, check the Check for bad blocks during format box, and press OK. This formats the partition and makes it active so Linux can use it.

Next, the program asks where you want your root partition to be, if you are performing a full install. If you are upgrading, the installation program will find it by itself.

If you have any partitions for other operating systems, the installation program asks you which ones are for what operating systems (see Figure 2.10).

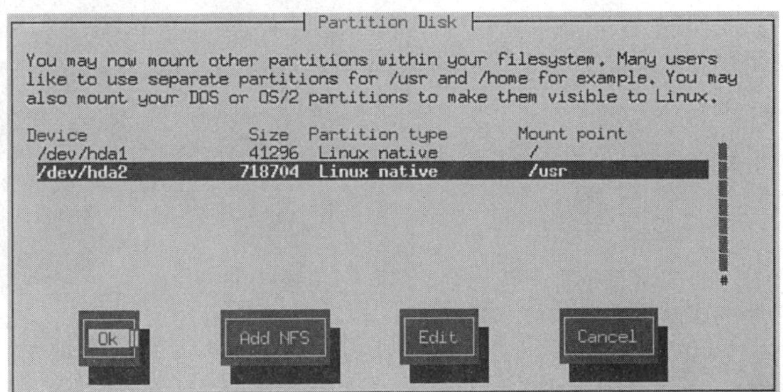

FIGURE 2.10.
The Partition Disk dialog box.

If you have any NFS filesystems to mount, you need to choose the Add NFS button at the bottom of the screen. A second dialog box is brought up that asks for the address of the NFS server, the NFS path, and the mount point, as shown in Figure 2.11.

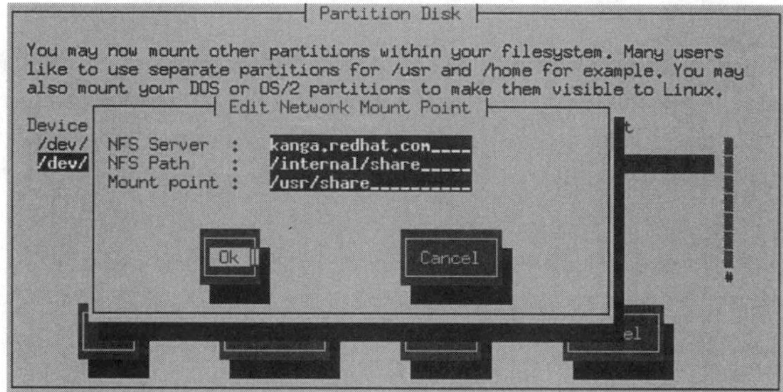

FIGURE 2.11.
NFS filesystem mounting.

The installation program now asks you which partitions you want to format. You should format them all unless there is some data you want to keep on any of them. It is a good idea to check the Check for bad blocks during format box also.

Installing Packages

After the partition(s) are formatted, you are ready to select the packages you want to be installed and start the installation. You first have to choose which system components you want to install (see Figure 2.12). Choose the components, and then you can go through and select or deselect each individual package of each component (see Figure 2.13).

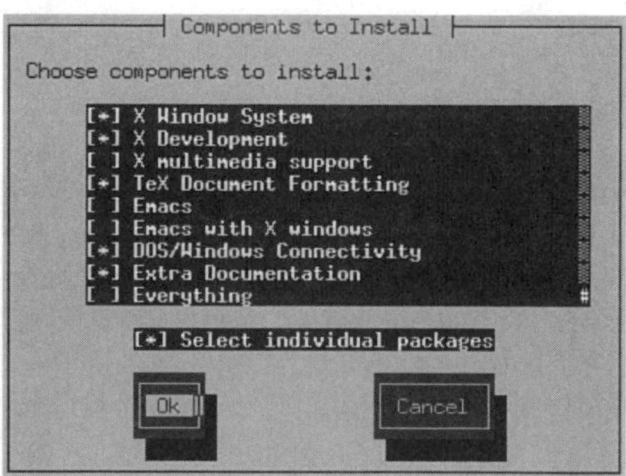

FIGURE 2.12.
Selecting components to install.

FIGURE 2.13.
Selecting packages.

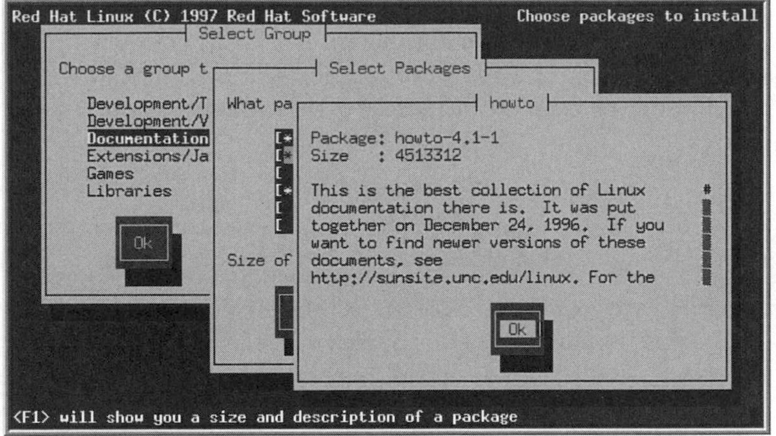

Sometimes, certain programs depend on others to work properly. These are called *dependencies*. If the installation program detects that some packages are missing that will be needed for another package, it brings up a dialog box that enables you to add the missing packages, as shown in Figure 2.14.

FIGURE 2.14.
The Unresolved Dependencies dialog box.

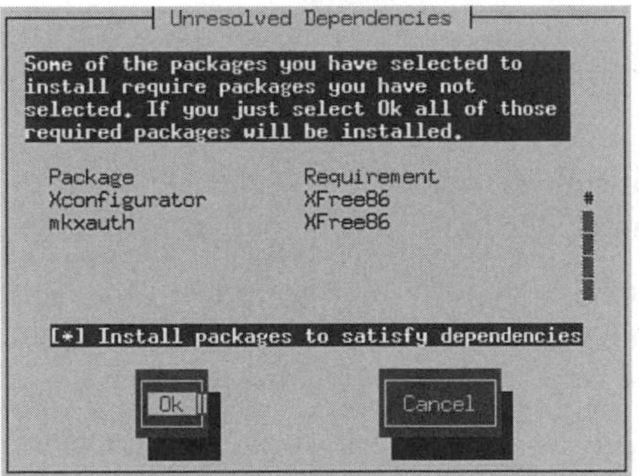

After the packages are installed, you need to configure your mouse, X Window (if installed), networking, printer, and clock.

The next dialog box asks what type of mouse you have. Most of the newest Microsoft mice use the Logitech protocol. If you choose a serial mouse, you are prompted for the COM port in which the mouse is plugged. If you have a mouse plugged in the PS/2 type port, you must select PS/2 Mouse, regardless of the type of mouse you have.

If you installed the X Window System, the installation program will start Xconfigurator. First, it prompts for your video card. If you don't see your video card and you have all the information on the card, you can select Unlisted Card and try to configure it yourself.

Second, Xconfigurator gives you a list of monitors from which to choose. Pick a monitor that will match yours exactly. If it does not match exactly, there is a possibility that you could destroy it by running it at a higher frequency than it was designed for. If you can't find your monitor and you know the frequencies of the monitor, you can select Custom and enter them yourself.

Next, you are asked about the amount of memory on your video card. Then you are presented with a menu of different video modes. Simply select the modes you want to be able to run in and press Enter. This information is written to `/etc/X11/XF86Config`.

After you have your X server configured, the installation program asks whether you want to configure networking. If you do not plan to connect your machine to a network, choose No. Otherwise, choose Yes and you will be presented with a dialog box that asks for your IP address, netmask, default gateway, and primary nameserver. You are then asked for your domain name, hostname, and any additional nameservers.

After you finish the network configuration, you are asked whether you want to set up a printer. (You don't have to install the printer at this time; it can be set up later.) The installation program asks what type of printer connection you are creating: Local, Remote, or LAN-Manager. You are then asked for the name of the queue you are creating, the name of the spool directory, the make and model of your printer, the size of paper your printer uses, and the depth of color you want to use if your printer is color.

If you are configuring a local printer, you also need to give the port to which your printer is connected.

If you are configuring a remote printer, you need to give the IP address of the host to which the printer is connected and the name of the queue in the remote host.

If you are configuring a LAN-Manager printer, you need to supply the name of the host to which the printer is connected, the IP number of the host, the name of the printer, the username you will use to access the printer, and the password.

You are now presented with a dialog box to set your clock. The program asks what time zone you are in and whether you want to set your CMOS clock to Greenwich Mean Time (also known as GMT or UTC). If you set the clock for local time, both Linux and another operating system (such as Windows 95) will use the clock. (Note that Windows 95 will reset your clock when your local time changes.) If you set the clock to UTC, Linux will handle time changes, but Windows 95 won't.

Setting Your Root Password

After you finish configuring the clock, you need to give your system a root password. The next dialog box asks for that password. It must be at least six characters long and should contain a mixture of upper- and lowercase letters and numbers. The password should not be based on anything that someone could guess (your name, phone number, birthday, and so on). You are asked to enter the password twice for verification that you typed it correctly. Do not forget this password, or you will not be able to log in to your system.

Finishing the Installation

After you set the root password, you are presented with a series of dialog boxes to set up LILO (see Figure 2.15). For details on this, see Chapter 3 on configuring and installing LILO.

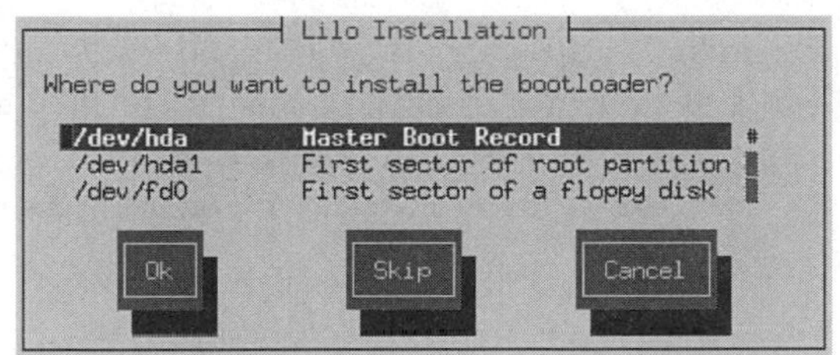

FIGURE 2.15.
The Lilo Installation dialog box.

After you install LILO, the installation program reboots your system. Press Enter at the `boot:` prompt. Enter `root` when prompted with `login:`, and enter the password you created during the installation when prompted with `password:`.

The Red Hat Package Manager

If you want to add packages to your Linux system in the future or upgrade current packages, you can use the Red Hat Package Manager (RPM). RPM technology is a very easy way to manage package installs and uninstalls. It keeps track of what is installed and any dependencies that are not met, and then it notifies you of them. There is also a graphical interface to RPM that can be accessed through the Control Panel while running X Window.

RPM Usage

The basic usage of the `rpm` command to install a package is the following:

```
rpm -I packagename.rpm
```

To uninstall a package you use the following:

```
rpm -u packagename.rpm
```

There are many other options available for RPM, but these two are the most commonly used options.

Packages for use with RPM are available at `ftp://ftp.redhat.com/pub/redhat/current/i386/RedHat/RPMS/` or any mirrors of this site.

Summary

The Red Hat Linux installation is the simplest and most straightforward installation available. After going through this chapter and following the step-by-step installation, you should now have a running Linux system. Keeping your system updated with the latest versions of utilities and libraries ensures compatibility with most new applications being developed for Linux and keeps your system operating efficiently.

If you do have problems, there are HOWTOs and FAQs on the CD-ROM that comes with this book. Most of them are in HTML format, so they can be viewed straight off the CD-ROM using a Web browser. In addition to the CD-ROM, the Red Hat Web site (`http://www.redhat.com`) contains installation documentation and errata sheets for Red Hat Linux.

CHAPTER

LILO

by Bill Ball and Jay Austad

IN THIS CHAPTER

Booting Linux requires you to install a program to load the kernel into your computer. Which program you use depends on the computer you're using: You'll use LILO for Intel-compatible PCs, MILO for Digital Equipment Corp. Alpha PCs, or SILO for SPARC-compatible workstations. Because the CD-ROM included with this book contains Red Hat Intel/Linux, this chapter will focus on LILO, which, according to its author, Werner Almesberger, stands for *Linux Loader*.

This chapter will help you if you chose not to install LILO when you first installed Red Hat Linux or if you need help in properly starting Linux with certain kernel options. You've probably already decided how you want to start Linux on your computer, but you should know that there are other ways to fire up your system.

Instead of using LILO, you can start Linux from DOS with `LOADLIN.EXE`, which is included on your CD-ROM under the `Dosutils` directory. I'll discuss `LOADLIN.EXE` later in this chapter in the section "Using `LOADLIN.EXE` to Boot Linux."

You can also use your computer as a diskless workstation by booting Linux over a network. A discussion on this subject is beyond the scope of this chapter, but you'll find the details on how to do this in Robert Nemkin's Diskless-HOWTO, under the `/usr/doc/HOWTO/mini` directory after you install Linux.

Yet another approach is to use a commercial boot loader, such as V Communications, Inc.'s System Commander, which can come in handy if you need to run other operating systems such as OS/2, Solaris, or Windows NT on your computer.

LILO has capabilities similar to commercial solutions, but it's free. For now, I'll assume that you're going to use LILO to boot in one of three traditional ways. You can use LILO to start Linux

- From the Master Boot Record (MBR) of your hard drive
- From the superblock of your root Linux partition on your hard drive
- From a floppy disk

In the following section, I'll show you a list of LILO's configuration parameters and its command-line arguments, and I'll point out some special features.

Installing and Configuring LILO

Although LILO is easy to install by using the `lilo` command (located under the `/sbin` directory), you should first take the time to read its documentation, which you'll find under `/usr/doc`. Along with the documentation, you'll also find a shell script called `QuickInst`, which can be used to replace an existing LILO installation or for a first-time install. LILO's documentation contains details of its features and provides important tips and workarounds for special problems, such as installing boot loaders on very large capacity hard drives or booting from other operating systems.

WARNING

Before trying anything with LILO, you should have an emergency boot disk. Having a system that won't boot is not much fun, and if you don't have a boot disk, you might think that there is no possible way to get back in and change things. Spending a few minutes to make yourself a boot disk can save you a big headache down the road. Whatever happens, don't panic! If you need to rescue your system, see Chapter 4, "System Startup and Shutdown," for details.

If you don't install LILO during your Red Hat install or decide not to use the `QuickInst` script, there are two basic steps to install LILO:

1. Configure `/etc/lilo.conf`.
2. Run `/sbin/lilo` to install LILO and make it active.

This discussion describes modifying an existing `lilo.conf` file. Before making any changes, do yourself a favor and create a backup of the file either in the same directory or on a separate disk. Several files are important to LILO and are created during an initial install:

- `/sbin/lilo`—A map installer; see `man lilo` for more information
- `/boot/boot.b`—A boot loader
- `/boot/map`—A boot map, which contains the location of the kernel
- `/etc/lilo.conf`—LILO's configuration file

Configuring LILO

Under Linux, your hard drives are abstracted to device files under the `/dev` directory. If you have one or more IDE drives, your first hard drive is referred to as `/dev/hda`, and your second hard drive is `/dev/hdb`. SCSI drives are referred to as `/dev/sda` and `/dev/sdb`. When you installed Linux, you most likely partitioned your hard drive. The first partition on your first drive would be `/dev/hda1` or `/dev/sda1`. Consequently, your second partition would be `/dev/hda2` or `/dev/sda2`, and so on.

Before configuring LILO, you should know which partitions have what operating system on them. You should also know where you want to install LILO. In almost all cases, you will want to put LILO on the MBR. You shouldn't do this, however, if you run OS/2. OS/2's boot loader should go on the MBR, and LILO should then be installed on the superblock of the root partition.

Before installing LILO, you should know where your Linux partition is, and if you have other operating systems, you must know where they are located. For example, your Linux partition might be at `/dev/hda1`, and your Windows 95 partition might be at `/dev/hda2`.

If Linux is the only operating system on your computer or if you have Windows 95 or Windows NT, you will want to install LILO as the MBR of the drive. If you have OS/2 also, you will want to install LILO on the root partition of your hard drive and use OS/2's boot loader on the MBR.

LILO is normally installed after you have partitioned your hard drives and after you have installed either Linux or other operating systems.

Armed with your information, you are now ready to edit LILO's configuration file, `/etc/lilo.conf`.

Editing `lilo.conf`

Editing `lilo.conf` is easy. Make sure that you're logged in as root, and load the file into your favorite editor, making sure to save your changes and to save the file as ASCII text. You'll edit `lilo.conf` for a number of reasons:

- You are testing a new kernel and want to be able to boot the same Linux partition with more than one kernel.
- You want to add password protection to a partition.
- You have a hardware setup that requires you to specify special options, such as booting a remote filesystem.
- Your kernel is called something other than `/vmlinuz` or is in a nonstandard place, such as `/etc`.

Listing 3.1 shows a sample `lilo.conf` file.

Listing 3.1. A sample `lilo.conf`.

```
# Start LILO global section
Boot = /dev/hda
Prompt
Vga = normal
Ramdisk = 0
# End LILO global section
image = /vmlinuz
  root = /dev/hda3
  label = linux
  read-only  # Non-UMSDOS filesystems should be mounted read-only for checking
other = /dev/hda1
  label = dos
  table = /dev/hda
```

You can add the parameters listed in Table 3.1 to your `/etc/lilo.conf` file. They could also be given at the boot prompt, but it is much simpler for them to reside in your `/etc/lilo.conf` file. Note that only 13 of LILO's 23 different options are listed here. See LILO's documentation for details.

Table 3.1. /etc/lilo.conf configuration parameters.

Parameter	*Description*
`boot=<boot_device>`	Tells the kernel the name of the device that contains the boot sector. If `boot` is omitted, the boot sector is read from the device that is currently mounted as root.
`linear`	Generates linear sector addresses instead of sector/head/cylinder addresses, which can be troublesome, especially when used with the compact option. See LILO's documentation for details.
`install=<boot_sector>`	Installs the specified file as the new boot sector. If `install` is omitted, `/etc/lilo/boot.b` is used as the default.
`message=<message_file>`	You can use this to display the file's text and customize the boot prompt, with a maximum message of up to 65,535 bytes. Rerun `/sbin/lilo` if you change this file.
`verbose=<level>`	Turns on progress reporting. Higher numbers give more verbose output, and the numbers can range from `1` to `5`. This also has a `-v` and `-q` option; see LILO's documentation for details.
`backup=<backup_file>`	Copies the original boot sector to `<backup_file>` (which can also be a device, such as `/dev/null`) instead of to `/etc/lilo/boot.<number>`.
`force-backup<backup_file>`	Similar to `backup`, this option will overwrite the current backup copy, but `backup` is ignored if `force-backup` is used.
`prompt`	Requires you to type a boot prompt entry.
`timeout=<tsecs>`	Sets a time-out (in tenths of a second) for keyboard input, which is handy if you want to boot right away or wait for longer than the default five seconds. Tip: To make LILO wait indefinitely for your keystrokes, use a value of `0`.
`serial=<parameters>`	Allows input from the designated serial line and the PC's keyboard to LILO. A break on the serial line mimics a Shift key press from the console. For security, password-protect all your boot images when using this option. The parameter string has the syntax `<port>,<bps><parity><bits>`, as in `/dev/ttyS1,8N1`. The components `<bps>`,

continues

Table 3.1. continued

Parameter	*Description*
	`<parity>`, and `<bits>` can be omitted. If one of these components is omitted, all the following components have to be omitted as well. Additionally, the comma has to be omitted if only the port number is specified. See LILO's documentation for details.
`ignore-table`	Ignore corrupt partition tables.
`password=<password>`	Use this to password protect your boot images.
`unsafe`	This keyword is placed after a definition for a partition. The keyword tells LILO not to attempt to read the MBR or that disk's partition table entry. You can declare all the partitions in your system as a log of all existing partitions and then place the `unsafe` keyword entry to prevent LILO from reading it.

After making your changes to `lilo.conf`, make sure to run `/sbin/lilo`. You should also *always* run `/sbin/lilo` after installing a new kernel.

LILO Boot Prompt Options

The following sample list of options can be passed to LILO at the boot prompt to enable special features of your system or to pass options to the Linux kernel to enable a proper boot. Knowing any needed options for your system is especially handy during the Red Hat Linux installation process because you'll be asked for any special options if you choose to install LILO then.

Although you'll normally type **`linux`** or **`dos`** at the `LILO:` prompt, you can also try one or two of the following. For a more up-to-date list of kernel messages or options, read Paul Gortmaker's BootPrompt-HOWTO under the `/usr/doc/HOWTO` directory.

- `rescue`—Boots Linux into single-user mode to allow system fixes (see Chapter 4 for details).
- `single`—Similar to `rescue`, but attempts to boot from your hard drive.
- `root=<device>`—Similar to the `/etc/lilo.conf` entry, this option allows you to boot from a CD-ROM or other storage device.
- `vga=<mode>`—Enables you to change the resolution of your console; try the `ask` mode.

Using LOADLIN.EXE to Boot Linux

`LOADLIN.EXE` is a program that uses the DOS MBR to boot Linux. This handy program, by Hans Lermen, will also pass along kernel options. `LOADLIN.EXE` is very helpful when you must boot from DOS in order to properly initialize modems or sound cards to make them work under Linux.

You need to do two things before using `LOADLIN.EXE`:

1. Copy `LOADLIN.EXE` to a DOS partition (for example, `C:\LOADLIN`).
2. Put a copy of your kernel image (`/vmlinuz`) on your DOS partition.

For example, to boot Linux, type the following from the DOS command line:

```
loadlin c:\vmlinuz root=/dev/hda3 ro
```

Make sure that you insert your root partition in the command line. The `ro` is for read-only. When you are first booting a Linux partition, it should be mounted as read-only or data loss could occur.

If you have a UMSDOS filesystem, you can type

```
loadlin c:\vmlinuz root=/dev/hda1 rw
```

The `rw` is for read/write. It is safe to start a UMSDOS filesystem this way. Again, make sure that you substitute your own partition in. `LOADLIN.EXE` accepts a number of options. See its documentation in the `LOADLIN.TGZ` file under the `Dosutils` directory on the book's CD-ROM.

How to Uninstall LILO

LILO can be uninstalled using the `lilo -u` command, or it can be disabled by making another partition active using `fdisk` under either Linux or MS-DOS.

If LILO has been installed as the MBR, you can restore the original MBR by booting under MS-DOS and using the commands `SYS c:` or `FDISK /MBR`.

Summary

This chapter covers the basics of configuring, installing, and using LILO, and introduces you to the `LOADLIN.EXE` boot utility. Hopefully, you've seen that using LILO can give you additional flexibility in the number of operating systems installed on your PC and that Linux can be used along with these other systems. Don't forget to read LILO's documentation, as you'll not only learn about how operating systems boot from your hard drive, but also how you can customize the Linux boot prompt.

Part II

IN THIS PART

Configuring Other Servers

CHAPTER 4

System Startup and Shutdown

by Bill Ball

IN THIS CHAPTER

This chapter explains how to start the Red Hat Linux system and how to properly shut it down. It also covers system crashes and what to do if your system won't boot.

Also, this chapter presents some tips on how to customize your system and how to avoid problems with system crashes.

The Boot Process

In Chapter 2, "Installation of Your Red Hat System," you learned how to install Linux, and in Chapter 3, "LILO," you found out how to install and use different loaders for different computers. There are a number of ways to start Linux with different computers, and a number of different ways to load in the Linux kernel. Intel Linux users will most likely use LILO, `LOADLIN`, `SYSLINUX`, or the commercial alternative, System Commander. SPARC users will use SILO, and Alpha users will probably use MILO. You'll find the basic steps outlined in your *Red Hat Linux Users Guide*, or through Red Hat at `http://www.redhat.com/linux-info`.

I'm assuming most readers will install Red Hat Linux/Intel, so here's a little background on how the Red Hat Linux startup process is different from that of other UNIX operating systems, such as BSD.

PCs start by looking at the first sector of the first cylinder of the boot drive, and then trying to load and execute code found there (which is how LILO works, as you found out in Chapter 3). This is also the case with other (but not all) hardware systems and versions of UNIX. You should be able to set the order in which your PC looks for the boot drive. This is usually done through a BIOS change in a setup menu you can invoke when you first turn on your machine. This can be handy if you never use a boot floppy. For example, laptop users with an external floppy can speed up the boot process by directing the computer to first look to the internal hard drive or CD-ROM.

You can also start Linux over a network and run a diskless Linux box. For more information on how to do this, see Robert Nemkin's "Diskless Linux Mini HOWTO," under `/usr/doc/HOWTO/mini`. Although Linux shares many similar traits with both System V and BSD UNIX, in the case of booting and starting the system, Linux is closer to the former. This means that Linux uses the `init` command and a similar directory structure of associated scripts to start running the system and loading processes.

According to the Red Hat folks, this approach is becoming the standard in the "Linux world" because it is "easier to use and more powerful and flexible." And you'll see why it is even easier for Red Hat Linux users when you learn about the `tksysv` client later in this chapter in the section "`tksysv` and Managing Your Services."

The Initialization Process and Startup Scripts

This section describes how Linux starts and details the functions of the different startup scripts used to prepare your system for use. An important concept to first note is the use of various runlevels or system states of Linux.

System states grew out of early versions of UNIX from the need to separate how the system ran according to the different forms of maintenance being performed on a system. This is similar to performing a software or hardware upgrade on older PCs, which generally requires a reboot or shutdown and restart of the computer. These days, however, this practice is partially obviated through new software and hardware technologies: "hot-swappable" hardware and software. This means you can change hard drives, PC cards, or associated software on-the-fly—while the system is running.

You'll find a description of these different runlevels in the `/etc/inittab` file, or initialization table. Although Linux differs from other versions of UNIX in several of the levels, Red Hat Intel/Linux mainly uses the following (as listed in `/etc/inittab`):

```
#   The runlevels used by RHS are:
#   0 - halt (Do NOT set initdefault to this)
#   1 - Single user mode
#   2 - Multiuser, without NFS (The same as 3, if you do not have networking)
#   3 - Full multiuser mode
#   4 - unused
#   5 - X11
#   6 - reboot (Do NOT set initdefault to this)
```

The next section describes these runlevels, including the first startup script in the initialization table, `/etc/rc.d/rc.sysinit`, or the system initialization script, which is run once at boot time by the `init` command. The `/etc/rc.d` directory structure and what some of these scripts do are also covered.

`init` and `/etc/inittab`

The `init` man page states, "`init` is the father of all processes." Its primary role is to create processes from a script stored in `/etc/inittab`. Much of how Linux starts its processes after loading the kernel comes from another UNIX, System V. In fact, the Linux `init` command is compatible with the System V `init` command, and the startup scripts model that approach. Although `init` starts as "the last step of the kernel booting," it is the first command that initializes and configures your system for use. `init` works by parsing `/etc/inittab` and running scripts in `/etc/rc.d` according to either a default or desired runlevel. Each script can start or stop a service, such as a networking, mail, news, or Web service.

Here's a listing of the `/etc/rc.d` directory:

```
init.d/
rc*
rc.local*
rc.news*
rc.sysinit*
rc0.d/
rc1.d/
rc2.d/
rc3.d/
rc4.d/
rc5.d/
rc6.d/
```

Under the `init.d` directory, you'll find a number of scripts used to start and stop services. I won't go into the details about each, but you should be able to guess at the function of some of them by their names. Here's a list:

```
amd.init*
cron.init*
functions*
gpm*
halt*
httpd.init*
inet*
keytable*
killall*
lpd.init*
mars_nwe.init*
named.init*
network*
news*
nfs*
nfsfs*
pcmcia*
portmap.init*
random*
sendmail.init*
single*
skeleton*
smb*
syslog*
yppasswd.init*
ypserv.init*
```

/etc/inittab and System States

One of the most important scripts in `/etc/inittab` is `rc.sysinit`, the system initialization script. When `init` parses `/etc/inittab`, this is the first script found and executed. This differs slightly from other versions of UNIX, which might include the system initialization commands directly in the `/etc/inittab` file.

However, much like other versions of UNIX, the Red Hat Linux `sysinit` script performs some or all of the following functions:

- Sets some initial `$PATH` variables
- Configures networking
- Starts up swapping for virtual memory
- Sets the system hostname
- Checks root filesystems for possible repairs
- Checks root filesystem quotas
- Turns on user and group quotas for root filesystem
- Remounts the root filesystem read/write

- Clears the mounted filesystems table, /etc/mtab
- Enters the root filesystem into mtab
- Readies the system for loading modules
- Finds module dependencies
- Checks filesystems for possible repairs
- Mounts all other filesystems
- Cleans out several /etc files: /etc/mtab, /etc/fastboot, /etc/nologin
- Deletes UUCP lock files
- Deletes stale subsystem files
- Deletes stale pid files
- Sets the system clock
- Turns on swapping
- Initializes the serial ports
- Loads modules

Whew! That's a lot of work just for the first startup script! But it's just the first step in a number of steps needed to start your system. So far, you've seen that after the Linux kernel is loaded, the init command is run. After the rc.sysinit is run by init, then init runs rc.local. If you look at the Red Hat Linux rc.local script, you'll see that it gets the operating system name and architecture of your computer and puts it into a file called /etc/issue, which is later used for display at the login prompt.

The next task of init is to run the scripts for each runlevel. If you look at the listing of the rc.d directory, you'll see the various rcX.d directories, where X is a number from 0 through 6. But if you look at the files under one of these directories, you'll find that each is merely a link to a script under init.d, with an associated name for a particular service. For example, under the rc3.d directory, you'll find

```
lrwxrwxrwx   1 root    root    17 Apr 10 09:11 S10network -> ../init.d/network*
lrwxrwxrwx   1 root    root    16 Apr 10 09:18 S30syslog -> ../init.d/syslog*
lrwxrwxrwx   1 root    root    19 Apr 10 09:22 S40cron -> ../init.d/cron.init*
lrwxrwxrwx   1 root    root    22 Apr 10 09:17 S40portmap -> ../init.d/portmap.init*
lrwxrwxrwx   1 root    root    16 Apr 10 09:16 S45pcmcia -> ../init.d/pcmcia*
lrwxrwxrwx   1 root    root    14 Apr 10 09:04 S50inet -> ../init.d/inet*
lrwxrwxrwx   1 root    root    20 Apr 10 09:06 S55named.init -> ../init.d/named.init*
lrwxrwxrwx   1 root    root    18 Jul 15 11:56 S60lpd.init -> ../init.d/lpd.init*
lrwxrwxrwx   1 root    root    13 Apr 10 09:16 S60nfs -> ../init.d/nfs*
lrwxrwxrwx   1 root    root    15 Apr 10 09:11 S70nfsfs -> ../init.d/nfsfs*
lrwxrwxrwx   1 root    root    18 Apr 10 09:11 S75keytable -> ../init.d/keytable*
lrwxrwxrwx   1 root    root    23 Apr 10 09:18 S80sendmail -> ../init.d/sendmail.init*
lrwxrwxrwx   1 root    root    13 Apr 10 09:10 S85gpm -> ../init.d/gpm*
lrwxrwxrwx   1 root    root    11 Apr 10 09:11 S99local -> ../rc.local*
```

Note the S in front of each name. This means to start a process or service. Now, if you look at the files under rc0.d, you'll see

```
lrwxrwxrwx  1 root  root    18 Apr 10 09:06 K08amd ->../init.d/amd.init*
lrwxrwxrwx  1 root  root    20 Apr 10 09:06 K10named.init -> ../init.d/named.init*
lrwxrwxrwx  1 root  root    15 Apr 10 09:11 K10nfsfs -> ../init.d/nfsfs*
lrwxrwxrwx  1 root  root    13 Apr 10 09:10 K15gpm -> ../init.d/gpm*
lrwxrwxrwx  1 root  root    13 Apr 10 09:16 K20nfs -> ../init.d/nfs*
lrwxrwxrwx  1 root  root    20 Apr 10 09:06 K25httpd -> ../init.d/httpd.init*
lrwxrwxrwx  1 root  root    21 Apr 10 09:11 K25news -> /etc/rc.d/init.d/news*
lrwxrwxrwx  1 root  root    23 Apr 10 09:18 K30sendmail -> ../init.d
➥sendmail.init*
lrwxrwxrwx  1 root  root    23 Apr 10 09:14 K32mars_nwe -> ../init.d/
➥mars_nwe.init*
lrwxrwxrwx  1 root  root    23 Apr 10 09:24 K33yppasswd -> ../init.d/
➥yppasswd.init*
lrwxrwxrwx  1 root  root    21 Apr 10 09:24 K35ypserv -> ../init.d/ypserv.init*
lrwxrwxrwx  1 root  root    14 Apr 10 09:04 K50inet -> ../init.d/inet*
lrwxrwxrwx  1 root  root    16 Apr 10 09:16 K52pcmcia -> ../init.d/pcmcia*
lrwxrwxrwx  1 root  root    19 Apr 10 09:22 K60cron -> ../init.d/cron.init*
lrwxrwxrwx  1 root  root    18 Jul 15 11:56 K60lpd.init -> ../init.d/lpd.init*
lrwxrwxrwx  1 root  root    22 Apr 10 09:17 K65portmap -> ../init.d/portmap.init*
lrwxrwxrwx  1 root  root    16 Apr 10 09:18 K70syslog -> ../init.d/syslog*
lrwxrwxrwx  1 root  root    16 Apr 10 09:11 K80random -> ../init.d/random*
lrwxrwxrwx  1 root  root    17 Apr 10 09:11 K99killall -> ../init.d/killall*
lrwxrwxrwx  1 root  root    14 Apr 10 09:11 S00halt -> ../init.d/halt*
```

Notice the `K` in front of each name. This means to kill a process or service. If you look under each of the different `rcX.d` directories, you'll see what services or processes are started or stopped in each runlevel. Later in this chapter I'll come back to some of the `rc.sysinit` tasks because some of the error-checking done when starting up can help pinpoint problems with your system. For now, however, the following sections explain the different runlevels and what basically happens in each.

Runlevel 0: /etc/rc.d/rc0.d

As you can see from the previous directory listing, this runlevel starts the shutdown sequence. Each script is run in the order listed. Some of the tasks run include

- Killing all processes
- Turning off virtual memory file swapping
- Unmounting swap and mounted filesystems

As shown in this section, and discussed later in this chapter, there are some important things done during a shutdown involving your computer, its services, and its filesystems. Although Linux is a robust operating system with system-checking safeguards, executing a proper shutdown is essential to maintaining the integrity of your computer's hard drive as well as any Linux volumes or partitions.

Runlevel 1: /etc/rc.d/rc1.d

This is the single-user mode, or administrative state, traditionally used by system administrators, or sysadmins, while performing software maintenance. No one else can log in during this mode, and networking is turned off, although filesystems are mounted.

Runlevel 2: /etc/rc.d/rc2.d

This is the multiuser state. Networking is enabled, although NFS is disabled.

Runlevel 3: /etc/rc.d/rc3.d

This is the default runlevel, which is specified as the first line in `/etc/inittab`. Remote file sharing is enabled, along with all other desired services.

Runlevel 4: /etc/rc.d/rc4.d

This directory is empty. As in other versions of UNIX, if you want to define your own runlevel, here's where you can add the appropriate links, with directions to selectively start or stop processes.

Runlevel 5: /etc/rc.d/rc5.d

This runlevel is much the same as the default, with the exception of `named`, the Internet domain nameserver. This is also the runlevel entered when running X11 under Linux.

Runlevel 6: /etc/rc.d/rc6.d

This is the reboot runlevel. The contents of this directory contain links similar to those in runlevel 0, but logic in the halt script under `init.d` determines whether or not the system is being shutdown or rebooted.

Keeping track of which process is started or stopped in which runlevel can be difficult. In the next section, you'll see one more reason why using Red Hat Linux can make your system administration tasks easier.

tksysv and Managing Your Services

One of the great things about Red Hat Linux is the number of tools included in the distribution to help you manage your system. One such handy tool is Donnie Barnes's `tksysv`, which can be called from a command line in a terminal window while you're running X, or through the control-panel client. You should use it for a number of reasons.

It is not only important to know how to properly shut down your system; you should also know how to properly start and stop services under Linux while the system is running. Although you can selectively "kill" processes with

```
# kill -9 pid
```

where `pid` is the number of the running process, this is a crude, ineffective, and potentially harmful way to stop processes. Using the information you have learned so far, you can also use the following approach (a handy tip from the `tksysv` help dialog), for example, to stop the Web server, `httpd`:

```
# /etc/rc.d/init.d/httpd.init stop
```

Both of these are manual approaches. But since the Red Hat folks have taken such great pains to make system administration easier, why not take advantage of point-and-click convenience? When you use `tksysv`, you can see at one glance which processes are going to be enabled or disabled at each runlevel.

The `tksysv` client, written in `tcl/tk`, is a runlevel editor. You simply select a service and then click the Add or Remove button. You can also select a service in the Start or Stop section of the dialog, and then click the Edit button to assign a number to the service in order to change the order in which the process is started or stopped when entering or leaving a particular runlevel.

Using `tksysv` sure beats doing everything by hand. But be careful! Making changes by hand-editing the default runlevel for `/etc/inittab` or using `tksysv` to change runlevels can put your system into an unusable state. Here's a handy tip from the help menu in `tksysv`:

"If you do mess up, you can get in to fix it by rebooting and doing

```
LILO boot: linux single
```

This should allow you to boot into single-user mode so you can fix it."

Shutting Down the Linux System

By now you've learned not only how Linux starts, but also a little bit about how it shuts down. If you look at the scripts in runlevel 0, you'll find a number of services being shut down, followed by the killing of all active processes, and finally, the halt script in `inet.d` executing the shutdown.

The halt script is used to either halt or reboot your system, depending on how it is called. But what happens during a shutdown? If you're familiar with other operating systems such as DOS, you remember that all you had to do was close any active application and then turn off the computer. Although Linux is easy to use, shutting down your computer is not as simple as turning it off. (Although you can try this if you wish, you do so at your own risk!) There are a number of processes that must take place before you or Linux turns off your computer. Let's take a look at some of the commands involved.

shutdown

Although many people use Linux as a single user on a single computer, many of us use computers either on a distributed or shared network. If you've ever been working under a tight deadline in a networked environment, then you know the dreadful experience of seeing the "System is going down in 5 minutes!" message from the system administrator. You might also know the frustration of working on a system on which the system administrator is trying to perform maintenance, suffering seemingly random downtimes or frozen tasks.

Luckily for most users, these jobs are performed during off hours, when most people are home with their loved ones, or fast asleep in bed. Unluckily for sysadmins, this is the perfect time for system administration or backups, and one of the top reasons for the `alt.sysadmin.recovery` newsgroup!

The primary command to stop Linux is the `shutdown` command. Like most UNIX commands, `shutdown` has a number of options. Curiously, no man page for the `shutdown` command is included in Red Hat Linux 4.2, but you can find its command-line syntax because it displays a small help message if you use an illegal option. Thanks to the programmer, here it is:

```
Usage:    shutdown [-krhfnc] [-t secs] time [warning message]
                -k:       don't really shutdown, only warn.
                -r:       reboot after shutdown.
                -h:       halt after shutdown.
                -f:       do a 'fast' reboot.
                -n:       do not go through "init" but go down real fast.
                -c:       cancel a running shutdown.
                -t secs: delay between warning and kill signal.
** the "time" argument is mandatory! (try "now") **
```

To properly shutdown your system immediately, use

```
# shutdown -h now
```

If you want to wait for a while, use the `-t` option. If you want to restart your computer, use

```
# shutdown -r now
```

The lack of documentation for shutdown in the Red Hat Linux can be troublesome, but even more curious is the presence of two text strings embedded in the program:

```
"You don't exist. Go away."
"(Well hello Mr. Tyler - going DOWN?)"
```

which were found by executing:

```
# strings /sbin/shutdown
```

Hint: To find out about `"You don't exist. Go away."`, see Ian Jackson's *Linux Frequently Asked Questions with Answers*. You should be able to find a copy at `ftp://sunsite.unc.edu/pub/Linux/docs/HOWTO`.

halt and reboot

There are two other commands that will also stop or restart your system: the `halt` and `reboot` commands. `reboot` is a symbolic link to `halt`. `halt` notifies the kernel of a shutdown or reboot. Although you should always use `shutdown` to restart your system, there is another command you can use: the Vulcan neck pinch, `ctrlaltdel`.

If you use the keyboard form of this command, you'll find that Linux uses the following command:

```
# shutdown -t3 -r now
```

If you use the command-line form of this approach, you have two options: hard or soft. Because a hard reset will restart your computer without calling the `sync` command, a soft reset is preferred. Why? Because `sync` updates the inodes of your files, or structure representations of each of your files. If you exit Linux without updating this information, Linux could lose track of your files on disk, and that spells disaster!

> **NOTE**
>
> The only time you'll want to risk shutting down Linux through a hard reset or the power-off switch on your computer is if you can't quickly kill a destructive process, such as an accidental `rm -fr /*`.

By now you should know that exiting Linux properly can help you avoid problems with your system. But what happens if something goes wrong? In the next section you'll learn about preventive measures, how to maintain your filesystem, and how to recover and overcome problems.

When the System Crashes

The best time to deal with a system crash is before the crash happens. This means being prepared with a good backup plan, good backups, emergency boot disks, or copies of important files. These issues are covered in this section, along with tips and hints for maintaining your filesystem integrity and system security.

First, here are some Do's and Don'ts to avoid problems:

- Don't use Linux as the root user.
- Do make a backup after a clean install and setup.
- Do create a set of emergency boot disks with your current kernel.
- Don't just turn off your computer when done.
- Do use the `shutdown` command.
- Do consider using an uninterruptible power supply.
- Don't disable `e2fsck` in `/etc/rc.d/rc.sysinit`.
- Do use `fsck` or `badblocks` to check floppies.
- Don't run `fsck` on mounted filesystems.
- Do make backups of important files on floppy disks.
- Don't worry about fragmentation of your Linux partitions.
- Do use your filesystem tools.
- Don't fill your hard drive with unnecessary programs.
- Do consider using flash RAM.
- Do read Lars Wirzenius's *Linux System Administrators' Guide 0.5*.

Running as Root

Don't use Linux as root all the time! Although you might be tempted, there are some very good reasons not to. First, even though you might have aliased the `rm` command to `rm -i` in your `.bashrc` file, a simple `# rm -fr /*` will not only wipe out your Linux system, but also any DOS or Windows partitions if mounted under `/mnt`. Instead, create a user for yourself and use the `su` command when you need to do things as the root operator. If you have programs that need to run SUID root, see Phil Hughes's article, "Safely Running Programs as `root`," in the May 1997 issue of *Linux Journal*.

Creating a Boot Disk

One of the first things you should do following a clean install and setup is to make a boot disk, using the current Linux kernel on your computer. You should always have a working copy in case you screw up when recompiling the kernel. Here's one quick way to not only make a copy of your current kernel, but also create an emergency boot disk. First, make sure your kernel points to your root device. You can check this on a recently built kernel with

```
# rdev zImage
```

Next, format a disk in your floppy drive using `fdformat` (assuming a 1.44MB drive A:):

```
# fdformat /dev/fd0H1440
```

Next, copy your kernel to the disk with

```
# dd if=zImage of=/dev/fd0
```

Now, assuming your computer is set to look at the floppy first, try rebooting with your boot disk with

```
# shutdown -r now
```

But you should also have a backup set of emergency boot disks that include not just the kernel, but also a minimal filesystem to get you started on the road to recovery. There are some excellent guides, scripts, and software to help you do this. (See "For More Information" at the end of this chapter.)

Generally, the approach is to create two disks, with one containing a kernel, and the other containing a compressed filesystem with a minimal directory of files, including file utilities. But guess what? Because you're a Red Hat Linux user, you don't have to! Read on to find out why.

Ackpht! Argggh! I've Deleted My Document!

If you accidentally delete a text file, don't panic! There's a handy tip, called "Desperate person's text file undelete," from Paul Anderson's "The Linux Tips HOWTO," courtesy of Michael Hamilton.

Assuming you remember some of the text, know which partition the file was on, and have a spare partition with some room, you should be able to recover a good portion of the file. Hamilton's approach uses the `egrep` and `strings` commands. For example, if you lose a 100-line file with the phrase "Xena," followed by "Lawless," and have room on your DOS partition:

```
# egrep -100 'Xena.+Lawless' /dev/hda3 > /mnt/dos/lucy
```

Then you can look for the text with

```
# strings /mnt/dos/lucy ¦ less
```

Your File Toolbox

You should also learn about and know how to use some of the file tools included with Red Hat Linux. While `e2fsck` is run automagically from the `rc.sysinit` script, it can be helpful in diagnosing and fixing problems. Other commands, such as `dumpe2fs` and `debugfs`, provide detailed technical information concerning your Linux filesystem, while others, such as `badblocks`, can be helpful if you have a non-IDE hard drive.

Here's a list of just some of the programs available:

e2fsck

Most Linux users choose to use the second extended filesystem, and with good reason: `e2fs` is robust, efficient, speedy, and relatively impervious to fragmentation. This command has a plethora of options aimed at helping you check and repair your filesystem. For safety's sake, unmount the partition and then try

```
# e2fsck -p /dev/hda3
```

to automatically repair the partition `/dev/hda3`.

badblocks

This command will search a device for bad blocks, and also has a number of options; but beware of the `-w` option, as it is a "write-mode" test and will destroy data on a partition.

fsck

This command is similar to `e2fsck`, as it checks and repairs Linux filesystems. Be sure to read its man page, as the `-P` option can be harmful.

dump and restore

The `dump` command can be used for filesystem backup, as it searches your files that need to be backed up. `dump` will also do remote backups. The companion program is `restore`, which also works across networks.

dumpe2fs

This command will dump your filesystem information. You'll get the inode count, block count, block size, last mount, and write time. Running `dumpe2fs` on a 450MB partition will generate a 26,000-character report. An interesting part of the report is the mount and maximum mount count, which determines when `e2fsck` is run on a partition when Linux starts.

tune2fs

If you just have to mess with your system's performance, you can use this command to adjust its tunable parameters—but only if you have an `ext2` filesystem. Use this command to adjust when `e2fsck` is run on your partition, but don't do it when the partition is mounted!

mke2fs

Linux hackers will be familiar with this program, which creates a Linux second extended filesystem on a partition. And you might need it too, if you want to create compressed filesystems on emergency disks, or if you install a new hard drive.

debugfs

This is an `ext2` filesystem debugger, with 34 built-in commands. If you call it with

```
# debugfs /dev/hda3
```

you can examine your filesystem in read-only mode.

Each of these utilities can help you maintain, diagnose, and repair a filesystem. But what if you can't boot? Read on!

Red Hat to the Rescue! When the System Won't Boot

There are a number of reasons why a Linux system might not boot. If you recall the earlier example of making a boot disk, you know that the `rdev` command is used to set the root device. Building a new kernel, and then trying to use LILO or `LOADLIN` to load the new kernel, won't work unless you've done this. You'll also have problems if you've rebuilt the kernel and hard-coded in the wrong root device.

I told you earlier that you'll appreciate being a Red Hat user. Here's another good reason: You get a set of emergency boot disks with your Red Hat distribution. If your system won't boot, here's how to possibly recover your system:

First, boot Linux from your Red Hat Linux boot disk. Next, at the `boot:` prompt, type `boot: rescue`, which will load a kernel from the disk. Follow the prompts, and when asked, insert the second disk, called "Supplemental Disk." A bar graph will show loading progress of a compressed filesystem, and you'll end up with a `#` prompt.

Under the sbin and usr/bin directories, you'll find a minimal set of programs. The idea is to at least get you to the point where you can try to check your existing partitions, and possibly mount your drive. For example, if you have a Linux partition on /dev/hda3, you can try

```
# mount -t ext2 /dev/hda3 tmp
```

to mount your partition under tmp, and then attempt a fix. If you've installed Red Hat Linux, and for some reason your system won't boot, and you don't have your Red Hat boot disks, you can also try booting from your Red Hat Linux CD-ROM. Reboot your computer to DOS, change directory to the CD-ROM and then DOSUTILS, and then type AUTOBOOT, which will execute the AUTOBOOT.BAT batch file and put you into the Red Hat installation process.

As a final note, you should remember that if you add another hard drive to your Linux system, be sure to make an entry for its partition in /etc/fstab so the drive will automatically be mounted when you next start your system.

For More Information

For information regarding the Linux boot process, a host of handy tips on building boot disks, pointers to boot disk packages, and a number of helpful scripts, see Tom Fawcett and Graham Chapman's "Linux Bootdisk HOWTO" under /usr/doc/HOWTO or at http://sunsite.unc.edu/mdw/linux.html.

You should also look for the following rescue packages and other helpful utilities at http://sunsite.unc.edu/pub/Linux/system/recovery:

- Scott Burkett's Bootkit
- Oleg Kibirev's CatRescue
- Thomas Heiling's Rescue Shell Scripts
- Karel Kubat's SAR—Search and Rescue
- Tom Fawcett's YARD

Read the man pages for the following commands on your Red Hat Linux system:

- badblocks
- debugfs
- dump
- dumpe2fs
- e2fsck
- fsck
- fstab
- halt
- hdparm
- init

- `inittab`
- `mke2fs`
- `mount`
- `rdev`
- `restore`
- `shutdown`
- `swapon`
- `tune2fs`

If you ever lose or destroy your copies of the Red Hat Linux boot disks, you can get replacements at `http://www.redhat.com/ftp.html`.

For details on how 4.4BSD boots, see Tabbed Section 1 of *4.4BSD System Manager's Manual.* For details about other UNIX boot processes, see *UNIX Unleashed: System Administrator's Edition.*

For loads of tips on maintaining your system, and background information about different Linux filesystems, see Lars Wirzenius's *Linux System Administrators' Guide 0.5.* You'll find a copy at `ftp://sunsite.unc.edu/pub/Linux/docs/LDP`.

If you're interested in a Linux filesystem defragmenter, check out Stephen Tweedie and Alexei Vovenko's defragmenter. You'll find it at `http://sunsite.unc.edu/pub/Linux/system/filesystems/defrag-0.6.tar.gz`.

Summary

This chapter covers a number of topics concerning starting and shutting down Linux, including the following:

- How Linux boots
- How Linux starts
- What runlevels are and when to use them
- How to start and stop processes properly
- How to use Red Hat's `tksysv` runlevel editor
- How to properly shut down your Linux system
- How to properly restart your Linux system
- The do's and don'ts of maintaining your system
- How to create a root disk and copy of your kernel
- How to possibly undelete a file
- How to possibly recover and remount a Linux partition

CHAPTER 5

Configuring and Building Kernels

by Steve Shah

IN THIS CHAPTER

The kernel is the program that is loaded at boot time which provides an interface between the user-level programs and the hardware. Its functionality includes performing the actual task switching that occurs in multitasking systems, handling requests to read and write to disks, dealing with the network interface, and managing memory. It is these functions that give Linux its underlying behavior seen throughout the system.

Technically, Linux is only the kernel. The programs that surround it, such as the compilers, editors, windowing managers, and so on, make up the distribution. (For example, Red Hat Linux is considered a *distribution* of Linux.) Therefore, several different distributions of Linux exist, but the kernel remains common among them.

The kernel is important because it is the glue that holds everything together. Working as a central command post for the system, it manages all the programs running, their memory allocation, their means of accessing the disk, and so on. Without the kernel, there is no Linux.

The default kernel that comes on the CD-ROM is the 2.0.30 kernel. This kernel, which is automatically installed, contains support for a large number of devices, thereby making it flexible. Unless you have a particularly unusual configuration, the standard issue kernel with Red Hat should work on your machine without any changes.

Although the standard issue kernel will work, you might need to add support for a new device or simply pare down the list of devices the kernel supports so that it takes less memory. Either way, you will need to step through the kernel configuration process.

WARNING

Recompiling a new kernel can be potentially dangerous. By doing so, you can easily deny yourself access to the system, so be sure to follow all the safety tips in this chapter. Being locked out of your own machine because of a silly mistake is one of the most frustrating results than can occur.

At the very least, you should have a boot disk ready. Test it and verify that it comes up as you expect it to. Be familiar with the commands necessary to mount the root partition, make changes to key files (for example, `/etc/lilo.conf`), and rerun LILO.

An Introduction to the Linux Kernel

Now that you have an understanding of what the kernel does, you might find a need to reconfigure and build it. In this section, I discuss the preamble to the process: acquiring the source code and installing it in the correct place.

Acquiring the Source Tree

The CD-ROM that comes with this book contains an RPM for the kernel source tree. To use it, simply install it using the `rpm` package. You can find updated versions of the kernel source at `www.redhat.com` or from one of the following:

- `http://www.kernel.org`
- `ftp://ftp.cdrom.com/pub/linux/sunsite/kernel`
- `ftp://sunsite.unc.edu/pub/Linux/kernel`
- `ftp://tsx-11.mit.edu/pub/linux/sources/system`

The source tree comes in one large file titled `linux-X.X.XX.tar.gz`, where `X.X.XX` is the version number of the kernel. For this example, you will use version 2.0.30.

NOTE

Version numbers in Linux have more significance than what may appear to you at first glance. To understand what I mean, look at the kernel used in this chapter–2.0.30.

The version number is broken up into three parts: the major number, the minor number, and the revision number. The major version number–2 in this kernel–rarely changes. Every time the number increases, major improvements have been made in the kernel, and upgrades are definitely warranted.

The minor number–0 in this kernel–indicates the kernel's stability. Even-numbered kernels (for example, 0, 2, 4, and so on) are considered stable production-quality kernels, whereas odd-numbered kernels (for example, 1, 3, 5, and so on) are development kernels. When a kernel reaches a production version, no more features are added, and the only changes made to it are to fix any last-minute bugs.

In contrast, odd-numbered kernels are actively being worked on. They contain experimental code and feature the latest developments. The side effect of these added features is the instability that may exist in them. Sometimes they are stable; other times they have critical flaws. Odd-numbered kernels should be used only on systems on which users are comfortable trying out new features and can accept downtime incurred by frequent kernel upgrades.

The last number, which is the revision number, indicates the current patch level for this version of the release. During the development phase, new versions can be released as often as twice a week.

If you decide to download a more recent source tree instead of using the version on the CD-ROM, you need to decompress and untar it. You should do so in the `/usr/src` directory because symbolic links from `/usr/include` have already been set up. By manipulating the

/usr/src directory so that /usr/src/linux always points to the most recent kernel, you don't have to fix the /usr/include directories every time you compile a new kernel. (See the following tip.)

To unpack the kernel, simply run

```
tar xzf linux-2.0.30.tar.gz
```

where linux-2.0.30.tar.gz is the name of the kernel you downloaded. This line decompresses and untars the kernel into the /usr/src/linux directory.

TIP

If you have an older kernel in place, you might not want to remove the previous source tree. After all, if you need to revert back to it, not having to download it again would be nice! Instead, create a new directory titled linux-2.0.30, where 2.0.30 is the version number of the new kernel. Then create a symbolic link from /usr/src/linux to /usr/src/linux-2.0.30. By doing so, you can easily repoint the symbolic link to new kernels as they are released. As a side benefit, your /usr/include directories can always remain pointed to /usr/src/linux.

If this is the first kernel you've compiled, be sure to take a few minutes to read the /usr/src/linux/README file. It contains up-to-the-minute details about the exact kernel you are working with as well as problem reporting information.

TIP

Due to the amount of concurrent development done in the Linux community, you might find that not all the drivers provided with the Linux kernel are the latest. If you have problems with a particular device, searching on the Internet to see whether a more recent version of the driver is available is often worthwhile.

For example, if you are having problems with the 3Com 3C59x driver, a quick peek at the source code shows that you can reach the author of the driver, Donald Becker, at linux-vortex@cesdis.gsfc.nasa.gov. Searching on the keywords linux vortex on the AltaVista search engine (www.altavista.digital.com) turns up the primary Web site for the development of this driver (http://cesdis.gsfc.nasa.gov/pub/linux/drivers/vortex.html) from which you can download the latest version and include it into your source tree.

Patching the Source Tree

As each new version of the source tree is released, a corresponding patch also is released containing the differences between the two versions. The patch, as you can imagine, is much smaller than the entire new source tree, thereby making it a much quicker upgrade.

When you're patching the Linux kernel, keep in mind that patches apply to only one particular version of the Linux kernel. For example, if you have the 2.0.27 kernel, the only patch that will apply to it is for the 2.0.28 kernel. If you want to bring your kernel up to version 2.0.30, you will need to apply three patches: 2.0.28, 2.0.29, and 2.0.30. The patch files are available in the same directories as the kernel sources at the FTP and Web sites mentioned previously in this chapter.

After you download a patch, you need to use a combination of the tar and patch programs to make the changes. Begin by moving the patch into the `/usr/src` directory. After it is there, run the commands

```
cd /usr/src
gzip -cd patch-XX.gz ¦ patch -p0
```

where *XX* is the version number of the patch you are applying. For example, you would apply the following to the 2.0.29 kernel:

```
cd /usr/src
gzip -cd patch-2.0.30.gz ¦ patch -p0
```

After you apply the patch, check for any files ending in `.rej` in the `/usr/src/linux` directory. If you find such files there, verify that you applied the patch correctly. If you are sure you patched correctly, watch for an update patch within a day or two. If an error occurs with the patch file, a new version of the patch will appear.

Modules

Modules are chunks of the kernel that are not permanently loaded into memory at boot time. Instead, they are loaded on demand and after a period of non-use are removed from memory. Modules are commonly used for networking code on a machine that is not permanently connected, supporting devices not often used, and so on. Although you can make even commonly used kernel code a module, you might find that the overhead in reloading it often outweighs the benefits of it being removed from memory when not in use.

The Linux kernel as of version 2.0 has easy-to-use support for modules. Modules have, for all practical purposes, become transparent in their operation. If you are curious about the details of their operation, read the documentation that comes with the `insmod`, `rmmod`, `ksyms`, and `lsmod` programs.

Configuring the Linux Kernel

Now that you have the kernel source tree unpacked and ready to go in `/usr/src/linux`, you can begin the configuration.

> **WARNING**
>
> Before making any key changes to a system, such as installing a new kernel, you should have a boot disk ready. In the unfortunate event that you misconfigure something (and everybody does eventually), you will need a way to get back into your system.
>
> If you are only compiling a new kernel and not making any other key changes, you can simplify the emergency rescue process by making a backup of the kernel and modules on the root partition. Modify the `/etc/lilo.conf` file to allow you to boot to your currently working kernel as an option. This step is important because not all new kernels work as advertised, especially if you are compiling a development kernel. Booting another kernel right off your root partition is substantially easier than booting off floppies to regain control.

You can configure the Linux kernel in one of three ways. The first (and original) method is to use the `make config` command. It provides you with a text-based interface for answering all the configuration options. You are prompted for all the options you need to set up your kernel.

The text-based interface is a good backup for instances in which you don't have fancy screen control (for example, your console is an old terminal for which you don't have a `termcap` setting); hence, you should be familiar with it.

More likely, however, you will have a standard PC console. If so, you can use the `make menuconfig` command, which provides all the kernel options in an easy-to-use menu. For the sample configuration in this chapter, you will use the `make xconfig` command, which provides a full graphical interface to all the kernel options.

Starting the Configuration

For the sample configuration, assume that the system is a generic Pentium class PC with an EIDE hard drive, IDE CD-ROM, an Adaptec 2940 SCSI card, and a 3Com 3C905 Ethernet card. The system is being configured as a server, so use a stock 2.0.30 kernel. (Remember: Never use development kernels on production systems!)

To start the configuration tool, change into the directory `/usr/src/linux` and invoke the following command:

```
make xconfig
```

After a brief pause (some text will scroll down your screen), a window like the one shown in Figure 5.1 appears.

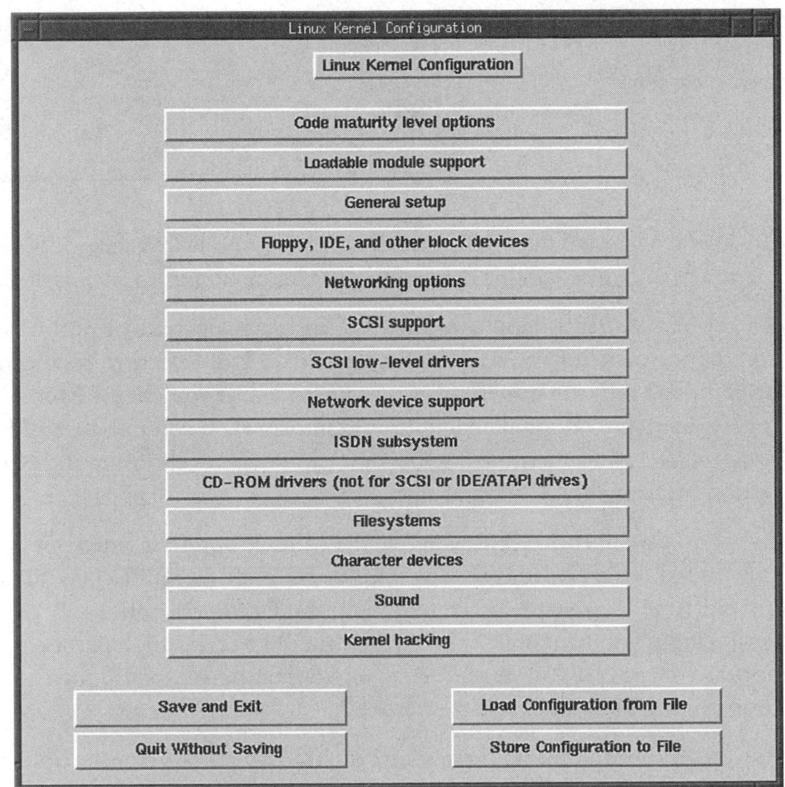

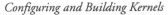

FIGURE 5.1.
Kernel configuration main menu.

The menu options, which are centered in the middle of the window, start with Code maturity level options and end with Kernel hacking. By using the four buttons below the menu, you can load or save configurations to disk for further work.

Stepping Through the Menus

Under each top-level menu in this opening window is a list of options that you can tag to either compile into the kernel, compile as a module, or not include at all. Remember that each option that you elect to compile into the kernel makes the kernel a little larger, thereby requiring more memory. Therefore, include only what you need, but be sure to include key system functions into the kernel such as network drivers and filesystem support for your boot drive. Essentially, you should add any feature you will need on a constant basis. Features that are not often used, such as PPP support, are best compiled as modules.

To start, take a close look at the menu under Code maturity level options. Begin by clicking that menu. This action brings up the Code maturity level options window, as shown in Figure 5.2.

FIGURE 5.2.
The Code maturity level options menu.

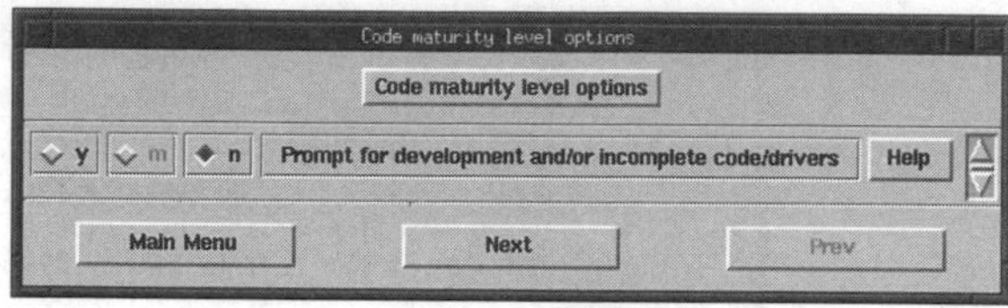

At the top of the window is the title of the menu, and below the title is the list of options. This menu has only one option, Prompt for development and/or incomplete code/drivers.

To the left of this window are your choices for this particular option. The three choices for each option are `y` for Yes, `m` for Module, and `n` for No. Selecting Yes means that the option will be compiled into the kernel and always be loaded. If you choose Module, the kernel will load that segment of code on demand. (For example, when you initiate a PPP connection, the corresponding PPP code is loaded.) As you can imagine, choosing the No option excludes this option from the kernel altogether.

As you can see in the current window, the Module option is faded out (grayed or dimmed). In this case, this particular option by itself doesn't add or remove anything from the kernel but instead serves as a guide to the rest of the configuration options. Because the kernel you are compiling is going for use in a server, you should not try any experimental code, so be sure this option is set to No. Any experimental sections of the kernel will then be automatically grayed, thus making them not available for use.

As you go through the configuration, you'll likely come across options that you don't know. As you upgrade kernels, you will find that these options are typically new ones that someone has recently added but that are not well publicized. You can select a help option that is located at the right of each option. Clicking the Help button opens another window describing the option. Simply click the OK button to close the help window.

After you finish working with this menu, you can take one of three actions. You can click the Main Menu button to close the current window and return to the menu shown in Figure 5.1, you can click the Next button to go to the next configuration submenu, or you can click the Prev button to go to the previous configuration submenu. Because Code maturity level options is the first configuration submenu, the Prev button is faded out in this window, leaving you access only to the Main Menu and Next buttons. Go ahead and click Next now.

Loadable Module Support

As I discussed earlier, loadable modules are chunks of the kernel that are loaded on demand. This feature gives you the benefit of being able to support features not often used without taking up additional memory during periods of non-use.

The Loadable module support submenu in this particular kernel version consists of three options, as you can see in Figure 5.3.

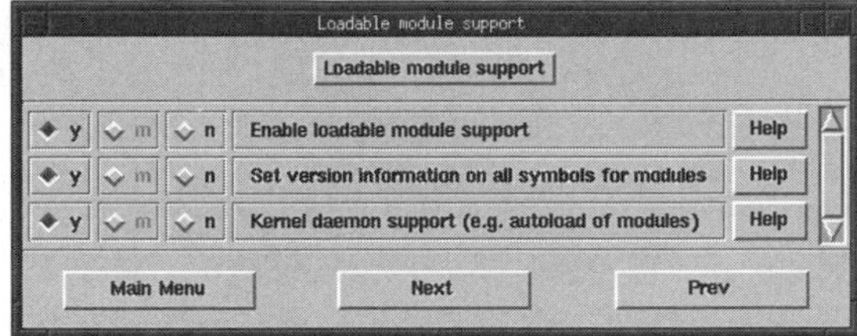

FIGURE 5.3.
The Loadable module support menu.

You need to choose the first option, Enable loadable module support, if you want to be able to make lesser-used features of the kernel loadable modules. Leave this option marked as Yes unless you have a specific reason not to have moduleless kernel. Tagging it No dims the other two options.

The next option, Set version information on all symbols for modules, allows you to use modules that were originally compiled for a different version of the kernel in the current kernel if they are compatible. You should leave this option tagged Yes.

The last option, Kernel daemon support, you'll definitely want to leave tagged Yes if you are using modules. This way, the `kerneld` program can automatically load modules on demand instead of forcing you to explicitly load and unload modules by hand.

General Setup

On the General setup submenu, shown in Figure 5.4, you can configure several key elements of the kernel. With these options, assume that they should be tagged Yes with the notable exception of Limit memory to low 16MB, which should be tagged No.

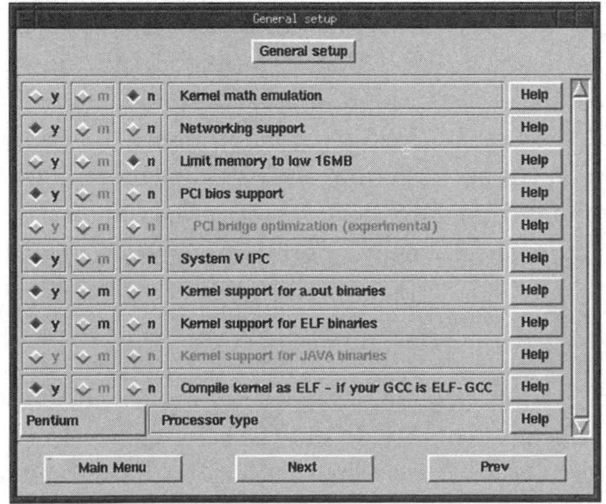

FIGURE 5.4.
The General setup menu.

You should turn on the first option, Kernel math emulation, only if you are compiling a kernel on a CPU with no math coprocessor chip. This feature is applicable only to systems with i386dx, i386sx, or i486sx chips and no corresponding math coprocessors. All Pentium class machines have math coprocessor support built into them. Selecting Yes for this option increases the kernel size by 45 kilobytes. Kernel math support cannot be compiled as a module.

If you plan to attach your machine to any kind of network, whether a LAN or via modem, you need to select Yes for Networking support. Because Networking support determines whether other options will be presented to you later and is not a feature in itself, you cannot select the Module option for it.

Some older motherboards had problems working with memory greater than 16MB. If your system exhibits this behavior, you should set Limit memory to low 16MB to Yes. Otherwise, leave it tagged No.

> **TIP**
>
> If you have over 64MB of memory in your system, you need to pass this information explicitly to the kernel. You do so by using the `mem=XXXM` option at the `boot:` prompt, where *XXX* is the amount of RAM you have in megabytes. See Chapter 3, "LILO," on configuring LILO to set this option as part of your default boot process.

Unless you know for sure that all the programs you plan to run on the system do not require InterProcess Communication (IPC, a method by which two programs running concurrently on one system can communicate with one another), you should set System V IPC to Yes. Many programs do not work unless this option is turned on. Because of the tight integration that is required between IPC and the kernel, this option cannot be compiled as a module.

When Linux was first created, programs that it could run had to in `a.out` format. (Programs are known as binaries in UNIX.) This format specifies how each program is structured internally and how the kernel needs to process the program while loading it into memory. For several reasons, the Linux development community decided to move to the ELF format. All recent development has been using the ELF with `a.out` quickly fading out of use. However, to ensure maximum compatibility with other programs, you should set both the Kernel support for `a.out` binaries and Kernel support for ELF binaries to Yes.

Because you opted not to use any experimental code in the Code maturity level options submenu, the option for kernel support of Java binaries is dimmed here.

The next-to-last option, Compile kernel as ELF - if your GCC is ELF-GCC, should be tagged Yes. GCC, which is the GNU C compiler, has supported the generation for ELF binaries for quite some time now. The version that ships with this book definitely has support.

The last option on this window, Processor type, is a little different from the others. As you can imagine, this option doesn't require a Yes/No answer but instead a list of processors for which the compiler can optimize the kernel. To select your processor type, click the button to the left of the option (in Figure 5.4, this button is labeled *Pentium*) to generate a drop-down box with a list of processors. Click the processor type you have (or the closest one), and you're set.

Floppy, IDE, and Other Block Devices

The Floppy, IDE, and other block devices submenu lists the options you have for basic device support for IDE and floppies as well as some older drive types (for example, MFM and RLL). As the kernel evolves, these options will change slightly.

You definitely should select Yes for Normal floppy disk support because you will have no way of accessing your floppy drives without it. Don't select No for this option because you're looking for a way to secure your floppies from nonroot users; instead change the permissions on `/dev/fd0` to `0600`.

If you have an IDE hard drive (like the sample system does), you should select Yes for Enhanced IDE/MFM/RLL disk/cdrom/tape support. Selecting No dims all the IDE options in the rest of the submenu. Because you're using this option, the next option (Old harddisk (MFM/RLL/IDE) driver) is dimmed.

The remainder of the IDE options are for support for specific chipsets. This information varies from machine to machine. When you're in doubt, selecting Yes for these options doesn't hurt, but it will result in a larger kernel. Each driver will automatically probe the system at boot time to determine whether it should or should not be activated.

You can select Yes for Loopback device support if you have a special need to mount a file as a filesystem (for example, for testing an ISO9660 image before burning it to a CD). You should also select Yes for Loopback device support if you intend on using the Common Desktop Environment. For most people, however, this option should be tagged No.

The Multiple devices driver support option turns on a special driver that allows you to connect multiple partitions (even on different disks) together to work as one large partition. Unless you are a systems administrator configuring this item, you should set this option to No. If you plan to set up this feature, be sure to read the `./drivers/block/README.md` file in the Linux source tree. The options for using Linear (append) mode and RAID-0 (striping) mode are applicable only if you plan to use Multiple devices driver support.

RAM disk support is provided in the kernel to allow you to create virtual filesystems in your system's memory. This feature is really useful only if you are creating a special kernel for use on boot disks. For most instances, select No for RAM disk support. Doing so automatically dims the Initial RAM disk (initrd) support option.

Unless you have a very old hard disk that you need to use with this machine, you should leave the XT harddisk support option tagged No. If you do need to support a very old hard disk, seriously consider making the investment in upgrading the device to something more current—if not for your performance, at least for the safety of the data.

Networking Options

Because of the rate at which network technology evolves, covering specifics is difficult because they become outdated too quickly. For this section on the Networking options, I'll cover the basics along with some security notes. For specific features, you should check the help box attached to each option on the Networking options submenu.

Before getting into details, you should have a clear idea of what sorts of networking features you expect your machine to offer. If your machine will spend a great deal of its time serving or as a user's desktop machine, you should keep the network configuration simple and not provide any elaborate services. On the other hand, if the machine is destined to become a gateway/proxy service, you should pay attention to the details.

NOTE

Because of the rapid developments in the networking industry, many options are still experimental code. As a result, many of the Networking options will be dimmed if you opted not to use any experimental code in the kernel. Don't be alarmed.

Assuming that you do want to join the network, you must turn on two of the options. The first, of course, is TCP/IP networking. Tagging this option No dims all the other options. The other option you must turn on is IP: syn cookies. Enabling this option is especially important if you are going to be attached to the Internet in one way or another because it provides protection against SYN attacks. (For additional details on SYN attacks as well as a various other security-related issues, visit the CERT home page at `http://www.cert.org`.)

The essence of many of the Networking options is the ability to configure Linux to act as either a router or a firewall. To access the firewalling options, be sure to enable the Network firewall, Network aliasing, and IP: forwarding/gatewaying options. If you plan to use your Linux machine in this fashion, you will probably want to enable the IP: accounting and IP: optimize as router not host options.

If you have trouble connecting to your Linux machine via Telnet from an older DOS system, you might want to select Yes for IP: PC/TCP compatibility mode. Turning on this option allows Linux to communicate with the older (and broken) software on the DOS side. The IP: Disable Path MTU Discovery (normally enabled) option can also be a cause of problems with older systems. Normally, Linux starts by sending larger packets of data across the network. If it finds a machine that cannot handle the larger size, it brings the size down until everyone is happy. Some older DOS machines with poorly written software don't handle this technique well and need to have this option disabled. If that is the case, check Yes for this option.

The IP: Reverse ARP option is useful if machines on the network use Address Resolution Protocol (ARP) to determine the network's IP address based on its Ethernet address. (Typically, this client is diskless.) Enabling this option allows Linux to answer such queries. Look into running `rarp` for further information about this protocol.

Another security issue you will need to contend with (especially if you are attached to the Internet) is source routed frames. IP allows for a machine originating a packet to specify the exact path of a packet from source to destination. This capability is rarely useful and is often used as a method of attacking machines across the Internet. Unless you are sure of what you're doing, you should select Yes for the IP: Drop source routed frames option.

Along with these TCP/IP-centric options are a few other protocol options such as IPX and AppleTalk. If you work in a heterogeneous environment with Macintoshes and Windows/Novell-based PCs, you might want to enable these options, but doing so isn't required as long as the other machines can talk TCP/IP. The most common use of enabling AppleTalk, for example, is to be able to use AppleTalk-based printers.

SCSI Support

If you plan to use any SCSI chains on your system, you should select either Yes or Module for all the options on the SCSI support submenu, as shown in Figure 5.5. (If you're using SCSI disks, Yes is a better option.)

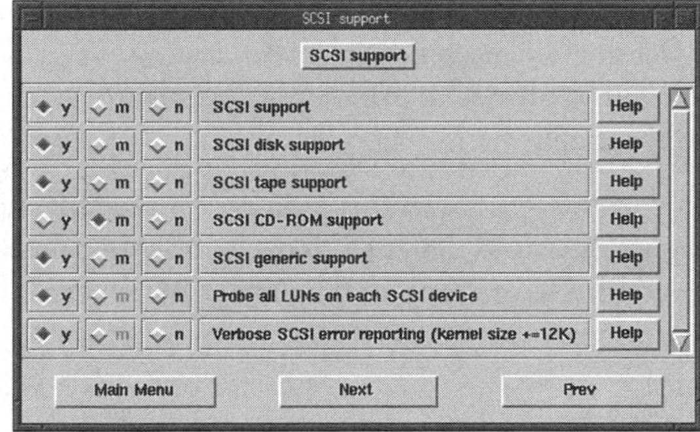

FIGURE 5.5.
The SCSI support menu.

The only option worth explicitly mentioning on this submenu is Verbose SCSI error reporting (kernel size +=12K), which, when enabled, gives detailed error messages in the event of a failure somewhere along the way. Although selecting this option costs some memory, it is often worthwhile when you need to debug an error condition quickly.

Because the sample system requires SCSI, select Yes for all options except SCSI CD-ROM support because you're using an IDE CD-ROM. If you are also using a SCSI CD-ROM, you might want to select the Module option because most systems access the CD-ROM infrequently.

SCSI Low-Level Drivers

Obviously, if you don't select Yes to SCSI in the SCSI support submenu, the SCSI low-level drivers submenu isn't relevant to you.

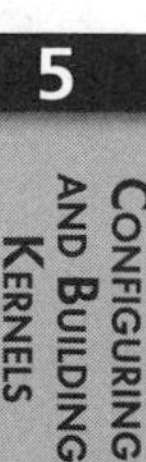

Like the submenu in Network support, the list of SCSI drivers supported by Linux increases regularly. For every SCSI card you have in your system, simply tag the option either as Yes if you intend to make heavy use of it or Module if it will have occasional only use (for example, a SCSI tape drive).

After you select the driver you want, be sure to read the corresponding help. It might contain information about where to obtain current drivers and bug fixes (if any are available).

Network Device Support

The Network device support submenu lists the drivers available for networking. This list includes the necessary drivers to control Ethernet cards, PPP connections, SLIP, Token Ring, and so on.

You must select Yes for the first option, Network device support, if you want to select any of the other options. Otherwise, checking No dims the other options.

The next option, Dummy net driver support, provides dummy network interfaces. This capability is often used for machines providing virtual domains in which each virtual interface receives its own IP address.

The last general option is for EQL support. EQL is a means by which two modems using PPP or SLIP can work together to provide double the transfer speed. Your choice for this option is based on the fact that the machine you are connecting to can also support this capability. Unless you know you will be providing this support, be sure to check No for the EQL (serial line load balancing) support option.

The remainder of the options in this submenu are for specific network interfaces. Note that some of them are questions designed to make other options available to you. For example, if you select Yes for the 3Com cards option, all the 3Com cards that are supported become available for you to select.

ISDN Subsystem

The ISDN subsystem submenu doesn't provide many options for ISDN users to configure. Most people should select No for the first option, ISDN support. Doing so dims the other options in the submenu.

If you do need ISDN support, begin by selecting Yes for the first option. This way, you can configure the other items on the submenu. Because of the nature of ISDN, be sure to find out whether your provider supports some of the options that Linux supports (for example, VJ-compression with synchronous PPP).

CD-ROM Drivers

On the CD-ROM drivers submenu, you can select the option to support non-SCSI/IDE/ATAPI CD-ROM drives. As with the other lists of drivers, you need to select Yes only for the devices that you have attached to your system.

Filesystems

Linux has a great deal of support for other filesystems, thereby allowing you to use disks from other systems without any conversion process. The most notable support is for the DOS-based filesystems.

As of the 2.0.30 kernel, the following filesystems on the Filesystems submenu are available for your use:

Filesystem	*Description*
Minix	This original Linux filesystem is still used by boot disks and common floppy disks. This option should be tagged Yes.
Extended fs	This first successor to the Minix is no longer used. There is no good reason to enable support for this filesystem.
Second extended fs	This is the current default Linux filesystem. You should definitely select Yes for this option. Remember: Your root filesystem cannot be a module.
`xiafs` filesystem	This filesystem was introduced at the same time as the Second extended fs as a replacement for the Extended fs; however, it never really caught on and is rarely used today. Unless you have a specific need, you should select No for this option.
DOS FAT fs	This particular option isn't a filesystem but a foundation for other FAT-based filesystems such as MS-DOS FAT, VFAT (Windows 95), and `umsdos` support.
MS-DOS FAT fs	If you want to be able to access DOS-based systems from Linux, you need to set this option to Yes. This capability is especially useful for dual boot systems.
VFAT (Windows 95) fs	VFAT is the upgrade from the original MS-DOS FAT structure; it includes support for long filenames. Again, if you are in a dual boot situation, having this capability is a good idea.
`umsdos`	This UNIX-like filesystem resides on top of the standard MS-DOS format. This capability is useful if you want to run Linux over your DOS partition occasionally. For a serious system, you should not need this support. (Red Hat Linux does not support running on a `umsdos` filesystem.)

continues

Filesystem	*Description*
/proc	To simplify access to system information, the /proc filesystem was created to provide an intuitive interface. Although it appears to exist on your hard disk, it doesn't take up any actual space. Many programs rely on your having this capability in place, so be sure to include support for it.
NFS	The Network File System (NFS) support is needed if you intend to access remote filesystems through this standard protocol. For a server, this capability is a must.
SMB	This network protocol was developed for Windows for Workgroups (also known as LanManager). This capability is useful only if you need to have direct access to Windows 95 or NT files as part of your filesystem. For most people, this option should be tagged No. For a server, you might want to select Module for this option because you never know where you're going to have to connect your machine.
NCP	NetWare support is done through the NCP protocol. Like SMB, this capability isn't terribly useful for most people; however, if you are in the process of transitioning away from NetWare, selecting this option is a useful way to provide a seamless transition.
ISO9660	The ISO9660 filesystem is necessary if you intend to use CD-ROMs because many CD-ROMs are encoded in this format. If you have a CD-ROM attached to your machine, be sure to select Yes for this option.
OS/2 HPFS	Support for the OS/2 filesystem, HPFS, is read-only under Linux. Most people should select No for this option.
System V and Coherent	These two filesystems are from very old versions of UNIX and are useful only as means of transitioning old data to new filesystems. Most people should select No for this option.
Amiga FFS	The Amiga support is still considered experimental code and should be used with caution.
UFS	UFS is available on several other UNIX systems, most notably Solaris and SunOS. (Under SunOS, it was known as 4.2.) The support for this filesystem is read-only.

NOTE

If you plan to access a filesystem over the network, you do not need to support the remote filesystem directly. You do need to support NFS, however. For example, if you intend to mount a disk residing on a Solaris system, you do not need UFS support, only NFS.

The Quota support option on this submenu is for people who need to limit the amount of disk space being used by each user. Currently, this capability is supported only with the second extended filesystem (`ext2`).

The last option in this submenu is for Mandatory lock support. Typically, file locking is done at the application level; however, there is an attempt to force locks on all files with this feature. As of the 2.0.30 kernel, the additional software to support this feature isn't available, so do not enable this option unless you are certain as to what you are doing.

Character Devices

Character devices work in a different manner than block devices. Block devices are typically disks, tape drives, and so on that transfer data in large chunks. In contrast, character devices transfer only one byte of data at a time; hence, they are typically keyboards, mice, serial ports, and so on.

As its name implies, the Character devices submenu is for the configuration of character devices in the kernel. This configuration is usually for your mouse, serial ports, and parallel ports, but a few unusual devices fall under this category as well.

To get basic support for your serial ports, you need to set the Standard/generic serial support option to Yes or Module. Unless you have a specific serial card such as an 8-port card, you do not need any additional serial support.

If you plan to use your printer or connect to a network via PLIP, be sure to set Parallel printer support to Yes also.

Mouse support comes in two flavors. You can use serial mice or bus mice. If you use serial mice, you do not need to explicitly turn on the Mouse Support option because the Standard/Generic serial support covers this capability. If you use a bus mouse, you need to set Mouse Support (not serial mice) to Yes and indicate which particular mouse you have attached to the machine.

The remaining options in the Character devices submenu are unusual and often unused features or hardware. Unless you explicitly know that your system uses them, select No for these options.

Sound

> **NOTE**
>
> Before you attempt to configure kernel support for your sound card, be sure you have the correct IRQ and I/O Base Memory address.

To enable sound card support in the kernel, begin by selecting Yes for the first option for Sound card support in the Sound submenu. By doing so, you can select which sound card you have in your system.

After you select Yes for the appropriate sound card in your system, scroll down to the section for providing the appropriate IRQ, DMA, and Base I/O address information. Although the information required varies from card to card, you should be able to get this information from the manual or the on-card jumper settings.

Kernel Hacking

Because the Linux kernel is available in source code form, many people have taken an interest in its underlying functionality for one reason or another. To facilitate these people, additional debugging information can be compiled into the kernel by selecting Yes for the Kernel profiling support option.

As part of the profiling support, many functions are invoked with the intention of trying to force them to fail. This capability is useful during development to ensure that all possible paths of execution are exercised and tested. The result is a kernel that is less stable; hence, unless you truly understand the hows and whys of the kernel, you should leave the Kernel profiling support option tagged No.

Final Notes About Configuration

Configuring a kernel can be tricky. Be ready to spend some time learning the options and the effects each option has on others. You can easily misconfigure a kernel, so don't feel bad if integrating a new feature correctly takes a few tries. As with any learning endeavor, as you gain experience, you will be able to get the job done right more quickly and with less heartache.

After you set all your options, be sure to save the configuration and not just quit without saving. The options are then written to a file that is read as part of the compilation. Based on your selections, only what is necessary is compiled.

Building the Kernel

Now that you have a configured kernel, you are ready to compile it. In comparison, the entire process, known as *building the kernel,* is much easier than the configuration process.

Before you begin, however, be prepared to wait. Depending on system speed, available memory, and other processes, compiling the kernel can take from 10 minutes for a fast Pentium to 1.5 hours for a slow i386. The process will also slow down your system for other tasks. If you are sharing CPU time with other people, you might want to wait until the CPU is less busy before embarking on this task.

The magic command to start the build is as follows:

```
make dep;make clean;make zImage
```

This line actually contains three commands in one. The first one, `make dep`, actually takes your configuration and builds the corresponding dependency tree. This process determines what gets compiled and what doesn't. The next step, `make clean`, erases all previous traces of a compilation so as to avoid any mistakes in which version of a feature gets tied into the kernel. Finally, `make zImage` does the full compilation. After the process is complete, the kernel is compressed and ready to be installed.

NOTE

As the kernel compiles, all the commands necessary to do the actual compilation will scroll down your screen. Although you don't need to understand the compilation process in detail, having some background in C programming and `Makefiles` is useful. Having this knowledge typically makes troubleshooting a little easier because the error messages make more sense. If you do not have this sort of background, look out for messages such as

```
make:***[directory/file.o] Error 1
```

where `[directory/file.o]` is the file at which the compilation failed. Take note of the first message starting with gcc after the preceding line. For example, if the output looks like

```
gcc -D__KERNEL__ -I/usr/src/linux/include -Wall -Wstrict-prototypes -O2
➥-fomit-frame-pointer -fno-strength-reduce -pipe -m486 -malign-loops=2
➥-malign-jumps=2 -malign-functions=2 -DCPU=586  -c -o init/main.o init/main.c
init/main.c:53: warning: function declaration isn't a prototype
init/main.c: In function `main':
init/main.c:53: storage class specified for parameter `_stext'
[...]
make:***[init/main.o] Error 1
```

you're interested in the line that says

```
init/main.c:53: warning function declaration isn't a prototype
```

Be sure to include this information when requesting help.

Before you can install the new kernel, you need to compile the corresponding modules. You do so by using the following command:

```
make modules
```

Again, watch for errors in the compilation.

Installing the Kernel

After the kernel and its corresponding modules are compiled, you're ready to start the installation.

Begin by checking the current `/boot` directory to see which kernels are presently installed. Most kernels' filenames begin with the `vmlinuz` string, but if you aren't sure, check the `/etc/lilo.conf` file to see which kernels are currently offered at boot time and their locations. (See Chapter 3 for additional information about LILO.)

After you know what the current kernels are, copy the file `/usr/src/linux/arch/i386/boot/zImage` from the kernel source tree to `/boot`, and give it an appropriate new name. For example, the sample kernel is the first kernel compiled with SCSI support in it, so you can use the following `copy` command:

```
cp /usr/src/linux/arch/i386/boot/zImage /boot/vmlinuz-2.0.30-scsi
```

The unique name enables you to see easily why that kernel is different from the others.

With the kernel in place, you're ready to start installing the appropriate kernel modules. As you do with the kernel, you should make a backup of the existing modules before installing the new ones.

To make a backup of the current modules, go into the `/lib/modules` directory and rename the current kernel version number to something else. For example, if the current version is 2.0.30, you can use the following:

```
cd /lib/modules
mv 2.0.30 2.0.30-working
```

This command renames the modules to `2.0.30-working` so that, in the event the new modules don't work as advertised, you can erase the new ones and rename this directory to `2.0.30` and regain control of the system.

After you back up the modules, change back into the kernel source directory and type

```
make modules_install
```

to install the modules into the `/lib/modules/`*`version_number`* directory, where *`version_number`* is the version number of the kernel you just compiled.

Finally, you need to edit the `/etc/lilo.conf` file to make your new kernel one of the boot time options. Do not remove the currently working kernel as an option! You will need it in case the new kernel doesn't work the way you expect it to. Remember to rerun LILO after making changes. Reboot and then test your results.

WARNING

When loading your kernel for the first time after a reboot, you might get the error that the kernel is too large. This happens because the kernel is compressed during the build procedure and then decompressed at boot time. Because of the nature of the Intel architecture, the kernel must be able to decompress within the first 1MB of memory, and if it can't, the system can't boot.

If you receive the "Kernel is too large" message, reboot and choose your old backup kernel to boot from.

At this point you have two choices: You can either go reconfigure your kernel and trim down unnecessary items by either not including them or using them as modules, or you can use `make bzImage` to build a kernel that can work around the kernel size limitation.

Recovering from Faulty Kernels

While you're learning the nuances of the Linux kernel and its parameters, you might make some mistakes and need to recover the system in its prior state. Having backed up your kernels and modules (you did that, right?), this process is relatively easy.

Begin by rebooting the system into single user mode. At the `lilo:` prompt, select the previously working kernel to boot with the kernel parameter `single`. As it boots up, you will notice errors as part of the process. Don't worry; the errors are caused by the mismatched modules in the `/lib/modules` directory.

After you log in, go to the `/lib/modules` directory and erase the current module installation. For example, if you renamed your old modules `2.0.30-working` and your new modules are `2.0.30`, then use the following command:

```
rm -rf 2.0.30
```

Using this command removes all the current modules for the broken kernel. With the broken programs gone, rename the stable kernel with its original name and reboot. This procedure should give you full control of your system again.

Summary

The kernel is the heart of Linux as well as one of its key features; other versions of UNIX have kernels three to four times the size without three to four times the functionality. Of course, this kernel provides the added benefit of the source code as well.

To keep up with the latest developments within the Linux community, you need to keep up with the latest kernel developments. The tools with which you configure and install the kernel have been refined a great deal, thereby making kernel upgrades and installation relatively straightforward tasks.

Like any other aspect of configuring Linux, understanding the details and nuances of the system are important to maintaining a healthy system. In particular, remember the following points:

- Be aware of which kernel version you install on systems. Critical systems should always get even version numbers.
- Make backups of both previous kernels and their corresponding modules. Locking yourself out of your system is a terrible way to waste an afternoon. In addition, keep a boot disk ready in case things go seriously wrong.
- Look for patches instead of downloading an entire new kernel. Using patches will save you a great deal of time.
- Read the `/usr/src/linux/README` file with each kernel distribution. This file will contain important information pertaining to the new release.
- Do not use any experimental code in a kernel destined for production use.
- Read the help information with each kernel option if you aren't sure about that option's functionality.
- Use `make dep;make clean;make zImage` to compile the kernel. Use `make modules;make modules_install` to compile and install modules.
- Compile lesser-used kernel features as modules to reduce kernel memory consumption. However, be sure to include key functions such as filesystem support for the root partition as part of the kernel—not a module.

Finally, don't be afraid of the kernel. Just be cautious, and you'll be fine.

CHAPTER 6

Common Desktop Environment

by Eric Goebelbecker

IN THIS CHAPTER

In 1993, several major software and hardware vendors joined together in an effort to eliminate many of the arbitrary and confusing discrepancies among the various versions of UNIX. These ranged from the monumental, such as key programming interfaces that made it difficult for software developers to support several UNIX versions, to the less complicated but no less bothersome or expensive issues, such as unnecessary variations in file locations, formats, and naming conventions. Regardless of how "big" these differences were, the vendors recognized that some standardization would have to take place if UNIX were to continue to withstand the tough competition provided by Microsoft's Windows NT, which was finally becoming a serious competitor to UNIX in the server arena.

As a solution to the problem of inconsistent user interfaces, the Common Desktop Environment (CDE) was presented in 1995 by Hewlett-Packard, Novell, IBM, and SunSoft (the software division of Sun Microsystems). The CDE addresses not only the problem of inconsistencies among versions of UNIX and among OEM versions of X Window, but also greatly increases the accessibility of UNIX to nontechnical users accustomed to environments such as Windows and Macintosh. The CDE not only presents the same "look and feel" on all supported platforms, but it also provides base applications—such as a networked workgroup calendar, a printer manager, context-sensitive help, and file and application managers—that enable a user to completely avoid the often intimidating shell prompt and occasionally confusing man pages. However, a power user can choose to turn off some of these features and interface directly with the shell and command-line tools while still enjoying a consistent interface if he or she has to use more than one UNIX variant. The CDE is so consistent in UNIX versions that many vendors even distribute much of the same documentation!

In this chapter, I will introduce the CDE implementation distributed by Red Hat Software and developed by TriTeal. This version is fully compliant with the standard developed by the major vendors and is delivered in Red Hat RPM format. Thus, any Red Hat user can easily install it and enjoy the benefits of an easy-to-use GUI interface that is virtually identical to that offered by commercial versions of UNIX, such as IBM's AIX, Hewlett-Packard's HP/UX, and Sun's Solaris, among others.

Installation

The Red Hat Package Manager (RPM) makes it easy to install any application delivered in the proper format. However, the TriTeal CDE is even simpler than most because the installation media supplied by Red Hat Software comes with a shell script that installs the packages for you. It is located in the top-level directory on the CDE CD-ROM and is named `install-cde`.

One reason for the shell script is that the CDE requires several other packages in order to operate properly. Another reason is to enable the user to easily alter the base installation directory. The RPM is fully capable of addressing both these issues, but because a significant part of the CDE's target market is the beginner or nontechnical user, the shell script is provided so that it can quietly handle the dependencies and interactively prompt the user for installation options. A script with the same name and interface is also supplied with other versions of the CDE, so its inclusion further provides consistency with other platforms and vendors.

The packages required by the CDE are typical of standard Red Hat installations. The required set includes the following:

- `pdksh`, which contains the public domain version of the Korn shell
- `libg++` and `gcc`, which provide the GNU compiler and standard C++ libraries
- Several packages for the support of login security, such as `crack` and `pam`
- `portmap`, which is needed for the CDE's network features

All these packages are included on the CDE media, so these dependencies are not an issue. The default root directory for the CDE software is `/usr/dt`, so it is important that the workstation have the required disk space, about 40MB, available in the appropriate partition. However, because the shell script asks the user if another directory should be used, it shouldn't be a problem if the required free space is only available in another partition.

CAUTION

The CDE packages configure the system to automatically start the CDE login manager after a system reboot. Because the login manager runs under X Window, it is important that X Window be configured correctly before the CDE is installed.

Getting Started with the CDE

After the installation script is run, the system should be rebooted. The CDE login manager starts in the last part of the initialization process. If you are watching the system as it initializes, you will see the normal console prompt, but don't bother trying to log in. The login manager will appear shortly, depending on how long it takes X Window to initialize on your system.

Logging in to the CDE

The login manager (`dtlogin`) screen is based on an older X Window application called `xdm`. With it, users are logged directly in to X Window, not only without having to run a shell script such as `startx`, but also with a default environment that can be configured in advance by the system administrator to suit the local environment. Much of this configurability is derived from `xdm`, but like much of the CDE, `dtlogin` adds a lot of new features. From the user's perspective, the login process is simple: Type in the username and press Enter. Then enter the password and press Enter again. `dtlogin` also enables a user to select the type of session he or she wants to start. These sessions can be specified by the administrator, but the default setup will probably suit most users' needs:

- Regular—The full-featured CDE session.
- FVWM-95-2—The `fvwm` window manager with the familiar Linux 95 style menu.
- FVWM—A minimally configured `fvwm` environment.
- Fail-safe—A single X terminal, with no window manager. This session is designed for addressing configuration problems.

These options, as well as `dtlogin`'s appearance, can be extensively modified. See the `dtlogin(1X)` manual page and the CDE documentation for details and examples.

In addition to the Fail-safe session, the Linux virtual terminal feature is still available. In order to change from the CDE to a virtual console, press Ctrl+Alt and F1+F6. In order to return, press Alt+F7.

When a regular session is started from the `dtlogin` screen, the CDE session manager (Xsession) takes over. Xsession executes the programs necessary to start the required desktop session, depending on the workstation and the user's individual configuration options. By modifying the scripts and configuration files processed by Xsession, a user or system administrator can customize CDE's appearance and specify what applications start at login and are available for use during the session. I will cover these options later in the chapter in the section "Customizing Your Session."

After the session is started, the user interacts with the Front Panel, Workspace Manager, Application Manager, and other CDE tools.

The Desktop Environment

When the desktop is finished loading, the first thing a new CDE user probably notices is the Front Panel, which is shown in Figure 6.1. Whereas the Motif and Open Look window managers offer only menus and the FVWM offers menus and simple icons, CDE provides a Front Panel with pop-up and breakaway icon panels, a virtual screen manager, a trash bin similar to that of the Macintosh, and predefined buttons for operations such as logging out, locking the screen, reading mail, and launching several desktop tools.

FIGURE 6.1.
The Front Panel.

After a close inspection of the Front Panel, a new user sees that the CDE offers a lot more than a program launch pad because it supplies its own set of desktop applications and context-sensitive help.

On the far left side of the default panel, the CDE supplies an analog clock, which displays the system time, and a calendar, which has an icon that displays the current date. The calendar is actually a sophisticated scheduling application that provides an appointment manager capable of notifying the user of appointments via sound, blinking video, pop-up windows, and e-mail. It also provides a To Do list manager and a wide variety of calendar views that should satisfy most users. But the real power of the desktop Calendar Manager lies in its network options. By taking advantage of the desktop's networking capabilities, it allows users to share their schedules with any other user of the CDE, regardless of whether they are using the same workstation and without having to copy or share any files. These sharing capabilities are completely configured from the application: No additional administrative work is required.

The next icon on the Front Panel is for the File Manager. This should look familiar to any Macintosh, Windows 95, or `xfm` user. Files can be viewed as icons or names and moved, copied, or deleted with the mouse. As with other file managers, files are moved when they are dragged with the mouse, copied when they are dragged with Shift or Ctrl pressed, and deleted when they are dragged to the Trash icon, which is located in the Control Panel. (All desktop applications share this Trash icon.)

The CDE also supports file associations, much like the Macintosh and Windows operating systems. These associations are governed by desktop actions, which are defined through the Application Manager and can be used in the File Manager. (I'll cover actions in more detail later in the chapter in the section "Customizing Your Session.") These actions enable a user to double-click a file and run the proper application, depending on how that type of file has been defined. The default set of actions provided with the CDE is already very powerful. For example, when a `tar` archive is double-clicked, a window pops up with a table of contents for the archive (a right-click provides an option to actually extract the contents), compressed files are decompressed, and text files are already associated with the desktop GUI editor (but can be reassociated with your favorite editor, such as `vi` or `xemacs`).

The next two icons launch the Text Editor and the Mailer, which are two more desktop tools supplied with the CDE. The Text Editor resembles most GUI text editors, with the addition of the CDE's ever-present help system and some nice little extras like word wrap and an integrated spell-checker. The Mailer uses the same spell-checker and offers a lot of other features, such as the ability to create mail templates and excellent mail folder features.

Above the editor icon is a small arrow that produces a subpanel when clicked (see Figure 6.2). Subpanels are one of the more advanced features of the CDE and also provide an easy method for users to customize their environment. Subpanels can be "torn off" and placed anywhere on the desktop, effectively extending the Front Panel and eliminating the need for the root menu. I'll cover how subpanels can be created in the "Customizing Your Session" section of this chapter.

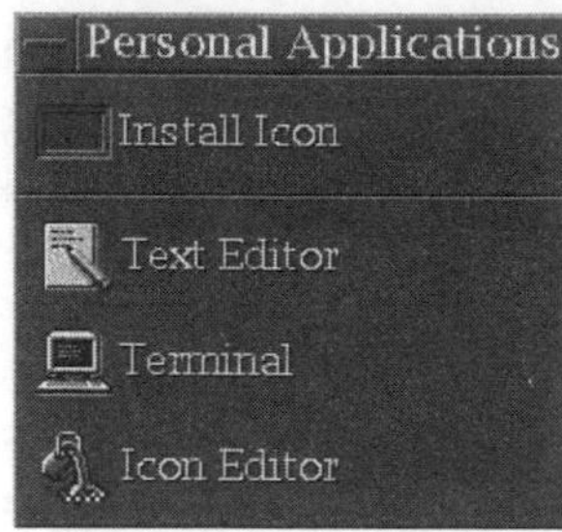

FIGURE 6.2.
A sample subpanel.

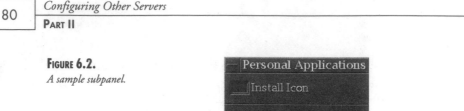

The subpanel located over the Text Editor has an icon for starting a Desktop Terminal (`dtterm`). It is a terminal that very closely resembles an `xterm` but has menus for operations such as changing the font size and cutting and pasting text, making it easier for new users to perform otherwise advanced operations at the shell prompt.

In the middle of the Front Panel, you see the Graphical Workspace Manager (GWM) and some smaller icons that are installed by default. The lock control locks the screen, the exit control logs you out, the green light indicates when the CDE is busy saving a configuration or launching a new application, and the fourth control brings up a separate Workspace Manager window.

The Workspace Manager has a virtual screen manager provided by TriTeal. TriTeal's version of the CDE has some features above and beyond those offered by the CDE. Although the CDE-specified desktop has buttons corresponding to virtual screens (the number of virtual screens defaults to four but can be easily altered; see the "Customizing Your Session" section), the Workspace Manager presents a graphical representation of each screen and its contents and allows windows to be manipulated from within the screen manager.

TIP

Another useful Workspace Manager tool is the application list. To display it, click the Workspace background (also referred to as the *root window*). This will activate the root menu. Select Application list. If you click an application name in this list, it will appear in front. If the application is running in another virtual workspace, it will also appear in front and you will be brought to that virtual screen.

Immediately to the right of the screen manager is the Printer Control, where you can view printers and manage documents. You can also drag documents to the Printer Control to be processed if the appropriate action has been configured for the application that created it.

The next three icons represent the heart of the CDE: the Style Manager, covered in the section "Customizing Your Session"; the Application Manager, also covered in "Customizing Your Session"; and the Help Viewer, explained in detail in "The Help Viewer."

Customizing Your Session

Although the default CDE session offers a lot, chances are you will want to customize your environment. When it comes to configuration options, the architects of the CDE stayed with the true UNIX spirit by supplying many different ways to accomplish the same thing. Most configuration preferences can be altered to suit a user's taste with a few simple clicks of the mouse; just about any aspect of the CDE can be managed through its configuration files at an individual user level, that is, without altering the entire system. This allows power users to tailor their environment as much as they want, while still giving less skilled users a very comfortable environment.

In addition, site administrators can easily tailor the desktop to suit their organization's needs by setting up configuration defaults in a shared system area (usually `/etc/dt`). Files in this area can not only make the necessary applications available, but they can also define what users can and cannot alter on their desktop.

The Style Manager

The Style Manager is one of the most convenient features of the CDE. Most X Window environments require changes to be made through the X resource configuration files, which is too complicated for the average user. Others provide limited configurability through menus and dialog boxes, such as modifying color schemes and basic window behavior, but still leave a bit to be desired when compared to user-friendly systems such as Windows and Macintosh. The CDE's Style Manager goes a long way toward addressing this issue.

The Style Manager, shown in Figure 6.3, is launched from the Front Panel by clicking the icon that resembles an artist's palette.

FIGURE 6.3.
The Style Manager.

With the Style Manager, you can configure various attributes of the CDE using the following options:

- Color—A color palette manager, which comes with more than thirty palettes already defined. Because the CDE is based on the Motif window manager, color can be changed dynamically. Therefore, you can view color changes as you select them. In addition, you can add, delete, or modify palettes. Instead of specifying colors for each display attribute (such as active window, inactive window, and so on), you can adjust the palette with a set of slide controls that affect all aspects of the color scheme as one.

- Font—Enables you to set the default font size for all applications.
- Backdrop—With this option, you can select a bitmap background from the 26 bitmaps that come with the desktop. For each virtual screen, you can choose an individual background to help you keep track of which screen is active.
- Keyboard—Offers the options to choose whether keys will repeat when held and to enable a "click" sound for each keypress.
- Mouse—The CDE offers a surprisingly complete set of options for the mouse. You can switch buttons for left- or right-handedness, adjust the click speed, and set the acceleration and threshold.
- Beep—Allows you to adjust the volume, tone, and length of the default "beep," usually intended as an alert or notifier of an error.
- Screen—Offers you the option of setting the screen to automatically blank after a specified period of inactivity. In addition, you can configure a screen saver that is activated after a similar interval. The screen saver has all the familiar `xlock` options, such as fireworks, fractals, and Conway's "game of life." The screen saver can also be activated from the Front Panel lock control.
- Window—Enables you to select window behavior, such as whether to activate a window by placing the mouse over it or by clicking it.
- Startup—The CDE's startup options are sometimes the source of confusion for new users. This option enables you to select a "home session" or specify that the state of the desktop when you last logged out be restored.

TIP

The CDE cannot restore applications that were started from a command-line session—only those that were started from a desktop application or menu.

The Front Panel

You can customize the Front Panel either from the desktop or by editing configuration files. This section covers the methods available from the desktop. In the section "Advanced Front Panel Customization," I will go over some of the configuration file settings.

The Workspace Manager

Unlike other versions of the CDE, TriTeal places a virtual window manager (called the Workspace Manager) on the front of the toolbar. From this manager, windows can be moved

between virtual workspaces by clicking and dragging with the mouse. However, in the Workspace Manager, windows cannot be dragged from the active workspace the way they can in `olvwm`.

You can configure the Workspace Manager by right-clicking it and selecting the Properties menu entry. From the Properties dialog, you can remove the Workspace Manager from the Front Panel. This will replace it with the default for all CDE versions—buttons that select each virtual workspace. Other options include the number of virtual workspaces and how they will be displayed within the Front Panel or its separate display window.

Subpanels

The initial Front Panel configuration supplies three subpanels: Help, Personal Printers, and Personal Applications. Adding panels is easy, as is adding additional icons to subpanels.

To add a panel, right-click the icons over which the new panel will be added and select the Add Subpanel option. A new panel is created, with two selections already defined: the icon that was already on the Front Panel and an Install Icon selection.

For example, add a subpanel above the Mail control. First, right-click (or left-click if your mouse is in left-handed mode) the Mail icon immediately left of the virtual screen manager. A small menu appears with three selections, the middle one being Add Subpanel. Select it by pointing the mouse at it and releasing the button. An up arrow will appear above the Mail icon. When you click this arrow, the subpanel pops up with the title Mail.

In order to display the use of the Install Icon icon, start the Application Manager by clicking the file drawer icon next to the Style Manager icon. The Application Manager window is shown in Figure 6.4.

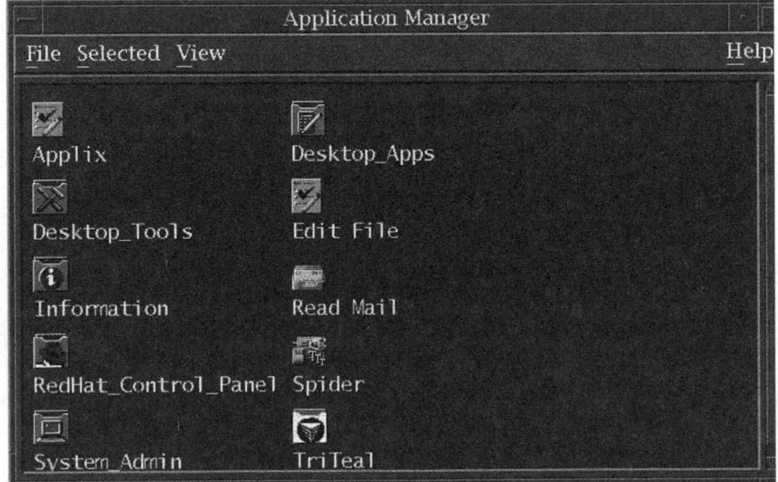

FIGURE 6.4.
The Application Manager.

With the new Mail subpanel still extended, drag the Information icon to the Install Icon control on the subpanel. The icon is added to the subpanel, and when it is clicked, the Information view of the Application Manager appears on the desktop.

To delete this new icon, click it and select Delete. To delete the new subpanel, click the Mail icon and select Delete Subpanel.

TIP

This is only the beginning of what is available via menus and the right mouse button. Don't be afraid to explore the Front Panel by yourself. If you are worried about making an irreversible change to the desktop, set up a home session (described in "The Style Manager" section) before you experiment. If you make a change that is too much to reverse, log out and log in again. When you have a configuration that you really like, save your home session again.

Advanced Customizations

Beyond the simple menu selections and drag and drop, there are customizations that require editing some configuration files and scripts.

Shell and Login Setup

Experienced users might be confused the first time they use the shell after logging into the CDE. Unless some adjustments have already been made, their `.profile` or `.login` scripts are not read. When a user logs into the CDE, the file `.dtprofile` is read instead.

Rather than force users to modify their environments, the CDE designers added a configuration parameter, `DTSOURCEPROFILE`, to the `.dtprofile`. If this variable is set to `true`, `dtlogin` will read the appropriate file, depending on the user's shell. The CDE is built upon `ksh`, so `dtlogin` expects `sh` or `ksh` syntax in `.dtprofile`. It will, however, accept `csh` syntax in `.login`. The default `.dtprofile` contains notes on how users can set up their environments to work well in and out of the desktop.

Another important setting in `.dtprofile` is session logging. Output generated by applications started within the desktop doesn't automatically go to the console as it does in most X Window environments. It is normally discarded. If viewing this output is necessary, direct it to a file (or the console) by setting the `dtstart_sessionlogfile` variable to a valid filename in `.dtprofile`. The default `.dtprofile` has comments explaining how to do this.

Logically, because `.dtprofile` is read in at login, you can make other adjustments to it to suit your needs, such as setting environment variables needed for applications and also modifying the search path. Because some changes might be necessary only within X Window, this provides a good mechanism for users who want to keep their non-GUI environment lean.

If you have no `.dtprofile` in your home directory (`$HOME`), the system uses the default version stored in `$CDEROOT/config/sys.dtprofile` (`$CDEROOT` is the base directory of the CDE installation, usually `/usr/dt`) and copies it into the your directory for the next time.

In the event that an administrator wants to make changes to the environment for an entire workstation, regardless of user, the system files listed can be copied into another directory, `/etc/dt/config`, and modified.

X Resources

Users who want to add personal X resources can simply create an `.Xdefaults` file in their home directory. For system administrators who want to set resources for entire systems, there is a shared file, `sys.resources`, you can modify and place in `/etc/dt/config/C/`.

Advanced Front Panel Customization

The Front Panel is controlled by a series of configuration files that are loaded dynamically each time the desktop is started. This dynamic loading process enables users to change their panel configuration without having root access to the system. Also, administrators can override default behavior and tailor the desktop to their needs without changing the default configuration files and without making things more difficult for advanced users.

The format of the Front Panel configuration files is described in detail in the `dtfpfile` manual page. (If this manual page is not available on your system, install the `TEDman` package from the CDE media.) I will cover enough of this file format in order to make some basic changes.

Configuration files are read from the *action database search path*, which consists of these locations, in this order:

- `$HOME/.dt/types/`
- `/etc/dt/appconfig/types/C/`
- `/usr/dt/appconfig/types/C/`

In the last two locations, `C` is the *language* directory. Another industry standard is the notion of *locales*. A locale is a set of display conventions and language files that make it possible to use an application effectively in different parts of the world. For example, one locale might display dates using the format MM/DD/YY, while another uses DD/MM/YY. Locales are part of the ISO standards for computing. Set the locale for the CDE with the `LANG` environment variable and by installing the proper locale support files. Support is included for Western Europe, Japanese, traditional Chinese, simplified Chinese, and Korean.

The generic `C` locale is the default and is generally the one used in the United States.

The order of the search path is important because in the event that two files specify the same name for two controls, the description that is read first is the one that is used. This enables a system administrator to override the CDE's behavior by placing control descriptions in the system location and enables users to override the administrator's control by placing their own definitions in their home directory.

TIP

All the changes you perform in this section will occur in the first location, the user's home directory. Any or all of them can be performed in either of the other two locations and will then affect all users on that system—this is how to integrate an application suite such as Applix or the Cygnus development tools into a company or departmentwide system. However, modifying the third directory, `/usr/dt`, is generally discouraged: An upgrade to a new version of CDE would remove the changes because a newer version of the configuration files would most likely be copied into the system!

For this reason, make any modifications to the default CDE configuration for an entire workstation or organization in the `/etc/dt` directory tree.

The Front Panel is divided into five different component types—panel, box, control, subpanel, and switch. The panel is the outermost container, the Front Panel itself. For this component, you need to set behavior such as whether a single or double-click activates controls and whether the Front Panel has a minimize button or default window menu.

A panel contains one or more boxes. A box contains one or more controls. The default configuration contains one box, which is adequate for most Front Panel setups.

A third container type is the subpanel, with which you are already familiar. In a configuration context, a subpanel contains controls, similar to a box.

Another container type, the switch, is the middle panel in the Front Panel, and it contains the virtual screen manager and the four small controls that immediately surround it.

A control is an icon like the Mail and Calendar icons discussed earlier in the chapter in the section "The Desktop Environment."

Let's go through the steps of removing a control from the default configuration of the Front Panel. Suppose you decide to delete the Mail control because you don't use the CDE mail reader.

The Mail control is a *built-in* control, which means that it comes in the default configuration and must be explicitly removed with a `DELETE` directive rather than simply left out of the configuration.

The first step is to create a new `.fp` file in your Front Panel configuration directory, which is `$HOME/.dt/types`. Almost all desktop modifications are made from the `types` branch of the directory tree:

```
cd $HOME/.dt/types
cp /usr/dt/appconfig/types/(LANGUAGE)/dtwm.fp ./mymail.fp
chmod +w mymail.fp
```

Next, edit mymail.fp using a text editor. Remove all the lines in the file except for the following, which start at approximately line 94:

```
CONTROL Mail
{
  TYPE                    icon
  CONTAINER_NAME          Top
  CONTAINER_TYPE          BOX
  POSITION_HINTS          5
  ICON                    DtMail
  LABEL                   Mail
  ALTERNATE_ICON          DtMnew
  MONITOR_TYPE            mail
  DROP_ACTION             Dtmail
  PUSH_ACTION             Dtmail
  PUSH_RECALL             true
  CLIENT_NAME             dtmail
  HELP_TOPIC              FPOnItemMail
  HELP_VOLUME             FPanel
}
```

This the default description for the Mail control. As you can see, there are a lot of configuration options available for a control. (See the dtfpfile manual page for a complete description.) In order to remove this control, you need to specify its name, its type, and the fact that you want it deleted in a file that will be read prior to /usr/dt/appconfig/types/C/dtwm.fp. You can actually cut the entry down to the following and place in it mymail.fp:

```
CONTROL Mail
{
  CONTAINER_NAME          Top
  CONTAINER_TYPE          BOX
  DELETE                  True
}
```

Save the file and restart the Workspace Manager, either by logging out and in again or by selecting Restart Workspace Manager from the root menu. As the CDE reinitializes, it will process the DELETE directive in your home directory and omit the Mail control.

However, the Front Panel looks a little strange now, so rather than omit the Mail icon completely, replace it with your preferred mail reader. You'll use elm for the sake of this exercise. Before you can add this to the Front Panel, you have to detour to the Application Manager and create a new action.

Creating New Actions

The CDE supplies a tool, Create Action, that is intended for, logically enough, creating actions. After an action is defined, it can be installed as an icon on the desktop, the Front Panel, or a subpanel. (Or all of them, if you wish.)

The Create Action tool is located in the Desktop_Apps section of the Application Manager. To start it, launch the Application Manager from the Front Panel, double-click the Desktop_Apps icon, and then double-click the Create Action icon.

TIP

If you don't use elm to read mail but want to complete this exercise, you can either replace elm with the name of your mail reader or complete the exercise and answer No when elm asks you whether it should create folders. Running elm like this has no permanent effect on your configuration. If you use an X Window-based mail reader, select a window type of Graphical.

In the Create Action dialog box, shown in Figure 6.5, you simply need to specify an action name; use Read Mail in the top text box and elm for the command to run. Also, select a window type of Terminal (Auto-Close). After these fields are filled in, select Save from the File menu.

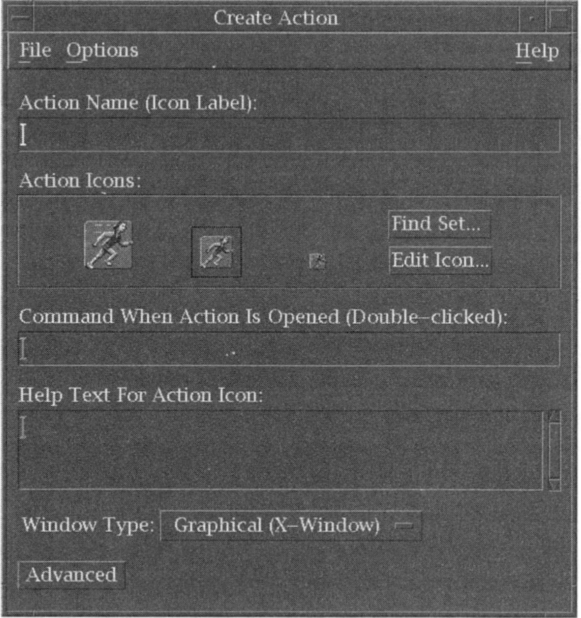

FIGURE 6.5.
The Create Action dialog box.

Now you have an icon called Read Mail in the root directory of Application Manager. If you want to, you can move this icon to another part of the directory tree. You also now have a desktop configuration file named `$HOME/.dt/types/Read_Mail.dt` that is read in as part of the Front Panel initialization process, creating an action `Read_Mail` that can be specified in `CONTROL` definitions.

Creating Controls

With this new action, you can now create a completely new control:

```
CONTROL MyOwnMail
{
  TYPE                    icon
  CONTAINER_NAME          Top
  CONTAINER_TYPE          BOX
  POSITION_HINTS          5
  ICON                    DtMail
  LABEL                   Mail
  ALTERNATE_ICON          DtMnew
  MONITOR_TYPE            mail
  PUSH_ACTION             Dtmail
  PUSH_RECALL             true
}
```

Place this in a file named `myownmail.fp` in the `$HOME/.dt/types` directory and restart the Workspace Manager. The Mail icon has returned and will launch `elm` in a `dtterm` window if clicked. When `elm` exits, the window closes because you selected an Auto-Close terminal in the Create Action dialog earlier.

This configuration contains a few fewer lines than the original Mail control. You removed the `HELP_TOPIC` and `HELP_VOLUME` directives because they are solely concerned with the help topics included for the desktop mail tool. You also removed the `DROP_ACTION` because `elm` is not prepared to handle drag-and-drop operations. However, you did retain the `MONITOR_TYPE` and `ALTERNATE_ICONS` directive because they will work together to notify you when new mail has arrived by changing the Front Panel icon. See the manual pages `dtfpfile` and `dtdtfile` for more details on component options.

Modifying Controls

Now that you have successfully created a new control, you can do it the easy way. Creating a completely new `MyOwnMail` control is not necessary.

Move `myownmail.fp` to `mymail.fp`. (It's important to actually move the file because if `myownmail.fp` still exists at the end of the exercise, you'll have two mail icons!)

Modify the file so that it reads this way:

```
CONTROL Mail
{
  TYPE                    icon
  CONTAINER_NAME          Top
  CONTAINER_TYPE          BOX
  POSITION_HINTS          5
  ICON                    DtMail
  LABEL                   Mail
  ALTERNATE_ICON          DtMnew
  MONITOR_TYPE            mail
  PUSH_ACTION             Dtmail
  PUSH_RECALL             true
}
```

When the desktop is restarted, the Front Panel remains the same. Because you specified a control name of Mail in your personal configuration, which is read in first, it overrode the default mail control.

Creating and Modifying Subpanels

Earlier you used the mouse to create new subpanels and add icons to them. When you make changes this way, they are added to the `fp_dynamic` subdirectory of `$HOME/.dt/types`. Do not edit these files by hand in order to make changes and additions to subpanels.

Creating Subpanels

A `SUBPANEL` definition looks very much like that of a `CONTROL`:

```
SUBPANEL Games
{
  CONTAINER_NAME          Date
  TITLE                   Games
}
```

This creates a subpanel named Games and places it above the Calendar control because the control name for Calendar is `Date` in the default configuration. The new panel has a single control for the calendar, which is created automatically by the Workspace Manager.

Now create an action called `Spider`, using the Create Action tool in the Application Manager. Then create a file in `$HOME/.dt/types` named `Spider.fp` that contains the following (a quick way would be to copy `mymail.fp` and edit it):

```
CONTROL Spider
{
  CONTAINER_NAME          Games
  CONTAINER_TYPE          SUBPANEL
  LABEL                   Spider
  ICON                    redhat_folder
  PUSH_ACTION             Spider
  PUSH_RECALL             true
}
```

When the desktop is restarted, a Red Hat icon appears in the Games subpanel. When it is clicked, the solitaire application Spider starts.

Modifying Subpanels

Like default controls, default subpanels can be modified.

To remove the Install Icon control, add

```
CONTROL_INSTALL False
```

To add a control to a subpanel, specify the subpanel as the container. For example, the following, when placed in an `.fp` file in the `$HOME/.dt/types` directory, will add a handy manual page control to the Help subpanel:

```
CONTROL Dtmanpageview
{
   TYPE file
   CONTAINER_TYPE        SUBPANEL
   CONTAINER_NAME        HelpSubpanel
   POSITION_HINTS        last
   ICON Dthover
   FILE_NAME     /usr/dt/appconfig/appmanager/C/Desktop_Apps/Dtmanpageview
   HELP_STRING  The Man Page Viewer (Dtmanpageview) action displays a
➥ man page in a Quick Help viewer window.
}
```

This is what the Install Icon tools insert into a file when the Man Page viewer icon is dragged into it. The two important directives are `CONTAINER_TYPE` and `CONTAINER_NAME`, which specify the container type, a `SUBPANEL`, and its name.

The Install Icon control is probably the best mechanism to use when possible because it avoids errors and installs nice extras, such as the help information shown in the preceding example.

Subpanel Behavior

When you click controls on subpanels, their default behavior is to close. You can override this but to do so, you must modify the default `PANEL` definition.

Create a file named `main.fp` file in `$HOME/.dt/types`. To `main.fp`, copy the default `PANEL` definition found in `/usr/dt/appconfig/types/C/dtwm.fp`. (It starts at approximately line 18.)

```
 PANEL FrontPanel
{
  DISPLAY_HANDLES         True
  DISPLAY_MENU            True
  DISPLAY_MINIMIZE        True
  CONTROL_BEHAVIOR        single_click
  DISPLAY_CONTROL_LABELS  False
  HELP_TOPIC              FPOnItemFrontPanel
  HELP_VOLUME             FPanel
}
```

Add the following directive:

```
SUBPANEL_UNPOST          False
```

This is a good example of how to take advantage of the way the Front Panel is dynamically constructed every time the CDE is initialized. A site administrator can add this modification, also, to the `/etc/dt/appconfig/types/C` area.

Restoring a Session When Something Goes Wrong

The Workspace Manager always saves a backup of the last session when it saves a new one. If something goes wrong, this backup session can be activated in order to restore a login to working order.

Log in as the user with either the Fail-safe or CommandLine Login, or by switching to one of the virtual terminals.

Change to the `$HOME/.dt/sessions` directory. The old session is in the `current.old` directory. Copy it to the `current` directory—for example,

```
cd current.old; find . ¦ cpio -pdmv ../current
```

Executing Applications and Commands at Login

When users log in to the desktop for the first time, the script `sys.session` in `/usr/dt/config/`*`language`*`/` is executed. It starts up a few desktop applications, including the Help Viewer.

Like most files that accompany the default CDE package, this copy of `sys.session` shouldn't be modified. Instead, users should place a new copy in `/etc/dt/config/`*`language`*`/` and modify it there. After a user logs out for the first time, he or she will have either a home or last session for the desktop to restore, so this script will not run again.

You might want to execute commands when you log in that cannot be set up via the CDE, such as daemon processes, or perhaps an application such as `xv` or `xsetroot` in order to place an alternative root window background. To do so, place a script named `sessionetc` in the directory named `$HOME/.dt/sessions`.

For example, the following script would place the file `companylogo.jpg` as the background at login:

```
#!/bin/sh
xv -root -rmode 5 -maxpect -quit $HOME/images/companylogo.jpg
```

> **NOTE**
>
> Backgrounds set by `xv` are only visible when `NoBackdrop` is selected in the CDE Style Manager.

`sessionetc` is executed as a shell script. Therefore, either `xv` must be in the user's search path, or the path must be fully qualified. In addition, the user must ensure that the path to the image is correct and that the script has the executable bit for owner set. Also, any programs run by `sessionetc` should either execute and exit in a timely manner or become background because the script is run in serial with the rest of the login process. Any programs remaining in the foreground for a long time will result in a delayed login.

Executing Commands at Logout

A similar script, `sessionexit`, can be placed in the same directory with commands to be executed on logout, such as cleaning up a temporary directory or backing up some files. Like `sessionetc`, the proper path must be available for any programs that are run, and the programs that are run should either exit quickly or be placed in the background.

The Help Viewer

The CDE help facility is a welcome sight to the new UNIX user. It provides fully indexed hyperlinks to topics about all the desktop applications and the desktop itself. It also provides context-sensitive help from all the applications.

Using the Help Viewer

The Help Viewer is effectively a replacement for "treeware" (paper) documentation. Help is divided into volumes, such as one for the File Manager, one for the Front Panel, and another for the Help Viewer itself. This, combined with the viewer's powerful search system, provides users with the ability to rapidly access exactly the information they need.

The top portion of the window always displays a table of contents for the volume currently in use (see Figure 6.6). The bottom portion displays the help document for the current topic. On the right are navigation buttons for bringing up an index or a history window, for backtracking to previously visited topics, and for jumping directly to the top-level topic in the currently selected volume.

The index is one of the more powerful features included in the Help Viewer. Help volumes are selected in a simple dialog box and can be displayed as tiered indexes or searched. From the index window, the desired help topic can be displayed.

The history window provides rapid access to the help topics visited in the current help session. It also organizes topics into volumes.

Context-Sensitive Help

All CDE controls have a Help option. Place the mouse over the Style Manager control, right-click with the mouse, and select the Help option.

The Help Viewer not only springs to life, but it displays a topic relevant to the control that has focus. This will also happen inside any CDE application. Try it from the Text Editor or Application Manager.

The control labeled On Item Help produces similar behavior as the F1 key if the control has focus. (When a control has focus, it is framed with a box.)

FIGURE 6.6.
A help window.

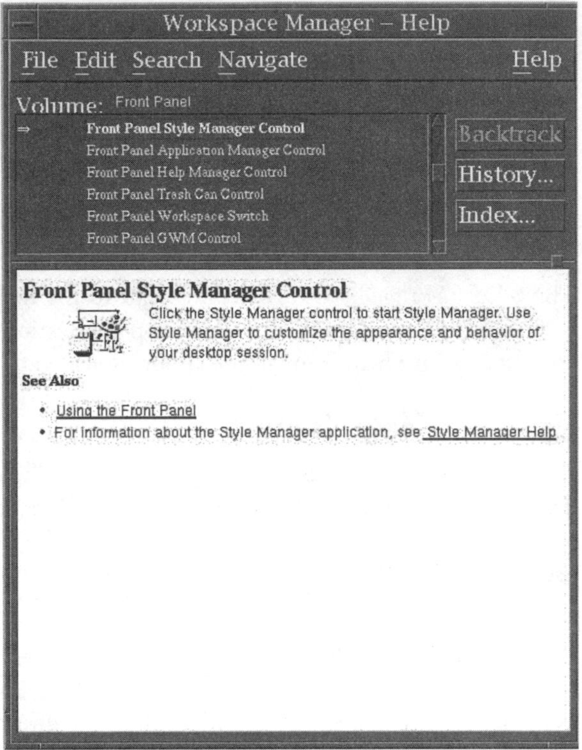

Adding Help to Icons

Modify the control you created earlier in `Spider.fp` to read as follows (you are adding a `HELP_STRING` configuration property):

```
CONTROL Spider
{
  CONTAINER_NAME        Games
  CONTAINER_TYPE        SUBPANEL
  LABEL                 Spider
  ICON                  redhat_folder
  PUSH_ACTION           Spider
  PUSH_RECALL           true
   HELP_STRING  Linux: What to drive.

}
```

Restart the desktop, go to the Spider control, and bring up the menu by right-clicking it. Select the Help option. The Help Viewer will appear, displaying the text you supplied in the control definition.

The Help Viewer can also be passed directives on what topic to bring up in an existing help file. If you take another look at the `FrontPanel` definition in the `main.fp` file you created earlier, you can see an example:

```
 PANEL FrontPanel
{
  DISPLAY_HANDLES         True
  DISPLAY_MENU            True
  DISPLAY_MINIMIZE        True
  CONTROL_BEHAVIOR        single_click
  DISPLAY_CONTROL_LABELS False
  HELP_TOPIC              FPOnItemFrontPanel
  HELP_VOLUME             FPanel
SUBPANEL_UNPOST           False
}
```

The two help directives, `HELP_TOPIC` and `HELP_VOLUME`, tell the desktop the name of the topic and the file that contains it in `$CDEROOT/appconfig/help/C`. This is good to know when you are modifying default icons. Again, for more information, see the manual pages included in the `TEDman` RPM.

Help Topics

The 18 help volumes included with the CDE contain a wealth of information useful for novice and advanced users and remove the need for anything more than the most basic of hard-copy manuals. They can be broken down into the following categories:

- Novice Help—Volumes such as “Introducing the Desktop,” “Desktop Help System,” and “File Manager” introduce the desktop to beginning users. They include basic topics such as how to use the mouse to more advanced operations such as managing files.
- Advanced Help—These volumes cover advanced topics such as creating and deleting actions, configuring the desktop for a network, customizing the Graphical Workspace Manager, and customizing the Front Panel, among many others.
- Application Help—Each desktop application, such as the Calendar, the Application Manager, DT Terminal, and the Style Manager, has a help volume.

Almost all the help volumes have a reference section that displays the volume’s contents in the format of a keyword and topic index, so you can quickly navigate within a topic without using the index window.

Summary

This chapter presents an overview to the TriTeal Network Desktop for Linux that is distributed by Red Hat Software. The desktop is an implementation of the Common Desktop Environment.

The CDE environment provides users with an easy-to-use, consistent, and stable interface, with all the amenities offered by commercial operating systems, such as drag and drop for files and printing, online context-sensitive help, and graphical desktop tools for reading mail, editing files, and even managing a schedule.

This chapter provides information on the following:

- The history of the CDE
- The installation of the CDE, using Red Hat's RPM system
- The initial CDE login process and use of several applications included with the desktop
- Customizing the CDE environment by using the Style Manager, making simple changes to the Front Panel, and altering the configuration files to make advanced changes
- The advanced help system provided with the CDE

The CDE, and TriTeal's version in particular, offers a lot more to UNIX systems than any one chapter can cover. With it, administrators can very easily provide a seamless environment to users of not only different workstations, but workstations running different versions of UNIX. They can also apply the sort of configuration changes discussed here to entire networks by making changes in one location, which not only makes performing the change easier, but also simplifies the change management process.

The CDE is one of the many mainstream commercial products available for Linux. This availability is yet another positive sign that Linux is finally receiving the acceptance that it deserves in the commercial arena.

SMTP and POP

by Jeff Smith, Chris Byers, and Steve Shah

IN THIS CHAPTER

Electronic mail (e-mail) is arguably the most used application of any data network such as the Internet. (Yes, even more so than the World Wide Web!) Early in the Internet's life, there were many proposed standards for e-mail between systems. These standards changed often, and the corresponding software changes were significant.

During this time of rapid change in e-mail protocols, a package emerged as a standard for mail transfer—`sendmail`. `sendmail`, written by Eric Allman of UC Berkeley, was an unusual program for its time because it thought of the e-mail problem in a different light. Instead of rejecting e-mail from different networks using so-called incorrect protocols, it massaged the message and fixed it so that the message could be passed on to its destination. The side effect of this level of configurability has been complexity. Several books have been written on the subject (the authoritative texts have reached over 1000 pages); however, for most administrators those are overkill.

One of the key features of `sendmail` that differentiated it from other mail transfer agents (MTAs) during the '80s was the separation of mail routing, mail delivery, and mail readers. `sendmail` performed mail routing functions only, leaving delivery to local agents that the administrator could select. This also allowed users to select their preferred mail readers as long as they could read the format of the messages written by the delivery software.

With the advent of larger heterogeneous networks, the need for mail readers that worked on network clients and connected to designated mail servers to send and receive mail gave way to the Post Office Protocol (POP). POP mail readers have since flourished with client software available for every imaginable platform and server software available for not only various implementations of UNIX (including Linux) but for other less robust operating systems as well.

This chapter covers the most recent work on `sendmail`, its underlying protocol SMTP, and the `qpopper` package which implements POP support for Linux.

SMTP

The Simple Mail Transfer Protocol (SMTP) is the established standard way of transferring mail over the Internet. The `sendmail` program provides the services needed to support SMTP connections for Linux.

This section covers the various details needed to understand the `sendmail` package, install it, and configure it. Before getting into the details, however, I'll take a moment to discuss the SMTP protocol in better detail and how the Domain Name System (DNS) (see Chapter 13, "TCP/IP Network Management," for details on DNS configuration) interacts with e-mail across the Internet.

Armed with a better understanding of the protocols, you can take on understanding `sendmail` itself beginning with the various tasks that `sendmail` performs (such as mail routing, header rewriting, and so on) as well as its corresponding configuration files.

WARNING

As with any large software package, sendmail has its share of bugs. Although the bugs that cause sendmail to fail or crash the system have been almost completely eliminated, security holes that provide root access are still found from time to time.

Like any software that provides network connectivity, you *must* keep track of security announcements from the Computer Emergency Response Team (CERT, www.cert.org) by either visiting its Web page, joining its mailing list, or reading its moderated newsgroup comp.security.announce.

Internet Mail Protocols

To understand the different jobs that sendmail performs, you need to know a little about Internet protocols. Protocols are simply agreed-upon standards that software and hardware use to communicate.

Protocols are usually layered, with higher levels using the lower ones as building blocks. For example, the Internet Protocol (IP) sends packets of data back and forth without building an end-to-end connection such as used by SMTP and other higher-level protocols. The Transmission Control Protocol (TCP), which is built on top of IP, provides for connection-oriented services such as those used by programs such as Telnet and the Simple Mail Transfer Protocol (SMTP). Together, TCP/IP provides the basic network services for the Internet. Higher-level protocols such as the File Transfer Protocol (FTP) and SMTP are built on top of TCP/IP. The advantage of such layering is that programs which implement the SMTP or FTP protocols don't have to know anything about transporting packets on the network and making connections to other hosts. They can use the services provided by TCP/IP for that job.

SMTP defines how programs exchange e-mail on the Internet. It doesn't matter whether the program exchanging the e-mail is sendmail running on an HP workstation or an SMTP client written for an Apple Macintosh. As long as both programs implement the SMTP protocol correctly, they can exchange mail.

The following example of the SMTP protocol in action might help demystify it a little. The user betty at gonzo.gov is sending mail to joe at whizzer.com:

```
$ sendmail -v joe@whizzer.com < letter
joe@whizzer.com... Connecting to whizzer.com via tcp...
Trying 123.45.67.1...  connected.
220-whizzer.com SMTP ready at Mon, 6 Jun 1997 18:56:22 -0500
220 ESMTP spoken here
>>> HELO gonzo.gov
250 whizzer.com Hello gonzo.gov [123.45.67.2], pleased to meet you
>>> MAIL From:<betty@gonzo.gov>
250 <betty@gonzo.gov>... Sender ok
>>> RCPT To:<joe@whizzer.com>
```

```
250 <joe@whizzer.com>... Recipient ok
>>> DATA
354 Enter mail, end with "." on a line by itself
>>> .
250 SAA08680 Message accepted for delivery
>>> QUIT
221 whizzer.com closing connection
joe@whizzer.com... Sent
$
```

The first line shows one way to invoke `sendmail` directly rather than let your favorite Mail User Agent (MUA) such as Elm, Pine, or Mutt do it for you. The `-v` option tells `sendmail` to be verbose and shows you the SMTP dialogue. The other lines show an SMTP client and server carrying on a conversation. Lines prefaced with >>> indicate the client (or sender) on `gonzo.gov`, and the lines that immediately follow are the replies of the server (or receiver) on `whizzer.com`. The first line beginning with `220` is the SMTP server announcing itself after the initial connection, giving its hostname and the date and time, and the second line informs the client that this server understands the Extended SMTP protocol (ESMTP) in case the client wants to use it. Numbers such as `220` are reply codes that the SMTP client uses to communicate with the SMTP server. The text following the reply codes is only for human consumption.

Although this dialogue might still look a little mysterious, it will soon be very familiar if you take the time to read RFC 821. Running `sendmail` with its `-v` option also helps you understand how an SMTP dialogue works.

The Domain Name System and E-mail

Names like `whizzer.com` are convenient for humans, but computers insist on using numeric IP addresses like `123.45.67.1`. The Domain Name System (DNS) provides this hostname to IP address translation and other important information.

In the old days when most of us walked several miles to school through deep snow, there were only a few thousand hosts on the Internet. All hosts were registered with the Network Information Center (NIC), which distributed a host table listing the hostnames and IP addresses of all the hosts on the Internet. Those simple times are gone forever. No one really knows how many hosts are connected to the Internet now, but they number in the millions, and an administrative entity like the NIC can't keep their names straight. Thus was born the DNS.

The DNS distributes authority for naming and numbering hosts to autonomous administrative domains. For example, a company called `whizzer.com` could maintain all the information about the hosts in its own domain. When the host `a.whizzer.com` wants to send mail or Telnet to the host `b.whizzer.com`, it sends an inquiry over the network to the `whizzer.com` nameserver, which might run on a host named `ns.whizzer.com`. The `ns.whizzer.com` nameserver would reply to `a.whizzer.com` with the IP address of `b.whizzer.com` (and possibly other information), and the mail would be sent or the Telnet connection made. Because `ns.whizzer.com` is authoritative for the `whizzer.com` domain, it can answer any inquiries about `whizzer.com` hosts regardless of where they originate; the authority for naming hosts in this domain has been delegated.

Now, what if someone on a.whizzer.com wants to send mail to joe@gonzo.gov? Ns.whizzer.com has no information about hosts in the gonzo.gov domain, but it knows how to find this information. When a nameserver receives a request for a host in a domain for which it has no information, it asks the root nameservers for the names and IP addresses of servers authoritative for that domain—in this case, gonzo.gov. The root nameserver gives the ns.whizzer.com nameserver the names and IP addresses of hosts running nameservers with authority for gonzo.gov. The ns.whizzer.com nameserver inquires of them and forwards the reply back to a.whizzer.com.

From the preceding description, you can see that the DNS is a large, distributed database containing mappings between hostnames and IP addresses, but it contains other information as well. When a program like sendmail delivers mail, it must translate the recipient's hostname into an IP address. This bit of DNS data is known as an A (address) record, and it is the most fundamental data about a host. A second piece of host data is the mail exchanger (MX) record. An MX record for a host like a.whizzer.com lists one or more hosts that are willing to receive mail for it.

What's the point? Why shouldn't a.whizzer.com simply receive its own mail and be done with the process? Isn't a postmaster's life complicated enough without having to worry about mail exchangers? Well, although it's true that the postmaster's life is often overly complicated, MX records serve useful purposes:

- Hosts not on the Internet (for example, UUCP-only hosts) can designate an Internet host to receive their mail and so appear to have Internet addresses. For example, suppose that a.whizzer.com is connected to ns.whizzer.com only once a day via a UUCP link. If ns.whizzer.com publishes an MX record for it, other Internet hosts can still send it mail. When ns.whizzer.com receives the mail, it saves the mail until a.whizzer.com connects. This use of MX records allows non-Internet hosts to appear to be on the Internet (but only to receive e-mail).
- Imagine a UNIX host pcserv.whizzer.com that acts as a file server for a cluster of personal computers. The PC clones have MUAs with built-in SMTP clients that allow them to send mail but not receive mail. If return addresses on the outbound mail look like someone@pc1.whizzer.com, how can people reply to the mail? MX records come to the rescue again. pcserv.whizzer.com publishes itself as the MX host for all the PC clones, and mail addressed to them is sent there.
- Hosts can be off the Internet for extended times because of unpredictable reasons ranging from lightning strikes to the propensity of backhoe operators to unexpectedly unearth fiber optic cables. Although your host is off the Internet, its mail queues on other hosts, and after a while it bounces back to the sender. If your host has MX hosts willing to hold its mail in the interim, the mail will be delivered when your host is available again. The hosts can be either on-site (that is, in your domain) or off-site, or both. The last option is best because backhoe operator disasters usually take your entire site off the Net, in which case an on-site backup does no good.

- MX records hide information and allow you more flexibility to reconfigure your local network. If all your correspondents know that your e-mail address is `joe@whizzer.com`, it doesn't matter whether the host that receives mail for `whizzer.com` is named `zippy.whizzer.com` or `pinhead.whizzer.com`. It also doesn't matter if you decide to change the name to `white-whale.whizzer.com`; your correspondents will never know the difference.

For the full details on configuring DNS for Linux, see Chapter 13.

Mail Delivery and MX Records

When an SMTP client delivers mail to a host, it must do more than translate the hostname into an IP address. First, the client asks for MX records. If any exist, it sorts them according to the priority given in the record. For example, `whizzer.com` might have MX records listing the hosts `mailhub.whizzer.com`, `walrus.whizzer.com`, and `mailer.gonzo.gov` as the hosts willing to receive mail for it (and the "host" `whizzer.com` might not exist except as an MX record, meaning that no IP address might be available for it). Although any of these hosts will accept mail for `whizzer.com`, the MX priorities specify which of these hosts the SMTP client should try first, and properly behaved SMTP clients will do so. In this case, the system administrator has set up a primary mail relay `mailhub.whizzer.com` and an on-site backup `walrus.whizzer.com`, and has arranged with the system administrator at `mailer.gonzo.gov` for an off-site backup. The administrators have set the MX priorities so that SMTP clients will try the primary mail relay first, the on-site backup second, and the off-site backup third. This setup takes care of the problems with the vendor who doesn't ship your parts on time as well as the wayward backhoe operator who severs the fiber optic cable that provides your site's Internet connection.

After collecting and sorting the MX records, the SMTP client gathers the IP addresses for the MX hosts and attempts delivery to them in order of MX preference. You should keep this fact in mind when debugging mail problems. Just because a letter is addressed to `joe@whizzer.com` doesn't necessarily mean that a host named `whizzer.com` exists. Even if such a host does exist, it might not be the host that is supposed to receive the mail.

Header and Envelope Addresses

The distinction between header and envelope addresses is important because mail routers can process them differently. An example will help explain the difference between the two.

Suppose you have a paper memo that you want to send to your colleagues Mary and Bill at the Gonzo Corporation, and Ted and Ben at the Whizzer company. You give a copy of the memo to your trusty mail clerk Alphonse, who notes the multiple recipients. Because he's a clever fellow who wants to save your company 32 cents, he makes two copies of the memo and puts each in an envelope addressed to the respective companies (instead of sending a copy to each recipient). On the cover of the Gonzo envelope, he writes Mary and Bill, and on the cover of the Whizzer envelope, he writes Ted and Ben. When Alphonse's counterparts at Gonzo and Whizzer receive the envelopes, they make copies of the memo and send them to Mary, Bill,

Ted, and Ben, without inspecting the addresses in the memo itself. As far as the Gonzo and Whizzer mail clerks are concerned, the memo itself might be addressed to the Pope; they care only about the envelope addresses.

SMTP clients and servers work in much the same way. Suppose that `joe@gonzo.gov` sends mail to his colleagues `betty@zippy.gov` and `fred@whizzer.com`. The recipient list in the letter's headers may look like this:

```
To: betty@zippy.gov, fred@whizzer.com
```

The SMTP client at `gonzo.gov` connects to the `whizzer.com` mailer to deliver Fred's copy. When it's ready to list the recipients (the envelope address), what should it say? If it gives both recipients as they are listed in the preceding `To:` line (the `header` address), Betty will get two copies of the letter because the `whizzer.com` mailer will forward a copy to `zippy.gov`. The same problem occurs if the `gonzo.gov` SMTP client connects to `zippy.gov` and lists both Betty and Fred as recipients. The `zippy.gov` mailer will forward a second copy of Fred's letter.

The solution is the same one that Alphonse and his fellow mail clerks used. The `gonzo.gov` SMTP client puts an envelope around the letter that contains only the names of the recipients on each host. The complete recipient list is still in the letter's headers, but they are inside the envelope, and the SMTP servers at `gonzo.gov` and `whizzer.com` don't look at them. In this example, the envelope for the `whizzer.com` mailer would list only `fred`, and the envelope for `zippy.gov` would list only `betty`.

Aliases illustrate another reason that header and envelope addresses differ. Suppose that you send mail to the alias `homeboys`, which includes the names `alphonse`, `joe`, `betty`, and `george`. In your letter, you write `To: homeboys`. However, `sendmail` expands the alias and constructs an envelope that includes all the recipients. Depending on whether the names are also aliases, perhaps on other hosts, the original message might be put into as many as four different envelopes and delivered to four different hosts. In each case, the envelope will contain only the name of the recipients, but the original message will contain the alias `homeboys` (expanded to `homeboys@`*`your.host.domain`* so replies will work).

A final example shows another way in which envelope addresses might differ from header addresses. `sendmail` allows you to specify recipients on the command line. Suppose that you have a file named `letter` that looks like this:

```
$ cat letter
To: null recipient <>
Subject: header and envelope addresses

testing
```

You send this letter with the following command (substituting your own login name for *`yourlogin`*):

```
$ sendmail yourlogin < letter
```

You will receive the letter even though your login name doesn't appear in the letter's headers because your address was on the envelope. Unless told otherwise (with the `-t` flag), `sendmail` constructs envelope addresses from the recipients you specify on the command line, and a correspondence doesn't necessarily exist between the header addresses and the envelope addresses.

`sendmail`'s Jobs

To better understand how to set up `sendmail`, you need to know what different jobs it does and how these jobs fit into the scheme of MUAs, MTAs, mail routers, final delivery agents, and SMTP clients and servers. `sendmail` can act as a mail router, an SMTP client, and an SMTP server. However, it does not do final delivery of mail.

`sendmail` as a Mail Router

`sendmail` is primarily a mail router, meaning it takes a letter, inspects the recipient addresses, and decides the best way to send it. How does `sendmail` perform this task?

`sendmail` determines some of the information it needs on its own, such as the current time and the name of the host on which it's running, but most of its brains are supplied by you, the postmaster, in the form of a configuration file, `sendmail.cf`. This somewhat cryptic file tells `sendmail` exactly how you want various kinds of mail handled. It is extremely flexible and powerful, and at first glance seemingly inscrutable. However, one of the strengths of V8 `sendmail` is its set of modular configuration file building blocks. Most sites can easily construct their configuration files from these modules, and many examples are included. Writing a configuration file from scratch is a daunting task, so you should avoid it if you can.

`sendmail` as an MTA—Client (Sender) and Server (Receiver) SMTP

As mentioned before, `sendmail` can function as an MTA because it understands the SMTP protocol (V8 `sendmail` also understands ESMTP). Because SMTP is a connection-oriented protocol, a client and a server (also known as a sender and a receiver) always exist. The SMTP client delivers a letter to an SMTP server, which listens continuously on its computer's SMTP port. `sendmail` can be an SMTP client or an SMTP server. When run by an MUA, it becomes an SMTP client and speaks client-side SMTP to an SMTP server (not necessarily another `sendmail` program). When your system boots and it starts in daemon mode, it runs continuously, listening on the SMTP port for incoming mail.

`sendmail` as a Final Delivery Agent (NOT!)

One thing `sendmail` doesn't do is final delivery. `sendmail`'s author wisely chose to leave this task to other programs. `sendmail` is a big, complicated program that runs with superuser privileges, an almost guaranteed recipe for security problems, and quite a few have occurred in `sendmail`'s past. The additional complexity of final mail delivery is the last thing `sendmail` needs.

sendmail's Auxiliary Files

sendmail depends on a number of auxiliary files to do its job. The most important are the aliases file and the configuration file, sendmail.cf. The statistics file, sendmail.st, can be created or not, depending on whether you want the statistics. sendmail.hf, which is the SMTP help file, should be installed if you intend to run sendmail as an SMTP server (most sites do). That's all that needs to be said about sendmail.st and sendmail.hf. (Other auxiliary files are covered in the *Sendmail Installation and Operating Guide*, or SIOG for short.) The aliases and sendmail.cf files, on the other hand, are important enough to be covered in their own sections.

The Aliases File

sendmail always checks recipient addresses for aliases, which are alternative names for recipients. For example, each Internet site is required to have a valid address postmaster to whom mail problems can be reported. Most sites don't have an actual account of that name but divert the postmaster's mail to the person or persons responsible for e-mail administration. For example, at the mythical site gonzo.gov, the users joe and betty are jointly responsible for e-mail administration, and the aliases file has the following entry:

```
postmaster: joe, betty
```

This line tells sendmail that mail to postmaster should instead be delivered to the login names joe and betty. In fact, these names could also be aliases:

```
postmaster: firstshiftops, secondshiftops, thirdshiftops
firstshiftops: joe, betty
secondshiftops: lou, emma
thirdshiftops: ben, mark, clara
```

In all these examples, the alias names are on the left side of the colon, and the aliases for those names are on the right side. sendmail repeatedly evaluates aliases until they resolve to a real user or a remote address. In the preceding example, to resolve the alias postmaster, sendmail first expands it into the list of recipients firstshiftops, secondshiftops, and thirdshiftops and then expands each of these aliases into the final list—joe, betty, lou, emma, ben, mark, and clara.

Although the right side of an alias can refer to a remote host, the left side cannot. The alias joe: joe@whizzer.com is legal, but joe@gonzo.gov: joe@whizzer.com is not.

Reading Aliases from a File—The :include: Directive

Aliases can be used to create mailing lists. (In the example shown in the preceding section, the alias postmaster is in effect a mailing list for the local postmasters.) For big or frequently changing lists, you can use the :include: alias form to direct sendmail to read the list members from a file. If the aliases file contains the line

```
homeboys: :include:/home/alphonse/homeboys.aliases
```

and the file /home/alphonse/homeboys.aliases contains

```
alphonse
joe
betty
george
```

the effect is the same as the alias

```
homeboys: alphonse, joe, betty, george
```

This directive is handy for mailing lists that change frequently or those managed by users other than the postmaster. If you find a user is asking for frequent changes to a mail alias, you might want to put it under his or her control.

Mail to Programs

The aliases file also can be used to send the contents of e-mail to a program. For example, many mailing lists are set up so that you can get information about the list or subscribe to it by sending a letter to a special address, *list*-request. The letter usually contains a single word in its body, such as help or subscribe, which causes a program to mail an information file to the sender. Suppose that the gonzo mailing list has such an address called gonzo-request:

```
gonzo-request: |/usr/local/lib/auto-gonzo-reply
```

In this form of alias, the pipe symbol (|) tells sendmail to use the program mailer, which is usually defined as /bin/sh. (See "The M Operator—Mailer Definitions" later in this chapter.) sendmail feeds the message to the standard input of /usr/local/lib/auto-gonzo-reply, and if it exits normally, sendmail considers the letter to be delivered.

Mail to Files

You can also create an alias that causes sendmail to send mail to files. An example is the alias nobody, which is common on systems running the Network File System (NFS):

```
nobody: /dev/null
```

Aliases that specify files cause sendmail to append its message to the named file. Because the special file /dev/null is the UNIX bit bucket, this alias simply throws mail away.

Setting Up sendmail

The easiest way to show you how to set up sendmail is to use a concrete example.

First, you must obtain the source and compile sendmail. Next, you must choose a sendmail.cf file that closely models your site's requirements and tinker with it as necessary. Then you must test sendmail and its configuration file. Finally, you must install sendmail, sendmail.cf, and other auxiliary files.

The preceding are the basic steps, but depending on where you install `sendmail`, you might also have to modify a file in the directory `/etc/init.d` so that `sendmail` will be started correctly when the system boots. In addition, if your system doesn't already have one, you must create an aliases file, often named `/usr/lib/aliases` or `/etc/mail/aliases` (the location of the aliases file is given in `sendmail.cf`, so you can put it wherever you want). You might also have to make changes to your system's DNS database, but that information is not covered here (see Chapter 13).

Obtaining the Source

Red Hat Linux ships with `sendmail` 8.8.5, and an RPM version is available from the `www.redhat.com` Web site to bring this up to version 8.8.7. Unfortunately, this isn't the latest version, and `sendmail` 8.8.7 has a serious security flaw that was recently published in `comp.security.announce`. If you are concerned with security (and you should be!), you will want to download the latest version of `sendmail`, 8.8.8.

`sendmail` version 8.8.8 is on the *Red Hat Linux Unleashed* CD-ROM. This is the most recent version available as this book goes to press, and it is the version documented in the O'Reilly book `sendmail`, 2nd Ed. (ISBN 1-56592-222-0). This version of `sendmail` is available from the site at `http://www.sendmail.org` or via FTP at `ftp://ftp.sendmail.org`. Using FTP, take the following steps to download it:

```
[root@gonzo src]# ftp ftp.sendmail.org
Connected to pub1.pa.vix.com.
220 pub1.pa.vix.com FTP server (Version wu-2.4(1) Fri Dec 29 06:15:49 GMT 1995)
ready.
Name (ftp.sendmail.org:root):anonymous
331 Guest login ok, send your complete e-mail address as password.
Password: mylogin@gonzo.gov <--- this will not be echo'ed back to you.
230 Guest login ok, access restrictions apply.
Remote system type is UNIX.
Using binary mode to transfer files.
ftp> cd ucb/src/sendmail
250-This directory contains sendmail 8.x source distributions.  The latest
250-production version is in sendmail.${VER}.tar.{Z,gz,sig} -- the .Z file
250-is compressed, the .gz file is the same bits gzipped, and the .sig file
250-is a PGP signature for the uncompressed bits in either of the first two
250-files.  Please take ONLY ONE of the .Z or .gz files.
250-
250-The status of various interesting ${VER}s is:
250-8.8.8  Many mostly minor fixes -- see RELEASE_NOTES for details.
250-8.8.7  Fixes a few problems where 8.8.6 was too paranoid.
250-8.8.6  Many mostly minor fixes -- see RELEASE_NOTES for details.
250-8.8.5  Fixes a critical security bug as well as several small problems.
250-8.8.4  Fixes several small bugs, including a potential security problem
250-       on some systems allowing local users to get the group permissions
250-       of other users, as well as a rare denial-of-service attack.  It
250-       also fixes the "HUP to smtpd" root shell vulnerability in 8.8.2
250-       described in CERT Advisory CA-96.24.
250-
```

```
250-The following versions are unsupported:
250-8.7.6  A security patch for CERT Advisory CA-96.20.
250-       *** SEE ALSO sendmail.8.7.6.patch.1 ***
250-       This version DOES NOT FIX the "HUP to smtpd" root shell problem.
250-
250-There is NO 8.6.* patch for CA-96.20.  8.6 is not supported, not secure,
250-and should not be run on any network-connected machine.
250-
250 CWD command successful.
ftp> bin
200 Type set to I.
ftp> get sendmail.8.8.8.tar.gz
local: sendmail.8.8.8.tar.gz remote: sendmail.8.8.8.tar.gz
200 PORT command successful.
150 Opening BINARY mode data connection for sendmail.8.8.8.tar.gz (1026343 bytes
).
226 Transfer complete.
1026343 bytes received in 717 secs (1.4 Kbytes/sec)
ftp> bye
221 Goodbye.
[root@gonzo src]#
```

Note that the exact name of the files to download differs depending on the current version of V8 `sendmail`, in this case version 8.8.8. Also, because the files are compressed, you must give FTP the `binary` command before transferring them. Note, too, that you should include your complete e-mail address as the password—for example, `mylogin@gonzo.gov`.

Unpacking the Source and Compiling sendmail

Now that you've got the source, you need to unpack it. (If you're using the version from the CD-ROM and the `sendmail` RPM package files, these steps are not necessary.) Because it's a compressed `tar` image, you must first decompress it and then extract the individual files from the `tar` archive. For this example, I'll assume that the file is currently in `/usr/local/src`.

```
[root@gonzo src]# tar -xzf sendmail.8.8.8.tar.gz
[root@gonzo src]# ls -l
drwxr-xr-x  13 30005    ver          1024 Nov  4 20:34 sendmail-8.8.8
-rw-r--r--   1 root     root      1026343 Nov  4 20:33 sendmail.8.8.8.tar.gz
```

Now you're almost ready to compile `sendmail`, but first read the following files, which contain the latest news pertinent to the specific release of `sendmail` you've downloaded:

```
FAQ
RELEASE_NOTES
KNOWNBUGS
READ_ME
```

Also take note that the *Sendmail Installation and Operation Guide* (SIOG) is in the `doc/op` subdirectory.

Now run `cd` and `ls` to see what files are in the source directory:

```
[root@gonzo src]# cd sendmail-8.8.8/src
[root@gonzo src]# ls
Makefile      collect.c     macro.c       parseaddr.c   srvrsmtp.c
Makefiles     conf.c        mailq.0       pathnames.h   stab.c
```

```
READ_ME         conf.h          mailq.1         queue.c         stats.c
TRACEFLAGS      convtime.c      mailstats.h     readcf.c        sysexits.c
alias.c         daemon.c        main.c          recipient.c     sysexits.h
aliases         deliver.c       makesendmail    safefile.c      trace.c
aliases.0       domain.c        map.c           savemail.c      udb.c
aliases.5       envelope.c      mci.c           sendmail.0      useful.h
arpadate.c      err.c           mime.c          sendmail.8      usersmtp.c
cdefs.h         headers.c       newaliases.0    sendmail.h      util.c
clock.c         ldap_map.h      newaliases.1    sendmail.hf     version.c
```

Thankfully, Eric Allman and the `sendmail` crew have done a fantastic job of making the installation process very straightforward. To compile your new version of `sendmail`, simply run

```
[root@gonzo src]# makesendmail
```

and watch it run. On the 2.0.30 kernel with Red Hat 4.2, `sendmail` compiles without any warnings or errors.

> **WARNING**
>
> Before installing the new `sendmail` configuration, be sure to make a backup of any files that you are going to replace, especially the old `sendmail` daemon you have. In the event the new `sendmail` doesn't work for you, you will need to restore the old versions while you troubleshoot the new version.

To install the new version of `sendmail`, first stop the currently running daemon with the following command:

```
[root@gonzo src]# /etc/rc.d/init.d/sendmail.init stop
```

Then simply copy the new binary to its proper place:

```
[root@gonzo src]# cp obj.Linux*/sendmail /usr/sbin/sendmail
```

It is also a good idea to copy the new man pages over too:

```
[root@gonzo src]# cp aliases.0 /usr/man/man5/aliases.5
[root@gonzo src]# cp mailq.0 /usr/man/man1/mailq.1
[root@gonzo src]# cp newaliases.0 /usr/man/man1/newaliases.1
[root@gonzo src]# cp sendmail.0 /usr/man/man8/sendmail.8
```

With everything in place, you can restart the new daemon with the following:

```
[root@gonzo src]# /etc/rc.d/init.d/sendmail.init start
```

`sendmail.cf`—The Configuration File

Now you've got a working `sendmail`, but like the Wizard of Oz's Scarecrow, it's brainless. The `sendmail.cf` file provides `sendmail` with its brains, and because it's so important, this section covers it in fairly excruciating detail. Don't worry if you don't understand everything in this section the first time through. It will make more sense upon rereading, and after you've had a chance to play with some configuration files of your own.

`sendmail`'s power lies in its flexibility, which comes from its configuration file, `sendmail.cf`. `sendmail.cf` statements comprise a cryptic programming language that at first glance doesn't inspire much confidence (but C language code probably didn't either the first time you saw it). However, learning the `sendmail.cf` language isn't very hard, and you won't have to learn the nitty-gritty details unless you plan to write a `sendmail.cf` from scratch—a bad idea at best. You do need to learn enough to understand and adapt the V8 `sendmail` configuration file templates to your site's needs.

General Form of the Configuration File

Each line of the configuration file begins with a single command character that tells the function and syntax of that line. Lines beginning with a `#` are comments, and blank lines are ignored. Lines beginning with a space or tab are continuations of the preceding line, although you should usually avoid continuations.

Table 7.1 shows the command characters and their functions. This table is split into three parts corresponding to the three main functions of a configuration file, which are covered later in the chapter in the section "A Functional Description of the Configuration File."

Table 7.1. `sendmail.cf` command characters.

Command Character	*Command Syntax and Example*	*Function*
`#`	`#` comments are ignored. Always use lots of comments.	A comment line.
	`# Standard RFC822 parsing`	
`D`	`D`*`X string`*	Defines a macro `X` to have the string value *`string`*.
	`DMmailhub.gonzo.gov`	
`C`	`CX` *`word1`*, *`word2`*, and so on.	Defines a class `X` as *`word1`*, *`word2`*, and so on.
	`Cwlocalhost myuucpname`	
`F`	`FX`*`/path/to/a/file`*	Defines a class `X` by reading it from a file.
	`Fw/etc/mail/host_aliases`	
`H`	`H?`*`mailerflag`*`?`*`name`*`:`*`template`*	Defines a mail header.
	`H?F?From: $q`	

Command Character	Command Syntax and Example	Function
O	`OX option arguments`	Sets option X. Most command-line options can be set in `sendmail.cf`.
	`OL9 # sets the log level to 9.`	
P	`Pclass=nn`	Sets mail delivery precedence based on the class of the mail.
	`Pjunk=-100`	
V	`Vn`	Tells V8 `sendmail` the version level of the configuration file.
	`V3`	
K	`Kname` class arguments.	Defines a key file (database map).
	`Kuucphosts dbm /etc/mail/uucphsts`	
M	`Mname,field_1=value_1,...`	Defines a mailer.
	`Mprog,P=/bin/sh,F=lsD,A=sh -c $u`	
S	`Snn`	Begins a new rule set.
	`S22`	
R	`Rlhs rhs comment`	Defines a matching / rewriting rule.
	`R$+ $:$>22 call ruleset 22`	

A Functional Description of the Configuration File

A configuration file does three things. First, it sets the environment for `sendmail` by telling it what options you want set and the locations of the files and databases it uses.

Second, a configuration file defines the characteristics of the mailers (delivery agents or MTAs) that `sendmail` uses after it decides where to route a letter. All configuration files must define local and program mailers to handle delivery to users on the local host; most also define one or more SMTP mailers; and sites that must handle UUCP mail define UUCP mailers.

Third, a configuration file specifies rulesets that rewrite sender and recipient addresses and select mailers. All rulesets are user-defined, but some have special meaning to `sendmail`. Ruleset 0, for example, is used to select a mailer. Rulesets 0, 1, 2, 3, and 4 all have special meaning to sendmail and are processed in a particular order. (See the section "The S and R Operators—Rulesets and Rewriting Rules" later in this chapter.)

The following sections cover the operators in more detail, in the order in which they appear in Table 7.1.

The D Operator—Macros

Macros are like shell variables. After you define a macro's value, you can refer to it later in the configuration file, and its value will be substituted for the macro. For example, a configuration file might have many lines that mention the hypothetical mail hub, mailer.gonzo.gov. Rather than type that name over and over, you can define a macro R (for relay mailer) as follows:

```
DRmailer.gonzo.gov
```

When sendmail encounters a $R in sendmail.cf, it substitutes the string mailer.gonzo.gov.

Macro names are always single characters. Quite a few macros are defined by sendmail and shouldn't be redefined except to work around broken software. sendmail uses lowercase letters for its predefined macros. Uppercase letters can be used freely. V8 sendmail's predefined macros are fully documented in section 5.1.2 of the SIOG.

The C and F Operators—Classes

Classes are similar to macros but are used for different purposes in rewriting rules. (See "The S and R Operators—Rulesets and Rewriting Rules" later in this chapter.) As with macros, classes are named by single characters. Lowercase letters are reserved to sendmail and uppercase letters for user-defined classes. A class contains one or more words. For example, you could define a class H containing all the hosts in the local domain as follows:

```
CH larry moe curly
```

For convenience, large classes can be continued on subsequent lines. The following definition of the class H is the same as the preceding one:

```
CH larry
CH moe
CH curly
```

You can also define a class by reading its words from a file:

```
CF/usr/local/lib/localhosts
```

If the file /usr/local/lib/localhosts contains the words larry, moe, and curly, one per line, this definition is equivalent to the preceding two.

Why use macros and classes? The best reason is that they centralize information in the configuration file. In the preceding example, if you decide to change the name of the mail hub from mailer.gonzo.gov to mailhub.gonzo.gov, you have to change only the definition of the $R macro remedy, and the configuration file will work as before. If the name mailer.gonzo.gov is scattered throughout the file, you might forget to change it in some places. Also, if important information is centralized, you can comment it extensively in a single place. Because configuration files tend to be obscure at best, a liberal dose of comments is a good antidote to that sinking feeling you get when, six months later, you wonder why you made a change.

The H Operator—Header Definitions

You probably won't want to change the header definitions given in the V8 `sendmail` configuration files because they already follow accepted standards. Here are some sample headers:

```
H?D?Date: $a
H?F?Resent-From: $q
H?F?From: $q
H?x?Full-Name: $x
```

Note that header definitions can use macros, which are expanded, when inserted into a letter. For example, the `$x` macro used in the preceding `Full-Name:` header definition expands to the full name of the sender.

The optional *`?mailerflag?`* construct tells `sendmail` to insert a header only if the chosen mailer has that mailer flag set. (See "The `M` Operator—Mailer Definitions" later in this chapter.)

Suppose that the definition of your local mailer has a flag `Q`, and `sendmail` selects that mailer to deliver a letter. If your configuration file contains a header definition like the following one, `sendmail` will insert that header into letters delivered through the local mailer, substituting the value of the macro `$F`:

```
H?Q?X-Fruit-of-the-day: $F
```

Why would you use the *`?mailerflag?`* feature? Different protocols can require different mail headers. Because they also need different mailers, you can define appropriate mailer flags for each in the mailer definition and use the *`?mailerflag?`* construct in the header definition to tell `sendmail` whether to insert the header.

The O Operator—Setting Options

`sendmail` has many options that change its operation or tell it the location of files it uses. Most of them can be given either on the command line or in the configuration file. For example, you can specify the location of the aliases file in either place. To specify the aliases file on the command line, you use the `-o` option:

```
$ sendmail -oA/etc/aliases [other arguments...]
```

To do the same thing in the configuration file, you include a line like this:

```
OA/etc/aliases
```

Either use is equivalent, but options such as the location of the aliases file rarely change, and most people set them in `sendmail.cf`. The V8 `sendmail` options are fully described in the SIOG.

The P Operator—Mail Precedence

Users can include mail headers indicating the relative importance of their mail, and `sendmail` can use those headers to decide the priority of competing letters. Precedences for V8 `sendmail` are given as follows:

```
Pspecial-delivery=100
Pfirst-class=0
Plist=-30
Pbulk=-60
Pjunk=-100
```

If users who run large mailing lists include the header `Precedence: bulk` in their letters, `sendmail` gives them a lower priority than letters with the header `Precedence: first-class`.

The V Operator—`sendmail.cf` Version Levels

As V8 `sendmail` evolves, its author adds new features. The `V` operator lets V8 `sendmail` know what features it should expect to find in your configuration file. Older versions of `sendmail` don't understand this command. The SIOG explains the different configuration file version levels in detail.

NOTE

The configuration file version level does not correspond to the `sendmail` version level. V8 `sendmail` understands versions 1 through 5 of configuration files, and no such thing as a version 8 configuration file exists.

The K Operator—Key Files

`sendmail` has always used keyed databases—for example, the aliases databases. Given the key `postmaster`, `sendmail` looks up the data associated with that key and returns the names of the accounts to which the postmaster's mail should be delivered. V8 `sendmail` extends this concept to arbitrary databases, including NIS maps (Sun's Network Information Service, formerly known as Yellow Pages or YP; see Chapter 13 for details). The `K` operator tells `sendmail` the location of the database, its class, and how to access it. V8 `sendmail` supports the following classes of user-defined databases: `dbm`, `btree`, `hash`, and `NIS`. The default used when compiling under Linux is the `dbm` format. See the SIOG for the lowdown on key files.

The M Operator—Mailer Definitions

Mailers are either MTAs or final delivery agents. Recall that the aliases file allows you to send mail to a login name (which might be aliased to a remote user), a program, or a file. A special mailer can be defined for each purpose. And even though the SMTP MTA is built in, it must have a mailer definition to tailor `sendmail`'s SMTP operations.

Mailer definitions are important because all recipient addresses must resolve to a mailer in ruleset 0. Resolving to a mailer is just another name for `sendmail`'s main function, mail routing. For example, resolving to the local mailer routes the letter to a local user via the final delivery agent defined in that mailer (such as `/bin/mail`) and resolving to the SMTP mailer routes the letter to another host via `sendmail`'s built-in SMTP transport, as defined in the SMTP mailer. A concrete example of a mailer definition will make this information clearer. Because `sendmail` requires a local mailer definition, look at the following:

```
Mlocal, P=/bin/mail, F=lsDFMfSn, S=10, R=20, A=mail -d $u
```

All mailer definitions begin with the `M` operator and the name of the mailer—in this case, `local`. Other fields follow, separated by commas. Each field consists of a field name and its value, separated by an equal sign (=). The allowable fields are explained in section 5.1.4 of the SIOG.

In the preceding local mailer definition, the `P=` equivalence gives the pathname of the program to run to deliver the mail, `/bin/mail`. The `F=` field gives the `sendmail` flags for the local mailer. (See also "The `H` Operator—Header Definitions" earlier in the chapter.) These flags are not passed to the command mentioned in the `P=` field but are used by `sendmail` to modify its operation depending on the mailer it chooses. For example, `sendmail` usually drops its superuser status before invoking mailers, but you can use the `S` mailer flag to tell `sendmail` to retain this status for certain mailers.

The `S=` and `R=` fields specify rulesets for `sendmail` to use in rewriting sender and recipient addresses. Because you can give different `R=` and `S=` flags for each mailer you define, you can rewrite addresses differently for each mailer. For example, if one of your UUCP neighbors runs obsolete software that doesn't understand domain addressing, you might declare a special mailer just for that site and write mailer-specific rulesets to convert addresses into a form its mailer could understand.

The `S=` and `R=` fields can also specify different rulesets to rewrite the envelope and header addresses. (See "Header and Envelope Addresses" earlier in this chapter.) A specification like `S=21/31` tells `sendmail` to use ruleset 21 to rewrite sender envelope addresses and ruleset 31 to rewrite sender header addresses. This capability comes in handy for mailers that require addresses to be presented differently in the envelope and the headers.

The `A=` field gives the argument vector (command line) for the program that will be run—in this case, `/bin/mail`. In this example, `sendmail` runs the command as `mail -d $u`, expanding the `$u` macro to the name of the user to whom the mail should be delivered:

```
/bin/mail -d joe
```

You could type this exact same command to your shell at a command prompt.

You might want to use many other mailer flags to tune mailers—for example, to limit the maximum message size on a per-mailer basis. These flags are all documented in section 5.1.4 of the SIOG.

The S and R Operators—Rulesets and Rewriting Rules

A configuration file is composed of a series of rulesets, which are somewhat like subroutines in a program. Rulesets are used to detect bad addresses, to rewrite addresses into forms that remote mailers can understand, and to route mail to one of `sendmail`'s internal mailers. (See the section "The `M` Operator—Mailer Definitions" earlier in this chapter.)

`sendmail` passes addresses to rulesets according to a built-in order. Rulesets also can call other rulesets not in the built-in order. The built-in order varies depending on whether the address being handled is a sender or receiver address, and what mailer has been chosen to deliver the letter.

Rulesets are announced by the `S` command, which is followed by a number to identify the ruleset. `sendmail` collects subsequent `R` (rule) lines until it finds another `S` operator, or the end of the configuration file. The following example defines ruleset 11:

```
# Ruleset 11
S11
R$+         $: $>22 $1      call ruleset 22
```

This ruleset doesn't do much that is useful. The important point to note is that `sendmail` collects ruleset number 11, which is composed of a single rule.

sendmail's Built-in Ruleset Processing Rules

`sendmail` uses a three-track approach to processing addresses: one to choose a delivery agent, another to process sender addresses, and one for receiver addresses.

All addresses are first sent through ruleset 3 for preprocessing into a canonical form that makes them easy for other rulesets to handle. Regardless of the complexity of the address, ruleset 3's job is to decide the next host to which a letter should be sent. Ruleset 3 tries to locate that host in the address and mark it within angle brackets. In the simplest case, an address like `joe@gonzo.gov` becomes `joe<@gonzo.gov>`.

Ruleset 0 then determines the correct delivery agent (mailer) to use for each recipient. For example, a letter from `betty@whizzer.com` to `joe@gonzo.gov` (an Internet site) and `pinhead!zippy` (an old-style UUCP site) requires two different mailers: an SMTP mailer for `gonzo.gov` and an old-style UUCP mailer for `pinhead`. Mailer selection determines later processing of sender and recipient addresses because the rulesets given in the `S=` and `R=` mailer flags vary from mailer to mailer.

Addresses sent through ruleset 0 must resolve to a mailer. This means that when an address matches the `lhs`, the `rhs` gives a triple of mailer, user, and host. The following line shows the syntax for a rule that resolves to a mailer:

```
Rlhs        $#mailer $@host $:user    your comment here...
```

The mailer is the name of one of the mailers you've defined in an M command—for example, smtp. The host and user are usually positional macros taken from the lhs match. (See "The Right-Hand Side (rhs) of Rules" later in the chapter.)

After sendmail selects a mailer in ruleset 0, it processes sender addresses through ruleset 1 (often empty) and then sends them to the ruleset given in the S= flag for that mailer.

Similarly, it sends recipient addresses through ruleset 2 (also often empty) and then to the ruleset mentioned in the R= mailer flag.

Finally, sendmail post-processes all addresses in ruleset 4, which among other things removes the angle brackets inserted by ruleset 3.

Why do mailers have different S= and R= flags? Consider the previous example of the letter sent to joe@gonzo.gov and pinhead!zippy. If betty@whizzer.com sends the mail, her address must appear in a different form to each recipient. For Joe, it should be a domain address, betty@whizzer.com. For Zippy, because whizzer.com expects old-style UUCP addresses (and assuming it has a UUCP link to pinhead and whizzer.com's UUCP hostname is whizzer), the return address should be whizzer!betty. Joe's address must also be rewritten for the pinhead UUCP mailer, and Joe's copy must include an address for Zippy that his mailer can handle.

Processing Rules Within Rulesets

sendmail passes an address to a ruleset and then processes it through each rule line by line. If the lhs of a rule matches the address, it is rewritten by the rhs. If it doesn't match, sendmail continues to the next rule until it reaches the end of the ruleset. At the end of the ruleset, sendmail returns the rewritten address to the calling ruleset or to the next ruleset in its built-in execution sequence.

If an address matches the lhs and is rewritten by the rhs, the rule is tried again—an implicit loop (but see the "$: and $@—Altering a Ruleset's Evaluation" section for exceptions).

As shown in Table 7.1, each rewriting rule is introduced by the R command and has three fields—the left-hand side (lhs, or matching side), the right-hand side (rhs, or rewriting side), and an optional comment—each of which must be separated by tab characters:

```
Rlhs        rhs         comment
```

Parsing—Turning Addresses into Tokens

sendmail parses addresses and the lhs of rules into tokens and then matches the address and the lhs, token by token. The macro $o contains the characters that sendmail uses to separate an address into tokens. It's often defined like this:

```
# address delimiter characters
Do.:%@!^/[]
```

All the characters in `$o` are both token separators and tokens. `sendmail` takes an address such as `rae@rainbow.org` and breaks it into tokens according to the characters in the `o` macro, like this:

```
"rae"      "@"      "rainbow"      "."      "org"
```

`sendmail` also parses the `lhs` of rewriting rules into tokens so they can be compared one by one with the input address to see whether they match. For example, the `lhs` `$-@rainbow.org` gets parsed as follows:

```
"$-"      "@"      "rainbow"      "."      "org"
```

(Don't worry about the `$-` just yet. It's a pattern-matching operator, similar to shell wildcards, that matches any single token and is covered later in the section "The Left-Hand Side [`lhs`] of Rules.") Now you can put the two together to show how `sendmail` decides whether an address matches the `lhs` of a rule:

```
"rae"      "@"      "rainbow"      "."      "org"
"$-"      "@"      "rainbow"      "."      "org"
```

In this case, each token from the address matches a constant string (for example, `rainbow`) or a pattern-matching operator (`$-`), so the address matches and `sendmail` would use the `rhs` to rewrite the address.

Consider the effect (usually bad!) of changing the value of `$o`. As shown previously, `sendmail` breaks the address `rae@rainbow.org` into five tokens. However, if the `@` character were not in `$o`, the address would be parsed quite differently, into only three tokens:

```
"rae@rainbow"      "."      "org"
```

You can see that changing `$o` has a drastic effect on `sendmail`'s address parsing, and you should leave it alone until you really know what you're doing. Even then, you probably won't want to change it because the V8 `sendmail` configuration files already have it correctly defined for standard RFC 822 and RFC 976 address interpretation.

The Left-Hand Side (`lhs`) of Rules

The `lhs` is a pattern against which `sendmail` matches the input address. The `lhs` can contain ordinary text or any of the pattern-matching operators shown in Table 7.2.

Table 7.2. `lhs` pattern-matching operators.

Operator	*Description*
`$-`	Matches exactly one token
`$+`	Matches one or more tokens
`$*`	Matches zero or more tokens
`$@`	Matches the null input (used to call the error mailer)

The values of macros and classes are matched in the lhs with the operators shown in Table 7.3.

Table 7.3. lhs macro and class-matching operators.

Operator	*Description*
$X	Matches the value of macro X
$=C	Matches any word in class C
$~C	Matches if token is not in class C

The pattern-matching operators and macro- and class-matching operators are necessary because most rules must match many different input addresses. For example, a rule might need to match all addresses that end with gonzo.gov and begin with one or more of anything.

The Right-Hand Side (rhs) of Rules

The rhs of a rewriting rule tells sendmail how to rewrite an address that matches the lhs. The rhs can include text, macros, and positional references to matches in the lhs. When a pattern-matching operator from Table 7.2 matches the input, sendmail assigns it to a numeric macro $n, corresponding to the position it matches in the lhs. For example, suppose the address joe@pc1.gonzo.gov is passed to the following rule:

```
R$+ @ $+        $: $1 < @ $2 >          focus on domain
```

In this example, joe matches $+ (one or more of anything), so sendmail assigns the string joe to $1. The @ in the address matches the @ in the lhs, but constant strings are not assigned to positional macros. The tokens in the string pc1.gonzo.gov match the second $+ and are assigned to $2. The address is rewritten as $1<@$2>, or joe<@pc1.gonzo.gov>.

$: and $@—Altering a Ruleset's Evaluation

Consider the following rule:

```
R$*  $: $1 < @ $j > add local domain
```

After rewriting an address in the rhs, sendmail tries to match the rewritten address with the lhs of the current rule. Because $* matches zero or more of anything, what prevents sendmail from going into an infinite loop on this rule? After all, no matter how the rhs rewrites the address, it will always match $*.

The $: preface to the rhs comes to the rescue; it tells sendmail to evaluate the rule only once.

Sometimes you might want a ruleset to terminate immediately and return the address to the calling ruleset or the next ruleset in sendmail's built-in sequence. Prefacing a rule's rhs with $@ causes sendmail to exit the ruleset immediately after rewriting the address in the rhs.

$>—Calling Another Ruleset

A ruleset can pass an address to another ruleset by using the `$>` preface to the `rhs`. Consider the following rule:

```
R$*         $: $>66 $1          call ruleset 66
```

The `lhs` `$*` matches zero or more of anything, so `sendmail` always does the `rhs`. As you learned in the preceding section, the `$:` prevents the rule from being evaluated more than once. `$>66 $1` calls ruleset 66 with `$1` as its input address. Because `$1` matches whatever was in the `lhs`, this rule simply passes the entirety of the current input address to ruleset 66. Whatever ruleset 66 returns is passed to the next rule in the ruleset.

Testing Rules and Rulesets—The -bt, -d, and -C Options

Debugging `sendmail.cf` can be a tricky business. Fortunately, `sendmail` provides several ways to test rulesets before you install them.

> **NOTE**
>
> The examples in this section assume that you have a working `sendmail`. If your system does not, try running these examples again after you have installed V8 `sendmail`.

The `-bt` option tells `sendmail` to enter its rule-testing mode:

```
$ sendmail -bt
ADDRESS TEST MODE (ruleset 3 NOT automatically invoked)
Enter <ruleset> <address>
>
```

> **NOTE**
>
> Notice the warning `ruleset 3 NOT automatically invoked`. Older versions of `sendmail` ran ruleset 3 automatically when in address test mode, which made sense because `sendmail` sends all addresses through ruleset 3 anyway. V8 `sendmail` does not, but invoking ruleset 3 manually is a good idea because later rulesets expect the address to be in canonical form.

The > prompt means `sendmail` is waiting for you to enter one or more ruleset numbers, separated by commas, and an address. Try your login name with rulesets 3 and 0. The result should look something like this:

```
> 3,0 joe
rewrite: ruleset  3   input: joe
rewrite: ruleset  3 returns: joe
rewrite: ruleset  0   input: joe
```

```
rewrite: ruleset  3   input: joe
rewrite: ruleset  3 returns: joe
rewrite: ruleset  6   input: joe
rewrite: ruleset  6 returns: joe
rewrite: ruleset  0 returns: $# local $: joe
>
```

The output shows how `sendmail` processes the input address `joe` in each ruleset. Each line of output is identified with the number of the ruleset processing it, the input address, and the address that the ruleset returns. The `>` is a second prompt indicating that `sendmail` is waiting for another line of input. When you're done testing, just press Ctrl+D.

Indentation and blank lines better show the flow of processing in this example:

```
rewrite: ruleset  3   input: joe
rewrite: ruleset  3 returns: joe

rewrite: ruleset  0   input: joe

     rewrite: ruleset  3   input: joe
     rewrite: ruleset  3 returns: joe

     rewrite: ruleset  6   input: joe
     rewrite: ruleset  6 returns: joe

rewrite: ruleset  0 returns: $# local $: joe
```

The rulesets called were 3 and 0, in that order. Ruleset 3 was processed and returned the value `joe`, and then `sendmail` called ruleset 0. Ruleset 0 called ruleset 3 again and then ruleset 6, an example of how a ruleset can call another one by using `$>`. Neither ruleset 3 nor ruleset 6 rewrote the input address. Finally, ruleset 0 resolved to a mailer, as it must.

Often you need more detail than `-bt` provides—usually just before you tear out a large handful of hair because you don't understand why an address doesn't match the `lhs` of a rule. You can remain hirsute because `sendmail` has verbose debugging built in to most of its code.

You use the `-d` option to turn on `sendmail`'s verbose debugging. This option is followed by a numeric code that tells which section of debugging code to turn on and at what level. The following example shows how to run `sendmail` in one of its debugging modes and the output it produces:

```
$ sendmail -bt -d21.12
ADDRESS TEST MODE (ruleset 3 NOT automatically invoked)
Enter <ruleset> <address>
> 3,0 joe
rewrite: ruleset  3   input: joe
--trying rule: $* < > $*
-- rule fails
--trying rule: $* < $* < $* < $+ > $* > $* > $*
-- rule fails
[etc.]
```

The `-d21.12` in the preceding example tells `sendmail` to turn on level 12 debugging in section 21 of its code. The same command with the option `-d21.36` gives more verbose output (debug level 36 instead of 12).

> **NOTE**
>
> You can combine one or more debugging specifications separated by commas, as in `-d21.12,14.2`, which turns on level 12 debugging in section 21 and level 2 debugging in section 14. You can also give a range of debugging sections, as in `-d1-10.35`, which turns on debugging in sections 1 through 10 at level 35. The specification `-d0-91.104` turns on all sections of V8 `sendmail`'s debugging code at the highest levels and produces thousands of lines of output for a single address.

The `-d` option is not limited for use with `sendmail`'s address testing mode (`-bt`); you can also use it to see how `sendmail` processes rulesets while sending a letter, as the following example shows:

```
$ sendmail -d21.36 joe@gonzo.gov < /tmp/letter
[lots and lots of output...]
```

Unfortunately, the SIOG doesn't tell you which numbers correspond to which sections of code. Instead, the author suggests that keeping such documentation current is a lot of work (which it is) and that you should look at the code itself to discover the correct debugging formulas.

The function `tTd()` is the one to look for. For example, suppose you want to turn on debugging in `sendmail`'s address-parsing code. The source file `parseaddr.c` contains most of this code, and the following command finds the allowable debugging levels:

```
$ egrep tTd parseaddr.c
        if (tTd(20, 1))
[...]
        if (tTd(24, 4))
        if (tTd(22, 11))
[etc.]
```

The `egrep` output shows that debugging specifications such as `-d20.1`, `-d24.4`, and `-d22.11` (and others) will make sense to `sendmail`.

If perusing thousands of lines of C code doesn't appeal to you, the O'Reilly book `sendmail`, 2nd Ed. documents the debugging flags for `sendmail`.

The `-C` option allows you to test new configuration files before you install them, which is always a good idea. If you want to test a different file, use `-C/path/to/the/file`. You can combine it with the `-bt` and `-d` flags. For example, a common invocation for testing new configuration files is

```
sendmail -Ctest.cf -bt -d21.12
```

> **WARNING**
>
> For security, `sendmail` drops its superuser permissions when you use the `-C` option. You should perform final testing of configuration files as the superuser to ensure that your testing is compatible with `sendmail`'s normal operating mode.

Testing sendmail and sendmail.cf

Before installing a new or modified `sendmail.cf`, you must test it thoroughly. Even small, apparently innocuous changes can lead to disaster, and as mentioned in the introduction to this chapter, people get really irate when you mess up the mail system.

The first step in testing is to create a list of addresses that you know should work at your site. For example, at `gonzo.gov`, an Internet site without UUCP connections, the following addresses must work:

```
joe
joe@pc1.gonzo.gov
joe@gonzo.gov
```

If `gonzo.gov` has a UUCP link, those addresses must also be tested. Other addresses to consider include the various kinds of aliases (for example, `postmaster`, an `:include:` list, an alias that mails to a file, and one that mails to a program), nonlocal addresses, source-routed addresses, and so on. If you want to be thorough, you can create a test address for each legal address format in RFC 822.

Now that you've got your list of test addresses, you can use the `-C` and `-bt` options to see what happens. At a minimum, you should run the addresses through rulesets 3 and 0 to make sure that they are routed to the correct mailer. An easy way to do so is to create a file containing the ruleset invocations and test addresses and then run `sendmail` on it. For example, if the file `addr.test` contains the lines

```
3,0 joe
3,0 joe@pc1.gonzo.gov
3,0 joe@gonzo.gov
```

you can test your configuration file `test.cf` by typing

```
$ sendmail -Ctest.cf -bt < addr.test
rewrite: ruleset  3   input: joe
rewrite: ruleset  3 returns: joe
[etc.]
```

You also might want to follow one or more addresses through the complete rewriting process. For example, if an address resolves to the `smtp` mailer and that mailer specifies `R=21`, you can test recipient address rewriting by using `3,2,21,4` *`test_address`*.

7 SMTP AND POP

If the `sendmail.cf` appears to work correctly so far, you're ready to move on to sending some real letters. You can do so by using a command like the following:

```
$ sendmail -v -oQ/tmp -Ctest.cf recipient < /dev/null
```

The `-v` option tells `sendmail` to be verbose so that you can see what's happening. Depending on whether the delivery is local or remote, you can see something as simple as `joe... Sent` or an entire SMTP dialogue.

The `-oQ/tmp` tells `sendmail` to use `/tmp` as its queue directory. Using this option is necessary because `sendmail` drops its superuser permissions when run with the `-C` option and can't write queue files into the normal mail queue directory. Because you are using the `-C` and `-oQ` options, `sendmail` also includes the following warning headers in the letter to help alert the recipient of possible mail forgery:

```
X-Authentication-Warning: gonzo.gov: Processed from queue /tmp
X-Authentication-Warning: gonzo.gov: Processed by joe with -C srvr.cf
```

`sendmail` also inserts the header `Apparently-to: joe` because, although you specified a recipient on the command line, none was listed in the body of the letter. In this case, the letter's body was taken from the empty file `/dev/null`, so no `To:` header was available. If you do your testing as the superuser, you can skip the `-oQ` argument, and `sendmail` won't insert the warning headers. You can avoid the `Apparently-to:` header by creating a file like

```
To: recipient

testing
```

and using it as input instead of `/dev/null`.

The recipient should be you so that you can inspect the headers of the letter for correctness. In particular, return address lines must include an FQDN for SMTP mail. That is, a header like `From: joe@gonzo` is incorrect because it doesn't include the domain part of the name, but a header like `From: joe@gonzo.gov` is fine.

You should repeat this testing for the same variety of addresses you used in the first tests. You might have to create special aliases that point to you for some of the testing.

The amount of testing you do depends on the complexity of your site and the amount of experience you have, but a beginning system administrator should test very thoroughly, even for apparently simple installations. Remember the flaming toaster.

POP

As much as you may love Linux, you have to deal with the reality that you must contend with other operating systems out there. Even worse, many of them aren't even UNIX based. Although the Linux community has forgiven the users of "other" operating systems, there is still a long way to go before complete assimilation will happen. In the meantime, the best thing that can happen is to use tools to tie the two worlds together.

The following sections cover the integration of the most-used application of any network: electronic mail (or e-mail for short). Because UNIX and "other" operating systems have a very different view of how e-mail should be handled, the Post Office Protocol (POP) was created. This protocol abstracts the details of e-mail to a system-independent level so that anyone who writes a POP client can communicate with a POP server.

Configuring a POP Server

The POP server you will configure on the sample systems is the freely available `qpopper` program. This package was originally written at Berkeley but is now maintained by the Eudora division of Qualcomm (`www.eudora.com/freeware`). If you also need client software for non-UNIX systems, check out the Eudora Light e-mail package also available from Qualcomm. Like `qpopper`, Eudora Light is available for free. (The Professional version does cost money, however.)

Red Hat has prepared an RPM of this package, which is available on the CD-ROM (`qpopper-2.3-1.i386.rpm`), or you can fetch it from Red Hat's Web site at `ftp://ftp.redhat.com/pub/contrib/i386/qpopper-2.3-1.i386.rpm`. To install it, simply run

```
rpm -i qpopper-2.3-1.i386.rpm
```

This way, you can install two programs: `/usr/sbin/in.qpopper` and `/usr/sbin/popauth`. `/usr/sbin/in.qpopper` is the actual server program that you will set up to run from `inetd`. `/usr/sbin/popauth` is used to configure clients that use APOP authentication.

Configuring `in.qpopper`

Most of `in.qpopper`'s (from this point on called just `qpopper`) options are configured at compile time; therefore, you don't have much of a say in how things are done unless you want to compile the package yourself. If you are interested in pursuing that route, you can fetch the complete package from Qualcomm's site at `http://www.eudora.com/freeware/servers.html`.

The default configuration items are fine for most sites. These defaults are as follows:

- Refusal to retrieve mail for anyone whose UID is below 10 (for example, root).
- Bulletin support in `/var/spool/mail/bulletins`.
- New users will receive the last bulletin posted.
- Verbose logging to `syslog`.
- APOP authentication uses `/etc/pop.auth` (see the section on `popauth` for details).

To allow `qpopper` to start from `inetd`, edit the `/etc/inetd.conf` file and add the following line:

```
pop-3     stream     tcp     nowait     root     /usr/sbin/tcpd in.qpopper
```

Don't forget to send the HUP signal to `inetd`. You can do so by issuing the following command:

```
kill -1 `cat /var/run/inetd.pid`
```

Now you're ready to test the connection. At a command prompt, enter

```
telnet popserver 110
```

where `popserver` is the name of the machine running the `qpopper` program.

You should get a response similar to the following:

```
+OK QPOP (version 2.3) at mtx.domain.com starting.
<14508.877059136@mtx.domain.com>
```

This result means that the POP server has responded and is awaiting an instruction. (Typically, this job is transparently done by the client mail reader.) If you want to test the authentication service, try to log in as yourself and see whether the service registers your current e-mail box. For example, to log in as `sshah` with the password `mars1031`, you enter

```
user sshah
+OK Password required for sshah
pass mars1031
+OK sshah has 5 messages (98031 octets).
quit
+OK Pop server at mtx.domain.com signing off.
```

The first line, `user sshah`, tells the POP server that the user for whom it will be checking mail is `sshah`. The response from the server is an acknowledgment that the user `sshah` exists and that a password is required to access the mailbox. You can then type `pass mars1031`, where `mars1031` is the password for the `sshah` user. The server acknowledges the correct password by responding with a statement indicating that five messages are currently in user `sshah`'s mail queue. Because you don't want to actually read the mail this way, you simply enter `quit` to terminate the session. The server sends a sign-off message and drops the connection.

Although the stock configuration of `qpopper` is ideal for most sites, you might want to adjust a few command-line parameters. To use a command-line parameter, simply edit your `inetd.conf` file so that the line invoking the `in.qpopper` program ends with the parameter you want to pass. For example, if you want to pass `-T 10` to the server, your `inetd.conf` entry would look like this:

```
pop-3     stream    tcp     nowait    root     /usr/sbin/tcpd in.qpopper -T 10
```

Don't forget to the send the HUP signal to the `inetd` program using the following command:

```
kill -1 `cat /var/run/inetd.pid`
```

The following parameters are available in `in.qpopper`:

Parameter	*Description*
`-d`	Enables the debugging messages to be sent to `SYSLOG`.
`-t` *`<tracefile>`*	Redirects the debugging information to be sent to *`<tracefile>`*, where *`<tracefile>`* is a log file on your system.

Parameter	Description
-s	Enables statistical information about each connection to be logged to SYSLOG.
-T <timeout>	Changes the time-out period for connections to <timeout> seconds. You might need to set this parameter to a higher value if your clients are connecting through slow connections (for example, PPP links).
-b <bulldir>	Specifies what directory to use to hold the bulletins. The default directory is /var/spool/mail/bulletins.

Using popauth

By default, the POP server sends all passwords in cleartext (not encrypted). If you are security conscious, using cleartext obviously is a bad idea, and a tighter control is needed on authentication. APOP support comes in at this point. APOP is a more security-minded way of authenticating users because the passwords are sent over the network already encrypted. qpopper supports APOP and keeps its APOP database in the /etc/pop.auth database. Because this database is kept in a binary format, you need to manipulate it using the popauth program.

When you installed qpopper, the /etc/pop.auth database was not created. Before you can begin using popauth, you need to initialize the database using the following command:

```
popauth -init
```

This command sets up the database and prepares it for further manipulation. popauth accepts the following three parameters to list, delete, and add users to its database:

Parameter	Description
-list	Displays the existing users in the database by their login names.
-delete <name>	Removes user <name> from the database, where <name> is that user's login.
-user <name>	Adds the user <name> to the database, where <name> is the user's login. When the parameter is invoked, you are prompted to enter the user's password twice (the second time to verify you typed it in correctly) to enable the entry.

For example, to add the user sshah to the database, you use the following:

```
[root@mtx /root]# popauth -user sshah
Changing POP password for sshah.
New password: scrubber
Retype new password: scrubber
```

To see that `sshah` was in fact added, you type

```
[root@mtx /root]# popauth -list
sshah
```

If you need to remove the user `sshah`, use the `-delete` option like this:

```
[root@mtx /root]# popauth -delete sshah
```

Warning: You will not be prompted for confirmation when deleting users from this database!

Managing Bulletins

Occasionally, you might need to send mail to all your users to alert them about changes to the system. (For example, you might send this message: `The servers will be offline on Sunday for maintenance.`) If most of your users use POP to read their mail, using bulletins will be much easier on your system.

A bulletin is a message that is sent to all users as they log in to read their mail. It isn't delivered to the users' server mail queues unless they have elected to keep their mail on the server instead of downloading it. By using bulletins for announcements instead of sending out mail, you can reduce the load on your mail server because it doesn't have to perform delivery to all your user's mail queues. Even better, this approach doesn't waste space on your server because the message is directly downloaded to the readers' machines.

To create a bulletin, simply create a new file in the `/var/spool/mail/bulletins` directory (or directory of your choice if you use the `-b` option on `in.qpopper`) with the filename beginning with a number, followed by a period, and then any arbitrary string. Consider this example:

```
1.welcome_to_our_pop_server
```

This bulletin could be the first one on your system. Each new bulletin must follow the numbering pattern in sequence. So the next bulletin, for example, could be titled

```
2.notice_of_downtime
```

Inside each file must be the necessary e-mail header information so that the client POP readers know how to handle the message. A minimal header consists of only a `From` line; however, the users will receive mail that appears to come from no one, with no subject, and no return address. Hence, better mail headers contain not only the `From` line, but also lines for the `From:`, `Date:`, `Subject:`, and `Reply-To:` headers.

The following is a sample message:

```
From sshah@domain.com Tue Sep 16 20:31:15 1997
From:     sshah@domain.com (Steve Shah)
Date:     Tue, 16 Sep 1997 20:31:15 -0700
Subject:     New compute server
    Reply-To: sysadmins@domain.com
```

```
Hello Everyone,

For your information, we have finally set up the new dual processor compute server.
(The old single processor server was getting lonely. ;) If you have any questions
or problems, feel free to send me mail or call me at x9433.
-Your Systems Group
```

After the file is in place, you do not need to alert the server because the server automatically sees the file and sends it to all users as they log in to read their mail.

Summary

In this chapter, you learned how to install, set up, and configure the `sendmail` and `qpopper` programs. The key things to remember about this process are the following:

- An MTA is a Mail Transfer Agent (what actually routes and delivers mail), and an MUA is a Mail User Agent (what the user uses to access her mail once it has been delivered). `sendmail` is an MTA *only*.
- The Simple Mail Transfer Protocol (SMTP) is the actual protocol used to transfer mail. `sendmail` is a program that uses this protocol to communicate with other mail servers. Other mail servers don't need to run `sendmail`, but they do need to communicate via SMTP.
- `sendmail` does NOT deliver mail once it has reached the destination system. A special program local to the system such as `/bin/mail` or `/usr/bin/procmail` is actually used to perform the delivery functions.
- The aliases file can either remap e-mail addresses to other usernames, redirect mail to files, or pass e-mail messages on to another program for processing.
- `sendmail` is a large program with a past history of security problems. Hence, be sure to keep up with the security bulletins.
- Whenever a new version of `sendmail` is released, download it from `ftp.sendmail.org` and install it.
- The Post Office Protocol (POP) is a protocol for allowing client machines to connect to a mail server and transfer mail. POP is not responsible for delivering mail to other users or systems.
- Although POP isn't nearly as large or complex as `sendmail`, it does have the potential to contain security problems as well. Watch for security announcements and upgrade accordingly.
- Bulletins are a handy way to distribute mail to all of your POP mail users at once without having to make copies for everyone.
- `popauth` is the means by which the POP protocol accepts passwords in an encrypted format.

Telling you all you must know about SMTP and POP in a single chapter is not possible, but as Yogi Berra (or maybe Casey Stengel) once said, "You could look it up," and you should. However, this chapter should give you a good basis for understanding the theory behind SMTP, V8 `sendmail`, and `qpopper`.

CHAPTER

FTP

by Steve Shah

IN THIS CHAPTER

Using the File Transfer Protocol (FTP) is a popular way to transfer files from machine to machine across a network. Clients and servers have been written for all the popular platforms, thereby often making FTP the most convenient way of performing file transfers.

You can configure FTP servers in one of two ways. The first is as a private user-only site, which is the default configuration for the FTP server; I will cover this configuration here. A private FTP server allows users on the system only to be able to connect via FTP and access their files. You can place access controls on these users so that certain users can be explicitly denied or granted access.

The other kind of FTP server is anonymous. An anonymous FTP server allows anyone on the network to connect to it and transfer files without having an account. Due to the potential security risks involved with this setup, you should take precautions to allow access only to certain directories on the system.

WARNING

Configuring an anonymous FTP server always poses a security risk. Server software is inherently complex and can therefore have bugs allowing unauthorized users access to your system. The authors of the FTP server you will configure in this chapter have gone to great lengths to avoid this possibility; however, no one can ever be 100 percent sure.

If you decide to establish an anonymous FTP server, be sure to keep a careful eye on security announcements from CERT (`www.cert.org`), and update the server software whenever security issues arise.

Depending on which packages you chose to install during the installation, you might already have the FTP server software installed. To determine whether you have the server software installed, check for the `/usr/sbin/in.ftpd` file. If it is there, you have the necessary software. If you don't, read the next section to learn how to install it.

Getting and Installing the FTP Server

Red Hat Linux uses the freely available `wu-ftpd` server. It comes as an RPM (Red Hat Package Manager) and is offered as an installation option during initial setup. If you decide that you want to run an FTP server but did not install the RPM, fetch `wu-ftpd-2.4.2b12-6.i386.rpm` from the CD-ROM, or check `www.redhat.com` for the latest edition.

To install the RPM, simply log in as root and run the following:

```
[root@denon /root]# rpm -i wu-ftpd-2.4.2b12-6.i386.rpm
```

If you plan to offer an anonymously accessible site, then be sure to install the `anonftp-2.3-3.i386.rpm` from the CD-ROM as well. As always, you can check for the latest version at `www.redhat.com`.

To install the anonymous FTP file, log in as root and run the following:

```
[root@denon /root]# rpm -i anonftp-2.3-3.i386.rpm
```

Now you have a working anonymous FTP server!

To test whether the installation worked, simply use the FTP client and connect to your machine. For the sample FTP server, `denon`, you would respond to the following:

```
[root@denon /root]# ftp denon
Connected to denon.domain.com.
220 denon.domain.com FTP server (Version wu-2.4.2-academ[BETA-12](1)
➥Wed Mar 5 12:37:21 EST 1997) ready.
Name (denon:root): anonymous
331 Guest login ok, send your complete e-mail address as password.
Password: sshah@domain.com             [This is not echoed on the screen]
230 Guest login ok, access restrictions apply.
Remote system type is UNIX.
Using binary mode to transfer files.
ftp>
```

To quit the FTP client software, simply enter `bye` at the `ftp>` prompt. If you want to test the private FTP server, rerun the FTP client but use your login instead of the anonymous login. Here's an example:

```
[root@denon /root]# ftp denon
Connected to denon.domain.com
220 denon.domain.com FTP server (Version wu-2.4.2-academ[BETA-12](1)
➥Wed Mar 5 12:37:21 EST 1997) ready.
Name (denon:root): sshah
331 Password required for sshah.
Password: mars1031               [This is not echoed on the screen]
230 User sshah logged in.
Remote system type is UNIX.
Using binary mode to transfer files.
ftp>
```


How the FTP Server Works

FTP service is controlled from the `/etc/inetd.conf` file and is automatically invoked whenever someone connects to the FTP port. (Ports are logical associations from a network connection to a specific service. For example, port 21 associates to FTP, port 23 associates to Telnet, and so on.) When a connection is detected, the FTP daemon (`/usr/sbin/in.ftpd`) is invoked and the session begins. In the `/etc/inetd.conf` file, the default Red Hat distribution contains the necessary line for this step to occur.

After the server is initiated, the client needs to provide a username and corresponding password. Two special usernames—`anonymous` and `ftp`—have been set aside for the purpose of allowing access to the public files. Any other access requires that the user have an account on the server.

If a user accesses the server by using his or her account, an additional check is performed to ensure that the user has a valid shell. If the user doesn't have a valid shell, he or she is denied access into the system. This check is useful if you want to allow users limited access to a server (for example, POP mail) but do not want them logging in via Telnet or FTP. For a shell to be valid, it must be listed in the `/etc/shells` file. If you decide to install a new shell, be sure to add it to your `/etc/shells` listing so that people using that shell can connect to the system via FTP.

Users accessing the FTP server are placed in their home directories when they first log in. At that point, they can change into any directories on the system to which they have permission. Anonymous users, on the other hand, have several restrictions placed on them.

Anonymous users are placed in the home directory for the FTP users. By default, this directory is set to `/home/ftp` by the `anonftp` RPM package. After the users get there, the FTP server executes a `chroot` system call. This call effectively changes the program's root directory to the FTP users' directory. Access to any other directories in the system, which includes the `/bin`, `/etc`, and `/lib` directories, is denied. This change in the root directory has the side effect of the server not being able to see `/etc/passwd`, `/etc/group`, and other necessary binaries such as `/bin/ls`. To make up for this change, the `anonftp` RPM package creates a `bin`, `etc`, and `lib` directory under `/home/ftp`, where necessary libraries and programs are placed (such as `ls`) and where the server software can access them even after the `chroot` system call has been made.

For security reasons, files placed under the `/home/ftp` directory have their permissions set such that only the server can see them. (This is done automatically during `anonftp`'s install.) Any other directories created under `/home/ftp` should be set up so that they are world readable. Most anonymous FTP sites place such files under the `pub` subdirectory.

Configuring Your FTP Server

Although the default configuration of the FTP server is reasonably secure, you can fine-tune access rights by editing the following files:

- `/etc/ftpaccess`
- `/etc/ftpconversions`
- `/etc/ftphosts`
- `/var/log/xferlog`

With all these files, you can have very fine control of who, when, and from where people can connect to your server as well as an audit trail of what they did after they did connect. The `/etc/ftpaccess` file is the most significant of these because it contains the most configuration options; however, misconfiguring any of the others can lead to denied service.

TIP

When editing any of the files in the /etc directory (FTP related or not), comment the file liberally. Keeping an edit history at the end of the file listing of who last edited the file, when they did it, and what they changed is a good way to track down problems as well as problem makers!

Controlling Access—The /etc/ftpaccess File

The /etc/ftpaccess file is the primary means of controlling who and how many users access your server. Each line in the file controls either defines an attribute or sets its value.

The following commands control access:

- class
- autogroup
- deny
- guestgroup
- limit
- loginfails
- private

The following commands control what information the server tells clients:

- banner
- email
- message
- readme

These commands control logging capabilities:

- log commands
- log transfers

The following are miscellaneous commands:

- alias
- cdpath
- compress
- tar
- shutdown

Permissions controls are set by the following commands:

- `chmod`
- `delete`
- `overwrite`
- `rename`
- `umask`
- `passwd-check`
- `path-filter`
- `upload`

Controlling User Access

The ability to control who may and may not enter your site is a critical component in fine-tuning your anonymous FTP server. The following commands define the criteria used to determine in which group each user should be placed.

class

The `class` command defines a class of users who can access your FTP server. You can define as many classes as you want. Each `class` line comes in the form

```
class <classname> <typelist> <addrglob> [<addrglob> ...]
```

where `<classname>` is the name of the class you are defining, `<typelist>` is the type of user you are allowing into the class, and `<addrglob>` is the range of IP addresses allowed access to that class.

The `<typelist>` is a comma-delimited list in which each entry has one of three values: `anonymous`, `guest`, or `real`. Anonymous users are, of course, any users who connect to the server as user `anonymous` or `ftp` and want to access only publicly available files. Guest users are special because they do not have accounts on the system per se, but they do have special access to key parts of the guest group. (See the description of the `guestgroup` command later in this chapter for additional details.) Real users must have accounts on the FTP server and are authenticated accordingly.

`<addrglob>` takes the form of a regular expression where `*` implies all sites. Several `<addrglob>`s can be associated with a particular class.

The line

```
class anonclass anonymous *
```

defines the class `anonclass`, which contains only anonymous users. They can originate their connections from anywhere on the network.

On the other hand, the line

```
class localclass real 192.168.42.*
```

allows only real users with accounts on the FTP server access to their accounts via FTP if they are coming from the local area network.

autogroup

The autogroup command is used to control access to anonymous users more tightly by automatically assigning them a certain group permission when they log in. The format of the autogroup line is

```
autogroup <groupname> <class> [<class> ...]
```

where *<groupname>* is the name of the group to which you want the anonymous users set, and *<class>* is a name of a class defined using the class command. You can have multiple *<class>* entries for an autogroup. Only the anonymous users referenced in *<class>* will be affected by autogroup.

Remember that the group to which you are giving the users permission must be in the /etc/group file.

deny

The deny command allows you to explicitly deny service to certain hosts based on either their names, IP addresses, or whether their hosts' names can be reverse-resolved via DNS. The format of the deny command is

```
deny <addrglob> <message_file>
```

where *<addrglob>* is a regular expression containing the addresses that are to be denied and *<message_file>* is the filename containing a message that should be displayed to the hosts when they connect.

The following is a sample deny line:

```
deny evilhacker.domain.com /home/ftp/.message.no.evil.hackers
```

This line displays the contents of the file /home/ftp/.message.no.evil.hackers to anyone trying to connect via FTP from evilhacker.domain.com. To deny users access based on whether their IP addresses can be reverse-resolved to their hostnames, use the string !nameserved for the *<addrglob>* entry.

guestgroup

The guestgroup command is useful when you have real users but want them to have only restrictive FTP privileges. The format of the command is

```
guestgroup <groupname> [<groupname> ...]
```

where *<groupname>* is the name of the group (as taken from /etc/group) that you want restricted.

When a user's group is restricted, the user is treated much like an anonymous visitor; hence, the same setups needed for anonymous visitors must be performed in this user's account. The user's password entry is also a little different in the directory field.

The field for the user's home directory is broken up by the `/./` characters. Before the split characters is the effective root directory, and after the split characters is the user's relative home directory. For example, consider the following password entry:

```
user1:encrypted password:500:128:User 1:/ftp/./user1:/bin/ftponly
```

Here, `/ftp` is the user's new relative root directory (`bin`, `etc`, and `lib` directories would need to be created under `/ftp` for the `ls` command and other necessary libraries), and `/ftp/user1` is the user's home directory.

limit

The `limit` command allows you to control the number of users who log in to the system via FTP by class and time of day. This capability is especially useful if you have a popular archive but the system needs to be available to your users during business hours. The format of the `limit` command is

```
limit <class> <n> <times> <message_file>
```

where `<class>` is the class to limit, `<n>` is the maximum number of people allowed in that class, `<times>` is the time during which the limit is in effect, and `<message_file>` is the file that should be displayed to the client when the maximum limit is reached.

The format of the `<times>` parameter is somewhat complex. The parameter is in the form of a comma-delimited string, where each option is for a separate day. Sunday through Saturday take the form `Su`, `Mo`, `Tu`, `We`, `Th`, `Fr`, and `Sa`, respectively, and all the weekdays can be referenced as `Wk`. Time should be kept in military format without a colon separating the hours and minutes. A range is specified by the dash character.

For example, to limit the class `anonfolks` to 10 from Monday through Thursday, all day, and Friday from midnight to 5:00 p.m., you would use the following `limit` line:

```
limit anonfolks 10 MoTuWeTh,Fr0000-1700 /home/ftp/.message.too_many
```

In this case, if the limit is hit, the contents of the file `/home/ftp/.message.too_many` are displayed to the connecting user.

loginfails

The `loginfails` command allows you to set the number of failed login attempts clients can make before disconnecting them. By default, this number is five; however, you can set it by using the command

```
loginfails <n>
```

where <*n*> is the number of attempts. For example, the following line disconnects a user from the FTP server after three failed attempts:

```
loginfails 3
```

private

You might find it convenient to be able to share files with other users via FTP without having to place the file in a 100 percent public place or having to give these users a real account on the server. The clients use the `SITE GROUP` and `SITE GPASS` commands so that they can change into privileged groups that require passwords.

For your FTP server to support this capability, you need to set the `private` flag using the command

```
private <switch>
```

where `<switch>` is either the string `YES` to turn it on or `NO` to turn it off.

Because you need to require passwords for these special groups, you need to use the `/etc/ftpgroups` file. The format of an access group in `/etc/ftpgroups` is

```
access_group_name:encrypted_password:real_group
```

where `access_group_name` is the name that the client uses to reference the special group, `encrypted_password` is the password users need to supply (via `SITE GPASS`) to access the group, and `real_group` is the actual group referenced in the `/etc/group` file.

> **TIP**
>
> To create the *encrypted_password* entry, use the UNIX `crypt` function. To make generating the encrypted password easier, use the following Perl script:
>
> ```
> #!/usr/bin/perl
> print "Enter password to encrypt: ";
> chop ($password=<STDIN>);
> print "The encrypted password is: ",crypt($password,$password);
> ```

Controlling Banner Messages

It is often useful to provide messages to FTP users when they connect to your site or specify a special action. These commands allow you to specify these instances as well as the corresponding messages. Using them is a great way to make your site self-documenting.

banner

The `banner` command allows you to display a sign onscreen before the client has to provide a login and password combination. The format of this command is

```
banner <path>
```

where <*path*> is the full pathname of the file you want to display. Consider this example:

```
banner /home/ftp/.banner
```

email

The `email` command allows you to specify the site maintainer's e-mail address. Some error messages or information requests provide the information given in this line on demand. The default value in the `/etc/ftpaccess` file is `root@localhost`.

The format of the `email` command is

```
email <address>
```

where <*address*> is the full e-mail address of the site maintainer.

Creating an e-mail alias "FTP" that forwards to the system administrators is generally good practice. Providing this kind of information in the sign-on banner is also a good idea so that users know whom to contact if they cannot log in to the system.

message

The `message` command allows you to set up special messages to be sent to the clients when they either log in or change into a certain directory. You can specify multiple messages. The format of this command is

```
message <path> <when> {<class> ...}
```

where <*path*> is the full pathname to the file to be displayed, <*when*> is the condition under which to display the message, and <*class*> is a list of classes to which this message command applies.

The <*when*> parameter should take one of two forms: either `LOGIN` or `CWD=`<*dir*>. If it is `LOGIN`, the message is displayed upon a successful login. If the parameter is set to `CWD=`<*dir*>, then the message is displayed when clients enter the <*dir*> directory.

The <*class*> parameter is optional. You can list multiple classes for a certain message. This capability is useful if you want only certain messages going to anonymous users and so on.

The message file itself (specified by <*path*>) can contain special flags that the FTP server substitutes with the appropriate information at runtime. These options are as follows:

Option	*Description*
`%T`	Local time
`%F`	Free space in the partition where <*dir*> is located
`%C`	Current working directory
`%E`	Site maintainer's e-mail address (specified by the `email` command)

Option	Description
%R	Client hostname
%L	Server hostname
%U	Username provided at login time
%M	Maximum number of users allowed in the specified class
%N	Current number of users in specified class

Remember that when messages are triggered by an anonymous user, the message path needs to be relative to the anonymous FTP directory.

An example message command is

```
message ./.toomany_anon LOGIN anonfolks
```

where the file `./.toomany_anon` contains

```
Sorry %R, but there are already %N users out of a maximum of %M users in
➥your class.  Please try again in a few minutes.
The FTP Administrator (%E)
```

If the limit of 25 users is reached at this site, for example, the client sees a message similar to the following:

```
Sorry, technics.domain.com, but there are already 25 out of a maximum
➥of 25 users in your class. Please try again in a few minutes.
The FTP Administrator (ftp@domain.com)
```


readme

The `readme` command allows you to specify the conditions under which clients are notified that a certain file in their current directory was last modified. This command can take the form

```
readme <path> <when> <class>
```

where *<path>* is the name of the file to alert the clients about (for example, `README`), *<when>* is similar to the *<when>* in the `message` command, and *<class>* is the classes for which this command applies. The *<when>* and *<class>* parameters are optional.

Remember that when you're specifying a path for anonymous users, the file must be relative to the anonymous FTP directory.

Controlling Logging

As with any complex network service, security quickly becomes an issue. In order to contend with possible threats, tracking connections made along with the corresponding commands is a necessity. The following commands allow you to determine how much, if any, logging should be done by the server software.

log commands

Often for security purposes, you might want to log the actions of your FTP users. You do so by using the `log commands` option. Each command invoked by the clients is sent to your log file. The format of the command is

```
log commands <typelist>
```

where *<typelist>* is a comma-separated list specifying which kinds of users should be logged. The three kinds of users recognized are anonymous, guest, and real. (See the description of the `class` command earlier in this chapter for each user type's description.) For example, to log all the actions taken by anonymous and guest users, you specify the following:

```
log commands anonymous,guest
```

log transfers

If you want to log only file transfers made by clients instead of their entire sessions with the `log commands` statement, you should use `log transfers` instead. The format of this command is

```
log transfers <typelist> <directions>
```

where *<typelist>* is a comma-separated list specifying which kinds of users should be logged (anonymous, guest, or real), and *<directions>* is a comma-separated list specifying which direction the transfer must take in order to be logged. The two directions you can choose to log are `inbound` and `outbound`.

For example, to log all anonymous transfers that are both `inbound` and `outbound`, you would use the following:

```
log transfers anonymous inbound,outbound
```

The resulting logs are stored in `/var/log/xferlog`. See the section on this file for additional information.

Miscellaneous Server Commands

The following set of commands provide some miscellaneous configuration items. Each command adds a good deal of flexibility to the server making it that much more useful to you as its administrator.

alias

The `alias` command allows you to define directory aliases for your FTP clients. They are activated when the clients use the `cd` command and specify the alias. This capability is useful to provide shortcuts to often requested files. The format of the command is

```
alias <string> <dir>
```

where *<string>* is the alias and *<dir>* is the actual directory the users should be transferred to. The following is an example of this command:

```
alias orb_discography /pub/music/ambient/orb_discography
```

Hence, if clients connect and use the command `cd orb_discography`, they are automatically moved to the `/pub/music/ambient/orb_discography` directory, regardless of their current locations.

cdpath

Similar to the UNIX `PATH` environment variable, the `cdpath` command lets you establish a list of paths to check whenever clients invoke the `cd` command. The format of the `cdpath` command is

```
cdpath <dir>
```

where *<dir>* is the directory on the server to be checked whenever clients use the `cd` command. Remember to use directories relative to the FTP home directory for your anonymous users. An example of the `cdpath` command is

```
cdpath /pub/music
cdpath /pub/coffee
```

If clients enter the command `cd instant`, the server examines the directories in the following order:

1. `./instant`
2. Aliases called `instant` (See the description of `alias` for more information.)
3. `/pub/music/instant`
4. `/pub/coffee/instant`

compress

The `wu-ftpd` server (the FTP server I have currently installed) offers a special feature that allows the server to compress or decompress a file before transmission: `compress`. This capability allows a client who might not have the necessary software to decompress a file to still be able to fetch it in a usable form. (For example, a file on your server is compressed using `gzip`, and a Windows client machine needs to get it but does not have the DOS version of `gzip` available.)

The format of the `compress` command is

```
compress <switch> <classglob>
```

where *<switch>* is either the string `YES` to turn on this feature or `NO` to turn off this feature. *<classglob>* is a comma-separated list of classes to which this compress option applies.

There is, of course, a catch to using this command. You need to configure the `/etc/ftpconversions` file so that the server knows which programs to use for certain file extensions. The default configuration supports compression by either `/bin/compress` or `/bin/gzip`.

Read the section on `/etc/ftpconversions` for details.

tar

Almost identical to the `compress` option, `tar` specifies whether the server will tar and untar files for a client on demand. The format of this command is

```
tar <switch> <classglob>
```

where `<switch>` is either the string `YES` to turn on this feature or `NO` to turn off this feature. The `<classglob>` option is a comma-separated list of classes that this `tar` command specifies.

Like the `compress` command, this feature is also controlled by the `/etc/ftpconversions` file. See the section on `/etc/ftpconversions` for details.

shutdown

The `shutdown` command tells the server to check for a particular file periodically to see whether the server will be shut down. By default, the RPMs you installed invoke the FTP server whenever there is a request for a connection; therefore, you don't really need this option if you plan to continue using it that way. On the other hand, if you intend to change the system so that the server software is constantly running in the background, you might want to use this option to perform clean shutdowns and to notify users accessing the site.

The format of the `shutdown` command is

```
shutdown <path>
```

where `<path>` is the full path of the file to check for shutdown information. When that file does become available, it is parsed out and the information gained from it dictates the behavior of the shutdown process as well as the `ftpshut` program (discussed later in the chapter in the section "`ftpshut`"). While there isn't any standard place for keeping this file, you might find it handy to keep in `/etc/ftpshutdown` because it will be obvious along with the other FTP configuration files. Make sure that the file is readable by root.

The format of the file is

```
<year> <month> <day> <hour> <minute> <deny_offset> <disconnect_offset> <text>
```

where `<year>` is any year after 1970; `<month>` is from 0 to 11 to represent January to December, respectively; `<day>` is from 0 to 30; `<hour>` is from 0 to 23; and `<minute>` is from 0 to 59. The `<deny_offset>` parameter specifies the time at which the server should stop accepting new connections in the form `HHMM`, where `HH` is the hour in military format and `MM` is the minute. `<disconnect_offset>` is the time at which existing connections are dropped; it is also in the form `HHMM`.

The `<text>` parameter is a free-form text block displayed to users to alert them of the impending shutdown. The text can follow the format of the `message` command (see the description of this command earlier in the chapter) and have the following special character sequences available:

Option	*Description*
`%s`	The time the system will shut down
`%r`	The time when new connections will be denied
`%d`	The time current connections will be dropped

Controlling Permissions

Along with controlling logins and maintaining logs, you will need to keep the permissions of the files placed in the archive under tight control. The following commands will allow you to specify what permissions should be set under certain conditions.

chmod

The `chmod` command determines whether a client has the permission to change permissions on the server's files using the client's `chmod` command. The format of this command is

```
chmod <switch> <typelist>
```

where `<switch>` is either `YES` to turn on the feature or `NO` to turn off the feature. `<typelist>` is the comma-separated list of user types affected by this command. The user types available are anonymous, guest, and real.

delete

The `delete` command tells the server whether client connections can delete files that are residing on the server via FTP. The format of the command is

```
delete <switch> <typelist>
```

where `<switch>` is either `YES` to turn on the feature or `NO` to turn off the feature. `<typelist>` is the comma-separated list of user types affected by this command. The user types available are anonymous, guest, and real.

overwrite

To control whether FTP clients can upload files and replace existing files on the server, you use the `overwrite` command. The format of this command is

```
overwrite <switch> <typelist>
```

where `<switch>` is either `YES` to turn on the feature or `NO` to turn off the feature. `<typelist>` is the comma-separated list of user types affected by this command. The user types available are anonymous, guest, and real.

rename

Client FTP software has the option of sending a `rename` request to the server to rename files. The `rename` command determines whether this request is acceptable. The format of this command is

```
rename <switch> <typelist>
```

where <*switch*> is either `YES` to turn on the feature or `NO` to turn off the feature. <*typelist*> is the comma-separated list of user types affected by this command. The user types available are anonymous, guest, and real.

umask

The `umask` command determines whether clients can change their default permissions in a similar fashion as the `umask` shell command. The format of the `umask` command is

```
umask <switch> <typelist>
```

where <*switch*> is either `YES` to turn on the feature or `NO` to turn off the feature. <*typelist*> is the comma-separated list of user types affected by this command. The user types available are anonymous, guest, and real.

passwd-check

Providing a valid e-mail address as your password is considered good manners when you're connecting to an anonymous FTP site. The `passwd-check` command lets you determine how strict you want to be with what string is submitted as an anonymous user's e-mail address. The format of the command is

```
passwd-check <strictness> <enforcement>
```

where <*strictness*> is one of three possible strings: `none`, `trivial`, or `rfc822`. <*enforcement*> is one of two possible strings: `warn` or `enforce`.

Selecting `none` for <*strictness*> will perform no check at all for the password. `trivial` is slightly more demanding by requiring that at least an `@` (at) symbol appear in the password. `rfc822` is the most strict, requiring that the e-mail address comply with the RFC 822 "Message Header Standard" (for example, `sshah@domain.com`).

Using `warn` as the <*enforcement*> warns the users if they fail to comply with the strictness requirement but allows them to connect with your server anyway. `enforce`, on the other hand, denies the users connections until they use acceptable passwords.

path-filter

If you allow users to upload files to your server via FTP, you might want to dictate what are acceptable filenames. (For example, control characters in filenames are not acceptable.) You can enforce this restriction by using the `path-filter` command. The format of this command is

```
path-filter <typelist> <mesg> <allowed-regexp> <denied-regexp>
```

where <*typelist*> is a comma-separated list of users this command affects; the user types available are anonymous, guest, and real. <*mesg*> is the filename of the message that should be displayed if the file does not meet this criteria. <*allowed-regexp*> is the regular expression that the filename must meet to be allowed in. <*denied-regexp*> is the regular expression that, if met, causes the file to be explicitly denied; <*denied-regexp*> is an optional parameter.

For example, the line

```
path-filter anonymous,guest /ftp/.badfilename UL* gif$
```

displays the file /ftp/.badfilename to anonymous or guest users if they upload a file that doesn't begin with the string UL or that ends with the string gif.

upload

You can use the upload command, along with path-filter, to control files placed onto your server. The upload command specifies what permissions the client has to place files in certain directories as well as what permissions the files will take on after they are placed there. The format of this command is

```
upload <directory> <dirglob> <switch> <owner> <group> <mode> <mkdir>
```

where *<directory>* is the directory that is affected by this command, *<dirglob>* is the regular expression used to determine whether a subdirectory under *<directory>* is a valid place to make an upload, and *<switch>* is either YES or NO, thereby establishing either an upload can or cannot occur there. The *<owner>*, *<group>*, and *<mode>* parameters establish the file's owner, group, and permissions after the file is placed on the server. Finally, you can specify the *<mkdir>* option as either dirs or nodirs, which allows the client to able to create or not create subdirectories under the specified directory.

Here is a sample entry:

```
upload /home/ftp * no
upload /home/ftp /incoming yes ftp ftp 0400 nodirs
```

This example specifies that the only location a file can be placed is in the /home/ftp/incoming directory (/incoming to the anonymous client). After the file is placed in this directory, its owner becomes ftp, group ftp, and the permission is 0400. The nodirs option at the end of the second line doesn't allow the anonymous client to create subdirectories under /incoming.

> **TIP**
>
> Setting uploads to read-only is a good idea so that the /incoming directory doesn't become a trading ground for questionable material—for example, illegal software.

Converting Files On-the-Fly—The /etc/ftpconversions File

The format of the /etc/ftpconversions file is

```
<1>:<2>:<3>:<4>:<5>:<6>:<7>:<8>
```

where <1> is the strip prefix, <2> is strip postfix, <3> is an add-on prefix, <4> is an add-on postfix, <5> is the external command to invoke to perform the conversion, <6> is the type of file, <7> is the option information used for logging, and <8> is a description of the action.

Confused? Don't be. Each of these options is actually quite simple. In the following sections, I describe them one at a time.

The Strip Prefix

The strip prefix is the string at the beginning of a filename that should be removed when the file is fetched. For example, if you want a special action taken on files beginning with `discography.`, where that prefix is removed after the action, you would specify `.discography` for this option. When the clients specify filenames, they should not include the strip prefix. That is, if a file is called `discography.orb` and a client issues the command `get orb`, the server performs the optional command on the file and then transfers the results back to the client.

The Strip Postfix

The strip postfix is the string at the end of the filename that should be removed when the file is fetched. The strip postfix is typically used to remove the trailing `.gz` from a gzipped file that is being decompressed before being transferred back to the client.

The Add-on Prefix

An add-on prefix is the string inserted before the filename when a file is transferred either to or from the server. For example, say you want to insert the string `uppercase.` to all files being pulled from the server that are getting converted to uppercase.

The Add-on Postfix

An add-on postfix is the string appended to a filename after an operation on it is complete. This type of postfix is commonly used when the client issues the command `get` *`largefile`*`.gz`, where the actual filename is only *`largefile`*; in this case, the server compresses the file using `gzip` and then performs the transfer.

The External Command

The key component of each line is the external command. This entry specifies the program to be run when a file is transferred to or from the server. As the file is transferred, it is filtered through the program where downloads (files sent to the client) need to be sent to the standard out and uploads (files sent to the server) will be coming from the standard in. For example, if you want to provide decompression with `gzip` for files being downloaded, the entry would look like the following:

```
gzip -dc %s
```

The `%s` in the line tells the server to substitute in the filename being requested by the user.

The Type of File

The type of file field for `/etc/ftpconversions` is a list of possible kinds of files that can be acted on, each type name separated by a pipe symbol (`|`). The three file types recognized are `T_REG`,

T_ASCII, and T_DIR, which represent regular files, ASCII files, and directories, respectively. An example of this entry is T_REG¦T_ASCII.

Options

The options field of /etc/ftpconversions is similar to the type of file field in that it is composed of a list of names separated by a pipe symbol (¦). The three types of options supported are O_COMPRESS, O_UNCOMPRESS, and O_TAR, which specify whether the command compresses files, decompresses files, or uses the tar command. A sample entry is O_COMPRESS¦O_TAR, which says that the file is both compressed and tarred.

The Description

The last parameter of /etc/ftpconversions, the description of the conversion, is a free-form entry in which you can describe what kind of conversion is done.

Example of an /etc/ftpconversions Entry

The following is a sample entry that compresses files using gzip on demand. This would allow someone who wants to get the file orb_discography.tar to instead request the file orb_discrography.tar.gz and have the server compress the file using gzip before sending it him. The configuration line that does this is as follows:

```
: : :.gz:/bin/gzip -9 -c %s:T_REG:O_COMPRESS:GZIP
```

The first two parameters are not necessary because you don't want to remove anything from the filename before sending it to the requester. The third parameter is empty because you don't want to add any strings to the beginning of the filename before sending it. The fourth parameter, though, does have the string .gz, which will result in the file having the .gz suffix added before being sent. The fifth parameter is the actual command used to compress the file, where the -9 option tells gzip to compress the file as much as it can, -c results in the compressed file being sent to the standard output, and %s is replaced by the server with the filename being requested (for example, orb_discography.tar). T_REG in the sixth parameter tells the server to treat the file being handled as a normal file rather than an ASCII file or directory. The second-to-last parameter, O_COMPRESS, tells the server that the action being taken is file compression, and finally, the last parameter is simply a comment for the administrator so that she can determine the action being taken at a glance.

A bit daunting, isn't it? Don't worry, examine the sample /etc/ftpconversions file that came with the wu-ftpd RPM package to see additional examples of using tar and gzip. In fact, most sites never need to add to this file because it covers the most popular conversion requests made.

Configuring Host Access—The /etc/ftphosts File

The /etc/ftphosts file establishes rules on a per-user basis defining whether users are allowed to log in from certain hosts or whether users are denied access when they try to log in from other hosts.

Each line in the file can be one of two commands:

```
allow <username> <addrglob>
```

or

```
deny <username> <addrglob>
```

where the `allow` command allows the user specified in `<username>` to connect via FTP from the explicitly listed addresses in `<addrglob>`. You can list multiple addresses.

The `deny` command explicitly denies the specified user `<username>` from the sites listed in `<addrglob>`. You can list multiple sites.

The FTP Log File—/var/log/xferlog

Although `/var/log/xferlog` isn't a configuration file, it is important nonetheless. In this file, all the logs generated by the FTP server are stored. Each line of the log consists of the following:

current-time	The current time in `DDD MMM dd hh:mm:ss YYYY` format, where `DDD` is the day of the week, `MMM` is the month, `dd` is the day of the month, `hh:mm:ss` is the time in military format, and `YYYY` is the year
transfer-time	The total time in seconds spent transferring the file
remote-host	The hostname of the client that initiated the transfer
file-size	The size of the file that was transferred
filename	The name of the file that was transferred
transfer-type	The type of transfer done, where `a` is an ASCII transfer and `b` is a binary transfer
special-action-flag	A list of actions taken on the file by the server, where `C` means the file was compressed, `U` means the file was uncompressed, `T` means the file was tarred, and `-` means that no action was taken
direction	A flag indicating whether the file was outgoing or incoming, represented by an `o` or `i`, respectively
access-mode	The type of user who performed the action, where `a` is anonymous, `g` is a guest, and `r` is a real user
username	The local username if the user was of type `real`
service-name	The name of the service being invoked (most often FTP)
authentication-method	The type of authentication used; `0` means no authentication was done (anonymous user), and `1` means the user was validated with RFC 931 Authentication Server Protocol
authenticated-user-id	The username by which this transfer was authenticated

FTP Administrative Tools

Several tools are available to help you administer your FTP server. These tools were automatically installed as part of the wu-ftp package when the wu-ftpd RPM was installed. These utilities help you see the current status of the server as well as control its shutdown procedure:

- ftpshut
- ftpwho
- ftpcount

ftpshut

The ftpshut command helps make shutting down the FTP server easier. This capability, of course, applies only if you are running the server all the time instead of leaving it to be invoked from inetd as needed. The format of ftpshut is

```
ftpshut -l <login-minutes> -d <drop-minutes> <time> <warning message>
```

where <login-minutes> is the number of minutes before the server shutdown that the server will begin refusing new FTP transactions. <drop-minutes> is the number of minutes before the server shutdown that the server will begin dropping existing connections. The default value for <login-minutes> is 10, and the default for <drop-minutes> is 5.

<time> is the time at which the server will be shut down. You can specify this time in one of three ways. The first is to specify the time in military format without the colon (for example, 0312 to indicate 3:12 a.m.). The second is to specify the number of minutes to wait before shutting down. The format of this method is +<min>, where <min> is the number of minutes to wait. (For example, +60 causes the server to shut down in 60 minutes.) The last option is the most drastic; by specifying the string now, the server shuts down immediately.

<warning message> is the message displayed on all the FTP clients that the server will be shut down. See the description of the shutdown command for the /etc/ftpaccess file earlier in this chapter for details on the formatting available for the warning message.

ftpwho

ftpwho displays all the active users on the system connected through FTP. The output of the command is in the format of the /bin/ps command. This format of this command is

```
<pid> <tty> <stat> <time> <connection details>
```

where <pid> is the process ID of the FTP daemon handling the transfer; <tty> is always a question mark (?) because the connection is coming from FTP, not Telnet; <stat> is the status of that particular instance of the daemon where S means it's sleeping, Z means it has crashed (gone "zombie"), and R means that it is the currently running process. <time> indicates how much actual CPU time that instance of the FTP has taken, and finally, <connection details> tells where the connection is coming from, who is the user, and what that user's current function is.

The following is an example of output from `ftpwho`:

```
Service class all:
10448  ?  S   0:00 ftpd: vestax.domain.com: anonymous/sshah@domain.com: IDLE
10501  ?  S   0:00 ftpd: toybox.domain.com: heidi: RETR mklinux-ALL.sit.bin
   -    2 users ( -1 maximum)
```

Here, you can see that two users are logged in (an unlimited number of users is allowed to connect). The first user is an anonymous user who claims to be `sshah@domain.com` and is currently not performing any functions. The second user, who has the username `heidi`, is currently retrieving the file `mklinux-ALL.sit.bin`.

ftpcount

`ftpcount`, which is a simplified version of `ftpwho`, shows only the total count of users logged in to the system and the maximum number of users allowed. A sample output from `ftpcount` shows the following:

```
Service class all                     -    2 users ( -1 maximum)
```

Summary

You might think that the proliferation of the World Wide Web would make FTP servers extinct; however, the last few years have shown us that quite the opposite is true. People are still deploying FTP sites in full force because of the ease of which they can be established and maintained. No cute HTML to do, no extra work—just put the file in the right place for download and let people get it.

This chapter covers a lot of detail on configuring the `wu-ftpd` server. The key points to remember when working with the FTP server are as follows:

- Keep a good watch on security announcements related to FTP servers, especially the `wu-ftpd` server.
- Monitor your logs for suspicious activity.
- Test your configuration carefully. With the large number of options available, you want to be sure that it behaves the way you intend it to.
- When setting up file owners and permissions, be sure that the permissions are correct.
- Use a lot of messages to help make your server self-documenting to outside users.

Apache Server

by Manuel Alberto Ricart, Eric Goebelbecker, and Richard Bowen

IN THIS CHAPTER

This chapter guides you through the installation and configuration of the Apache Web server using Red Hat's RPM system. Red Hat includes the current version of Apache with its overall Linux product. However, if the latest version of Red Hat Linux is a few months old, a more recent version of Apache can be found in the `/pub/contrib` area of Red Hat's FTP server. For information about the latest version of Apache, such as what bug fixes and new features have been added, see the Apache group's Web server, `http://www.apache.org`, or the Apache Week Web site at `http://www.apacheweek.org`.

The current version of Red Hat Linux, version 4.2, includes Apache version 1.1.3. The latest stable release of Apache available at the time of this printing is 1.2.4, and 1.3 is available in beta form. Version 1.2.4 is available in RPM format on Red Hat's FTP server.

There is a lag between the release of new and beta versions of Apache and its corresponding RPM packages. Installing Apache from source code is possible on Red Hat Linux, but is beyond the scope of this chapter because the installer has to either alter the directory structure of the workstation or imitate the directory structure of a previous Apache RPM.

Server Installation

The Apache RPM can either be found on the Red Hat Linux installation media or on the Red Hat FTP server. It can be installed like any other RPM with the command-line `rpm` tool or with `glint`, the X Window package management utility. To install the package using `rpm`, execute

```
rpm -i latest_apache.rpm
```

where *`latest_apache.rpm`* is the name of the latest Apache RPM.

TIP

If Apache has already been installed on your system, this command will fail. To force `rpm` to install the latest version, use this command:

```
rpm -i --force apache-1.2.4-5.i386.rpm
```

The Apache RPM installs files in the following directories:

- `/etc/httpd/conf`—This directory contains all the Apache configuration files.
- `/etc/rc.d/`—The tree under this directory contains the system startup scripts. The Apache RPM installs a complete set for the Web server. These scripts can be used to start and stop the server from the command line and will also automatically start and stop the server when the workstation is halted, started, or rebooted.
- `/home/httpd`—The RPM installs the default server icons and CGI scripts in this location.

- `/usr/doc` and `/usr/man`—The RPM contains manual pages and `readme` files, which are placed in these directories. As is the case for most RPM packages, the `readme` and other related documentation is placed in a directory under `/usr/doc` that is named for the server version.
- `/usr/sbin`—The executable programs are placed in this directory.

Runtime Server Configuration Settings

Apache reads its configuration settings from three files: `access.conf`, `httpd.conf`, and `srm.conf`. Primarily, this organization has been developed to maintain backward compatibility with the NCSA server, but the reasoning behind it makes good sense. The configuration files reside in the `conf` subdirectory of the server distribution. Backup copies of the configuration files are included in the software distribution; they are named `access.conf-dist`, `httpd.conf-dist`, and `srm.conf-dist`, respectively.

Runtime configuration of your server is done by way of *configuration directives*. Directives are commands that set some option; you use them to tell the server about various options that you want to enable, such as the location of files important to the server configuration and operation. Configuration directives follow this syntax:

```
directive option option...
```

Directives are specified one per line. Some directives only set a value such as a filename; others let you specify various options. Some special directives, called *sections*, look like HTML tags. Section directives are surrounded by angle brackets, such as `<directive>`. Sections usually enclose a group of directives that apply only to the directory specified in the section:

```
<Directory somedir/in/your/tree>
  directive option option
  directive option option
</directive>
```

All sections are closed with a matching section tag that looks like `</directive>`. You will see some of these constructs in the `conf/access.conf` and in your `conf/httpd.conf` files. Note that section tags, like any other directives, are specified one per line.

Editing `httpd.conf`

`httpd.conf` contains configuration directives that control how the server runs, where its logfiles are found, the user ID (UID) it runs under, the port that it listens to, and so on. You need to edit some of the default configuration values to settings that make sense in your site. I kept most of the defaults found on my `httpd.conf`, with the exception of the following:

`ServerAdmin`	The `ServerAdmin` directive should be set to the address of the Webmaster managing the server. It should be a valid e-mail address or alias, such as *`webmaster@your.domain`*.

Setting this value to a valid address is important because this address will be returned to a visitor when a problem occurs (see Figure 9.1).

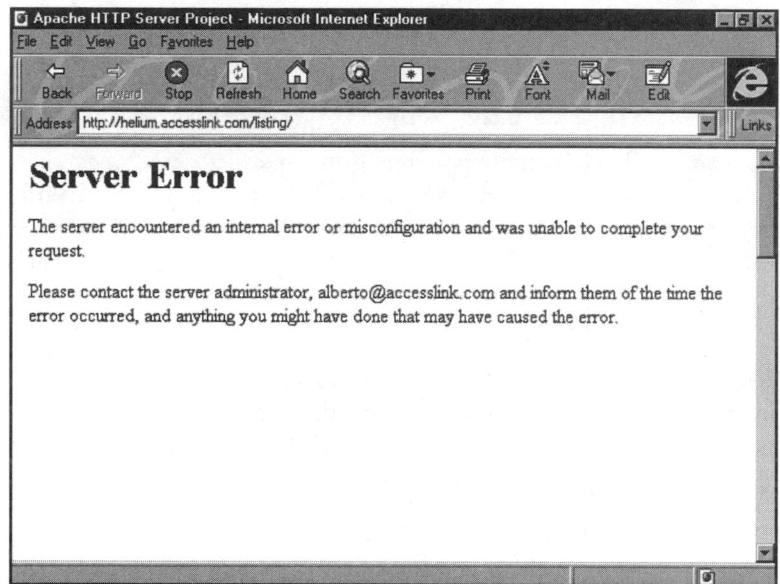

FIGURE 9.1.
One of the error messages the server returns if an error occurs. Note that the `ServerAdmin` *was set to* `alberto@accesslink.com`.

`User` and `Group`

The `User` and `Group` directives set the UID and group ID (GID) that the server will use to process requests. I kept these settings as the defaults: `nobody` and `nogroup`. Verify that the names `nobody` and `nogroup` exist in your `/etc/passwd` and `/etc/group` files, respectively. (They are provided by Red Hat Linux, so they should already be defined.) If you want to use a different UID or GID, go ahead; however, be aware that the server will run with the permissions you define here. The permissions for the specified UID and GID should be limited because, in case of a security hole, whether on the server or (more likely) in your own CGI programs, those programs will run with the assigned UID. If the server runs as root or some other privileged user, someone can exploit the security holes and do nasty things to your site. Instead of specifying the `User` and `Group` directives using names, you can specify them by using the UID and GID numbers. If you use numbers, be sure that the numbers you specify correspond to the user and group you want, and that they are preceded by the pound (#) symbol.

Here's how these directives would look if specified by name:

```
User nobody
Group nogroup
```

Here's the same specification, but by UID and GID:

```
User #-1
Group #-1
```

`ServerName`

The `ServerName` directive sets the hostname the server will return. Set it to a fully qualified domain name (fqdn). If this value is not set, the server will try to figure out the name by itself and set it to its canonical name. However, you might want the server to return a friendlier address such as `www.your.domain`. Whatever you do, `ServerName` should be a real Domain Name System (DNS) name for your network. If you are administering your own DNS, remember to add a `CNAME` alias for your host. If someone else manages the DNS for you, ask that person to set this name for you.

Your `ServerName` entry should look like this:

```
ServerName www.your.domain
```

TIP

If you want to install a Web server for test purposes on a standalone machine, you can do so by specifying a `ServerName` of `localhost`. You can then access the server as `http://www.localhost` from within the standalone machine. This approach can be useful for trying new configurations or Internet Web servers.

`ServerRoot`

This directive sets the absolute path to your server directory. This directive tells the server where to find all the resources and configuration files. Many of these resources are specified in the configuration files relative to the `ServerRoot` directory.

Your `ServerRoot` directive should read:

```
ServerRoot /etc/httpd
```

Editing `srm.conf`

The `srm.conf` file is the resource configuration file. It controls settings related to the location of your Web document tree, the CGI program directories, and other resource configuration issues that affect your Web site. I kept most of the defaults found on my `srm.conf` file. The most important directives on this configuration file are as follow:

`DocumentRoot`	Set this directive to the absolute path of your document tree. Your document tree is the top directory from which Apache will serve files. By default, it is set to `/home/httpd/html`.
`UserDir`	This directive defines the directory relative to a local user's home directory where that user will put public HTML documents. It's relative because each user will have his or her own HTML directory. The default setting for this directive is `public_html`, so each user will be able to create a directory called `public_html` under his or her home directory, and HTML documents placed in that directory will be available as `http://servername/~username`, where *`username`* is the username of the particular user.

Allowing individual users to put Web content on your server poses several important security considerations. If you are operating a Web server on the Internet rather than on a private network, you should read the WWW Security FAQ by Lincoln Stein. You can find a copy at `http://www.genome.wi.mit.edu/WWW/faqs/www-security-faq.html`.

A copy of the boilerplate `conf/srm.conf` file has been included at the end of this chapter in Listing 9.2.

Editing `access.conf`

`access.conf` is the global *access control file*; it configures the type of access users have to your site and the documents you make available, as well as security issues defining the extent to which users can alter the security settings you might have defined. The default configuration provides unrestricted access to documents in your `DocumentRoot`. I kept all the defaults found in my `access.conf` file.

If you want to provide a more restrictive site, you might want to verify that all `<Directory` *`path`*`>` sections match the directories they list in your installation. The `Directory` sections specify a set of options, usually involving security issues, on a per-directory basis. In particular, you might want to remove the `Indexes` option that follows the `Options` directive on the section that looks like this:

```
<Directory /home/httpd/cgi-bin>
Options Indexes FollowSymLinks
</Directory>
```

Actually, the example given here is a very bad one because it turns on two options for the `cgi-bin` directory that no decent system administrator would ever allow. The `Indexes` option allows for server-generated directory listings. You probably don't want anyone peeking at the contents of your `cgi-bin` directories. The `FollowSymLinks` directive allows the Web server to follow symbolic links to other directories. This directive is a potential security problem because it could allow the server to "escape" from the server directories and could potentially allow users to access files that you do not want them to see.

Options that you implement on your global configuration files can be overridden by the use of an `.htaccess` file. `.htaccess` files allow you to set server directives on a per-directory basis. This capability is particularly useful for user directories, where the user does not have access to the main server configuration files. You can disable all `.htaccess` overrides by setting the directive `AllowOverride` to `None`, as follows. This directive is, by default, set to allow all overrides.

```
AllowOverride None
```

Configuring an inetd Server

Normally, Apache runs in standalone mode or daemon mode. How it is run by the system depends on how it is configured by the `ServerType` directive in `conf/httpd.conf`.

A *standalone server* offers superior performance over `inetd`-run servers because usually a server process is ready to serve a request. When run under `inetd` (the Internet daemon), a new server is started every time a request is received on the HTTP port. A considerable amount of overhead is involved in starting a new server process with each new request.

The default setting for `ServerType` is standalone; unless you have an extremely light traffic site, you should stick with this setting. `inetd` servers are good for information you want to make available but for which you don't want to dedicate a computer.

> **TIP**
>
> An `inetd` server is great for testing configuration settings because the server rereads all its settings every time it receives a request. On a standalone server, you need to restart the server manually before it sees any changes you made to the configuration files.

To run a server from `inetd`, you need to modify `conf/httpd.conf` once more and change the `ServerType` directive from standalone to `inetd`, as follows:

```
ServerType inetd
```

The `Port` directive has no effect on an `inetd` server. A standalone server uses this configuration information to learn which port it should be listening to. Because `inetd` does the binding between the port and the software, this setting has no effect on an `inetd` configuration.

Configuring inetd

`inetd` is the "Internet superserver." It gets started when the machine boots by `/etc/rc`. After it is launched, `inetd` listens for connections on Internet socket ports. When it finds a connection, it starts the program responsible for managing that port. When the request is served and the program exits, `inetd` continues to listen for additional requests on that port.

To make Apache work from `inetd`, you need to edit `/etc/inetd.conf` and `/etc/services`. Configuring an `inetd` server requires a bit more system configuration than a standalone server.

First, you need to edit your `/etc/services` file. The `/etc/services` database contains information about all known services available on the Internet. Each service is represented by a single line listing the following information:

Official service name

Port number

Protocol name

Aliases by which the service is known

Each entry is separated by a tab or spaces. An entry describing `httpd` looks like this:

```
http portnumber/tcp httpd httpd
```

TCP/IP RESERVED PORTS

TCP/IP ports range from 0 to 65,535; however, the first 1,024 ports are reserved. A reserved port is controlled and assigned by the IANA and, on most systems, can be used only by system (or root) processes or by programs executed by privileged users. (The IANA is the Internet Assigned Numbers Authority. More details about the IANA and reserved ports are available at `http://www.sockets.com/services.htm#WellKnownPorts`.) If you want to run the server at port 80 (the default for `httpd`), the superuser must start `httpd`.

Set *portnumber* to the port number on which you want to run the server. Typically, this port will be port 80 for a standalone server. `inetd` servers run better at port 8080, so your entry will look like this:

```
http 8080/tcp httpd httpd
```

If you are running NetInfo, you can type this line into a temporary file, such as /tmp/services, and then run

```
niload services . < /tmp/services
```

Next, you need to edit /etc/inetd.conf to configure inetd to listen for httpd requests. Each line in inetd.conf contains the following information:

Service name

Socket type

Protocol

Wait/no wait

User the server program will run as

Server program

Server program arguments

My completed entry looks like this:

```
httpd  stream  tcp  nowait nobody  /sbin/httpd httpd -f /etc/httpd/conf/httpd.conf
```

WARNING

The preceding example starts the server as nobody. Typically, you will want a standalone server to be started by the root user so that the server can bind to port 80, the standard HTTP port, and be able to change the UID and GID of its children processes. When the standalone server starts, it forks children processes. These children processes run with a UID of nobody and a GID of nogroup, unless you specified a different setting with the User and Group directives. The children processes handle the HTTP requests. The main process, owned by root, has as its duty the creation and destruction of its children processes. This makes the standard, standalone server secure.

If you specify the root UID in this example with the intention of running the inetd server on port 80, the process handling the request is owned by root. This setup can create security problems; unlike a standalone server, the inetd server doesn't fork any children processes, so it handles requests with the UID and GID of the process owner.

After adding the httpd entry to /etc/inetd.conf, you need to restart inetd. You can easily do so by finding out the inetd process number by using ps and sending it a HANGUP signal:

```
# kill -HUP InetdProcessID
```

Replace the *InetdProcessID* with the process number listed by the ps command. If the PID listed is 86, you would type kill -HUP 86.

inetd then restarts, rereading the configuration file that instructs it to listen for a request for port 8080.

Running the Web Server for the First Time

Before you can run the server for the first time, you need to create an HTML document. The standard Apache distribution includes such a file, but I have created another file that is more useful, and I am sure that you'll use it time and time again. Using your favorite text editor, create a file called `index.html` inside the `htdocs` directory with this content:

```
<HTML>
<HEAD>
<TITLE>Red Hat Linux Unleashed</TITLE>
</HEAD>
<BODY BGCOLOR="#ffffff" LINK="#000080" VLINK="#000080">
<H1><CENTER>Red Hat Linux Unleashed </CENTER></H1>
<H2><CENTER>Congratulations! Your Apache server was successfully
installed.</CENTER></H2>

<H3>Here are some interesting sites that host information about
the Apache server: </H3>

<UL>
<LI>The official homepage for the
<A HREF="http://www.apache.org">Apache Group</A>

<LI>The official homepage for
<A HREF="http://www.us.apache-ssl.com">Community Connexion</A>
developers of Stronghold: Apache-SSL-US (A Netscape compatible
SSL server based on Apache)

<LI>The official homepage for
<A HREF="http://www.algroup.co.uk/Apache-SSL">Apache-SSL</A>
(A Netscape compatible SSL server based on Apache - only available
to users outside of the United States).

<LI><A HREF="http://www.zyzzyva.com/server/module_registry/">
Apache Module Registry</A>, the place where you can find information
about 3<SUP>rd</SUP> party Apache modules and other development stuff.

<LI><A HREF="http://www.apacheweek.com">The Apache Week Home</A>,
here you will find an essential weekly guide dedicated to Apache server
➥information.

<LI><A HREF="http://www.ukweb.com">UK Web's Apache Support Center</A>

<LI><A HREF="http://www.fastcgi.com">The FastCGI Website</A>
</UL>

<P>
<STRONG>Deja News a very handy USENET news search engine:</STRONG>
<FORM ACTION="http://search.dejanews.com/dnquery.xp" METHOD=POST>

<P>
<CENTER>
<STRONG>Quick Search For:</STRONG> <INPUT NAME="query" VALUE="Apache" SIZE="37">
<INPUT TYPE="submit" VALUE="Search!"><INPUT NAME="defaultOp" VALUE="AND"
➥TYPE="hidden">
<INPUT NAME="svcclass" VALUE="dncurrent" TYPE="hidden">
<INPUT NAME="maxhits" VALUE="20" TYPE="hidden">
```

```
</CENTER>
</FORM>

</BODY>
</HTML>
```

Put this file in your `htdocs` directory. At this point, you are ready to test the server.

Starting a Standalone Server

If you are running a standalone server, you need to start `httpd` manually. You do so by entering the following line:

```
# /sbin/httpd -f /etc/httpd/conf/httpd.conf
```

Note that I started the standalone server from the root account, indicated by the pound sign (`#`) at the beginning of the line. You need to start standalone servers by root so that two important events occur:

- If your standalone server uses the default HTTP port (port 80), only the superuser can bind to Internet ports that are lower than 1025.
- Only processes owned by root can change their UID and GID as specified by the `User` and `Group` directives. If you start the server under another UID, it will run with the permissions of the user starting the process.

Starting an `inetd` Server

As you probably guessed, you don't need to start an `inetd` server. `inetd` starts `httpd` every time a request is received in the port assigned to the server. `inetd` servers make good development platforms because configuration settings are reread every time you send a request.

Starting and Stopping the Server

The Apache server, `httpd`, has a few command-line options you can use to set some defaults specifying where `httpd` will read its configuration directives. The Apache `httpd` executable understands the following options:

```
httpd [-d ServerRoot] [-f ConfigurationFile] [-x] [-v] [-?]
```

The `-d` option overrides the location of the *`ServerRoot`* directory. It sets the initial value of the *`ServerRoot`* variable (the directory where the Apache server is installed) to whatever path you specify. This default is usually read from the *`ServerRoot`* directive in `httpd.conf`.

The `-f` flag specifies the location of the main configuration file, `conf/httpd.conf`. It reads and executes the configuration commands found on *`ConfigurationFile`* on startup. If the *`ConfigurationFile`* is not an absolute path (doesn't begin with a `/`), its location is assumed to be relative to the path specified in the *`ServerRoot`* directive in `httpd.conf`. By default, this value is set to *`ServerRoot`*`/conf/httpd.conf`.

The -x option is used by the developers of Apache as a debugging aid and should not be used under normal server operation. It runs a single server process that does not create any children.

The -v option prints the development version of the Apache server and terminates the process.

The -? option prints the following usage information for the server:

```
Usage: httpd [-d directory] [-f file] [-v]
-d directory : specify an alternate initial ServerRoot
-f file : specify an alternate ServerConfigFile
```

The start Script

I have developed a small start script that launches the server with all the command-line settings I use. This script saves me a little typing when I'm trying tasks that require me to start and stop the server. Here's the listing for the start script:

```
#!/bin/sh
/sbin/httpd -f /etc/httpd/conf/httpd.conf
```

You can create such a script by just typing it into a file (one per script). After you finish entering it, to turn it into executable, type

```
cd WhereEverYouEnterThem
chmod 755 start stop restart
```

You might want to store the script in a place where it is convenient, such as /usr/local/bin.

The Apache RPM installs a script in /etc/rc3.d named S85httpd that will start the server with the default configuration file.

The stop Script

The server is designed to stop gracefully when it is sent a TERM (terminate) signal. When the server starts, it spawns several children processes; it therefore becomes more difficult to terminate. Apache automatically kills any children processes when the main process is killed. Luckily, the developers of Apache put the process ID of the main process in a file where you can easily obtain the ID. My stop script makes use of the PidFile (/usr/local/etc/httpd/logs/PidFile) file.

The following is the listing for the stop script:

```
#!/bin/sh
#Stop Apache Script
kill 'cat /var/log/httpd/httpd.pid'
```

The Apache RPM installs a script named K25httpd in /etc/rc0.d/ that will stop the server.

The restart Script

The server is designed to restart if it receives a -HUP (hang-up) signal. On receiving this type of signal, the server stops and immediately restarts, rereading its configuration files.

Here's the listing for the `restart` script:

```
#!/bin/sh
#Restart Apache Script
kill -HUP 'cat /var/log/httpd/logs/httpd.pid'
```

This convenient script automates the process. Any time you modify any of the configuration files, you need to restart the server to enable the changes. Using `htrestart` makes performing this process easy.

Configuration File Listings

For your convenience, I have provided listings of the various configuration files I talked about in this chapter. You might notice some differences between the files listed here and configuration files of source you download from the Internet. These differences are normal because newer versions of the server might have been released since this printing.

Listing 9.1 shows the server configuration file.

Listing 9.1. `conf/httpd.conf`.

```
# This is the main server configuration file. See URL http://www.apache.org/
# for instructions.

# Do NOT simply read the instructions in here without understanding
# what they do, if you are unsure consult the online docs. You have been
# warned.

# Originally by Rob McCool

# ServerType is either inetd, or standalone.

ServerType standalone

# If you are running from inetd, go to "ServerAdmin".

# Port: The port the standalone listens to. For ports < 1023, you will
# need httpd to be run as root initially.

Port 80

# HostnameLookups: Log the names of clients or just their IP numbers
#   e.g.   www.apache.org (on) or 204.62.129.132 (off)
HostnameLookups on

# If you wish httpd to run as a different user or group, you must run
# httpd as root initially and it will switch.

# User/Group: The name (or #number) of the user/group to run httpd as.
#  On SCO (ODT 3) use User nouser and Group nogroup
User nobody
Group #-1
```


continues

Listing 9.1. continued

```
# ServerAdmin: Your address, where problems with the server should be
# e-mailed.

ServerAdmin you@your.address

# ServerRoot: The directory the server's config, error, and log files
# are kept in

ServerRoot /etc/httpd

# BindAddress: You can support virtual hosts with this option. This option
# is used to tell the server which IP address to listen to. It can either
# contain "*", an IP address, or a fully qualified Internet domain name.
# See also the VirtualHost directive.

#BindAddress *

# ErrorLog: The location of the error log file. If this does not start
# with /, ServerRoot is prepended to it.

ErrorLog logs/error_log

# TransferLog: The location of the transfer log file. If this does not
# start with /, ServerRoot is prepended to it.

TransferLog logs/access_log

# PidFile: The file the server should log its pid to
PidFile logs/httpd.pid

# ScoreBoardFile: File used to store internal server process information
ScoreBoardFile logs/apache_status

# ServerName allows you to set a host name which is sent back to clients for
# your server if it's different than the one the program would get (i.e. use
# "www" instead of the host's real name).
#
# Note: You cannot just invent host names and hope they work. The name you
# define here must be a valid DNS name for your host. If you don't understand
# this, ask your network administrator.

#ServerName new.host.name

# CacheNegotiatedDocs: By default, Apache sends Pragma: no-cache with each
# document that was negotiated on the basis of content. This asks proxy
# servers not to cache the document. Uncommenting the following line disables
# this behavior, and proxies will be allowed to cache the documents.

#CacheNegotiatedDocs

# Timeout: The number of seconds before receives and sends time out
#  n.b. the compiled default is 1200 (20 minutes !)

Timeout 400
```

```
# KeepAlive: The number of Keep-Alive persistent requests to accept
# per connection. Set to 0 to deactivate Keep-Alive support

KeepAlive 5

# KeepAliveTimeout: Number of seconds to wait for the next request

KeepAliveTimeout 15

# Server-pool size regulation.  Rather than making you guess how many
# server processes you need, Apache dynamically adapts to the load it
# sees --- that is, it tries to maintain enough server processes to
# handle the current load, plus a few spare servers to handle transient
# load spikes (e.g., multiple simultaneous requests from a single
# Netscape browser).

# It does this by periodically checking how many servers are waiting
# for a request.  If there are fewer than MinSpareServers, it creates
# a new spare.  If there are more than MaxSpareServers, some of the
# spares die off.  These values are probably OK for most sites ---

MinSpareServers 5
MaxSpareServers 10

# Number of servers to start --- should be a reasonable ballpark figure.

StartServers 5

# Limit on total number of servers running, i.e., limit on the number
# of clients who can simultaneously connect --- if this limit is ever
# reached, clients will be LOCKED OUT, so it should NOT BE SET TOO LOW.
# It is intended mainly as a brake to keep a runaway server from taking
# Unix with it as it spirals down...

MaxClients 150

# MaxRequestsPerChild: the number of requests each child process is
#  allowed to process before the child dies.
#  The child will exit so as to avoid problems after prolonged use when
#  Apache (and maybe the libraries it uses) leak.  On most systems, this
#  isn't really needed, but a few (such as Solaris) do have notable leaks
#  in the libraries.

MaxRequestsPerChild 30

# Proxy Server directives. Uncomment the following line to
# enable the proxy server:

#ProxyRequests On

# To enable the cache as well, edit and uncomment the following lines:

#CacheRoot /usr/local/etc/httpd/proxy
#CacheSize 5
#CacheGcInterval 4
#CacheMaxExpire 24
#CacheLastModifiedFactor 0.1
```

continues

Listing 9.1. continued

```
#CacheDefaultExpire 1
#NoCache adomain.com anotherdomain.edu joes.garage.com

# Listen: Allows you to bind Apache to specific IP addresses and/or
# ports, in addition to the default. See also the VirtualHost command

#Listen 3000
#Listen 12.34.56.78:80

# VirtualHost: Allows the daemon to respond to requests for more than one
# server address, if your server machine is configured to accept IP packets
# for multiple addresses. This can be accomplished with the ifconfig
# alias flag, or through kernel patches like VIF.

# Any httpd.conf or srm.conf directive may go into a VirtualHost command.
# See also the BindAddress entry.

#<VirtualHost host.foo.com>
#ServerAdmin webmaster@host.foo.com
#DocumentRoot /www/docs/host.foo.com
#ServerName host.foo.com
#ErrorLog logs/host.foo.com-error_log
#TransferLog logs/host.foo.com-access_log
#</VirtualHost>
```

Listing 9.2 shows the resource configuration file.

Listing 9.2. conf/srm.conf.

```
# With this document, you define the name space that users see of your http
# server.  This file also defines server settings which affect how requests are
# serviced, and how results should be formatted.

# See the tutorials at http://www.apache.org/ for
# more information.

# Originally by Rob McCool; Adapted for Apache

# DocumentRoot: The directory out of which you will serve your
# documents. By default, all requests are taken from this directory, but
# symbolic links and aliases may be used to point to other locations.

DocumentRoot /home/httpd/html

# UserDir: The name of the directory which is appended onto a user's home
# directory if a ~user request is received.

UserDir public_html

# DirectoryIndex: Name of the file or files to use as a pre-written HTML
# directory index.  Separate multiple entries with spaces.

DirectoryIndex index.html
```

```
# FancyIndexing is whether you want fancy directory indexing or standard

FancyIndexing on

# AddIcon tells the server which icon to show for different files or filename
# extensions

AddIconByEncoding (CMP,/icons/compressed.gif) x-compress x-gzip

AddIconByType (TXT,/icons/text.gif) text/*
AddIconByType (IMG,/icons/image2.gif) image/*
AddIconByType (SND,/icons/sound2.gif) audio/*
AddIconByType (VID,/icons/movie.gif) video/*

AddIcon /icons/binary.gif .bin .exe
AddIcon /icons/binhex.gif .hqx
AddIcon /icons/tar.gif .tar
AddIcon /icons/world2.gif .wrl .wrl.gz .vrml .vrm .iv
AddIcon /icons/compressed.gif .Z .z .tgz .gz .zip
AddIcon /icons/a.gif .ps .ai .eps
AddIcon /icons/layout.gif .html .shtml .htm .pdf
AddIcon /icons/text.gif .txt
AddIcon /icons/c.gif .c
AddIcon /icons/p.gif .pl .py
AddIcon /icons/f.gif .for
AddIcon /icons/dvi.gif .dvi
AddIcon /icons/uuencoded.gif .uu
AddIcon /icons/script.gif .conf .sh .shar .csh .ksh .tcl
AddIcon /icons/tex.gif .tex
AddIcon /icons/bomb.gif core

AddIcon /icons/back.gif ..
AddIcon /icons/hand.right.gif README
AddIcon /icons/folder.gif ^^DIRECTORY^^
AddIcon /icons/blank.gif ^^BLANKICON^^

# DefaultIcon is which icon to show for files which do not have an icon
# explicitly set.

DefaultIcon /icons/unknown.gif

# AddDescription allows you to place a short description after a file in
# server-generated indexes.
# Format: AddDescription "description" filename

# ReadmeName is the name of the README file the server will look for by
# default. Format: ReadmeName name
#
# The server will first look for name.html, include it if found, and it will
# then look for name and include it as plaintext if found.
#
# HeaderName is the name of a file which should be prepended to
# directory indexes.

ReadmeName README
HeaderName HEADER
```

continues

Listing 9.2. continued

```
# IndexIgnore is a set of filenames which directory indexing should ignore
# Format: IndexIgnore name1 name2...

IndexIgnore */.??* *~ *# */HEADER* */README* */RCS

# AccessFileName: The name of the file to look for in each directory
# for access control information.

AccessFileName .htaccess

# DefaultType is the default MIME type for documents which the server
# cannot find the type of from filename extensions.

DefaultType text/plain

# AddEncoding allows you to have certain browsers (Mosaic/X 2.1+) uncompress
# information on the fly. Note: Not all browsers support this.

AddEncoding x-compress Z
AddEncoding x-gzip gz

# AddLanguage allows you to specify the language of a document. You can
# then use content negotiation to give a browser a file in a language
# it can understand.  Note that the suffix does not have to be the same
# as the language keyword --- those with documents in Polish (whose
# net-standard language code is pl) may wish to use "AddLanguage pl .po"
# to avoid the ambiguity with the common suffix for perl scripts.

AddLanguage en .en
AddLanguage fr .fr
AddLanguage de .de
AddLanguage da .da
AddLanguage el .el
AddLanguage it .it

# LanguagePriority allows you to give precedence to some languages
# in case of a tie during content negotiation.
# Just list the languages in decreasing order of preference.

LanguagePriority en fr de

# Redirect allows you to tell clients about documents which used to exist in
# your server's namespace, but do not anymore. This allows you to tell the
# clients where to look for the relocated document.
# Format: Redirect fakename url


# Aliases: Add here as many aliases as you need (with no limit). The format is
# Alias fakename realname

#Alias /icons/ /usr/local/etc/httpd/icons/

# ScriptAlias: This controls which directories contain server scripts.
# Format: ScriptAlias fakename realname
```

```
#ScriptAlias /cgi-bin/ /usr/local/etc/httpd/cgi-bin/

# If you want to use server side includes, or CGI outside
# ScriptAliased directories, uncomment the following lines.

# AddType allows you to tweak mime.types without actually editing it, or to
# make certain files to be certain types.
# Format: AddType type/subtype ext1

# AddHandler allows you to map certain file extensions to "handlers",
# actions unrelated to filetype. These can be either built into the server
# or added with the Action command (see below)
# Format: AddHandler action-name ext1

# To use CGI scripts:
#AddHandler cgi-script .cgi

# To use server-parsed HTML files
#AddType text/html .shtml
#AddHandler server-parsed .shtml

# Uncomment the following line to enable Apache's send-asis HTTP file
# feature
#AddHandler send-as-is asis

# If you wish to use server-parsed imagemap files, use
#AddHandler imap-file map

# To enable type maps, you might want to use
#AddHandler type-map var

# Action lets you define media types that will execute a script whenever
# a matching file is called. This eliminates the need for repeated URL
# pathnames for oft-used CGI file processors.
# Format: Action media/type /cgi-script/location
# Format: Action handler-name /cgi-script/location

# For example to add a footer (footer.html in your document root) to
# files with extension .foot (e.g. foo.html.foot), you could use:
#AddHandler foot-action foot
#Action foot-action /cgi-bin/footer

# Or to do this for all HTML files, for example, use:
#Action text/html /cgi-bin/footer

# MetaDir: specifies the name of the directory in which Apache can find
# meta information files. These files contain additional HTTP headers
# to include when sending the document

#MetaDir .web

# MetaSuffix: specifies the file name suffix for the file containing the
# meta information.

#MetaSuffix .meta
```


continues

Listing 9.2. continued

```
# Customizable error response (Apache style)
#  these come in three flavors
#
#    1) plain text
#ErrorDocument 500 "The server made a boo boo.
#  n.b.  the (") marks it as text, it does not get output
#
#    2) local redirects
#ErrorDocument 404 /missing.html
#  to redirect to local url /missing.html
#ErrorDocument 404 /cgi-bin/missing_handler.pl
#  n.b. can redirect to a script or a document using server-side-includes.
#
#    3) external redirects
#ErrorDocument 402 http://other.server.com/subscription_info.html
#
```

Listing 9.3 shows the global access configuration file.

Listing 9.3. conf/access.conf.

```
# access.conf: Global access configuration
# Online docs at http://www.apache.org/

# This file defines server settings which affect which types of services
# are allowed, and in what circumstances.

# Each directory to which Apache has access can be configured with respect
# to which services and features are allowed and/or disabled in that
# directory (and its subdirectories).

# Originally by Rob McCool

# This should be changed to whatever you set DocumentRoot to.

<Directory /home/httpd/html>

# This may also be "None", "All", or any combination of "Indexes",
# "Includes", "FollowSymLinks", "ExecCGI", or "MultiViews".

# Note that "MultiViews" must be named *explicitly* — "Options All"
# doesn't give it to you (or at least, not yet).

Options Indexes FollowSymLinks

# This controls which options the .htaccess files in directories can
# override. Can also be "All", or any combination of "Options", "FileInfo",
# "AuthConfig", and "Limit"

AllowOverride None

# Controls who can get stuff from this server.
```

```
order allow,deny
allow from all

</Directory>

# /usr/local/etc/httpd/cgi-bin should be changed to wherever your ScriptAliased
# CGI directory exists, if you have that configured.

<Directory /home/httpd/cgi-bin>
AllowOverride None
Options None
</Directory>

# Allow server status reports, with the URL of http://servername/status
# Change the ".nowhere.com" to match your domain to enable.

#<Location /status>
#SetHandler server-status

#order deny,allow
#deny from all
#allow from .nowhere.com
#</Location>

# You may place any other directories or locations you wish to have
# access information for after this one.
```

Summary

Congratulations! At this point, you should have a properly configured Apache server running. Several advanced options are available for Web sites running Apache, so you should check out the online documentation available at `http://www.apache.org/docs/` and the periodic articles available at `http://www.webweek.com/`. You can also subscribe to a weekly mailing from *Web Week* that will keep you informed about the latest developments in the Apache project. Reading about the Apache project itself, at `http://www.apache.org/ABOUT_APACHE.html`, is also particularly interesting. You can also find some fascinating information about the development of the World Wide Web at `http://www.webhistory.org/`. If you are interested in Perl and CGI programming, you might want to take a look at the Apache/Perl integration project at `http://perl.apache.org/`. Finally, if you have other operating systems on other machines, remember that Apache is available for a variety of other platforms, including OS/2 and, very soon now, Windows. (The beta version of Apache 1.3 does have Windows support, but this product isn't in its final and stable form yet.) Of course, real Web sites run on Red Hat!

CHAPTER 10

X Window

by Kamran Husain

IN THIS CHAPTER

This chapter details the way to configure the X Window System for Linux. This version of X Window for Linux is called XFree86 version 3.3.1.

This chapter covers the following topics with regard to configuring your X Window System:

- How to configure XFree86 on your system
- Working with the `xf86config` program and the `XF86Config` file
- What the `.xinitrc` file is
- Your personal X resource file
- Using `xdm`
- Configuration of the window manager

Setting Up Your XFree86 System

This section covers another one of the most difficult, time-consuming, and frustrating parts of installing XFree86: setting up an `XF86Config` file.

If you have XFree86 3.3.1 and your graphic card is listed in the `Hardware-HOWTO` file, you should use the `xf86config` program to do your configuration. This `xf86config` program is a comfortable and safe way to set up your system. If your graphics card is not listed, you have some work ahead of you.

The XF86Config File

To be able to set up an `XF86Config` file, you need to read these files from `/usr/X11R6/lib/X11/doc`: `README`, `README.Config`, `VideoModes.doc`, and `README.Linux`. You also need to read the man pages on the following topics: `XF86Config`, `XFree86`, and the server you are using.

The `XF86Config` file can be located in several places:

- `/usr/X11R6/lib/X11`. This is the standard location for the sample `XF86Config` file, but in some cases you cannot use it (for example, a read-only `/usr` partition).
- `/etc`.
- In your `home` directory.
- As `XF86Config.eg` in `/usr/X11R6/lib/X11`.

The Linux filesystem standard places the `XF86Config` file in `/etc/X11`. The XFree86 servers will not "expect" an `XF86Config` file at this location, so there must be a link from one of the places in the preceding list to `/usr/X11R6/lib/X11`. Find this link first and use it to access the file. This way, you can be sure your changes take effect.

To give you some hints, here is a list of what you need to set up the `XF86Config` file correctly:

- The server suitable for your system. To get a hint as to which is the correct one, run the `SuperProbe` program that comes with XFree86. It will identify your chipset, and you can look at the `XFree86HOWTO` file on the CD-ROM at the back of this book to see which server supports this chipset. Note that `SuperProbe` can detect far more hardware than XFree86 supports.

- Your monitor's specifications, most importantly the maximum horizontal and vertical scan frequency ranges and the bandwidth. This information can be obtained from your monitor's datasheet.
- The name of the chipset for your video card. For example, Tseng Labs, ET3000, ET4000, and so on.
- The available dot clocks for your card or (if supported) the name of the programmable dot clock generator. Learn how to obtain these by reading the file `/usr/X11R6/lib/X11/doc/README.Config`. Running `XF86Config` sets your system's dot clocks.
- "Mouse type" refers to the protocol the mouse is using, not to the manufacturer. For example, a serial Microsoft mouse connected to the PS/2 port uses the PS/2 protocol, not the Microsoft protocol.
- The type of device your mouse is connected to: serial or bus. (Usually you can use `/dev/mouse`.)
- Whether you want to use a national keyboard map or if you want to run the generic U.S. key table.

CAUTION

Do not share `XF86Config` files with people who do not have the same configuration (graphics card and monitor). By sharing, you could fry your monitor.

It isn't so hard to figure out modes for multisync monitors. Don't ever use a mode that you haven't verified as being within your monitor's specs. Even if you have exactly the same setup as the computer you're sharing the file with, check all modes before trying them. There are many people who run their computers from specs that may not damage their hardware but could damage yours.

Using Xconfigurator

Red Hat Linux comes with a utility called `Xconfigurator`. This is a menu-driven tool that will ask questions about your video card, monitor, and mouse, and then create an `XF86Config` file for you. `Xconfigurator` will ask some fairly in-depth questions about your video card and monitor. Gather up all your documentation about your machine's hardware before running `Xconfigurator`.

Examining the XF86Config File

The `XF86Config` file contains all the configuration parameters for your X Window installation. Space does not permit me to print the whole file. You will have to look in the directory

/usr/lib/X11 for the XF86Config.eg file. Copy this XF86Config.eg file to XF86Config. Then edit the XF86Config file. The format of the XF86Config file consists of different sets that are listed in the following sections:

- Files (file pathnames)
- Font paths
- Keyboard type
- Pointer (including mouse type)
- Server flags (miscellaneous server options)
- Monitor (video modes)
- Device
- Screen

Each of these sections describes your hardware configuration, location of files, or both, to the X server. Each section is enclosed by the words:

```
Section "SectionName"
< information for the section >
EndSection
```

The File Pathnames

There is no reason to fiddle with the standard paths as provided in the sample XF86Config file. In fact, any distribution that provides a different path structure should have edited this section of the XF86Config.sample or the template XF86Config file for xf86config. You do have to know where these paths are pointing to in case of difficulties.

Your XF86Config file should look similar to the lines from my XF86Config file, as shown in Listing 10.1.

Listing 10.1. Font paths.

```
#
# Multiple FontPath entries are allowed (which are concatenated together),
# as well as specifying multiple comma-separated entries in one FontPath
# command (or a combination of both methods)
#
FontPath       "/usr/X11R6/lib/X11/fonts/misc/"
FontPath       "/usr/X11R6/lib/X11/fonts/Type1/"
FontPath       "/usr/X11R6/lib/X11/fonts/Speedo/"
FontPath       "/usr/X11R6/lib/X11/fonts/75dpi/"
# FontPath     "/usr/X11R6/lib/X11/fonts/100dpi/"
```

To see whether these lines are correct, look into each of the directories mentioned in Listing 10.1 to see whether they have files in them. If these directories are empty, you do not have the fonts installed, or they may be at another location.

The Keyboard Section

You should specify the `ServerNumlock` option. This is an easy way to specify your keyboard for XFree86. Otherwise, only those keyboard modifications needed for international keyboard support have to be set manually. In a typical `XF86Config` file, this section looks like the one shown in Listing 10.2.

Listing 10.2. Keyboard selection.

```
#
# Keyboard and various keyboard-related parameters
#
Section "Keyboard"
  AutoRepeat 500 5
  ServerNumLock
#  Xleds      1 2 3
#  DontZap
#
# To set the LeftAlt to Meta, RightAlt key to ModeShift,
# RightCtl key to Compose, and ScrollLock key to ModeLock:
#
#  LeftAlt     Meta
#  RightCtl    Compose
#  ScrollLock  ModeLock

# EndSection
```

The Pointer Section

The pointer section keyword is the name for the protocol the mouse uses. The available protocol names are listed in the `XF86Config` man page.

The Logitech serial mouse uses several keywords. The MouseMan uses the MouseMan keyword. The more recent Logitech serial mouse uses the Microsoft keyword. The older Logitech serial mouse uses the Logitech keyword.

Any mouse connected to the PS/2 port uses the PS/2 keyword even if it is in fact a serial mouse.

TIP

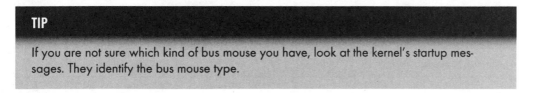

If you are not sure which kind of bus mouse you have, look at the kernel's startup messages. They identify the bus mouse type.

CAUTION

Ensure that the kernel bus mouse driver is using the same IRQ as the bus mouse. If not, you have to change the IRQ and rebuild the kernel. The IRQ for bus mouse devices is given in `/usr/src/linux/include/linux/busmouse.h`. The macro `MOUSE_IRQ` contains this IRQ and is set to `5` by default.

The following is a list of device names for the mouse selection:

- `/dev/inportbm`—Use for the Microsoft bus mouse. Note that this uses the bus mouse protocol, not the Microsoft protocol.
- `/dev/logibm`—Use this for the Logitech bus mouse. Note that this uses the bus mouse protocol, not the Logitech protocol.
- `/dev/psaux`—Select for a PS/2 or quick port mouse. This uses the PS/2 protocol.
- `/dev/atibm`—For the ATI XL bus mouse. Note that the ATI GU bus mouse is a Logitech or Microsoft bus mouse, depending on the version you have.
- Other supported mice are serial mice; therefore, the device names are the same as the serial devices (`/dev/ttyS?` or `/dev/ttyS??` for Linux).

TIP

If you have a two-button mouse, you might want to emulate the third button by setting `Emulate3Buttons` in the mouse section. Emulation is accomplished by pressing both buttons simultaneously. There are quite a number of other settings available, but they usually are not needed. Look at the `XF86Config` man page for a list of available settings.

You have to select one type of mouse and its baud rate if it's serial. Note in Listing 10.3 that I have "uncommented" the Microsoft mouse selection for my mouse and the 1200-baud rate line, and you will have to uncomment the line that matches your mouse selection. The 1200-baud rate seems to work fine with older mice and using the 9600 rate did not result in a speed difference for newer mice. Your results may vary.

Listing 10.3. Mouse selection.

```
#
Section "Pointer"
# Mouse definition and related parameters
#
#MouseSystems "/dev/mouse"
Microsoft     "/dev/mouse"
#MMSeries     "/dev/mouse"
#Logitech     "/dev/mouse"
```

```
#MouseMan      "/dev/mouse"
#Busmouse      "/dev/mouse"
  BaudRate     1200
#  BaudRate    9600
#  SampleRate 150
#  Emulate3Buttons
... <deleted some stuff here > ...
EndSection
```

The Server Section

If you want to identify the chipset your graphics card uses, run `SuperProbe`, a program that comes with XFree86 and is capable of identifying a wide range of graphics hardware. Note that `SuperProbe` can probe far more hardware than XFree86 supports.

Listing 10.4 shows a plain setting for a 640×480 monitor for X with a virtual space of 800×600. A virtual space is an area where the display portion of your monitor is mapped onto. Your monitor is a window into this space.

Listing 10.4. Server selection.

```
#
# First the 8-bit color SVGA driver
#
vga256

#
# To disable SpeedUp, use NoSpeedUp
#
#  NoSpeedUp
#  Virtual    1152 900

  # Virtual   800 600
  Virtual     640 480
  ViewPort      0 0
  # Modes               "640x480" "800x600" "1024x768"
  # Modes               "640x480" "800x600"
  Modes                 "640x480"

#
# Next the 1-bit mono SVGA driver
#
vga2

  Virtual     800 600
  ViewPort      0 0
  Modes                 "640x480"
  # Modes          "800x600" "640x480"
```

Setting Up Video Modes

This is the hardest part. Please read `VideoModes.doc` before beginning. If you are using `xf86config` (which I strongly recommend) and your monitor is not in the database, choose the generic modes and start making your own modes from there. If you do not have `xf86config`, read the tutorial on building modes in the `README.Config` file.

> **NOTE**
>
> I know this entire chapter is full of warnings. Please do not be alarmed. Just be careful and read the instructions for each step before taking it.

The XFree86 distribution includes a neat utility, `xvidtune`, to tune video modes. Because there is no check on the usability of a mode, you have to check the mode data against your monitor's specifications before testing the mode. The first line of the tuning modes screen gives you information on the specifications of the mode. You have to continuously check that these values are within your monitor's capabilities before testing that mode.

See Listing 10.5 for the common video modes for XFree86.

Listing 10.5. Video modes.

```
Section "Device"
    Identifier "Generic VGA"
    VendorName "Unknown"
    BoardName "Unknown"
    ChipSet "generic"
#   VideoRam 256
#   Clocks 25.2 28.3
EndSection

# **********************************************************************
# Screen sections
# **********************************************************************

# The color SVGA server

Section "Screen"
    Driver      "svga"
    Device      "Generic SVGA"
    Monitor     "Generic Monitor"
    Subsection      "Display"
        Depth       8
        Modes      "640x480"
        ViewPort    0 0
        Virtual     800 600
    EndSubsection
EndSection

# The 16-color VGA server
```

```
Section "Screen"
    Driver      "vga16"
    Device      "Generic VGA"
    Monitor     "Generic Monitor"
    Subsection "Display"
        Modes       "640x480"
        ViewPort     0 0
        Virtual      800 600
    EndSubsection
EndSection

# The Mono server

Section "Screen"
    Driver      "vga2"
    Device      "Generic VGA"
    Monitor     "Generic Monitor"
    Subsection "Display"
        Modes       "640x480"
        ViewPort     0 0
        Virtual      800 600
    EndSubsection
EndSection
```

The Mode line in a video section can have up to 10 values. Be very careful when modifying these values because a wrong setting may wind up destroying your monitor! It does not matter if these are not present because defaults can be used. A typical line to override defaults for a monitor would be:

```
"640x400" 28 640 480 728 776 480 480 482 494
```

The 10 values in order from left to right are shown in the following section. These values only make sense to video engineers or those folks who have to work with a monitor not defined in the default modes. Check your monitor's hardware specifications and get the values from there to fill in these ten parameters. The following are the fields to set:

- Label for screen resolution; for example, 640×480 or 1024×768.
- The clock frequency in mHz.
- The Horizontal Display End in number of visible dots per line on the screen.
- The Start Horizontal Retrace value. This specifies the number of pulses before the video sync pulse starts.
- The End Horizontal Retrace value defines the end of the sync pulse.
- The Horizontal Total value. This is the total number of dots per line invisible and visible.
- The Vertical Display End value. The number of visible lines on the screen.
- The Start Vertical Retrace value. The number of lines before the sync pulse starts.
- The End Vertical Retrace value is the number of lines at the end of the sync pulse.
- The Vertical Total value. The total number of lines, invisible plus visible, on the screen.

Multiscan monitors handle frequencies of 15 to 40 mHz. Some monitors work at 72 mHz vertical scan to prevent the flicker. You have to be able to calculate the frequency from the monitor's specification and come up with these numbers. A good place to start would be the `XFree86-HOWTO` document on how to get these values. Keep in mind that your video monitor is just a glorified television. You give it wrong values and you can fry it.

International Keyboard Layout for XFree86

XFree86 servers are able to read the key table from the Linux kernel, so you need to set up only one keyboard layout file (for the kernel). There are some restrictions, though; the kernel can support more keyboard functions than X11. X11 can only modify one of the four key tables. This modifier is called `ModeShift`.

Configurable keys for the `ModeShift` modifier are `LeftAlt`, `RightAlt` (`=AltGr`), `RightCtl`, and `ScrollLock`.

Usually the `AltGr` key is used for international keyboard modifications. To enable the XFree86 server to read the `AltGr` key table from the kernel, you should put the following line in the `.olvwmrc` file:

```
RightAlt "ModeShift"
```

Besides supporting only one additional key map, X11 cannot use *dead* keys. A key is called *dead* if when it is typed, it does not print a character until a second character is typed. A typical example is an accent key. Such keys are not supported by X11, so you need to replace all dead-key symbols with non-dead equivalents. Table 10.1 lists what you have to change.

Table 10.1. Key symbols.

Dead	*Non-Dead*
`dead_tilde`	ASCII tilde
`dead_grave`	grave
`dead_circumflex`	ASCII circum
`dead_acute`	apostrophe
`dead_diaeresis`	diaeresis

Instead of supporting dead keys, XFree86 supports a `Compose` key. This feature is described in the `XFree86kbd` man page and can be modified by assigning the `Compose` function to one of the keys. By default the `ScrollLock` key has the `Compose` function.

If you still want to have the dead keys on the console, you will have to use an `xmodmap` file to map the keys to the correct symbols under X. This is also the method that must be used with earlier versions of XFree86. On `sunsite` in the directory `/pub/Linux/X11/misc`, you can find sample `xmodmap` files for several languages. Note that you have to set the `ModeShift` modifier to get the right key table working.

Please read the kbd.FAQ that comes with the kbd package for Linux. You will find many hints for modifying your keyboard layout on the console, as well as for X.

The .xinitrc File

To use X, you need a startup file that calls the local modifications, the window manager, and an application you want to use right after X has started. If you are using startx (or runx) to start X, this startup file is called xinitrc. There is a standard xinitrc file, /usr/lib/X11/xinit/xinitrc, which is the traditional location for this file. The Linux filesystem standard places this file in /etc/X11/xinit/xinitrc in order to allow a read-only mounted /usr partition, so look in that location first.

If you are not content with what this file does (for instance, if you want to use a different window manager), you should copy it to the file .xinitrc in your home directory. After copying the file, you can edit it. Look at the man pages for startx and xinit for more information.

Note that both the .xinitrc and the .Xresources files must be readable and executable, so run the following commands on these files after editing them. You only have to run the chmod command once on the application.

```
$ chmod u+rx .xinitrc .Xresources
```

This command makes these files executable.

See Listing 10.6 for a sample .xinitrc file.

Listing 10.6. A sample .xinitrc file.

```
#!/bin/sh
# $XConsortium: xinitrc.cpp,v 1.4 91/08/22 11:41:34 rws Exp $
# modified by obz

userresources=$HOME/.Xresources
usermodmap=$HOME/.Xmodmap
sysresources=/usr/lib/X11/xinit/.Xresources
sysmodmap=/usr/lib/X11/xinit/.Xmodmap

# merge in defaults and keymaps

if [ -f $sysresources ]; then
    xrdb -merge $sysresources
fi

if [ -f $sysmodmap ]; then
    xmodmap $sysmodmap
fi

if [ -f $userresources ]; then
    xrdb -merge $userresources
fi
```

continues

Listing 10.6. continued

```
18 if [ -f $usermodmap ]; then
19     xmodmap $usermodmap
20 fi

21 # Set the background to a dull gray
22 if [ -f /usr/bin/X11/xsetroot ]; then
23 xsetroot -solid gray32
24 fi

25 if [ -f /usr/bin/X11/xclock ]; then
26       xclock -geometry 80x80 &
27 fi

28 olvwm &
29 # fvwm &

30 xterm  -e /bin/bash
```

The line numbers in this listing have been added for your benefit. Let's look at these lines in greater detail.

Lines 4–7 set the resource environment variables for the X Window installation for your system. Change these to the path of your system's X Window System distribution.

Lines 9 through 20 check for the existence of these resources and then run the appropriate program, `xmodmap` or `xrdb`, with these resources as parameters. For now you can use this the way it stands.

Lines 22–24 check for the `xsetroot` program, and if present, execute it to set the background to a solid color, `gray32`.

The `olvwm &` command in line 28 starts the OPEN LOOK window manager for you. If you want to use `fvwm` instead of `olvwm`, uncomment line 29 and comment line 28 instead. The window manager must be run in the background if you have more commands following this one.

Line 30 starts a terminal to work with. Because this is the last line in the `.xinitrc` file, exiting this terminal causes your X session to stop. If you want to start more `xterms`, you can start them from within this `xterm`.

A simpler `.xinitrc` file to start with would be the following:

```
xterm -name Console &
olvwm
```

You can then enhance this `.xinitrc` file with what you want.

The Personal X Resource File

Sometimes you won't be content with default settings for applications that don't have a configuration file of their own. You can change some of these defaults by setting X resources in the `.Xresources` file in your `home` directory.

NOTE

You should know what effects setting the resources will have on the programs you use. Read the man pages for the program and for `xrdb` before editing the `.Xresources` file.

A resource file looks like an application default file. The difference is that in the resource file, resources for several applications are set. You should use the full names (*Progname.Resourcename*) instead of abbreviating the program name with an asterisk. Examples of application default files can be found in the `/usr/X11R6/lib/X11/app-defaults` directory. The resources available for a single application are usually shown in the man pages for that application.

If you are running a color server, you might want to put the following lines into your `.Xresources` file if some programs start in black and white:

```
#ifdef COLOR
*customization: -color
#endif
```

If this change is made, the program *foo* will read both the *Foo* and the *Foo-color* application default file from `/usr/X11R6/lib/X11/app-defaults`. The usual behavior is for *Foo* only to be read.

NOTE

If you are running a color server, the preceding code definitely should be added to the system `.Xresources` file. You might mention that to the person or entity who maintains the program you are running.

Note that the black-and-white color scheme of a program may be caused by the program rather than its resources.

The `-xrm` can be used with most X programs to override the parameters set in your `.Xresources` file. The usage is

```
-xrm "resource"
```

Alternatively, you can use the `xrdb` *<filename>* command to enforce any changes you have made in *<filename>* that apply to your current session.

Using xdm

If you want to run X on your system all the time, you could run `xdm` from the system startup. `xdm` is preconfigured on most systems, so you should not have to edit any of the `xdm` configuration files. Usually a runlevel is attached to an X-only system (look at `/etc/inittab`). All you have to do to get it working is change the default runlevel. On systems that use an `init` without runlevels (run `man init` to see whether your system uses an `init`), you should look into the `/etc/rc` and `/etc/rc.d/rc.local` files; you usually only have to remove comment signs at the beginning of a line that calls `xdm`. If no such line is present, you probably have a system that has no preconfigured `xdm`. In any event, `xdm` by default runs your `.xinitrc` file for you.

Configuration of the Window Manager

Window managers are a user- and site-specific issue. Several window managers are available for Linux. The configuration of one window manager is quite different from that of another. The window manager used in the configuration is usually explained in your `.xinitrc` file, so look there. The most commonly used window managers for Linux are

- `olwm` or `olvwm` for the OPEN LOOK Window manager. (It is on the CD-ROM at the back of this book.)
- `mwm` for the Motif window manager, possibly the most common commercial window manager. You have to buy it along with Motif.
- `twm`. (It is part of the XFree86 distribution on the CD-ROM at the back of this book.)
- `fvwm95`. (This seems to be the most popular freely available window manager and is on the CD-ROM at the back of this book.)

I discuss `mwm` in greater detail in Chapter 26, "Motif Programming."

Compiling Programs That Use X

Before compiling any programs for X, please read the `GCC-HOWTO` file. This file can be found in the `pub/Linux/docs/HOWTO` directories of `sunsite` or under `/usr/doc`. Many questions on compiling programs with Linux are answered here.

If you have the source code for a program that uses X11, it is usually shipped with an `Imakefile` instead of a `Makefile`.

`Imakefiles` are files that create `Makefiles` for your system. Discussing `Imakefiles` is beyond the scope of this book; however, you will have to work with `Imakefiles` if you work at all with X sources. Just remember the shell script `xmkmf`, and you should be okay.

TIP

`xmkmf` is an abbreviation for `X Make Makefile`.

CAUTION

The `xmkmf` shell script actually runs the `imake` command with a set of arguments. The most common argument is the `-DUseInstalled` argument. If you examine `xmkmf` (look in `/usr/X11R6/bin/`), you will see that the `xmkmf` script is a basic wrapper around a call to `imake`. It's very tempting to use `imake` on a command line by itself. Do not do so. Run the `imake` command with the `-DUseInstalled` argument if you must run `imake` on the command line.

Of course, before ever running `xmkmf`, you should read the documentation that usually comes with such packages.

Run `xmkmf` in the directory that contains the `Imakefile`. If there is a hierarchy of directories with `Imakefiles`, you usually only have to run `xmkmf` in the root directory of that hierarchy.

The `xmkmf` command builds the `Makefiles` in all directories in the hierarchy.

Then you should run the `make` command with an argument to let `make` resolve its dependencies, using the following command:

```
$ make depend
```

TIP

Don't be afraid if `include` files, such as `stddef.h`, `varargs.h`, and so on, are not found. They are `gcc` proprietary header files, and therefore not in the standard `include` directories.

After that, you can `make` the program by running `make`, and you can install your new utility (usually in `/usr/X11R6/bin`) by running this line:

```
$ make install
```

The installation of the man pages is accomplished by running

```
$ make install.man
```

Some Common Problems

Some of the problems you might see when you work with XFree86 are outlined in the following:

- No windows—all you get is a gray background and no windows. This is due to running without a window manager. Running X only starts the X server, not the window manager. You should use the `startx` script in `usr/X11/R6/bin/startx`.

- Your Logitech serial mouse does not work. The keyword `Logitech` is reserved for older Logitech serial mice. Use the keyword `MouseMan` (or `Microsoft`) for newer mice. Logitech serial mice plugged into a PS/2 port require the keyword `PS/2`.
- You get errors about not finding any font files. First check the `XF86Config` file to see whether the directories in the font path are named correctly and contain fonts. If they are correct, run `mkfontdir` in each of those directories to set them up for use with X.
- After leaving X, your screen fonts are not restored. This is a known bug with some servers. There are utilities called `runx` or `restoretext` included with `svgalib` that can help you in most cases. You can get them from `sunsite.unc.edu` in the file `/pub/Linux/libs/graphics/svgalib-1.2.10.tar.gz`.
- You will have some problems on uncommon, extremely new, or extremely old cards. This is what you have to live with when you are dealing with freeware.
- The server dies with the message `Cannot find a free VT`. XFree86 needs a free virtual terminal (VT) on which to run. So if you have put a `getty` process on every virtual console in your `/etc/inittab`, XFree86 is not able to start. The common practice is to leave `/dev/tty8` (for kernel messages) and `/dev/tty7` (for XFree86) free of a `getty` process.

This is not an exhaustive list. Read the `HOWTO` documents in `/usr/docs` on the CD-ROM for more information about other video card problems that are too specific to list here.

Compiling Sources for XFree86

You do not typically want to compile sources for XFree86 unless you really want to make changes to the sources because something is not working. You will need a lot of disk space and CPU time to do a complete build of the XFree86 system. Anything you need to know for compiling XFree86, you can find in the following files (in `/usr/X11R6/lib/X11/doc`): `INSTALL`, `README`, and `README.Linux`.

Note that you should not compile XFree86 to get rid of hard-coded restrictions (on the maximal pixel clock, for example) because without these restrictions, your hardware will probably break down.

To build a server that includes only those drivers you need, you should use the `LinkKit` instead of compiling the complete system. This is a little easier than trying to build it from scratch. The `LinkKit` package is specific and complicated and is therefore beyond the scope of this chapter.

Read `/usr/X11R6/lib/Server/README` for a description of how to use `LinkKit`. This file is not included in the standard XFree86 `tar` files but is part of the file that includes the `LinkKit`. You can find the `LinkKit` at `www.xfree86.org`.

For adding drivers to the SVGA servers, you need the `LinkKit` only.

The documentation on how to build servers can be found in the `/usr/X11R6/lib/Server/VGADriverDoc` directory after installing the `LinkKit` package.

Summary

This chapter covers the topic of configuring the XFree86 system. After reading this chapter, you should have an idea of how to set up your `XF86Config` file to generate your X environment. Just remember to start with the basic configuration settings for VGA cards and then make enhancements. Keep backups of your work and do not change the video settings unless you know what you are doing. If nothing works despite your best efforts, you have the recourse of knowing where to look for answers in FAQs, newsgroups, and FTP sites on the Internet for HOWTO and other documents on Linux.

Part III

Hardware Connectivity and Devices

IN THIS PART

CHAPTER 11

Filesystems, Disks, and Other Devices

by James Youngman

IN THIS CHAPTER

One of the simplest and most elegant aspects of UNIX (and Linux) design is the way that everything is represented as a file. Even the devices on which files are stored are represented as files.

Hardware devices are associated with drivers that provide a file interface; the special files representing hardware devices (or just *devices*) are kept in the directory `/dev`. Devices are either block devices or character devices.

A *character device* is one from which you can read a sequence of characters—for example, the sequence of keys typed at a keyboard or the sequence of bytes sent over a serial line. A *block device* is one that stores data and offers access to all parts of it equally; floppy and hard disks are block devices. Block devices are sometimes called *random access devices,* just as character devices are sometimes called *sequentially accessed devices.* With the latter, you can get data from any random part of a hard disk, but you have to retrieve the data from a serial line in the order it was sent.

When you perform some operation on a file, the kernel can tell that the file involved is a device by looking at its file mode (not its location). The device nodes are distinguished by having different major and minor device numbers. The *major device number* indicates to the kernel which of its drivers the device node represents. (For example, a block device with major number 3 is an IDE disk drive, and one with the major device number 8 is a SCSI disk.) Each driver is responsible for several instances of the hardware it drives, and these are indicated by the value of the minor device number. For example, the SCSI disk with the minor number 0 represents the whole "first" SCSI disk, and the minor numbers 1 to 15 represent fifteen possible partitions on it. The `ls` command prints the major and minor device numbers for you:

```
$ ls -l --sort=none /dev/sda{,?,??} /dev/sdb
brw-rw----   1 root     disk       8,   0 Sep 12  1994 /dev/sda
brw-rw----   1 root     disk       8,   1 Sep 12  1994 /dev/sda1
brw-rw----   1 root     disk       8,   2 Sep 12  1994 /dev/sda2
brw-rw----   1 root     disk       8,   3 Sep 12  1994 /dev/sda3
brw-rw----   1 root     disk       8,   4 Sep 12  1994 /dev/sda4
brw-rw----   1 root     disk       8,   5 Sep 12  1994 /dev/sda5
brw-rw----   1 root     disk       8,   6 Sep 12  1994 /dev/sda6
brw-rw----   1 root     disk       8,   7 Sep 12  1994 /dev/sda7
brw-rw----   1 root     disk       8,   8 Sep 12  1994 /dev/sda8
brw-rw----   1 root     disk       8,   9 Sep 12  1994 /dev/sda9
brw-rw----   1 root     disk       8,  10 Sep 12  1994 /dev/sda10
brw-rw----   1 root     disk       8,  11 Sep 12  1994 /dev/sda11
brw-rw----   1 root     disk       8,  12 Sep 12  1994 /dev/sda12
brw-rw----   1 root     disk       8,  13 Sep 12  1994 /dev/sda13
brw-rw----   1 root     disk       8,  14 Sep 12  1994 /dev/sda14
brw-rw----   1 root     disk       8,  15 Sep 12  1994 /dev/sda15
brw-rw----   1 root     disk       8,  16 Sep 12  1994 /dev/sdb
```

The obscure options to this `ls` command ensure that the devices are presented in this order. If just `ls -l` had been used, the entries would have been sorted alphabetically, and `/dev/sda10` would have come before `/dev/sda2`.

The b at the far left indicates that all of these are block devices. (Character devices are indicated by a c.) The major and minor device numbers appear just before the time field, separated by commas. (This is the position normally occupied in `ls -l` output by the file's size.)

Block Devices

If you had just one file of data to store, you could put it directly on a block device and read it back. Block devices have some fixed capacity, though, and you would need some method of marking the end of your data. Block devices behave in most respects just like ordinary files, except that although an ordinary file has a length determined by how much data is in it, the "length" of a block device is just its total capacity. If you wrote a megabyte to a 100MB block device and read back its contents, you would get the 1MB of data followed by 99MB of its previous contents. Bearing in mind this restriction, there are still several UNIX utilities that encode the amount of data available in the file's data rather than the file's total length, and hence are suitable for storing data directly on block devices—for example, `tar` and `cpio`, which are suitable for everybody; and `dump`, which is suitable only for the system administrator (because it requires read access to the block device underlying the data to be backed up). To back up the entire contents of your home directory to floppy disk, you would type the following:

```
$ tar cf /dev/fd0 $HOME
```

or

```
$ find $HOME -print0 | cpio --create -0 --format=crc >/dev/fd0
```

The `-print0` and `-0` options for `find` and `cpio` ensure that the names of the files to be backed up that `find` sends to `cpio` are separated by ASCII NULs, rather than newlines. This ensures that any filenames containing a newline are correctly backed up.

NOTE

The only characters that are illegal in UNIX filenames are the slash and the ASCII NUL.

These backup utilities are written specifically to write their backups to any kind of file; in fact, they were designed for sequentially accessed character devices—for example, tape drives.

Filesystems

When you have more than one item of data, it is necessary to have some method of organizing files on the device. These methods are called *filesystems*. Linux enables you to choose any organizational method to marshal your files on their storage device. For example, you can use the MS-DOS filesystem on a floppy, or the faster `ext2` filesystem on your hard disk.

Many different filesystems are supported by Linux; the `ext2` filesystem is used most because it is designed for Linux and is very efficient. Other filesystems are used for compatibility with other systems; for example, it's common to use the `msdos` and `vfat` filesystems on floppies. (These are the native filesystems of MS-DOS and Windows 95.) Under Red Hat Linux 4.2, some filesystems are built into the kernel:

```
$ cat /proc/filesystems
        ext2
        msdos
nodev   proc
```

And some filesystems are available as loadable modules:

```
$ ls /lib/modules/`uname -r`/fs
ext.o     isofs.o   ncpfs.o   smbfs.o   ufs.o     vfat.o
hpfs.o    minix.o   nfs.o     sysv.o    umsdos.o  xiafs.o
```

Some of these (`nfs`, `ncpfs`, and `smbfs`) are network filesystems that don't depend on block devices. Network filesystems are covered in Chapter 13, "TCP/IP Network Management." There are more filesystems that are supported by Linux but not provided by the standard kernel (for example, NTFS).

The `mount` Command

To mount a block device into the filesystem, use the `mount` command. You need to specify what device contains the filesystem, what type it is, and where in the directory hierarchy to mount it.

A `mount` command looks like this:

```
mount [-t type] [-o options] device mount-point
```

`device` must be a block device, or, if it contains a colon, it can be the name of another machine from which to mount a filesystem (see Chapter 13). *`mount-point`* should be an existing directory; the filesystem will appear at this position. (Anything previously in that directory will be hidden.) The filesystem type and options are optional, and the variety and meaning of options depend on the type of filesystem being mounted. If the filesystem you want to mount is specified in the `/etc/fstab` file, you need to specify only the mount point or the device name; the other details will be read from `/etc/fstab` by `mount`. Here is an example of the `mount` command being used:

```
# mount /dev/fd1 -t vfat /mnt/floppy
mount: block device /dev/fd1 is write-protected, mounting read-only
# ls /mnt/floppy
grub-0.4.tar.gz
# umount /mnt/floppy
# ls /mnt/floppy
filesystem not mounted
```

In this example, I mounted a floppy containing a `vfat` filesystem at the mount point `/mnt/floppy` (and got an informational message). The directory `/mnt/floppy` already existed. I used `ls` to see what was on the disk and unmounted it again. I then ran `ls` again and the response I got was simply the name of a file that I leave in the directory `/mnt/floppy` on my hard disk to remind me that there currently is nothing mounted there. This enables me to distinguish this from having an empty floppy mounted.

Mounting a `vfat` floppy like this caused the Linux kernel to automatically load the `vfat` driver into the kernel while it was needed. These drivers are loaded by the system daemon `kerneld`, and when they become unused after the filesystem is unmounted, they are unloaded to recover the memory that they occupied. See Chapter 5, "Configuring and Building Kernels," for more information about kernel modules.

Any one of several things can cause the `mount` command to fail. It is possible to specify an incorrect device name (that is, a device file that does not exist or one for which a driver is not available in the kernel or for which the hardware is not present). Other error conditions include unreadable devices (for example, empty floppy drives or bad media) and insufficient permissions (`mount` commands other than those sanctioned by the administrator by listing them with the option `user` in `/etc/fstab` are forbidden to ordinary users). Trying to mount a device at a mount point that does not already exist will also not work. Still more error conditions are possible but unlikely (for example, exceeding the compiled-in limit to the number of mounted filesystems) or self-explanatory (for example, most usage errors for the `mount` command itself). There are some more unlikely error messages that chiefly relate to the loopback devices.

In order to mount a filesystem, the point at which it is to be mounted (that is, the mount point) must be a directory. This directory doesn't have to be empty, but after the filesystem is mounted, anything "underneath" it will be inaccessible. Linux provides a *singly rooted* filesystem, in contrast to those operating systems that give each filesystem a separate drive letter. Although this might seem less flexible, it is *more* flexible, because the size of each block device (that is, hard disk or whatever) is hidden from programs, and things can be moved around. For example, if you have some software that expects to be installed in `/opt/umsp`, you can install it in `/big-disk/stuff/umsp` and make `/opt/umsp` a symbolic link. There is also no need to edit a myriad of configuration files that are now using the wrong drive letter after you install a new disk drive, for example.

There are many options governing how a mounted filesystem behaves; for example, it can be mounted read-only. There are options for filesystems such as `msdos` that don't have any concept of users. The filesystems enable you to give each file a particular file mode (for security or to allow access by everyone). When you mount an `nfs` filesystem, there is so much flexibility available that the options have a separate manual page (`man nfs`), although the defaults are perfectly reasonable. The `nfs` filesystem is explained in more detail in Chapter 13.

Table 11.1 contains options useful for `mount`, given in alphabetical order. Unless otherwise indicated, these options are valid for all filesystem types, although asking for asynchronous writes to a CD-ROM is no use! Options applicable only to NFS filesystems are not listed here; refer to the `nfs` manual page for those.

Table 11.1. mount options.

mount *Option*	*Description*
async	Write requests for the filesystem normally should wait until the data has reached the hardware; with this option, the program continues immediately instead. This does mean that the system is slightly more prone to data loss in the event of a system crash, but, on the other hand, crashes are very rare with Linux. This option speeds up NFS filesystems by a startling extent. The opposite of this option is sync.
auto	Indicates to mount that it should mount the device when given the -a flag. This flag is used by the startup scripts to make sure that all the required filesystems are mounted at boot time. The opposite of this option is noauto.
defaults	Turns on the options rw, suid, dev, exec, auto, nouser, and async.
dev	Allows device nodes on the system to be used. Access to devices is completely determined by access rights to the on-disk device node. Hence, if you mount an ext2 filesystem on a floppy and you have previously placed a writable /dev/kmem device file on the disk, then you've just gained read/write access to kernel memory. System administrators generally prevent this from happening by mounting removable filesystems with the nodev mount option.
exec	Indicates to the kernel that it should allow the execution of programs on the filesystem. This option is more frequently seen as noexec, which indicates to the kernel that execution of programs on this filesystem shouldn't be allowed. This is generally used as a security precaution or for NFS filesystems mounted from another machine that contain executable files of a format unsuitable for this machine (for example, being intended for a different CPU).
noauto	Opposite of auto; see above.
nodev	Opposite of dev; see above.
noexec	Opposite of exec; see above.
nosuid	Opposite of suid; see below.
nouser	Opposite of user; see below.

mount *Option*	*Description*
remount	Allows the mount command to change the flags for an already-mounted filesystem without interrupting its use. You can't unmount a filesystem that is currently in use, and this option is basically a workaround. The system startup scripts, for example, use the command mount -n -o remount,ro / to change the root filesystem from read-only (it starts off this way) to read/write (its normal state). The -n option indicates to mount that it shouldn't update /etc/fstab because it can't do this while the root filesystem is still read-only.
ro	Mounts the filesystem read-only. This is the opposite of the option rw.
rw	Mounts the filesystem read/write. This is the opposite of the option ro.
suid	Allows the set user ID and set group ID file mode bits to take effect. The opposite of this option is nosuid. The nosuid option is more usual; it is used for the same sorts of reasons that nodev is used.
sync	All write operations cause the calling program to wait until the data has been committed to the hardware. This mode of operation is slower but a little more reliable than its opposite, asynchronous I/O, which is indicated by the option async (see above).
user	Allows ordinary users to mount the filesystem. When there is a user option in /etc/fstab, ordinary users indicate which filesystem they want to mount or unmount by giving the device name or mount point; all the other relevant information is taken from the /etc/fstab file. For security reasons, user implies the noexec, nosuid, and nodev options.

Options are processed by the mount command in the order they appear on the command line (or in /etc/fstab). Thus, it is possible to allow users to mount a filesystem and then run set user ID executables by using the options user, suid in that order. Using them in reverse order (suid, user) wouldn't work because the user option would turn the suid option off again.

There are many other options available, but these are all specific to particular filesystems. All the valid options for mount are detailed in its manual page. An example is the umask flag for the vfat and fat filesystems, which allows you to make all the files on your MS-DOS or Windows partitions readable (or even writable if you prefer) for all the users on your Linux system.

Setting Up Filesystems

When the kernel boots, it attempts to mount a root filesystem from the device specified by the kernel loader, LILO. The root filesystem is initially mounted read-only, and the boot process proceeds as described in Chapter 4, "System Startup and Shutdown." During the boot process, the filesystems listed in the filesystem table `/etc/fstab` are mounted. This file specifies which devices are to be mounted, what kinds of filesystems they contain, at what point in the filesystem the mount takes place, and any options governing *how* they are to be mounted. The format of this file is described in `fstab`.

The Red Hat File System Manager

An easy way of setting up filesystem entries in `/etc/fstab` is the configuration tool File System Manager in the Red Hat Control Panel (though you can invoke it separately as `fstool`). The File System Manager is shown in Figure 11.1.

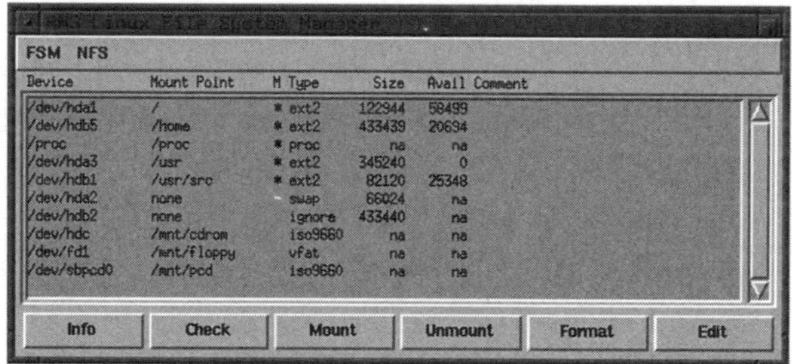

FIGURE 11.1.
The File System Manager.

When you start `fstool`, it produces a window that contains all the entries in `/etc/fstab`. Each entry shows the device name, mount point, filesystem type, size, space used, and space available. Additionally, each mounted filesystem is marked with an asterisk. The Info button displays extra information about the highlighted filesystem (the same information as is indicated in `/etc/fstab` and in the output of the `df` command).

Filesystems can be mounted or unmounted with the two buttons Mount and Unmount. Any errors that occur are shown in a dialog box; this can happen if, for example, you try to mount a CD-ROM when there is no disk in the drive. (Go ahead and try it.) The Format button works only for hard disk partitions; for these, it runs `mkfs` (see the section "Creating New Filesystems," later in this chapter). Other media (for example, floppy disks) are formatted differently (see the section "Floppy Disks," later in this chapter).

The Check button works only for `ext2` and `minix` filesystems. If you get the error `fsck: command not found`, this just means that the directory `/sbin` is not on your path, and you should be able to fix this by running `su - root`. (You might also need to do `export DISPLAY=:0.0`, if that is necessary.) Checking a filesystem can take a while, and the result is shown in a dialog box afterward. It is very unusual for errors to be shown for hard disk filesystems here because these are checked at boot time and don't get corrupted during the normal operation of Linux.

The NFS menu is used to add and remove NFS network mounts, which are explained in Chapter 13. You can exit the File System Manager by selecting the Quit option from the FSM menu.

Editing /etc/fstab Manually

The filesystem table `/etc/fstab` is just a text file; it is designed to have a specific format that is readable by humans and not just computers. It is separated into columns by tabs or spaces (it doesn't matter which you use). You can edit it with your favorite text editor—it doesn't matter which. You must take care, however, if you modify it by hand, because removing or corrupting an entry will make the system unable to mount that filesystem next time it boots. For this reason, I make a point of saving previous versions of this file using the Revision Control System (a very useful program—see the manual page for `rcs`).

My `/etc/fstab` looks like this:

```
#
# /etc/fstab
#
# You should be using fstool (control-panel) to edit this!
#
#<device> <mountpoint> <filesystemtype> <options>    <dump> <fsckorder>

/dev/hda1      /              ext2      defaults          1       1
/dev/hdb5      /home          ext2      defaults,rw       1       2
/dev/hda3      /usr           ext2      defaults          1       2
/dev/hdb1      /usr/src       ext2      defaults          1       3

/dev/hdc       /mnt/cdrom     iso9660   user,noauto,ro    0       0
/dev/sbpcd0    /mnt/pcd       iso9660   user,noauto,ro    0       0
/dev/fd1       /mnt/floppy    vfat      user,noauto       0       0

/proc          /proc          proc      defaults
/dev/hda2      none           swap      sw
```

The first four entries are the `ext2` filesystems comprising my Linux system. When Linux is booted, the root filesystem is mounted first; all the other local (that is, nonnetwork) filesystems are mounted next. Filesystems appear in `/etc/fstab` in the order they are mounted; `/usr` must appear before `/usr/src`, for example, because the mount point for one filesystem exists on the other. The following three filesystems are all removable filesystems (two CD-ROMs and a floppy drive). These have the `noauto` option set so that they are not automatically mounted at boot time. The removable devices have the `user` option set so that I can mount and unmount them without having to use su all the time. The CD-ROMs have the filesystem type `iso9660`, which is the standard filesystem for CD-ROMs, and the floppy drive has the filesystem type `vfat`, because I often use it for interchanging data with MS-DOS and Windows systems.

The last two filesystems are special; the first (`/proc`) is a special filesystem provided by the kernel as a way of providing information about the system to user programs. The information in the `/proc` filesystem is used in order to make utilities such as `ps`, `top`, `xload`, `free`, `netstat`, and so on work. Some of the "files" in `/proc` are really enormous (for example, `/proc/kcore`) but don't worry—all the information in the `/proc` filesystem is generated on-the-fly by the Linux kernel as you read it; no disk space is wasted. You can tell that they are not real files because, for example, root can't give them away with `chown`.

The final "filesystem" isn't, in fact, a filesystem at all; it is an entry that indicates a disk partition used as swap space. Swap partitions are used to implement virtual memory. Files can also be used for swap space. The names of the swap files go in the first column where the device name usually goes.

The two numeric columns on the right relate to the operation of the `dump` and `fsck` commands, respectively. The `dump` command compares the number in column five (the *dump interval*) with the number of days since that filesystem was last backed up so that it can inform the system administrator that the filesystem needs to be backed up. Other backup software—for example, Amanda—can also use this field for the same purpose. (Amanda can be found at the URL `http://www.cs.umd.edu/projects/amanda/amanda.html`.) Filesystems without a dump interval field are assumed to have a dump interval of zero, denoting "never dump." For more information, see the manual page for `dump`.

The sixth column is the `fsck pass` and indicates which filesystems can be checked in parallel at boot time. The root filesystem is always checked first, but after that, separate drives can be checked simultaneously, Linux being a multitasking operating system. There is no point, however, in checking two filesystems on the same hard drive at the same time, because this would result in lots of extra disk head movement and wasted time. All the filesystems that have the same pass number are checked in parallel, from 1 upward. Filesystems with a 0 or missing pass number (such as the floppy and CD-ROM drives) are not checked at all.

Creating New Filesystems

When you install Red Hat Linux, the installation process makes some new filesystems and sets the system up to use them. When you later come to set up new filesystems under Linux, you will be coming to it for the first time.

Many operating systems don't distinguish between the preparation of the device's surface to receive data (formatting) and the building of new filesystems. Linux does distinguish between the two, principally because only floppy disks need formatting in any case, and also because Linux offers as many as half a dozen different filesystems that can be created (on any block device). Separately providing the facility of formatting floppy disks in each of these programs would be poor design and would require you to learn a different way of doing it for each kind of new filesystem. The process of formatting floppy disks is dealt with separately (see the section "Floppy Disks," later in this chapter).

Filesystems are initially built by a program that opens the block device and writes some structural data to it so that, when the kernel tries to mount the filesystem, the device contains the image of a pristine filesystem. This means that both the kernel and the program used to make the filesystem must agree on the correct filesystem structure.

Linux provides a generic command, `mkfs`, that enables you to make a filesystem on a block device. In fact, because UNIX manages almost all resources with the same set of operations, `mkfs` can be used to generate a filesystem inside an ordinary file! Because this is unusual, `mkfs` asks for confirmation before proceeding. When this is done, you can even mount the resulting filesystem using the loop device (see the section "Mounting Filesystems on Files," later in this chapter).

Because of the tremendous variety of filesystems available, almost all the work of building the new filesystem is delegated to a separate program for each; however, the generic `mkfs` program provides a single interface for invoking them all. It's not uncommon to pass options to the top-level `mkfs` (for example, `-V` to make it show what commands it executes or `-c` to make it check the device for bad blocks). The generic `mkfs` program also enables you to pass options to the filesystem-specific `mkfs`. There are many of these filesystem-dependent options, but most of them have sensible defaults, and you normally would not want to change them. The only options you might want to pass to `mke2fs`, which builds `ext2` filesystems, are `-m` and `-i`. The `-m` option specifies how much of the filesystem is reserved for root's use (for example, for working space when the system disk would otherwise have filled completely). The `-i` option is more rarely exercised and is used for setting the balance between inodes and disk blocks; it is related to the expected average file size. As stated previously, the defaults are reasonable for most purposes, so these options are used only in special circumstances:

```
# mkfs -t ext2 /dev/fd1
mke2fs 1.10, 24-Apr-97 for EXT2 FS 0.5b, 95/08/09
Linux ext2 filesystem format
Filesystem label=
360 inodes, 1440 blocks
72 blocks (5.00) reserved for the super user
First data block=1
Block size=1024 (log=0)
Fragment size=1024 (log=0)
1 block group
8192 blocks per group, 8192 fragments per group
360 inodes per group

Writing inode tables: done
Writing superblocks and filesystem accounting information: done
# mount -t ext2 /dev/fd1 /mnt/floppy
# ls -la /mnt/floppy
total 14
drwxr-xr-x   3 root     root         1024 Aug  1 19:49 .
drwxr-xr-x   7 root     root         1024 Jul  3 21:47 ..
drwxr-xr-x   2 root     root        12288 Aug  1 19:49 lost+found
# umount /mnt/floppy
```

Here, you see the creation and mounting of an `ext2` filesystem on a floppy. The structure of the filesystem as specified by the program's defaults are shown. There is no volume label, and there are 4096 bytes (4KB) per inode (360 × 4 = 1440). The block size is 1KB and 5 percent of the disk is reserved for root. These are the defaults (which are explained in the `mke2fs` manual page). After you have created a filesystem, you can use `dumpe2fs` to display information about an `ext2` filesystem, but remember to pipe the result through a pager such as `less` because this output can be very long.

After creating the filesystem on this floppy, you can include it in the filesystem table by changing the existing line referring to a `vfat` filesystem on `/dev/fd1` to the following:

```
/dev/fd1       /mnt/floppy    ext2   user,sync,errors=continue 0 0
```

The first three columns are the device, mount point, and filesystem type, as shown previously. The options column is more complex than previous ones. The `user` option indicates that users are allowed to mount this filesystem. The `sync` option indicates that programs writing to this filesystem wait while each write finishes, and only then continue. This might seem obvious, but it is not the normal state of affairs. The kernel normally manages filesystem writes in such a way as to provide high performance (data still gets written to the device of course, but it doesn't necessarily happen immediately). This is perfect for fixed devices such as hard disks, but for low-capacity removable devices such as floppy disks it's less beneficial. Normally, you write a few files to a floppy and then unmount it and take it away. The unmount operation must wait until all data has been written to the device before it can finish (and the disk can then be removed). Having to wait like this is off-putting, and there is always the risk that someone might copy a file to the floppy, wait for the disk light to go out, and remove it. With asynchronous writes, some buffered data might not have yet been written to disk. Hence, synchronous writes are safer for removable media.

The `ext2` filesystem has a configurable strategy for errors. If an `ext2` filesystem encounters an error (for example, a bad disk block) there are three possible responses to the error:

Remount the device read-only—For filesystems that contain mostly nonessential data (for example, `/tmp`, `/var/tmp`, or news spools), remounting the filesystem read-only so that it can be fixed with `fsck` is often the best choice.

Panic—Continuing regardless in the face of potentially corrupted system configuration files is unwise, so a kernel panic (that is, a controlled crash—or emergency landing, if you prefer) can sometimes be appropriate.

Ignore it—Causing a system shutdown if a floppy disk has a bad sector is a little excessive, so the `continue` option tells the kernel to "carry on regardless" in this situation. If this actually does happen, the best thing to do is to use the `-c` option of `e2fsck`, for example, with `fsck -t ext2 -c /dev/fd1`. This runs `e2fsck`, giving it the `-c` option, which invokes the command `badblocks` to test the device for bad disk blocks. After this is done, `e2fsck` does its best to recover from the situation.

Repairing Filesystems

Some disk data is kept in memory temporarily before being written to disk, for performance reasons (see the previous discussion of the `sync` mount option). If the kernel does not have an opportunity to actually write this data, the filesystem can become corrupted. This can happen in several ways:

- The storage device (for example, a floppy disk) can be manually removed before the kernel has finished with it.
- The system might suffer a power loss.
- The user might mistakenly turn off the power or accidentally press the reset button.

As part of the boot process, Linux runs the `fsck` program, whose job it is to check and repair filesystems. Most of the time the boot follows a controlled shutdown (see the manual page for `shutdown`), and in this case, the filesystems will have been unmounted before the reboot. In this case, `fsck` says that they are "clean." It knows this because before unmounting them, the kernel writes a special signature on the filesystem to indicate that the data is intact. When the filesystem is mounted again for writing, this signature is removed.

If, on the other hand, one of the disasters listed takes place, the filesystems will not be marked "clean," and when `fsck` is invoked, as usual, it will notice this and begin a full check of the filesystem. This also occurs if you specify the `-f` flag to `fsck`. To prevent errors creeping up on it, `fsck` also enforces a periodic check; a full check is done at an interval specified on the filesystem itself (usually every 20 boots or 6 months, whichever comes sooner), even if it was unmounted cleanly.

The boot process (see Chapter 4) checks the root filesystem and then mounts it read/write. (It's mounted read-only by the kernel; `fsck` asks for confirmation before operating on a read/write filesystem, and this is not desirable for an unattended reboot.) First, the root filesystem is checked with the following command:

```
fsck -V -a /
```

Then all the other filesystems are checked by executing this command:

```
fsck -R -A -V -a
```

These options specify that all the filesystems should be checked (`-A`) except the root filesystem, which doesn't need checking a second time (`-R`), and that operations produce informational messages about what it is doing as it goes (`-V`), but that the process should not be interactive (`-a`). The latter is done because, for example, there might not be anyone present to answer any questions from `fsck`.

In the case of serious filesystem corruption, the approach breaks down because there are some things that `fsck` will not do to a filesystem without your say-so. In this case, it returns an error value to its caller (the startup script), and the startup script spawns a shell to allow the administrator to run `fsck` interactively. When this has happened, this message appears:

```
*** An error occurred during the file system check.
*** Dropping you to a shell; the system will reboot
*** when you leave the shell.
Give root password for maintenance
(or type Control-D for normal startup):
```

This is a very troubling event, particularly because it might well appear if you have other problems with the system—for example, a lockup (leading you to press the reset button) or a spontaneous reboot. None of the online manuals are guaranteed to be available at this stage, because they might be stored on the filesystem whose check failed. This prompt is issued if the root filesystem check failed, or the filesystem check failed for any of the other disk filesystems.

When the automatic `fsck` fails, you need to log in by specifying the root password and run the `fsck` program manually. When you have typed in the root password, you are presented with the following prompt:

```
(Repair filesystem) #
```

You might worry about what command to enter here, or indeed what to do at all. At least one of the filesystems needs to be checked, but which one? The preceding messages from `fsck` should indicate which, but it isn't necessary to go hunting for them. There is a set of options you can give `fsck` that tells it to check *everything* manually, and this is a good fallback:

```
fsck -A -V ; echo == $? ==
```

This is the same command as the previous one, but the `-R` option is missing, in case the root filesystem needs to be checked, and the `-a` option is missing, so `fsck` is in its "interactive" mode. This might enable a check to succeed just because it can now ask you questions. The purpose of the `echo == $? ==` command is to unambiguously interpret the outcome of the `fsck` operation. If the value printed between the equals signs is less than 4, all is well. If this value is `4` or more, more recovery measures are needed. The meanings of the various values returned are as follows:

`0`	No errors
`1`	Filesystem errors corrected
`2`	System should be rebooted
`4`	Filesystem errors left uncorrected
`8`	Operational error
`16`	Usage or syntax error
`128`	Shared library error

If this does not work, this might be because of a *corrupted superblock*—`fsck` starts its disk check and if this is corrupted, it can't start. By good design, the `ext2` filesystem has many backup superblocks scattered regularly throughout the filesystem. Suppose the command announces that it has failed to clean some particular filesystem—for example, `/dev/fubar`. You can start `fsck` again, using a backup superblock by using the following command:

```
fsck -t ext2 -b 8193 /dev/fubar
```

8193 is the block number for the first backup superblock. This backup superblock is at the start of block group 1 (the first is numbered 0). There are more backup superblocks at the start of block group 2 (16385), and block group 3 (24577); they are spaced at intervals of 8192 blocks. If you made a filesystem with settings other than the defaults, these might change. `mke2fs` lists the superblocks that it creates as it goes, so that is a good time to pay attention if you're not using the default settings. There are further things you can attempt if `fsck` is still not succeeding, but these are very rare and usually indicate hardware problems so severe that they prevent the proper operation of `fsck`. Examples include broken wires in the IDE connector cable and similar nasty problems. If this command still fails, you might seek expert help or try to fix the disk in a different machine.

These extreme measures are very unlikely; a manual `fsck`, in the unusual circumstance where it is actually required, almost always fixes things. After the manual `fsck` has worked, the root shell that the startup scripts provide has done its purpose. Type `exit` to exit it. At this point, in order to make sure that everything goes according to plan, the boot process is started again from the beginning. This second time around, the filesystems should all be error-free and the system should boot normally.

Hardware

There are block devices under Linux for representing all sorts of random access devices—floppy disks, hard disks (XT, EIDE, and SCSI), Zip drives, CD-ROM drives, ramdisks, and loopback devices.

Hard Disks

Hard disks are large enough to make it useful to keep different filesystems on different parts of the hard disk. The scheme for dividing these disks up is called *partitioning*. Although it is common for computers running MS-DOS to have only one partition, it is possible to have several different partitions on each disk. The summary of how the disk is partitioned is kept in its *partition table*.

The Partition Table

A hard disk might be divided up like this:

Device Name	*Disk*	*Partition*	*Filesystem*	*Mounted At*
/dev/hda1	1	1	ext2	/
/dev/hda3	1	3	ext2	/usr
/dev/hdb1	2	1	ext2	/usr/src
/dev/hdb5	2	5	ext2	/home

Note that the partitions on the first disk have names starting with `/dev/hda`, and those on the second have names starting with `/dev/hdb`. These prefixes are followed by the number of the partition.

NOTE

All is not quite as simple as it could be in the partition table, however. Early hard disk drives on PCs were quite small (about 10MB), so there was a need for only a small number of partitions and the format of the partition table originally allowed for only four partitions. Later on, this became a restriction, and the *extended partition* was introduced as a workaround.

Inside each extended partition is another partition table. This enables this extended partition to be divided, in the same way, into four *logical partitions*. Partitions that aren't inside an extended partition are sometimes referred to as *primary partitions*.

Running `fdisk -l` shows that my first hard disk is divided up like this:

Device	*Begin*	*Start*	*End*	*Blocks*	*ID*	*System*
/dev/hda1	1	1	244	122944	83	Linux native
/dev/hda2	245	245	375	66024	82	Linux swap
/dev/hda3	376	376	1060	345240	83	Linux native

In this case, there are three primary partitions, of which one is a swap partition.

Disk Geometry

The units of the table in the last section are *cylinders*. The partition table allocates a consecutive block of cylinders to each partition. The term *cylinder* itself dates from the days when it was possible to remove a disk pack from a UNIX machine and point to the various parts. That can't be done here, so here's another way of looking at it.

Imagine that a hard disk is in fact a stack of pizzas. Each of the pizzas is a *platter*, a disk-shaped surface with a magnetic coating designed to hold magnetic encodings. Both sides of these platters are used. These rotate around the spindle, like the spindle in a record player. (Don't put pizzas on a record player!) The hard disk has a movable arm containing several *disk heads*. Each side of each platter has a separate disk head. If you were to put your fingers between the pizzas while keeping them straight, this would be the same as the arrangement of the heads on the arm. All the parts of the platters that the heads pass over in one rotation of the disk is called a *cylinder*. The parts of a single platter that one head passes over in one rotation is called a *track*. Each track is divided into *sectors*, as if the pizzas had been already sliced for you. The layout of a disk, its *geometry*, is described by the number of cylinders, heads, and sectors comprising the disk. Another important feature is the rotational speed of the disk—generally, the faster this is, the faster the hard disk can read or write data.

You can discover the geometry of one of your hard disks by using the `hdparm` command, and typical output might look like this:

```
# /sbin/hdparm -g /dev/hdc

/dev/hdc:
 geometry     = 6232/16/63, sectors = 6281856, start = 0
```

NOTE

IBM PCs with older BIOSes can have difficulty with large disks; see the Linux Large-Disk mini-HOWTO.

Floppy Disks

Floppy disks are removable low-capacity storage media. As storage devices, they are far slower than hard disks, but they have the advantage that they are removable and make good media for transporting modest amounts of data.

The block devices corresponding to the floppy disks begin with the letters `fd`; `/dev/fd0` is the first, and any additional ones have increasing numbers. There are many possible formats for a floppy disk, and the kernel needs to know the format (geometry) of a disk to read it properly. Linux can usually work out the correct format so the automatic devices `/dev/fd0` (plus `/dev/fd1` and so on for extra floppy drives) are usually sufficient, but if for some reason it is necessary to specify the exact format, further device names are provided for indicating this. The device `/dev/fd0H1440`, for example, denotes a 1.44MB high-density floppy. There are many more devices indicating obscure formats, both older lower-capacity formats and other nonstandard extra–high-capacity formats. You can even create your own floppy disk formats, using the `serfdprm` program.

The most common reason to use the specific-format device names is that you are formatting a floppy for the first time. In this situation, the disk is not yet readable, so the kernel will not be able to autoprobe an existing format. You need to use the name `/dev/fd0H1440`, for example, to denote a high-density 3.5-inch disk in the first floppy drive. For device names representing other formats, refer to the `fd` manual page. Section 4 of the manual is the section devoted to devices and so on.

The process of formatting a floppy is completely destructive to the data on it, and because it requires writing to the actual device itself, it requires root privileges. It is done like this:

```
# fdformat /dev/fd0H1440
Double-sided, 80 tracks, 18 sec/track. Total capacity 1440 kB.
Formatting ... done
Verifying ... done
```

After you have formatted a floppy, please don't forget to use `mkfs` to build a filesystem on it (see the section "Creating New Filesystems," earlier in this chapter).

Another popular way of accessing floppy disks is to use the `mtools` package, which is a suite of programs designed to enable the user to manipulate DOS-format disks without needing to mount them. The commands are designed specifically to be similar to MS-DOS commands. Windows 95 filesystems are also supported. You will find an introduction to the use of `mtools` in the `mtools` manual page. `mtools` can also be used to access hard disks and disk image files, and it supports many nonstandard disk formats.

CD-ROM Drives

The CD-ROM drive is fundamentally just another kind of read-only block device. These are mounted in just the same way as other block devices. CD-ROMs almost always contain standard ISO 9660 filesystems, often with some optional extensions. There is no reason, however, why any other filesystem should not be used. Once you have mounted your CD-ROM, it behaves like any other read-only filesystem.

You can set up and mount your CD-ROM drive using the Red Hat File System Manager, as explained previously, or by using the following `mount` command:

```
# mount /dev/cdrom -t iso9660 /mnt/cdrom
```

The directory `/mnt/cdrom` is a very common place to mount one's CD-ROM drive under Red Hat Linux, because this is where the graphical package manager Glint expects to find the contents of the Red Hat installation CD-ROM, for example.

The device name `/dev/cdrom` is commonly used as a symbolic link to the actual device name corresponding to the CD-ROM, because at the time the CD-ROM drive became available for the PC, there was no cheap standard interface for these devices. Each manufacturer chose or invented an interfacing scheme that was incompatible with everyone else's. For this reason, there are about a dozen different drivers for CD-ROM drives available in the Linux kernel. SCSI would have been a sensible standard to have been used, but although SCSI CD-ROM drives are available, they're not particularly popular.

The ATAPI standard arrived in time to ensure that all non-SCSI CD-ROM drives at quad speed or faster use a standard interface, so the situation is far simpler for new CD-ROM drives. Support for ATAPI CD-ROMs is taken care of by one driver for all drives. The ATAPI standard also provides for very large hard disk drives and tape drives. ATAPI CD-ROM drives are attached to IDE interfaces, just like hard disks, and they have the same set of device names as hard disk devices.

Because CD-ROMs come already written, there is no need to partition them. They are accessed using the device names for whole-disk devices: `/dev/hda`, `/dev/hdb`, and so on.

The ISO 9660 standard specifies a standard format for the layout of data on CD-ROMs. It restricts filenames to no more than 32 characters, for example. Most CD-ROMs are written with very short filenames, for compatibility with MS-DOS. To support certain UNIX features such as symbolic links and long filenames, a set of extensions called *Rock Ridge* was developed, and the Linux kernel will automatically detect and make use of the Rock Ridge extensions.

CD-ROM drives also usually support the playing of audio CDs, and there are many Linux programs for controlling the CD-ROM drive, in just the same way as one might control a CD player. The multimedia package on the Red Hat 4.2 CD-ROM contains the `xplaycd` program, which can be used for playing CDs. To make it work, you need to set the `/dev/cdrom` symbolic link to point to your real CD-ROM device.

Loopback Devices

Loopback devices enable new filesystems to be stored inside regular files. You might want to do this to prepare an emulated hard disk image for DOSEMU, an install disk, or just to try out a filesystem of a new type or an ISO9660 CD-ROM image before writing it to the CD writer.

Mounting Filesystems on Files

Under UNIX, root permissions are needed to change the system's filesystem structure; even if you own a file and the mount point on which you want to mount it, only root can do this, unless the `user` option has been specified in `/etc/fstab` for this filesystem.

When a filesystem is mounted using the loopback driver, the file containing the filesystem plays the role of the block device in the `mount` command and `/etc/fstab`. The kernel talks to the block device interface provided by the loopback device driver, and the driver forwards operations to the file:

```
# mount $(pwd)/rtems.iso -t iso9660 -o ro,loop /mnt/test
# ls -F /mnt/test
INSTALL   LICENSE   README   SUPPORT   c/   doc/   rr_moved/
# mount ¦ grep loop ¦ fold -s
/home/james/documents/books/Sams/Linux-Unleashed-2/ch9/tmp/rtems.iso on
/mnt/test type iso9660 (ro,loop=/dev/loop0)
# umount /mnt/test
```

Once the loopback filesystem is mounted, it's just a normal filesystem.

Using Encrypted Filesystems

Loopback filesystems offer even more—encryption, for example. A loopback filesystem can be configured to decrypt data from the block device on-the-fly so that the data on the device is useless to people even if they can read it—unless they have the password. The `mount` command prompts for the password at the appropriate time. To make this work, first you have to use `mkfs` to generate a filesystem on the encrypted block device; `losetup` is used to associate a loop device and encryption method with the block device you want to use (in the following case, a floppy drive):

```
# /sbin/losetup -e DES /dev/loop0 /dev/fd1
Password:
Init (up to 16 hex digits):
# /sbin/mkfs -t ext2 -m0 /dev/loop0
mke2fs 1.10, 24-Apr-97 for EXT2 FS 0.5b, 95/08/09
Linux ext2 filesystem format
Filesystem label=
360 inodes, 1440 blocks
0 blocks (0.00) reserved for the super user
First data block=1
Block size=1024 (log=0)
Fragment size=1024 (log=0)
1 block group
8192 blocks per group, 8192 fragments per group
360 inodes per group

Writing inode tables: done
Writing superblocks and filesystem accounting information: done
# losetup -d /dev/loop0
```

As shown previously, the `losetup`'s `-e` option associates an encryption method and block device with a loopback device. The `-d` option deletes this association and erases the stored encryption key.

When the filesystem has been created on the encrypted device, it can be mounted in a manner similar to the normal case:

```
# /sbin/losetup -d /dev/loop0
# mount /dev/fd1 -t ext2 -o loop=/dev/loop0,encryption=DES /mnt/test
Password:
Init (up to 16 hex digits):
# ls /mnt/test
lost+found
```

Usually, the whole process of using an encrypted filesystem can be set up for ordinary users by adding the appropriate line to `/etc/fstab`:

```
$ mount /mnt/test
Password:
Init (up to 16 hex digits):
$ ls -ld /mnt/test
drwxrwxrwx   3 james  root    1024 Sep 14 22:04 /mnt/test
```

In this example, root has enabled users to mount encrypted filesystems by including

```
/dev/fd1    /mnt/test    ext2    user,loop,encryption=DES
```

in /etc/fstab. Additionally, ownership of the top-level directory on the floppy disk has been given to the user james because presumably it is his floppy disk. If root had not done this, james would have been able to mount his filesystem but not read it. It was essential to do that, but it turns out that in this example, root has made a fatal mistake. As well as changing the ownership of the filesystem's root directory, root has changed the directory's mode as well. This means that once the unsuspecting james has supplied his very secret password, any user on the system can read and write the files on the floppy! This underlines the fact that encryption alone is not sufficient for safety. Careful thought is also essential.

In the previous case, the file ownerships and permissions have turned out to me more of a hindrance than a help. It would probably be better to use an MS-DOS filesystem on the encrypted device, because ownership is automatically given away to the user mounting the disk and the file modes are set correctly:

```
$ ls -ld  /mnt/floppy/
drwxr-xr-x 2 james  users   7168 Jan  1  1970 /mnt/floppy/
```

However there are *still* two problems with this strategy. First, it is not possible to make an encrypted filesystem easily on a floppy, because the mkfs.msdos program needs to know the geometry for the device on which it is creating the filesystem and the loopback device drivers don't really have geometries. Second, once your encrypted ext2 filesystem is mounted, the superuser can *still* read your data.

The encryption methods outlined previously are not available in standard kernels because most useful forms of encryption technology are not legally exportable from the United States. However, they are already available outside the United States at the URL ftp://ftp.replay.com/pub/linux/all/linux-crypt-kernelpatches.tar.gz.

This site is in Holland. You need to apply these patches to your kernel and recompile it in order to use the DES and IDEA encryption methods with loopback devices. The patches were made against version 2.0.11 of the Linux kernel, but they work perfectly well with the kernel supplied with Red Hat Linux 4.2.

To summarize, encrypted filesystems can be useful for some kinds of data (for example, for storing digital signatures for important system binaries in such a way that they can't be tampered with), but their usefulness to users other than root is limited. However, of course all the ordinary file encryption mechanisms are still available to and useful for ordinary users.

Other Block Devices

Although hard disks, floppy disks, and CD-ROM drives are probably the most heavily used block devices, there are other kinds of block devices too. These include ramdisks and Zip drives.

Ramdisks

Ramdisks are block devices that store their data in RAM rather than on a disk. This means they are very fast; nevertheless, ramdisks are rarely used with Linux because Linux has a very good disk caching scheme, which provides most of the speed benefit of a ramdisk but not the fixed cost in memory.

The most common use for ramdisks, then, is to serve as a root filesystem while Linux is being installed. A compressed filesystem image is loaded into a ramdisk, and the installation process is run from this disk. The ramdisk's filesystem can be larger than a single floppy, because the image is compressed on the floppy.

Although ramdisks are useful with operating systems lacking effective disk buffering, they offer little performance advantage under Linux. Should you want to try out a ramdisk, they work just like any other block device. For example, to mount a ramdisk as `/tmp`, you would add

```
/dev/ram     /tmp         ext2     defaults     0 0
```

to `/etc/fstab` and then create and mount an `ext` filesystem with the following:

```
/sbin/mkfs -t ext2 /dev/ram
mount /tmp
```

Any performance benefits from doing this are hard to find, but you might find that this helps in unusual circumstances.

The principal advantage of ramdisks is that they enable great flexibility in the boot process. Although it is possible to recompile a kernel including support for your hardware, this makes the initial installation process difficult. Historically, this problem has been worked around by the provision of dozens of different installation boot disks, each providing support for one or two items of boot hardware (SCSI cards and CD-ROM drives, for example).

A simpler solution is to exploit loadable kernel modules. Instead of having separate boot disks for each type of hardware, all containing different kernels, it is simple to provide just one boot disk containing a modular kernel and the module utilities themselves.

A compressed filesystem is loaded from the floppy disk into a ramdisk by the kernel loader, LILO, at the same time the kernel is loaded. The kernel mounts this filesystem and runs a program (`/linuxrc`) from it. This program then mounts the "real" root filesystem and exits, enabling the kernel to remount the real root filesystem on `/`. This system is convenient to set up, and the process of creating initial ramdisks had been automated by Red Hat Software (see the manual page for `mkinitrd`). Red Hat Linux systems whose root filesystem is on a SCSI device have a modular kernel and boot by this method.

Zip Drives

Zip drives are drives providing removable 100MB cartridges. They come in three varieties: parallel port (PPA), IDE, and SCSI. All are supported, but the parallel port version is slowest; it is also a SCSI drive but with a proprietary parallel port interface, for which the Linux kernel provides a driver. Hence, both kinds of drive appear as SCSI disks.

Because they're just standard (but removable) SCSI or IDE disks, most aspects of their use are just as for other block devices. Red Hat Linux 4.2 comes with support for both the SCSI and

PPA varieties. Further information can be found in the Zip-Drive mini-HOWTO (which explains how to install your Zip drive), and the Zip-Install mini-HOWTO, which explains how to install Red Hat Linux onto a Zip drive.

Character Devices

Character devices offer a flow of data that must be read in order. Whereas block devices enable a seek to select the next block of data transferred, for example, from one edge or the other of a floppy disk, character devices represent hardware that doesn't have this capability. An example is a terminal, for which the next character to be read is whatever key you type at the keyboard.

In fact, because there are only two basic types of devices, block and character, all hardware is represented as one or the other, rather like the animal and vegetable kingdoms of biological classification. Inevitably, this means that there are a few devices that don't quite fit into this classification scheme. Examples include tape drives, generic SCSI devices, and the special memory devices such as `/dev/port` and `/dev/kmem`.

NOTE

Network interfaces are represented differently; see Chapter 13.

Parallel Ports

Parallel ports are usually used for communicating with printers, although they are versatile enough to support other things too—for example, Zip drives, CD-ROM drives, and even networking.

The hardware itself offers character-at-a-time communication. The parallel port can provide an interrupt to notify the kernel that it is now ready to output a new character, but because printers are usually not performance-critical on most PCs, this interrupt is often borrowed for use by some other hardware, often sound hardware. This has an unfortunate consequence: The kernel often needs to poll the parallel hardware, so driving a parallel printer often requires more CPU work than it should.

The good news, though, is that if your parallel printer interrupt is not in use by some other hardware, it can be enabled with the printer driver configuration program, `tunelp`. The `-i` option for `tunelp` sets the IRQ for use with each printer device. You might set the IRQ for the printer port to 7 like this:

```
# /usr/sbin/tunelp /dev/lp1 -i 7
/dev/lp1 using IRQ 7
```

If this results in the printer ceasing to work, going back to the polling method is easy:

```
# /usr/sbin/tunelp /dev/lp1 -i 0
/dev/lp1 using polling
```

The best way to test a printer port under Red Hat Linux is from the Control Panel's Printer Configuration tool (`/usr/bin/printtool`). The Tests menu offers the option of printing a test page directly to the device rather than via the normal printing system. This is a good starting point. More information on setting up printers can be found in Chapter 12, "Printing with Linux."

Tape Drives

Tape drives provide I/O of a stream of bytes to or from the tape. While most tape drives can be repositioned (that is, rewound and wound forward like audio or video tapes), this operation is very slow by disk standards. While access to a random part of the tape is at least feasible, it is very slow, and so the character device interface is workable for using tape drives.

For most UNIX workstations, the interface of choice for tape drives is SCSI because this fits in well with the SCSI disks and so on. SCSI provides the ability to just plug in a new device and start using it. (Of course, you can't do this with the power on.) SCSI has traditionally been more expensive than most other PC technologies, so it wasn't used for many tape drives developed for use with PCs. There have been several interfaces used for tape drives for IBM PCs, and these include the following:

Type	*Device Names*	*Major Number*
SCSI	`/dev/st*`	9
Floppy	`/dev/rft*`	27
QIC-02	`/dev/rmt`	12
IDE	`/dev/ht*`	37
Parallel Port	(Currently unsupported)	

All these tape drives have the feature that when the device is closed, the tape is rewound. All these drives except the QIC-02 drive have a second device interface with a name prefixed with `n`—for example `/dev/nst0`, `/dev/nst3`, or `/dev/nht0`. All these devices support the magnetic tape control program, `mt`, which is used for winding tapes past files, rewinding them, and so on. Many commands, particularly the more advanced `mt` commands, are only available for SCSI tape drives.

Apart from the `mt` command for the basic control of a tape drive, there are many commands that you can use for storing and retrieving data on tape. Because the character devices are "just files," you could use `cat` to store data on the tape, but this is not very flexible. There are a great many programs particularly or partly designed with tape drives in mind, including the following:

`tar` This is widely used for creating archives in regular files but was originally created for making tape backups. In fact, `tar` stands for *tape archiver*. Archives made by `tar` can be read on a wide variety of systems.

`cpio` Another program principally intended for backups and so on, `cpio` stands for copy in–out. The GNU version of `cpio`, which is used by Linux distributions, supports eight different data formats—some of which are varieties of its "native" format, two are varieties of `tar` archives, and some are obsolete. If you want to unpack an unknown archive, `cpio`, along with `file` and `dd`, is very useful.

`dump` The `dump` utility is of use only to system administrators because it backs up an `ext2` filesystem by raw access to the block device on which the filesystem exists. (For this reason, it is better to do this when the filesystem is either not mounted or is mounted read-only.) This has the advantage, among other things, that the access times of the backed-up directories are left unmodified. (GNU `tar` will also do this.) Although tapes written with `dump` are not always readable on other versions of UNIX, unlike those written by `tar` and `cpio`, this is a popular choice.

`dd` Designed for blockwise I/O, `dd` is a general-purpose tool for doing file manipulations and can often be very useful.

`afio` A variant of `cpio` that compresses individual files into the backup. For backups, this is preferable to `tar`'s compression of the whole archive because a small tape error can make a compressed `tar` archive useless, although a `tar` archive that isn't compressed doesn't have this vulnerability. This isn't very widely used outside the Linux world.

Amanda Amanda is a powerful backup system that schedules, organizes, and carries out backups for you. It uses either `tar` or `dump` to do the actual work, and will effortlessly allow you to automate all the backups for one machine or a multitude. One of its most useful features is its capability to do fast backups across the network from several client machines to a single server machine containing a tape drive. More information about Amanda is available at the URL `http://www.cs.umd.edu/projects/amanda/`; RPMs of Amanda are available on the Red Hat FTP site.

BRU BRU (Backup and Restore Utility) is a commercial product for making backups.

Terminals

The *terminal* is the principal mode of communication between the kernel and the user. When you type keystrokes, the terminal driver turns them into input readable by the shell, or whatever program you are running.

For many years, UNIX ran only on serial terminals. While most computers now also have video hardware, the terminal is still a useful concept. Each window in which you can run a shell provides a separate *pseudo-terminal*, each one rather like a traditional serial terminal. Terminals are often called `ttys` because the device nodes for many of them have names like `/dev/tty*`.

The terminal interface is used to represent serial lines to "real" terminals, to other computers (via modems), mice, printers, and so on. The large variety of hardware addressed by the terminal interface has led to a wide range of capabilities being offered by the terminal device driver, and hence explaining all the facilities offered could easily occupy an entire chapter. This section just offers an overview of the facilities.

For more complete information on terminals and serial I/O, refer to the Linux Documentation Project's excellent HOWTO documents. These are provided on the Red Hat Linux 4.2 CD-ROM and are also available on the Web at `http://sunsite.unc.edu/LDP/`. Specific HOWTOs dealing with this are the Serial-HOWTO, section 9 of the Hardware-HOWTO, and the Serial Port Programming mini-HOWTO. There are many documents dealing with using modems for networking. These are mentioned later in the chapter in the section "Using Modems."

The Terminal Device Driver

The terminal device driver gathers the characters that you type at the keyboard and sends them on to the program you're working with, after some processing. This processing can involve gathering the characters into batches a line at a time and taking into account the special meanings of some keys you might type.

Some special keys of this sort are used for editing the text that is sent to the program you're interacting with. Much of the time, the terminal driver is building a line of input that it hasn't yet sent to the program receiving your input. Keys that the driver will process specially include the following:

Return (CR) or Line feed (LF)	CR is usually translated into LF by the terminal driver (see the `icrnl` option in the manual page for `stty`). This ends the current line, which is then sent to the application (it is waiting for terminal input, so it wakes up).

Backspace/Delete	Only one of these two keys can be selected as the erase key, which erases the previous character typed. For more information, read the Linux Keyboard Setup mini-HOWTO.
End-of-File, usually Ctrl+D	When a program is reading its standard input from the keyboard, and you want to let it know that you've typed everything that you're going to, you press Ctrl+D.
Word-erase, usually Ctrl+W	Deletes the last word you typed.
Kill-Line, usually Ctrl+U	This kills the entire line of input so that you can start again.
Interrupt, usually Ctrl+C	Kills the current program. Some programs block this at times when the program might leave the terminal in a strange state if it were unexpectedly killed.
Suspend, usually Ctrl+Z	This key sends a suspend signal to the program you're using. The result is that the program is stopped temporarily, and you get the shell prompt again. You can then put that program (job) in the background and do something else. See Chapter 21, "Shell Programming," for more information.
Quit, usually Ctrl+\ (Ctrl+Backslash)	Sends a Quit signal to the current program; programs that ignore Ctrl+C can often be stopped with Ctrl+\, but programs ignoring Ctrl+C are often doing so for a reason.
Stop, usually Ctrl+S, and Start, usually Ctrl+Q	These stop and restart terminal output temporarily, which can be useful if a command produces a lot of output, although it can often be more useful just to repeat the command and pipe it through `less`.

There are many other terminal modes and settings; these can be examined with the `stty` command. This command has a built-in set of sensible settings for terminals, and normally when you just type `stty` to find the current settings, it just shows you the differences from its "sane" settings:

```
$ stty
speed 9600 baud; line = 0;
```

TIP

If you ever find that your terminal state has been messed up, then you can usually fix this with the command `stty sane` and Ctrl+J. Note that the command is ended with Ctrl+J, rather than Enter (which is the same as Ctrl+M). This is because the `icrnl` option might have been turned off. This is fixed again with `stty sane`. GNU `bash` will always cope with CRs that have not been converted to LF anyway, but some other programs won't.

If this still doesn't work, and the screen font appears to have been changed, try typing `echo`, pressing Ctrl+V and Esc, typing `c`, and pressing Ctrl+J. You press Ctrl+V to make the terminal driver pass the next key through without processing. You can get a similar effect by typing `reset` and pressing Ctrl+J, but the program `reset` is only available if the `ncurses` package is installed.

Programs can turn off the processing that the line driver does by default; the resulting behavior (raw mode) allows programs to read unprocessed input from the terminal driver (for example, CR is not mapped to LF), and control characters don't produce the signals described in the table earlier in this section. The `stty sane` command will return things to normal.

Serial Communications

Although the terminal interfaces used most commonly under Linux are the console driver and the pseudo-terminals driven by programs like `xterm`, `script`, and `expect`, the original terminal interface involved serial communications. In fact, this still lingers on; a pseudo-`tty` associated with an `xterm` window still has an associated baud rate as shown in the example in the section "The Terminal Device Driver." Changing this baud rate has no actual effect, though. For real serial ports, however, the baud rate and many other parameters have a direct relevance. The device nodes relating to the serial ports are composed of two "teams," with the names `/dev/cua*` and `/dev/ttyS*`. These allow the same serial hardware to be used for both incoming and outgoing serial connections, as explained later in the section "Using Modems."

Configuring the Serial Ports

Serial port configuration is mostly done either with the `stty` command or directly by programs using the interface outlined in the `termios` manual page. The `stty` command offers almost all the configuration possibilities provided by `termios`; however, there are configuration issues for serial hardware that are not addressed by `stty`. The `setserial` command allows the configuration of the correct IRQ settings for each serial port and of extra-fast baud rates that the standard `termios` specification doesn't provide. For more detailed information, refer to the Linux Serial-HOWTO and the manual page for `setserial`.

Using Modems

Modems (other than "WinModems") are very flexible devices. They allow dial-up terminal access and wide area networking, and they also often allow the sending and receiving of faxes or voice-mail. The two "teams" of serial device nodes mentioned earlier are intended specifically for good modem support, and they look like this:

```
$ ls -l /dev/ttyS* /dev/cua* /dev/mo*
crw-rw----   1 root     uucp       5,  64 Jan  1  1980 /dev/cua0
crw-rw----   1 root     uucp       5,  65 Jan  1  1980 /dev/cua1
crw-rw----   1 root     uucp       5,  66 Jan  1  1980 /dev/cua2
crw-rw----   1 root     uucp       5,  67 Jan  1  1980 /dev/cua3
lrwxrwxrwx   1 root     uucp            4 Jun  7 14:16 /dev/modem -> cua2
lrwxrwxrwx   1 root     root           10 Sep  6  1996 /dev/mouse -> /dev/ttyS0
crw-r--r--   1 root     root       4,  64 Nov  1 08:56 /dev/ttyS0
crw-r--r--   1 root     root       4,  65 May 29  1995 /dev/ttyS1
crw-r--r--   1 root     root       4,  66 Jan  1  1980 /dev/ttyS2
crw-r--r--   1 root     root       4,  67 Jan  1  1980 /dev/ttyS3
```

The `/dev/cua*` devices are intended for use for dialing out, and the `/dev/ttyS*` devices are intended for dialing in. A process such as `getty` can be waiting for an `open` system call to complete (that is, waiting for the modem to signal that there is an incoming call) on the `/dev/ttyS0` device while you are opening the corresponding device `/dev/cua0`, which refers to the same hardware. Because there can't be an incoming call on that line while you're using the modem, `getty` continues to wait. Lock files keep everyone from trying to use the same device at the same time.

These days, internetworking is the most common use for modems by far. There are many resources that will help you set up your machine for Internet access via a modem. See the section "Connecting to the Net with PPP" in Chapter 13. Other resources include the Red Hat PPP-Tips document, which can be found in the support section of Red Hat's Web site, the EzPPP package, and the ISP-HOOKUP and PPP HOWTOS. There are also a large number of useful mini-HOWTOs that each help with more specific things; these include the Diald, Dip+SLiRP+CSLIP, Dynamic-IP-Hacks, IP-Masquerade, PPP-over-ISDN, PPP-over-minicom, SLIP+proxyARP, and Tiny-News Linux mini-HOWTOs. If, on the other hand, you send and receive e-mail by UUCP rather than Internet protocols, you should start by reading the Linux UUCP HOWTO and the Linux Sendmail+UUCP mini-HOWTO.

Generic SCSI Devices

Not all SCSI devices are hard disks, CD-ROM drives, or tape drives. Some are optical scanners, CD-ROM recorders, or even electron microscopes. The kernel can't possibly abstract the interfaces for all possible SCSI devices, so it gives user programs direct access to SCSI hardware via the generic SCSI devices. These enable programs to send arbitrary SCSI commands to hardware. Although this offers the opportunity of wreaking havoc by mistake, it also offers the capability of driving all sorts of interesting hardware, of which the principal examples are CD-ROM recorders. The SCSI device nodes all have names starting with `/dev/sg`. SCSI commands are sent to the devices by writing data to the device, and the results are read back by reading from the device.

CD-ROM Recorders

CD-ROM recorders are devices for recording data on special media that can be read in ordinary CD-ROM drives. There are two stages in the writing of a CD: the generation of the CD image and the writing of that image to the media.

The surface of a CD-R (recordable CD) is only writable once, so if `mkisofs` worked like the other `mkfs` tools it would always generate image files representing empty CDs. For this reason, `mkisofs` populates the filesystem with files as it generates the image file.

The CD image file is produced by the `mkisofs` program, which generates the structures for an ISO9660 filesystem and populates it with the files from a directory tree. CDs are not writable in the same sense as block devices; this is why they are not *actually* block devices. The image file must be written to the CD-R with a specialized program, `cdwrite`, which understands all the various proprietary schemes used for driving CD writers. All the CD writers supported by Linux (as of version 2.0.30 of the kernel) are SCSI devices, so the kernel accommodates this by providing access to the generic SCSI device interface that enables a program to send SCSI commands to these devices.

While *burning* (writing) a CD, it is usually important that the flow of data to the writer keeps up with the speed at which the writer is going; otherwise, if the writer runs out of data to write, the CD-R is ruined. For this reason, it is usual to use `mkisofs` to generate an image file and then separately use `cdwrite` to write this image file to the CD writer.

It is possible to use a pipe to send the data from `mkisofs` directly to `cdwrite`. This often works either because a fast machine can ensure that `mkisofs` supplies the data fast enough to keep the CD writer busy or because the CD writer is not sensitive to data underruns. (Some of the more expensive ones have internal hard disks to which the data is written as an intermediate stage.) This technique is not recommended, however, because the generation of the intermediate image file has other benefits; it enables you to test your CD image before the final writing of the data takes place.

Testing CD Images

Just as you can use `mkfs` to create a filesystem inside an ordinary file, you can mount filesystems contained in ordinary files by using the loopback device driver described previously. The first example of mounting a loopback filesystem is a demonstration of how you can test a CD image.

Other Character Devices

There are several other varieties of character devices, some which are used frequently. For example, `/dev/null` is used very frequently.

The Controlling Terminal Device—/dev/tty

Most processes have a controlling terminal, particularly if they were started interactively by a user. The *controlling terminal*, which I'll refer to as simply `/dev/tty`, is used for initiating a conversation directly with the user (for example, to ask them something). An example is the `crypt` command:

```
$ fmt diary.txt | crypt | mail -s Diary confidant@linux.org
Enter key:
$
```

Here, the `crypt` command has opened `/dev/tty` in order to obtain a password. It was not able to use its own standard output to issue the prompt and its standard input to read the password because these are being used for the data to be encrypted.

> **NOTE**
>
> Of course, it's unusual to send e-mail encrypted with `crypt`. A better choice is probably PGP. PGP is available in RPM format from `ftp://ftp.replay.com//pub/linux/redhat`.

More useful examples of this are commands that need to ask the operator something even if their input and output are redirected. A case in point is the `cpio` command, which prompts the operator for the name of a new tape device when it runs out of space. See the section "`/dev/null` and Friends" later in this chapter for another example.

Nonserial Mice

Many computers have bus or PS/2 mice instead of serial mice. This has the advantage of keeping both of the two standard serial ports free, but the disadvantage of using up another IRQ. These devices are used by `gpm` and the X Window System, but most other programs don't interact with them directly. Setting up your system with these mice is quite easy; the Red Hat Linux installation process pretty much takes care of it for you. Should you have problems with your mouse, though, you should read the manual page for `gpm` and the Linux BusMouse-HOWTO.

Audio Devices

There are several audio-related device nodes on Linux systems, and they include the following:

`/dev/sndstat`	Indicates the status of the sound driver
`/dev/audio*`	Sun-compatible audio output device
`/dev/dsp*`	Sound sampling device
`/dev/mixer`	For control of the mixer hardware on the sound card
`/dev/music`	A high-level sequencer interface

`/dev/sequencer*`	A low-level sequencer interface
`/dev/midi*`	Direct MIDI port access

Setting up the sound driver under Linux can sometimes be quite difficult, but the Linux Sound-HOWTO provides useful advice.

Random Number Devices

Many aspects of computing require the generation of apparently random sequences. Examples include games, numerical computations, and various computer security related applications. Numerical computing with random numbers requires that the sequence of random numbers be repeatable but also that the sequence "looks" random. Games require apparently random numbers too, but the quality of the random numbers used is not quite as critical as for numerical computation programs. The system libraries produce repeatable sequences of "pseudo-random" numbers that satisfy these requirements well.

On the other hand, there are many aspects of computer security in which it is advantageous to generate numbers that really are random. Because you can assume that an attacker has access to the same sorts of random number generators that you do, using these is usually not very safe—an attacker can use these generators to figure out what random number you'll come out with next. Sequences that are genuinely random must in the end be produced from the real world, and not from the internals of some computer program. For this reason, the Linux kernel keeps a supply of random numbers internally. These numbers are derived from very precise timings of the intervals between "random" external events—for example, the user's keypresses on the keyboard, mouse events, and even some interrupts (such as from the floppy disk drive and some network cards). These "real" random numbers are used in security-critical contexts—for example, the choosing of TCP sequence numbers.

NOTE

The Linux kernel uses these methods to produce TCP sequence numbers that are more difficult to guess than those of any other implementation at the time of writing. This improves the security of TCP connections against "hijacking."

The two random number devices differ in what happens when the rate of reading exceeds the rate at which random data is collected inside the kernel. The `/dev/random` device makes the calling program wait until some more randomness arrives, and the `/dev/urandom` device falls back on the difficult-to-guess MD5 hash to produce a stream of random data. When more random information arrives later, this is added to the randomness of `/dev/urandom`. To summarize, `/dev/random` doesn't sacrifice quality in favor of speed, but `/dev/urandom` does.

/dev/null and Friends

In the following, the special devices `/dev/full` and `/dev/null` first simulate a tape-full condition and then discard the output:

```
$ echo diary.txt ¦ cpio -o >/dev/full
Found end of tape.  To continue, type device/file name when ready.
/dev/null
52 blocks
```

In the real world, when the tape on `/dev/st0` became full, you would probably just have changed the tape in the drive and typed `/dev/st0` a second time. However, `/dev/full` is occasionally useful for testing purposes, and `/dev/null` is used all the time for discarding unwanted output. The device `/dev/zero` produces a stream of zero bytes when read. (`/dev/null`, on the other hand, produces no output at all.)

Memory Devices

The memory devices have the same major device number as `/dev/null` and `/dev/full`, but are used very differently. They are as follows:

`/dev/mem`	Provides access to physical memory
`/dev/kmem`	Provides access to the kernel's virtual memory
`/dev/port`	Provides access to I/O ports

These devices are not frequently used in many programs; the X Window System's X server uses memory mapping on `/dev/mem` to access the video memory, and many programs use `/dev/port` to access I/O ports on those architectures that have a separate I/O space. (Many modern processors do not.)

Virtual Console Screen Devices

The virtual console screen devices exist to provide screen capture capabilities for virtual consoles (VCs). They are not readable by ordinary users; hence, other users cannot eavesdrop on your session.

There are two sets of device nodes for this purpose:

```
$ ls -l /dev/vcs[012] /dev/vcsa[012]
crw--w----    1 root     tty        7,   0 Sep 27  1995 /dev/vcs0
crw--w----    1 root     tty        7,   1 Sep 27  1995 /dev/vcs1
crw--w----    1 root     tty        7,   2 Sep 27  1995 /dev/vcs2
crw--w----    1 root     tty        7, 128 Sep 27  1995 /dev/vcsa0
crw--w----    1 root     tty        7, 129 Sep 27  1995 /dev/vcsa1
crw--w----    1 root     tty        7, 130 Sep 27  1995 /dev/vcsa2
```

Each set is numbered from 0 to 63, corresponding to the numbering system for the `/dev/tty*` console devices. The device `/dev/vcs0`, like the device `dev/tty0`, always refers to the currently selected VC.

The /dev/vcs* files provide a snapshot of what is in view on the corresponding VC. This contains no newlines because there are none actually on the screen; a newline character just moves the cursor after all. To make the captured data into the kind of thing you usually see in text files or send to printers, you need to add newlines in the appropriate places. This can be done with dd:

```
$ dd cbs=80 conv=unblock </dev/vcs1 ¦ lpr
```

This command works only if the screen is 80 columns wide. This is not always true; the kernel can set up a different video mode at boot time, and the SVGATextMode command can be used to change it at any time.

This problem can be overcome by using the other set of devices, /dev/vcsa*. Reading from these devices gives a header, followed by the screen data with attribute bytes. The header consists of two bytes indicating the screen size (height first), followed by two bytes indicating the cursor position. The screen data is provided two bytes per character cell, the first containing the attribute byte and the second containing the character data (as with /dev/vcs*). This can be used to provide full-color screen dumps and so on. The following script uses /dev/vcsa1 to determine the width of the VC and to get the conversion of /dev/vcs1 right:

```
#! /bin/sh

# Insist on exactly one argument (the VC number to dump)
[ $# -eq 1 ] ¦¦ { echo "usage: $0 [vc-number]" >&2; exit 1 }

vc=$1 # Which VC to dump.

# Extract the VC's width from the second byte of the vcsa device.
# Th "unpack" expression extracts the value of the second
# character of the input (the vcsa device).
width=`perl -e 'print unpack("x%C",<>);' < /dev/vcsa${vc}`

# Use dd(1) to convert the output now that we know the width.
dd cbs=${width} conv=unblock </dev/vcs${vc}
```

Summary

This chapter introduces the topics of character and block devices and filesystem administration, with an overview of the hardware accessed via the special files in the directory /dev. Further information can be obtained from the Linux Documentation Project material at http://sunsite.unc.edu/LDP. Much of the LDP material is also provided on the CD-ROM accompanying this book.

CHAPTER 12

Printing with Linux

by Bill Ball

IN THIS CHAPTER

This chapter shows you how to use your printer with Linux. A number of programs, files, and directories are integral to supporting printing under Linux, but you'll find that with little effort, you'll be able to get to work and print nicely formatted documents or graphics.

If you can print to your printer from DOS, Windows 95, or Windows NT, don't worry! You'll be able to print under Linux, and will probably be pleasantly surprised by the additional printing capabilities you won't find in the commercial operating system installed on your PC.

As a Red Hat Linux user, you'll be especially pleased because the kind folks in North Carolina have hidden the ugly and gory details of installing and using a printer, and have made the process a snap!

Printer Devices

Under Linux, each piece of your computer's hardware is abstracted to a device file (hopefully with an accompanying device driver in the kernel; see Chapter 11, "Filesystems, Disks, and Other Devices," for more details). Printer devices, traditionally named after line printers, are character mode devices, and will be found under the `/dev` directory. Some of these are shown in Table 12.1.

Table 12.1. Parallel printer devices.

Device Name	*Printer*	*Address*
`/dev/lp0`	First parallel printer	`0x3bc`
`/dev/lp1`	Second parallel printer	`0x378`
`/dev/lp2`	Third parallel printer	`0x278`

Serial printers are assigned to serial devices such as `/dev/ttySX`, where `X` is a number from 0 to 3. There are quite a few `tty` devices listed in `/dev`. Generally, if you're going to use a serial printer, you'll have to use the `setserial` command to make sure the printer's serial port is set to the fastest baud rate your printer supports.

There are some special cases, such as using an old Apple LaserWriter as a serial printer (it has a Diablo print-wheel emulation mode using the Courier font), when you must define your own printer or edit an entry in the `/etc/printcap` database. Sometimes you can manipulate the printer to get a higher speed. For example, here's a 10-year-old trick to increase the serial port speed of the Apple LaserWriter Plus to 19200, by Dale Carstensen, and posted to the `comp.laser-printers` newsgroup:

```
%!
0000 % Server Password
statusdict begin 25 sccbatch 0 ne exch 19200 ne or
{ serverdict begin exitserver} {pop end stop} ifelse
statusdict begin
```

```
25 19200 0 setsccbatch
end % note--next line has an actual CTRL-D
```

See Appendix D in the *RedBook*, Adobe's PostScript language reference manual, for more information about LaserWriters, or peruse `comp.laser-printers` for hints on setting up your laser printer. Also check the `/usr/lib/ghostscript/doc` directory for information about 25 different PostScript printer utilities included in the Ghostscript distribution.

Most users, however, have a printer attached to the parallel printer port, so I'll concentrate on `/dev/lp`.

How Do I Print?

First, check to see that your printer is plugged in, turned on, and attached to your computer's parallel port. Pass-through parallel port cables shouldn't pose a problem, but don't expect to be able to use your printer while you're using your CD-ROM, QuickCam, SCSI adapter, or tape, ZIP, or SyQuest drive if attached to a pass-through cable.

For starters, try a simple

```
# ls >/dev/lp1
```

Chances are your printer will activate and its print head will move, but when you look at the printout, you might see a staircase effect, with each word on a separate line, moving across the page. Don't worry! This is normal, and tells you that you can at least access your printer. Later in this chapter, you'll find out how to fine-tune your printing.

If you're unable to print, then try using

```
# cat /proc/devices
```

to see if the `lp` device driver loaded or compiled into your kernel. You should see something like the following:

```
Character devices:
 1 mem
 2 pty
 3 ttyp
 4 ttyp
 5 cua
 6 lp
 7 vcs
10 misc
14 sound
63 pcmcia
Block devices:
 1 ramdisk
 2 fd
 3 ide0
 9 md
22 ide1
```

You can also try the `tunelp` command, which sets various parameters to "tune" your printer port or lets you know if your printer device is using interrupts or polling for printing. Try using

```
# tunelp /dev/lp1
```

and you might see something like the following:

```
/dev/lp1 using polling
```

Or you can try

```
# tunelp /dev/lp1 -s
```

and you might see

```
/dev/lp1 status is 223, on-line
```

If `tunelp` reports "No such device or address," or if you do not find an `lp` character device, see Chapter 5, "Configuring and Building Kernels."

The RHS Linux Print System Manager

If you want to install, modify, or delete a local, remote, or LAN printer, you're going to love the `printtool` program. Found in `/usr/bin`, `printtool` is a graphical interface printer setup program you can call up from the command line or through the Red Hat `control-panel` program.

The `control-panel` and `printtool` programs run under X, so you'll have to first fire up X and then type

```
# printtool
```

from a terminal window. The main `printtool` dialog will then come up (see Figure 12.1). First, click the Add button. You'll be asked to select a local, remote, or LAN manager printer.

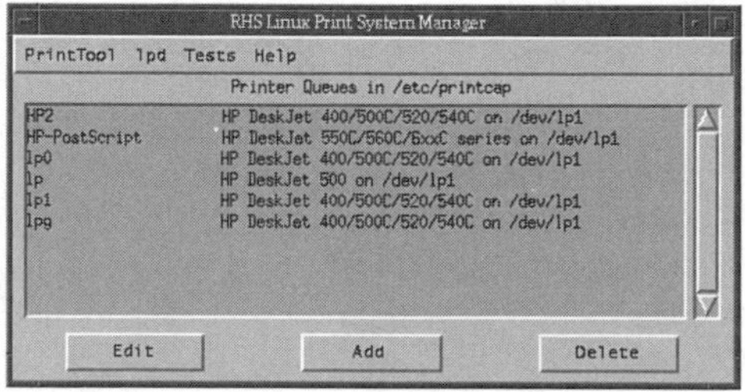

FIGURE 12.1.
The main `printtool` *dialog.*

Remote and LAN Printers

To set up a remote printer, you'll need the following, according to the `printtool` program's help information:

- The hostname of the remote machine hosting the printer
- The printer queue name of the printer on the remote machine

This means that you can send documents to other printers anywhere. Using Red Hat's `printtool` command to set up remote printing will create a remote printer entry in `/etc/printcap`. For details about a remote printer entry, see the `printcap` man page and look for the `rm` and `rp` capabilities. But you should also know there are other, possibly easier ways to print to remote printers, such as using the `rlpr` command. For more information, read Grant Taylor's Linux Printing HOWTO under `/usr/doc`.

To set up a LAN printer, you'll need the following (according to `printtool`):

- Printer server name
- Printer server IP number
- Printer name
- Printer user
- Printer password

This information is entered in a dialog that pops up after you select the type of printer you want to set up. If you want detailed instructions on how to print from Red Hat Linux to a printer on a Windows 95 system or to print on a Linux printer from Windows 95, browse to `http://www.redhat.com/support/docs/rhl/Tips`.

Local Printers

For now, I'll assume you're going to set up a parallel port printer attached directly to your computer. To do so, run `printtool`, then click the Add button, select Local, and then click the OK button.

An Info dialog will appear, telling you which parallel printer devices have been detected. Click OK and then click the Select button in the Edit Local Printer Entry dialog. You'll be presented a large dialog called Configure Filter, with a list of 32 popular printers to choose from (see Figure 12.2). Pick your printer, or a printer close to yours, and then click the OK button.

The dialog will disappear, and you can then click OK on the Edit Local Printer Entry dialog. The printer you defined will appear under the list of Printer Queues in the main `printtool` dialog. Select it and then select an ASCII or PostScript test from the Tests menu.

The ASCII test page prints two lines of text, followed by a centered paragraph of text. The PostScript test page prints a half-inch and one-inch border, a logo, and color scale (grayscale on a black-and-white printer).

`printtool` works by first defining your printer and then inserting the definition, along with a pointer to a filter script (written in `bash`) in the `/var/spool/lpd` directory, into an `/etc/printcap` entry. The filter and associated scripts reside in a directory, or printer queue, under `/var/spool/lpd`, with either a name you choose, or an assigned default, such as `lp0`. See the sample `/etc/printcap` database file later in this chapter.

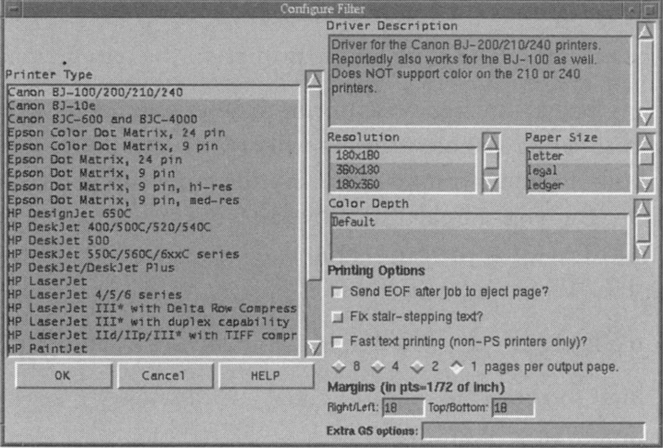

FIGURE 12.2.
The Configure Filter dialog.

You can use `printtool` to add, edit, or delete different printers. Another nice feature is the ability to assign a size limit to spooled files, which can be helpful if you have limited disk space or don't want users to fill up your filesystem. If you have a printer that requires you to change the print cartridge in order to print black-and-white or color pages, you'll find `printtool` indispensable. Try it!

By the way, although the current version of `printtool`, 3.2, creates a backup of your `/etc/printcap` database each time you make a change, it does not delete the associated printer queue, or spool directory, when you delete a printer. One disconcerting `printtool` bug is that while you're printing, at least with a kernel using polling, your printer's parallel port will not be detected if you run `printtool` to install a printer. Perhaps this will be fixed in a newer version.

Linux Printing Commands

Of course, you don't have to use the `printtool` command to set up your printer. You can edit `/etc/printcap` directly, but you should know what you're doing and understand `printcap`'s format. This file, an ASCII database of your system's local and networked printers, describes the capabilities of each printer in detail. For full details, see the `printcap` man page for commands, and the `termcap` man page for the file's layout.

In fact, you can have multiple entries for each printer, which is helpful is you want to print different size papers, print color or black-and-white documents, or change printer trays.

Linux uses the 4.3BSD line printer spooling system. This system has a number of features and associated programs to support background printing, multiple local and networked printers, and control of the printers and queued documents.

The main files used in the Linux printer spooling system are as follows:

```
/etc/printcap
/usr/sbin/lpd
/usr/sbin/lpc
```

```
/usr/bin/lpr
/usr/bin/lprm
/usr/bin/lpq
/dev/printer
```

When you first boot Linux, the shell script `lpd.init`, under `/etc/rc.d/init.d/`, starts `lpd`, the printer daemon. This program, a printer server, runs in the background, waiting for print requests. When a request is detected (on `/dev/printer`), a copy of `lpd` is created, while the original continues to wait for more requests.

Print requests are started with the `lpr` command. For example, the command line

```
# lpr myfile.txt
```

will print your document to a file in the `/var/spool/` directory. There are also print spooling commands to help you track your request. If you're printing a large document, or a number of smaller files, you can see a list of print jobs running by using the `lpq` command. For example, to print a number of files at once, use

```
# lpr .x*
```

followed by

```
# lpq
```

This outputs the following:

```
Rank   Owner      Job  Files                               Total Size
active root       301  .xboing-scores, .xinitrc            1366 bytes
```

If you want to stop the preceding print job, use the `lprm` command, followed by the job number, as in the following:

```
# lprm 301
dfA071Aa01088 dequeued
dfB071Aa01088 dequeued
cfA071Aa01088 dequeued
```

This shows that `lprm` has removed the spool files from the printer's spool directory under `/var/spool/lpd`.

If you want to disable or enable a printer and its spooling queue, rearrange the order of any print jobs, or find out the status of printers, you can use `lpc` from the command line or interactively. But you must be logged in as root or as a superuser (through the `su` command). See the `lpc` man page for details.

Simple Formatting

Of course, printing directory listings or short text files is fine, but default printouts of longer files require formatting with borders, headers, and footers. To get a nicer document with text files, use the `pr` command.

The pr command has 19 different command-line options to help you format documents for printing. For example,

```
# pr +9 -h CONFIDENTIAL DOCUMENT -o 5 < myfile.txt ¦ lpr
```

will print your document, starting at page 9, with a header containing the date, time, words "CONFIDENTIAL DOCUMENT," and page number, with a left margin of 5 spaces.

Another text formatter you might want to try is the fmt command; see its man page for details.

Other Helpful Printer Programs and Filters

Printer filters work by defining and inserting printer definitions into your /etc/printcap file. Embedded in each printer description is a pointer (pathname) to a script or program containing the filter that is run before output to the printer. See the printcap man page and the sample /etc/printcap listing later in this chapter.

APSfilter

Even if, as a Red Hat user, you're spoiled with the printtool program, there might be times when you need to use other programs or scripts to help set up or manage printing. If you can't or don't want to run X, but want to easily install printing services for HP or PostScript printers, one great solution is the printing filter package called APSfilter, by Andreas Klemm and Thomas Bueschgens. Installing APSfilter is a snap, and it's even easier to use.

APSfilter works well with all Linux printing applications. Two added benefits are that it prints two formatted pages in Landscape mode on a single page when you print text documents, saving you paper, and automagically recognizes the following documents: xfig, pbm, pnm, tiff, jpeg, gif, Sun rasterfile, PostScript, dvi, raw ASCII, gzip, and compressed.

One downside is that APSfilter's printing of grayscale is not as good as the grayscale printing offered by the printtool program's setup (at least on HP deskjets). Hopefully, this will be fixed in the next version.

BubbleTools

If you have a Canon Bubble Jet, IBM Proprinter X24E, Epson LQ1550, or Epson Stylus, Olav Wolfelschneider's BubbleTools printer drivers can help you. This filter program converts a number of graphics formats, including Group 3 Fax, for this series of 360-dpi printers.

magicfilter

Another printer filter similar to APSfilter is H. Peter Anvin's magicfilter, which detects and converts documents for printing through a combination of a compiled C filter and printer configuration file.

You can find APSfilter, BubbleTools, and magicfilter, along with other Linux printing utilities at sunsite.unc.edu/pub/Linux/system/Printing.

PostScript Printers

If you want a print spooler specifically designed for PostScript printers, give Dave Chappell's PPR a try. PPR works with printers attached to parallel, serial, and AppleTalk (LocalTalk) ports, along with other network interfaces. PPR also works much like other non-PostScript printer filters, and converts different graphics file formats for printing.

You can find PPR at `ftp://ppr-dist.trincoll.edu/pub/ppr/`.

Enhanced Printer Spooler

The future of Linux printing has arrived, and its name is `LPRng`. This print spooler software, descended from the 4.3BSD release, but totally rewritten from the ground up, offers a host of benefits and features in the areas of distribution, setup, use, and security. Some of these are as follows:

- GNU GPL distribution for freedom from restrictive copyrights
- Backwards printer filter compatibility
- Enhanced security with a permissions database
- Improved diagnostics
- Multiple printers on a single queue
- Simplified client and server printer configuration files
- Simplified printer database

You will find the latest copy of `LPRng` at the site `ftp://dickory.sdsu.edu/pub/LPRng` (along with other neat printing utilities).

System Accounting

Want to know how much printing you or your users have been doing and at what cost? Should your printer's name be "TreeEater"? See the man pages for the `pac` command, which you can use to track usage and costs. You'll also need to read the man pages for the `printcap` database to see how to enable printer use accounting.

Some Program Tips

The following are some helpful tips to help you print documents or set up applications for easier printing.

emacs

Want to print directly from `emacs`? You can print the entire buffer, unformatted or formatted, by pressing Esc+X, typing **`lpr-buffer`**, and hitting Enter, or by pressing Esc+X, typing **`print-buffer`**, and hitting Enter. Just make sure that you set your `lpr-switches` variable in your `.emacs` file to point to the correct printer in your `/etc/printcap` file.

You'll find `emacs`, along with its help files and documentation, on your Red Hat Linux CD-ROM.

Applixware for Linux

Applixware, a fully integrated suite of office tools and development environment, is a newcomer to the Linux scene, but is a veteran UNIX application. If you want to create, import, edit, and print documents with ease, this product is a good bet.

However, here's a tip on how to set up your printer for Applixware you won't find in the program's manuals. Go to Applixware Preferences and select Printing. In the Printing Preferences dialog that comes up, set Default Printer Type to PostScript, as shown in Figure 12.3. Then scroll down the list of preferences at the bottom of the dialog to Pathname of Your Printer Aliases File. Click in the Value text area, and enter the path of the file (`/etc/printers`). Then create a simple ASCII file containing a list of printers defined in your `/etc printcap` file. (You are using X so that you can do a lot of different things at once, aren't you?)

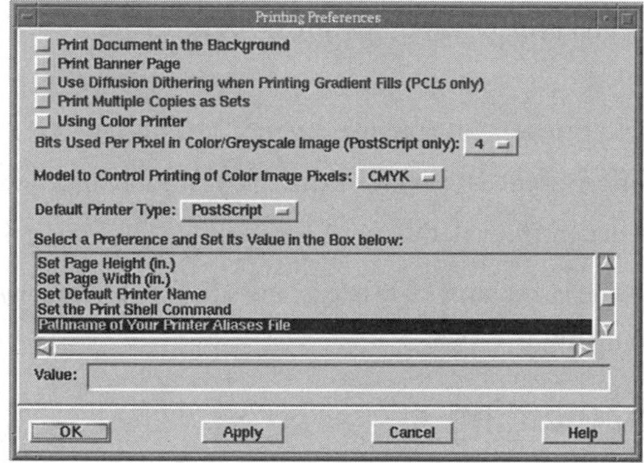

FIGURE 12.3.
The Printer Preferences dialog.

For example, here's a sample `/etc/printcap` for an HP DeskJet 500, created following installation and setup using `printtool`. Note that `printtool` offers four different modes for the printer (normal black-and-white printing, normal color printing with color cartridge, Floyd-Steinberg black-and-white print for better grayscale, and Floyd-Steinberg color printing for best, but slow):

```
### /etc/printcap
###
### Please don't edit this file directly unless you know what you are doing!
### Be warned that the control-panel printtool requires a very strict format!
### Look at the printcap(5) man page for more info.
###
### This file can be edited with the printtool in the control-panel.
##
##PRINTTOOL3## LOCAL cdj500 300x300 letter {} DeskJet500 8 1
DJ500greyscale:\
    :sd=/var/spool/lpd/lp0:\
    :mx#0:\
```

```
    :sh:\
    :lp=/dev/lp1:\
    :if=/var/spool/lpd/lp0/filter:
##PRINTTOOL3## LOCAL cdj500 300x300 letter {} DeskJet500 24 {}
DJ500colorbest:\
    :sd=/var/spool/lpd/lp0:\
    :mx#0:\
    :sh:\
    :lp=/dev/lp1:\
    :if=/var/spool/lpd/lp0/filter:
##PRINTTOOL3## LOCAL cdj500 300x300 letter {} DeskJet500 3 {}
DJ500colornormal:\
    :sd=/var/spool/lpd/lp0:\
    :mx#0:\
    :sh:\
    :lp=/dev/lp1:\
    :if=/var/spool/lpd/lp0/filter:
##PRINTTOOL3## LOCAL cdj500 300x300 letter {} DeskJet500 1 1
DJ500mononormal:\
    :sd=/var/spool/lpd/lp0:\
    :mx#0:\
    :sh:\
    :lp=/dev/lp1:\
    :if=/var/spool/lpd/lp0/filter:
```

From this listing, create and save the file `/etc/printers` with the following four lines:

```
DJ500greyscale
DJ500colorbest
DJ500colornormal
DJ500mononormal
```

Then, under Applixware, save the preferences by clicking the OK button and then the Dismiss button.

Now, when you go to print from, say, Applix Words, you'll see these four printers listed in your Print dialog box. Select an appropriate printer, make sure that PostScript is selected in the Class pop-up menu, and uncheck the Print to File box. When you hit OK, your file will immediately print using the fonts and formatting of your Applix Words document.

Other Helpful Programs

The following are short descriptions of just a couple of the programs offering handy printing services available either in your Red Hat distribution or for Linux. You'll find some of these indispensable.

XV

One great tool that does a lot more than just print graphics is John Bradley's program, `xv`, which runs under X. It can read and export nearly 18 different graphics file formats, and even comes in a scanner-driver version so you can scan and immediately print. You can print a quick copy of a graphic with the click of a button.

pbm Utilities

To translate or manipulate your graphics files into a multitude of different formats or effects for printing, try one of Jef Poskanzer's numerous `pbm` utilities. At last count there were nearly 40 different programs. See the `pbm` man page for pointers.

Ghostview

Although most of the convenience of having PostScript documents print automagically on cheap inkjet printers under Linux is due to Aladdin Enterprises' interpreter, `gs`, or Ghostscript, Tim Theisen's X client, Ghostview is another one of those "insanely great" programs that come with nearly every Linux distribution.

You can use Ghostview to preview or print `.ps` files. This program features multiple levels of magnification, landscape and portrait modes, and prints PostScript files too.

For More Information

See the man pages for `tunelp`, `printcap`, `lpd`, `lpr`, `lpq`, `lprm`, and `lpc`. Curiously, there is no man page for the `printtool` program, but its Help menu shows some general information and troubleshooting tips.

Information on how to use APSfilter is under `aps/doc` in a number of files.

For information about the BSD printing system, read Ralph Campbell's abstract "4.3BSD Line Printer Spooler Manual," which is part of the 4.4BSD *System Manager's Manual*, tabbed section 7.

For an excellent introduction to `LPRng`, see Patrick Powell's abstract "LPRng—An Enhanced Printer Spooler." This 13-page document, in PostScript or text format, includes the history, architecture, configuration, operation, and algorithm of the spooler software. You can find it at `http://ltpwww.gsfc.nasa.gov/ltpcf/about/unix/Depotdoc/LPRng` or look at the files `Intro.txt` or `Intro.ps` in the `DOC` directory of the `LPRng` sources.

To join the `LPRng` mailing list, send a subscribe message to `plp-request@iona.com`.

For detailed information about printing under Linux, you'll need to read The Linux Printing HOWTO by Grant Taylor. The Linux Printing HOWTO contains a host of great tips, tricks, traps, and hacks concerning printing under Linux, including setups for serial printers, and network printing.

Also read The Linux Printing Usage HOWTO, by Mark Komarinski, under `/usr/doc`.

And don't forget to peruse the following newsgroups for information about printers, PostScript, or Linux printing:

```
comp.lang.postscript
comp.laser-printers
comp.os.linux.hardware
```

```
comp.os.linux.setup
comp.periphs.printers
comp.sources.postscript
comp.sys.hp.hardware
```

Summary

In this chapter, you've learned about Linux printer devices and how to print simple files. I've also shown you the RHS Linux Print System Manager and some Linux printing commands for simple formatting of text files. Hopefully, you'll also try some of the other printer programs and filters. Use this chapter's information as a starting point to explore the printing features of Red Hat Linux, and push your printer to the max!

CHAPTER 13

TCP/IP Network Management

by Steve Shah

IN THIS CHAPTER

Although a standalone system can be quite interesting and very useful, you cannot harness the true power of a UNIX system until you attach it to a network. This chapter covers the various means and tools you will need to do so.

An Introduction to Networking

TCP/IP (Transmission Control Protocol/Internet Protocol) was the first widely used networking protocol under UNIX and has been an integral part of Linux since its creation. The success of TCP/IP was the result of a combination of many things. The three that had the most to do with this success were the United States Department of Defense's involvement in creating the protocol and establishing a wide area network with it (the predecessor to what has become the Internet), the fact that the protocol specifications are freely available to anyone in the world, and finally, the nature of TCP/IP itself: robust and untied to any particular physical medium.

What Is an IP Number?

An IP number is what uniquely identifies a network interface. If your network is private, you only need to worry about address uniqueness within your own network. If, however, your network is attached to the Internet, you do need to worry about having a unique address across the entire Internet.

An IP address consists of four numbers, ranging from 0 to 255, separated by dots. A valid address looks something like `192.168.3.12`. This is sometimes called the *dotted* address; however, it is most frequently referred to as the *IP address*. Although coming up with an address might appear simple, you need to be aware of some restrictions.

TIP

You might have noticed that I've specified that IP addresses need to be unique to a network interface, not a host. This is because it is possible for a single host to have multiple network interfaces. You should keep this distinction in mind. In most cases, the two terms mean the same thing and therefore are used interchangeably. In all the examples in this chapter, each host has only one network interface; hence, I use the term *host* more often.

A TCP/IP Primer

The range of addresses available has been broken up into three segments: class A, B, and C. Each class is determined by the first number in the IP address. (More accurately, it is determined by the first few bits of the address, but as you can imagine, picking out the ranges in decimal is much easier for us humans.) The classes are shown in Table 13.1.

Table 13.1. IP ranges.

Class	*Range*	*Comment*
A	1 to 126	Each class A network is capable of holding 16 million addresses.
B	128 to 191	Each class B network is capable of holding 65 thousand addresses.
C	192 to 223	Each class C network is capable of holding 254 addresses.
Reserved	224 to 255	

Within these class ranges there are several special addresses. The one you will see most frequently is `127.0.0.1`, the *loopback address*. The loopback address, also known as *localhost*, is a network address that points back to the machine it originated from. This is useful for establishing and testing network services on a machine without having to really connect to a network.

Depending on the class, a network can hold a varying number of hosts within it. For class A networks, the first number in dotted notation shows which network. The subsequent three numbers identify the hosts. In class B networks, the first two dotted numbers identify the network, leaving the last two dotted numbers to identify the hosts. Finally, class C networks use the first three numbers to identify the network and the last number to identify the hosts.

If the host part of the network address is all zeros, that address refers to the entire network, not just one host. Hence, a host's IP address should not have a zero in it.

Within each address class, special addresses are designated for internal networks, networks which are not directly connected to the Internet. Machines that are behind firewalls, for example, can use these addresses for communicating with one another. The ranges for these addresses are

Class A:	`10.0.0.0`
Class B:	`172.16.0.0` to `172.31.0.0`
Class C:	`192.168.0.0` to `192.168.255.0`

For all the examples in this chapter, I use the class C network `192.168.42.0`.

Determining which IP address to use is highly site-dependent. If you are attaching your machine to an established network, you will need to contact your network administrator to establish which IP address you should use. This includes connecting to an Internet Service Provider (ISP) that will be assigning you an address.

If, on the other hand, you are establishing a local area network at home or behind a firewall, you should use one of the established private ranges. These are chunks of IP addresses that have been put aside by the InterNIC so that no publicly accessible network can use them.

NOTE

So far, I've used only IP addresses to identify machines on a network. How is it, then, that you can use names to find machines across the Internet? Simple. Most sites set up a special mapping between hostnames and their IP numbers. Many programs are designed to automatically use names instead of IP addresses because they are much easier for humans to digest. Imagine trying to remember `192.168.42.7` instead of `www.domain.com`!

The Domain Name Service (DNS), which makes this possible, is covered later in this chapter in the section "The Domain Name Service."

TIP

Details into the theory of TCP/IP are beyond the scope of this chapter. For additional information regarding TCP/IP theory, check out the Sams book *TCP/IP Blueprints* (ISBN: 0-672-31055-4) by Robin Burk, Martin Bligh, Thomas Lee, et al.

Subnetworking

Imagine trying to network a site with hundreds, if not thousands, of machines. Now try to imagine the resulting mess of network addresses, cables, and traffic. Attempting to manage such a beast will only leave you with a migraine and a fist full of hair.

Realizing this would eventually happen, the creators of TCP/IP designed in the ability to break a network down into subnetworks for easier management. Each subnetwork, or subnet for short, has its own *broadcast address* and *network mask*. The broadcast address is used to send messages to all of the machines within a particular subnet. The network mask, or netmask for short, tells you how many machines are in a subnet and their corresponding network addresses.

If you are joining an existing network, you should be given this information. If, on the other hand, you are setting up your own network, you will need to determine these numbers on your own.

Computing Netmasks

An IP address is composed of a total of 32 bits. Every 8 bits makes up one number in the dotted address. While many sites set up their netmasks across an 8-bit boundary, smaller sites are finding it necessary to allocate fewer than 254 addresses to a site. This means less intuitive netmasks.

As I mentioned earlier, IP addresses are broken up into two parts, the network address and the host address. Depending on the class of the address, there can be anywhere from 254 to 16 million addresses in a particular network. In order to subnet these address ranges, a certain part of the host address must be allocated to the subnetwork address. By counting the number of bits it takes to compose the network and subnet address, you can figure out how many bits are in the netmask.

For example, if you are in the network `192.168.42.0` (equal to `11000000.10101000.00101010.00000000`) and you don't need to subnet at all, you would see that it takes 24 bits to make the netmask. Hence, the netmask for this network is `255.255.255.0` (equal to `11111111.11111111.11111111.00000000` in binary).

Let's say that you do want to subnet the network, and want to break this down into 8 subnets, each with 32 addresses. Remember that for each subnet, you need one network address and one broadcast address. Hence, each subnet would really only be able to contain 30 addresses. Table 13.2 shows how to determine the netmask based on how many subnets you have.

Table 13.2. Subnet netmasks.

Subnets	*Hosts on the Subnet*	*Netmask*
2	126	`255.255.255.128 (11111111.11111111.11111111.10000000)`
4	62	`255.255.255.192 (11111111.11111111.11111111.11000000)`
8	30	`255.255.255.224 (11111111.11111111.11111111.11100000)`
16	14	`255.255.255.240 (11111111.11111111.11111111.11110000)`
32	6	`255.255.255.248 (11111111.11111111.11111111.11111000)`
64	2	`255.255.255.252 (11111111.11111111.11111111.11111100)`

Although it is entirely possible to encode your netmask such that the subnet part of the address does not consume the bits in the suggested order, figuring out each host's address becomes very tricky and cumbersome. It is not a recommended practice.

Determining the Broadcast Address

After you have the network mask determined, it is very easy to determine the broadcast address.

Begin by taking the network address along with the subnetwork component. In your sample network, this would be `192.168.42.0`. Because you need 24 bits (the first three dotted numbers) to identify the network, hold those bits constant and make the remainder bits all 1. This turns the sample address into `192.168.42.255`.

The Next Generation of IP, IPv6

If you're quick with figures, you might have realized that IP numbers have 32 bits, thereby providing us with 4+ billion possible IP addresses. Quite a few addresses, isn't it? In fact, we should be set for a long time!

Not quite. Because of the way addresses are segmented between classes A, B, C, and reserved and because of the problem with liberal policies on IP address assignment early in the Internet's life, we're quickly running out of available IP addresses. Between every new movie having a new IP address for its domain name and network connectivity becoming cheap enough for small businesses, it is predicted that we will run out of IP addresses not too long after the year 2000.

Luckily, a solution has been developed to cope with this. IPv6 is the successor to the current IPv4 standard. (IPv5 was an experimental real-time stream protocol.) IPv6 addresses many of the problems of IPv4, such as inadequate address space, no security, an overly complex structure, no support for a large number of options, and no special tags indicating the type of service in use.

IPv6 solves the address space problem by expanding the address field to 128 bits. The idea behind this was that the address space should allow for an inefficient scheme of address assignment (similar to the idea behind class A, B, and C addresses in IPv4) but still allow for billions of possible hosts on each subnetwork.

A resolution for the security issue was something else that was designed into IPv6. With commerce on the Internet growing at phenomenal rates, the need for security mechanisms needed to be integrated into the network protocol itself instead of letting it remain above the protocol. Authentication and privacy were serious considerations in IPv6's design.

Multimedia has also been taking the Internet by storm. Entertainment services are looking to broadcast their services in real-time audio and video. By tagging the packets of data with a datatype field, the routers across the Internet know to give priority to those packets needing real-time transmission. (If this subject interests you, look into the RSVP protocol at `http://www.ietf.org`.)

The last major revision with IPv6 was to simply include the information needed in each packet of data. This allows routers to be able to process more packets per second without needing to use faster (and more costly) hardware.

As of this writing, Red Hat Linux doesn't support IPv6 because most people are sticking with IPv4 for their connectivity needs. There is an IPv6 package available for Linux if you are interested in experimenting with it or possibly joining the 6Bone, a small network of IPv6 systems on the Internet. (Check out the site at `http://www-6bone.lbl.gov/6bone`.)

Getting a New IP Address

If you're planning to join the Internet with your new Linux box for the first time, you will need to have two things:

- An Internet Service Provider (ISP) who is providing a connection to the Internet
- An unused IP range and domain name

Often, your ISP will assist you with all of the steps involved in getting your machine connected, but it is always a good idea to know the steps involved.

The easiest way to join the Internet is to have an existing account on someone else's network. A good start would be the ISP you're planning to join. This will give you an opportunity to evaluate its services and determine if its connection to the Internet is fast enough for your needs. (See information on the `traceroute` command later in this chapter in the section "The Software of DNS" to help you determine the quality of your connection.)

When you've decided to go with a particular ISP, the ISP will need to set up its machines to respond to connection requests for your desired domain name. (Note that your ISP doesn't need to provide content, just the name service.) With your ISP ready to handle the domain, you begin your registration with the InterNIC.

The InterNIC is an organization that keeps track of all the domain names allocated and their corresponding IP address ranges. Whenever a new site wants to have its own domain name, it must be allocated from the InterNIC. If the new site also needs an IP range allocated to it, the InterNIC will take care of that as well. (Typically, the InterNIC will allocate IP ranges to ISPs, and the ISPs will pass them on to you.)

Not too long ago, you could simply ask the InterNIC to allocate a domain name, and it would do it. However, with the recent boom of commercialization, the rules have changed so that you must have an ISP responding to your desired domain name before InterNIC will allocate the domain. (In other words, you cannot request `my-new-domain.com` without having a server ready to respond to requests made on that domain.) Along with each new domain is an annual fee of $100.

To request a new domain name, visit the InterNIC's Web site at `http://www.internic.net`. You will have to work with your ISP when doing this. It can take up to one week for the InterNIC to process your request and allocate the domain name.

When your new domain name is allocated and the InterNIC has announced it to all of the nameservers across the Internet, your site will be ready to accept connections.

The Network Card Solution

If you are using a network card to join a network, configuring it is a straightforward task. This section shows how to use the `netcfg`, `ifconfig`, and `route` commands to do this.

NOTE

All the commands used in this section must be run as the root user because they change kernel parameters. Some of these programs can be run as a normal user for gaining status information; I point out these programs.

Stock Network Configuration

Red Hat Linux comes with networking enabled. The easiest way to get started with networking is to configure it as part of your installation. If you are not familiar with the information requested, you can skip it and reconfigure it later with the `netcfg` program.

Begin by starting up the X Window environment and running `netcfg` from an `xterm` window. The opening window should look something like Figure 13.1.

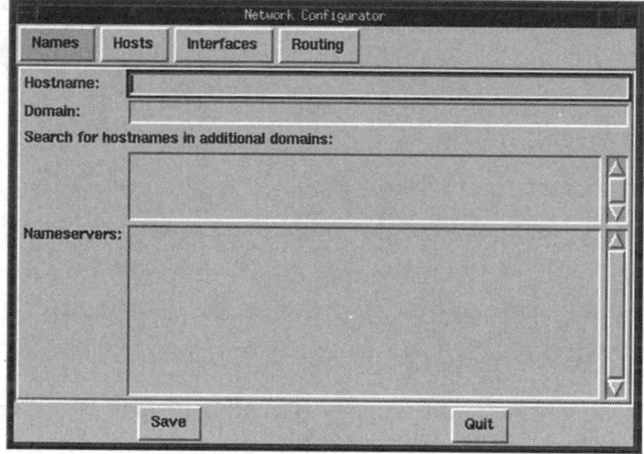

FIGURE 13.1.
The Network Configurator Names menu.

If your Hostname: and Domain: entries already have entries in them, don't worry. That just means you've already set those values during the installation. If not, enter the appropriate information for your hostname and domain name. If you are unsure of these, contact your local network administrator to find out.

The Search for hostnames in additional domains: box should be left blank unless you want to be able to specify hostnames from multiple domains without having to use their fully qualified domain names. This is usually a bad idea.

The Nameservers: box is important. This will tell your network where to resolve hostnames that are not local to your network. Each line should contain the IP address of every DNS server you want to query (with a maximum of three). If you do not know this information, again, contact your network administrator and ask. If you are the network administrator, read the section on setting up a DNS server, "The Domain Name Service."

When you are done entering this information, click the Hosts button at the top of the window. The window will change to look like Figure 13.2.

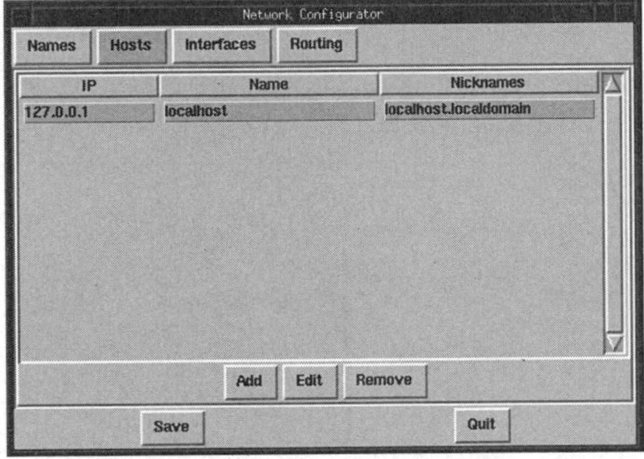

FIGURE 13.2.
The Network Configurator Hosts menu.

This is what will become the `/etc/hosts` file. (See the section "The Domain Name Service," later in this chapter, for detailed information.) This file essentially provides a mapping from hostnames to IP numbers. At the very least, you should provide mappings for any machines on your network necessary as part of your boot procedure (such as servers). For example, if you wanted to add an entry for the host `vestax` whose IP address is `192.168.42.7`, you would do the following:

1. Click the Add button, which is toward the bottom of the window. This brings up the Edit `/etc/hosts` window; it has three entries.
2. In the first box for the IP number, enter `vestax`'s IP address.
3. In the Name box, enter the name `vestax`.
4. If `vestax` has any aliases, you can enter them in the Nicknames box. If there are no aliases, leave that box blank.
5. Click Done to finish adding this entry. The Edit `/etc/hosts` window will close and the main window will show your addition in the table.

After you have entered all the hosts your system needs to know at boot time, click the button labeled Interfaces at the top of the window. The window will change to look like Figure 13.3.

You can configure an Ethernet device from this window. To configure your Ethernet card, do the following:

1. Click the Add button at the bottom of the screen to bring up the Choose Interface window.
2. In the Choose Interface window, click the button to select Ethernet and then click OK. The Choose Interface window will disappear and a new window titled Edit Ethernet/Bus Interface will appear.

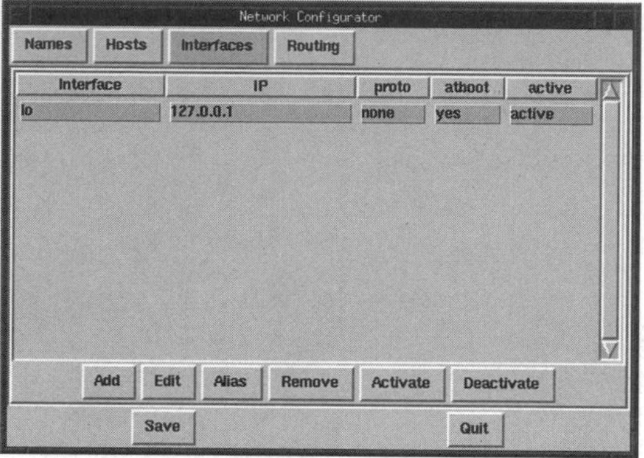

FIGURE 13.3.
The Network Configurator Interfaces menu.

3. In the Edit Ethernet/Bus Interface window, click the IP box and enter the IP address of your machine. The Netmask: box will automatically fill in, based on the address you provide in the IP box. If this is not correct, click the Netmask: box and make the necessary corrections.
4. If you want this interface to automatically start at boot time, click the Activate interface at boot time button. Leave the Allow any user to (de)activate interface box unselected. It is a very bad practice to allow nonroot users to configure network settings.
5. The Interface Configuration Protocol enables you to select alternative methods (BOOTP or DHCP) to configure your network interface. Unless you have been instructed by a network manager to use these protocols, leave this box blank. Click Done to bring up a new window asking whether you want to save the current configuration. Click Save to keep your addition. Both windows will close, leaving you back with the original Network Configurator window, this time showing your new network interface.

With your interface defined, you can now set routes and gateways for your machine. Click the button labeled Routing at the top of the window. This will change the Network Configurator window to look like Figure 13.4.

To set up your routing information, follow these steps:

1. Click in the Gateway box and enter the IP address of your gateway to rest of the network. If you do not have a gateway machine (for example, you're configuring a local area network without an Internet connection), you can leave this blank.
2, If you do have a gateway, enter the device name from which the gateway will be accessed. Most likely, this will be the device name that was configured in the Interfaces part of the Network Configurator window. If you are using a Ethernet card, this will most likely be `eth0`.

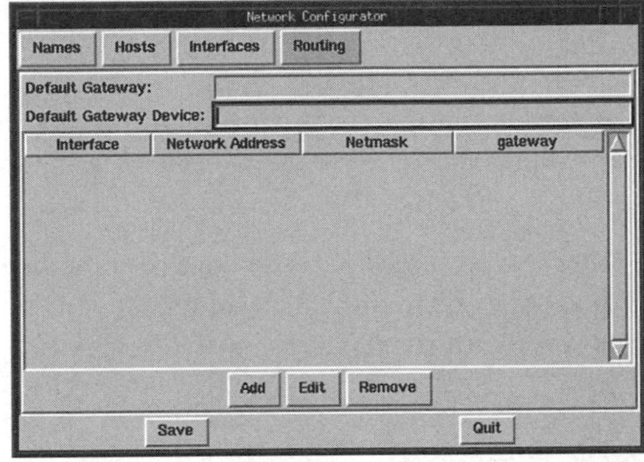

FIGURE 13.4.
The Network Configurator Routing menu.

3. Click Save at the bottom of the window and then click Quit, which is also at the bottom. This will exit the `netcfg` program.

Your system now has the necessary scripts configured to establish your network connection. Before you can claim victory, you need to test the connection. Enter the following command to start the network connection:

```
/etc/rc.d/init.d/network stop;/etc/rc.d/init.d/network start
```

This will restart your network connection. Try pinging a machine in your immediate network using the `ping` command, like this:

```
ping IP_Address
```

where *`IP_Address`* is the IP address of the machine you are trying to ping. If you placed the IP address to hostname mapping in the Hosts section in `netcfg`, then you can use the hostname instead. This should return output similar to this:

```
PING 192.168.42.1 (192.168.42.1): 56 data bytes
64 bytes from 192.168.42.1: icmp_seq=0 ttl=255 time=1.0 ms
64 bytes from 192.168.42.1: icmp_seq=1 ttl=255 time=3.5 ms
-- 192.168.42.1 ping statistics --
2 packets transmitted, 2 packets received, 0% packet loss
round-trip min/avg/max = 1.0/24.4/47.8 ms
```

Note that in order to get `ping` to stop, you need to press Ctrl+C.

If you have an Internet connection, try pinging a machine outside of your network. This should result in output similar to the preceding, with the notable exception that the time measurements will be longer. If the ping fails at this point, try another host; it could be the other machine that has failed and not yours.

If the pings fail, restart `netcfg` and verify the information you provided it.

Using ifconfig

`ifconfig` is the tool used to set up and configure your network card. If you used the Red Hat installation package, you might already have this configured for you. You should, however, understand this command in the event you need to configure the network by hand after a system crash.

The purpose of `ifconfig` is to set up and configure the network interfaces. Typically, this is done early in the boot sequence so that any other network services that need to be started know how to communicate with the rest of the world.

The format of the `ifconfig` command is as follows:

```
ifconfig interface IP_address options
```

> **NOTE**
>
> The `ifconfig` command takes parameters in a slightly different way than most commands. Each parameter should not be prefixed by a minus sign (`-`) unless you are turning that function off. If you are setting a parameter, such as the netmask, simply use `netmask` followed by the netmask you want to set—for example, `netmask 255.255.255.0`.

`interface` is the network device that you want to set up. If you are using Ethernet, this will be `eth` followed by a number designating which Ethernet card you are using. The numbering starts from zero (the first Ethernet card in your system will be `eth0`). *`IP_address`* is the address that you want to assign to your machine. Use dotted notation and remember not to assign it the network address or broadcast address.

These are the only required options for configuring a network device. `ifconfig` will use the default netmask and broadcast address based on the class of your *`IP_address`* setting. The default netmask and broadcast addresses, however, will only be correct if you are subnetting along an 8-bit boundary.

To set the netmask and broadcast address, use the parameters `netmask` and `broadcast`, respectively, followed by the address you want to set for them.

Here is a sample `ifconfig`:

```
ifconfig eth0 192.168.42.2 netmask 255.255.255.0 broadcast 192.168.42.255
```

As with most other UNIX commands, there is no output if it is successful. To see what the currently configured cards are, simply run `ifconfig` without any parameters:

```
[root@vestax /root]# ifconfig
```

```
lo        Link encap:Local Loopback
          inet addr:127.0.0.1  Bcast:127.255.255.255  Mask:255.0.0.0
          UP BROADCAST LOOPBACK RUNNING  MTU:3584  Metric:1
          RX packets:10984 errors:0 dropped:0 overruns:0
          TX packets:10984 errors:0 dropped:0 overruns:0

eth0      Link encap:10Mbps Ethernet  HWaddr 00:60:97:C3:D0:C9
          inet addr:192.168.42.2 Bcast:192.168.42.255 Mask:255.255.255.0
          UP BROADCAST RUNNING MULTICAST  MTU:1500  Metric:1
          RX packets:1995581 errors:1 dropped:1 overruns:0
          TX packets:1361726 errors:0 dropped:0 overruns:0
          Interrupt:11 Base address:0x6100
```

The first network card listed here is the `lo` device, which is the loopback device. I'm not terribly interested in that entry, although it should be there. The second entry shows how the `eth0` network card is currently configured. The `Link encap` tells you that it is configured as a 10Mbps Ethernet card. The `HWaddr` tells you the hardware address of that particular Ethernet card (also known as the MAC address). On the second line of the output is the `inet addr`. This is the address you have configured the card to answer to. On the same line are the respective broadcast and netmask addresses. The third line of the output shows which options have been enabled on the card from the `ifconfig` command. You should recognize the `BROADCAST` option because you explicitly set it. The others are default options that are covered shortly. The fourth line contains information regarding the number of packets that have been received. In this example, about 1.9 million packets have been received, 1 packet had an error, 1 packet was dropped, and no packets were overruns. (Overruns are packets that are too long.) In the line below it is the same information for packets transmitted. The last line provides the configuration information for the hardware.

Optional Parameters to `ifconfig`

The following parameters are optional on the `ifconfig` command line:

`up` — This tells `ifconfig` to activate the network interface and begin sending and receiving packets.

`down` — This option enables you to shut the interface down after it has been activated. This is useful for shutting down an active card when troubleshooting network-related problems.

`arp` — ARP (Address Resolution Protocol) enables you to map a network card's hardware address to its IP address. Protocols such as DHCP use this to find machines on a subnet without having to know an IP address first. Note that the ARP will work only within your immediate subnet and will not transfer through routers. By default, this option is turned on. To turn it off, place a minus sign in front of it (`-arp`).

`mtu N` — The MTU (Maximum Transfer Unit) sets the size of each Ethernet packet to *N*, where *N* is the number of bytes in each packet. For Ethernet, this defaults to `1500`, and you shouldn't change it unless you are sure about what you are doing.

Using route

In order to communicate with machines outside your local area network, you need to use a router. This device is the link between your network and the rest of the world. When you need to communicate to a machine outside of your LAN, your host will send the message to the router, which will forward it on through the outside network. The same is true for packets coming in from the outside network. The router will receive the packet and forward it to your host.

If you used the Red Hat installation procedure for configuring your network, this has already been configured for you. For a host connected to the Internet, you should have at the very least three possible routes: a loopback, a route to your LAN, and a default route to your router. By running `route` without any parameters, you can see your current routing table. The format of the `route` command is

```
route cmd type target_ip netmask gateway options
```

where *cmd* is either `add` or `del` depending on whether you want to add or delete a route, respectively. If you use `del`, you then only need the *target_ip* parameter, which specifies the IP address for which you are routing.

If, on the other hand, you used the `add` command, you need to specify *type* to be either `-net` or `-host`, where `-net` is a network that you are routing to and `-host` is a specific host you are routing to.

The *target_ip* address specifies either the network or host IP address to which you are routing. There is a special keyword for this option: `default`. If you specify `default` instead of an actual IP address, all packets that do not have a specific route listed in the route table will be sent to this route.

`netmask` allows you to specify the netmask to the network you are routing to. Note that this applies only when using the `-net` option. The `netmask` option is used like this: `netmask` *mask_number* where *mask_number* is the actual netmask in dotted notation.

gateway specifies which gateway to use for sending packets to *target_ip*. For example, if your default route points to the Internet (a likely situation), then your gateway setting should point to your router connecting to the Internet. For example, if the router were `192.168.42.1`, this option would be specified as `gw 192.168.42.1`. You can use hostnames if you want to, so long as they appear in the `/etc/hosts` file. (See the section "The Domain Name Service," later in this chapter, for details.)

The options available in addition to the ones already stated are as follows:

`-n`	Uses numerical addresses instead of trying to resolve IP addresses to hostnames. This is used when invoking `route` without either the `add` or `del` parameter so you can see which routes are currently set.

`dev ethn` Specifies the device onto which a routed packet should go. This is useful only if you have a multihomed system (a machine with multiple network cards). The `ethn` parameter specifies the interface's name. This option should always be at the end of the command line.

Examples of Using `route`

In this example, the default route is set up to go to `192.168.42.1`, your router:

```
route add -net default gw 192.168.42.1
```

(You'll find that many routers are set up such that their IP addresses end in `.1`. This isn't a rule, but a common practice.) Because this is a `-net`, the netmask is automatically computed.

Assuming your machine is set up as `192.168.42.12` with a netmask of `255.255.255.0`, this route points to your own local area network:

```
route add -net 192.168.42.0 dev eth0
```

This keeps the router from having to send packets back to your network after they've sent to it as the default route. The last parameter, `dev eth0`, specifies that the `192.168.42.0` network is connected to the first Ethernet device in the system.

Understanding the `route` Table

When `route` is invoked without a parameter, it displays your current routing table. The output should look something like this:

```
[root@denon /root]# route
Kernel IP routing table
Destination     Gateway         Genmask         Flags   Metric   Ref   Use   Iface
192.168.42.0    *               255.255.255.0   U       0        0     2     eth0
loopback        *               255.0.0.0       U       0        0     3     lo
default         192.168.42.1    0.0.0.0         UG      0        0     0     eth0
```

`Destination` is the destination network or host address for packets, and `Gateway` is the gateway host (typically a router) used to get to the destination. An `*` character is displayed if no gateway is set. Flags describe the characteristic of the route. It is possible to have more than one characteristic, as in the default route. The possible flags are

`U` The route is up.

`H` The route is a host.

`G` The route is through a gateway.

`Metric` gives the route a weight, a lower weight being a faster route. This is useful only for dynamic routing, so you will almost always see this as `0`. The `Ref` column states the number of references to the route. Because this information is not used in the Linux kernel, it is always `0`. `Use` tells you how many times this route has been looked up by your system. `Iface` is the network interface the route uses.

The Domain Name Service

Up until now, I've been referring to hosts by their IP addresses. Although this might be terribly convenient for the computers to use, we humans work much better with names. Obviously, some sort of translation table is needed to convert IP addresses to hostnames. But with millions of machines on the Internet and new ones popping up every day, it would be impossible for everyone to keep this sort of table up-to-date. This is where DNS comes in.

The Domain Name Service (DNS) is the protocol by which each site maintains only its own mapping of IP addresses to machine names. Each site makes this mapping a publicly queriable database so that when people from around the world want to find the corresponding IP address, they simply query the correct database and get their answer.

In order to access this database, you need to run a DNS server for your site. (A DNS server is also known as a nameserver or NS for short.) These servers come in three varieties: primary, secondary, and caching. If you are connecting to an existing network (through your campus network, for example), you will need to run only a caching server. If, on the other hand, you are setting up a new site to be accessed through the Internet, you will need to set up a primary server. Secondary servers become important as your site grows to the point that the primary server can no longer handle the load and queries to it need to be broken up across different machines.

Before DNS—The `/etc/hosts` File

As your machine gets started, it will need to know the mapping of some hostnames to IP addresses (for example, your NIS servers) before DNS can be referenced. This mapping is kept in the `/etc/hosts` file.

Following is a sample `/etc/hosts` file:

IP Address	*Hostname*	*Alias*
127.0.0.1	localhost	
192.168.42.7	vestax	www
192.168.42.8	mailhub	mailhub.domain.com
192.168.42.6	technics	

The leftmost column is the IP address to be resolved. The next column is that host's name. Any subsequent columns are aliases for that host. In the second line, for example, the address `192.168.42.7` is for the host `vestax`. Another name for `vestax` is www. The domain name is automatically appended to the hostname by the system; however, many people append it themselves for clarity (for example, `www.domain.com`).

At the very least, you need to have the entries for

- Localhost
- Your NIS server
- Any systems from which you NFS mount disks
- The host itself

In this example, `localhost` is the first line, followed by `vestax`, your WWW server. `mailhub` is the machine with which `sendmail` communicates for mail, and finally there is `technics`, the name of the machine from which the `/etc/hosts` file came.

Configuring the DNS Client: `/etc/resolv.conf`

Every machine in your network is a DNS client. In order to know which DNS server to use, you need to configure the `/etc/resolv.conf` file. This file should look something like

```
search domain.com
nameserver 192.168.42.1
```

where `domain.com` is the domain name of your site and the IP address listed after `nameserver` is the address of the DNS server with which you will be communicating. You can have up to three `nameserver` entries, each of which will be tried sequentially until one of them returns an answer.

> **NOTE**
>
> You must supply the nameserver's IP address, not its hostname. After all, how is the resolver going to know what the nameserver's IP address is until it finds the nameserver?

The Software of DNS

While configuring DNS for your site, you will need to be familiar with the following tools:

- `named`
- The resolver library
- `nslookup`
- `traceroute`

`named` is the daemon that needs to run on DNS servers to handle queries. If it cannot answer a query, it is its responsibility to forward the request on to a server that can. Along with queries, `named` is responsible for performing zone transfers. Zone transferring is the method by which changed DNS information is propagated across the Internet. You will need to install the `named` daemon from the `BIND` distribution, available from `http://www.redhat.com` or on the CD-ROM that comes with this book (filename `bind-4.9.5p1-2.i386.rpm`).

The resolver library enables client programs to perform DNS queries. This library is built into the standard library under Linux.

`nslookup` is a utility invoked from the command line to ensure both the resolver and the DNS server being queried are configured correctly. `nslookup` does this by resolving either a hostname into an IP address or an IP address into a domain name. To use `nslookup`, simply provide the address you want to resolve as the parameter to `nslookup`—for example,

```
nslookup rane.domain.com
```

The result should look something like this:

```
[root@vestax /root]# nslookup rane.domain.com
Server: numark.domain.com
Address: 192.168.42.1

Non-authoritative answer:
Name: rane.domain.com
Address: 192.168.42.8
```

The `traceroute` utility allows you to determine the path a packet is taking across your network and into other networks. This is very useful for debugging network connection problems, especially when you suspect the trouble is located in someone else's network.

Using the ICMP protocol (same as `ping`), `traceroute` looks up each machine along the path to a destination host and displays the corresponding name and IP address for that site. With each name is the number of milliseconds each of the three tiers took to get to the destination.

To use `traceroute`, use the destination hostname or IP address as the parameter—for example,

```
traceroute www.hyperreal.org
```

would return something similar to the following:

```
traceroute to hyperreal.org (204.62.130.147), 30 hops max, 40 byte packets
 1  fe0-0.cr1.NUQ.globalcenter.net (205.216.146.77)  0.829 ms  0.764 ms  0.519 ms
 2  pos6-0.cr2.SNV.globalcenter.net (206.251.0.30)  1.930 ms  1.839 ms  1.887 ms
 3  fe1-0.br2.SNV.globalcenter.net (206.251.5.2)  2.760 ms  2.779 ms  2.517 ms
 4  sl-stk-17-H10/0-T3.sprintlink.net (144.228.147.9)  5.117 ms  6.160 ms  6.109 ms
 5  sl-stk-14-F0/0.sprintlink.net (144.228.40.14)  5.453 ms  5.985 ms  6.157 ms
 6  sl-wired-2-S0-T1.sprintlink.net (144.228.144.138)  10.987 ms  25.130 ms  11.831
   ➥ms
 7  sf2-s0.wired.net (205.227.206.22)  30.453 ms  15.800 ms  21.220 ms
 8  taz.hyperreal.org (204.62.130.147)  16.745 ms  14.914 ms  13.018 ms
```

If you see any start characters (such as `*`) instead of a hostname, that machine may likely be unavailable for a variety of reasons (network failure and firewall protection being the most common). Also be sure to note the time it takes to get from one site to another. If you feel your connection is going excessively slow, it might just be one connection in the middle that is slowing you down and not the site itself.

`traceroute` is also a good way to measure the connectivity of a site. If you are in the process of evaluating an ISP, try doing a `traceroute` from its site to a number of other sites, especially to large communications companies such as Sprint (`www.sprint.net`) and MCI. Count how many hops as well as how much time per hop it takes to reach its network. This is often reasonable grounds for comparing one ISP to another.

Configuring DNS Servers

As mentioned earlier, DNS comes in three flavors: primary, secondary, and caching.

Primary DNS is the most authoritative of the three. When a DNS server is primary for a domain, it is considered to have the most up-to-date records for all the hosts in that site.

Secondary DNS is not quite as authoritative as primary, but it is considered authoritative. Typically, backup or offsite DNS servers for a domain are configured as secondary; hence, they don't receive the updates as quickly as the primary servers do. For all practical purposes though, they are considered authoritative.

Caching DNS servers are not authoritative at all. When a query is made to a caching server for the first time, the query is forwarded to an authoritative server. If that server is not authoritative over the domain being queried, the request is forwarded until the authoritative server answers the query and returns it back to the caching server. The caching server keeps the entry in its local cache and continues to return that answer until the entry expires.

All DNS servers should be configured to perform caching functions.

Depending on your site's configuration, you might not even need a nameserver of your own. For instance, if you are connecting to an already existing network, there might already be a nameserver for you to use. On the other hand, if you are setting up a new department, you might want to set up a caching server for your local machines to reduce load on your site's primary server.

> **TIP**
>
> If you plan on setting up and using a PPP connection, you should definitely set up your own caching DNS server. This will reduce the load on your PPP connection.

The `/etc/named.boot` File

This is the file that is read in when `named` is started. Each line in the `named.boot` file begins with a keyword or a semicolon indicating that line to be a comment. The format of the file is

```
; Comments begin with the semicolon
directory   directory_name
cache       .              filename
primary     domain         filename
secondary   domain         ip_addr filename
forwarders  ip_addr        [...]
```

The `directory` keyword tells `named` where any filenames mentioned in the configuration are located in the system.

The `cache` keyword makes `named` perform caching functions. The file listed at the end of the cache line contains a list of all the root DNS servers on the Internet. These root servers are needed to prime `named`'s cache. You can get the latest list of root servers from the InterNIC at `ftp://rs.internic.net/domain/named.cache`.

Lines beginning with `primary` indicate that the server is a primary DNS server for the listed *`domain`*. The entries for that server are listed in the file noted at the end of the line.

As you can predict, lines beginning with `secondary` make `named` behave as a secondary DNS server for the specified *`domain`*. This entry requires two parameters for a given domain: the IP address of the primary server and the file into which it should cache the entries pulled from the primary server. Depending on how the primary server is configured, the cached data is updated periodically via a zone transfer.

The `forwarders` line tells `named` to whom DNS queries should be forwarded if it cannot resolve queries on its own. If you are running a caching-only server, this should be your secondary or primary server for your site. If you are primary for your site, this should forward to your ISP's DNS server.

Primary Nameserver Configuration Files

As shown in the preceding section, the primary line in the `/etc/named.boot` file points to a file that contains the information needed by `named` in order to be primary for the specified domain. The file format for these configuration files are unfortunately a bit tricky and require care when setting up. Be especially careful with periods. A misplaced period can quickly become difficult to track down.

The format of each line in the configuration file is as follows:

```
name    IN    record_type    data
```

`name` is the hostname you are dealing with. Any hostnames that do not end in a period automatically get the domain name appended to them. The second column, `IN`, is actually a parameter telling `named` to use the Internet class of records. Two other classes exist: `CH` for ChaosNet and `HS` for Hesiod. ChaosNet has been long obsolete and HS was meant to be a replacement for NIS but has been overshadowed by NIS+.

The third and fourth columns, *`record_type`* and *`data`*, respectively, indicate what kind of record you are dealing with and the parameters associated with it. There are eight possible records:

- `SOA`—Start of authority
- `NS`—Nameserver
- `A`—Address record
- `PTR`—Pointer record

- MX—Mail exchanger
- CNAME—Canonical name
- RP and TXT—The documentation entries

SOA—Start of Authority

The SOA record starts the description of a site's DNS entries. The format of this entry is as follows:

```
domain.com. IN ns1.domain.com. hostmaster.domain.com. (
    1997082401        ; serial number
    10800             ; refresh rate in seconds (3 hours)
    1800              ; retry in seconds (30 minutes)
    1209600           ; expire in seconds (2 weeks)
    604800 )          ; minimum in seconds (1 week)
```

The first line begins with the domain for which this SOA record is authoritative. This entry is followed by IN to indicate that the Internet standard is being used. The column after the IN is the primary nameserver for this domain. Finally, the last column specifies the e-mail address for the person in charge. Note that the e-mail address is not in the standard *user@domain.com* form, but instead has the @ symbol replaced by a period. It is good practice to create the mail alias hostmaster at your site and have all mail sent to it forwarded to the appropriate people.

TIP

Remember how I said that periods were important in DNS records? You should have then noticed that all of the fully qualified hostnames were suffixed with a period. Incorrectly placed periods anywhere in DNS-related files will cause grief and be difficult to track down later.

At the end of the first line is an open parenthesis. This tells named that the line continues onto the next line, thereby making the file easier to read.

The five values presented in subsequent lines detail the characteristics of this record. The first line is the record's serial number. Whenever you make a change to any entry in this file, you need to increment this value so that secondary servers know to perform zone transfers. Typically, the current date in the form YYYYMMDDxx is used, where YYYY is the year, MM is the month, DD is the day, and xx is the revision done that day. (This allows for multiple revisions in one day.)

The second value is the refresh rate in seconds. This value tells the secondary DNS servers how often they should query the primary server to see if the records have been updated at all.

The third value is the retry rate in seconds. If the secondary server tries to contact the primary DNS server to check for updates but cannot contact it, the secondary server tries again after *retry* seconds.

The fourth value indicates to secondary servers that have cached the entry that if they cannot contact the primary server for an update, they should discard the value after the specified number of seconds. One to two weeks is a good value for this.

The final value, the `minimum` entry, tells caching servers how long they should wait before expiring an entry if they cannot contact the primary DNS server. Five to seven days is a good guideline for this entry.

Don't forget to place a closing parenthesis after the fifth value.

NS—Nameserver

The `NS` record specifies the authoritative nameservers for a given domain. A sample line for this is

```
IN NS     ns1.domain.com.
IN NS     ns2.domain.com.
```

Note that if the domain name for the nameserver applies to the current `SOA` record, you do not need to specify the `name` field in the DNS record.

In this example, there are two nameservers for the domain, `domain.com`: `ns1.domain.com` and `ns2.domain.com`. These are fully qualified hostnames, so they need to have the period to suffix them. Without the period, `named` will evaluate their value to be `ns1.domain.com.domain.com`, which is *not* what you're looking for.

A—Address Record

The address record is used for providing translations from hostnames to IP addresses. There should be an `A` record for all your machines you want to have a known hostname. A sample entry using the `A` record is

```
toybox     IN A         192.168.42.59
```

In this example, the address is specified for the host `toybox`. There is not a period after its name, so `named` will assume its domain from the current SOA record, thereby making it `toybox.domain.com.`

PTR—Pointer Record

The pointer record, also known as reverse resolution record, tells `named` how to turn an IP address into a hostname. `PTR` records are a little odd, however, in that they should not be in the same `SOA` as your `A` records. You will see why when you configure a small primary DNS server later in this section.

A `PTR` record looks like this:

```
59.42.168.192.  IN PTR  toybox.domain.com.
```

Notice that the IP address to be reverse-resolved is in reverse order and is suffixed with a period.

MX—Mail Exchanger

The mail exchanger record enables you to specify which host in your network is in charge of receiving mail from the outside. `sendmail` uses this record to determine the correct machine mail needs to be sent to. The format of an `MX` record looks like this:

```
domain.com.     IN MX 10     mailhub
                IN MX 50     mailhub2
```

The first column indicates the hostname for which mail is received. In this case, it is for `domain.com`. Based on the previous examples, you might have noticed that you have yet to specify a machine that answers to `domain.com.` only, yet the sample `MX` record shows that you can accept mail for it. This is an important feature of DNS: You can specify a hostname for which you accept mail without that hostname having an `A` record.

As expected, the `IN` class is the second column. The third column specifies that this line is an `MX` record. The number after the `MX` indicates a priority level for that entry. Lower numbers mean higher priority. In this example, `sendmail` will try to communicate with `mailhub` first. If it cannot successfully communicate with `mailhub`, it will then try `mailhub2`.

CNAME—Canonical Name

The `CNAME` record makes it possible to alias hostnames via DNS. This is useful for giving common names to servers. For example, we are used to Web servers having the hostname `www`, as in `www.domain.com`. However, you might not want to name the Web server this at all. On many sites, the machines have a theme to the naming of hosts and placing `www` in the middle of that might appear awkward.

To use a `CNAME`, you must have another record such as an `A` or `MX` record for that host that specifies its real name—for example,

```
toybox     IN A         192.168.42.59
www        IN CNAME     toybox
```

In this example, `toybox` is the real name of the server and `www` is its alias.

RP and TXT—The Documentation Entries

It is often useful to provide contact information as part of your database—not just as comments, but as actual records that can be queried by others. This can be accomplished by using the `RP` and `TXT` records.

`TXT` records are a free form text entry that allow you to place whatever information you deem fit. Most often, you will only want to give contact information. Each `TXT` record must be tied to a particular hostname—for example,

```
domain.com.     IN TXT "Contact: Heidi S."
                IN TXT "Systems Administrator/"
                IN TXT "               Ring Master"
                IN TXT "Voice: (800) 555-1212"
```

Because TXT records are free form, they do not force you to place contact information there. As a result, the RP record was created, which explicitly states who is the responsible person for the specified host—for example,

```
domain.com.         IN RP heidis.domain.com. domain.com.
```

The first column states which host the responsible party is set for. The second column, IN, defines this record to use the Internet class. RP designates this to be a responsible party record. In the fourth column is the e-mail address of the person who is actually responsible. Notice that the @ symbol has been replaced by a period in this address, much like in the SOA record. The last column specifies a TXT record that gives additional information. In this example, it points back to the TXT record for domain.com.

Configuring a Caching DNS Server

In order to get a caching nameserver running, you need two files in place. The first is the /etc/named.boot file, which should look like this:

```
directory /etc/dns
cache     .     root-servers
```

This configuration communicates that the data files are kept in the /etc/dns directory and the root-servers file (kept in /etc/dns) contains the IP addresses of the root DNS servers for priming the cache. You can obtain the most recent list of root servers from ftp://rs.internic.net/domain/named.cache.

Note that this configuration does not forward any queries it cannot answer to another server. If you have a primary server at your site, you might want to add a forwarders line to your /etc/named.boot file.

When you have the necessary files in place, all you need to do is restart the nameserver with the following command:

```
/usr/sbin/named.restart
```

Configuring a Primary and Secondary DNS Server

In this example, you will configure a primary DNS server for domain.com. Your sample domain has a handful of hosts in it and does secondary DNS for an ally company. For this configuration, it will need four files in addition to the /etc/named.boot file.

The /etc/named.boot file for this server is

```
directory /etc/dns
cache     .                                        root-servers
primary      domain.com                            domain.hosts
primary      42.168.192.IN-ADDR.ARPA               domain.reverse
primary      0.0.127.IN-ADDR.ARPA                  local.reverse
secondary    ally.com             172.16.1.1       ally.hosts.cache
secondary    16.172.IN-ADDR.ARPA 172.16.1.1        ally.reverse.cache
```

The first two lines are straight from your caching server. This was done so that it would perform the caching functions necessary for better performance. The third line specifies the domain for which you are primary and the file containing the corresponding DNS records.

The fourth line is related to the `PTR` record mentioned earlier. So far, your `/etc/named.boot` file has only specified the DNS records that enable the translation of names into IP addresses. However, it is a good practice to allow for the reverse translation to take place. In fact, some sites on the Internet will not allow you to connect with them unless they can make that reverse resolution.

The second column in the fourth line specifies the network for which you are providing reverse resolution. All reverse mappings exist in the `IN-ADDR.ARPA` domain, thereby eliminating any possible confusion regarding the number's purpose. The network and subnetwork parts of the IP address are placed in reverse order to follow the standard way domain names are written. (Domain names describe the hostname, then the subnetwork, and then the network, whereas IP addresses describe the network, subnetwork, and finally hostname.) By placing the IP address in reverse, it follows the convention established by the actual host and network names.

The last column in the fourth line simply tells you which file contains the reverse mapping information. Because reverse mappings require their own `SOA` record, they need to be kept in a separate file than the forward mappings.

The fifth line of the `/etc/named.boot` file is the reverse mapping information for the localhost.

The sixth and seventh lines specify that your server does secondary DNS for `ally.com`. The third column makes these entries a little different because they specify the primary DNS server for `ally.com`. It is this specified server from which your secondary server will fill its cache. The last column specifies where the cache files for `ally.com` will stay on the system.

TIP

It is common for sites to pick a naming scheme for all their hosts. This tends to make remembering their names easier, especially as the site grows in size. For example, the east wing of the office might use famous music bands to name their machines while the west wing uses names of musical instruments. This makes locating a machine by its name easier.

Listing 13.1 contains the `domain.hosts` file.

Listing 13.1. The `domain.hosts` file.

```
; forward mappings for the domain.com. hosts file
; update history:
;    August 6, 1997 - sshah@domain.com
;        Setup primary DNS for domain.com.
```

continues

Listing 13.1. continued

```
@               IN SOA      domain.com. hostmaster.domain.com. (
                            1997080600    ; serial number
                            10800       ; refresh rate (3 hours)
                            1800           ; retry (30 minutes)
                            1209600       ; expire (2 weeks)
                            604800 )       ; minimum (1 week)
                IN NS       ns1.domain.com
                IN NS       ns2.domain.com
                IN MX 10    mailhub.domain.com
numark          IN A        192.168.42.1
ns1             IN CNAME    numark
domain.com.     IN CNAME    numark
mtx             IN A        192.168.42.2
ns2             IN CNAME    mtx
pioneer         IN A        192.168.42.3
denon           IN A        192.168.42.4
atus            IN A        192.168.42.5
technics        IN A        192.168.42.6
vestax          IN A        192.168.42.7
www             IN CNAME    vestax
rane            IN A        192.168.42.8
mailhub         IN CNAME    rane
```

Notice the use of the `@` symbol instead of the domain name? This is a shortcut you can use because the domain name is specified in the `/etc/named.boot` file.

An additional note regarding names. As mentioned in the preceding tip, using themes in naming machines is helpful from a management perspective. Listing 13.1 uses the names of companies that make professional audio gear. In keeping with this sort of theme, however, you might run into the instance where outsiders expect certain names for your systems such as your Web server. By default, most people expect Web servers to begin with `www`, as in `www.domain.com`. While you can name the machine `www`, two issues arise: First, the naming theme is broken. If your site is large enough, this can become a problem. Second, if you want to start using a new Web server, you have to change all the machines' configurations accordingly. It is much easier to change the `CNAME` entry in your DNS to point to a new Web server instead.

Listing 13.2 contains the `domain.reverse` file.

Listing 13.2. The `domain.reverse` file.

```
; reverse mappings for domain.com
; revision history: sshah@domain.com, Aug. 6, 1997
@                 IN SOA    domain.com. hostmaster.domain.com. (
                            1997080600    ; serial number
                            10800       ; refresh rate (3 hours)
                            1800           ; retry (30 minutes)
                            1209600       ; expire (2 weeks)
                            604800 )       ; minimum (1 week)
                  IN NS     ns1.domain.com
                  IN NS     ns2.domain.com
```

```
192.168.42.1      IN PTR     numark
192.168.42.2      IN PTR     mtx
192.168.42.3      IN PTR     pioneer
192.168.42.4      IN PTR     denon
192.168.42.5      IN PTR     atus
192.168.42.6      IN PTR     technics
192.168.42.7      IN PTR     vestax
192.168.42.8      IN PTR     rane
```

Finally, Listing 13.3 contains the `local.reverse` file.

Listing 13.3. The `local.reverse` file.

```
; local.reverse
@            IN SOA     domain.com. hostmaster.domain.com. (
                        1997080600     ; serial number
                        10800         ; refresh rate (3 hours)
                        1800             ; retry (30 minutes)
                        1209600         ; expire (2 weeks)
                        604800 )         ; minimum (1 week)
             IN NS      ns1.domain.com
             IN NS      ns2.domain.com
1            IN PTR     localhost.domain.com.
```


The Network Information Service

The Network Information Service (NIS) is a simple client/server database system. The protocol itself is generic and can be used for anything. Under Linux, however, the most common uses of it are the sharing of password and group files across the network. This section covers the setup of both master and slave NIS servers as well as the configuration needed to make clients use them.

A Brief History

NIS, developed by Sun Microsystems as part of their SunOS operating system, was originally known as "The Yellow Pages," or YP for short. Unfortunately, the name "Yellow Pages" had already been trademarked and the resulting lawsuit forced the name to be changed to NIS. You will soon see, however, that all of the NIS commands are still prefixed with `yp`.

The NIS protocol was made public and implementations of it quickly spread to other variations of UNIX. Linux has had support for NIS from its onset. Because Linux follows the NIS standard, it can work with other flavors of UNIX as either the NIS server or client.

Recently, NIS has been updated in the form of NIS+. NIS+ addresses many of the concerns with NIS, most notably in the areas of security. As of this writing, however, Linux support for NIS+ through the NIS libraries has been weak. Server support is not ready, and the client software isn't complete. Because it is still developmental, NIS+ is not covered here.

Understanding NIS

As you configure your network, you will find that some of your configuration files are not host specific, but they require frequent updating. `/etc/passwd` and `/etc/group` are two that quickly come to mind. NIS enables you to set up a master server where these files are stored and then configure each machine on your network as clients to this server. Whenever a client needs to fetch an entry from the `/etc/passwd` file, it consults the NIS server instead.

In order for a file to be sharable via NIS, two prerequisites must be met. First, the file must be tabular with at least one entry that is unique across the entire file. In the `/etc/passwd` file, this entry is either the login or UID. Second, the file in its raw form must be a straight text file.

With the criteria met, these files are converted into DBM files, a simple database format allowing for quick searches. A separate DBM needs to be created for each key to be searched. In the `/etc/passwd` file, for instance, you need the database to be searchable by login and by UID. The result is the DBM files `passwd.byname` and `passwd.byuid`.

The original text file, along with the DBM files created from it, are maintained at the NIS master server. Clients that connect to the server to obtain information do not cache any returned results.

NIS Domains

NIS servers and clients must be in the same NIS domain if they want to communicate with one another. Note that the NIS domain is not the same as a DNS domain, although it is valid for them to share the same name.

TIP

You should maintain separate names for your NIS and DNS domains for two reasons: First, it is easier for you to differentiate what you're talking about when discussing problems with anyone else. Second, it makes it just that much more difficult for potential intruders to understand the internal workings of your machines from the outside.

Both the clients and servers bind themselves to a domain; hence, a client can belong to only one NIS domain at a given time. Once bound, clients send a broadcast to find the NIS server for the given domain.

The Different Servers

So far, you might have noticed that I've referenced the NIS server explicitly as the "master" server. This is because there are two kinds of NIS servers: master servers and slave servers.

Master NIS servers are the actual truthholders. They contain the text files used to generate the DBM files, and any changes to the database must be made to these files.

Slave NIS servers are designed to supplement master NIS servers by taking some of the load off of them. When a file is updated on the server, a server push is initiated, and the slave NIS server gets an updated copy of the DBM files.

Configuring a Master NIS Server

By default, the Red Hat distribution does not come with an NIS server. You can either download it from `http://www.redhat.com` or use the distribution on the CD-ROM that comes with this book. The filename for the NIS server on the CD-ROM is `ypserv-1.1.7-1.i386.rpm`.

Before you configure the server software, you need to decide whether you are going to set up any slave servers. If you are, you need to know their hostnames before continuing. Along with the names of your NIS servers, you will need to decide on a domain name at this point. Remember that this domain name is not the same as your DNS domain name and for clarity purposes should be set differently.

With this information at hand, you are ready to begin. First, you need to set the domain name. This is done with the `domainname` command—for example,

```
[root@vestax /etc]# domainname audionet.domain.com
```

Although this will work for the moment, you do need to change a startup configuration file so that this will be done every time your system reboots. The `/etc/rc.d/init.d/ypserv.init` script that was installed as part of the RPM looks for the domain name to be set in the `/etc/sysconfig/network` file. Simply add the following line:

```
NIS_DOMAIN=audionet.domain.com
```

With the domain name set, you can now decide what files you want to share via NIS as well as their filenames. This is done by editing `/var/yp/Makefile`. As the name implies, NIS maintains its maps by using the `make` utility. While familiarity with how this tool works is useful, it isn't mandatory to configure NIS.

Begin by loading `/var/yp/Makefile` into your favorite editor. Scroll down past the lines that read

```
# These are files from which the NIS databases are built. You may edit
# these to taste in the event that you don't wish to keep your NIS source files
# separate from your NIS server's actual configuration files.
```

Below this segment of text you will see lines that resemble the following:

```
GROUP      = $(YPPWDDIR)/group
PASSWD     = $(YPPWDDIR)/passwd
etc...
```

This section tells NIS where your database files are located. The `$(YPPWDDIR)` string is a variable that was set to `/etc` at the top of the `Makefile`. Although it is possible to change this to another directory, you will most likely want to keep it there for consistency. The string that comes after `$(YPPWDDIR)` is the name of the file in `/etc` that will become shared through NIS.

Most of these entries can remain the same. The few that you will want to change are `GROUP`, `PASSWD`, `SHADOW`, `ALIASES`, and possibly `HOSTS`.

The `GROUP` line shows that the file for controlling group information is at `/etc/group`. You might want to keep your local group file on the server separate from your NIS group file because your local group file could contain server-specific groups that you don't want to share across NIS, such as the `www` group for your Web server.

The same holds true for the other lines as well, especially the `PASSWD` line. A simple convention you might want to use to indicate that the file is being shared across NIS is to suffix it with a `.yp`. The resulting line looks something like the following:

```
PASSWD          = $(YPPWDDIR)/passwd.yp
```

With the filenames you want set, you can now determine which files to distribute. Scroll down the `Makefile` past the following block:

```
# If you don't want some of these maps built, feel free to comment
# them out of this list.
# Note that we don't build the eithers or bootparams maps by default
# since /etc/ethers and /etc/bootparams are not likely to be present
# on all systems
#
```

Your cursor should be at the following line:

```
all: passwd hosts group netid networks protocols rpc services netgrp
➥mail shadow ypservers publickey ethers # amd.home bootparams
```

This line specifies which maps will be made available via NIS. The `#` symbol after `ethers` is the comment symbol. The `amd.home` and `bootparams` maps are commented out at the moment.

Before making any changes to this line, you should make a copy of it and comment the copy out. The result looks something like the following:

```
#all: passwd hosts group netid networks protocols rpc services netgrp
#mail shadow ypservers publickey ethers # amd.home bootparams

all: passwd hosts group netid networks protocols rpc services netgrp
➥mail shadow ypservers publickey ethers # amd.home bootparams
```

By commenting out the line, you can retain a copy of it just in case something goes wrong. You can always look back to it and see how it looked before things were changed. With the copy in place, go ahead and begin your changes.

The only files you need to distribute for your network are the `passwd`, `hosts`, `group`, `netid`, `protocols`, `rpc`, `services`, `mail`, and `ypservers`. To indicate this change, edit the uncommented version of the line to read:

```
all: passwd hosts group netid protocols rpc services mail ypservers
```

Unless you are comfortable with `Makefiles`, you should leave the remainder of the file alone. Save the `Makefile` and quit the editor.

You are now ready to initialize your NIS database. This is done with the /usr/lib/yp/ypinit command. When invoked, it will prompt for the name of any NIS slave servers you want to set up. For this example, select denon to be the slave NIS server.

Remember that you do not have to set up a slave NIS server. Setting up a slave server is only useful if you have a large number of NIS clients and need to distribute the load they generate.

To initialize the master server, use the following:

```
[root@vestax /root]# /usr/lib/yp/ypinit -m
At this point, we have to construct a list of the hosts which will run NIS
servers. vestax is in the list of NIS server hosts. Please continue to add
the names for the other hosts, one per line. When you are done with the
list, type a <control D>.
    next host to add:  vestax
    next host to add:  denon
    next host to add: <CTRL-D>
The current list of NIS servers looks like this:

vestax
denon

Is this correct?  [y/n: y]  y
We need some minutes to build the databases...
Building /var/yp/audionet.domain.com/ypservers...
Running /var/yp/Makefile...
NIS Map update started on Mon May  5 22:16:53 PDT 1997
make[1]: Entering directory '/var/yp/audionet.domain.com'
Updating passwd.byname...
Updating passwd.byuid...
Updating hosts.byname...
Updating hosts.byaddy...
Updating group.byname...
Updating group.bygid...
Updating netid.byname...
Updating protocols.bynumber...
Updating protocols.byname...
Updating rpc.byname...
Updating rpc.bynumber...
Updating services.byname...
Updating mail.aliases...
make[1]: Leaving directory '/var/yp/audionet.domain.com'
NIS Map update completed
```

If anywhere in the middle of the output you received a message like the following instead

```
make[1]:***No rule to make target '/etc/shadow', needed by 'shadow.byname'. Stop.
make[1]: Leaving directory '/var/yp/audionet.domain.com'
```

it means that you are missing one of the files you listed in the Makefile. Go back and check that you edited the Makefile as you intended and then check to make sure that the files you selected to be shared via NIS actually do exist. After you've made sure of these, you do not need to rerun ypinit but instead can just rerun cd /var/yp;make.

Congratulations! You now have an NIS master server! Time to test the work with an NIS client.

Configuring an NIS client

Compared to configuring an NIS server, NIS clients are trivial. There are only four files you need to deal with, one of which is only one line long.

Begin by creating the `/etc/yp.conf` file. This file needs only two lines, one to specify the NIS domain name and the other to specify the NIS server hostname. The format of this file is

```
domainname domainname
ypserver nis_server
```

where *`domainname`* is the name of your NIS domain and *`nis_server`* is the server's hostname. For this example, this file should look like the following:

```
domainname audionet.domain.com
ypserver vestax.domain.com
```

The next step is to modify the startup scripts so that your `domainname` gets set every time you boot. To do this, edit the `/etc/rc.d/rc.local` script and add the following lines to it:

```
#
# Setup NIS domain name
#
if [ -f /etc/domainname ]; then
    domainname 'cat /etc/domainname'
    echo "NIS domain: 'domainname'"
fi
```

This modification checks for the file `/etc/domainname`. If `/etc/domainname` is found, the NIS domain is set to the contents of that file.

In order to get the modification to `/etc/rc.d/init.d/rc.local` to be useful, you need to create the `/etc/domainname` file. The content of the file should be only the NIS domain name on the first line with no subsequent lines. For the sample network, this looks like the following:

```
audionet.domain.com
```

The last file that needs to be changed is the `/etc/nsswitch.conf` file. This is slightly more involved than the previous files; however, a default file comes as part of the Red Hat installation. This file is used to configure which services are to be used to determine information such as hostnames, password files, and group files.

Begin by opening `/etc/nsswitch.conf` with your favorite editor. Scroll down past the comments (those lines beginning with the `#` symbol). You should see something like this:

```
passwd:    files nis
shadow:    files nis
group:     files nis

hosts:     files nis dns

services:      files [NOTFOUND=return] nis
etc...
```

The first column indicates the file in question. In the first line, this is `passwd`. The next column indicates the source for the file. This can be one of six options:

Option	*Description*
`nis`	Uses NIS to determine this information.
`yp`	Uses NIS to determine this information (alias for `nis`).
`dns`	Uses DNS to determine this information (applicable only to hosts).
`files`	Uses the file on the local machine to determine this information (for example, `/etc/passwd`).
`[NOTFOUND=return]`	Stops searching if the information has not been found yet.
`nis+`	Uses NIS+. (You won't use this because of the incomplete support for NIS+ under Linux.)

The order these are placed in the `/etc/nsswitch.conf` file determines the search order used by the system. For example, in the `hosts` line, the order of the entries are files `nis dns`, indicating that hostnames are first searched for in the `/etc/hosts` file, then via NIS in the map `hosts.byname`, and finally by DNS via the DNS server specified in `/etc/resolv.conf`.

In almost all instances, you want to search the local file before searching through NIS or DNS. This allows a machine to have local characteristics (such as a special user listed in `/etc/passwd`) while still using the network services being offered. The notable exception to this is the netgroup file that by its very nature should come from NIS.

Modify the order of your searches to suit your site's needs and save the configuration file.

NOTE

If you are familiar with NIS from an older version of Linux or another UNIX altogether, you might be wondering why I haven't mentioned the `ypbind` daemon.

Red Hat's standard C library comes with the NIS resolver built into it. This allows for NIS functions to work without the need of an extra daemon on the client workstation. A side effect of this is that the `ypwhich` program, which normally states which NIS server is being used, does not work. While it's a slight nuisance, you can still test the configuration with `ypcat`, as you will see shortly.

Because of the way NIS works under Red Hat, you do not need to reboot in order to start NIS client functions. By simply running

```
domainname 'cat /etc/domainname'
```

you can establish a connection to the NIS server and test your client software without having to reboot.

As a precautionary measure, you should schedule a reboot while you are with the machine to ensure that it does come up and configure the NIS information correctly. After all, your users will not be very happy if after a power failure, your machine does not come back up correctly without assistance.

With the NIS client and server configured, you are ready to test your work. Try the following:

```
ypcat passwd
```

If your configuration is working, you should see the contents of your NIS server's `/etc/passwd.yp` file displayed on your screen. (Assuming, of course, that you chose that file to be shared via NIS for your `passwd` file.) If you received a message such as

```
No such map passwd.byname. Reason: can't bind to a server which serves domain
```

you need to go back and double-check that your files have been properly configured.

TIP

A difference between the NIS that comes with Red Hat and other UNIXes' NIS packages is that Red Hat does not need the `/etc/passwd` file to have the string `+:*:0:0:::` appended to it. You might, however, want to add that anyway because the finger daemon, `fingerd`, does need that line in order to check NIS maps for user information.

Configuring an NIS Secondary Server

After you've decided to configure a machine to be an NIS secondary server, you need to start by configuring it as an NIS client machine. Verify that you can access the server maps via the `ypcat` command.

Begin configuring the secondary server by installing the `ypserv` RPM from either `http://www.redhat.com` or from the CD-ROM (filename `ypserv-1.1.7-1.i386.rpm`).

When you have the `ypserv` program installed, go ahead and start it up by running `/etc/rc.d/init.d/ypserv.init start`. It isn't doing anything useful yet, but you will need to have it running shortly.

Next, either download `ypbind-3.0-1.src.rpm` from `http://www.redhat.com` or copy it from the CD-ROM. After it's installed, you will need to compile it as follows:

1. Go to the directory `/usr/src/redhat/SOURCES` and run `tar -xvzf ypbind-3.0.tar.gz`. This will uncompress and untar the archive into the `/usr/src/redhat/SOURCES/ypbind` directory.
2. Type **`cd ypbind`** to go into the `ypbind` directory. You are now ready to apply the patch that came with the distribution. Type **`patch < ../ypbind-3.0-glibc.diff`** to apply the patch.

3. The `Makefile` distributed with this package assumes you use the `nsl` libraries. Red Hat doesn't use this library, so you need to remove it from the `Makefile` by running the following: `mv Makefile Makefile.nsl;grep -v nsl Makefile.nsl > Makefile`.
4. Run `make` to build the distribution. Ignore any warnings about `'rcsid'` defined but not used. When it is completed, you should have the `ypbind` binary in the current directory.
5. Copy the `ypbind` binary to the `/usr/lib/yp` directory and be sure its permissions are set to `0700`.
6. Start `ypbind` on the client machine and test it by running `ypwhich -m`. It should list all of the maps being served from the current NIS master.

If you remember the details on NIS clients, you might remember not needing `ypbind` because it is built into the resolver library under Red Hat Linux. However, the `ypinit` program that you'll be using soon requires it in order to communicate with the master server. `ypbind` will not become part of the startup sequence.

Now you are ready to tell the master server that a slave server exists. To do this, edit the `/var/yp/ypservers` file so that the slave server you are setting up is included in the list. If you configured your master server with the name of the slave server during the `ypinit -m` phase, you do not need to do this.

Although `ypbind` will not be part of startup, you do need to make a small change in the startup sequence in order to set the NIS domain name. This is done by editing the `/etc/sysconfig/network` file and adding the line `NIS_DOMAIN=`*`nisdomain.com`* where *`nisdomain.com`* is your NIS domain name. In the sample network, this would be `audionet.domain.com`.

In order to set the domain name without having to reboot for the purpose of installing the NIS slave server, set the NIS domain name explicitly by using the `domainname` command, such as

```
domainname nisdomain.com
```

where *`nisdomain.com`* is the NIS domain name of your choice.

You can now initialize the slave server by running the command

```
/usr/lib/yp/ypinit -s master
```

where *`master`* is the hostname for the NIS master server. In this example, it's `vestax`. The output of this should look something like the following:

```
We will need some minutes to copy the databases from vestax.
Transferring mail.aliases...
Trying ypxfrd ... not running
Transferring services.byname...
Trying ypxfrd ... not running
Transferring rpc.bynumber...
Trying ypxfrd ... not running
[etc...]
```

```
denon.domain.com's NIS database has been set up.
If there were warnings, please figure out what went wrong, and fix it.

At this point, make sure that /etc/passwd and /etc/group have
been edited so that when the NIS is activated, the databases you
have just created will be used, instead of the /etc ASCII files.
```

Don't worry about the `Trying ypxfrd...not running` message. This happens because you haven't set the NIS master server to run the YP map transfer daemon `rpc.ypxfrd`. In fact, you never set it up to do so—instead use a server push method where the NIS master server pushes the maps to all the NIS slaves whenever there is an update.

In order to set the NIS master to do the actual push, you need to change its `Makefile` a little. On the master server, edit the `Makefile` so that the line `NOPUSH="True"` is changed to read `#NOPUSH="True"` and the line that reads `DOMAIN = 'basename \'pwd\''` is changed to `DOMAIN= '/bin/domainname'`.

Now for the big test. On the NIS master server, run `cd /var/yp;make all` to force all the maps to be rebuilt and pushed. The output should look something like the following:

```
Updating passwd.byname....
Pushed passwd.byname map.
Updating passwd.byuid...
Pushed passwd.byuid map.
Updating hosts.byname...
Pushed hosts.byname.
Updating hosts.byaddr...
Pushed hosts.byaddr.
[etc...]
```

On the NIS slave server, change the `/etc/yp.conf` file so that the `ypserver` is set to point to the slave server. Try running the command `ypcat passwd` and see if your NIS password file is displayed. If so, you're set! The NIS slave server is configured.

If you're having problems, go back and trace through your steps. Also, be sure to reboot the machine and see if your NIS slave server still works correctly. If it doesn't come back up, be sure that the changes you made to the boot sequence when installing `ypserv` were correct.

TIP

If your NIS client or slave server seems to have a hard time finding other hosts on the network, be sure that the `/etc/nsswitch.conf` file is set to resolve hosts by file before NIS. Then be sure that all the important hosts needed for the NIS servers to set themselves up are in their own local `/etc/hosts` file.

Using NIS-isms in Your /etc/passwd File

The most popular use of NIS is to keep a global user database so that it is possible to grant access to any machine at your site to any user. Under Red Hat Linux, this behavior is implicit for all NIS clients.

There are times, however, when you do not want everyone accessing certain systems, such as those used by personnel. This can be fixed by using the special token + in your /etc/passwd file. By default, NIS clients have the line +:::::: at the end of their /etc/passwd file, thereby allowing everyone in NIS to log in to the system. In order to change this so that the host remains an NIS client but does not grant everyone permission, the line +::::::/bin/false should be explicitly added to the end of your /etc/passwd file. This will allow only people with actual entries in the /etc/passwd file for that host (for example, root) to log in.

In order to allow a specific person to log in to a host, you can add a line to the /etc/passwd file granting this access. The format of the line is *+username*:::::: where *username* is the login of the user you want to grant access to. NIS will automatically grab the user's passwd entry from the NIS server and use the correct information for determining the user information (for example, UID, GID, GECOS, and so on). You can override particular fields by inserting the new value in the *+username*:::::: entry. For example, if the user sshah uses /usr/local/bin/tcsh as his shell, but the host he needs to log in to keeps it in /bin/tcsh, his /etc/passwd entry can be set to +sshah::::::/bin/tcsh.

Using Netgroups

Netgroups are a great way to group people and machines into nice neat names for access control. A good example of this is for a site where users are not allowed to log in to server machines. A netgroup for the system administrators can be created and those in the group let in through a special entry in the /etc/passwd file.

Netgroup information is kept in the /etc/netgroup file and shared via NIS.

The format of a netgroups file is

```
groupname member-list
```

where *groupname* is the name of the group being defined and the *member-list* is comprised of other group names or tuples of specific data. Each entry in the *member-list* is separated by a whitespace.

A tuple containing specific data comes in the form

```
(hostname, username, domain name)
```

where *hostname* is the name of the machine for which that entry is valid, *username* is the login of the person being referenced, and *domain name* is the NIS domain name. Any entry left blank is considered a wildcard; for example, (technics,,,) implies everybody on the host technics. An entry with a dash in it (-) means that there are no valid values for that entry. For example, (-,sshah,) implies the user sshah and nothing else. This is useful for generating a list of users or machine names for use in other netgroups.

In files where netgroups are supported (such as /etc/passwd), they are referenced by placing an @ sign in front of them. So if you wanted to allow the netgroup sysadmins consisting of (-,sshah,) (-,heidis,) permission to log in to a server, you would add the line

```
+@sysadmins
```

to your `/etc/passwd` file.

An example of a full netgroups file is as follows:

```
sysadmins        (-,sshah,) (-,heidis)
servers        (numark,-,) (vestax,-,)
clients        (denon,-,) (technics,-,) (mtx,-,)
research-1       (-,boson,) (-,jyom,) (-,weals,) (-,dave,)
research-2       (-,scora,) (-,dan,) (-,david,) (-,barth,)
consultants       (-,arturo,)
allusers        sysadmins research-1 research-2 consultants
allhosts        servers clients
```

The Network File System

The Network File System, or NFS, is the means by which UNIX systems share their disk resources with one another. By abstracting the details of the filesystem to this level, it is possible for other systems (both UNIX and non-UNIX alike) to follow the NFS protocol and share disks across one another.

The success of NFS is due to a number of its key features, the first and foremost being that its specifications have been made publicly available from Sun Microsystems from its initial development onward. At the same time, Sun began shipping all of its workstations with this capability. During the '80s and early '90s, the Sun UNIX (SunOS and later Solaris) made heavy use of the protocol and many other UNIX vendors followed suit. Linux supported NFS before even version 1.0 was released.

Another key feature is NFS's robust nature. It is a *stateless protocol* meaning that each request made between the client and server is complete in itself and does not require knowledge of prior transactions. Because of this, NFS cannot tell the difference between a very slow host and a host that has failed altogether. This allows for servers to go down and come back up without having to reboot the clients.

NOTE

NFS works by using a protocol called remote procedure calls, or RPC for short. RPCs are a well-defined protocol for allowing two hosts to communicate with each other. In order for RPC to work, however, a central registry for all the RPC programs running on a system needs to be established. This registry then listens for RPC calls over the network and relays them to the appropriate program. Under Linux, this registry is called `rpc.portmapper` and is discussed in the next section, "Installing NFS."

WARNING

NFS's design by nature is, unfortunately, insecure. While there are some steps that provide a moderate level of security to protect you from the common user pretending to be an evil hacker, there is not much more you can do. Any time you share a disk via NFS with another machine, you need to give the users of that machine (especially the root user) a certain amount of trust. If you believe that the person you are sharing the disk with is untrustworthy, you need to explore alternatives to NFS for sharing data and disk space.

Be sure to keep up with security bulletins from both Red Hat and the Computer Emergency Response Team (CERT). You can find these on Red Hat's site at `www.redhat.com`, CERT's site at `www.cert.org`, or the moderated newsgroup `comp.security.announce`.

Installing NFS

Although the NFS software that comes with Red Hat Linux does come preinstalled, you do need to be aware of what the software is and what each specific program does. This is important when trying to troubleshoot problems and configure NFS-related tools such as the `automounter`.

There are three programs used to provide NFS server services:

`rpc.portmapper` This program does not directly provide NFS services itself; however, it maps calls made from other machines to the correct NFS daemons.

`rpc.nfsd` This daemon is what translates the NFS requests into actual requests on the local filesystem.

`rpc.mountd` This daemon's services requests to mount and unmount filesystems.

NOTE

The `rpc.nfsd` and `rpc.mountd` programs need only run on your NFS servers. In fact, you might find it prudent to not have them run at all on your client machines for security concerns and to free up resources that might otherwise be consumed by them. NFS clients do not need any special NFS software to run. They should, however, run the `rpc.portmapper` program because it provides RPC functionality to programs other than NFS as well.

By default, these programs are installed and loaded at boot time for you. To check for this, use the `rpcinfo` command as follows:

```
rpcinfo -p
```

This will display all the registered RPC programs running on your system. To check which RPC programs are registered on a remote host, use `rpcinfo` such as

```
rpcinfo -p hostname
```

where *hostname* is the name of the remote host you want to check. The output for a Linux host running NFS appears something like the following:

```
[root@vestax /root]# rpcinfo -p
  program    vers    proto    port
   100000       2      tcp     111    portmapper
   100000       2      udp     111    portmapper
   100005       1      udp     821    mountd
   100005       1      tcp     823    mountd
   100003       2      udp    2049    nfs
   100003       2      tcp    2049    nfs
```

Note the number specified after `rpc.nfsd` and `rpc.mountd`. Those numbers tell each program how many instances it should start up at once. Having several instances of each daemon improves network performance up to a point. Having too many started will degrade performance. Unfortunately, there is no magic formula for determining the ideal number to use for your system as it varies depending on your own usage. Typically, most sites start with four and adjust later.

NOTE

Currently, multiple NFS servers running in parallel is still experimental. The key limitation is that when running more than one instance of `rpc.nfsd`, the filesystem can only be shared read-only. This is useful for disks that hold large quantities of read-only information such as Usenet news spools, but not much else.

Starting and Stopping the NFS daemons

You might run across instances when you need to stop NFS and restart it later. You can do this by using the startup scripts that are executed at boot time and shutdown. NFS's scripts are `/etc/rc.d/init.d/nfs`.

To start the NFS services, run the following as root:

```
[root@vestax /root]# /etc/rc.d/init.d/nfs start
```

To stop NFS services, run the following as root:

```
[root@vestax /root]# /etc/rc.d/init.d/nfs stop
```

Configuring NFS

The two key files to NFS are the `/etc/exports` and `/etc/fstab` files. The `exports` file is configured on the server side. This file specifies which directories are to be shared with which clients and each client's access rights. The fstab file is configured on the client side and specifies which servers to contact for certain directories as well as where to place them in the directory tree.

Setting Up the /etc/exports File

The /etc/exports file specifies which directories to share with which hosts on the network. This file needs only to be set up on your NFS servers.

The /etc/exports file follows the following format:

```
/directory/to/export     host1(permissions) host2(permissions)
                         ➥host3(permissions) host4(permissions)
#
# Comments begin with the pound sign and must be at the start of
# the line
#
/another/dir/to/export    host2(permissions) host5(permissions)
```

In this example, */directory/to/export* is the directory you want to make available to other machines on the network. You must supply the absolute pathname for this entry. On the same line, the hosts that can access this directory are listed. If the list is longer than the line size permits, you can use the standard continuation character (the backslash, \) to continue onto the next line. Each host is given a set of access permissions. They are as follows:

rw	Read and write access.
ro	Read-only access.
no_root_squash	Acknowledge and trust the client's root account.

If you are familiar with the export file configurations of other flavors of UNIX, you know that this is not similar. Whether one is better than the other is a holy war discussion best left to Usenet newsgroups.

After you have set up your /etc/exports file, run the exportfs command with the -a option—for example,

```
exportfs -a
```

This sends the appropriate signals to the rpc.nfsd and rpc.mountd daemons to reread the /etc/exports file and update their internal tables.

13 TCP/IP NETWORK MANAGEMENT

TIP

It is considered good convention to place all the directories you want to export in the /export hierarchy. This makes their intent clear and self-documenting. If you need the directory to also exist elsewhere in the directory tree, use symbolic links. For example, if your server is exporting its /usr/local hierarchy, you should place the directory in

continues

continued

/export, thereby creating /export/usr/local. Because the server itself will need access to the /export/usr/local directory, a symbolic link from /usr/local should be created pointing to the real location, /export/usr/local.

Using mount to Mount an Exported Filesystem

To mount a filesystem, use the mount command

```
mount servername:/exported/dir /dir/to/mount
```

where *servername* is the name of the server from which you want to mount a filesystem, */exported/dir* is the directory listed in its /etc/exports file, and */dir/to/mount* is the location on your local machine where you want to mount the filesystem. For example, to mount /export/home from the NFS server denon to the directory /home, you would use

```
mount denon:/export/home /home
```

Remember that the directory must exist in your local filesystem before anything can be mounted there.

There are options that can be passed to the mount command. The most important characteristics are specified in the -o options. These characteristics are as follows:

rw	Read/write.
ro	Read-only.
bg	Background mount. Should the mount initially fail (the server is down, for instance), the mount process will background itself and continue trying until it is successful. This is useful for filesystems mounted at boot time because it keeps the system from hanging at that mount should the server be down.
intr	Interruptible mount. If a process is pending I/O on a mounted partition, it will allow the process to be interrupted and the I/O call to be dropped.
soft	By default, NFS operations are "hard," meaning that they require the server to acknowledge completion before returning to the calling process. The soft option allows the NFS client to return a failure to the calling process after retrans number of retries.
retrans	Specifies the maximum number of retried transmissions to a soft-mounted filesystem.

Here's an example of these parameters in use:

```
mount -o rw,bg,intr,soft,retrans=6 denon:/export/home /home
```

To unmount the filesystem, use the `umount` command—for example,

```
umount /home
```

This will unmount the `/home` filesystem.

There is, of course, a caveat. If users are using files on a mounted filesystem, you cannot unmount it. All files must be closed before this can happen, which on a large system can be tricky, to say the least. There are three ways to handle this:

- Use the `lsof` program (available at `ftp://vic.cc.purdue.edu/pub/tools/unix/lsof`) to list the users and their open files on a given filesystem. Then either wait until they are done, beg and plead for them to leave, or kill their processes off. Then unmount the filesystem. Often, this isn't very desirable.
- Use `umount` with the `-f` option to force the filesystem to unmount. This is often a bad idea as it will leave the programs (and users) accessing the filesystem confused. Files that are in memory that have not been committed to disk might be lost.
- Bring the system to single-user mode and then unmount the filesystem. Although this is the largest inconvenience, it is the safest way because no one loses any work.

Configuring the `/etc/fstab` File to Mount Filesystems Automatically

At boot time, the system will automatically mount the root filesystem with read-only privileges. This will allow it to load the kernel and read critical startup files. However, after the system has bootstrapped itself, it will need guidance. Although it is possible for you to jump in and mount all the filesystems, it isn't realistic because you would then have to finish bootstrapping the machine yourself and worse, the system could not come back online by itself. (Of course, if you enjoy coming into work at 2 a.m. to bring a system back up…)

To get around this, Linux uses a special file called `/etc/fstab`. This file lists all the partitions that need to be mounted at boot time and the directory where they need to be mounted. Along with that information, you can pass parameters to the `mount` command.

> **NOTE**
>
> NFS servers can also be NFS clients. For example, a Web server that exports part of its archive to, say, an FTP server, can NFS mount from the server containing home directories at the same time.

Each filesystem to be mounted is listed in the `fstab` file in the following format:

```
/dev/device        /dir/to/mount      ftype parameters fs_freq fs_passno
```

The following make up this line:

/dev/device	The device to be mounted. In the case of mounting NFS filesystems, this comes in the form of *servername:/dir/exported*, where *servername* is the name of the NFS server, and */dir/exported* is the directory that is exported from the NFS server—for example, `denon:/export/home`, where `denon` is the hostname of your NFS server and `/export/home` is the directory that it specified in the `/etc/exports` directory as being shared.
/dir/to/mount	The location at which the filesystem should be mounted on your directory tree.
ftype	The filesystem type. Usually, this is `ext2` for your local filesystems; however, NFS mounts should use the `nfs` filesystem type.
parameters	These are the parameters you passed to `mount` by using the `-o` option. They follow the same comma-delimited format. An example entry would look like `rw,intr,bg`.
fs_freq	This is used by `dump` to determine whether a filesystem needs to be dumped.
fs_passno	This is used by the `fsck` program to determine the order to check disks at boot time.

Any lines in the `fstab` file that start with the pound symbol (`#`) are considered comments.

If you need to mount a new filesystem while the machine is live, you will need to perform the mount by hand. If you want to have this mount automatically active the next time the system is rebooted, you should be sure to add it to the `fstab` file.

There are two notable partitions that don't follow the same set of rules as normal partitions. They are the swap partition and `/proc`, which use filesystem types `swap` and `proc`, respectively.

Mounting the swap partition is not done using the `mount` command. It is instead managed by the `swapon` command. In order for a swap partition to be mounted, it needs to be listed in the `fstab` file. Once there, use `swapon` with the `-a` parameter, followed by the partition on which you've allocated swap space.

The `/proc` filesystem is even stranger because it really isn't a filesystem. It is an interface to the kernel abstracted into a filesystem format.

TIP

If you need to remount a filesystem that already has an entry in the `fstab` file, you don't need to type in the `mount` command with all the parameters. Instead, simply pass the directory to `mount` as the parameter, as in

```
mount /dir/to/mount
```

where */dir/to/mount* is the directory that needs to be mounted. `mount` will automatically look to the `fstab` file for all the details, such as which partition to mount and which options to use.

If you need to remount a large number of filesystems that are already listed in the `fstab` file, you can use the `-a` option in `mount` to try to remount all the entries in `fstab` like this:

```
mount -a
```

If it finds that a filesystem is already mounted, no action on that filesystem will be performed. If, on the other hand, it finds that an entry is not mounted, it will automatically mount it with the appropriate parameters.

WARNING

When setting up servers that mount filesystems from other servers, be wary of *cross mounting*. Cross mounting happens when two servers mount each other's filesystems. This can be dangerous if you do not configure the `/etc/fstab` file to mount these systems in the background (via the `bg` option) because it is possible for these two machines to deadlock during their boot sequence as each host waits for the other to respond.

For example, let's say you want `host1` to mount `/export/usr/local` from `host2`, and `host2` to mount `/export/home/admin` from `host1`. If both machines are restarted after a power outage, `host1` will try to mount the directory from `host2` before turning on its own NFS services. `host2` is, at the same time, trying to mount the directory from `host1` before it turns on its NFS services. The result is both machines waiting forever for the other machine to start.

If you use the `bg` option in the `/etc/fstab` entry for both hosts, they would fail on the initial mount, background the mount, and continue booting. Eventually, both machines would start their NFS daemons and allow each other to mount their respective directories.

Complete Sample Configuration Files

Listing 13.4 contains a complete `/etc/exports` file for a server.

Listing 13.4. A complete /etc/exports file.

```
#
# /etc/exports for denon
#
# Share the home dirs:
/export/home        technics(rw) pioneer(rw) vestax(rw)
                    ➥atus(rw) rane(rw)

#
# Share local software
#
/export/usr/local     technics(rw,no_root_squash)
                      ➥vestax(rw,no_root_squash)
                      ➥pioneer(rw,no_root_squash)
                      ➥atus(rw,no_root_squash)
                      ➥rane(rw,no_root_squash)
```

Listing 13.5 contains a complete `/etc/fstab` file for a client.

Listing 13.5. A complete /etc/fstab file.

```
#
# /etc/fstab for technics
#

/dev/hda1                   /                   ext2 rw                 0 0
/dev/hda2                   swap                swap
/dev/hda3                   /usr                ext2 rw                 0 0
/dev/hda4                   /var                ext2 rw                 0 0
denon:/export/home          /home               nfs  rw,bg,intr,soft 0 0
denon:/export/usr/local     /usr/local          nfs  rw,bg,intr,soft 0 0
rane:/export/mail           /var/spool/mail     nfs  rw,bg,intr,soft 0 0
```

Connecting to the Net with PPP

Red Hat Linux has made connecting to the Internet through PPP (Point to Point Protocol) a much simplified process complete with a GUI interface. Before continuing, you need to be sure of the following:

- You have X Window working. This is necessary for the tools you are going to use to configure PPP.
- You have established an account with a local ISP. The ISP should have provided a phone number, login, password, and IP addresses to its DNS server.
- PPP service has been compiled into your kernel. If you are using the kernel that came with the Red Hat distribution, you do not need to make any changes.
- Your modem has been attached and configured with `modemtool`. `modeltool` simply sets a symbolic link from the `/dev/modem` file to the appropriate device name for your modem port.

- You do not have a default route. If you do have a default route set on `boot`, edit the `/etc/sysconfig/network` file so that the `GATEWAY` line reads `GATEWAY=` and reboot.

After you have these necessities set up, you can begin configuring PPP.

NOTE

Unless otherwise specified, all the commands in this section must be run as the root user.

Simple Client

If your Red Hat machine is a standalone unit with no other network configured or if you only want your Red Hat machine to connect to the Internet via the PPP connection, this is all the configuration you need. On the other hand, if you are planning a more elaborate network with your Red Hat machine being your interface to the Internet, this section is only the beginning, but necessary.

Begin by starting the `netcfg` tool for configuring your network. If you have already configured your DNS, the information for your host will be displayed (see Figure 13.5).

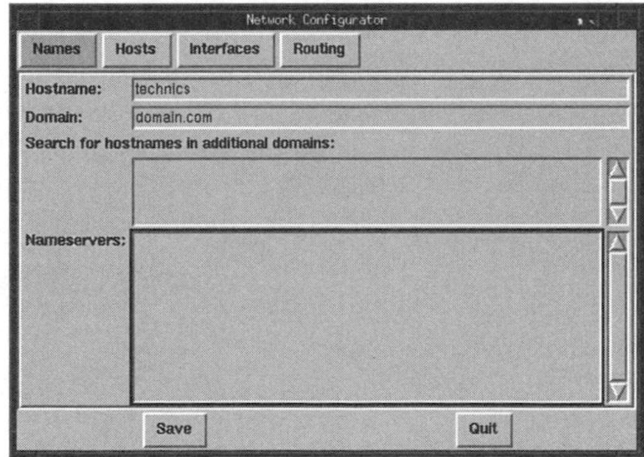

FIGURE 13.5.
The Network Configurator Names menu with hostname and domain information.

To configure the information in this window, perform the following steps:

1. If you haven't specified a hostname for yourself, click in the Hostname: box and enter one.
2. In the Domain: box, enter the domain name of your ISP.
3. Leave the Search for hostnames in additional domains: box blank and skip to the Nameservers: box below it. In here, enter the DNS server IP address your ISP provided you (one IP address to a line).

You are now ready to configure the PPP device. To do this, click the Interfaces button at the top of the window. The window will change to look like Figure 13.6.

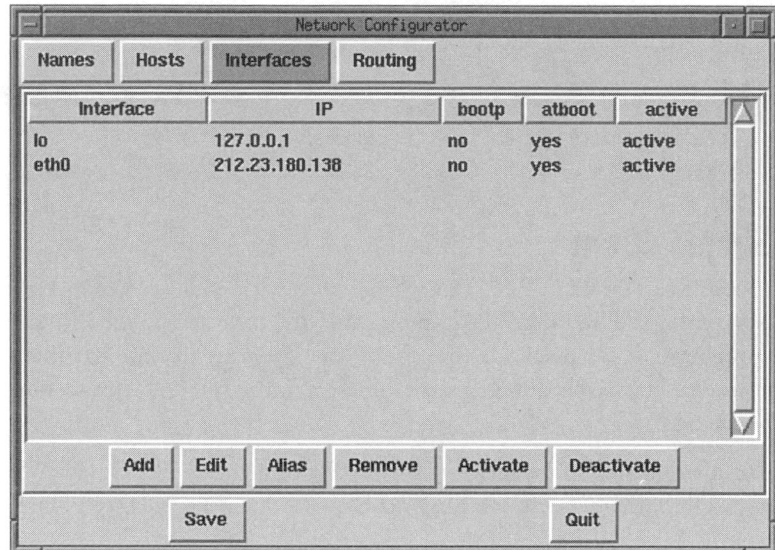

FIGURE 13.6.
The Network Configurator Interfaces menu before configuring PPP.

4. Click the Add button at the bottom of the window. Another window listing your interface options will appear. Select PPP as the Interface Type and click OK. The Interface Options window will close and the Create PPP Interface window will appear (see Figure 13.7).

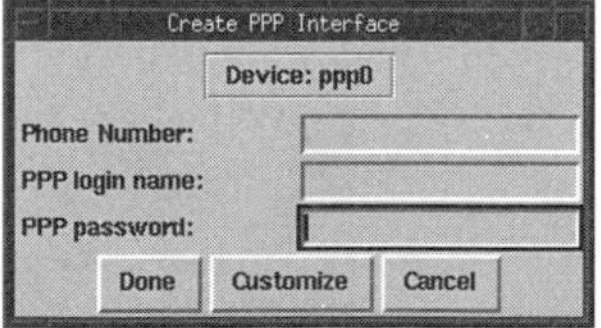

FIGURE 13.7.
The Network Configurator Create PPP Interface menu.

Before continuing, be sure that no one with whom you don't want to share your PPP password is watching. At the PPP password prompt, the password will be shown on the screen in clear text and anyone reading over your shoulder will be able to see it.

5. Click in the Phone Number: box and enter the phone number for your ISP. Be sure to include any special dialing prefixes you need to either disable call waiting or get to an outside line.
6. Skip the Use PAP Authentication button unless your ISP requires it. Enter the appropriate information in the PPP login name: box and the PPP password: box.

7. After you have the PPP information typed in, click the Customize button at the bottom of the Create PPP Interface window. The Create PPP Interface window closes, and the Edit PPP Interface window appears (see Figure 13.8).

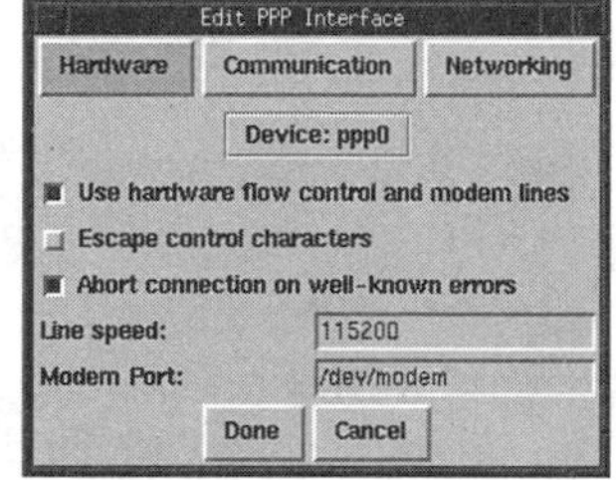

FIGURE 13.8.
The Network Configurator Edit PPP Interface Hardware menu.

8. Make sure that the Use hardware flow control and modem lines entry and the Abort connection on well-known errors entry are set and that Escape control characters and Allow any user to (de)activate interface are not set.
9. In the Line speed: box, select the highest speed your computer can communicate with the modem, not the highest speed the modem can communicate with another modem. For most modems, this should be `115200`.
10. For the Modem Port: box, use `/dev/modem`. If you have not configured your modem with the `modemtool` program yet, this is the time to do it.

At this point, your hardware is configured. Now to tackle the network aspects of the configuration. Click the Networking button in the Edit PPP Interface window. The window will change to look something like Figure 13.9.

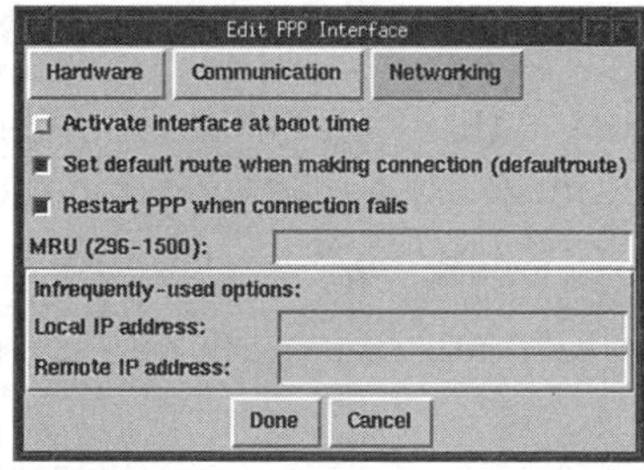

FIGURE 13.9.
The Network Configurator Edit PPP Interface Networking menu.

You now have to make some important decisions:

- Do you want the PPP connection to automatically restart if it drops?
- Do you want the PPP connection to automatically start at boot time?

If you answer yes to the first question, you will be unable to drop the PPP connection until the system shuts down or you kill the `pppd` daemon with the `kill` command. For a flaky connection, this is a very useful option because it will keep you from having to constantly restart your connection.

Answering yes to the second question is useful only if your account with your ISP is a 24-hours-a-day connection.

To set your desired parameters, do the following:

1. In the current Edit PPP Interface window, set the Activate interface at boot time option and Restart PPP when connection fails option to your preferences. Keep the second option, Set default route when making connection (defaultroute), set.
2. The MRU box stands for Maximum Receive Unit, which is similar to the MTU of a network card. This option sets how much data is contained in a packet between you and your ISP within the range of 296 bytes and 1500 bytes. If your telephone lines are clear, set this number higher. Conversely, if your telephone line often has a lot of static, you will want to set it to a lower number.
3. The last two options in the current Edit PPP Interface window let you specify your IP address and your server's IP address. In most instances, your IP address is dynamically assigned by your ISP; however, some ISPs offer a plan that gives you a static IP address for a higher monthly cost. (This is useful if you need to keep a continuous network connection going.) If you do have a static IP plan, your ISP will provide these two numbers for you. Otherwise, leave them blank.

To complete the PPP setup, click Done. Another window will come up asking if you want to save the current configuration. Click the Save button. The Edit PPP Interface window will disappear and your original Network Configurator window will show the PPP interface, as shown in Figure 13.10.

You are now ready to test your PPP connection. Click the Activate button at the bottom of the Network Configurator window to start your PPP connection. You should hear your modem dialing and connecting within a few moments. After it is connected, test the connection by pinging your ISP's nameserver. A valid connection should look something like this:

```
[root@technics /root]# ping -c 5 207.155.59.1
PING 207.155.59.1 (207.155.59.1): 56 data bytes
64 bytes from 207.155.59.1: icmp_seq=0 ttl=254 time=141.8 ms
64 bytes from 207.155.59.1: icmp_seq=1 ttl=254 time=140.4 ms
64 bytes from 207.155.59.1: icmp_seq=2 ttl=254 time=150.4 ms
64 bytes from 207.155.59.1: icmp_seq=3 ttl=254 time=140.3 ms
64 bytes from 207.155.59.1: icmp_seq=4 ttl=254 time=140.4 ms

--- 207.155.59.1 ping statistics ---
5 packets transmitted, 5 packets received, 0% packet loss
round-trip min/avg/max = 140.3/142.6/150.4 ms
```

When you are done with your connection, click the Deactivate button in the Network Configurator window. Be sure to click Save one last time before you click Quit.

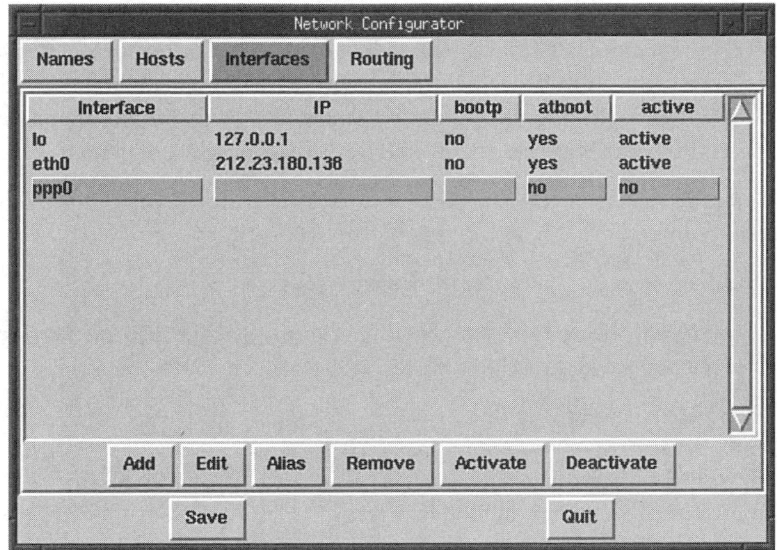

FIGURE 13.10.
The Network Configurator Interfaces menu with PPP information.

To bring your connection back up, simply run `netcfg`, select Interfaces from the top menu, highlight the `ppp` interface, and click Activate.

TIP

Instead of having to start the `netcfg` program every time you want to activate your PPP connection, you can use command-line scripts in the `/etc/sysconfig/network-scripts` directory. The command for starting PPP is

```
./ifup-ppp ifcfg-ppp0 &
```

The command to shut down your PPP connection is

```
./ifdown-ppp ifcfg-ppp0 &
```

On-Demand Dialing

As you become more Net savvy, you might find it useful to have your machine automatically dial out to your ISP and log in whenever it detects a packet destined to a particular IP address, for example, your ISP's nameserver.

When the kernel tries to connect to an IP that it doesn't have a route for, it invokes the script `/sbin/request-route` with the destination IP address. `request-route` checks to see if it has a script corresponding to that address. If it does, the script is invoked, which presumably starts the necessary connection to establish the desired route. In most instances, this would be the PPP connection.

There is, however, a slight limitation in the current setup. If you attempt to connect to an IP that requires the PPP connection be up, but was not specifically set with `request-route` so that the connection is started, the kernel will return an error to the calling program. To circumvent this, you can use a slightly modified script that establishes a default script to invoke for all IPs that cannot be reached. This feature is especially useful if you run your own nameserver.

Before using a new `request-route` script, make a backup copy of the original with the following command:

```
cp /sbin/request-route /sbin/request-route-orig
```

Should you decide to return back to the original script, you can simply copy the `/sbin/request-route-orig` script back to `/sbin/request-route`.

Next, add the following line

```
if [ ! -f $chatfile ] ; then chatfile=/etc/ppp/chat-default; fi
```

to `request-route` after the line that reads

```
chatfile=/etc/ppp/chat.$1
```

With `request-route` ready, you need to provide it the script files necessary to invoke the PPP connection. You've already configured PPP with the `netcfg` tool, so the script is already done and just needs to be copied to `/etc/ppp` like so:

```
cp /etc/sysconfig/network-scripts/chat-ppp0 /etc/ppp/chat-default
```

Doing this will set up your default PPP service. If for some reason you need to set up a different network connection for a particular IP address, you can create a specific chat script for that address and name it `/etc/ppp/chat.`*`xxx.xxx.xxx.xxx`*, where *`xxx.xxx.xxx.xxx`* is the IP address. The `request-route` script will automatically pick the IP-specific script over the default script.

By default, the PPP connection will automatically shut itself down after five minutes of inactivity. You can change this by editing the `request-route` script and changing the number after the string `idle-disconnect` to however many seconds you want it to wait for before automatically disconnecting.

If you want to force a disconnection before the idle out period, you can simply kill the `pppd` daemon. Do not use the `-9` option on `kill` when doing so, however, because `pppd` intercepts the standard termination signal and does cleanup work before exiting.

Summary

As you've seen in this chapter, adding network access and networking tools to your system is a fantastic asset. And with Red Hat Linux, sharing data through these networking tools is relatively straightforward, which is impressive considering the power they add to your system.

Here's a summary of this chapter's main points:

- An IP address is the number that uniquely identifies a machine across a network.
- The `netcfg` tool is used to configure basic network services such as setting up the network card or PPP connection, establishing routes, setting the hostname and DNS information, and setting up the `/etc/hosts` file.
- Should you need to hand-configure your network interface, use the `ifconfig` command to set up the IP number, netmask, and broadcast address.
- When configuring a network by hand, don't forget to set the routing table with the `route` command. Without it, your machine will not know where to send packets!
- The Domain Name System (DNS) is used for resolving hostnames across the Internet to their actual IP numbers. DNS servers are often called nameservers.
- When establishing a small network, it is a good idea to configure a caching nameserver to reduce load on your connection to other networks.
- The Network File System (NFS) is used to share disks from machine to machine. It is a very powerful tool enabling you to keep one copy of data and have all your machines on the network access it.
- If you share a disk with another host via NFS, you should have complete trust in the administrator of that host. NFS security relies on good deal of trust.
- The Network Information System (NIS) is used for sharing common files on the network. This is most often used for sharing user information (such as `/etc/passwd`, `/etc/group`).
- If you have several NIS clients, you should set up NIS slave servers and have them share the load.
- Use netgroups if you want to cluster users into manageable groups for access control.
- PPP is used to enable your machine to connect to an Internet Service Provider through a modem. Red Hat Linux has all the necessary support for doing this and is easily configured through the `netcfg` program.

After you have your machine configured and accessing the network, HAVE FUN WITH IT! You will quickly find uses for the network access that you could never even dream about on a standalone system. A word of warning, though—after you have put your machine onto a network, you will never want to take it offline.

IN THIS PART

System Administration and Management

CHAPTER 14

Getting Started with Red Hat Linux

by Sriranga R. Veeraraghavan

IN THIS CHAPTER

This chapter covers the basics of getting started on a Red Hat Linux installation and takes a look at the organization of the file on a system along with the installation of packaged software using Red Hat Package Manager.

Organization

A Red Hat Linux installation is usually very nicely organized and fully featured, in comparison with other UNIX and Linux distributions. This is because Red Hat complies with the Linux filesystem standard (FSSTND). A complete description of the standard is available at `http://www.pathname.com/fhs/`.

A feature of FSSTND is that the root directory, `/`, is very clean and only holds the most essential files. My `/` looks something like the following:

```
bin/          etc/          lost+found/  sbin/         var/
boot/         home/         mnt/         tmp/
dev/          lib/          proc/        usr/
```

The following sections cover the types of files contained in most of these directories. The `/dev`, `/proc`, and `/boot` directories and their contents are covered in Chapter 11, "Filesystems, Disks, and Other Devices."

`/bin` and `/sbin`

Most of the essential programs for using and maintaining a UNIX or Linux system are stored in the `/bin` and `/sbin` directories. The `bin` in the names of these directories comes from the fact that executable programs are binary files.

The `/bin` directory is usually used to hold the most commonly used essential user programs, such as

- `login`
- Shells (`bash`, `ksh`, `csh`)
- File manipulation utilities (`cp`, `mv`, `rm`, `ln`, `tar`)
- Editors (`ed`, `vi`)
- Filesystem utilities (`dd`, `df`, `mount`, `umount`, `sync`)
- System utilities (`uname`, `hostname`, `arch`)

In addition to these types of programs, the `/bin` directory might also contain GNU utilities like `gzip` and `gunzip`.

The `/sbin` directory is used to hold essential maintenance or system programs such as the following:

- `fsck`
- `fdisk`

- `mkfs`
- `shutdown`
- `lilo`
- `init`

The main difference between the programs stored in `/bin` and `/sbin` is that the programs in `/sbin` are executable only by root.

/etc

The `/etc` directory is normally used to store the systemwide configuration files required by many programs. Some of the important files in `/etc` are as follows:

- `passwd`
- `shadow`
- `fstab`
- `hosts`
- `motd`
- `profile`
- `shells`
- `services`
- `lilo.conf`

The first two files in this list, `/etc/passwd` and `/etc/shadow`, are files that define the authorized users for a system. The `/etc/passwd` file contains all of the information about a user except for the encrypted password, which is contained in `/etc/shadow`. This is done for security reasons. Manually editing these files is not recommended. To add or change user information, follow the procedures covered in Chapter 19, "User Accounts and Logins."

The next file on the list, `/etc/fstab`, contains a list of devices that the system knows how to mount automatically. A line from this file looks something like the following:

```
/dev/hda1        /                  ext2     defaults 1 1
```

The first part, `/dev/hda1`, indicates the device to mount (in this case the first partition of the internal hard drive, `hda`). The second part, `/`, indicates where to mount the device. The entry, `ext2`, indicates what type of filesystem the device contains, while the rest of the entries are mount options (the default options are specified for this device).

This file will contain at least two other entries, one for `swap` and another for `/proc`. On many systems, `/etc/fstab` also contains entries for CD-ROMs, floppy disks, Zip disks, and other mountable media.

To add, delete, or change mount information, use Red Hat's `fstool`, covered in Chapter 11.

The file `/etc/hosts` contains a list of IP addresses and the corresponding hostnames (and aliases). This list is used to resolve the IP address of a machine when its name is given. A sample entry might look like the following:

```
10.8.11.2        kanchi
```

`/etc/motd` is the file in which the system administrator puts the message of the day (hence the name `motd`). Usually, it contains information related to the system such as scheduled downtime or upgrades of software, but it can contain anything. The contents of this file are usually displayed at login.

`/etc/profile` is the default initialization file for users whose shell is either `sh`, `ksh`, or `bash`. Mostly it is used for settings variables like `PATH` and `PS1`, along with things like the default `umask`. It is not meant to be used in place of personal initialization files and should be kept small because it is used by scripts as well as users.

The file `/etc/shells` also pertains to shells. It is a list of "approved" shells for users. One of its primary uses is to prevent people from accidentally changing their shells to something unusable.

In `/etc/services` is a list of all of the services that run on the various ports on the system. The entries will look something like the following:

```
telnet          23/tcp
http            80/tcp
```

The first entry is the name of the service, the second entry is the port on which the service runs, and the final entry is the type of service. From the preceding lines you can see that Telnet runs on port 23 and HTTP runs on port 80, which are the standard ports for those services.

The last file on the list is `/etc/lilo.conf`. This file contains a description of the behavior of the system at boot time, along with listing all the bootable images on the system.

There are also two important subdirectories in `/etc`:

- `X11`
- `rc.d`

The `X11` subdirectory of `/etc` contains the configuration files for the X server and the various window managers like `fvwm`, `mwm`, and `twm`. Most window manager packages will add their configuration files into a directory located under `/etc/X11`. An exception to this is a Red Hat Linux installation with the CDE (Common Desktop Environment) installed. The CDE is covered in Chapter 6, "Common Desktop Environment."

The `rc.d` subdirectory of `/etc` contains initialization scripts that run when Linux is loaded or shut down. Some of the scripts contain commands to load modules, while others handle general boot behavior.

In addition to the files discussed, many other configuration files are found in the /etc directory. The process of modifying and maintaining configuration files is covered in Chapter 15, "Essential System Administration," and Chapter 16, "Advanced System Administration."

/home

The /home directory is where all the home directories for all the users on a system are stored. This includes home directories for actual users (people) and for users such as HTTPD. An interesting feature of Linux is that the home directory for the user root is usually stored as /home/root. This is different from many UNIX systems, where / is the home directory for the user root.

/mnt

By convention, the /mnt directory is the directory under which removable media such as CD-ROMs, floppy disks, Zip disks, or Jaz disks are mounted. Usually the /mnt directory contains a number of subdirectories, each of which is a mount point for a particular device type. On my system, the /mnt directory looks like the following:

```
cdrom/      floppy/     zip/
```

By using subdirectories under /mnt to house all the mounted removable media, you keep the / directory clean.

/tmp and /var

The /tmp and /var directories are used to hold temporary files or files with constantly varying content.

The /tmp directory is usually a dumping ground for files that only need to be used briefly and can afford to be deleted at any time. It usually is quite unstructured, but on a multiuser system, most users abide by the convention of creating a personal directory (named the same as their username) in /tmp for storing their temporary files. The most common use of /tmp (other than as a location for throwaway files) is as a starting point for building and installing programs.

The /var directory is a bit more structured than /tmp and usually looks something like the following:

```
catman/    local/     log/       nis/       run/       tmp/
lib/       lock/      named/     preserve/  spool/     yp/
```

Of these directories, the /var/log directory is one of the directories with which all users should be familiar, as most of the messages generated by the system are stored in it. On my system, /var/log contains the following files:

```
./            dmesg         maillog       savacct       spooler       wtmp
../           httpd/        messages      secure        usracct
cron          lastlog       pacct         sendmail.st   uucp/
```

Of these files, the following are very helpful when attempting to diagnose system problems:

- `dmesg` contains the messages displayed when the system was last booted.
- `messages` contains all the messages displayed at boot time since the system was first booted.

/usr

By convention, the `/usr` directory is where most programs and files directly relating to users of the system are stored. It is in some ways a miniversion of the `/` directory. On my system, the `/usr` directory looks like the following:

```
X11/            etc/             libexec/        share/
X11R6/          games/           local/          src/
X386@           i486-linuxaout/  man/            tmp@
bin/            include/         openwin/
dict/           info/            opt/
doc/            lib/             sbin/
```

The contents of the various directories are briefly described in the following paragraphs.

The `/usr/bin` and `/usr/sbin` directories hold the vast majority of the executables available on a system. The function and type of the executables placed into these directories follow the same general convention as for `/bin` and `/sbin`.

The `/usr/opt` directory under Linux is equivalent to the `/opt` directory in Solaris. It is the location where optional software packages are usually installed. For example, the Caldera Internet-Office Suite is usually installed into `/usr/opt`.

The `/usr/X11` and `/usr/X11R6` directories and subdirectories contain all of the X Window–related files, such as man pages, libraries, and executables. Most Red Hat Linux systems contain only `/usr/X11R6`, the 6 revision of the X Window version 11, but some older systems might contain `/usr/X11R5` or even `/usr/X11R4`, the 5 and 4 revisions of X Window version 11.

Although X is the primary windowing environment under Linux, most installations will also contain the `/usr/openwin` directory for storing files that use open windows. This includes programs like `olwm`, `textedit`, and `workman`.

The `/usr/local` directory is the location where local programs, man pages, and libraries are installed. At many sites, most of the directories in `/usr` are kept the same on every computer, but anything that needs to be installed on a particular machine is placed in `/usr/local`, thus identifying those files as local files. This makes maintenance of large numbers of systems easier.

Finally, one of the most useful directories under `/usr` is `/usr/dict`. This is where the local dictionary, called `/usr/dict/words`, for the system is stored. Most versions of `/usr/dict/words` contain about 25,000 words, but some can be as large as a hundred thousand or more.

RPM

One of the most powerful and innovative utilities available in Red Hat Linux is RPM, the Red Hat Package Manager. It can be used to install, uninstall, upgrade, query, verify, and build software packages.

A software package built with RPM is an archive of files and some associated information, such as a name, a version, and a description. A few of the advantages of RPM packages over the traditional `tar.gz` method of software distribution are as follows:

- Upgrading—A new version of the software can be installed without losing customization files.
- Uninstalling—A software package that installs files in several locations can be cleanly removed.
- Verification—Once installed, a package can be verified to be in working order.
- Querying—Information about what package a file belongs to can be easily obtained.

In addition to these features, RPM is available for many flavors of Linux and UNIX, making it one of the emerging utilities for distributing software packages.

Major Modes and Common Options

The major modes in which RPM can be run are the following:

- Install (`rpm -i`)
- Uninstall (`rpm -e`)
- Query (`rpm -q`)
- Verify (`rpm -V`)

The options to invoke the major modes are given in parentheses. These major modes are covered in detail in subsequent sections.

All of these major modes understand the following options:

`-vv`	Prints out all debugging information; useful to see what exactly RPM is doing
`--quiet`	Prints out very little information, only error messages

In addition to these, there are a few other "minor" modes that are useful. These are as follows:

- Version (`rpm --version`)
- Help (`rpm --help`)
- Showrc (`rpm --showrc`)
- Rebuilddb (`rpm --rebuilddb`)

The version mode, invoked as

```
rpm --version
```

prints out a line containing version information, similar to this:

```
RPM version 2.3.11
```

The help mode prints out an extensive help message and is invoked as follows:

```
rpm --help
```

Because the message is long, it is handy to have a large `xterm` or to pipe the output to `more`. To get a shorter help message, just type

```
rpm
```

This prints out a usage message. The showrc mode

```
rpm --showrc
```

prints out a list of variables that can be set in the files `/etc/rpmrc` and `$HOME/.rpmrc`. The default values are adequate for most installations.

The rebuilddb option is used to rebuild the database that RPM uses to keep track of which packages are installed on a system. It is invoked as follows:

```
rpm --rebuilddb
```

The database files are usually stored `in /var/lib/rpm/`. In most cases the database files do not need to be rebuilt very often.

Installing Packages

One of the major uses of RPM is to install software packages. The general syntax of an `rpm` install command is

```
rpm -i [options] [packages]
```

where *`options`* can be one of the common options given earlier or one of the install options covered in the following list, and *`packages`* is the name of one or more RPM package files. Some of the install options are as follows:

`-v`	Prints out what RPM is doing.
`-h` or `--hash`	Prints out 50 hash marks (#) as the package is installed.
`--percent`	Prints out percentages as files are extracted from the package.
`--test`	Goes through a package install, but does not install anything; mainly used to catch conflicts.

`--excludedocs`	Prevents the installation of files marked as documentation, such as man pages.
`--includedocs`	Forces files marked as documentation to be installed; this is the default.
`--nodeps`	No dependency checks are performed before installing a package.
`--replacefiles`	Allows for installed files to be replaced with files from the package being installed.
`--replacepkgs`	Allows for installed packages to be replaced with the packages being installed.
`--oldpackage`	Allows for a newer version of an installed package to be replaced with an older version.
`--force`	Forces a package to be installed.

When giving options to RPM, regardless of the mode, all the single-letter options can be lumped together in one block. For example, the command

```
rpm -i -v -h kernel-2.0.30-3.i386.rpm
```

is equivalent to

```
rpm -ivh kernel-2.0.30-3.i386.rpm
```

All options starting with `--` must be given separately, however.

Now let's look at a couple of examples of installing RPM packages. The first example installs `vim` (the improved version of `vi`) from the package:

```
vim-4.5-2.i386.rpm
```

This package follows the standard naming convention for RPM packages, which is

```
name-version-release.arch.rpm
```

where *`name`* is the package's name, *`version`* is the package's version, *`release`* is the package's release level, *`arch`* is the hardware architecture the package is for, and `rpm` is the default extension. This naming scheme is quite handy because some of the essential information about a particular package can be determined from just looking at its name.

For the `vim` package, say you are installing `vim` version 4.5, release 2 for a computer with the i386 architecture. Let's go ahead and install this package. With the Red Hat CD-ROM on `/mnt/cdrom`, the package you want is

```
/mnt/cdrom/RedHat/RPMS/vim-4.5-2.i386.rpm
```

First, `cd` into the appropriate directory; then to install it type the following at the prompt (`#`):

```
# rpm -ivh vim-4.5-2.i386.rpm
```

As the package is installed, the output will look like the following:

```
vim                           ################
```

When the install is finished, 50 hash marks will be displayed.

In this example I used the hash character (#) to indicate the root prompt because only root can properly install packages for an entire system. If you try to install this package as a user other than root, an error similar to the following will be generated:

```
failed to open //var/lib/rpm/packages.rpm
error: cannot open //var/lib/rpm/packages.rpm
```

Now to install the X11 version of `vim` from the package:

```
/mnt/cdrom/RedHat/RPMS/vim-X11-4.2-8.i386.rpm
```

If you try using

```
rpm -ivh vim-X11-4.2-8.i386.rpm
```

you will get the following error:

```
package vim-X11-4.2-8 is already installed
error: vim-X11-4.2-8.i386.rpm cannot be installed
```

To install this package, use the `--replacepkgs` option:

```
rpm -ivh --replacepkgs vim-X11-4.5-2.i386.rpm
```

Occasionally, the files that one package installs conflicts with the files of a previously installed package. If you had `vim` version 4.2 installed, the following message would have been generated:

```
/bin/vim conflicts with file from vim-4.2-8
/usr/share/vim/vim_tips.txt conflicts with file from vim-4.2-8
error: vim-4.5-2.i386.rpm cannot be installed
```

If you wanted to install these files anyway, the `--replacefiles` option could be added to the command.

Another type of conflict that is sometimes encountered is a dependency conflict. This happens when a package that is being installed requires certain other packages to function correctly. For example, when I try to install the package

```
# rpm -ivh dosemu-0.66.2-1.i386.rpm
```

I get the following dependency errors:

```
failed dependencies:
kernel >= 2.0.28 is needed by dosemu-0.66.2-1
dosemu = 0.64.1 is needed by xdosemu-0.64.1-1
```

This indicates two things. I need to upgrade to my kernel 2.0.28, and if I install a newer version of `dosemu`, I will also need to install a newer version of `xdosemu`. Although it is usually not a good idea to ignore dependency problems, using the `--nodeps` option will cause RPM to ignore these errors and install the package.

Upgrading Packages

RPM's upgrade mode provides an easy way to upgrade existing software packages to newer versions. Upgrade mode is similar to install mode:

```
rpm -U [options] [packages]
```

`options` can be any of the install options or any of the general options.

Here is an example of how to upgrade packages. On my system I am currently running `emacs` version 19.31, but I want to upgrade to the newer `emacs` version 19.34. To upgrade, I use the following command:

```
# rpm -Uvh emacs-19.34-4.i386.rpm
```

The upgrade mode is really a combination of two operations, uninstall and install. First, RPM uninstalls any older versions of the requested package and then installs the newer version. If an older version of the package does not exist, RPM will simply install the requested package.

An additional advantage of upgrade over manual install and uninstall is that upgrade automatically saves configuration files. For these reasons, some people prefer to use upgrade rather than install for all package installations.

Uninstalling Packages

The uninstall mode of RPM provides for a clean method of removing files belonging to a software package from many locations.

Many packages install files in `/etc`, `/usr`, and `/lib`, so removing a package can be confusing, but with RPM an entire package can be removed as follows:

```
rpm -e [options] [package]
```

`options` is one of the options listed later in this section, and *`package`* is the name of the package to be removed. For example, if I want to remove the package for `dosemu`, the command is as follows:

```
rpm -e dosemu
```

The name specified here for the package is just the name of the package, not the name of the file that was used to install the package. If I had asked for

```
rpm -e dosemu-0.64.1-1.i386.rpm
```

the following error would have been generated:

```
package dosemu-0.64.1-1.i386.rpm is not installed
```

Another common error encountered while trying to uninstall packages is a dependency error. This occurs when a package that is being uninstalled has files required by another package. For example, when I try to remove `dosemu` from my system, I get the following error:

```
removing these packages would break dependencies:
dosemu = 0.64.1 is needed by xdosemu-0.64.1-1
```

This means that the package `xdosemu` would not function properly if the package `dosemu` were removed. If I still wanted to remove this package, RPM could be given the `--nodeps` option to make it ignore dependency errors.

The other useful option is the `--test` option, which causes RPM to go through the motions of removing a package without actually removing anything. Usually there is no output from an uninstall, so the `-vv` option is given along with the `--test` option to see what would happen during an uninstall. For example,

```
rpm -e -vv --test xdosemu
```

produces the following output on my system:

```
D: counting packages to uninstall
D: opening database in //var/lib/rpm/
D: found 1 packages to uninstall
D: uninstalling record number 1650520
D: running preuninstall script (if any)
D: would remove files test = 1
D: /usr/man/man1/xtermdos.1 - would remove
D: /usr/man/man1/xdos.1 - would remove
D: /usr/bin/xtermdos - would remove
D: /usr/bin/xdos - would remove
D: /usr/X11R6/lib/X11/fonts/misc/vga.pcf - would remove
D: running postuninstall script (if any)
D: script found - running from file /tmp/02695aaa
+ PATH=/sbin:/bin:/usr/sbin:/usr/bin:/usr/X11R6/bin
+ export PATH
+ [ -x /usr/X11R6/bin/mkfontdir ]
+ cd /usr/X11R6/lib/X11/fonts/misc
+ /usr/X11R6/bin/mkfontdir
D: would remove database entry
```

As you can see, the files that would have been removed are clearly indicated in the output.

Querying Packages

The querying mode in RPM allows for determining the various attributes of packages. The basic syntax for querying packages is

```
rpm -q [options] [packages]
```

where *options* is one or more of the query options listed later in this section. The most basic query is one similar to

```
rpm -q kernel
```

On my system, this prints out the following line for the kernel package:

```
kernel-2.0.27-5
```

In a manner similar to uninstall, RPM's query mode uses the name of the package, not the name of the file that the package came in, for queries.

Now for a few more sample queries. If you wanted to get a list of all the files "owned" by the kernel package, you can use the `-l` option:

```
rpm -ql kernel
```

This outputs the following list of files on my system:

```
/boot/System.map-2.0.27
/boot/module-info
/boot/vmlinuz-2.0.27
```

In addition to getting a list of the files, you can determine their state by using the `-s` option:

```
rpm -qs kernel
```

This option gives the following information about the state of files in my kernel package:

```
normal        /boot/System.map-2.0.27
normal        /boot/module-info
normal        /boot/vmlinuz-2.0.27
```

If any of these files reported a state of `missing`, there would probably be problems with the package.

In addition to the state of the files in a package, the documentation files and the configuration files can be listed. To list the documentation that comes with the `dosemu` package, use the following:

```
rpm -qd dosemu
```

This produces the following list:

```
/usr/man/man1/dos.1
```

To get the configuration files for the same package, you would use the following query:

```
rpm -qc dosemu
```

This results in the following list:

```
/etc/dosemu.conf
/var/lib/dosemu/hdimage
```

In addition to these queries, complete information about a package can be determined by using the `info` option. For example,

```
rpm -qi kernel
```

gives the following information about the installed kernel package:

```
Name        : kernel              Distribution: Red Hat Linux Vanderbilt
Version     : 2.0.27              Vendor: Red Hat Software
Release     : 5                   Build Date: Sat Dec 21 21:06:28 1996
Install date: Thu Jul 17 14:10:52 1997    Build Host: porky.redhat.com
Group       : Base/Kernel         Source RPM: kernel-2.0.27-5.src.rpm
Size        : 565900
Summary     : Generic linux kernel
Description : This package contains the Linux kernel that is
➥used to boot and run your system. It contains few device
➥drivers for specific hardware. Most hardware is instead
➥supported by modules loaded after booting.
```

Here is a summary of the query options:

`-l`	Lists all the files in a package
`-s`	Lists the state of files in a package
`-d`	Lists all files in a package that are marked as documentation
`-c`	Lists all files in a package that are marked as configuration
`-i`	Lists the complete information for a package

If any of these options, except for `-i`, are given along with a `-v` option, then the files are listed in `ls -l` format. For example,

```
rpm -qlv kernel
```

outputs the following:

```
-rw-r--r---     root     root     104367 Dec 21 21:05 /boot/System.map-2.0.27
-rw-r--r---     root     root      11773 Dec 21 21:05 /boot/module-info
-rw-r--r---     root     root     449760 Dec 21 21:05 /boot/vmlinuz-2.0.27
```

In addition to the preceding query options, RPM also understands the following query options:

`-a`	Lists all installed packages
`-f` *file*	Lists the package that owns the specified file
`-p` *package*	Lists the package name of the specified package

Verifying Packages

Verifying packages is an easy way to determine if there are any problems with an installation. In verification mode, RPM compares information about an installed package against information about the original package, which is stored in the package database at install time.

The basic syntax for verifying a package is as follows:

```
rpm -V [package]
```

If a package is verified correctly, RPM will not output anything. If RPM detects a difference between the installed package and the database record, it outputs an 8-character string, where tests that fail are represented by a single character and tests that pass are represented by a period (.). The characters for failed tests are as follows:

Character	*Failed Test*
5	MD5 Sum
S	File Size
L	Symlink
T	Mtime
D	Device
U	User
G	Group
M	Mode (permissions and file type)

For example, on my system, verifying the `bash` package using

```
rpm -V bash
```

fails as follows:

```
.M..L...  /bin/bash
....L...  /bin/sh
```

This indicates that the size of my `bash` is different from the information stored in the database. This is okay on my system because I have recompiled `bash`.

In addition it is possible to use the query option `-f` to verify a package containing a particular file, which is helpful when diagnosing problems with programs. For example, if `ksh` were behaving peculiarly,

```
rpm -Vf /bin/ksh
```

would verify the package that `ksh` came in. If any of the tests fail, you will be closer to understanding the source of the problems.

Introduction to glint

The most common way most users interact with RPM is via `glint`, the graphical Linux installation tool. `glint` is an X-based interface for RPM that allows for installing, uninstalling, querying, and verifying packages via a graphical "File Manager" interface.

`glint` is accessible from the command line or the Control Panel application that comes with Red Hat Linux. To launch `glint`, simply type

```
glint
```

at the prompt. `glint` accepts no command-line options. When `glint` is loading, a message such as

```
Glint Graphical Package Manager -- version 2.1.5 Copyright (d) 1996
➥Red Hat Software
➥This may be freely redistributed under the terms of the GNU Public License
```

will appear in the terminal window. After `glint` has loaded, a window similar to Figure 14.1 will appear.

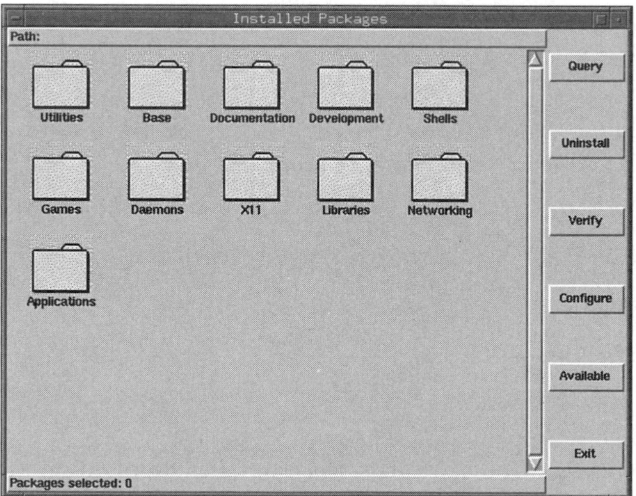

FIGURE 14.1.
The primary `glint` *window.*

From this window, different packages can be selected and queried, verified, uninstalled, or installed. When you click the Available button, all packages available for installation from the default location (`/mnt/cdrom/RedHat/RPMS`) will be listed in the Available Packages window, as shown in Figure 14.2.

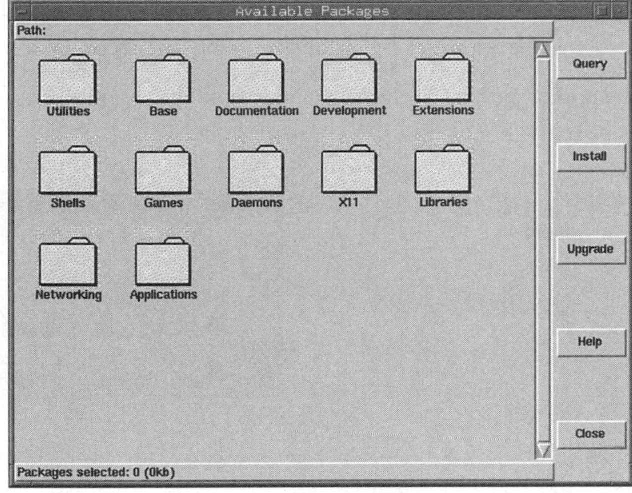

FIGURE 14.2.
The Available Packages `glint` *window.*

By navigating through the folders, you can select and install different packages. As an example, let's take a look at installing the `vim` package.

To install the `vim` package, first launch `glint`; then in the Installed Packages window, click the Available button. When the Available Packages window appears, select the Applications folder and then the Editors folder. Then, click the package `vim-4.5-2`, which becomes highlighted (see Figure 14.3).

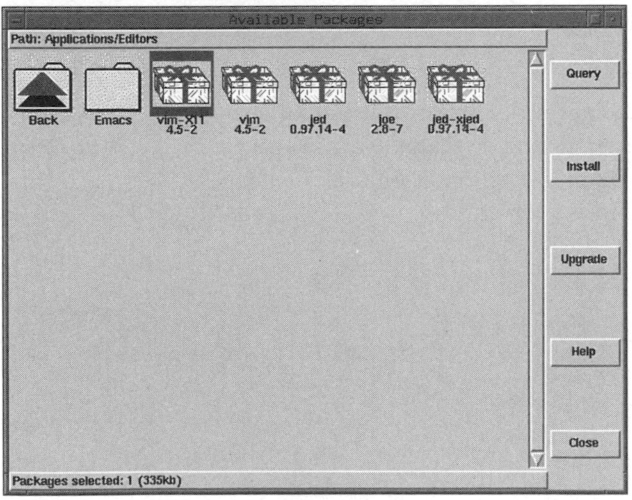

FIGURE 14.3.
Available Packages with `vim` *selected.*

When a package is highlighted, it can be installed by clicking the Install button. You can install many packages at once by highlighting more than one package.

When you click the Install button, the Installing dialog box appears (see Figure 14.4). This dialog shows the progress of the installation.

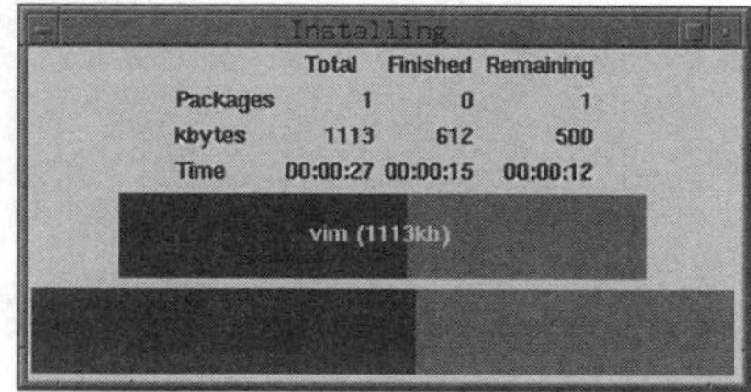

FIGURE 14.4.
The Installing dialog.

When `vim` has been installed, it will be removed from the Available Packages window.

In this example, I assumed that the available packages were stored in the default location mentioned earlier. Often that is not the case. You can change this location by first clicking the Configure button in the primary `glint` window (refer to Figure 14.1). Then, enter the different location where the package files are located in the Configuration dialog that appears (see Figure 14.5).

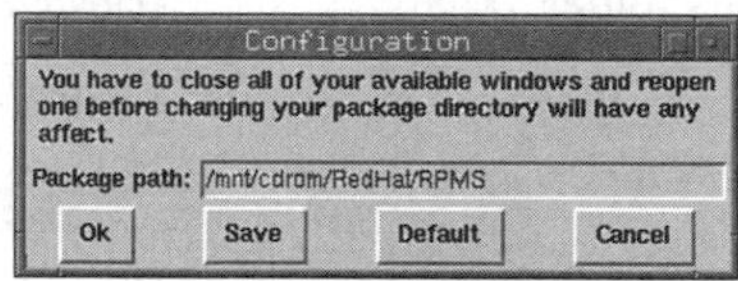

FIGURE 14.5.
Changing the package location.

`glint` also provides a nice front end for querying packages. `glint` executes most of the queries automatically and displays the results in a tabular form. For example, a query of the `vim` package looks similar to Figure 14.6.

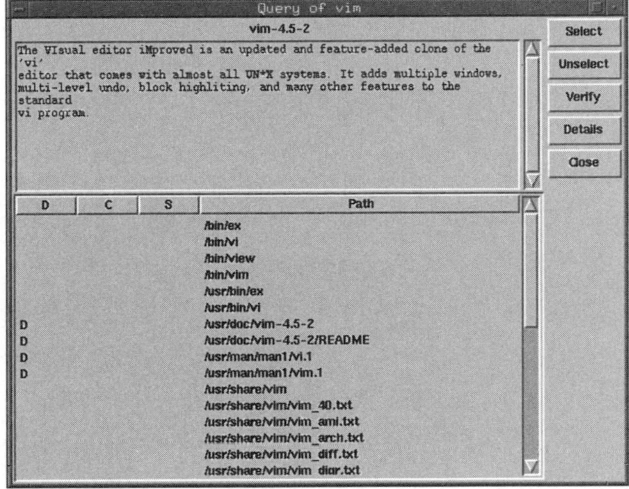

FIGURE 14.6.
Query of the `vim` *package.*

In this format, the description of the package and all its files marked by type are clearly visible. In some respects, it is easier to use than the command-line queries.

Summary

This chapter covers the basic structure of a Red Hat Linux installation along with using RPM, the Red Hat Package Manager. From this starting point, the rest of the Linux world waits to be explored and enjoyed.

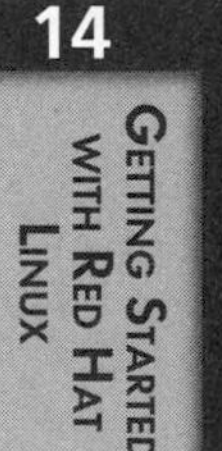

CHAPTER

Essential System Administration

by David Pitts

IN THIS CHAPTER

Today, system administrators are at a premium. They are demanding high salaries, and are receiving them. It does not matter whether the systems are Windows NT, Novell NetWare, or UNIX. Part of the reason for this premium is simply supply and demand. The number of knowledgeable system administrators is low, and the demand for them is high. The other reason for this premium I have already alluded to. This reason is "*knowledgeable* system administrators." The market is becoming flooded with system administrators with little skills or training. People are entering the field because of the high pay. Many of them come with a willingness to learn, but unfortunately, training them is a several-year and multi-thousand dollar investment that corporations are incurring with no guarantee of a return on their investment. This is particularly true when it comes to UNIX systems.

UNIX is a very large and complicated operating system. It is also very powerful. Every aspect of the system is under the direct control of the system administrator. But, what is it a system administrator does? Here is a breakdown of the tasks that a system administrator must deal with on a day-to-day basis:

- Account management
- Assisting programmers
- Assisting users with problems
- Data backup and restoration
- Meetings, both formal and informal
- Problem determination
- Software installation and configuration
- System automation
- System configuration and management
- System integrity and other security issues
- System startup and shutdown
- User education

Handling the All-Powerful Root Account

Although system administrators do all the things in the preceding list, they don't do them as system administrators, per se; they do them as a special user called root, also known as the superuser (`su`). Root is a special user account that is on every UNIX system. This special user has full access to the system. The system ignores all permissions when dealing with root, providing read, write, and execute permissions to every file and device known to the system.

What does this mean in practical terms? This means that the command `rm -r /` run as root will delete the entire system. It also means that root has access to all data. This is important when it comes to backing up and restoring data, performing systems maintenance, and even for security tasks. There are many commands that, with certain parameters, would be ideal to hand off to the users; bringing up print queues is a good example. Unfortunately, the same command, with different parameters, takes down the print queues or could delete other users' printouts. The root account is all powerful. It can be used to keep the system up and running as a stable environment; it can also destroy the system and all data contained therein.

It is because of this ability to manipulate the system that, as the system administrator, you should take great care when you are using the root account—not only when you are dealing with the system, but also when you are dealing with passwords. A password is the only identification that the computer has for determining if people attempting to log on with a certain user ID are who they say they are. Thus, anyone who gets root's password can control the system. This also means that a Red Hat Linux system left unsecured can be booted from disk and the root password changed.

That is correct—you can change the root password this easily:

1. Boot the system with the boot disk.
2. Mount the root partition.
3. Edit the `/etc/passwd` file to remove any password for root.
4. Reboot from the hard disk.
5. Set a new password for root.

This is nice, and convenient, if the Red Hat system happens to be on a system in someone's home with no other purpose than teaching the user how to use UNIX. But this is a problem for a Red Hat system being used as an ISP in an unsecured location in a public building.

Because of the power of the root account, each user on the system who has access to the root password should not log in as root. When a task that requires root authority is needed, the users should `su` to root (this is explained in greater detail in Chapter 19, "User Accounts and Logins"), perform the task, and then return to their normal account. This procedure helps to ensure two things. First, it helps to keep users from accidentally performing actions that they did not intend to, but which are allowed by root. Second, it provides logging. The `/etc/login.defs` is the file that defines, among other things, the `su` log, the failed login log, and the list of who logged in last. Although logging does not stop an action, it will at least help to determine who was performing the action.

Maintaining the System—Implementing Changes

The overall function of any system administrator is to keep the system up and running. Not only does this mean applying the latest updates of software, adding and replacing hardware, and adding new software, but it also means being part soothsayer, part instructor, and part detective. The system administrator must

- Understand how things work
- Know where to find things

- Plan processes
- Have a back-out plan and know when to use it
- Make changes in small increments
- Test all changes
- Communicate effectively and in a timely fashion

Each of these seven items can, in and of themselves, be daunting. For example, it takes years of training and practice to understand how everything works, and, just about the time you figure everything out, it changes. The learning curve is steep and the changes are inevitable, but does this mean that you ignore this area? Of course it doesn't. Without an understanding of how things work, none of the other items can be accomplished effectively. As a system administrator, you must be careful not to spend too little or too much time in any one of these areas.

Fortunately, the first two items can be documented and referred to at a later time. As two of the primary reasons for this book, they are covered throughout it. The other five items are examined in more detail in the following sections.

Planning Processes

Red Hat is a complicated operating system. Many files and processes are dependent upon other files and processes. Therefore, when you are preparing to make a change to the system, it only makes sense to define a process for the task. The amount of planning and documenting required for the task should, obviously, depend on the complexity of the task. It should, though, at least touch on the following items.

First, some kind of description of the task should be listed. Second, there should be documentation of how this task is going to affect the system, including, but not limited to, the files and processes affected. The third item should be a test plan. Finally, there should be some way to back out of the change—to restore the system to its previous configuration.

Creating a Back-Out Plan

Creating the back-out plan is the most important part of making a change to a system. In determining the back-out plan, consider how long the task will take, how long testing will take, and how long it will take to back out of the current process and return to the former process. An important part of the back-out plan is a decision point—a predetermined point when you decide to continue with the current process or to implement the back-out plan. This could be a decision based on a time limit, a lack of system resources, malfunctioning equipment, poorly written software, or any other problem that requires returning to the old process.

Making Changes in Small Increments

It is easier to back out of small changes than it is to back out of big and multiple changes. It is also easier to plan a series of smaller changes than it is to plan one large change. Diagnosing problems is considerably easier when fewer things are changed than when a large number of things are changed. If a task can be broken down into several small tasks, each with individual test plans and back-out plans, then the job becomes much simpler.

Developing a Test Plan

Each change to a system needs to be tested. Even a small change, such as moving a file from one location to another, should have a test plan. The test plan should be appropriate to the task. In the example of moving a file, the test plan could be as simple as the following:

1. Are there users or processes dependent upon the file?
2. If yes, can the users or processes still access the file?
3. If no, then make it available (change permissions, add directory to path, create link, and so on).
4. Does it do what it is supposed to do?
5. If yes, okay; if no, then fix it.

A task as simple as moving a file requires five steps to properly test. Imagine the difficulty of testing a large change.

Communicating Effectively and in a Timely Manner

Communicating the result of changes to the system is the final element of a successful system change. Success does not necessarily mean that the task was completed without errors. In fact, it could mean that the task could not be completed and the back-out plan was successfully implemented. Communication also means letting the users know in advance of a change that affects them.

Communication, on a larger level, is any information passed between one user and another, be it one-way communication or a dialog back and forth. Although it is imperative to have this communication before, during, and after a system change, communication does not have to nor should it stop there. Some system administrators communicate birthdays, local news, jokes, and just about anything else to users on a regular basis.

Many different tools can be used to communicate to users. In order to decide which tool to use, you need to determine the purpose of the communication. For example, if you are about to shut down a system, then that information needs to be communicated only to the users currently logged on to the system. If, on the other hand, you want to announce a birthday, then that information needs to be announced either to all users, or to all users who log on to the system that day. Or, perhaps a user is remotely logged on to a system and is having problems. A user with only one phone line cannot call in the problem without disconnecting. This situation requires an entirely different form of communication. In the following sections, several different tools for communication are discussed; some are commands, and others are concepts. In addition, examples are given to illustrate which tool would be best given the particular need. The following are the communication tools that are discussed in the upcoming sections:

- write: One-way communication with another user currently logged on the system.
- Echo to the device: One-way communication with another user currently logged on the system.
- wall: One-way communication with all other users currently logged on the system.
- talk: Interactive two-way communication with another user currently logged on the system.
- mesg: Controls message reception (talk and write) from other nonroot users currently logged on the system.
- motd: Message of the day received by users when they log on the system.
- Electronic mail: For sending messages to and receiving messages from users whether or not they are currently logged on the system.
- Pre-login message /etc/issue: The message is displayed on a terminal at time of login. User does not have to log on to see this message.

write

The write command enables a user to write a message to a terminal. The syntax is the command followed by the user ID of the person to whom you want to write. This places you in a write shell. Anything you type, until you hit Ctrl+C, will be echoed to that user's display. For example, I tried to write a message to my friend Rich, who was logged on to mk.net:

```
shell:/home/dpitts$ write rbowen
Hello Rich.  How are you today?
shell:/home/dpitts$
```

I didn't receive a reply.

I wasn't sure that I was doing it right, so, I tried to send a message to myself. Before I did, though, I turned off my mesg (mesg n). Here's what happened:

```
shell:/home/dpitts$ write dpitts
write: you have write permission turned off.
```

So, as a further test, I turned my mesg on (mesg y) and tried again:

```
shell:/home/dpitts$ mesg y
shell:/home/dpitts$ write dpitts

Message from dpitts@shell on ttyp0 at 20:10 ...
hello
hello
It enters what I type, and then echoes it back to me.
It enters what I type, and then echoes it back to me.
type <ctrl>c
type <ctrl>c
EOF
shell:/home/dpitts$
```

It is displaying everything that I type, and then echoing it back to me with `write`. That is why there are two identical lines. Had this gone to another terminal, then I would have seen what I typed, and when I hit Enter, it would have been sent to the user I had indicated.

You will notice that when I received the message, I got an initial line that told me who the message was from, the `tty` (terminal type) I was on, and the time (local to the server):

```
Message from dpitts@shell on ttyp0 at 20:10 ...
```

After I had held down the Ctrl key and pressed the C key, it disconnected me from the `write` program, indicated by the last line showing the end of the file (`EOF`).

NOTE

The `write` command writes to a terminal. The operating system doesn't think that it is input from the person being written to. Therefore, even in an editing session when text gets overwritten by the `write` command, the text is not really there. (On most editors Ctrl+L will restore the original screen.) This also means that a person cannot send commands to your terminal and have the computer execute them. It is strictly an output operation on the receiver's end.

Echo to the Device

Echoing to a device is similar to the `write` command. It has a similar result in that it writes output to a device (such as a terminal), but it uses a different mechanism, and thus, potentially, has different results. Let me see if I cannot send some output to someone's terminal as I log on to `mk.net`.

First, I look to see who is logged on:

```
shell:/home/dpitts$ who -u
root     ttyp1    Aug 13 10:01 00:05 (laptop.mk.net)
rbowen   ttyp2    Aug 13 17:29 00:44 (rbowen.is.lex.da)
dpitts   ttyp3    Aug 13 18:13   .   (d13.dialup.seane)
```

I am logged on (`dpitts`), the system administrator is logged on (`root`) and my good friend Rich Bowen is logged on (`rbowen`).

Next, I try to echo a comment and send it to my terminal type:

```
shell:/home/dpitts$ echo hello >/dev/tty/p3
bash: /dev/tty/p3: Not a directory
```

Oops, I did it wrong. I should have sent it to `/dev/ttyp3`, like this:

```
shell:/home/dpitts$ echo hello /dev/ttyp3
hello /dev/ttyp3
```

Nope, that was wrong again, although it did go to my terminal (because of the `echo` command); what I needed to do was to take the output and send it to the device `/dev/ttyp3`, not have it echo `/dev/ttyp3` back to me. Therefore, I should have done it like this:

```
shell:/home/dpitts$ echo hello> /dev/ttyp3
hello
```

Well, I finally got it right. Now to send it to Rich:

```
shell:/home/dpitts$ echo hello rich > /dev/ttyp2
bash: /dev/ttyp2: Permission denied
```

Permission denied! I wonder why that happened? Let me look at the permissions on his device:

```
shell:/home/dpitts$ ls -la /dev/ttyp2
crw--w----   1 rbowen   tty       3,   2 Aug 13 18:14 /dev/ttyp2
```

Well, I am not the owner of the device, and I am not in the group `tty`. The permissions for the rest of the world is no read, write, or execute. That is why I did not have permission to write to his terminal type.

So, even though I could `write` to `rbowen`, I did not have the permission to send something directly to his terminal.

wall

Sometimes administrators need to send a message to all the users currently logged on the system. This type of communication is typically used when the administrator needs to inform everyone about something that affects them. One time the `wall` command is typically used is when a system is about to shut down. The system administrator, instead of just blowing everyone off the system, might want to give them time to close their applications and save their data. The `wall` command stands for *write all.* Just like the `write` command, it only sends the text to the terminal, and the computer does not treat it as input from that user. The standard for `wall` is that it gets its information to display from a file. You can either do this or use a less than sign to send it information from the command line. In the following example, I have a small file that says "system shutting down!" The system was not really shutting down, so I made sure no one was logged on first (I didn't want to upset anyone). When a `wall` command is issued, the output goes to everyone currently logged in, including the person issuing the command.

Here's how I checked to see who was logged on:

```
shell:/home/dpitts$ who
dpitts   ttyp1    Aug 24 00:10 (d4.dialup.seanet)
```

Good, I was the only one logged on. Therefore, I issued the following command:

```
shell:/home/dpitts$ wall test

Broadcast Message from dpitts@shell
        (/dev/ttyp1) at 0:11 ...

system shutting down!
```

Note that the output tells that it is a Broadcast Message from `dpitts@shell`. It also tells what terminal I am on and the current time. It then gives the message. This information is important if something unfortunate were about to happen and you wanted to respond. If the output was anonymous (as it is when writing to a device), then the people receiving the information would not know to whom to respond.

talk

Writing to a device, either with `write`, `wall`, or literally to the device, is strictly one-way communication. This has its benefits, but also has its drawbacks. For example, what if the person receiving the data wanted to respond to the message? This could be done with a series of `write` commands, or with the `talk` command. The `talk` command notifies the second person that you want to talk. The command tells the other person what to type to finish initializing a `talk` session.

When the session is established, each person receives a split window. When the first person types information on the top window, it is echoed in the bottom window of the second person's display and vice versa. Also, displaying in both windows happens as each letter is typed. So, as one person types, the other person sees the information.

mesg

The `mesg` command was briefly mentioned in the discussion on `write`. The `mesg` command is used to allow or disallow others from writing or walling messages to you. Of course, root overrides this authority. The syntax for that command is `mesg y` or `mesg n`. The `y` parameter allows the communication and the `n` parameter disallows the communication with normal users.

motd

The `motd` (*message of the day*) command is a good way of passing information to whomever happens to log in that particular day. Typically, this is a reminder or an announcement of some type. Many companies use it to announce birthdays and other days of significance or to remind users of an event or telephone number to call. The `motd` command is a good way to communicate if the information is either not that important or is only important to a person if he or she logs in.

The `motd` is actually a file that has its contents displayed upon login. The file is kept in the `/etc` directory and is called `motd` (`/etc/motd`). For example, when I log in to `mk.net`, I get the following message:

```
Welcome to shell.mk.net!
```

Electronic Mail

Electronic mail is quickly becoming the medium from which much communication is passing between people these days. Many companies now consider e-mail to be a necessary element in accomplishing their business and spend great amounts of money making sure that people receive their electronic mail.

Electronic mail is a great way of communicating with others when time is not a critical factor. It can be sent to individuals or to entire lists of people. One of the benefits of electronic mail is that information can be passed to one or more individuals whenever they happen to log in and check their mail. Another benefit of electronic mail is that it can be sent to other people on other servers. If you are connected to the Internet, then the mail can be sent practically anywhere.

Pre-Login Message

The `/etc/issue` file contains the message that is displayed when a Telnet session is initiated. Following the issue statement, the session prompts for the login and password. This pre-login message is a good place to put something that you want everyone to see before they log in to the system. This could include things like a notice that printers are not working or an explanation of the purpose of the workstation that they are trying to log on to. The following example is the pre-login message I get when I log on to `mk.net`:

```
/etc/issue pre-login message
******************************
**  MK Computer Associates  **
******************************
**    UNIX shell server     **
**      (shell.mk.net)      **
******************************
** Login on this machine is **
**  restricted to web site  **
**  development activities  **
**     ONLY, thank you.     **
******************************

shell login:
```

As you can see from the pre-login message, this particular server is restricted to Web site development activities (`ONLY`). I know, in this case, that I should not use this server to perform engineering computations, for example.

Although the `/etc/issue` file can be as long as you want it to be, it is best to keep it short. The reason for this is that if it is too long people won't read it and it will scroll off their screen, and those who might have read it will probably not take the time to scroll back to see what, if anything, they missed.

Getting Help

One of the things that all system administrators realize at some point is that they cannot possibly know everything about the operating system; it is too complex and changes on a regular basis. A good system administrator, though, knows where to turn to get help. Because you are reading this book, you have at least started on your way to being a good system administrator. This book unleashes many of the tools and "secrets" of the Red Hat Linux operating system. With a book of this type, the index becomes very important. A book like this is not bought to be read from cover to cover, like a good C. S. Lewis novel, but is intended to be a resource guide—a place to go to find specific answers to specific questions. The following sections discuss the places you can turn to get help.

Man Pages

The man pages are like the Marines. They are your first lines of defense. Man pages contain the online version of the Red Hat UNIX reference manuals. They provide definitions and explanations of commands. In addition, they provide optional parameters for commands to perform specific functions. After all of the explanations are examples, and finally, other commands that are similar or relate to the command you looked up.

The format of the man pages is as follows:

- NAME
- SYNOPSIS
- DESCRIPTION
- COMMAND-LINE OPTIONS
- SEE ALSO
- BUGS

Over time, especially in Linux, people have customized the man pages to include other optional fields. Some of these fields are AUTHOR, SORT KEYS, UPDATING, and NOTES. The additions have been added to enhance the pages. For example, the AUTHOR section many times includes an e-mail address of the author. This is good if the command is not working as you expected it to. (Remember, none of Linux was taken from AT&T's UNIX, so small differences do exist, even in the "standard" commands.)

Probably the one thing to point out to new man page users is the syntax used for showing the SYNOPSIS of the command. There are several standards that are followed in writing commands that are used in the man pages. Here's the SYNOPSIS for the ps command:

```
SYNOPSIS
       ps  [-]  [lujsvmaxScewhrnu]  [txx]  [O[+¦-]k1[[+¦-]k2...]] [pids]
```

Anything in square brackets ([]) is optional. Note that the only thing not optional in this command is the command itself. Therefore, you can issue the ps command without any options, and you will receive a snapshot of the current processes.

The [-] means that the - is an optional argument. Many commercial versions of UNIX require a dash to indicate that what follows are arguments. This is not true for the Red Hat Linux version of the ps command. The next set of characters (between the next set of square brackets) indicates that any of these parameters can be added to the ps command. For example, a common set of parameters to add to the ps command is -la, which will display a long listing of all (including hidden) files.

The man pages are not a singular file or directory of Linux manuals. Instead, the man pages are a set of directories, each containing a section of the man pages. These directories contain the raw data for the man pages. In Red Hat Linux, there are eight sections of man pages. In addition, each section has corresponding `catn` subdirectories that store processed versions of the man pages. When a man page is accessed, the program that formats the man pages saves a copy of the formatted man page in the `catn` (`/etc/catn`) directories. This saves time in the future because the next time a user requests a man page for a specific subject, if that subject had been accessed before, then the formatting does not have to be repeated, but can be displayed from the previously formatted page. The following shows what information is found within each section:

Section	*Content*
1	User commands
2	System calls
3	Functions and library routines
4	Special files, device drivers, and hardware
5	Configuration files and file formats
6	Games and demos
7	Miscellaneous: character sets, filesystem types, datatype definitions, and so on
8	System administration commands and maintenance commands

The `man` command searches the sections in a predefined order: 1, 6, 8, 2, 3, 4, 5, and 7. It checks for commands first, followed by system calls and library functions, and then the other sections.

There is a special way of accessing the man pages so that all pages listing a certain piece of data are displayed. This is the keyword search for man pages (`man -k`). In order to use this searching capability, the command `catman -w` must be issued first. This command (which takes a little while) indexes the man pages so that the keyword search will work.

One of the benefits of man pages is that you can add your own local man pages. A friend of mine did not know how to do this, so he wrote a Perl program called `man.pl` that performed a similar function. It was a shame that he didn't have this book to tell him it could be done! Adding man pages is a wonderful way of documenting tools that you write for use at your site. Two directories are left blank for that purpose. They are the `mann` directory and the `cat` directory (`/usr/man/mann` and `/usr/man/cat`).

The simplest way of making a man page is to place some text in a file describing the command or topic. However, it is fairly easy to make a more elaborate page that looks like a normal man page. Man pages are designed for the `nroff` text formatter, and have text and `nroff` directives intermingled.

The best way to figure out what the different directives do is to look at a man page and see how it is laid out. To do this with Linux, you must first gunzip the file. Once gunzipped, the file can be looked at with a text editor. All the different directives begin with a period (or dot). Table 15.1 lists many of the `nroff` directives and an explanation of what they do.

Table 15.1. `nroff` directives.

Directive	*Explanation*
`.B`	Uses bold type for the text (entire line is bolded).
`.fi`	Starts autofilling the text (adjusting the text on the lines).
`.I`	Uses italicized type for the text (entire line is italicized).
`.IP`	Starts a new indented paragraph.
`.nf`	Stops autofilling the text (adjusting the text on the lines).
`.PP`	Starts a new paragraph.
`.R`	Uses Roman type for text given as its arguments.
`.SH`	Section heading (names are uppercase by convention).
`.TH`	Title heading (arguments are command name and section).
`.TP`	Tagged paragraph (uses a hanging indent).
`.TP` *n*	The *n* specifies the amount to indent.

When testing the man page, you can simulate an actual man page call to the file with the following command:

```
$ nroff -man <file> ¦ more
```

The man pages are not the only place that a resourceful system administrator can turn for answers. There is also the Internet. Within the Internet there are e-mail, Web pages describing how to do things, and newsgroups.

E-mail

With e-mail, you can send questions to people that you know who are doing similar work. For example, when I get stuck writing Perl scripts, I send a note off to Rich. He drops everything and responds immediately to my questions (yeah, right!). The point is, there are those that you associate with who can assist you with your problems or point you on your way to success. If you don't know anyone who is working with Red Hat Linux, you can do two things. First, find new friends—obviously the ones you have are holding you back; and secondly, you can e-mail newsgroups.

Red Hat Mailing Lists and Newsgroups

Many mailing lists and newsgroups are available to assist you with your problems. After you have been doing Linux for a while, there might even be questions that you can answer. Newsgroups are a great source of information. Before I list newsgroups that are available to you, I want to first mention the Red Hat mailing lists (`http://www.redhat.com/support/mailing-lists`).

> **NOTE**
>
> A *newsgroup* is a place where postings are and you can go get them. When you are on a *mailing list*, you are sent postings either in bulk or as they come in.

These lists are maintained by Red Hat, and they are also monitored by Red Hat. Currently, there are thirteen different lists. Direct from Red Hat's Web page, here they are:

- `redhat-list`

  For the general discussion of topics related to Red Hat Linux.
- `redhat-digest`

  This is the digest version of the `redhat-list`. Instead of getting mail that goes to the `redhat-list` as individual messages, subscribers to this list receive periodic volumes that include several posts at once.
- `redhat-announce-list`

  This is the most important list. All Red Hat users should make it a point to subscribe. Here, security updates and new RPMs are announced. It is very low traffic and moderated for your convenience.
- `redhat-install-list`

  For the general discussion of installation-related topics only. This can include appropriate hardware, problems with hardware, package selection, and so on.
- `redhat-ppp-list`

  For the general discussion of PPP under Red Hat. This includes configuration, installation, changes, and so on.
- `redhat-devel-list`

  This is for general discussion of software development under Red Hat Linux. This is where Red Hat will announce the availability of alpha- and beta-quality software that is being made available for testing purposes (with the exception of RPM; it has its own list).

- `sparc-list`

  This is for SPARC-specific issues only. This can be kernel development, SILO, and so on.
- `axp-list`

  This is for alpha-specific issues only. This can be kernel development, MILO, and so on.
- `rpm-list`

  This is for discussion of RPM-related issues. This can be RPM usage in general, RPM development using `rpmlib`, RPM development using shell scripts, porting RPM to non-Linux architectures, and so on.
- `applixware-list`

  For Applixware discussion only. Mostly related to installation, usage, macro writing, and so on.
- `cde-list`

  For CDE discussion only. Mostly related to installation and usage.
- `forsale-list`

  This list is for posting for sale and wanted items of a computer nature. This includes software and hardware and should be limited to items that work with Linux.
- `post-only`

  This "list" is a fake list. It has no posting address, only a request address (`post-only-request@redhat.com`). You can subscribe to this list and then you will be allowed to post to any of the Red Hat mailing lists without receiving any mail from those lists. This is because Red Hat doesn't allow posts from folks who aren't subscribed to the list, but frequently people want to read the list via local gateways and so forth and don't need to subscribe themselves. This way you just subscribe to post-only and you are allowed to post to any list.

So, how do you subscribe? For each of the preceding lists there is a subscription address. It is the list address with `-request` on the end of it. For example, for `redhat-list`, you would send your subscription or unsubscription request to `redhat-list-request@redhat.com`. For the RPM list, you would use `rpm-list-request@redhat.com`. All you need to send is the word subscribe in the subject line of your message to subscribe, and unsubscribe in the subject line to unsubscribe. You can leave the body of the message empty.

NOTE

To unsubscribe from the `redhat-digest`, please send your request to `redhat-digest-request@redhat.com`, NOT `redhat-list-request`.

Other Newsgroups

Other newsgroups require a newsreader to read them. Most of the current browsers supply some kind of newsreader. There are somewhere around fifteen to twenty thousand newsgroups. Following is a list of some that are of interest to Linux users:

```
alt.os.linux.caldera                  alt.os.linux
alt.fido.linux                        alt.uu.comp.os.linux.questions
comp.os.linux.announce                comp.os.linux.advocacy
comp.os.linux.development.apps        comp.os.linux.answers
comp.os.linux.hardware                comp.os.linux.development.systems
comp.os.linux.misc                    comp.os.linux.m68k
comp.os.linux.setup                   comp.os.linux.networking
linux.act.680x0                       comp.os.linux.x
linux.act.apps                        linux.act.admin
linux.act.chaos_digest                linux.act.bbsdev
linux.act.configs                     linux.act.compression
linux.act.debian                      linux.act.c-programming
linux.act.doc                         linux.act.dec_alpha
linux.act.fsf                         linux.act.findo
linux.act.fsstnd                      linux.act.gcc
linux.act.ibcs2                       linux.act.interviews
linux.act.kernal                      linux.act.linux-bbs
linux.act.linuxnews                   linux.act.localbus
linux.act.mca                         linux.act.mips
linux.act.mumail                      linux.act.newbie
linux.act.normal                      linux.act.ftp
linux.act.hams                        linux.act.ibsc2
linux.act.japanese                    linux.act.laptops
linux.act.linuxbsd                    linux.act.linuxss
linux.act.lugnuts                     linux.act.mgr
linux.act.msdos                       linus.act.net
linux.act.new-channels                linux.act.nys
linux.act.oasg-trust                  linux.act.oi
linux.act.pkg                         linux.act.postgres
linux.act.ppp                         linux.act.promotion
```

linux.act.qag	linux.admin.isp
linux.act.serial	linux.act.scsi
linux.act.sound	linux.act.seyon
linux.act.sysvpkg-project	linux.act.svgalib
linus.act.term	linux.act.tape
linux.act.userfs	linux.act.tktools
linux.act.wabi	linux.act.uucp
linux.act.x11	linux.act.word

The preceding list consists of maybe a third of the actual newsgroups specifically dealing with Linux. Most of the others are similar to those listed. It is probably best to scan the newsgroups that you have access to for `Linux`.

In addition to newsgroups, there are myriad Web pages devoted to Linux, and specifically, Red Hat. When I performed a search on WebCrawler (`www.webcrawler.com`) for `Linux`, I got back 9107 documents; and searching on `Linux AND Redhat`, I got back 294 documents. With so many to choose from and considering the volatility of the Web, it might be helpful if I point out and briefly describe a few Web resources I feel will be around a while.

The first one, which should be obvious, is Red Hat's home page. It is located at `http://www.redhat.com`. It is, of course, the first place to look for any information concerning Red Hat Linux.

Another great source for information about Linux (as well as every other type of UNIX) is `http://www.ugu.com`. This is the UNIX Guru Universe page. According to the site's front page, it is "the largest single point UNIX resource on the Net!" This Web site is highly configurable and provides a great deal of information on everything of value to the UNIX community.

The Linux Documentation Project (`http://sunsite.unc.edu/LDP/linux.html`) has a tremendous number of links providing everything from general Linux information, to Linux user groups, to Linux development projects. Although I do not think there is much, if anything, unique about this site, it is complete. It has information on just about everything there is associated with Linux.

Knowing how much the Web changes on a day-to-day basis, I am reluctant to share any more Web sites. If you go to the three listed, I think that if they cannot answer your questions, they will, somewhere between the three, have a current link to the location that can.

Problem Solving—Logs

Many times, when trying to diagnose a problem, it is helpful to look at log files of various activities. As an example, consider the following scenario:

You are the administrator of a server connected to the Internet. When you try to log in with your user ID (after all, you don't log in as root, but su to root), you find that you cannot log in.

Perhaps the problem is as simple as you mistyped your password. In this case, a simple second attempt at logging in will fix the problem. Of course if that were the problem, you wouldn't be reading this book.

Perhaps you forgot your password. This is a common error, especially when a password has just been changed.

NOTE

Writing down new passwords is not a good idea as it gives other people access to your account.

If it was a forgotten password, you could simply log in as root (or get the system administrator) and change the password.

Perhaps someone logged on to your system, as you, and changed your password. How would you know this? This is one of the places where logs come in handy. Certain logs can be examined, depending upon the information needed. Probably the first file to check is the `login.access` file.

`login.access`

The `login.access` file is used to control login access (hence, its name). The file is nothing more than a table that is checked each time a person attempts to log in. The table is scanned for the first entry that matches the user/host or user/`tty` combination. The table is a colon-delimited list of permissions, users, and origins (host or `tty`).

The permission is either a plus sign (+) or a minus sign (-). A plus sign indicates that the user has permission to access, and a minus sign indicates that the user does not have permission to access.

The user is the user ID of the person either being restricted or allowed access to the machine from that location. The option `ALL` would indicate all users. The `ALL` option can be used in conjunction with the `EXCEPT` option. The `EXCEPT` option allows for certain users to be excluded from the `ALL` option. Groups can also be included as valid users. This would be a way of restricting or allowing access to the system for users who have similar job functions. The group file is searched only when the name does not match the user logged in. An interesting twist to this is that it does not check primary groups, but instead checks secondary groups in the `/etc/groups` file.

The origin is where the user is logging in from. The option `ALL` would indicated all locations. The `ALL` option can be used in conjunction with the `EXCEPT` option to allow exceptions to the `ALL` option.

This file is used many times to restrict access to the console. Following are some examples of allowing access and denying access to various groups. The first example is used to restrict access to the console to all but a few accounts:

```
-:ALL EXCEPT admin shutdown sync:console
```

The next example disallows nonlocal logins to the privileged accounts in the group wheel:

```
-:wheel:ALL EXCEPT LOCAL
```

The following is an example of disallowing certain accounts to log in from anywhere:

```
-:bertw timp wess lorenl billh richb chrisb chrisn:ALL
```

This last example would allow all other accounts to log in from anywhere.

Other Files That Deny or Allow Users or Hosts

Another file that will deny hosts from accessing the computer is the `/etc/hosts.deny` file. The `hosts.deny` file describes the names of the hosts that are not allowed to use the local INET services. These INET services are defined by the `/usr/sbin/tcpd` server.

The `/etc/hosts.lpd` file describes the names of the hosts that are considered "equivalent" to the current host. This "equivalence" means that the hosts listed are trusted enough to allow `rsh` commands. Typically a system that is directly connected to the Internet has only an entry of `localhost`.

syslog

The `syslog` is a good file to check on a regular basis. Although most of the information should be standard repeats for your system, you aren't looking for these. What you are looking for are anomalies. Anomalies are things that show when the system noticed something out of the ordinary. The following example comes from a fictitious `syslog`. The bolded items are the ones that I would be curious about:

```
Aug  8 19:51:53 shell sendmail[333]: gethostbyaddr(268.266.81.253) failed: 1
Aug  8 19:51:53 shell sendmail[333]: gethostbyaddr(268.266.81.254) failed: 1
Aug  8 19:52:56 shell mountd[324]:
➥Unauthorized access by NFS client 208.206.80.2.
Aug  8 19:52:56 shell mountd[324]:
➥Blocked attempt of 268.266.80.2 to mount /var/spool/mail
Aug  8 19:52:57 shell mountd[324]:
➥Unauthorized access by NFS client 268.266.80.2.
Aug  8 19:52:57 shell mountd[324]:
➥Blocked attempt of 268.266.80.2 to mount /home
Aug  8 19:54:19 shell in.qpopper[371]:
➥warning: can't get client address: Connection reset by peer
Aug  8 19:54:52 shell mountd[324]:
➥Unauthorized access by NFS client 268.266.80.2.
Aug  8 19:54:52 shell mountd[324]:
➥Blocked attempt of 268.266.80.2 to mount /home
Aug  8 20:00:30 shell inetd[410]: execv /usr/sbin/nmbd: No such file or directory
Aug  8 20:00:30 shell inetd[319]: /usr/sbin/nmbd: exit status 0x1
```

```
Aug  8 20:00:42 shell last message repeated 11 times
Aug  8 20:01:56 shell last message repeated 23 times
Aug  8 20:02:37 shell last message repeated 15 times
Aug  8 20:04:23 shell inetd[319]: /usr/sbin/nmbd: exit status 0x1
Aug  8 20:05:21 shell last message repeated 11 times
Aug  8 20:13:39 shell sendmail[577]: gethostbyaddr(268.266.80.11) failed: 1
Aug  8 20:13:39 shell sendmail[577]: gethostbyaddr(268.266.80.12) failed: 1
```

In this portion of the `syslog`, the bolded lines show where some system tried to access certain files by mounting the filesystems to its machine. Now, this could very well be a case where a legitimate user was trying to mount certain files, but it might not be. This is where a familiarity of the particular system helps. Is the IP of the system trying to mount the filesystems a known IP? If it is a known IP, perhaps it is just an error; if it is not, then it might be indicative of an attempted security breach. (See Chapter 20, "System Security," for more on this topic.)

There are many other logs that can be made active to give you more information. Many of these files are defined in the `/etc/login.defs` file. This file controls the configuration definitions for login. They include setting the location for failed logins (`/var/log/faillog`), whether to enable additional passwords for dial-up access (`/etc/dialups`), whether to allow time restrictions to logins (`/etc/porttime`), defining the superuser log (`/var/log/sulog`), and many other configurations. It is up to you as the system administrator to decide which, if any, of these functions to turn on. Actually, the "if any" part of the previous statement is not true. There are many configurations within the `/etc/login.defs` file that are mandatory. One such example is the location for the mail queue (`/var/spool/mail`).

The point is, this is one powerful file. Take a few minutes to get acquainted with it and understand how it works (it is well documented). It will save you a lot of time when you know that the `/var/log/lastlog` file contains the information on the last person logged in to the system.

Wine—Accessing Windows Applications Under Linux

The most common way to access applications under Linux is with the product called Wine. Wine is both a program loader and an emulation library that enables UNIX users to run MS Windows applications on an *x*86 hardware platform running under some UNIXes. The program loader will load and execute an MS Windows application binary, while the emulation library will take calls to MS Windows functions and translate these into calls to UNIX/X, so that equivalent functionality is achieved.

MS Windows binaries will run directly; there will be no need for machine-level emulation of program instructions. Sun has reported better performance with their version of WABI than is actually achieved under MS Windows, so theoretically the same result is possible under Wine.

There is a great discussion as to what Wine stands for. The two most common rumors are that it stands for Windows emulator, or that it stands for Wine is not an emulator.

New Releases of Wine

Wine has been in perpetual alpha stage since it first came out. New releases/versions are released about once a month. Several newsgroups track the latest release of Wine, including `comp.emulators.ms-windows.wine`. The different versions are referred to according to when they were released. The file format would be `Wine-`*`<yearmonthday>`*`.tar.gz`. It is doubtful, at least to this author, that Wine will ever be anything other than an alpha product. This is because volunteers develop it, and Windows is changing enough to keep the volunteers busy until the cows come home.

Where to Get Copies of Wine

Wine comes on the CD-ROM with this book. It can also be downloaded from numerous sites. Some of the more common sites for downloading Wine are

```
sunsite.unc.edu://pub/Linux/ALPHA/wine/development/Wine-970804.tar.gz
tsx-11.mit.edu://pub/linux/ALPHA/Wine/development/Wine-970804.tar.gz
ftp.infomagic.com://pub/mirrors/linux/wine/development/Wine-970804.tar.gz
aris.com://pub/linux/ALPHA/Wine/development/Wine-970804.tar.gz
```

Patches are also available. If you have previously loaded a version, the same locations should have files with the same name, but with a `diff` instead of the `tar`. For example, on Sunsite's site, I found the following:

```
Wine-970629.diff.gz     29-Jun-97 14:07    32k
Wine-970629.tar.gz      29-Jun-97 14:08   1.4M
Wine-970720.diff.gz     20-Jul-97 13:51    83k
Wine-970720.tar.gz      20-Jul-97 13:51   1.4M
Wine-970804.diff.gz     04-Aug-97 13:18    68k
Wine-970804.tar.gz      04-Aug-97 13:19   1.4M
```

There were actually versions dating back to March, but this shows the difference between the two types of files, particularly in the file size.

Installation and Problems Running Windows Applications

Installation of Wine is simple. After you gunzip the file and untar the file, follow the directions in the `README` file. Included in the `README` file is how to compile the source code as well as how to configure it.

Running Wine is also a simple process. Assuming you already have X running, open an `xterm` window, and, at the shell prompt, type the following:

```
wine [program name]
```

I know that Solitaire works under Wine, so let me give you an example of how to run Solitaire. Solitaire is located in the `/windows` directory on my C: drive. Under Red Hat Linux, the C:

drive is referred to as `/doc/c`. Therefore, to run the Solitaire program (`sol.exe`) under Linux, I simply type the following:

```
wine /dos/c/windows/sol.exe
```

And, poof, just like magic, a window pops up, and I can now play Solitaire!

The most common problem I have seen when trying to run a Windows application, especially for the first time, is that the MS-DOS partition is not mounted under my Red Hat Linux filesystem.

The easiest check for this is to check your mounts with the `mount` command. If it is not mounted, try mounting it manually. If it will mount, you might want to consider placing it in your `/etc/fstab` file so that it will automatically get mounted during startup of Linux.

If the filesystem is mounted and it still does not work, check the path statements in the `wine.conf` file. All letters in the path must be lowercase.

Summary

This chapter gives you a glimpse of the importance of planning an activity and providing all of the necessary steps involved in changing a system. These steps are even more vital in a production system. As a reminder, a system administrator should

- Understand how things work
- Know where to find things
- Plan processes
- Have a back-out plan and know when to use it
- Make changes in small increments
- Test all changes
- Communicate effectively and in a timely fashion

Communication is the key to success in system administration, as it is with life. You have many tools to enable you to communicate with other users on the system.

The chapter takes a brief look at problem determination. Although without knowing specifics it is difficult to get too much into the problems, knowing where to look for the log information is a good start. As a matter of fact, knowing where to look for help (such as mailing lists, man pages, and newsgroups) is also a good place to start. As a side note, understanding permissions is another one of the keys to system administration.

As a bonus, this chapter presents a look at Wine. As the system that you are using is probably an Intel-based box, you do have the ability to run Windows applications. The Wine application enables the use of some Windows applications under the Linux environment.

CHAPTER 16

Advanced System Administration

by David Pitts

IN THIS CHAPTER

A large portion of this book is devoted to advanced system administration, including script and automation development, configuring and building kernels, network management, security, and many other tasks. One task not addressed thus far is performance analysis. This chapter, then, looks at the initial steps of performance analysis, showing how to determine CPU, memory, and paging space usage. Two tools are examined: `vmstat` and `top`.

Basic Performance Analysis

Basic performance analysis is the process of identifying performance bottlenecks and involves a number of steps. The first step is to look at the big picture: Is the problem CPU or I/O related? If it is a CPU problem, what is the load average? You should probably check to see what processes are running and who is causing the problem. If it is an I/O problem, then is it paging or normal disk I/O? If it is paging, increasing memory might help. You can also try to isolate the program or the user causing the problem. If it is a disk problem, then is the disk activity balanced? If you have only one disk, perhaps you might want to install a second.

The next section looks at several tools that can be used to determine the answers to the preceding questions.

Determining CPU Usage

CPU usage is the first test on the list. There are many different ways to obtain a snapshot of the current CPU usage. The one I am going to focus on here is `vmstat`. The `vmstat` command gives you several pieces of data, including the CPU usage. The following is the syntax for the command:

```
$ vmstat interval [count]
```

`interval` is the number of seconds between reports, and *`count`* is the total number of reports to give. If the count is not included, `vmstat` will run continuously until you stop it with Ctrl+C or kill the process.

Here is an example of the output from `vmstat`:

```
shell:/home/dpitts$ vmstat 5 5
 procs                  memory     swap        io     system          cpu
 r b w   swpd   free   buff cache  si  so   bi   bo   in   cs  us  sy  id
 0 0 0   1104   1412 10032 36228   0   0   10    8   31   15   7   4  24
 0 0 0   1104   1736 10032 36228   0   0    0    3  111   18   1   1  99
 0 0 0   1104   1816 10032 36228   0   0    0    1  115   23   2   2  96
 0 1 0   1104   1148 10096 36268   8   0    7    4  191  141   4   6  91
 0 0 0   1104   1868  9812 35676   6   0    2   10  148   39  25   4  70
```

The first line of the report displays the average values for each statistic since boot time. It should be ignored. For determining CPU used, you are interested in the last three columns, as indicated by the `cpu` heading. They are `us`, `sy`, and `id` and are explained in the following table.

CPU	*Description*
`us`	Percentage of CPU cycles spent on performing user tasks.
`sy`	Percentage of CPU cycles spent as system tasks. These tasks include waiting on I/O, performing general operating system functions, and so on.
`id`	Percentage of CPU cycles not used. This is the amount of time the system was idle.

Just because the CPU time is high (or the idle time low) is not necessarily indicative of an overall CPU problem. It could be that there are a number of batch jobs running that just need to be rearranged. In order to determine that there is actually a CPU problem, it is important to monitor the CPU percentages for a significant period of time. If the percentages are high during this time, there is definitely a problem.

Next, look at a different section of the `vmstat` output. If the problem is not CPU related, look to see whether it is a problem with paging or normal disk I/O. To determine whether it is a memory problem, look at the headings `memory` and `swap`:

```
shell:/home/dpitts$ vmstat 5 5
 procs                      memory    swap          io     system         cpu
 r b w   swpd   free   buff cache  si  so    bi    bo   in    cs   us  sy  id
 1 0 0   1096   1848   4580 37524   0   0     9     8    8    17    7   3  29
 1 0 0   1096   1424   4580 37980   0   0    92    10  125    24   94   4   3
 2 0 0   1096    864   4536 38408   0   0   112    31  146    42   93   2   5
 2 0 0   1096    732   4360 38480  10   0    98     7  146    48   97   3   1
```

Memory	*Description*
`swpd`	The amount of virtual memory used (KB)
`free`	The amount of idle memory (KB)
`buff`	The amount of memory used as buffers (KB)
`cache`	The amount of memory left in the cache (KB)

Swap	*Description*
`si`	The amount of memory swapped in from disk (KB/s)
`so`	The amount of memory swapped to disk (KB/s)

The most important of these fields is the `swap in` column. This column shows paging that has previously been swapped out, even if it was done before the `vmstat` command was issued.

The io section is used to determine if the problem is with blocks sent in or out of the device:

```
shell:/home/dpitts$ vmstat 5 5
 procs                  memory    swap          io     system         cpu
 r b w  swpd  free  buff cache  si  so    bi    bo   in   cs  us  sy  id
 1 0 0  1096  1848  4580 37524   0   0     9     8    8   17   7   3  29
 1 0 0  1096  1424  4580 37980   0   0    92    10  125   24  94   4   3
 2 0 0  1096   864  4536 38408   0   0   112    31  146   42  93   2   5
 2 0 0  1096   732  4360 38480  10   0    98     7  146   48  97   3   1
```

The io section is described in the following table.

IO	*Description*
bi	The blocks sent to a block device (blocks/s)
bo	The blocks received from a block device (blocks/s)
cs	The number of context switches per second

These fields run from several to several hundred (maybe even several thousands). If you are having a lot of in and out block transfers, the problem is probably here. Keep in mind, though, that a single reading is not indicative of the system as a whole, just a snapshot of the system at that time. There are three states in which the processes can exist. They are runtime, uninterrupted sleep, and swapped out. These are defined in the following table.

Procs	*Description*
r	The number of processes waiting for runtime
b	The number of processes in uninterrupted sleep
w	The number of processes swapped out but otherwise able to run

The number of processes waiting for runtime is a good indication that there is a problem. The more processes waiting, the slower the system. More than likely, you won't be looking at vmstat unless you already know there is a bottleneck somewhere, so the r field doesn't give you much vital information.

top

The top command provides another tool for identifying problems with a Linux system. The top command displays the top CPU processes. More specifically, top provides an ongoing look at processor activity in real time. It displays a listing of the most CPU-intensive tasks on the system and can provide an interactive interface for manipulating processes. The default is to update every five seconds. The following is an example of the output from top:

```
  1:36am  up 16 days,  7:50,  3 users,  load average: 1.41, 1.44, 1.21
60 processes: 58 sleeping, 2 running, 0 zombie, 0 stopped
CPU states: 89.0% user,  8.5% system, 92.4% nice,  3.9% idle
Mem:  63420K av, 62892K used,   528K free, 32756K shrd,  6828K buff
Swap: 33228K av,  1096K used, 32132K free                38052K cached
PID USER     PRI  NI  SIZE  RSS SHARE STATE  LIB %CPU %MEM   TIME COMMAND
```

The following table explains what each field means.

Field	*Description*
`up`	The time the system has been up and the three load averages for the system. The load averages are the average number of processes ready to run during the last 1, 5, and 15 minutes. This line is just like the output of `uptime`.
`processes`	The total number of processes running at the time of the last update. This is also broken down into the number of tasks that are running, sleeping, stopped, and zombied.
`CPU states`	The percentage of CPU time in user mode, system mode, niced tasks, and idle. (*Niced* tasks are only those whose `nice` value is negative.) Time spent in niced tasks will also be counted in system and user time, so the total will be more than 100 percent.
`Mem`	Statistics on memory usage, including total available memory, free memory, used memory, shared memory, and memory used for buffers.
`Swap`	Statistics on swap space, including total swap space, available swap space, and used swap space. This and `Mem` are just like the output of `free`.
`PID`	The process ID of each task.
`USER`	The username of the task's owner.
`PRI`	The priority of the task.
`NI`	The `nice` value of the task. Negative `nice` values are lower priority.
`SIZE`	The size of the task's code plus data plus stack space, in kilobytes.
`RSS`	The total amount of physical memory used by the task, in kilobytes.
`SHARE`	The amount of shared memory used by the task.
`STATE`	The state of the task, either `S` for sleeping, `D` for uninterrupted sleep, `R` for running, `Z` for zombies, or `T` for stopped or traced.
`TIME`	Total CPU time the task has used since it started. If cumulative mode is on, this also includes the CPU time used by the process's children that have died. You can set cumulative mode with the `S` command-line option or toggle it with the interactive command `S`.
`%CPU`	The task's share of the CPU time since the last screen update, expressed as a percentage of total CPU time.

continues

Field	*Description*
%MEM	The task's share of the physical memory.
COMMAND	The task's command name, which will be truncated if tasks have only the name of the program in parentheses (for example, "(getty)").

As you can probably tell from the server used to obtain the data, there are no current bottlenecks in the system.

`free` is another good command for showing the amount of memory that is used and is, as you can imagine, free:

```
shell:/home/dpitts$ free
             total       used       free     shared    buffers     cached
Mem:         63420      61668       1752      23676      13360      32084
-/+ buffers:            16224      47196
Swap:        33228       1096      32132
```

The first line of output (`Mem:`) shows the physical memory. The `total` column does not show the physical memory used by the kernel, which is usually about a megabyte. The `used` column shows the amount of memory used. The `free` column shows the amount of free memory. The `shared` column shows the amount of memory shared by several processes. The `buffers` column shows the current size of the disk buffer cache. The `cached` column shows how much memory has been cached off to disk.

The last line (`Swap:`) shows similar information for the swapped spaces. If this line is all zeroes, your swap space is not activated.

To activate a swap space, use the `swapon` command. The `swapon` command tells the kernel that the swap space can be used. The location of the swap space is given as the argument passed to the command. The following example shows starting a temporary swap file:

```
$ swapon /temporary_swap
```

To automatically use swap spaces, list them in the `/etc/fstab` file. The following example lists two swap files for the `/etc/fstab`:

```
/dev/hda8 none swap sw 0 0
/swapfile none swap sw 0 0
```

To remove a swap space, use the `swapoff` command. Usually, this is necessary only when using a temporary swap space.

WARNING

If swap space is removed, the system will attempt to move any swapped pages into other swap space or to physical memory. Should there not be enough space, the system will freak out but will eventually come back. During the time that it is trying to figure out what to do with these extra pages, the system will be unavailable.

How Much Swap Is Enough?

A common question asked by people who are designing a system for the first time is, "How much swap space is enough?" Some people just estimate that you should have twice as much swap space as you have physical memory. Following this method, if you have a system with 16MB of memory, you will set up 32MB of swap space. Depending on how much physical memory you have, this number can be way out of line. For example, my system has 64MB of physical memory, so I should configure 124MB of paging space. I would say that this is unnecessary. I prefer to use a slightly more complex strategy for determining the amount of swap space needed.

Determining the amount of swap space you need is a simple four-step program. First, admit that you have a memory problem. No, sorry, that is a different program. The four steps are as follows:

1. Estimate your total memory needs. Consider the largest amount of space you will need at any given time. Consider what programs you will be running simultaneously. A common way of determining this is to set up a bogus swap space (quite large) and load as many programs as you estimate will be run at the same time. Then, check how much memory you have used. There are a few things that typically don't show up when a memory check is performed. The kernel, for example, will use about a megabyte of space.
2. Add a couple megabytes as a buffer for those programs that you did not think you would be using but found out later that, in fact, you will.
3. Subtract the amount of physical memory you have from this total. The amount left is the amount of swap space needed to run your system with all the memory in use.
4. If the total from step 3 is more than approximately three times the amount of physical memory you have, there will probably be problems. If the amount is greater than three times the cost, then it is worthwhile to add more physical memory.

Sometimes these calculations show that you don't need any swap space; my system with 64MB of RAM is an example. It is a good policy to create some space anyway. Linux uses the swap space so that as much physical memory as possible is kept free. It swaps out memory pages that have not been used for a while so that when the memory is needed, it is available. The system will not have to wait for the memory to be swapped out.

Momma Always Said to Be Nice!

I grew up with two older brothers and one younger one. There were many times when Momma said to one or more of us to be nice! Sometimes the same is true for our processes. The `renice` command is used to alter the priority of running processes.

By default in Red Hat Linux, the `nice` value is `0`. The range of this is `-20` to `20`. The lower the value, the faster the process runs. The following example shows how to display the `nice` value by using the `nice` command. My shell is running at the default value of `0`. To check this another way, I issue the `ps -l` command. The `NI` column shows the `nice` value:

```
shell:/home/dpitts$ nice
0
shell:/home/dpitts$ ps -l
 FLAGS   UID   PID  PPID PRI  NI   SIZE   RSS WCHAN       STA TTY TIME COMMAND
   100   759  3138  3137   0   0   1172   636 force_sig   S   p0  0:00 -bash
100000   759  3307  3138  12   0    956   336             R   p0  0:00 ps -l
```

I change the `nice` value by using the `renice` command. The syntax of the command is as follows:

```
renice priority [[-p] pid ...] [[-g] pgrp ...] [[-u] user ...]
```

In the following example, the shell's `nice` value is changed to a value of `5`. This means that any process with a lower value will have priority on the system.

```
shell:/home/dpitts$ renice 5 3138
3138: old priority 0, new priority 5
shell:/home/dpitts$ nice
5
shell:/home/dpitts$ ps -l
 FLAGS   UID   PID  PPID PRI  NI   SIZE   RSS WCHAN       STA TTY TIME COMMAND
   100   759  3138  3137   5   5   1172   636 force_sig   S N p0  0:00 -bash
100000   759  3319  3138  14   5    968   368             R N p0  0:00 ps -l
```

The owner of the process (and root) has the ability to change the `nice` value to a higher value. Unfortunately, the reverse is not also true:

```
shell:/home/dpitts$ renice -5 3138
renice: 3138: setpriority: Permission denied
```

Only root has the capability to lower a `nice` value. This means that even though I set my shell to a `nice` value of `5`, I cannot lower it even to the default value.

The `renice` command is a wonderful way of increasing the apparent speed of the system for certain processes. This is a trade-off, though, because the processes that are raised will now run slower.

Summary

Computers slow down significantly when they run out of memory. Also, if they try to do too much at one time, they seem slow. As a system administrator, your job is to determine whether the system is really slow or just seems slow. The difference is significant. If the system seems slow, the problem is usually a matter of adjusting the times certain processes are run. Using `cron` and `at` helps to schedule certain activities when the system is otherwise idle.

If the system is really slow, that is, waiting on processes all the time, with consistent IO waits, then it is time to invest in more equipment. The other option is to just live with it. (Get your users to buy off on that one!) As system administrator, your job is to keep performance at an acceptable level. With tools such as `vmstat` and `top`, this task is much simpler.

Sacrificing speed in certain processes is another way of increasing the apparent speed of other processes. The basic concept is that each process gets a certain piece of the processing pie. Certain processes can have a smaller, or root can give them a larger, piece of the processing pie. The amount of processing that can be completed never changes. The change is in how much processing time each process gets. Mainframes call this *cycles*. The lower your `nice` value, the more cycles you get each time the processor comes to do your work.

CHAPTER 17

GNU Project Utilities

by Sriranga R. Veeraraghavan

IN THIS CHAPTER

GNU (which stands for "GNU's not UNIX") is a UNIX-compatible software system that is being developed by Richard Stallman. The GNU project utilities are the GNU implementation of familiar UNIX programs like `mv`, `cp`, and `ls`.

The GNU versions of these programs generally run faster, provide more options, have fewer arbitrary limits, and are generally POSIX.2-compliant.

The GNU project utilities are distributed in several parts. The `bin` utilities, `diff` utilities, and `shar` (shell archive) utilities are primarily used in development work. The most frequently used utilities are the file utilities, find utilities, shell utilities, and text utilities; these are covered in this chapter.

The true power of the GNU project utilities is that they enable a user to break down complex tasks and solve them piece by piece, quickly and easily.

File Utilities

This section covers the major GNU file management utilities. The following is a complete list of the programs included in the GNU file utilities distribution:

`chgrp`	`ls`
`chown`	`mkdir`
`chmod`	`mvdir`
`cp`	`mkfifo`
`dd`	`mknod`
`df`	`mv`
`du`	`rm`
`install`	`rmdir`
`ln`	`sync`
`dir`	`touch`
`vdir`	

Listing Directory Contents

The GNU file utilities include three programs for listing directory contents and information about files: `ls`, `dir`, and `vdir`. The biggest difference between these three programs is in their default behavior; `dir` is equivalent to `ls -C`, and `vdir` is equivalent to `ls -l`.

The default behavior of `ls` (invoked with no arguments) is to list the contents of the current directory. If a directory is given as an argument, then its contents are listed nonrecursively (files starting with a period (`.`) are omitted). For filename arguments, just the name of the file is printed. By default, the output is listed alphabetically.

The GNU version of ls supports all the standard options and also introduces the major feature of color-coding files.

The variable $LS_COLOR (or $LS_COLOUR) is used to determine the color scheme. If $LS_COLOR is not set, the color scheme is determined from the system default stored in the file /etc/DIR_COLORS. This variable can be set by hand, but it is much easier to have the program dircolors set it by issuing the following command:

```
eval `dircolors`
```

To aid in customizing the color scheme, dircolors supports a -p option that prints out the default configuration. Redirecting the output to a file creates a valid dircolors init file. So,

```
dircolors -p > .dircolorsrc
```

will create a file .dircolorsrc, which can be customized. After the file .dircolorsrc is customized, $LS_COLORS can be set by issuing the following command:

```
eval `dircolors .dircolorsrc`
```

Putting this line in an init file (.profile or .cshrc) and then having the alias

```
alias ls="ls --colors" (sh,bash,ksh)
alias ls "ls --colors" (csh,tcsh)
```

will ensure that the custom color scheme is used for ls.

Listing 17.1 is an excerpt from a .dircolorsrc file that implements bold text for directories and normal text for all other types of files. If any of these file types are left out, default values are substituted for them. The comments describe the different color values that can be used.

Listing 17.1. Excerpt from a .dircolorsrc file.

```
# Below are the color init strings for the basic file types. A color init
# string consists of one or more of the following numeric codes:
# Attribute codes:
# 00=none 01=bold 04=underscore 05=blink 07=reverse 08=concealed
# Text color codes:
# 30=black 31=red 32=green 33=yellow 34=blue 35=magenta 36=cyan 37=white
# Background color codes:
# 40=black 41=red 42=green 43=yellow 44=blue 45=magenta 46=cyan 47=white
NORMAL 00      # global default
FILE   00      # normal file
DIR    01      # directory
LINK   00      # symbolic link
FIFO   00      # pipe
SOCK   00      # socket
BLK    00      # block device driver
CHR    00      # character device driver
ORPHAN 00      # symlink to nonexistent file
EXEC   00      # executables
```

To implement colors, simply specify the scheme as

```
FILE_TYPE attribute codes;text codes;background codes
```

This line indicates all links are red with a white background:

```
LINK 00;31;47
```

Another feature of the `--color` option is that files with extensions can also be colorized. For example, to make all `.jpg` files underlined, put the line

```
.jpg 04
```

into the `.dircolors` file. Any file extension can be used. Some people like to have archive files (`.uu`, `.tar`, `.tar.gz`, `.gz`, `.Z`, `.z`, `.tgz`) in one color and picture files (`.jpg`, `.jpeg`, `.gif`) in another.

File Operations

The next set of commands in the file utilities are the utilities that are used for basic file operations, such as copying and moving files.

The file operations commands like `cp`, `mv`, `rm`, and `ln` are familiar to all UNIX users. The GNU versions of these commands support all the standard options along with a few additional options for safety and convenience. These options are as follows:

`-b` or `--backup`	Makes backups of files that are about to be overwritten or removed. Without this option, the original versions are destroyed. (Not available in `rm`.)
`-s suffix` or `--suffix=suffix`	Appends suffix to each backup file made if a backup option is specified. (Not available in `rm`.)
`-v` or `--verbose`	Prints out the filename before acting upon it.

In terms of safety, the backup options are like the `-i` option (interactive mode); they frequently prevent mishaps.

By default, the suffix for the backups is the tilde (~), but this can easily be changed by setting the variable `$SIMPLE_BACKUP_SUFFIX`. Setting this variable also avoids having to give the `-s` option each time.

Another command that is useful for copying files is the `install` command. It is frequently used to install compiled programs and is familiar to programmers who use `make`, but it also can be useful for the casual user because it can be used to make copies of files and set attributes for those files.

Changing File Attributes

In addition to having a name, contents, and a file type, every file in UNIX has several other pieces of information associated with it. The most commonly encountered of these are the file's owner, a group, permissions, and timestamps. All the pieces of information stored about a file make up its attributes.

The four commands chown, chgrp, chmod, and touch enable users to change file attributes.

The chown command is used to change the owner and/or group of a file, depending on how it is invoked. The basic syntax is

```
chown [options] [owner] [ [:.] [group] ] [files]
```

where either owner or group is optional and the separator can be either a . or a :. Thus, a command of the form

```
chown ranga:users *
```

or

```
chown ranga.users *
```

changes the owner of all files in the current directory to ranga and the group of all the files in the current directory to users, provided that ranga was a valid username and users was a valid group name. To find out which usernames and group names are valid, check in the files /etc/passwd and /etc/group.

In addition to giving usernames and group names, uid (user IDs) and gid (group IDs) can be given to chown. The command

```
chown 500:100 foo.pl
```

changes the owner of foo.pl to the user with uid 500 and the group of foo.pl to the group with gid 100. When using numeric IDs, make sure that the IDs are valid, as chown only works for valid names.

If only the owner of a file (or files) needs to be changed, then the group name or group ID can be omitted. For example,

```
chown larry: camel.txt llama.txt
```

changes only the owner of the files camel.txt and llama.txt to larry.

Similarly, if only the group of a file (or files) needs to be changed, the username or uid can be omitted. Thus,

```
chown :100 bar.sh
```

changes only the group of `bar.sh` to `100`. If only a group change is required, the `chgrp` command can be used. Its basic syntax is

```
chgrp [options] [group] [files]
```

where *group* can be either the `gid` or a group name. To change the group of `bar.sh` to `100` with the `chgrp` command, the command would be

```
chgrp 100 bar.sh
```

In addition to changing the owner and group of a file, it is often necessary to change the permissions that the owner, group, and the "world" have in respect to files. This is done via the `chmod` command. The basic syntax is

```
chmod [options][[g][u][o][a]][-/+/=][[r][w][x]][files]
```

where the letters `g`, `u`, `o`, and `a` (called the user part) specify whose access to the file is modified; the `-`, `+`, and `=` operators (called the operator part) specify how the access is changed; and the letters `r`, `w`, and `x` (called the permissions part) specify the permissions.

The letters in the user part have the following meanings:

`u`	The user who owns the file
`g`	Other users who are in the file's group
`o`	All other users
`a`	All users; the same as `ugo`

The functions of the operators are as follows:

`+`	Adds the specified permissions to the file
`-`	Removes the specified permissions from a file
`=`	Sets the permissions on a file to the specified permissions

The letters in the permissions part have the following meanings:

`r`	Permission to read the file
`w`	Permission to write to the file
`x`	Permission to execute the file

Here are a few examples to illustrate the usage of `chmod`. In order to give the world read access to all files in a directory, use this:

```
chmod a+r *
```

Instead of `a`, `guo` could also be used. To stop anyone except the owner of `.profile` from writing to it, use this:

```
chmod go-w .profile
```

To be a file miser, use this:

```
chmod go-rwx ~/*
```

When specifying the user part or the permissions part, the order in which the letters are given is irrelevant. Thus the commands

```
chmod guo+rx *
```

and

```
chmod uog+xr *
```

are equivalent.

If more than one set of permissions changes need to be applied to a file or files, a comma-separated list can be used: For example,

```
chmod go-w,a+x a.out
```

removes the groups and world write permission on `a.out`, and adds the execute permission for everyone.

The commands `chown`, `chgrp`, and `chmod` accept the following options:

`-c` or `--changes`	Describes files to which a change was made
`-f`, `--silent`, or `--quiet`	Prints no output or errors
`-v` or `--verbose`	Describes the actions done to each file
`-R` or `--recursive`	Recursively applies changes to a directory and its contents

The final file attribute that often needs to be changed is the timestamp. This is done via the `touch` command. The `touch` command is normally used to change the access or modification times of a file, but can also be used to create empty files. The basic syntax is

```
touch [options] [files]
```

By default `touch` will change the access and modification times of a file to the current time and will create files that do not exist. For example,

```
touch foo bar blatz
```

results in the files `foo`, `bar`, and `blatz` having their access and modification times changed to the current time. If either `foo`, `bar`, or `blatz` do not exist, then `touch` will try to create the file. The only limitation is that `touch` cannot change files that the current user does not own or does not have write permissions for.

Some of the options that `touch` understands are as follows:

`-a`, `--time=atime`, or `--time=access`	Changes access time only
`-c`	Doesn't create files that don't exist

`-m`, `--time=mtime`, or `--time=modify`	Changes modification time only
`--date=time`	Uses `time` instead of current time
`-r file` or `--reference=file`	Uses the times from `file` instead of the current time

One of the common uses of `touch` is to create a large number of files quickly for testing scripts that read and process filenames.

Disk Usage

The GNU disk usage utilities, `df` and `du`, are quite similar to their UNIX counterparts, but implement a few nice options that make their output much easier to read and understand.

By default, both programs produce output in terms of blocks, which varies depending on the local machine (strict POSIX machines use 512 bytes per block, while others use 1024 bytes per block), but their output can be changed to be in kilobytes, megabytes, or gigabytes. The output options are as follows:

`-k` or `--kilobytes`	Prints in 1KB (1024-byte) blocks
`-m` or `--megabytes`	Prints in 1MB (1,048,576 bytes) blocks
`-h` or `--human-readable`	Appends a letter to indicate size (`K` for kilobytes, `M` for megabytes, `G` for gigabytes)

Find Utilities

The find utilities enable the user to find files that meet given criteria and perform actions on those files. The three main utilities are `locate`, `find`, and `xargs`. The `locate` and `find` commands are used to locate files, and `xargs` is used to act upon those files.

locate

The `locate` command is the simplest and fastest command available for finding files. It does not actually search the filesystem; instead, it searches through filename databases that contain a list of files that were in particular directory trees when the databases were last updated. Typically, the databases are updated nightly, and thus are reasonably up-to-date for executables and libraries.

The basic syntax for `locate` is

```
locate [string1 ... stringN]
```

Any number of files can be specified and `locate` will run through the database files and print out a list of matches. For example,

```
locate bash emacs
```

prints out a list of files that contain the string `bash` or `emacs`. Some matches on my system include

```
/usr/bin/bashbug
/usr/local/bin/bash
/usr/local/man/man1/bash.1
/usr/lib/zoneinfo/Africa/Lumumbashi
/usr/doc/minicom-1.75-2/doc/Todo.emacskey.dif
/usr/local/bin/emacs
/usr/share/emacs/19.34/etc/emacs.1
```

In addition, `locate` will also properly handle shell wildcards. Thus,

```
locate *[mM]akefile
```

prints out a list of `makefiles` on the system.

If the filename databases are not being updated regularly on a system, the system administrator can update the databases by running the `updatedb` command manually. Usually simply running `updatedb` without any options and waiting for it to finish is adequate, but sometimes it is necessary to specify the directories that should and should not be included. To facilitate this, `updatedb` understands the following options:

`--localpaths=path`	A list of nonnetwork directories to put in the database; the default is `/`.
`--netpaths=path`	A list of network directories to put in the database; the default is `none`.
`--prunepaths=path`	A list of directories not to put in the database; the default is `'/tmp /usr/tmp /var/tmp /afs'`

find

The `find` command is much more powerful than `locate` and can be given extensive options to modify the search criteria. Unlike `locate`, `find` actually searches the disk (local and/or remote); thus, it is much slower, but provides the most up-to-date information. The basic syntax of `find` is

```
find directory [options]
```

The most basic usage of `find` is to print out the files in a directory and its subdirectories:

```
find directory -print
```

After learning about the `find` command, many new users quickly implement an alias or function as a replacement for `locate`:

```
find / -print | grep $1
```

Generally, this is a bad idea because most systems may have network drives mounted, and `find` will end up trying to access them, causing not only the local machine to slow down, but also remote machines. The correct way to get output like `locate` from `find` is the following:

```
find directories -name name -print
```

For example, use this line to find all `makefiles` in `/usr/src/`:

```
find /usr/src -name "[mM]akefile" -print
```

The `-name` option accepts all shell metacharacters. An alternative to the preceding method for finding all files named `Makefile` or `makefile` is to use the case-insensitive `-iname` option instead of `-name`. For the truly adventurous, `find` also supports a `-regex` option.

In addition to specifying which filenames to find, `find` can be told to look at files of a specific size, type, owner, or permissions.

To find a file by size, the following option is used:

```
-size n[bckw]
```

where *n* is the size and the letters stand for

`b`	512-byte blocks (default)
`c`	Bytes
`k`	Kilobytes (1024 bytes)
`w`	2-byte words

For example, to find all files in `/usr` over 100KB, use

```
find /usr -size 100k
```

To find by files by type, the following option is used:

```
-type x
```

where *x* is one of the following letters:

`b`	Block (buffered) special
`c`	Character (unbuffered) special
`d`	Directory
`p`	Named pipe (FIFO)
`f`	Regular file
`l`	Symbolic link
`s`	Socket

Therefore, to find all the symbolic links in /tmp, use the following:

```
find /tmp -type l
```

In addition to simply printing out the filename, find can be told to print out file information by specifying the -ls option. For example,

```
find /var -name "log" -ls
```

produces the following output:

```
42842 1 drwxr-xr-x 2 root root 1024 Jul 17 14:29 /var/log/httpd
157168 1 -rw-r--r-- 1 root nobody 4 Aug 14 17:44 /var/run/httpd.pid
```

The output is similar in form to the output from ls -il.

The last option of interest for find is the -exec option, which allows for the execution of a command on each filename that matches the previous criteria. The basic syntax of the -exec option is

```
-exec [command [options]] '{}' ';'
```

The -exec option uses the string '{}' and replaces it with the name of the current file that was matched. The ';' string is used to tell find where the end of the executed command is. For example, the following makes a list of all the files that contain the word foo in the Linux source files:

```
find /usr/src/linux -name "*.c" -exec grep -l foo '{}' ';'
```

Note that the preceding command should appear all on one line.

xargs

One of the biggest limitations of the -exec command is that it can only run the specified command on one file at a time. The xargs command solves this problem. It enables the user to run a single command on many files at one time. In general, it is much faster to run one command on many files because this cuts down on the number of commands that need to be started. Here's how to modify the preceding example to count the number of files with foo in them:

```
find /usr/src/linux -name "*.c" -exec grep -l foo '{}' ';' ¦ wc -l
```

Note that this command, also, should appear all on one line.

In my version of the sources (780 files), there were 27 files with the word foo in them, and it took about 44 seconds to find that out.

Now let's modify it to run with xargs. First, you need to replace the -exec grep foo '{}' ';' part with an xargs so to avoid having to start up new greps for each file. The basic syntax for xargs is

```
xargs [options] [command [options]]
```

17

GNU PROJECT UTILITIES

There is no need to specify filenames to `xargs` because it reads these from the standard input, so the `xargs` command will be

```
xargs grep -l foo
```

To get a list of files for `xargs` to give to `grep`, use `find` to list the files in `/usr/src/linux` that end in `.c`:

```
find /usr/src/linux -name "*.c"
```

Then attach the standard output of `find` to the standard input of `xargs` with a pipe:

```
find /usr/src/linux -name "*.c" | xargs grep -l foo
```

Finally, tack on a `wc -l` to get a count and you have

```
find /usr/src/linux -name "*.c" | xargs grep -l foo | wc -l
```

On my system this took about 29 seconds, which is considerably faster. The difference becomes even greater when more complex commands are run and the list of files is longer.

You need to be careful about filenames that contain spaces in them. Many people believe that spaces are not valid characters in UNIX filenames, but they are, and handling them correctly is becoming an issue of greater importance because today many machines are able to mount and read disks from systems that frequently use spaces in filenames.

I routinely mount Mac HFS disks (Zip, floppy, hard disk) and many files on these disks have spaces in their filenames. This will confuse `xargs` because it uses the newline character (`\n`) and the space character as filename delimiters. The GNU version of `xargs` provides a pretty good workaround for this problem with the `--null` and `-0` options, which tell `xargs` to use the `null` character (`\0` or `\000`) as the delimiter. In order to generate filenames that end in `null`, `find` can be given the `-print0` option instead of `-print`.

As an illustration, here is an `ls` of my Mac's Zip Tools disk:

```
./              .resource/      Desktop DB*     System Folder/ ../
.rootinfo       Desktop DF*     Utilities/ .finderinfo/     Applications/    Icon:0d*
```

Notice that the `Desktop DB` and the `Desktop DF` files have spaces in them, as does the `System Folder` directory. If I wanted to run through this Zip disk and remove all files that end in `prefs copy`, I would normally try

```
find /mnt/zip -name "*prefs copy" -print | xargs rm
```

However, this won't work because I have a filename with spaces, but if I add `-print0`, I can do this with no problems:

```
find /mnt/zip -name "*prefs copy" -print0 | xargs rm
```

Two other options that are useful for `xargs` are the `-p` option, which makes `xargs` interactive, and the `-n args` option, which makes `xargs` run the specified command with only `args` number of arguments.

Some people wonder why the -p option. The reason is that xargs runs the specified command on the filenames from its standard input, so interactive commands like cp -i, mv -i, and rm -i don't work right. The -p option solves that problem. In the preceding example, the -p option would have made the command safe because I could answer yes or no to each file. So the real command I typed was the following:

```
find /mnt/zip -name "*prefs copy" -print0 ¦ xargs -p rm
```

Many users frequently ask why xargs should be used when shell command substitution archives the same results. The real drawback with commands such as

```
grep -l foo `find /usr/src/linux -name "*.c"`
```

is that if the set of files returned by find is longer than the system's command-line length limit, the command will fail. The xargs approach gets around this problem because xargs runs the command as many times as is required, instead of just once.

Shell Utilities

The GNU shell utilities are a package of small shell programming utilities. The following programs are included in the package:

```
basename        printenv
chroot          printf
date            pwd
dirname         seq
echo            sleep
env             stty
expr            su
factor          tee
false           test
groups          true
hostname        tty
id              uname
logname         users
nice            who
nohup           whoami
pathchk         yes
```

Who's Who in GNU

One of the first things many people do when they log on to a new machine is to see who else is logged on. The GNU shell utilities provide the commands who and users to give information about which users are currently logged on and what they are doing. The users command just prints out a list of names of people who are logged on. The who command is much more sophisticated.

In addition to giving information about who is logged on, who makes it possible to find out how long people have been idle, when they logged on, and if they are allowing other people to talk. Some of the options that who recognizes are as follows:

-H or --heading	Prints a heading
-T, -w, or --mesg	Adds user message status as +, -, or ?
-i, -u, or --idle	Adds user idle time as HOURS:MINUTES, . (less than a minute), or old (greater than a day)

One of the useful features of who over users is that because who outputs one user entry per line, it can be used with commands like grep or sed to process and format its output with ease.

The id Commands

The next set of frequently used commands are the id commands.

Knowing your own uid and gid and having the ability to determine other users' uids and gids are very handy skills.

Almost all users know about the commands whoami and groups, but many have never heard of id, which encompasses their functionality and adds the ability to determine user information about other people on the system.

By default, the id command prints out all the identification information about the current user. When I run id on my system, I get (as myself)

```
uid=500(ranga) gid=100(users) groups=100(users)
```

But, I can also run id on my brother's login name:

```
id vathsa
```

and I get

```
uid=501(vathsa) gid=100(users) groups=500(vathsa)
```

I could have determined all the preceding information by looking in /etc/passwd, but id is a much easier way of accomplishing the task.

In addition, the output of id can be tailored using the following options:

-g or --group	Prints only the group ID
-G or --groups	Prints only the supplementary groups
-n or --name	Prints a name instead of a number

`-r` or `--real`	Prints the real ID instead of the effective ID
`-u` or `--user`	Prints only the user ID

Thus, `groups` is really just `id -Gn` and `whoami` is just `id -un`.

A related command is `logname`, used to determine the username that was used to log in. The `logname` command becomes useful if a user (usually the sysadmin) logs into the system as different people and uses `su` extensively.

Checking What System You're Running

Everyone should know how to check what system they are running. The command to use is `uname`, and it comes with a whole host of options. Usually, the most useful option is `-a`, which prints all the information `uname` knows about. On my computer, `uname -a` prints

```
Linux kanchi 2.0.29 #4 Sat Jul 19 10:36:15 PDT 1997 i586
```

This is a complete summary of my system and even includes the version of the kernel I am running and when I last complied it, along with my current architecture. Some of the other options for `uname` are

`-m` or `--machine`	Prints the machine (hardware) type
`-n` or `--nodename`	Prints the machine's network node hostname (usually the same as hostname)
`-r` or `--release`	Prints the operating system release
`-s` or `--sysname`	Prints the operating system name
`-v`	Prints the operating system version

Environment Variables and Shell Functions

The *environment* is a list of variables and shell functions that the shell passes to every process that is started. It is important to know about the environment and manage it properly because it affects the execution of many programs.

The two main commands for getting information and controlling the environment are `printenv` and `env`. If invoked without arguments, both commands will print a list of all the current environment variables and shell functions.

The difference between the two is that `env` is used to manipulate the environment given to a process, and `printenv` is used to simply list information about the environment.

The primary use of `env` is to start a subshell or process in a clean environment when the current environment needs to be preserved. For example,

```
env -i $0
```

starts another shell in a clean environment. The `env` command can also be used to set the environment:

```
env DISPLAY=kanchi:0.1 netscape &
```

The preceding line starts up Netscape on my second display without affecting my environment. The options that `env` understands are as follows:

`-u` or `--unset=NAME`	Removes named variable from the environment
`-i` or `--ignore-environment`	Starts with an empty environment

Text Utilities

The GNU text utilities contain programs that enable the easy manipulation of large amounts of text. The programs in this distribution are as follows:

`cat`	`od`
`cksum`	`paste`
`comm`	`pr`
`csplit`	`sort`
`cut`	`split`
`expand`	`sum`
`fmt`	`tac`
`fold`	`tail`
`head`	`tr`
`join`	`unexpand`
`md5sum`	`uniq`
`nl`	`wc`

The `head` and `tail` Commands

What's a cat without a head and a tail? A very bad deal. Every `cat` should come with a `head` and a `tail`. Every GNU `cat` comes with them, so if you have one of those old system V cats, upgrade (it's easier than bathing your cat).

Seriously, there are certain times when it is nice to be able to output entire files at once, or to squeeze multiple blank lines in a file into one line, but most often more control over which lines are displayed is required. The `head` and `tail` commands provide this control.

The `head` command shows the first 10 (or `n` if `-n` is given) lines of its standard input. This is useful for viewing the tops of large `README` files, but its real power is in daily applications.

Take the following problem. Every day a list of the five largest mail spool files needs to be generated. What is the easiest solution? It's easier to see if the problem is broken down. First, to generate a list of the mail spool files and their sizes, use

```
ls -1 /var/spool/mail
```

Next, to sort the list by size, give `ls` the `-S` (sort by size) option:

```
ls -1S /var/spool/mail
```

To get a list of the five largest mail spool files, pipe the output of `ls` into `head -5`:

```
ls -1S ¦ head -5
```

On my system, I get this list:

```
root
ranga
vathsa
amma
anna
```


Say you also want the five oldest mail spool files. Start with `ls -1` again, but this time give the `-t` (sort by last accessed time) option instead of the `-S` option:

```
ls -1t /var/spool/mail
```

To get the bottom five, use `tail` instead of `head`:

```
ls -1t /var/spool/mail ¦ tail -5
```

On my system, I get (there are only five users on my system) this list:

```
anna
root
amma
vathsa
ranga
```

As a quick check with `ls -l` reveals, in this list the files are listed newest to oldest; to reverse the order, use `tac` (the reverse of `cat`):

```
ls -1t /var/spool/mail ¦ tail -5 ¦ tac
```

On my system, I get this list:

```
ranga
vathsa
amma
root
anna
```

There is one other handy feature of `tail`: the `-f` option, which allows for examining files while they are growing. Often I have to look at the log files generated by programs that I am debugging, but I don't want to wait for the program to finish, so I start the program and then `tail -f` the log file. Another common use for `tail -f` is

```
tail -f /var/log/httpd/access_log
```

which can be used to watch the HTTP requests made for their system.

The split Command

The split command is probably one of the handiest commands for transporting large files around. One of its most common uses is to split up compressed source files (to upload in pieces or fit on a floppy). The basic syntax is

```
split [options] filename [output prefix]
```

where the options and output prefix are optional. If no output prefix is given, split uses the prefix of x and output files are labeled xaa, xab, xac, and so on. By default, split puts 1000 lines in each of the output files (the last file can be fewer than 1000 lines), but because 1000 lines can mean variable file sizes, the -b or --bytes option is used. The basic syntax is

```
-b bytes[bkm]
```

or

```
--bytes=bytes[bkm]
```

where *bytes* is the number of bytes of size:

b	512 bytes
k	1KB (1024 bytes)
m	1MB (1,048,576 bytes)

Thus,

```
split -b1000k JDK.tar.gz
```

will split the file JDK.tar.gz into 1000KB pieces. To get the output files to be labeled JDK.tar.gz., you would use the following:

```
split -b1000k JDK.tar.gz JDK.tar.gz.
```

This would create 1000KB files that could be copied to a floppy or uploaded one at a time over a slow modem link.

When the files reach their destination, they can be joined by using cat:

```
cat JDK.tar.gz.* > JDK.tar.gz
```

A command that is useful for confirming whether or not a split file has been joined correctly is the cksum command. Historically, it has been used to confirm if files have been transferred properly over noisy phone lines.

cksum computes a cyclic redundancy check (CRC) for each filename argument and prints out the CRC along with the number of bytes in the file and the filename. The easiest way to compare the CRC for the two files is to get the CRC for the original file:

```
cksum JDK.tar.gz > JDK.crc
```

and then compare it to the output cksum for the joined file.

Counting Words

Counting words is a handy thing to be able to do, and there are many ways to do it. Probably the easiest is the `wc` command, which stands for word count, but `wc` only prints the number of characters, words, or lines. What about if you need a breakdown by word? It's a good problem, and one that serves to introduce the next set of GNU text utilities.

Here are the commands you need:

`tr`	Transliterate; changes the first set of characters it is given into the second set of characters it is given; also deletes characters
`sort`	Sorts the file (or its standard input)
`uniq`	Prints out all the unique lines in a file (collapses duplicates into one line and optionally gives a count)

I used this chapter as the text for this example. First, this line gets rid of all the punctuation and braces, and so on, in the input file:

```
tr '!?":;[]{}(),.' ' ' < ~/docs/ch16.doc
```

This demonstrates the basic usage of `tr`:

```
tr 'set1' 'set2'
```

This takes all the characters in `set1` and transliterates them to the characters in `set2`. Usually, the characters themselves are used, but the standard C escape sequences work also (as you will see).

I specified `set2` as `' '` (the space character) because words separated by those characters need to remain separate. The next step is to transliterate all capitalized versions of words together because the words *To* and *to, the* and *The*, and *Files* and *files* are really the same word. To do this, tell `tr` to change all the capital characters `'A-Z'` into lowercase characters `'a-z'`:

```
tr '!?":;[]{}(),.' ' ' < ~/docs/ch16.doc ¦
tr 'A-Z' 'a-z'
```

I broke the command into two lines, with the pipe character as the last character in the first line so that the shell (`sh`, `bash`, `ksh`) will do the right thing and use the next line as the command to pipe to. It's easier to read and cut and paste from an `xterm` this way, also. This won't work under `csh` or `tcsh` unless you start one of the preceding shells.

Multiple spaces in the output can be squeezed into single spaces with

```
tr '!?":;[]{}(),.' ' ' < ~/docs/ch16.doc ¦
tr 'A-Z' 'a-z' ¦  tr -s ' '
```

To get a count of how many times each word is used, you need to sort the file. In the simplest form, the `sort` command sorts each line, so you need to have one word per line to get a good sort. This code deletes all of the tabs (`\t`) and the newlines (`\n`) and then changes all the spaces into newlines:

```
tr '!?":;[]{}(),.' ' ' < ~/docs/ch16.doc ¦
tr 'A-Z' 'a-z' ¦ tr -s ' ' ¦ tr -d '\t\n' ¦ tr ' ' '\n'
```

Now you can sort the output, so simply tack on the `sort` command:

```
tr '!?":;[]{}(),.' ' ' < ~/docs/ch16.doc ¦
tr 'A-Z' 'a-z' ¦ tr -s ' ' ¦ tr -d '\t\n' ¦ tr ' ' '\n' ¦ sort
```

You could eliminate all the repeats at this point by giving the `sort` the `-u` (unique) option, but you need a count of the repeats, so use the `uniq` command. By default, the `uniq` command prints out "the unique lines in a sorted file, discarding all but one of a run of matching lines" (man page `uniq`). `uniq` requires sorted files because it only compares consecutive lines. To get `uniq` to print out how many times a word occurs, give it the `-c` (count) option:

```
tr '!?":;[]{}(),.' ' ' < ~/docs/ch16.doc ¦
tr 'A-Z' 'a-z' ¦ tr -s ' ' ¦ tr -d '\t\n' ¦
tr ' ' '\n' ¦ sort ¦ uniq -c
```

Next, you need to sort the output again because the order in which the output is printed out is not sorted by number. This time, to get `sort` to sort by numeric value instead of string compare and have the largest number printed out first, give sort the `-n` (numeric) and `-r` (reverse) options:

```
tr '!?":;[]{}(),.' ' ' < ~/docs/ch16.doc ¦
tr 'A-Z' 'a-z' ¦ tr -s ' ' ¦ tr -d '\t\n' ¦
tr ' ' '\n' ¦ sort ¦ uniq -c ¦ sort -rn
```

The first few lines (ten actually, I piped the output to `head`) look like this:

```
389 the
164 to
127 of
115 is
115 and
111 a
 80 files
 70 file
 69 in
 65 '
```

Note that the tenth most common word is the single quote character, but I said we took care of the punctuation with the very first `tr`. Well, I lied (sort of); we took care of all the characters that would fit between quotes, and a single quote won't fit. So why not just backslash escape that sucker? Well, not all shells will handle that properly.

So what's the solution?

The solution is to use the predefined character sets in `tr`. The `tr` command knows several character classes, and the punctuation class is one of them. Here is a complete list (names and definitions) of class names, from the man page for `uniq`:

`alnum`	Letters and digits
`alpha`	Letters

`blank`	Horizontal whitespace
`cntrl`	Control characters
`digit`	Digits
`graph`	Printable characters, not including space
`lower`	Lowercase letters
`print`	Printable characters, including space
`punct`	Punctuation characters
`space`	Horizontal or vertical whitespace
`upper`	Uppercase letters
`xdigit`	Hexadecimal digits

The way to invoke `tr` with one of these character classes is `'[:classname:]'`. To get rid of punctuation, use the `punct` class:

```
tr '[:punct:]' ' ' < ~/docs/ch16.doc |
tr 'A-Z' 'a-z' | tr -s ' ' | tr -d '\t\n' |
tr ' ' '\n' | sort | uniq -c | sort -rn
```

Here's some of the new output:

```
405 the
170 to
136 a
134 of
122 and
119 is
 80 files
 74 file
 72 in
 67 or
```

The numbers are different for some of the words because I have been running the commands and writing the chapter at the same time.

I could also have replaced `'A-Z'` and `'a-z'` with the `upper` and `lower` classes, but there is no real advantage to using the classes, and the ranges are much more illustrative of the process.

Summary

This chapter covers the four major GNU utilities packages and the major commands in each of these packages. As you have seen in the various examples, the real power of these packages lies in their capability to help the user break down complex tasks and solve them quickly.

Backup and Restore

by David Pitts

IN THIS CHAPTER

Data is important. Both the time it took to create it and the uniqueness of the data make it valuable. Therefore, care should be taken that data is not lost.

Data can be lost several different ways. The first is through carelessness. I do not know how many times I have restored data for people who have been in the wrong directory when they issued an `rm -r` command. The second way that data can be lost is through hardware failure. Although newer hard drives are more reliable than the older ones, they still fail, and data is lost. A third way that data is lost is faulty software. Too many times I have programmed a tool to perform a task, only to have the tool destroy my data instead of manipulating it. The rule of thumb these days is that programs are released before they are ready. If there is a bug, then the people who developed the software will put out a patch. Still the data, and time it took, are both gone. Finally, the earth can just swallow up entire buildings; or there can be earthquakes, or tornadoes, or volcanoes, or hurricanes, or aliens from outer space.

Backups can protect that investment in time and in data, but only if they are actually successful in backing up and keeping the information. Therefore, part of a successful backup procedure is a test strategy to spot check backups. The easiest way to spot check your backups is to perform a restore with them. This is something you should attempt *before* you *need* to perform a restore with them.

Backups can take on many forms. I worked for a company once that had six servers. Their backup method was to `tar` servers and store a copy of that `tar` on another server. In addition, they did tape backups of the servers, which included the online version of the backups. These tape backups were used for disaster recovery purposes and kept offsite. This example actually shows a couple different ways of performing backups: One way is to store tarred copies on other machines, and the other is to store copies on tape backup (and to keep the copies offsite). The combination of these two methods provides a fairly reliable way of doing backups in that it covers everything from the simple "Oops, I accidentally deleted your database!" to "Godzilla just stepped on our building, and we need the data back in less than two days!"

This chapter covers what the qualities of a good backup are and the process of selecting a good backup medium and a backup tool. Finally, backup strategies are considered, including incremental and full backups and when to perform each.

Qualities of a Good Backup

Obviously, in the best of all possible worlds, backups would be perfectly reliable, always available, easy to use, and really fast. In the real world, this is not the case. There are trade-offs to be made. For example, backups stored offsite are good for disaster recovery, but would not always be available.

Above all, backups need to be reliable. A reliable backup medium should last for several years. Of course, if the backups are never successfully written to the backup medium, then it does not matter how good the medium is.

Speed is more or less important, depending upon the system. If there is a time window when the system is not being utilized, and the backup can be automated, then speed is not an issue. On the other hand, the restoration might be an issue. The time it takes to restore the data is as important as how critical it is to have the data available.

Availability is a necessary quality. It does no good to perform regular backups if, when they are needed, they are unavailable. Backups for disaster recovery would not be available to restore a single file that a user accidentally deleted. A good backup and recovery scheme includes both a local set of backups for day-to-day restores and an offsite set of backups for disaster recovery purposes.

It does no good to have fast, available, reliable backups if they are not usable. The tools used for backup and restoration need to be easy to use. This is especially important for restoration. In an emergency, the person who normally performs the backup and restores might be unavailable. A nontechnical user might have to perform the restoration. Obviously, documentation is a part of usability.

Selecting a Backup Medium

Today the three common backup options are floppies, tapes, and hard drives. Table 18.1 rates these media in terms of reliability, speed, availability, and usability.

Table 18.1. Backup medium comparison.

Media	*Reliability*	*Speed*	*Availability*	*Usability*
Floppies	Good	Slow	High	With small data—good; with large data—bad
Tapes	Good	Medium to fast	High	Depending on the size of the tape, can be highly usable
Hard drives	Excellent	Fast	High	Highly usable

Of course, there are other options, including CDs and floptical disks. Writable CDs are good for archival purposes, but they cannot be overwritten; therefore, the expense tends to be high. Flopticals, with attributes of both floppies and optical disks, tend to have the good qualities of floppies and tapes. They are good for single file restoration, and they can hold a lot of data.

Selecting a Backup Tool

Many tools are available for making backups. In addition to numerous third-party applications, Red Hat Linux comes with some standard tools for performing this task. This section examines two of them, `tar` and `cpio`.

`tar` and `cpio` are very similar. Both are capable of storing and retrieving data from almost any media. In addition, both `tar` and `cpio` are ideal for small systems, which Red Hat Linux systems often are. For example, the following `tar` command saves all files under `/home` to the default tape drive:

```
$ tar -c /home
```

The `-c` option tells `tar` which directory it is gathering files from—`/home` in the preceding example.

`cpio`, while similar, has several advantages. First it packs data more efficiently than does the `tar` command. Second, it is designed to back up arbitrary sets of files (`tar` is designed to back up subdirectories). Third, `cpio` is designed to handle backups that span over several tapes. Finally, `cpio` skips over bad sections on a tape and continues, while `tar` crashes and burns.

Backup Strategy

The simplest backup strategy is to copy every file from the system to a tape. This is called a full backup. Full backups by themselves are good for small systems, such as those typically used by Red Hat Linux users.

The downside of a full backup is that it is time-consuming. Restoring a single file is almost too cumbersome to be of value. There are times when a full backup is the way to go, and times when it is not. A good backup and recovery scheme will identify when a full backup is necessary and when incremental backups are preferred.

Incremental backups tend to be done more frequently. With an incremental backup, only those files that have changed since the last backup are backed up. Therefore, each incremental builds upon previous incremental backups.

UNIX uses the concept of a backup level to distinguish different kinds of backups. A full backup is designated as a level 0 backup. The other levels indicate the files that have changed since the preceding level. For example, on Sunday evening you might perform a level 0 backup (full backup). On Monday night, you would perform a level 1 backup, which backs up all files changed since the level 0 backup. Tuesday night would be a level 2 backup, which backs up all files changed since the level 1 backup, and so on. This gives way to two basic backup and recovery strategies. Here is the first:

Sunday	Level 0 backup
Monday	Level 1 backup
Tuesday	Level 1 backup
Wednesday	Level 1 backup
Thursday	Level 1 backup
Friday	Level 1 backup
Saturday	Level 1 backup

The advantage of this backup scheme is that it requires only two sets of tapes. Restoring the full system from the level 0 backup and the previous evening's incremental can perform a complete restore. The negative side is that the amount backed up grows throughout the week, and additional tapes might be needed to perform the backup. Here is the second strategy:

Sunday	Level 0 backup
Monday	Level 1 backup
Tuesday	Level 2 backup
Wednesday	Level 3 backup
Thursday	Level 4 backup
Friday	Level 5 backup
Saturday	Level 6 backup

The advantage of this backup scheme is that each backup is relatively quick. Also, the backups stay relatively small and easy to manage. The disadvantage is that it requires seven sets of tapes. Also, to do a complete restore, you must use all seven tapes.

When deciding which type of backup scheme to use, you need to know how the system is used. Files that change often should be backed up more often than files that rarely change. Some directories, such as `/tmp`, never need to be backed up.

Performing Backups with tar and cpio

A full backup with `tar` is as easy as

```
$ tar -c /
```

An incremental backup takes a bit more work. Fortunately, the `find` command is a wonderful tool to use with backups. The `find` command can be used to find all files that have changed since a certain date. It can also find files that are newer than a specified file. With this information, it is easy to perform an incremental backup. The following command finds all files that have been modified today, and backs up those files with the `tar` command to an archive on `/dev/rmt1`:

```
$ tar c1 `find / -mtime -1 ! -type d -print`
```

`! -type d` says that if the object found is a directory, don't give it to the `tar` command for archiving. This is done because `tar` follows the directories, and you don't want to back up an entire directory unless everything in it has changed. Of course, the `find` command can also be used for the `cpio` command. The following command performs the same task as the preceding `tar` command:

```
$ find / -mtime -1 ¦ cpio -o >/dev/rmt1
```

As mentioned, the `find` command can find files that are newer than a specified file. The `touch` command updates the time of a file. Therefore, it is easy to touch a file after a backup has completed. Then, at the next backup, you simple search for files that are newer than the file you touched. The following example searches for files that are newer than the file `/tmp/last_backup` and performs a `cpio` to archive the data:

```
$ find / -newer /tmp/last_backup -print ¦ cpio -o > /dev/rmt0
```

With `tar`, the same action is completed this way:

```
$ tar c1 `find / -newer /tmp/last_backup -print`
```

NOTE

You will want to touch the file before you start the backup. This means that you have to use different files for each level of backup, but it ensures that the next backup gets any files that are modified during the current backup.

Restoring Files

Backing up files is a good thing. But, backups are like an insurance policy. When it is time for them to pay up, you want it all, and you want it now! In order to get the files, you must restore them. Fortunately, it is not difficult to restore files with either `tar` or `cpio`. The following command restores the file `/home/alana/bethany.txt` from the current tape in the drive:

```
$ tar -xp /home/alana/bethany.txt
$ cpio -im `*bethany.txt$` < /dev/rmt0
```

The `-p` in `tar` and the `-m` in `cpio` ensures that all the file attributes are restored along with the file. By the way, when restoring directories with `cpio`, the `-d` option will create subdirectories. The `tar` command does it automatically.

What Is on the Tape?

When you have a tape, you may or may not know what is on it. Perhaps you are using a multiple level backup scheme and you don't know which day the file was backed up. Both `tar` and `cpio` offer a way of creating a table of contents for the tape. The most convenient time to create this file, of course, is during the actual backup. The following two lines show how to perform a backup and at the same time create a table of contents file for that tape:

```
$ tar -cv / > /tmp/backup.Monday.TOC
$ find / -print ¦ cpio -ov > /dev/rmt0 2> /tmp/backup.Monday.TOC
```

The `cpio` backup automatically sends the list to standard error. Therefore, this line just captures standard error and saves it as a file. By the way, if the > in the `tar` command is replaced with the word `tee`, then the table of contents will not only be written to the file; it will also be printed to standard output (the screen).

Summary

Backups are important, but being able to restore the files is more important. There is nothing that will cause the lump in the throat to appear faster than trying to restore a system, only to find that the backups failed. As with any administrative task performed on a system, backups require a good plan, proper implementation, good documentation, and lots of testing. An occasional spot check of a backup could save hours, if not days, of time.

PART

Dealing with Others

CHAPTER 19

User Accounts and Logins

by David Pitts

IN THIS CHAPTER

In order to run a process, there must be a process owner. That process owner is a user account. In some instances, the user account is a default system username (such as `daemon`, `bin`, or `sys`), but in most instances, the user account is an actual person who logs on to a system, performs tasks, and logs off the system.

Even in a single user environment, it is important to know how to create accounts. Most duties do not require the use of the default user, root. Therefore, one of the first tasks that should be done when setting up a new system is to make a user account under which much of the tasks will be done. Only when absolutely necessary should someone log on to root to perform a task (and even then, the person should use the `su` command to switch to root, not log on as root).

This chapter shows how to add and remove users. In addition, it gives you a look at the components that make up a user, discusses passwords, and covers a few tools for identifying the users on the system.

Adding Users

There are two ways to add users to a system. The first is to use a script that prompts for the requested information. The second is to manually edit the `/etc/passwd` file and the `/etc/group` file. The use of a script is the preferred method. First, it limits the mistakes (always a good idea!). Second, you don't have to understand the process or be familiar with the editor. But, because you are reading this book, the second reason—understanding the process and familiarization with the editor—becomes moot.

Adding a user is a simple process, involving the following six steps:

1. Edit `/etc/passwd`.
2. Edit `/etc/group`.
3. Create a home directory.
4. Copy files from `/etc/skel` to the new home.
5. Change ownerships and permissions.
6. Set the password.

Editing `etc/passwd`

The first task is to edit the `/etc/passwd` file, adding the new user to the list. Technically, it is the second thing you should do. The real first thing you should do is copy the `/etc/passwd` file to a backup file in case you make a mistake. The `/etc/passwd` file should be owned by root and the group ID set to zero (root or system). The permissions for the file should be set so that root has read and write permissions and everyone else (including group) should only have read access (`644` in hex).

Each user must have a distinct username and password from a security perspective. Each should also have a unique user ID number. The rest of the information associated with a user doesn't have to be unique, and in some cases, is exactly the same as that of other users. The format of the /etc/passwd file is a series of seven segments delimited by colons:

username : password : user ID : group ID : comment : home directory : login command

The default /etc/passwd file looks like this when Red Hat Linux is first installed:

```
root::0:0:root:/root:/bin/bash
bin:*:1:1:bin:/bin:
daemon:*:2:2:daemon:/sbin:
adm:*:3:4:adm:/var/adm:
lp:*:4:7:lp:/var/spool/lpd:
sync:*:5:0:sync:/sbin:/bin/sync
shutdown:*:6:0:shutdown:/sbin:/sbin/shutdown
halt:*:7:0:halt:/sbin:/sbin/halt
mail:*:8:12:mail:/var/spool/mail:
news:*:9:13:news:/usr/lib/news:
uucp:*:10:14:uucp:/var/spool/uucppublic:
operator:*:11:0:operator:/root:/bin/bash
games:*:12:100:games:/usr/games:
man:*:13:15:man:/usr/man:
postmaster:*:14:12:postmaster:/var/spool/mail:/bin/bash
nobody:*:-1:100:nobody:/dev/null:
ftp:*:14:50::/home/ftp:/bin/bash
```

If there is nothing to be entered into a field, then that field is left blank (see the ftp entry). There will still be a colon delimiting the field from the other fields. Following is a short description of each of the fields:

username	A unique identifier for the user
password	The user's encrypted password
user ID (UID)	The unique number that identifies a user to the operating system
group ID (GID)	The unique number that identifies the user's group
comment	The information displayed when a person is fingered; usually the user's name
home directory	The directory in which the user is placed upon login
login command	The command executed when the user logs in; usually a shell

The following sections give more detailed descriptions of the contents of these fields.

The Username

The username is a single string. Usually it is eight characters or less. This username uniquely identifies the user, and it should be easy for the user to identify and remember. The system identifies the user by this name. Typically, a combination of the letters of the first and last name is used (mine is dpitts on many systems).

Although there are traditions (corporate folklore) as to how the username is designated, the computer does not care what the username is, as long as it is unique. In fact, underscores, periods, numbers, and some special characters can be used in the username. Also, case makes a difference; `dpitts` is different from `dpittS` or `DPitts`.

Passwords

The system stores the user's encrypted password in this field. If the system is using a shadow password system, the value placed in this field will be an `x`. A value of `*` blocks login access to the account, as `*` is not a valid character for an encrypted field. This field should never be edited (after it is set up) by hand, but a program such as `passwd` should be used so that proper encryption takes place. If this field is changed by hand, the old password is no longer valid and, more than likely, will have to be changed by root.

If the system is using a shadow password system, a separate file exists called `/etc/shadow` that contains passwords (encrypted, of course).

The User ID

Every username has a number associated with it. This number, also called the UID, is used by the system to identify everything owned by the user. All processes, files, and so on associated with the user are identified in this manner. The valid range for the user ID is zero and up. Therefore, the account `nobody` from the `/etc/passwd` file listing earlier in this chapter, has an invalid UID, because it is `-1`.

Comments

This field is used by other programs to identify the user. Typically, the user's real name is placed in this field. Many times the user's telephone number is also placed here. One thing to keep in mind concerning this field is that anyone can read it. This means that you should not put anything in this field that you do not want everyone who has access to your system to see. This field is sometimes called the GECOS field, after the operating system that first used it.

In addition to users having access to this field, certain utilities use this field as an identifier as well. `sendmail`, for example, can access this field to show who is sending the mail. `finger` displays this information upon request.

The Home Directory

The home directory field tells the system where to dump the user, if the login is successful. Typically, this directory is the home directory of the user, but it does not have to be. The system does not care where the directory points, as long as that user can enter it.

Typically, the home directories are grouped together for convenience. The standard directory, under which all users are placed, is `/home`. So, my directory might be `/home/dpitts`; and `rbowen`'s directory would be `/home/rbowen`. Some systems, and some companies, use a different location for grouping home directories. Some alternative locations I have seen are `/u`, `/user`, `/s`, and `/usr`.

The Login Command

The login command is the command that is executed when the user first logs in. In most cases this is a shell command. In other cases it might be a front-end interface or a single application. If this field is left blank, the system will default to `/bin/bash` shell.

Red Hat allows two different ways for the users to change the login command: the `chps` command and the `passwd -s` command. Both of these commands look exactly alike in their implementation. Both ask for a password and then ask what to change the login command to. Before your security hairs on the back of your neck start to stand straight up, there is a file called `/etc/shells` that has the same ownership and permissions as the `/etc/passwd` file. In this file, the system administrator defines which login commands are acceptable. Because of the permissions, every user has access to read the file, but not to change it. The following is an example of an `/etc/shells` file:

```
shell:/home/dpitts$ cat /etc/shells
/bin/sh
/bin/bash
/bin/tcsh
/bin/csh
/bin/ash
/bin/zsh
```

As you can see, the only login command the user can change to are shells. Following is an example of both the `chsh` command and the `passwd -s` command. As always, the password is not displayed.

```
shell:/home/dpitts$ chsh
Password:
Changing the login shell for dpitts
Enter the new value, or press return for the default

        Login Shell [/bin/bash]:
shell:/home/dpitts$ passwd -s
Password:
Changing the login shell for dpitts
Enter the new value, or press return for the default

        Login Shell [/bin/bash]: /bin/bash
shell:/home/dpitts$
```

Editing /etc/group

After the `/etc/passwd` file has been set up, the next step is to define the groups that that user is associated with. Every user is associated with at least one group. A group is a collection of users thrown together for a particular purpose. This purpose could be job function—programmer, system administrator, accountant, or engineer—or the users could all have access to a special device—scanner, color printer, or modem.

There is no limit to the number of groups on a system. In fact, the default `/etc/group` file contains eighteen groups:

```
root::0:root
bin::1:root, bin, daemon
daemon::2:root,bin,daemon
sys::3:root,bin,adm
tty::5:
disk::6:root,adm
lp::7:lp
mem::8:
kmem::9:
wheel::10:root
floppy::11:root
mail::12:mail
news::13:news
uucp::14:uucp
man::15:man
users::100:games
nogroup::-1:
```

Each line contains four segments and, like the `passwd` file, is delimited by colons:

`group name : password : group ID : users`

If there is nothing to be entered into a field, that field is left blank (notice the *`password`* field). There will still be a colon delimiting the field from the other fields. Following is a short description of each of the fields:

`group name`	A unique identifier for the group
`password`	Usually left blank or an `*`, but a password can be assigned
`group ID`	The unique number that identifies a group to the operating system
`users`	A list of all user IDs that belong to that group

Like the `/etc/passwd` file, there are two ways of editing this file. The first way is with a script, such as `addgroup` or `groupadd`; the second way is to manually edit the file with a text editor. (By the way, always make sure you make a backup copy of the file before you edit it!) When adding groups to this file, just follow the format of the other files. Add a unique group, assign it a password if necessary, give it a unique group ID, and then list the users associated with that group. The users, by the way, are separated with commas. If the line is not in the correct format or is incorrect in some other way, the users might not be able to use that group ID.

If the system were using a shadow password system, the password field would be moved to `/etc/shadow.group`, and an `x` would be assigned to the field.

When finished editing the `/etc/group` file, double-check its permissions. It should be owned by root, and its group should be root or sys (group ID of `0`). The permissions should be read and write for owner and read for everyone else (`644` in hex).

The list of groups does not have to be in any particular order. The list of users in each group is also irrelevant. Red Hat Linux will search the entire file until it comes to the line it is looking for.

Although users can be in several groups, Linux only allows them to be active in a single group at any given time. The starting group, commonly called the primary group, is the group identified in the `/etc/passwd` file. If a user wants to switch to another group (and he or she is in the group according to `/etc/group`), the user must issue the `newgrp` command to switch.

Removing a group or a user from a group is as simple as editing the `/etc/group` file and removing either the entire line or the particular user you want removed. You should also check the `/etc/passwd` file to make sure that there are no users defined to the group you just deleted.

Creating a Home Directory and Copying Files to the New Home

After a new user has been added to the `/etc/passwd` file and the `/etc/group` file, the next step is to create the user's new home directory. For the rest of this chapter, assume that the home directory is `/home/`*`username`*.

To create the directory, go to the `/home` directory (`cd /home`), and issue the `mkdir` command. The parameter passed to the `mkdir` command is the directory you wish to correct. In the following example, I am creating a user directory for `tpowell`:

```
shell:/home/dpitts$ cd /home
shell:/home/dpitts$ mkdir tpowell
```

I now have a directory for my friend Tim. Now that I have the directory, I need to copy the files from `/etc/skel` to the new home. This is accomplished with the `cp` command, as shown in the following example:

```
shell:/home/dpitts$ cp /etc/skel/*  /home/tpowell
```

Changing Ownerships and Permissions

Now that the basic files are placed in the new user's account, it is time to give the files and the new home directory to the new user, and to give the files the correct file permissions. Of course, an individual site might differ as to the security placed on the files and directories. The following is a general guideline of the commands that need to be executed:

1. `cd /home/new_users_name ex. cd /home/tpowell`
2. `chown -R username.group ex. chown -R tpowell.user`
3. `chmod -R go=u, go-w`
4. `chmod go= .`

Setting the Password

Issue the `passwd` command as root and set the password of the new user. After you have set this password, the account will work. If you are creating dummy accounts, you might not want to set the password.

Changing User Properties

There are a few commands for changing various properties of an account. The `chsh` command, used to change the login command, is mentioned earlier in this chapter. In addition to it (and the `passwd -s`), there are two other commands that can be used:

`chfn`	Changes the full name field (the comment field)
`passwd`	Changes the password

The superuser (root) can use these commands to change the properties of any account. Normal users (those whose UIDs do not correspond to 0) can only change the properties of their own account.

Temporarily Disabling a User

Sometimes it is necessary to temporarily disable a user's account. Many times you do not want to remove it, just make it inaccessible. One of the ways that I have seen people do this is to change the user's password. Although this works, it also causes confusion for the user, who doesn't know what is going on.

A better way of disabling the account is to change the login command set in the `/etc/passwd` file. Make a special program called a `tail` script:

```
#!/usr/bin/tail +2
This account has been temporarily closed due to <whatever reason>.
Please call the system administrator at 555-1212 to discuss this situation.
```

The first two characters of the first line (`#!`) tell the kernel that the rest of the line is a command that needs to be run to interpret this file. (If you are accustomed to shell programming or Perl programming, this ought to look familiar.) The `tail` command outputs the last two lines of the file (which happens to be everything except the first line that executed the program).

If our friend `tpowell` has not logged in to his account for 90 days, the system administrator would do something like this:

```
# chsh -s /usr/local/lib/no-login/old tpowell
# su - tpowell
This account has been closed due to inactivity.
Please call the system administrator at 555-1212 to discuss this situation.
#
```

By using the `su` command to switch to `tpowell`, I was able to test and make sure that I had done the command correctly, and that it said what I wanted it to say. It worked.

The Login and How to Become a Specific User

When logging in via a terminal, `init` makes sure there is a `getty` program for the terminal connection. `getty` listens at the terminal and waits for the user to notify that he or she is ready to log in. When it notices a user, `getty` outputs a welcome message (`/etc/issue`), prompts for a username, and runs the `login` program. The `login` program checks for the existence of the `/etc/nologin` file. If it exists, logins are disabled. If it does not exist, the `login` program gets the username as a parameter and prompts the user for the password. The password is compared to the password on file for the user. If all of this matches up, `login` starts the login command identified in the `/etc/passwd` file. If it does not match up, the program will either allow the user another chance to enter the user ID and password, or the program will terminate the process. When `init` notices that the process terminated, it starts a new `getty` for the terminal.

After the login command is run, and assuming there is a place to send standard output, the `login` program outputs the contents of `/etc/motd` and checks for electronic mail. These two steps can be turned off by placing an empty file in your home directory called `.hushlogin`. This can be done with the following command:

```
shell:/home/dpitts$touch .hushlogin
shell:/home/dpitts$
```

The `touch` command says to update the file passed as a parameter with the current date and time. If that file does not exist, it creates it with nothing in it. It is this second part that had the desired effect.

> **NOTE**
>
> If the file `/etc/nologin` exists, logins are disabled. This file is usually created by shutdown. All failed login attempts are logged in the system log file (`syslog`). It also logs all logins by root. Current logins are listed in the `/var/run/utmp` file and logged in the `/var/log/wtmp`. file.

The su Command

The su command (su stands for switch user) is used to switch from one user to another. If no user is given as a parameter, the su command assumes a switch to the root user account. If the - parameter is used, all environment variables for the user switched to are read. If not, the environment variables of the real user are kept. The su command switches the effective username. It does not change the actual username.

If a normal user switches to another user, the system will ask for the password of the user being switched to. If root attempts to switch to another user, the system switches to that user without the necessary password.

Searching

Sometimes when you are on a system, it is nice to know who else is on the system. Other times it is nice to know other information about a user, such as whether or not the user is currently logged on the system. The next sections discuss the `who` command and the `finger` command, lists possible reasons they are used, and explains where the information comes from.

who

The `who` command checks the `/var/run/utmp` file to create its information. The `/var/run/utmp` command keeps track of who is currently logged on. Other than for mere curiosity's sake, there are other reasons why you might care who is logged on. One possible reason is system performance. If you are getting really bad system performance, you will probably want to see who is logged on and what the logged-on user is doing. The `who` command tells who, and the `ps` command tells what. Of course, to communicate with users with `write` or `talk`, you need to know if that user is logged on.

The `-u` parameter for `who` adds the column for how long it has been since that login has been active. In the following example, there are two users. The first has not done anything for fifteen minutes. The second, me, is currently running a command (gee, I bet it is the `who -u` command).

```
shell:/home/dpitts$ who -u
wsheldah  ttyp0    Sep  1 12:55 00:15 (d3.dialup.lexne)
dpitts   ttyp1    Sep  1 17:06   .   (a20.dialup.seane)
```

The output is a space-delimited line with the following elements (`who -u`):

user id <space> *terminal logged in* <space> *Date logged in (month and day)* <space>
time logged in <space> *inactive time* <space> *where logged in from*

finger

The `finger` command checks some system and user-defined files and reports the information it finds. After the following example of a `finger` command, the output is explained:

```
shell:/home/dpitts$ finger dpitts
Login: dpitts                          Name: MCA Financial Systems
Directory: /home2/dpitts               Shell: /bin/bash
On since Mon Sep  1 17:06 (EDT) on ttyp1 from a20.dialup.seane
Mail forwarded to dpitts@seanet.com
No mail.
Plan:

David Pitts
Systems Administrator, Consultant, Author

shell:/home/dpitts$
```

First, the `finger` command reads and interprets the `/etc/passwd` file. From that file, it gives the login ID, the comment field, the home location, and the login command issued. In addition, it checks the `/var/run/utmp`, and if the person is logged in, it displays how long, on which terminal, and from where. After it gives this information, it then checks for the existence of a `.forward` file. If one exists, it displays its information. Next, it checks to see if the user has any mail waiting to be read. It then checks for a .plan file in the user's home directory. The .plan file contains information that the user wishes to have displayed when another user looks him or her up. This can be any ASCII information.

As you can tell, the finger command gives quite a bit of publicly available information. The files that are accessed (passwd, .plan, and .forward) need to have information in them that is appropriate for any user that can access the system to see.

Summary

Regardless of the size of the system, user and account management is an essential part of system administration. Using tools such as who and finger, users can identify other users, and with tools such as chsh, chfn, and passwd, the user is able to change information associated with the /etc/passwd file without the assistance of the system administrator.

This chapter looks at the numerous users and groups that are necessary to run a system. The system uses the user and the group to identify ownership of processes and files. This same user and group information enables the user to manipulate files and initiate processes.

CHAPTER 20

System Security

by David Pitts

IN THIS CHAPTER

Security is one of the hottest topics in any system debate. How do you make your site more secure? How do you keep hackers out of your system? How do you make sure that your data is safe from intruders? How do you keep your company's secrets, secret?

Your system is as secure as its weakest point. This is an old saying, and one that is still true. I am reminded of an old Andy Griffith TV show in which the town drunk is sleeping off another episode in the jail. After he is sober, he looks around at the bars on the windows, the barred walls, and the gate. "A pretty secure jail," I thought; then the town drunk pushed open the door, said good-bye to Barney, and left. So much for the security!

Many times, systems are as secure as that jail. All the bars and locks are in place, but the door is left open. This chapter takes a look at what some of the bars and locks are, and explains how to lock the door. More importantly, though, you will learn how to conduct a security audit and where to go to get more information.

Security comes in many forms. Passwords and file permissions are your first two lines of defense. After that, things get difficult. Security breaches take on many forms. To understand your particular system and the security issues relevant to your system, you should first develop a security audit.

Thinking About Security—An Audit

There are three basic parts of a security audit, each with many things to think about. First, you need to develop a plan, a set of security aspects to be evaluated. Second, you need to consider the tools that are available for assisting in evaluating the security aspects and choose ones that are suitable to your system. The third part of a security audit is knowledge gathering—not only knowledge of how to use the system, but what the users are doing with the system, break-in methods for your system, physical security issues, and much more. The following sections look at each of these three pieces of the audit and offer some direction about where to go for more information.

A Plan

The plan can be as complex as a formal document, or as simple as a few notes scribbled on the back of a java receipt. Regardless of the complexity, the plan should at least list what aspects of the system you are going to evaluate, and how. This means asking two questions:

- What types of security problems could we have?
- Which ones can we (or should we) attempt to detect or fix?

To answer these questions, it might be necessary to ask a few more questions concerning the following areas:

- Accountability
- Change control and tracking

- Data integrity, including backups
- Physical security
- Privacy of data
- System access
- System availability

Based on the discussion of these topics, a more detailed plan can be developed. As always, there will be trade-offs. For example, privacy of data could mean that only certain people could log on to the system, which affects system access for the users. System availability is always in contention with change control. For example, when do you change that failing hard drive on a 7×24 system? The bottom line is that the detailed plan that is developed should include a set of goals; a way of tracking the progression of the goals, including changes to the system; and a knowledge base of what types of tools are needed to do the job.

Tools

Having the right tools always makes the job easier. That is especially true when you are dealing with security issues. A number of tools are available on the Internet, including tools to check passwords, check system security, and protect your system. Some major UNIX-oriented security organizations assist the UNIX/Red Hat Linux user groups in discussing, testing, and describing tools available for use. CERT, CIAC, and the Linux Emergency Response Team are excellent sources of information for both the beginner and advanced system administrator.

The following list introduces many of the available tools. This should be a good excuse, though, to surf the Net and see what else is available!

`cops` — A set of programs; each checks a different aspect of security on a UNIX system. If any potential security holes do exist, the results are either mailed or saved to a report file.

`crack` — A program designed to find standard UNIX eight-character DES-encrypted passwords by standard guessing techniques.

`deslogin` — A remote login program that can be used safely across insecure networks.

`findsuid.tar.Z` — Finds changes in `setuid` (set user ID) and `setgid` (set group ID) files.

`finger` daemon — Secure `finger` daemon for UNIX. Should compile out-of-the-box nearly anywhere.

`freestone` — A portable, fully functional firewall implementation.

`gabriel` — A `satan` detector. `gabriel` gives the system administrator an early warning of possible network intrusions by detecting and identifying `satan`'s network probing.

`ipfilter`	A free packet filter that can be incorporated into any of the supported operating systems, providing IP packet-level filtering per interface.
`ipfirewall`	An IP packet filtering tool, similar to the packet filtering facilities provided by most commercial routers.
`kerberos`	A network authentication system for use on physically insecure networks. It allows entities communicating over networks to prove their identities to each other while preventing eaves-dropping or replay attacks.
`merlin`	Takes a popular security tool (such as `tiger`, `tripwire`, `cops`, `crack`, or `spi`) and provides it with an easy-to-use, consistent graphical interface, simplifying and enhancing its capabilities.
`npasswd`	`passwd` replacement with password sanity check.
`obvious-pw.tar.Z`	An obvious password detector.
`opie`	Provides a one-time password system for POSIX-compliant, UNIX-like operating systems.
`pcheck.tar.Z`	Checks format of `/etc/passwd`; verifies root default `shell` and `passwd` fields.
Plugslot Ltd.	PCP/PSP UNIX network security and configuration monitor.
`rsaeuro`	A cryptographic toolkit providing various functions for the use of digital signatures, data encryption, and supporting areas (PEM encoding, random number generation, and so on).
`rscan`	Allows system administrators to execute complex (or simple) scanner scripts on one (or many) machines and create clean, formatted reports in either ASCII or HTML.
`satan`	The security analysis tool for auditing networks. In its simplest (and default) mode, it gathers as much information about remote hosts and networks as possible by examining such network services as `finger`, NFS, NIS, `ftp` and `tftp`, `rexd`, and others.
`ssh`	Secure shell—a remote login program.
`tcp` wrappers	Monitor and control remote access to your local `tftp`, `exec`, `ftp`, `rsh`, `telnet`, `rlogin`, `finger`, and `systat` daemon.
`tiger`	Scans a system for potential security problems.
`tis` firewall toolkit	Includes enhancements and bug fixes from V1.2, and new proxies for HTTP/Gopher and X11.
`tripwire`	Monitors system for security break-in attempts.

`xp-beta`	An application gateway of X11 protocol. It is designed to be used at a site that has a firewall and uses SOCKS and/or CERN WWW Proxy.
`xroute`	Routes X packets from one machine to another.

There are, as you can see, a few tools for your use. If you want a second reason for looking at these tools, keep in mind that people trying to break into your system know how to, and do, use these tools. This is where the knowledge comes in.

Knowledge Gathering

Someone once said a little knowledge goes a long way. As stated in the chapter opening, all the bells and whistles can be there, but if they are not active, they do no good. It is, therefore, important that the system staff, the users, and the keepers of the sacred root password all follow the security procedures put in place—that they gather all the knowledge necessary to adhere to those procedures.

I was at the bank the other day, filling out an application for a car loan. The person assisting me at the bank was at a copy machine in another room (I could see her through the window). Another banking person, obviously new, could be heard from his office. He was having problems logging in to the bank's computer. He came out and looked around for the bank employee helping me. He did not see her. I got his attention and pointed him toward the copy area. He thanked me and went to her and asked for the system's password because he could not remember it. She could not remember the password. He went back to his desk, checked a list of telephone numbers hanging on the wall by his phone, entered something into the computer, and was in. About that time, my bank person came out of the copy area, stuck her head in his office, and said that she recalled the password. He said he had it. She asked if he had done with the password what they normally do. He looked at his phone list and said yes. She left and returned to me at her desk.

This scenario is true. The unfortunate thing about it, besides the fact that at least two customers, the person with the employee trying to log in to the system, and I, saw the whole thing, is that they didn't know, nor did they care that others might be listening. To them it was business as usual. What can be learned from this? DON'T WRITE DOWN PASSWORDS!!!!!

Not only should passwords not be written down, but they should also not be easily associated with the user. I'll give you two examples that illustrate this point. The first involves a wonderful man from the Middle East with whom I worked on a client site. He has three boys. As a proud father, he talks about them often. When referring to them individually, he uses their first names. When referring to them cumulatively, he calls them "three boys." His password (actually, he uses the same password for all his accounts) is `threeboys`.

The second example comes from one of the sweetest people I have met in the industry. She is an unmarried person with no children. On her desk is a little stuffed cow, named Chelsea. I do not remember the significance of the name, but I remember that she really likes dairy cows. Her password is, you guessed it, `chelsea`. These peoples' passwords are probably still `threeboys` and `chelsea`.

File security is another big issue. The use of `umask` (file creation masks) should be mandated. It should also be set to the maximum amount possible. It is easy to change a particular file to give someone else access to it. It is difficult, if not impossible, to know who is looking at your files. The sensitivity of the data, of course, would certainly determine the exact level of security placed on the file. In extremely sensitive cases, such as employees' personnel records, it might be necessary to also encrypt the files.

After an audit has been done, you should have an excellent idea of what security issues you need to be aware of and which issues you need to track. The next section shows you how to track intruders.

Danger, Will Robins, Danger!

I used to love watching *Lost in Space*. On that show there was a life-sized robot that would declare, "Danger, Will Robins, danger!" when there was some danger. Unfortunately, there is no such robot to declare when there is danger on our systems. (There are some tools, but they are nowhere near as consistent as the robot was!)

If you have a lot of extra disk space, you can turn on auditing. Auditing records all user connects and disconnects from your system. If you don't rely on auditing, you should scan the logs often. As an alternative, it might be worthwhile to write a quick summary script that gives an account of the amount of time each user is on the system.

Unfortunately, there are too many holes to block them all. Measures can be placed to plug the biggest of them, but locking a computer in a vault, allowing no one access to it and no connectivity outside of the vault, is the only way to keep a system secure. The bottom line is, if users want into your system, and they are good enough, they can get in. What you have to do is prepare for the worst.

Preparing for the Worst

There are basically three things that can be done to a system, short of physically removing it. These are stealing data, destroying data, and providing easier access for next time. Physically, an intruder can destroy or remove equipment, or, if very creative, could even add hardware. Short of chaining the system to the desk, there is not much that can be done about theft. The physical security is beyond the scope of this book, anyway. What is within the scope of this book is dealing with the data, and dealing with additional access measures.

Data should be backed up on a regular basis. The backed-up information, depending on how secure it needs to be, can be kept on a shelf next to the system or kept in a locked vault at an alternative location. This is the best way of getting back data that has been destroyed.

Most of the time, though, data is not just destroyed. A more common problem is that the data is captured. This could be actual company secrets or system configuration files. It is very important to keep an eye on the system files. It is also a good idea to occasionally search for programs that have `suid` or `sgid` capability. It might be wise to search for `suid` and `sgid` files when the system is first installed. Then, later searches can be compared to this initial list.

suid and sgid

Many people talk about `suid` (set user ID) and `sgid` (set group ID) without really understanding them. The concept behind these powerful, yet dangerous, tools is that a program (not a script) is set so that it is run as the owner or group set for the program, not the person running the program. For example, say you have a program with `suid` set, and its owner is root. Anyone running the program runs that program with the permissions of the owner instead of his or her own permissions. The `passwd` command is a good example of this. The file `/etc/passwd` is writable by root, and readable by everyone. The `passwd` program has `suid` turned on. Therefore, anyone can run the `passwd` program and change their password. Because the program is running as the user root, not the actual user, the `/etc/passwd` file can be written to.

The same concept holds true for `sgid`. Instead of the program running with the permissions and authority of the group associated with the person calling the program, the program is run with the permissions and authority of the group that is associated with the program.

How to Find suid and sgid Files

The `find` command once again comes in handy. With the following command, you can search the entire system looking for programs with their `suid` or `sgid` turned on:

```
find / -perm -200 -o -perm -400 -print
```

It is probably best to run the preceding `find` command when you first load a system, saving its output to a file readable only by root. Future searches can be performed and compared to this "clean" list of `suid` and `sgid` files. This will ensure that only the files that are supposed to have these permissions really do.

Setting suid and sgid

The set user ID and set group ID can be powerful tools for giving users the ability to perform tasks without the other problems that could arise with the user having the actual permissions of that group or user. However, these can be dangerous tools as well. When considering changing the permissions on a file to be either `suid` or `sgid`, keep in mind these two things:

- Use the lowest permissions needed to accomplish the task.
- Watch for back doors.

Using the lowest permissions means not giving a file an `suid` of root if at all possible. Often, a less privileged person can be configured to do the task. The same goes for `sgid`. Many times setting the group to the appropriate non-sys group will accomplish the same task while limiting other potential problems.

Back doors come in many forms. A program that allows a shell is a back door. A program that has multiple entrances and exits are back doors. Keep in mind that if a user can run an `suid` program set to root and the program contains a back door (the user can get out of the program to a prompt without actually exiting the program), then the system keeps the effective user ID as what the program is set to (root), and the user now has root permissions.

With that said, how do you set a file to have the effective user be the owner of the file, or the effective group be the group of the file, instead of running as the user ID or the user's group ID of the person invoking the file? The permissions are added with the `chmod` command, as follows:

```
chmod u+s file(s)
chmod g+s file(s)
```

The first example sets `suid` for the file(s) listed. The second example sets `sgid` to the file(s) listed. Remember, `suid` sets the effective ID of the process to the owner associated with the file, and `sgid` sets the effective group's ID of the process to the group associated with the file. These cannot be set on nonexecutables.

File and Directory Permissions

As stated in the introduction to this chapter, file and directory permissions are the basics for providing security on a system. These, along with the authentication system, provide the basis for all security. Unfortunately, many people do not know what permissions on directories mean, or they assume they mean the same thing they do on files. The following section describes the permissions on files; after that, the permissions on directories are described.

Files

The permissions for files are split into three different sections: the owner of the file, the group associated with the file, and everyone else (the world). Each section has its own set of file permissions. These permissions provide the ability to read, write, and execute (or, of course, to deny the same). These permissions are called a file's *filemode*. Filemodes are set with the `chmod` command.

There are two ways to specify the permissions of the object. You can use the numeric coding system or the letter coding system. Using the letter coding system, the three sections are referred to as `u` for user, `g` for group, and `o` for other or `a` for all three. There are three basic types of permissions: `r` for read, `w` for write, and `x` for execute. Combinations of `r`, `w`, and `x` with the three groups provide the permissions for files. In the following example, the owner of the file has read, write, and execute permissions, while everyone else has read access only:

```
shell:/home/dpitts$ ls -l test
-rwxr--r--   1 dpitts   users           22 Sep 15 00:49 test
```

The command `ls -l` tells the computer to give you a long (`-l`) listing (`ls`) of the file (`test`). The resulting line is shown in the second code line, and it tells you a number of things about the file. First, it tells you the permissions. Next, it tells you how many links the file has. It then tells you who owns the file (`dpitts`) and what group is associated with the file (`users`). Following the ownership section, the date and timestamp for the last time the file was modified is given. Finally, the name of the file is listed (`test`). The permissions are actually made up of four sections. The first section is a single character that identifies the type of object that is listed out. Check Table 20.1 to determine what the different options are for this field.

Table 20.1. Object type identifier.

Character	*Description*
-	Plain file
b	Block special file
c	Character special file
d	Directory
l	Symbolic link
p	Named pipe
s	Socket

Following the file type identifier are the three sets of permissions: `rwx` (owner), `r--` (group), and `r--` (other).

NOTE

A small explanation needs to be made as to what read, write, and execute actually mean. For files, a user who has read capability can see the contents of the file, a user who has write capability can write to it, and a user who has execute permission can execute the file. If the file to be executed is a script, then the user must have read and execute permissions to execute the file. If the file is a binary, then just the execute permission is required to execute the file.

Directories

The permissions on a directory are the same as those used by files: read, write, and execute. The actual permissions, though, mean different things. For a directory, read access provides the ability to list the names of the files in the directory. It does not allow the other attributes to be seen (owner, group, size, and so on). Write access provides the ability to alter the directory contents. This means that the user could create and delete files in the directory. Finally, execute access lets the user make the directory the current directory.

Table 20.2 summarizes the differences between the permissions for a file and those for a directory.

Table 20.2. File permissions versus directory permissions.

Permission	*File*	*Directory*
`r`	View the contents	Search the contents
`w`	Alter file contents	Alter directory contents
`x`	Run executable file	Make it the current directory

Combinations of these permissions also allow certain tasks. For example, I already mentioned that it takes both read and execute permission to execute a script. This is because the shell must first read the file to see what to do with it. (Remember that `#! /local/bin/perl` tells it to execute the `/local/bin/perl` executable, passing the rest of the file to the executable.) There are other combinations that allow certain functionality. Table 20.3 describes the different combinations of permissions and what they mean, both for a file and for a directory.

Table 20.3. Comparison of file and directory permission combinations.

Permission	*File*	*Directory*
`---`	Cannot do anything with it.	Cannot access it or any of its subdirectories.
`r--`	Can see the contents.	Can see the contents.
`rw-`	Can see and alter the contents.	Can see and alter the contents.
`rwx`	Can see and change the contents, as well as execute the file.	Can list the contents, add or remove files, and make the directory the current directory (`cd` to it).
`r-x`	If a script, can execute it. Otherwise, provides read and execute permission.	Provides ability to change to directory and list contents, but cannot delete or add files to directory.
`--x`	Can execute if a binary.	User can execute a binary that he or she already knows about.

As stated, the permissions can also be manipulated with a numeric coding system. The basic concept is the same as the letter coding system. As a matter of fact, the permissions look exactly alike. The difference is the way the permissions are identified. The numeric system uses binary counting to determine a value for each permission and sets them. Also, the `find` command can accept the permissions as an argument using the `-perm` option. In that case, the permissions must be given in their numeric form.

With binary, you count from the right to the left. Therefore, if you look at a file, you can easily come up with its numeric coding system value. The following file has full permissions for the owner and read permissions for the group and the world:

```
shell:/home/dpitts$ ls -la test
-rwxr--r--   1 dpitts   users          22 Sep 15 00:49 test
```

This would be coded as `744`. Table 20.4 explains how this number was achieved.

Table 20.4. Numeric permissions.

Permission	*Value*
Read	4
Write	2
Execute	1

Permissions use an additive process. Therefore, a person with read, write, and execute permissions to a file would have a `7` (`4+2+1`). Read and execute would have a value of `5`. Remember, there are three sets of values, so each section would have its own value.

Table 20.5 shows both the numeric system and the character system for the permissions.

Table 20.5. Comparison of numeric and character permissions.

Permission	*Numeric*	*Character*
Read-only	4	`r--`
Write-only	2	`-w-`
Execute-only	1	`--x`
Read and write	6	`rw-`
Read and execute	5	`r-x`
Read, write, and execute	7	`rwx`

Permissions can be changed using the `chmod` command. With the numeric system, the `chmod` command must be given the value for all three fields. Therefore, to change a file to read, write, and execute by everyone, the following command would be issued:

```
$ chmod 777 <filename>
```

To perform the same task with the character system, the following command would be issued:

```
$ chmod a+rwx <filename>
```

Of course, more than one type of permission can be specified at one time. The following command adds write access for the owner of the file, and adds read and execute access to the group and everyone else:

```
$ chmod u+w,og+rx <filename>
```

The advantage that the character system provides is that you do not have to know what the previous permissions are. You can selectively add or remove permissions without worrying about the rest. With the numeric system, each section of users must always be specified. The downside of the character system is when complex changes are being made. Looking at the preceding example (`chmod u+w,og+rx <filename>`), it might have been easier to use the numeric system and replace all those letters with three numbers: `755`.

How `suid` and `sgid` Fit into This Picture

The special-purpose access modes `suid` and `sgid` add an extra character to the picture. Before looking at what a file looks like with the different special access modes, check Table 20.6 for the identifying characters for each of the modes and a reminder as to what they mean.

Table 20.6. Special-purpose access modes.

Code	*Name*	*Meaning*
`s`	`suid`	Sets process user ID on execution
`s`	`sgid`	Sets process group ID on execution

`suid` and `sgid` are used on executables. Therefore, the code is placed where the code for the executable would normally go. The following file has `suid` set:

```
$ ls -la test
-rwsr--r--   1 dpitts   users          22 Sep 15 00:49 test
```

The difference between the `suid` being set and the `sgid` being set is the placement of the code. The same file with `sgid` active would look like this:

```
$ ls -la test
-rwxr-sr--   1 dpitts   users          22 Sep 15 00:49 test
```

To set the `suid` with the character system, the following command would be executed:

```
$ chmod u+s <filename>
```

To set the `sgid` with the character system, the following command would be executed:

```
$ chmod g+s <filename>
```

To set the suid and the sgid using the numeric system, use these two commands:

```
$ chmod 2### <filename>
$ chmod 4### <filename>
```

In both instances, the ### is replaced with the rest of the values for the permissions. The additive process is used to combine permissions; therefore, the following command would add suid and sgid to a file:

```
$ chmod 6### <filename>
```

> **NOTE**
>
> A sticky bit is set using chmod 1### <filename>. If a sticky bit is set, the executable is kept in memory after it has finished executing. The display for a sticky bit is a t, placed in the last field of the permissions. Therefore, a file that has been set to 7777 would have the following permissions: -rwsrwsrwt.

The Default Mode for a File or Directory

The default mode for a file or directory is set with the umask. The umask uses the numeric system to define its value. To set the umask, you must first determine the value that you want the files to have. For example, a common file permission set is 644. The owner has read and write permission, and the rest of the world has read permission. After the value is determined, then it is subtracted from 777. Keeping the same example of 644, the value would be 133. This value is the umask value. Typically, this value is placed in a system file that is read when a user first logs on. After the value is set, all files created will set their permissions automatically using this value.

Passwords—A Second Look

The system stores the user's encrypted password in the /etc/passwd file. If the system is using a shadow password system, the value placed in this field will be x. A value of * blocks login access to the account, as * is not a valid character for an encrypted field. This field should never be edited (after it is set up) by hand, but a program such as passwd should be used so that proper encryption takes place. If this field is changed by hand, the old password is no longer valid and, more than likely, will have to be changed by root.

> **NOTE**
>
> If the system is using a shadow password system, a separate file exists called /etc/shadow that contains passwords (encrypted, of course).

A password is a secret set of characters set up by the user that is known only by the user. The system asks for the password, compares what is inputted to the known password, and, if there is a match, confirms that the user is who she says she is and lets her access the system. It cannot be said enough—do not write down your password! A person who has a user's name and password is, from the system's perspective, that user, with all the rights and privileges thereof.

Related WWW Sites

Table 20.7 shows the more standard locations to find some of the tools discussed in this chapter. Other Web sites have these tools as well, but these were chosen because they will probably still be around when this book is published and you are looking for the information.

Table 20.7. WWW sites for tools.

Tool	*Address*
`cops`	`ftp://ftp.cert.org/pub/tools/cops`
`crack`	`ftp://ftp.cert.org/pub/tools/crack`
`deslogin`	`ftp://ftp.uu.net/pub/security/des`
`findsuid.tar.Z`	`ftp://isgate.is/pub/unix/sec8/findsuid.tar.Z`
`finger` daemon	`http://www.prz.tu-berlin.de/~leitner/fingerd.html`
`freestone`	`ftp.soscorp.com/pub/sos/freestone`
`freestone`	`ftp://ftp.cs.columbia.edu/pub/sos/freestone`
`gabriel`	`ftp://ftp.best.com/pub/lat`
`ipfilter`	`http://cheops.anu.edu.au/~avalon/ip-filter.html`
`ipfirewall`	`ftp://ftp.nebulus.net/pub/bsdi/security`
`kerberos`	`http://www.contrib.andrew.cmu.edu/usr/db74/kerberos.html`
`merlin`	`http://ciac.llnl.gov/`
`npasswd`	`ftp://wuarchive.wustl.edu/usenet/comp.sources.unix/volume25/npasswd`
`obvious-pw.tar.Z`	`ftp://isgate.is/pub/unix/sec7/obvious-pw.tar.Z`
`opie`	`ftp://ftp.nrl.navy.mil/pub/security/nrl-opie/`
`pcheck.tar.Z`	`ftp://isgate.is/pub/unix/sec8/pcheck.tar.Z`
Plugslot Ltd	`http://www.var.org/~greg/PCPPSP.html`
`rsaeuro`	`ftp://ftp.ox.ac.uk/pub/crypto/misc/`
`rscan`	`http://www.umbc.edu/rscan/`
`satan`	`http://www.fish.com/satan`
Secure Telnet	`ftp://idea.sec.dsi.unimi.it/cert-it/stel.tar.gz`

Tool	*Address*
ssh	http://www.cs.hut.fi/ssh/
tcp wrappers	ftp://ftp.win.tue.nl/pub/security/
telnet (encrypted)	ftp.tu-chemnitz.de/pub/Local/informatik/sec_tel_ftp/
tiger	ftp://wuarchive.wustl.edu/packages/security/TAMU/
tis firewall toolkit	ftp://ftp.tis.com/pub/firewalls/toolkit/
tripwire	ftp://wuarchive.wustl.edu/packages/security/tripwire/
xp-beta	ftp://ftp.mri.co.jp/pub/Xp-BETA/
xroute	ftp://ftp.x.org/contrib/utilities/

Summary

Security is only as good as the users' willingness to follow the policies. This is, on many systems and in many companies, where the contention comes in. The users just want to get their job done. The administrators want to keep the undesirables out of the system. The corporate management wants to keep the corporate secrets secret. Security is, in many ways, the hardest area to get users to cooperate, but is, in fact, the most important. Users who write down or share passwords, poorly written software, and maliciousness are the biggest security problems.

For the administrator in charge of the system, the only advice that can be offered is this: The best user will only follow the policies that you follow. If you have poor security habits, they will be passed along. On the other hand, people generally rise to the minimum level they see exhibited or see as expected. It is the job of the administrator to go beyond the call of duty and gently point out improvements while at the same time fighting the dragons at the back gate trying to get into the system.

Shell Programming

by Sanjiv Guha

IN THIS CHAPTER

When you enter commands from the command line, you are entering commands one at a time and getting the response from the system. From time to time you will need to execute more than one command, one after the other, and get the final result. You can do so with a *shell program* or *shell script*. A shell program is a series of Linux commands and utilities that have been put into a file using a text editor. When you execute a shell program, each command is interpreted and executed by Linux, one after the other.

You can write shell programs and execute them like any other command under Linux. You can also execute other shell programs from within a shell program if they are in the search path. A shell program is like any other programming language and has its own syntax. You can have variables defined and assign various values and so on. These are discussed in this chapter.

Creating and Executing a Shell Program

Say you want to set up a number of aliases every time you log on. Instead of typing all the aliases every time you log on, you can put them in a file using a text editor, such as `vi`, and then execute the file.

Here is a list of what is contained in a sample file created for this purpose, `myenv`:

```
alias ll 'ls -l'
alias dir 'ls'
alias copy 'cp'
```

`myenv` can be executed in a variety of ways under Linux.

You can make `myenv` executable by using the `chmod` command as follows, and then execute it as you would any other native Linux command:

```
chmod +x myenv
```

This turns on the executable permission of `myenv`. There is one more thing you need to ensure before you can execute `myenv`. The file `myenv` must be in the search path. You can get the search path by executing

```
echo $PATH
```

If the directory where the file `myenv` is located is not in the current search path, then you must add the directory name in the search path.

Now you can execute the file `myenv` from the command line, as if it were a Linux command:

```
myenv
```

NOTE

You must ensure that the first line in your shell program starts with a pound sign (#). The pound sign tells the shell that the line is a comment. Following the pound sign, you must have an exclamation point (!), which tells the shell to run the command following the exclamation point and to use the rest of the file as input for that command. This is common practice for all shell scripting.

A second way to execute myenv under a particular shell, such as pdksh, is as follows:

```
pdksh myenv
```

This invokes a new pdksh shell and passes the filename myenv as a parameter to execute the file.

You can also execute myenv from the command line as follows:

Command	*Environment*
. myenv	pdksh and bash
source myenv	tcsh

The dot (.) is a way of telling the shell to execute the file myenv. In this case, you do not have to ensure that execute permission of the file is set. Under tcsh, you have to use the source command instead of the dot (.) command.

After executing the command myenv, you should be able to use dir from the command line to get a list of files under the current directory, and ll to get a list of files with various attributes displayed.

Variables

Linux shell programming is a full-fledged programming language and as such supports various types of variables. There are three major types of variables: environment, built-in, and user.

Environment variables are part of the system environment, and you do not have to define them. You can use them in your shell program; some of them, like PATH, can also be modified within a shell program.

Built-in variables are provided by the system; unlike environment variables, you cannot modify them.

User variables are defined by you when you write a shell script. You can use and modify them at will within the shell program.

A major difference between shell programming and other programming languages is that in shell programming, variables are not typecast; that is, you do not have to specify whether a variable is a number or a string and so on.

Assigning a Value to a Variable

Say you want to use a variable called `lcount` to count the number of iterations in a loop within a shell program. You can declare and initialize this variable as follows:

Command	*Environment*
`lcount=0`	`pdksh` and `bash`
`set lcount = 0`	`tcsh`

NOTE

Under `pdksh` and `bash`, you must ensure that the equal sign (=) does not have space before and after it.

As shell programming languages do not use typed variables, it is possible that the same variable can be used to store an integer value one time and a string another time. However, this is not recommended. You should be careful not to do this.

To store a string in a variable, you can use the following:

Command	*Environment*
`myname=Sanjiv`	`pdksh` and `bash`
`set myname = Sanjiv`	`tcsh`

The preceding can be used if the string does not have embedded spaces. If a string has embedded spaces, you can do the assignment as follows:

Command	*Environment*
`myname='Sanjiv Guha'`	`pdksh` and `bash`
`set myname = 'Sanjiv Guha'`	`tcsh`

Accessing Variable Values

You can access the value of a variable by prefixing the variable name by a `$` (dollar sign). That is, if the variable name is `var`, you can access the variable by using `$var`.

If you want to assign the value of var to the variable lcount, you can do that as follows:

Command	*Environment*
`lcount=$var`	`pdksh` and `bash`
`set lcount = $var`	`tcsh`

Positional Parameters

It is possible to write a shell script that takes a number of parameters at the time you invoke it from the command line or from another shell script. These options are supplied to the shell program by Linux as *positional parameters*. The positional parameters have special names provided by the system. The first parameter is stored in a variable called `1` (number 1) and can be accessed by using `$1` within the program. The second parameter is stored in a variable called `2` and can be accessed by using `$2` within the program, and so on. It is possible to omit one or more of the higher numbered positional parameters while invoking a shell program. For example, if a shell program `mypgm` expects two parameters—such as a first name and a last name—then you can invoke the shell program with only one parameter, the first name. However, you cannot invoke it with only the second parameter, the last name.

Here's a shell program called `mypgm1`, which takes only one parameter (a name) and displays it on the screen:

```
#Name display program
if [ $# == 0]
then
   echo "Name not provided"
else
   echo "Your name is "$1
```

In `pdksh` and `bash`, if you execute `mypgm1` as follows:

```
. mypgm1
```

you will get the output:

```
Name not provided
```

However, if you execute `mypgm1` as follows:

```
. mypgm1 Sanjiv
```

then you will get the following output:

```
Your name is Sanjiv
```

The shell program `mypgm1` also illustrates another aspect of shell programming, the built-in variables. In `mypgm1`, the variable `$#` is a built-in variable and provides the number of positional parameters passed to the shell program.

Built-in Variables

Built-in variables are a special type of variable that Linux provides to you. These variables can be used to make decisions within a program. You cannot modify the values of these variables within the shell program.

Some of these variables are

`$#`	Number of positional parameters passed to the shell program
`$?`	Code of the last command or shell program executed within the shell program
`$0`	The name of the shell program
`$*`	A single string of all arguments passed at the time of invocation of the shell program

To show these built-in variables in use, here is a sample program called `mypgm2`:

```
#my test program
echo "Number of parameters is "$#
echo "Program name is "$0
echo "Parameters as a single string is "$*
```

In `pdksh` and `bash`, if you execute `mypgm2` from the command line, as follows:

```
. mypgm2 Sanjiv Guha
```

you will get the following result:

```
Number of parameters is 2
Program name is mypgm2
Parameters as a single string is Sanjiv Guha
```

Special Characters

Some characters have special meaning to Linux shells, so using them as part of variable names or strings will cause your program to behave incorrectly. If a string contains such special characters, then you also have to use escape characters to indicate that the special characters should not be treated as special characters.

Some of these special characters are shown in the following table.

Character	*Explanation*
`$`	Indicates the beginning of a shell variable name
`¦`	Pipes standard output to the next command
`#`	Starts a comment
`&`	Executes a process in the background
`?`	Matches one character

Character	*Explanation*
*	Matches one or more characters
>	Output redirection operator
<	Input redirection operator
`	Command substitution (the backquote or backtick—the key above the Tab key)
>>	Output redirection operator (to append to a file)
[ ]	Lists a range of characters
`[a-z]`	Means all characters a through `z`
`[a,z]`	Means characters a or `z`
`. filename`	Executes the file `filename`
Space	Delimiter between two words

There are a few special characters that deserve special note. They are the double quotes ("), the single quote ('), the backslash (\), and the backtick (`). They are discussed in the following sections.

Double Quotes

If a string contains embedded spaces, you can enclose the string in double quotes (") so that the shell interprets the whole string as one entity instead of more than one. For example, if you assigned the value of `abc def` (`abc` followed by one space followed by `def`) to a variable called `x` in a shell program as follows:

Command	*Environment*
`x=abc def`	`pdksh` and `bash`
`set x = abc def`	`tcsh`

you would get an error as the shell would try to execute `def` as a separate command. What you need to do is surround the string in double quotes as follows:

Command	*Environment*
`x="abc def"`	`pdksh` and `bash`
`set x  = "abc def"`	`tcsh`

The double quotes resolve all the variables within the string. Here is an example for `pdksh` and `bash`:

```
var ="test string"
newvar="Value of var is $var"
echo $newvar
```

Here is the same example for tcsh:

```
set var = "test string"
set newvar = "Value of var is $var"
echo $newvar
```

If you execute a shell program containing these three lines, you will get the following result:

```
Value of var is test string
```

Single Quote

You can use the single quote (') to surround a string in order to stop the shell from resolving a variable. In the following example, the double quotes in the preceding example have been changed to single quotes.

pdksh and bash:

```
var ='test string'
newvar='Value of var is $var'
echo $newvar
```

tcsh:

```
set var = 'test string'
set newvar = 'Value of var is $var'
echo $newvar
```

If you execute a shell program containing these three lines, you will get the following result:

```
Value of var is $var
```

As you can see, the variable var did not get resolved.

Backslash

You can use a backslash (\) before a character to stop the shell from interpreting the following character as a special character. Say you want to assign a value of $test to a variable called var. If you use the following command:

Command	*Environment*
var=$test	pdksh and bash
set var = $test	tcsh

then a null value will be stored in var. This is because the shell will interpret $test as the value of the variable test, and as test has not been assigned any value, var will contain null. You should use the following command to correctly store $test in var:

Command	*Environment*
`var=\$test`	`pdksh` and `bash`
`set var = \$test`	`tcsh`

The backslash (`\`) before the dollar sign (`$`) signals to the shell to interpret the `$` as any other ordinary character and not to associate any special meaning to it.

Backtick

You can use the backtick (`` ` ``) character to signal the shell to execute the string delimited by the backtick. This can be used in shell programs when you want the result of execution of a command to be stored in a variable. For example, if you want to count the number of lines in a file called `test.txt` in the current directory and store the result in a variable called `var`, then you can use the following command:

Command	*Environment*
``var=`wc -l test.txt` ``	`pdksh` and `bash`
``set var = `wc -l test.txt` ``	`tcsh`

Comparison of Expressions

The logical comparison of two operators (numeric or string) is done slightly differently, depending on which shell you are in. In `pdksh` and `bash`, a command called `test` can be used to achieve comparisons of expressions. In `tcsh`, you can write an expression to accomplish the same thing.

pdksh and bash

This section covers comparisons using the `pdksh` or `bash` shells. Later in the chapter, the section "`tcsh`" contains a similar discussion for the `tcsh` shell.

The syntax of the `test` command is as follows:

```
test expression
```

or

```
[ expression ]
```

Both these forms of `test` commands are processed the same way by `pdksh` and `bash`. The `test` commands support the following types of comparisons:

- String comparison
- Numeric comparison

- File operators
- Logical operators

String Comparison

The following operators can be used to compare two string expressions:

`=`	To compare if two strings are equal
`!=`	To compare if two strings are not equal
`-n`	To evaluate if the string length is greater than zero
`-z`	To evaluate if the string length is equal to zero

Next are some examples comparing two strings, `string1` and `string2`, in a shell program called `compare1`:

```
string1="abc"
string2="abd"
if [ string1 = string2 ] then
   echo "string1 equal to string2"
else
   echo "string1 not equal to string2"
fi

if [ string2 != string1 ] then
   echo "string2 not equal to string1"
else
   echo "string2 equal to string2"
fi

if [ string1 ] then
   echo "string1 is not empty"
else
   echo "string1 is empty"
fi

if [ -n string2 ] then
   echo "string2 has a length greater than zero"
else
   echo "string2 has length equal to zero"
fi

if [ -z string ]
   echo "string1 has a length equal to zero"
else
  echo "string1 has a length greater than zero"
fi
```

If you execute `compare1`, you will get the following result:

```
string1 not equal to string2
string2 not equal to string1
string1 is not empty
string2 has a length greater than zero
string1 has a length greater than zero
```

If two strings are not equal in size, the system will pad the shorter string with trailing spaces for comparison. That is, if `string1` has value of `abc` and that of `string2` is `ab`, then for comparison purposes, `string2` will be padded with trailing spaces—that is, it will have a value of `ab `.

Number Comparison

The following operators can be used to compare two numbers:

`-eq`	To compare if two numbers are equal
`-ge`	To compare if one number is greater than or equal to the other number
`-le`	To compare if one number is less than or equal to the other number
`-ne`	To compare if two numbers are not equal
`-gt`	To compare if one number is greater than the other number
`-lt`	To compare if one number is less than the other number

The following examples compare two numbers, `number1` and `number2`, in a shell program called `compare2`:

```
number1=5
number2=10
number3=5

if [ number1 -eq number3 ] then
   echo "number1 is equal to number3"
else
   echo "number1 is not equal to number3"
fi

if [ number1 -ne number2 ] then
   echo "number1 is not equal to number2"
else
   echo "number1 is equal to number2"
fi

if [ number1 -gt number2 ] then
   echo "number1 is greater than number2"
else
   echo "number1 is not greater than number2"
fi

if [ number1 -ge number3 ] then
   echo "number1 is greater than or equal to number3"
else
   echo "number1 is not greater than or equal to number3"
fi

if [ number1 -lt number2 ] then
   echo "number1 is less than number2"
```

```
else
   echo "number1 is not less than number2"
fi

if [ number1 -le number3 ] then
   echo "number1 is less than or equal to number3"
else
   echo "number1 is not less than or equal to number3"
fi
```

When you execute the shell program `compare2`, you will get the following results:

```
number1 is equal to number3
number1 is not equal to number2
number1 is not greater than number2
number1 is greater than or equal to number3
number1 is less than number2
number1 is less than or equal to number3
```

File Operators

These operators can be used as file comparison operators:

`-d`	To ascertain if a file is a directory
`-f`	To ascertain if a file is a regular file
`-r`	To ascertain if read permission is set for a file
`-s`	To ascertain if the name of a file has a length greater than zero
`-w`	To ascertain if write permission is set for a file
`-x`	To ascertain if execute permission is set for a file

Assume that in a shell program called `compare3`, there is a file called `file1` and a subdirectory `dir1` under the current directory. Assume that `file1` has a permission of `r-x` (read and execute permission) and `dir1` has a permission of `rwx` (read, write, and execute permission).

The code for `compare3` would look like this:

```
if [ -d dir1 ] then
   echo "dir1 is a directory"
else
   echo "dir1 is not a directory"
fi

if [ -f dir1 ] then
   echo "file1 is a regular file"
else
   echo "file1 is not a regular file"
fi

if [ -r file1 ] then
   echo "file1 has read permission"
else
   echo "file1 does not have read permission"
fi
```

```
if [ -w file1 ] then
   echo "file1 has write permission"
else
   echo "file1 does not have write permission"
fi

if [ -x dir1 ] then
   echo "dir1 has execute permission"
else
   echo "dir1 does not have execute permission"
fi
```

If you execute the file compare3, you will get the following results:

```
dir1 is a directory
file1 is a regular file
file1 has read permission
file1 does not have write permission
dir1 has execute permission
```

Logical Operators

Logical operators are used to compare expressions using the rules of logic; the characters represent NOT, AND, and OR:

!	To negate a logical expression
-a	To logically AND two logical expressions
-o	To logically OR two logical expressions

tcsh

As stated earlier, the comparisons are different under tcsh than they are under pdksh and bash. This section explains the same concepts as the section "pdksh and bash" but uses the syntax necessary for the tcsh shell environment.

String Comparison

Operators that can be used to compare two string expressions are as follows:

==	To compare if two strings are equal
!=	To compare if two strings are not equal

The following examples compare two strings, string1 and string2, in the shell program compare1:

```
set string1 = "abc"
set string2 = "abd"

if  (string1 == string2)  then
   echo "string1 equal to string2"
else
   echo "string1 not equal to string2"
endif
```

```
if  (string2 != string1)  then
   echo "string2 not equal to string1"
else
   echo "string2 equal to string1"
endif
```

If you execute compare1, you will get the following results:

```
string1 not equal to string2
string2 not equal to string1
```

Number Comparison

These operators can be used to compare two numbers:

>=	To compare if one number is greater than or equal to the other number
<=	To compare if one number is less than or equal to the other number
>	To compare if one number is greater than the other number
<	To compare if one number is less than the other number

The next examples compare two numbers, number1 and number2, in a shell program called compare2:

```
set number1 = 5
set number2 = 10
set number3 = 5

if  (number1 > number2)  then
   echo "number1 is greater than number2"
else
   echo "number1 is not greater than number2"
endif

if  (number1 >= number3) then
   echo "number1 is greater than or equal to number3"
else
   echo "number1 is not greater than or equal to number3"
endif

if  (number1 < number2)  then
   echo "number1 is less than number2"
else
   echo "number1 is not less than number2"
endif

if  (number1 <= number3) then
   echo "number1 is less than or equal to number3"
else
   echo "number1 is not less than or equal to number3"
endif
```

Executing the shell program compare2, you will get the following results:

```
number1 is not greater than number2
number1 is greater than or equal to number3
number1 is less than number2
number1 is less than or equal to number3
```

File Operators

These operators can be used as file comparison operators:

`-d`	To ascertain if a file is a directory
`-e`	To ascertain if a file exists
`-f`	To ascertain if a file is a regular file
`-o`	To ascertain if a user is the owner of a file
`-r`	To ascertain if read permission is set for a file
`-w`	To ascertain if write permission is set for a file
`-x`	To ascertain if execute permission is set for a file
`-z`	To ascertain if a file size is zero

The following examples are based on a shell program called `compare3` that contains a file called `file1` and a subdirectory `dir1` under the current directory. Assume that `file1` has a permission of `r-x` (read and execute permission) and `dir1` has a permission of `rwx` (read, write, and execute permission).

The following is the code for the `compare3` shell program:

```
if  (-d dir1) then
   echo "dir1 is a directory"
else
   echo "dir1 is not a directory"
endif

if (-f dir1)  then
   echo "file1 is a regular file"
else
   echo "file1 is not a regular file"
endif

if (-r file1) then
   echo "file1 has read permission"
else
   echo "file1 does not have read permission"
endif

if (-w file1) then
   echo "file1 has write permission"
else
   echo "file1 does not have write permission"
endif

if (-x dir1) then
   echo "dir1 has execute permission"
else
   echo "dir1 does not have execute permission"
endif

if (-z file1) then
   echo "file1 has zero length"
```

```
else
   echo "file1 has greater than zero length"
endif
```

If you execute the file `compare3`, you will get the following results:

```
dir1 is a directory
file1 is a regular file
file1 has read permission
file1 does not have write permission
dir1 has execute permission
file1 has greater than zero length
```

Logical Operators

Logical operators are used with conditional statements. These operators are used to perform logical ANDs and ORs, and the third operator is used to negate a logical expression:

`!`	To negate a logical expression
`&&`	To logically AND two logical expressions
`¦¦`	To logically OR two logical expressions

Iteration Statements

The iteration statements are used to repeat a series of commands contained within the iteration statement to be executed multiple times.

The `for` Statement

There are a number of formats of the `for` statement. The first format is as follows:

```
for curvar in list
do
    statements
done
```

This form should be used if you want to execute *`statements`* once for each value in *`list`*; for each iteration, the current value of the list is assigned to `vcurvar`. *`list`* can be a variable containing a number of items or a list of values separated by spaces. This format of the `for` statement is used by `pdksh` and `bash`.

The second format is as follows:

```
for curvar
do
    statements
done
```

In this form, the *`statements`* are executed once for each of the positional parameters passed to the shell program. For each iteration, the current value of the positional parameter is assigned to the variable `curvar`.

This form can also be written as follows:

```
for curvar in "$@"
do
    statements
done
```

Remember that `$@` provides you a list of positional parameters passed to the shell program, all stringed together.

Under `tcsh`, the `for` statement is called `foreach`. The format is as follows:

```
foreach curvar (list)
    statements
end
```

In this form, *`statements`* are executed once for each value in *`list`*, and for each iteration, the current value of *`list`* is assigned to `curvar`.

Suppose you want to create a backup version of each file in the directory to a subdirectory called `backup`. You can do the following in `pdksh` and `bash`:

```
for filename in `ls`
do
   cp $filename backup/$filename
   if [ $? -ne 0 ] then
      echo "copy for $filename failed"
   fi
done
```

In the preceding example, a backup copy of each file is created, and if the copy fails, a message is generated.

The same example in `tcsh` is as follows:

```
foreach filename (`ls`)
   cp $filename backup/$filename
   if $? -ne 0 then
      echo "copy for $filename failed"
   fi
end
```

The `while` Statement

The `while` statement can be used to execute a series of commands while a specified condition is true. The loop will terminate as soon as the specified condition evaluates to false. It is possible that the loop will not execute at all if the specified condition evaluates to false right at the beginning. You should be careful with the `while` command, as the loop might never terminate if the specified condition never evaluates to false.

In `pdksh` and `bash`, the following format is used:

```
while expression
do
    statements
done
```

In tcsh, the following format is used:

```
while (expression)
    Statements
end
```

If you want to add the first five even numbers, you can use the following shell program in pdksh and bash:

```
loopcount=0
result=0
while [ $loopcount -lt 5 ]
do
   loopcount = `expr $loopcount + 1`
   result = `$result + ($loopcount * 2)`
done

echo "result is $result"
```

In tcsh, this program can be written as follows:

```
set loopcount = 0
set result = 0
while ( $loopcount < 5 )
   set loopcount  =  `expr $loopcount + 1`
   set result  =  `$result + ($loopcount * 2)`
end

echo "result is $result"
```

The until Statement

The until statement can be used to execute a series of commands until a specified condition is true. The loop will terminate as soon as the specified condition evaluates to true.

In pdksh and bash, the following format is used:

```
until expression
do
    statements
done
```

As you can see, the format is similar to the while statement.

If you want to add the first five even numbers, you can use the following shell program in pdksh and bash:

```
loopcount=0
result=0
until [ $loopcount -ge 5 ]
do
   loopcount = `expr $loopcount + 1`
   result = `$result + ($loopcount * 2)`
done

echo "result is $result"
```

The example here is identical to the example for the `while` statement, except that the condition being tested is just the opposite of the condition specified in the `while` statement.

The `tcsh` command does not support the `until` statement.

The `repeat` Statement (`tcsh`)

The `repeat` statement is used to execute only one command a fixed number of times.

If you want to print a hyphen (-) 80 times on the screen, you can use the following command:

```
repeat  80 echo '-'
```

The `select` Statement (`pdksh`)

The `select` statement is used to generate a menu list if you are writing a shell program that expects input from the user online. The format of `select` statement is as follows:

```
select  item in itemlist
do
    Statements
done
```

`itemlist` is optional. If not provided, then the system will iterate through the entries in `item` one at a time. If, however, *`itemlist`* is provided, then the system will iterate for each entry in *`itemlist`*, and the current value of *`itemlist`* is assigned to `item` for each iteration, which then can be used as part of the statements being executed.

If you want to write a menu that gives the user a choice of picking a `Continue` or a `Finish`, then you can write the following shell program:

```
select  item in Continue Finish
do
   if [ $item = "Finish" ] then
      break
   fi
done
```

When the `select` command is executed, the system will display a menu with numeric choices to the user—in this case, `1` for `Continue` and `2` for `Finish`. If the user chooses `1`, the variable `item` will contain a value of `Continue`, and if the user chooses `2`, the variable `item` will contain a value of `Finish`. When `2` is chosen by the user, the `if` statement will be executed and the loop will terminate.

The `shift` Statement

The `shift` statement is used to process the positional parameters, one at a time, from left to right. As you remember, the positional parameters are identified as `$1`, `$2`, `$3`, and so on. The effect of the `shift` command is that each positional parameter is moved one position to the left and the current `$1` parameter is lost.

The format of the `shift` command is as follows:

```
shift  number
```

The parameter *number* is the number of places to be shifted and is optional. If not specified, the default is `1`; that is, the parameters are shifted one position to the left. If specified, then parameters are shifted *number* positions to the left.

The `shift` command is useful when you are writing shell programs in which a user can pass different options. Depending on the specified option, the parameters that follow can mean different things or might not be there at all.

Conditional Statements

Conditional statements are used in shell programs to decide which part of the program to execute depending on specified conditions.

The `if` Statement

The `if` statement evaluates a logical expression to make a decision. An `if` condition has the following format in `pdksh` and `bash`:

```
if [ expression ] then
    Statements
elif [expression ] then
    Statements
else
    Statements
fi
```

The `if` conditions can be nested. That is, an `if` condition can contain another `if` condition within it. It is not necessary for an `if` condition to have an `elif` or `else` part. The `else` part is executed if none of the expressions specified in the `if` statement and optional in subsequent `elif` statements are true. The word `fi` is used to indicate the end of the `if` statements. This is very useful if you have nested `if` conditions. In such a case you should be able to match `fi` to `if` to ensure that all the `if` statements are properly coded.

In the following example, a variable `var` can have two values: `Yes` and `No`. Any other value is an invalid value. This can be coded as follows:

```
if [ $var = "Yes" ] then
   echo "Value is Yes"
elif [ $var = "No" ] then
   echo "Value is No"
else
   echo "Invalid value"
fi
```

In `tcsh`, the `if` statement has two forms. The first form, similar to the one for `pdksh` and `bash`, is as follows:

```
if (expression) then
    Statements
else if (expression) then
    Statements
else
    Statements
endif
```

The if conditions can be nested. That is, an if condition can contain another if condition within it. It is not necessary for an if condition to have an else part. The else part is executed if none of the expressions specified in any of the if statements are true. The optional if (else if (*expression*) then) part of the statement is executed if the condition following it is true and the previous if statement is not true. The word endif is used to indicate the end of the if statements. This is very useful if you have nested if conditions. In such a case you should be able to match endif to if to ensure that all the if statements are properly coded.

Remember the example of the variable var having only two values, Yes and No, for pdksh and bash? Here is how it would be coded with tcsh:

```
if ($var == "Yes") then
   echo "Value is Yes"
else if ($var == "No" ) then
   echo "Value is No"
else
   echo "Invalid value"
endif
```

The second form of if condition for tcsh is as follows:

```
if (expression) command
```

In this format, only a single command can be executed if the expression evaluates to true.

The case Statement

The case statement is used to execute statements depending on a discrete value or a range of values matching the specified variable. In most cases, you can use a case statement instead of an if statement if you have a large number of conditions.

The format of a case statement for pdksh and bash is as follows:

```
case str in
   str1 | str2)
      Statements;;
   str3|str4)
      Statements;;
   *)
      Statements;;
esac
```

You can specify a number of discrete values—such as str1, str2, and so on—for each condition, or you can specify a value with a wildcard. The last condition should be * (asterisk) and will be executed if none of the other conditions are met. For each of the specified conditions, all the associated statements until the double semicolon (;;) are executed.

You can write a script that will echo the name of the month if you provide the month number as a parameter. If you provide a number other than one between 1 and 12, then you will get an error message. The script is as follows:

```
case $1 in
   01 | 1) echo "Month is January";;
   02 | 2) echo "Month is February";;
   03 | 3) echo "Month is March";;
   04 | 4) echo "Month is April";;
   05 | 5) echo "Month is May";;
   06 | 6) echo "Month is June";;
   07 | 7) echo "Month is July";;
   08 | 8) echo "Month is August";;
   09 | 9) echo "Month is September";;
   10) echo "Month is October";;
   11) echo "Month is November";;
   12) echo "Month is December";;
   *) echo "Invalid parameter";;
esac
```

It is important that you end the statements under each condition with a double semicolon (`;;`). If you do not do that, then the statements under the next condition will also be executed.

The format for a `case` statement for `tcsh` is as follows:

```
switch (str)
   case str1|str2:
      Statements
      breaksw
   case str3|str4:
      Statements
      breaksw
   default:
      Statements
      breaksw
endsw
```

You can specify a number of discrete values—such as `str1`, `str2`, and so on—for each condition, or you can specify a value with a wildcard. The last condition should be `default` and will be executed if none of the other conditions are met. For each of the specified conditions, all the associated statements until `breaksw` are executed.

The example that echoes the month when a number is given, shown earlier for `pdksh` and `bash`, can be written in `tcsh` as follows:

```
switch  ( $1 )
   case 01 | 1:
      echo "Month is January"
      breaksw
   case 02 | 2:
      echo "Month is February"
      breaksw
   case 03 | 3:
      echo "Month is March"
      breaksw
```

```
    case 04 ¦ 4:
        echo "Month is April"
        breaksw
    case 05 ¦ 5:
        echo "Month is May"
        breaksw
    case 06 ¦ 6:
        echo "Month is June"
        breaksw
    case 07 ¦ 7:
        echo "Month is July"
        breaksw
    case 08 ¦ 8:
        echo "Month is August"
        breaksw
    case 09 ¦ 9:
        echo "Month is September"
        breaksw
    case 10:
        echo "Month is October"
        breaksw
    case 11:
        echo "Month is November"
        breaksw
    case 12:
        echo "Month is December"
        breaksw
    default:
        echo "Invalid parameter"
        breaksw
endsw
```

It is important that you end the statements under each condition with `breaksw`. If you do not, the statements under the next condition will also be executed.

Miscellaneous Statements

There are two other statements that you should be aware of. These are the `break` statement and the `exit` statement.

The break Statement

The `break` statements can be used to terminate an iteration loop. The loop can be a `for`, `until`, or `repeat` command, for example.

The exit Statement

`exit` statements can be used to exit a shell program. You can optionally use a number after `exit`. If the current shell program has been called by another shell program, then the calling program can check for the code and make a decision accordingly.

Functions

As do other programming languages, shell programs also support *functions*. A function is a piece of shell program that does a particular process that can be used more than once in the shell program. Writing a function will help you write shell programs without duplication of code.

Following is the format of a function definition in `pdksh` and `bash`:

```
func(){
   Statements
}
```

You can call a function as follows:

```
func param1 param2 param3
```

The parameters, *`param1`*, *`param2`*, and so on, are optional. You can also pass the parameters as a single string, for example, `$@`. A function can parse the parameters as if they were positional parameters passed to a shell program.

An example is a function that displays the name of the month or an error message if you pass a month number. Here is the example, in `pdksh` and `bash`:

```
Displaymonth() {
   case $1 in
      01 | 1) echo "Month is January";;
      02 | 2) echo "Month is February";;
      03 | 3) echo "Month is March";;
      04 | 4) echo "Month is April";;
      05 | 5) echo "Month is May";;
      06 | 6) echo "Month is June";;
      07 | 7) echo "Month is July";;
      08 | 8) echo "Month is August";;
      09 | 9) echo "Month is September";;
      10) echo "Month is October";;
      11) echo "Month is November";;
      12) echo "Month is December";;
      *) echo "Invalid parameter";;
   esac
}

displaymonth 8
```

The preceding program will display the following:

```
Month is August
```

Summary

In this chapter, you have learned how to write a shell program. Shell programs can be used to write programs that can be used to do simple things such as setting a number of aliases when you log on as well as complicated things such as customizing your shell environment.

Part VI

Automation, Programming, and Modifying Source Code

IN THIS PART

CHAPTER 22

Automating Tasks

by Cameron Laird

IN THIS CHAPTER

"[T]he three great virtues of a programmer: *laziness*, *impatience*, and *hubris*."

Wall & Schwartz, in *Programming Perl*

Automation enlists a machine—a Linux computer, in the present case—to perform jobs. What makes this definition live, though, and the true subject of this chapter, is *attitude*. The most important step you can take in understanding mechanisms of automation under Red Hat Linux is to adopt the attitude that the computer works for *you*. After you've done that, when you realize you're too lazy to type in a telephone number that the machine should already know, or too impatient to wait until midnight to start backups, and when you have enough confidence in your own creativity to teach the machine a better way, the technical details will work themselves out. This chapter offers more than a dozen examples of how small, understandable automation initiatives make an immediate difference. Let them lead you to your own successes.

First Example—Automating Data Entry

How can the details work out? Let's look at an example from yesterday (the day before I started to write this chapter).

Problem and Solution

A client wanted to enhance an online catalog to include thumbnail pictures of the merchandise. After a bit of confusion about what this really meant, I realized that I needed to update a simple database table of products to include a new column (or attribute, or value) that would specify the filenames of the thumbnails. The database management system has a couple of interactive front ends, and I'm a swift typist, so it probably would have been quickest to point and click my way through the two hundred picture updates. Did I do that? Of course not—what happened later proved the wisdom of this decision. Instead, I wrote a shell script to automate the update, which is shown in Listing 22.1.

Listing 22.1. A shell script that updates a database.

```
# picture names seem to look like {$DIR/137-13p.jpg,$DIR/201-942f.jpg,...}  The
#     corresponding products appear to be {137-13P, 201-942F, ...}
DIR=/particular/directory/for/my/client

      # Will we use .gif-s, also, eventually?  I don't know.
for F in $DIR/*.jpg
do
            # BASE will have values {137-13p,201-942f, ...}
      BASE=`basename $F .jpg`
            # The only suffixes I've encountered are 'p' and 'f', so I'll simply
            #     transform those two.
            # Example values for PRODUCT:  {137-13P, 201-942F, ...}
      PRODUCT=`echo $BASE | tr pf PF`
            # one_command is another shell script, that passes a line of SQL to
              ➥the DBMS.
      one_command update catalog set Picture = "'$DIR/$BASE.jpg'" where Product
      ➥= "'$PRODUCT'"
done
```

As it turned out, the team decided within a couple days that the pictures needed to be in a different directory, so it was only a few seconds' work to update the penultimate line of the script and add a comment, such as

```
    ...
        # Do *not* include a directory specification in Picture; that will be
        # known only at the time the data are retrieved.
    one_command update catalog set Picture = "'$BASE.jpg'" where Product =
➥"'$PRODUCT'"
done
```

and rerun it. It's inevitable we'll someday have more pictures to add to the database or will want reports on orphaned pictures (those that haven't been connected yet to any product), and this same script, or a close derivative of it, will come into play again.

Analysis of the Implementation

Let's work through the example in Listing 22.1 in detail, to practice the automation mentality.

Do you understand how the script in Listing 22.1 works? Chapter 21, "Shell Programming," explains shell processing, and Appendix B, "Top 50 Linux Commands and Utilities," presents everything you're likely to need about the most commonly used UNIX utilities. You can always learn more about these by reading the corresponding man pages or any of the fine books available on shell programming. The most certain way to learn, of course, is to experiment on your own. For example, if you have any question about what `man tr` means by "...translation...," it's an easy matter to experiment, such as with

```
tr pf PF <<HERE
abcopqOPQ
FfpPab
HERE
```

and conclude that you're on the right track when you see the following:

```
abcoPqOPQ
FFPPab
```

This is one of the charms of relying on shells for automation; it's easy to bounce between interaction and automation, which shapes a powerful didactic perspective and a check on understanding.

The sample product catalog script in Listing 22.1 is written for `sh` processing. I strongly recommend this be your target for scripts, rather than `ksh`, `csh`, or `bash`. I much prefer any of the latter for interactive, command-line use. In automating, though, when I'm often connecting to hosts that don't use Red Hat Linux, availability and esoteric security issues have convinced me to code using constructs that `sh`, and therefore all the shells, recognizes. Default Red Hat Linux installations link `/bin/sh` and `/bin/bash`. All the work in this chapter, though, is written so that it will function properly no matter what the details are of your host's configuration. Chapter 21 gives more details on the differences among shells, and the page http://starbase.neosoft.com/~claird/comp.unix.shell/shell.html supplements this with a few remarks targeted particularly to readers of this chapter. Incidentally, if you have a question that the URLs given here don't answer, e-mail me at claird@neosoft.com, and I'll update the pages available on the World Wide Web.

Did I really include the in-line comments, the lines that begin with #, when I first wrote the script in Listing 22.1? Yes. I've made this level of source code documentation a habit, and it's one I recommend to you. If your life is at all like mine, telephones ring, coworkers chat, and power supplies fail; I find it easier to type this much detail as I'm thinking about it, rather than risk having to re-create my thoughts in case of an interruption. Also, it's *much* easier to pick up the work again days or weeks later. Writing for human readability also eases the transition when you pass your work on to others.

Listing 22.1 begins by assigning a shell variable DIR in line 3. It's good practice to make such an assignment, even for a variable (apparently) used only once. It contributes to self-documentation and generally enhances maintainability; it's easy to look at the top of the script and see immediately on what magic words or configuration in the outside environment (/particular/directory/for/my/client, in this case; see line 3) the script depends.

Many of the jobs you'll want to accomplish involve a quantifier: "change all...," "correct every...," and so on. The shell's looping constructs, for and while, are your friends. You'll make almost daily use of them.

basename and tr are universally available and widely used. tr, like many UNIX utilities, expects to read standard input. If you have information in shell variables, you can feed tr the information you want, either through a pipe from echo, as in

```
echo $VARIABLE ¦ tr [a-z] [A-Z]
```

or an equivalent, or with a so-called HERE document, such as

```
tr [a-z] [A-Z] <<HERE
$VARIABLE
HERE
```

or perhaps by creating a temporary file:

```
echo $VARIABLE >$TMPFILE
tr [a-z] [A-Z] $TMPFILE
```

one_command, as invoked in line 15 of Listing 22.1, is a two-line shell script I had written earlier in the day to process SQL commands. Why not in-line the body of that script here? Although that's technically feasible, I have a strong preference for small, simple programs that are easy to understand and correspondingly easy to implement correctly. one_command already has been verified to do one small job reliably, so the script lets it do that job. This fits with the UNIX tradition that counsels combining robust toolkit pieces to construct grander works.

In fact, notice that the example in Listing 22.1 shows the shell's nature as a "glue" language. There's a small amount of processing within the shell in manipulating filenames, and then most of the work is handed off to other commands; the shell just "glues" together results. This is typical, and a correct style you should adopt for your own scripting.

Certainly it was pleasant when the filenames changed and I realized I could rework one word of the script, rather than retyping the two hundred entries. As satisfying as this was, the total benefit of automation is still more profound. Even greater than saving my time are the improvements in quality, traceability, and reusability this affords. With the script, I control the data entering the database at a higher level and eliminate whole categories of error: mistyping, accidentally pushing a wrong button in a graphical user interface, and so on. Also, the script in Listing 22.1 records my procedure, in case it's later useful to audit the data. Suppose, for example, that next year it's decided I shouldn't have inserted any of these references to the database's `Picture` attribute. How many will have to be backed out? Useful answers—at most, the count of `$DIR/*.jpg`—can be read directly from the script; there's no need to rely on memory or speculate.

Tips for Improving Automation Technique

You're in charge of your career in automation. Along with everything else this chapter advises, you'll go farthest if you do the following:

- Improve your automation technique.
- Engineer well.

These tips have specific meaning in the rest of this chapter. Look for ways to apply them in all that follows.

Continuing Education

There are three important ways to improve your skill with these techniques, which apply equally well whether you're using Perl, `cron`, Expect, or another mechanism:

- Scan the documentation.
- Read good scripts.
- Practice writing scripts.

Documentation has the reputation of being dry and even unreadable. It's very important you learn how to employ it. All the tools presented here have man pages, which you need to be comfortable using. Read these documents and reread them. Authors of the tools faced many of the challenges you do. Often, reading through the lists of options or keywords, you'll realize that particular capabilities apply exactly to your situation. Study the documentation with this in mind; look for the ideas that you can use. Give particular attention to commands you don't recognize. If some of them—`cu`, perhaps, or `od`—are largely superannuated, you'll realize in reading about others—such as `tput`, `ulimit`, `bc`, `nice`, or `wait`—that earlier users were confronted with just the situations that confound your own work. Stand on their shoulders and see farther.

It's important to read good programming. Aspiring literary authors find inspiration in Pushkin and Pynchon, not grammar primers; similarly, you'll go farthest when you read the best work of the best programmers. Look in the columns of computer magazines and, most importantly, the archives of software with freely available source. Good examples of coding occasionally turn up in Usenet discussions. Prize these; read them and learn from the masters.

All the examples in this chapter are written to be easy to use. They typically do one small task completely; this is one of the best ways to demonstrate a new concept. Although exception handling, and argument validation in particular, is important, it is beyond the scope of this chapter.

Crystallize your learning by writing your own scripts. All the documents you read will make more sense after you put the knowledge in place with your own experience.

Good Engineering

The other advice for those pursuing automation is to practice good engineering. This always starts with a clear, well-defined goal. Automation isn't an absolute good; it's only a method for achieving human goals. Part of what you'll learn in working through this chapter is how much, and how little, to automate.

When your goal is set, move as close to it as you can with components that are already written. "Glue" existing programs together with small, understandable scripting modules. Choose meaningful variable names. Define interfaces carefully. Write comments.

Shell Scripts

You already learned many of the elements of automation in Part IV, "System Administration and Management," particularly in Chapter 14, "Getting Started with Red Hat Linux"; and Appendix B supplements it. Let's look at a few additional examples of scripts that are often useful in day-to-day operation.

chstr

Users who maintain source code, client lists, and other records often want to launch a find-and-replace operation from the command line. It's useful to have a variant of `chstr` on UNIX hosts. Listing 22.2 gives one example.

Listing 22.2. `chstr`—a simple find-and-replace operation.

```
########
#
# See usage() definition, below, for more details.
#
# This implementation doesn't do well with complicated escape
#     sequences. That has been no more than a minor problem in
```

```
#     the real world.
#
########
usage() {
     echo \
"chstr BEFORE AFTER <filenames>
     changes the first instance of BEFORE to AFTER in each line of <filenames>,
     and reports on the differences.
Examples:
     chstr TX Texas */addresses.*
     chstr ii counter2 *.c"
     exit 0
}

case $1 in
     -h¦-help)     usage;;
esac

if test $# -lt 3
then
     usage
fi

TMPDIR=/tmp
     # It's OK if more than one instance of chstr is run simultaneously.
     #     The TMPFILE names are specific to each invocation, so there's
     #     no conflict.
TMPFILE=$TMPDIR/chstr.$$

BEFORE=$1
AFTER=$2

     # Toss the BEFORE and AFTER arguments out of the argument list.
shift;shift

for FILE in $*
do
     sed -e "s/$BEFORE/$AFTER/" $FILE >$TMPFILE
     echo "$FILE:"
     diff $FILE $TMPFILE
     echo ""
     mv $TMPFILE $FILE
done
```

Most interactive editors permit a form of global search-and-replace, and some even make it easy to operate on more than one file. Perhaps that's a superior automation for your needs. If not, `chstr` is a minimal command-line alternative that is maximally simple to use.

WWW Retrieval

A question that arises frequently is how to automate retrieval of pages from the World Wide Web. This section shows the simplest of many techniques.

FTP Retrieval

Create a shell script, retrieve_one, with the contents of Listing 22.3 and with execution enabled (that is, command chmod +x retrieve_one).

Listing 22.3. retrieve_one—automating FTP retrieval.

```
# Usage:  "retrieve_one HOST:FILE" uses anonymous FTP to connect
#     to HOST and retrieve FILE into the local directory.

MY_ACCOUNT=myaccount@myhost.com
HOST=`echo $1 | sed -e "s/:.*//"`
FILE=`echo $1 | sed -e "s/.*://"`
LOCAL_FILE=`basename $FILE`

     # -v:  report all statistics.
     # -n:  connect without interactive user authentication.
ftp -v -n $HOST << SCRIPT
     user anonymous $MY_ACCOUNT
     get $FILE $LOCAL_FILE
     quit
SCRIPT
```

retrieve_one is useful for purposes such as ordering a current copy of a FAQ into your local directory; start experimenting with it by making a request with the following:

```
retrieve_one rtfm.mit.edu:/pub/usenet-by-hierarchy/comp/os/linux/answers/linux/faq/
➥part1
```

HTTP Retrieval

For an HTTP interaction, let the Lynx browser do the bulk of the work. The Lynx browser that comes as part of the Red Hat distribution is adequate for all but the most specialized purposes. In those cases, pick up a binary executable of the latest Lynx and simple installation directions at http://www.crl.com/~subir/lynx/bin. Although most Lynx users think of Lynx as an interactive browser, it's also handy for dropping a copy of the latest headlines, with live links, in a friend's mailbox with

```
lynx -source http://www.cnn.com | mail someone@somewhere.com
```

To create a primitive news update service, script

```
NEW=/tmp/news.new
OLD=/tmp/news.old
URL=http://www.cnn.com
while true
do
     mv $NEW $OLD
     lynx -dump -nolist $URL >$NEW
     diff $NEW $OLD
          # Wait ten minutes before starting the next comparison.
     sleep 600
done
```

and launch it in the background. Any changes in the appearance of CNN's home page will come to your screen every ten minutes. This simple approach is less practical than you might first expect because CNN periodically shuffles the content without changing the information. It's an instructive example, though, and a starting point from which you can elaborate your own scripts.

Conclusions on Shell Programming

Shells are "glue"; if there's a way to get an application to perform an action from the command line, there's almost certainly a way to "wrap" it in a shell script that gives you power over argument validation, iteration, and input-output redirection. These are powerful techniques and well worth the few minutes of study and practice it takes to begin learning them.

Even small automations pay off. My personal rule of thumb is to write tiny disposable one-line shell scripts when I expect to use a sequence even twice during a session. For example, although I have a sophisticated set of reporting commands for analyzing World Wide Web server logs, I also find myself going to the trouble of editing a disposable script such as `/tmp/r9`,

```
grep claird `ls -t /usr/cern/log/* ¦ head -1` ¦ grep -v $1 ¦ wc -l
```

to do quick, ad hoc queries on recent hit patterns; this particular example reports on the number of requests for pages that include the string `claird` and exclude the first argument to `/tmp/r9`, in the most recent log.

cron and at Jobs

Linux comes with several utilities that manage the rudiments of job scheduling. `at` schedules a process for later execution, and `cron` (or `crontab`—it has a couple of interfaces, and different engineers use both these names) periodically launches a process.

cron and find—Exploring Disk Usage

One eternal reality of system administration is that there's not enough disk space. The following sections offer a couple little expedients recommended for keeping on top of what's happening with your system.

Cores

`cron` use always involves a bit of setup. Although Appendix B gives more details on `cron`'s features and options, I'll go carefully through an example here, one that helps track down core clutter.

You need at least one external file to start using the `cron` facility. Practice `cron` concepts by commanding first

```
echo "0,5,10,15,20,25,30,35,40,45,50,55 * * * * date > `tty`" >/tmp/experiment
```

then,

```
crontab /tmp/experiment
```

and finally,

```
crontab -l
```

The last of these gives you a result that looks something like the following:

```
0,5,10,15,20,25,30,35,40,45,50,55 * * * * date > /dev/ttyxx
```

Every five minutes, the current time will appear in the window from which you launched this experiment.

For a more useful example, create a `/tmp/entry` file with the single line

```
0 2 * * * find / -name "core*" -exec ls -l {} \;
```

Next, use the command

```
crontab /tmp/entry
```

The result is that each morning, at 2:00, `cron` launches the core-searching job and e-mails you the results when finished. This is quite useful because Linux creates files `core*` under certain error conditions. These core images are often large and can easily fill up a distressing amount of real estate on your disk. With the preceding sequence, you'll have a report in your e-mail inbox each morning, listing exactly the locations and sizes of a collection of files that are likely doing you no good.

User Space

Suppose you've experimented a bit and have accumulated an inventory of `cron` jobs to monitor the health of your system. Now, along with your other jobs, you want your system to tell you every Monday morning at 2:10 which ten users have the biggest home directory trees (`/home/*`). First, enter

```
crontab -l >/tmp/entries
```

to capture all the jobs you've scheduled, and append the line

```
10 2 * * 1 du -s /home/* ¦ sort -nr ¦ head -10
```

to the bottom of `/tmp/entries`. Make the request

```
crontab /tmp/entries
```

and `cron` will e-mail the reports you seek.

at: Scheduling Future Events

Suppose you write a weekly column on cycles in the material world, which you deliver by e-mail. To simplify legal ramifications involving financial markets, you make a point of delivering it at 5:00 Friday afternoon. It's Wednesday now, you've finished your analysis, and you're almost through packing for the vacation you're starting tonight. How do you do right by your subscribers? It only takes three lines at scripting:

```
at 17:00 Friday << COMMAND
     mail -s "This week's CYCLES report." mailing_list < analysis.already_written
COMMAND
```

This schedules the `mail` command for later processing. You can log off from your session, and your Linux host will still send out the mail `at 17:00 Friday`, just as you instructed. In fact, you can even shut down your machine after commanding it `at ...`, and, as long as it's rebooted in time, your scheduled task will still be launched on the schedule you dictated.

Other Mechanisms: Expect, Perl, and More

Are you ready to move beyond the constraints of the UNIX shell? There are several alternative technologies that are free, easy to install, easy to learn, and more powerful—that is, with richer capabilities and more structured syntax—than the shell. A few examples will suggest what they have to offer.

Comparing Technologies

I'm often asked to compare different technologies for automation; as a service to readers, I've launched the page `http://starbase.neosoft.com/~claird/comp.lang.misc/portable_scripting.html`, which answers questions about choosing among different scripting languages. The most important principles are as follows:

- Choose a language that your friends (acquaintances, coworkers, correspondents, and so on) use.
- Choose a language that feels good to you.

With few exceptions, the capabilities of different languages are close enough that the social and psychological factors dominate.

Expect

Expect "is a must-know tool for system administrators and many others," according to a user testimonial that appears on the back cover of *Exploring Expect*, its standard reference. Why? Expect automates interactions, particularly those involving terminal control and time delays, that no other tool has attempted. Many command-line applications have the reputation for being unscriptable because they involve password entry and refuse to accept redirection of standard input for this purpose. That's no problem for Expect, though. After you install Expect (`http://starbase.neosoft.com/~claird/comp.lang.tcl/expect.html`), create a script `hold` with the contents of Listing 22.4.

Listing 22.4. `hold`—a "keep-alive" written in Expect.

```
#!/usr/local/bin/expect

# Usage:  "hold HOST USER PASS".
# Action:  login to node HOST as USER.  Offer a shell prompt for
#     normal usage, and also print to the screen the word HELD
#     every five seconds, to exercise the connection periodically.
#     This is useful for testing and using WANs with short time-outs.
#     You can walk away from the keyboard, and never lose your
#     connection through a time-out.
# WARNING:  the security hazard of passing a password through the
#     command line makes this example only illustrative.  Modify to
#     a particular security situation as appropriate.
set hostname [lindex $argv 0]
set username [lindex $argv 1]
set password [lindex $argv 2]

     # There's trouble if $username's prompt is not set to "...} ".
     #     A more sophisticated manager knows how to look for different
     #     prompts on different hosts.
set prompt_sequence "} "

spawn telnet $hostname

expect "login: "
send "$username\r"
expect "Password:"
send "$password\r"

     # Some hosts don't inquire about TERM.  That's another
     #     complexification to consider before widespread use
     #     of this application is practical.
     # Note use of global [gl] pattern matching to parse "*"
     #     as a wildcard.
expect -gl "TERM = (*)"
send "\r"

expect $prompt_sequence
send "sh -c 'while true; do; echo HELD; sleep 5; done'\r"
interact
```

I work with several telephone lines that are used with short time-outs, as a check on out-of-pocket expenses. I use a variant of the script in Listing 22.4 daily, for I often need that to hold one of the connections open.

Expect is an extension to `tcl`, so it is fully programmable with all the `tcl` capabilities that Chapter 25, "`tcl` and `tk` Programming," presents. For a perspective on `tcl` that emphasizes the automation themes of this chapter, see the pages `http://starbase.neosoft.com/~claird/comp.lang.tcl/tcl.html` and `http://starbase.neosoft.com/~claird/comp.lang.tcl/expect.html`.

Perl

Chapter 24, "Perl Programming," presents Perl as the most popular scripting language for Red Hat Linux, apart from the shell. Its power and brevity take on particular value in automation contexts, as the page `http://starbase.neosoft.com/~claird/comp.lang.perl.misc/perl.html` emphasizes. For example, if `/usr/local/bin/modified_directories.pl` contains

```
#!/usr/local/bin/perl

# Usage:  "modified_directories.pl DIR1 DIR2 ... DIRN"
# Output:  a list of all directories in the file systems under
#     DIR1 ... DIRN, collectively.  They appear, sorted by the
#     interval since their last activity, that is, since a file
#     within them was last created, deleted, or renamed.
# Randal Schwartz wrote a related program from which this is
#     descended.
use File::Find;
@directory_list = @ARGV;

     # "-M" abbreviates "time since last modification", while
     #      "-d" "... is a directory."
find (sub {$modification_lapse(File::Find::name} = -M if -d;}, @directory_list);
foreach (sort{$modification_lapse{$a} <=> $modification_lapse{$b}} keys %size) {
          # Tabulate the results in nice columns.
     printf "%5d:  %s\n", $modification_lapse{$_}, $_;
}
```

and you adjoin an entry such as

```
20 2 * * * /usr/local/bin/modified_directories.pl /
```

to your `crontab`, then each morning you'll receive an e-mail report on the date each directory on your host was last modified. This can be useful both for spotting security issues when read-only directories have been changed (they'll appear unexpectedly at the top of the list) and for identifying dormant domains in the filesystem (at the bottom of the list) that might be liberated for better uses.

Other Tools

Many other general-purpose scripting languages effectively automate operations. Apart from Perl and `tcl`, Python deserves the most attention. As of fall 1997, Java (see the page `http://starbase.neosoft.com/~claird/comp.lang.java/java.html`) is *not* such a language; its support of Linux is too immature, and it's too "heavy" for automation projects. This is likely to change in the future. Until then, put your energies into other projects, or realize that you're working at "the bleeding edge," that is, with a technology that is more educational than it is directly useful.

Several special-purpose tools are also important in automation, such as Python, Emacs, `procmail`, and `calendar`.

Python

Python can be of special interest to Red Hat Linux users. Python is object-oriented, modern, clean, portable, and particularly easy to maintain. If you are a full-time system administrator looking for a scripting language that will grow with you, consider Python. The official home page for Python is `http://www.python.org`.

Emacs

Emacs is one of the most polarizing lightning rods for religious controversy among computer users. Emacs has many intelligent and zealous users who believe it the ideal platform for all automation efforts. Its devotees have developed what was originally a screen editor into a tool with capabilities to manage newsgroup discussion, Web browsing, application development, general-purpose scripting, and much more. For the purposes of this chapter, what you need to know about Emacs is as follows:

- It's an editor that you ought to try at some point in your career.
- If you favor integrated development environments, Emacs can do almost anything you imagine. As an editor, it emulates any other editor, and its developers ensure that it always offers state-of-the-art capabilities in language-directed formatting, application integration, and development automation.

Even if the "weight" of Emacs (it's slow on startup and seems to require quite a bit of education and configuration) sways you against its daily use, keep it in mind as a paragon of how sophisticated programming makes common operations more efficient.

procmail

Computer use has exploded in the Internet era. The most indispensable, most used Internet function is e-mail. Can e-mail be automated?

Yes, of course, and it's perhaps the single best return on your invested time to do so. Along with aliases, distribution lists, startup configurations, and the plethora of mail agents or clients with their feature sets, you'll want to learn about `procmail`. Suppose that you receive a hundred messages a day, that a fifth of them can be handled completely automatically, and that it takes at least three seconds of your time to process a single piece of e-mail; those are conservative estimates, from the experience of the computer workers I know. A bit of `procmail` automation will save you at least a minute a day, or six hours a year. Even conservative estimates make it clear that an hour of setting up `procmail` pays for itself many times over.

Along with the `man procmail*` pages, serious study of `procmail` starts with the page `http://www.faqs.org/faqs/mail/filtering-faq`, Nancy McGough's "Filtering Mail FAQ." This gives detailed installation and debugging directions. To supplement it, I've launched the page `http://starbase.neosoft.com/~claird/comp.mail.misc/procmail.html` to keep you updated on the latest procmail news. Because your Red Hat Linux machine will almost certainly have a correctly configured procmail, you can immediately begin to program your personal use of it. As a first experiment, create exactly these files: ~/.procmailrc, with contents

```
VERBOSE=on
MAILDIR=$HOME/mail
PMDIR=$HOME/.procmail
LOGFILE=$PMDIR/log
INCLUDERC=$PMDIR/rc.testing
```

~/.procmail/rc.testing, holding

```
:0:
* ^Subject:.*HOT
SPAM.HOT
```

and ~/.forward, with

```
"¦IFS=' ' && exec /usr/local/bin/procmail -f ¦¦ exit 75 #YOUR_EMAIL_NAME"
```

After you create these three, set necessary permissions with the following:

```
chmod 644 ~/.forward
chmod a+x ~/.
```

Now exercise your filter with the following:

```
echo "This is the first message." ¦ mail -s "Example of HOT SPAM." YOUR_EMAIL_NAME
echo "This is the second message." ¦ mail -s "Desired message." YOUR_EMAIL_NAME
```

What you now see in your mailbox is only one new item, the one with the subject Desired message. You also have a new file in your home directory, SPAM.HOT, holding ... the first message.

procmail is a robust, flexible utility you can program to achieve even more useful automations than this. When you gain familiarity with it, it will become natural to construct rules that, for example, automatically discard obvious spam, sort incoming mailing-list traffic, and perhaps even implement pager forwarding, remote system monitoring, or FAQ response. This can save you considerable time each day.

calendar

calendar is quite specialized, easy to use, and, because it matches a real-world need particularly well, very useful. calendar takes responsibility for sending messages to your screen to remind you of events or responsibilities. You can download calendar from ftp://ftp.redhat.com/pub/contrib/i386, file calendar-8.4-3.i386.rpm. Experiment with calendar by creating a local file called calendar (the command and the specification file have the same name, in general) with the following contents:

```
#include "/usr/lib/gcal-lib/calendar.holid"
Monday\tTake out trash.
```

```
Tuesday\tFeed dolphin.
Wednesday\tRe-synchronize orgone collector.
Thursday\tKaryotype produce from refrigerator.
Friday\tTake out trash.
Saturday\tPractice polo.
Sunday\tClimb Matterhorn.
```

Run `calendar`. You'll see a few historical events with current anniversaries, and your own applicable daily chores. Three aspects of `calendar` give it dramatic power:

- You can run `calendar` automatically, using the techniques you've learned so far: For example, have `cron` put a reminder in your e-mail every morning or invoke `calendar` from your shell's startup file so that it's run each time you log in.
- `calendar` has a sophisticated knowledge of calendars. It will, on request, remind you when it's the second Tuesday of the month, the day after Easter, or Mother's Day. See `man calendar` for details.
- The `#include` mechanism permits information-sharing. If your `calendar` begins

  ```
  #include "/some/centrally/maintained/directory/calendar.bigboss"
  #include "/some/centrally/maintained/directory/calendar.cafetaria"
  /* My own stuff follows ... */
  ```

  the first reminders `calendar` gives you will be those for the company president and the lunch-time menu, with your personal events after.

Although `calendar` does a small job, it does it efficiently. Consider whether its capability to focus attention on the upcoming days' priorities matches your needs.

Internal Scripts

One more element of the automation attitude is to be on the lookout for opportunities within every application you use. Scripting has become a pervasive theme, and almost all common applications have at least a rudimentary macro or scripting capability. IRC users know about bots, Web browsers typically expose at least a couple of scripting interfaces, all modern PPP clients are scriptable, and even such venerable tools as `vi` and `ftp` have configuration, shortcut, and macro capabilities that enormously magnify productivity. If you use a tool regularly, take a few minutes to reread its presentation in this volume; chances are, you'll come up with a way to make your work easier and more effective.

Concluding Challenge for an Automater—Explaining Value

You've become knowledgeable and experienced in scripting your computer so that it best serves you. You know how to improve your skills in script-writing. You've practiced different approaches enough to know how to solve problems efficiently. The final challenge in your automation career is this: How do you explain how good you have become?

This is a serious problem, and, as usual, the solution begins with attitude. You no longer pound at the keyboard to bludgeon technical tasks into submission; now you operate in a more refined way and achieve correspondingly grander results. As an employee, you're much more valuable than the system administrators and programmers who reinvent wheels every day. In your recreational or personal use of Red Hat Linux, the computer is working for you, not the other way around, as it might have been when you started. Your attitude needs to adjust to the reality you've created by improving your productivity. Invest in yourself, whether by attending technical conferences where you can further promote your skills, or negotiating a higher salary, or simply taking the time in your computer work to get things right. It's easy in organizations to give attention to crises and reward those visibly coping with emergencies. It takes true leadership to plan ahead, organize work so emergencies don't happen, and use techniques of automation to achieve predictable and manageable results on schedule.

One of the most effective tools you have in taking up this challenge is *quantification*. Keep simple records to demonstrate how much time you put into setting up backups before you learned about `cron`, or run a simple experiment to compare two ways of approaching an elementary database maintenance operation. Find out how much of your online time goes just to the login process and decide whether scripting that is justified. Chart a class of mistakes that you make and see whether your precision improves as you apply automation ideas.

In all cases, keep in mind you are efficient, perhaps extraordinarily efficient, because of the knowledge you apply. Automation feels good!

Summary

Automation offers enormous opportunities for using your Linux computer to achieve the goals you set. The examples in this chapter demonstrate that every Linux user can begin immediately to exploit the techniques and attitude of automation.

CHAPTER 23

C and C++ Programming

by Robin Burk, revised by David B. Horvath, CCP

IN THIS CHAPTER

UNIX shells support a wide range of commands that can be combined, in the form of scripts, into reusable programs. Command scripts for shell programs (and utilities such as `gawk` and Perl) are all the programming that many UNIX users need in order to customize their computing environment.

Script languages have several shortcomings, however. To begin with, the commands that a user types into a script are read and evaluated only when the script is being executed. Interpreted languages are flexible and easy to use, but they are also inefficient because the commands must be reinterpreted each time the script is executed. Interpreted languages are also ill-suited to manipulate the computer's memory and I/O devices directly. Therefore, the programs that process scripts (such as the various UNIX shells, the `awk` utility, and the Perl interpreter) are themselves written in the C and C++ languages, as is the UNIX kernel.

Many users find it fairly easy to learn a scripted, interpreted language because the commands can usually be tried out one at a time, with clearly visible results. Learning a language such as C or C++ is more complex and difficult because you must learn to think in terms of machine resources and the way in which actions are accomplished within the computer, rather than in terms of user-oriented commands.

This chapter introduces you to the basic concepts of C and C++ and demonstrates how to build some simple programs. Even if you don't go on to learn how to program extensively in either language, you will find that the information in this chapter will help you to understand how kernels are built and why some of the other features of UNIX work the way they do. Additional resources are listed at the end of the chapter in the section "Additional Resources."

Introduction to C

C is the programming language most frequently associated with UNIX. Since the 1970s, the bulk of the operating system and its applications have been written in C. Because the C language doesn't directly rely on any specific hardware architecture, UNIX was one of the first portable operating systems. In other words, the majority of the code that makes up UNIX doesn't know and doesn't care about knowing what computer it is actually running on. Machine-specific features are isolated in a few modules within the UNIX kernel, which makes it easy for you to modify these when porting to a different hardware architecture.

C was first designed by Dennis Ritchie for use with UNIX on DEC PDP-11 computers. The language evolved from Martin Richard's BCPL, and one of its earlier forms was the B language, which was written by Ken Thompson for the DEC PDP-7. The first book on C was *The C Programming Language* by Brian Kernighan and Dennis Ritchie and was published in 1978.

In 1983, the American National Standards Institute (ANSI) established a committee to standardize the definition of C. The resulting standard is known as *ANSI C*, and it is the recognized standard for the language grammar and a core set of libraries. The syntax is slightly different from the original C language, which is frequently called K&R—for Kernighan and Ritchie. In this chapter, I will primarily address ANSI C.

Programming in C: Basic Concepts

C is a compiled, third-generation procedural language. *Compiled* means that C code is analyzed, interpreted, and translated into machine instructions at some time prior to the execution of the C program. These steps are carried out by the C compiler and, depending on the complexity of the C program, by the `make` utility. After the program is compiled, it can be executed over and over without recompilation.

The phrase *third-generation procedural* describes computer languages that clearly distinguish the data used in a program from the actions performed on that data. Programs written in third-generation languages take the form of a series of explicit processing steps, or procedures, which manipulate the contents of data structures by means of explicit references to their location in memory and which manipulate the computer's hardware in response to hardware interrupts.

Functions in C Programs

In the C language, all procedures take the form of functions. Just as a mathematical function transforms one or more numbers into another number, a C function is typically a procedure that transforms some value or performs some other action and returns the results. The act of invoking the transformation is known as *calling* the function.

Mathematical function calls can be nested, as can function calls in C. When function calls are nested, the results of the innermost function are passed as input to the next function, and so on. Table 23.1 shows how nested calls to the square root function are evaluated arithmetically.

Table 23.1. Nested operations in mathematics.

Function	*Value*
`sqrt(256)`	16
`sqrt( sqrt(256) ) = sqrt(16)`	4
`sqrt( sqrt( sqrt(256) ) ) = sqrt(4)`	2

Figure 23.1 shows the way that function calls are nested within C programs. In the figure, the `Main` function calls `Function 1`, which calls `Function 2`. `Function 2` is evaluated first, and its results are passed back to `Function 1`. When `Function 1` completes its operations, its results are passed back to the `Main` function.

Nonfunctional procedures in other languages often operate on data variables that are shared with other code in the program. For instance, a nonfunctional procedure might update a programwide `COUNT_OF_ERRORS` whenever a user makes a keyboard mistake. Such procedures must be carefully written, and they are usually specific to the program for which they were first created because they reference particular shared data variables within the wider program.

A function, however, receives all the information it needs (including the location of data variables to use in each instance) when it is called. The function neither knows nor cares about the wider program context that calls it; it simply transforms the values found within the input variables (parameters), whatever they might be, and returns the result to whatever other function invokes it.

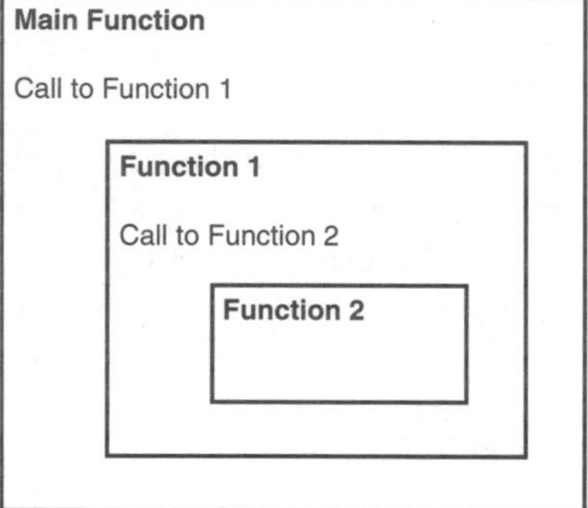

FIGURE 23.1.
Nesting function calls within C programs.

Because procedures written in C are implemented as functions, they don't need to know whether (or how deeply) they will be nested inside other function calls. This enables you to reuse C functions in many different programs without modifying them. For example, `Function 2` in Figure 23.1 might be called directly by the `Main` logic in a different C program.

An entire C program is itself a function that returns a result code, when executed, to the program that invokes it. This is usually a shell in the case of applications, but might also be any other part of the operating system or any other UNIX program. Because C programs are all structured as functions, they can be invoked by other programs or nested inside larger programs without needing to be rewritten in any way.

> **NOTE**
>
> C's feature of structuring programs as functions has heavily shaped the look and feel of UNIX. More than in most other operating environments, UNIX systems consist of many small C programs that call one another, are combined into larger programs, and are invoked by the user as needed. Instead of using monolithic, integrated applications, UNIX typically hosts many small, flexible programs. Users can customize their working environments by combining these tools to do new tasks.

Data in C Programs

The two kinds of data that are manipulated within C programs are *literal values* and *variables*. *Literal values* are specific, actual numbers or characters, such as `1`, `4.35`, or `a`. *Variables* are names associated with a place in memory that can hold data values. Each variable in C is typed; that is, each variable can hold only one kind of value. The basic datatypes include integers, floating-point (real) numbers, characters, and arrays. An *array* is a series of data elements of the same type; the elements are identified by the order in which they appear (by their place within the series).

You can define complex data structures as well. Complex data structures are used to gather a number of related data items together under one name. A terminal communications program, for example, might have a terminal control block (TCB) associated with each user who is logged on. The TCB typically contains data elements identifying the communications port, the active application process, and other information associated with that terminal session.

All the variables in a C program must be explicitly defined before they can be used.

Creating, Compiling, and Executing Your First Program

The development of a C program is an iterative procedure. Many UNIX tools familiar to software developers are involved in this four-step process:

1. Using an editor, write your code into a text file.
2. Compile the program.
3. Execute the program.
4. Debug the program.

Repeat the first two steps until the program compiles successfully. Then begin the execution and debugging. When I explain each of these steps in this chapter, you might find that some of the concepts seem strange, especially if you're a nonprogrammer. Remember that this chapter serves as only an introduction to C as a programming language. For more in-depth coverage of C, check out one of the resources listed at the end of this chapter in the section "Additional Resources."

The typical first C program is almost a cliché—the Hello, World program, which prints the simple line `Hello, World`. Listing 23.1 contains the source code of the program.

Listing 23.1. Source code of the Hello, World program.

```
main()
{
printf("Hello, World\n");
}
```

This program can be compiled and executed as follows:

```
$ gcc hello.c
$ ./a.out
Hello, World
$
```

NOTE

If the current directory is in your path, you could have executed `a.out` by typing

`a.out`

The Hello, World program is compiled with the `gcc` command, which creates a file `a.out` if the code is correct. Just typing `a.out` will run it. Notice that Listing 23.1 includes only one function, `main`. Every C program must have a `main` function; `main` is where the program's execution begins. The only statement in Listing 23.1 is a call to the `printf` library function, which passes the string `Hello, World\n`. (Functions are described in detail later in this chapter in the section "Functions.") The last two characters of the string, `\n`, represent the newline character.

NOTE

`a.out` is the default filename for executables (binaries) created by the C compiler under UNIX. This can be changed through the use of a command-line switch (see the section "GNU C/C++ Compiler Command-Line Switches" later in this chapter).

An Overview of the C Language

As with all programming languages, C programs must follow certain rules. These rules include how a program should appear and what the words and symbols mean; altogether, these are called the *syntax* of a programming language. Think of a program as a story. Within a story, each sentence must have a noun and a verb, put together with a particular syntax. Sentences form paragraphs, and the paragraphs tell the story. Similarly, C statements constructed with the correct syntax can form functions and programs.

Elementary C Syntax

Like all languages, C deals primarily with the manipulation and presentation of data. The language C evolved from, BCPL, dealt with data only as data. C, however, goes one step further by using the concept of *datatypes*. The three basic datatypes are integers, floating-point numbers, and characters. Other datatypes are built from these.

Integers are the basic mathematical datatype. They can be classified as `long` and `short` integers, and their size is implementation dependent. With a few exceptions, integers are four bytes in length, and they can range from -2,147,483,648 to 2,147,483,647. In ANSI C, these values are defined in a header (`limit.h`) as `INT_MIN` and `INT_MAX`. The qualifier `unsigned` moves the range one bit higher, to the equivalent of `INT_MAX` minus `INT_MIN`.

Floating-point numbers are used for more complicated mathematics, whereas integer mathematics is limited to integer results. For example, with integers, 3/2 equals 1. Floating-point numbers give a greater amount of precision to mathematical calculations than integers can; with floating-point numbers, 3/2 equals 1.5. Floating-point numbers can be represented by a decimal number, such as 687.534, or with scientific notation, such as 8.87534E+2. For larger numbers, scientific notation is preferred. For even greater precision, the type `double` provides a greater range. Again, specific ranges are implementation dependent.

Characters are usually implemented as single bytes, although some international character sets require two bytes. One common set of character representations is ASCII, which is found on most U.S. computers.

You use arrays for sequences of values that are often position dependent. An array is particularly useful when you need a range of values of a given type. Related to the array is the pointer. Variables are stored in memory, and a *pointer* is the physical address of that memory. In a sense, a pointer and an array are similar, except when a program is invoked. The space needed for an array's data is allocated when the routine that needs the space is invoked. For a pointer, the space must be allocated by the programmer, or the variable must be assigned by dereferencing a variable. The ampersand (`&`) is used to indicate dereferencing, and an asterisk (`*`) is used to indicate when the value pointed at is required. Here are some sample declarations:

`int i;`	Declares an integer
`char c;`	Declares a character
`char *ptr;`	Declares a pointer to a character
`double temp[16];`	Declares an array of double-precision floating-point numbers with 16 values

Listing 23.2 shows an example of a program with pointers.

Listing 23.2. An example of a program with pointers.

```
int i;
int *ptr;

i=5;
ptr = &i;
printf("%d %x %d\n", i,ptr,*ptr);
```

The output of this program is as follows:

```
5 f7fffa6c 5
```

NOTE

The middle value, `f7fffa6c`, is an address. This might be different on your system because the pointer variable will change from version to version of the libraries.

A pointer is just a memory address and will tell you the address of any variable.

There is no specific type for a string. An array of characters is used to represent strings. They can be printed using an `%s` flag, instead of `%c`.

Simple output is created by the `printf` function. `printf` takes a format string and the list of arguments to be printed. A complete set of format options is presented in Table 23.2. Format options can be modified with sizes. Check the `gcc` documentation (man page or info file) for the full specification.

Table 23.2. Format conversions for `printf`.

Conversion	*Meaning*
`%%`	Percentage sign
`%E`	Double (scientific notation)
`%G`	Double (format depends on value)
`%X`	Hexadecimal (letters are capitalized)
`%c`	Single character
`%d`	Integer
`%e`	Double (scientific notation)
`%f`	Double of the form `mmm.ddd`
`%g`	Double (format depends on value)
`%i`	Integer
`%ld`	Long integer
`%n`	Count of characters written in current `printf`
`%o`	Octal
`%p`	Print as a pointer
`%s`	Character pointer (string)
`%u`	Unsigned integer
`%x`	Hexadecimal

Some characters cannot be included easily in a program. Newlines, for example, require a special escape sequence because there cannot be an unescaped newline in a string. Table 23.3 contains a complete list of escape sequences.

Table 23.3. Escape characters for strings.

Escape Sequence	*Meaning*
`\"`	Double quote
`\'`	Single quote

Escape Sequence	*Meaning*
`\?`	Question mark
`\\`	Backslash
`\a`	Audible bell
`\b`	Backspace
`\f`	Form feed (new page)
`\n`	Newline
`\ooo`	Octal number
`\r`	Carriage return
`\t`	Horizontal tab
`\v`	Vertical tab
`\xhh`	Hexadecimal number

A full program is a compilation of statements. Statements are separated by semicolons, and they can be grouped in blocks of statements surrounded by curly braces. The simplest statement is an assignment, in which a variable on the left side is assigned the value of an expression on the right.

Expressions

At the heart of the C programming language are *expressions*. These are techniques to combine simple values into new values. The three basic types of expressions are comparison, numerical, and bitwise.

Comparison Expressions

The simplest expression is a comparison. A comparison evaluates to a `true` or a `false` value. In C, `true` is a nonzero value, and `false` is a zero value. Table 23.4 contains a list of comparison operators.

Table 23.4. Comparison operators.

Operator	*Meaning*
`<`	Less than
`>`	Greater than
`==`	Equal to
`<=`	Less than or equal to
`>=`	Greater than or equal to

continues

Table 23.4. continued

Operator	*Meaning*
`¦¦`	Logical OR
`&&`	Logical AND
`!`	Logical NOT

You can combine simple comparisons with ANDs and ORs to make complex expressions. For example, consider the definition of a leap year. In words, it is any year divisible by 4, except a year divisible by 100 unless that year is divisible by 400. Using `year` as the variable, you can define a leap year with the following expression:

```
((((year%4)==0)&&((year%100)!=0))¦¦((year%400)==0))
```

On first inspection, this code might look complicated, but it isn't. The parentheses group the simple expressions with the ANDs and ORs to make a complex expression.

Mathematical Expressions

One convenient aspect of C is that expressions can be treated as mathematical values, and mathematical statements can be used in expressions. In fact, any statement—even a simple assignment—has values that can be used in other places as an expression.

The mathematics of C is straightforward. Barring parenthetical groupings, multiplication and division have higher precedence than addition and subtraction. The operators are standard and are listed in Table 23.5.

Table 23.5. Mathematical operators.

Operator	*Meaning*
`+`	Addition
`-`	Subtraction
`*`	Multiplication
`/`	Division
`%`	Integer remainder

There are also unary operators, which affect a single variable. These are `++` (increment by one) and `--` (decrement by one). These are shorthand for `var = var + 1` and `var = var - 1`, respectively.

There are also shorthands for situations in which you want to change the value of a variable. For example, if you want to add an expression to a variable called a and assign a new value to a, the shorthand a += *expr* is the same as a=a+*expr*. The expression can be as complex or as simple as required.

NOTE

Most UNIX functions take advantage of the truth values and return 0 for success. This enables a programmer to write code such as

```
if (function())
        {
        error condition
        }
```

The return value of a function determines whether the function worked.

Bitwise Operations

Because a variable is just a string of bits, many operations work on those bit patterns. Table 23.6 lists the bit operators.

Table 23.6. Bit operators.

Operator	*Meaning*
&	Bitwise AND
|	Bitwise OR
~	Negation (one's complement)
<<	Bit shift left
>>	Bit shift right

A bitwise AND compares the individual bits in place. If both are 1, the value 1 is assigned to the expression. Otherwise, 0 is assigned. For a logical OR, 1 is assigned if either value is a 1. Bit shift operations move the bits a number of positions to the right or left. Mathematically, this is the same as multiplying or dividing by 2, but circumstances exist where the bit shift is preferred.

Bit operations are often used for masking values and for comparisons. A simple way to determine whether a value is odd or even is to perform a bitwise AND with the integer value 1. If it is true, the number is odd.

Statement Controls

With what you've seen so far, you can create a list of statements that are executed only once, after which the program terminates. To control the flow of commands, three types of loops exist in C. The simplest is the while loop. The syntax is

```
while (expression)
      statement
```

As long as the expression between the parentheses evaluates as nonzero—or `true` in C—the statement is executed. *`statement`* actually can be a list of statements blocked off with curly braces. If the expression evaluates to zero the first time it is reached, the statement is never executed. To force at least one execution of the statement, use a `do` loop. The syntax for a `do` loop is

```
do
        statement
        while (expression);
```

The third type of control flow is the `for` loop. This is more complicated. The syntax is

```
for(expr1;expr2;expr3) statement
```

When this expression is reached for the first time, *`expr1`* is evaluated, and then *`expr2`* is evaluated. If *`expr2`* is nonzero, *`statement`* is executed, followed by *`expr3`*. Then *`expr2`* is tested again, followed by the statement and *`expr3`*, until *`expr2`* evaluates to zero. Strictly speaking, this is a notational convenience because a `while` loop can be structured to perform the same actions, as in the following:

```
expr1;
while (expr2) {
        statement;
        expr3
        }
```

Loops can be interrupted in three ways. A `break` statement terminates execution in a loop and exits it. `continue` terminates the current iteration and retests the loop before possibly reexecuting the statement. For an unconventional exit, you can use `goto`. `goto` changes the program's execution to a labeled statement. According to many programmers, `goto` is poor programming practice, and you should avoid using it.

Statements can also be executed conditionally. Again, there are three different formats for statement execution. The simplest is an `if` statement. The syntax is

```
if (expr) statement
```

If the expression *`expr`* evaluates to nonzero, *`statement`* is executed. You can expand this with an `else`, the second type of conditional execution. The syntax for `else` is

```
if (expr) statement else statement
```

If the expression evaluates to zero, the second statement is executed.

NOTE

The second statement in an `else` condition can be another `if` statement. This situation might cause the grammar to be indeterminate if the structure

```
if (expr) if (expr) statement else statement
```

is not parsed cleanly.

> As the code is written, the `else` is considered applicable to the second `if`. To make it applicable with the first `if`, surround the second `if` statement with curly braces, as in the following:
>
> ```
> if (expr) {if (expr) statement} else statement
> ```

The third type of conditional execution is more complicated. The `switch` statement first evaluates an expression. Then it looks down a series of `case` statements to find a label that matches the expression's value and executes the statements following the label. A special label `default` exists if no other conditions are met. If you want only a set of statements executed for each label, you must use the `break` statement to leave the `switch` statement.

This covers the simplest building blocks of a C program. You can add more power by using functions and by declaring complex datatypes.

If your program requires different pieces of data to be grouped on a consistent basis, you can group them into structures. Listing 23.3 shows a structure for a California driver's license. Note that it includes integer, character, and character array (string) types.

Listing 23.3. An example of a structure.

```
struct license {
        char name[128];
        char address[3][128];
        int zipcode;
        int height, weight, month, day, year;
        char license_letter;
        int license_number;
        };

struct license newlicensee;
struct license *user;
```

Because California driver's license numbers consist of a single character followed by a seven-digit number, the license ID is broken into two components. Similarly, the new licensee's address is broken into three lines, represented by three arrays of 128 characters.

Accessing individual fields of a structure requires two different techniques. To read a member of a locally defined structure, you append a dot to the variable and then the field name, as in the following example:

```
newlicensee.zipcode=94404;
```

When using a pointer to a structure, you need `->` to point to the member (to reference the individual members):

```
user->zipcode=94404;
```

Interestingly, if the structure pointer is incremented, the address is increased not by `1`, but by the size of the structure.

Functions

Functions are an easy way to group statements and to give them a name. These are usually related statements that perform repetitive tasks such as I/O. `printf`, described earlier, is a function. It is provided with the standard C library. Listing 23.4 illustrates a function definition, a function call, and a function.

NOTE

The three-dot ellipsis simply means that some lines of sample code are not shown here in order to save space.

Listing 23.4. An example of a function.

```
int swapandmin( int *, int *);          /* Function declaration */

...

int i,j,lower;

i=2; j=4;
lower=swapandmin(&i, &j);              /* Function call */

...

int swapandmin(int *a,int *b)          /* Function definition */
{
int tmp;

tmp=(*a);
(*a)=(*b);
(*b)=tmp;
if ((*a)<(*b)) return(*a);
return(*b);
}
```

ANSI C and K&R differ most in function declarations and calls. ANSI C requires that function arguments be prototyped when the function is declared. K&R required only the name and the type of the returned value. The declaration in Listing 23.4 states that a function `swapandmin` will take two pointers to integers as arguments and that it will return an integer. The function call takes the addresses of two integers and sets the variable named `lower` to the return value of the function.

When a function is called from a C program, the values of the arguments are passed to the function. Therefore, if any of the arguments will be changed for the calling function, you can't pass only the variable—you must pass the address, too. Likewise, to change the value of the argument in the calling routine of the function, you must assign the new value to the address.

In the function in Listing 23.4, the value pointed to by `a` is assigned to the `tmp` variable. `b` is assigned to `a`, and `tmp` is assigned to `b`. `*a` is used instead of `a` to ensure that the change is reflected in the calling routine. Finally, the values of `*a` and `*b` are compared, and the lower of the two is returned.

If you include the line

```
printf("%d %d %d",lower,i,j);
```

after the function call, you will see `2 4 2` as output.

This sample function is quite simple, and it is ideal for a macro. A macro is a technique used to replace a token with different text. You can use macros to make code more readable. For example, you might use `EOF` instead of `(-1)` to indicate the end of a file. You can also use macros to replace code. Listing 23.5 is the same as Listing 23.4 except that it uses macros.

Listing 23.5. An example of macros.

```
#define SWAP(X,Y) {int tmp; tmp=X; X=Y; Y=tmp; }
#define MIN(X,Y) ((X<Y) ? X : Y )

...

int i,j,lower;

i=2; j=4;
SWAP(i,j);
lower=MIN(i,j);
```

When a C program is compiled, macro replacement is one of the first steps performed. Listing 23.6 illustrates the result of the replacement.

Listing 23.6. An example of macro replacement.

```
int i,j,lower;

i=2; j=4;
{int tmp; tmp=i; i=j; j=tmp; };
lower= ((i<j) ? i : j );
```

The macros make the code easier to read and understand.

CAUTION

Macros can have side effects. Side effects occur because the programmer expects a variable to be evaluated once when it is actually evaluated more than once. Replacing the variable `i` with `i++` changes things dramatically:

```
lower=MIN(i++,j);
```

is converted to

```
lower= ((i++ < j) ? i++ : j );
```

As a result, the variable `i` can be incremented twice instead of once as the programmer expects.

Creating a Simple Program

For the next example, you'll write a program that prints a chart of the first ten integers and their squares, cubes, and square roots.

Writing the Code

Using the text editor of your choice, enter all the code in Listing 23.7 and save it in a file called `sample.c`.

Listing 23.7. Source code for `sample.c`.

```
#include <stdio.h>
#include <math.h>

main()
{
int i;
double a;

for(i=1;i<11;i++)
        {
        a=i*1.0;
        printf("%2d. %3d %4d %7.5f\n",i,i*i,i*i*i,sqrt(a));
        }
}
```

The first two lines are header files. The `stdio.h` file provides the function definitions and structures associated with the C input and output libraries. The `math.h` file includes the definitions of mathematical library functions. You need it for the square root function.

The `main` loop is the only function that you need to write for this example. It takes no arguments. You define two variables: One is the integer `i`, and the other is a double-precision floating-point number called `a`. You don't have to use `a`, but you can for the sake of convenience.

The program is a simple `for` loop that starts at 1 and ends at 11. It increments `i` by 1 each time through. When `i` equals 11, the `for` loop stops executing. You also could have written `i<=10` because the expressions have the same meaning.

First, you multiply `i` by 1.0 and assign the product to `a`. A simple assignment would also work, but the multiplication reminds you that you are converting the value to a double-precision floating-point number.

Next, you call the `print` function. The format string includes three integers of widths `2`, `3`, and `4`. After the first integer is printed, you print a period. After the next integer is printed, you print a floating-point number that is seven characters wide with five digits following the decimal point. The arguments after the format string show that you print the integer, the square of the integer, the cube of the integer, and the square root of the integer.

Compiling the Program

To compile this program by using the GNU C compiler, enter the following command:

```
gcc sample.c -lm
```

This command produces an output file called `a.out`. This is the simplest use of the C compiler. `gcc` is one of the most powerful and flexible commands of a UNIX system.

A number of different flags can change the compiler's output. These flags are often dependent on the system or compiler. Some flags are common to all C compilers. These are described in the following paragraphs.

The `-o` flag tells the compiler to write the output to the file named after the flag. The `gcc -o sample sample.c` command puts the program in a file named `sample`.

NOTE

The output discussed here is the compiler's output, not the sample program. Compiler output is usually the program, and in every example here, it is an executable program.

The `-g` flag tells the compiler to save the symbol table (the data used by a program to associate variable names with memory locations) in the executable, which is necessary for debuggers. Its opposite is the `-O` flag, which tells the compiler to optimize the code—that is, to make it more efficient. You can change the search path for header files with the `-I` flag, and you can add libraries with the `-l` and `-L` flags.

The compilation process takes place in several steps:

1. First, the C preprocessor parses the file. To parse the file, it sequentially reads the lines, includes header files, and performs macro replacement.

2. The compiler parses the modified code for correct syntax. This builds a symbol table and creates an intermediate object format. Most symbols have specific memory addresses assigned, although symbols defined in other modules, such as external variables, do not.
3. The last compilation stage, linking, ties together different files and libraries and links the files by resolving the symbols that hadn't previously been resolved.

Executing the Program

The output from this program appears in Listing 23.8.

Listing 23.8. Output from the `sample.c` program.

```
$ sample
 1.    1     1 1.00000
 2.    4     8 1.41421
 3.    9    27 1.73205
 4.   16    64 2.00000
 5.   25   125 2.23607
 6.   36   216 2.44949
 7.   49   343 2.64575
 8.   64   512 2.82843
 9.   81   729 3.00000
10.  100  1000 3.16228
```

NOTE

To execute a program, just type its name at a shell prompt. The output will immediately follow.

Building Large Applications

C programs can be broken into any number of files, as long as no single function spans more than one file. To compile this program, you compile each source file into an intermediate object before you link all the objects into a single executable. The `-c` flag tells the compiler to stop at this stage. During the link stage, all the object files should be listed on the command line. Object files are identified by the `.o` suffix.

Making Libraries with ar

If several different programs use the same functions, they can be combined in a single library archive. The `ar` command is used to build a library. When this library is included on the compile line, the archive is searched to resolve any external symbols. Listing 23.9 shows an example of building and using a library.

Listing 23.9. Building a large application.

```
gcc -c sine.c
gcc -c cosine.c
gcc -c tangent.c
ar c libtrig.a sine.o cosine.o tangent.o

gcc -c mainprog.c
gcc -o mainprog mainprog.o libtrig.a
```

Large applications can require hundreds of source code files. Compiling and linking these applications can be a complex and error-prone task of its own. The `make` utility is a tool that helps developers organize the process of building the executable form of complex applications from many source files.

Debugging Tools

Debugging is a science and an art unto itself. Sometimes, the simplest tool—the code listing—is best. At other times, however, you need to use other tools. Three of these tools are `lint`, `gprof`, and `gdb`. Other available tools include `escape`, `cxref`, and `cb`. Many UNIX commands have debugging uses.

`lint` is a command that examines source code for possible problems. The code might meet the standards for C and compile cleanly, but it might not execute correctly. `lint` checks type mismatches and incorrect argument counts on function calls. `lint` also uses the C preprocessor, so you can use similar command-like options as you would for `gcc`. The GNU C compiler supports extensive warnings that might eliminate the need for a separate `lint` command.

The `gprof` command is used to study where a program is spending its time. If a program is compiled and linked with `-p` as a flag, when it executes, a `mon.out` file is created with data on how often each function is called and how much time is spent in each function. `gprof` parses and displays this data. An analysis of the output generated by `gprof` helps you determine where performance bottlenecks occur. Whereas optimizing compilers can speed your programs, `gprof`'s analysis will significantly improve program performance.

The third tool is `gdb`—a symbolic debugger. When a program is compiled with `-g`, the symbol tables are retained, and a symbolic debugger can be used to track program bugs. The basic technique is to invoke `gdb` after a core dump and get a stack trace. This indicates the source line where the core dump occurred and the functions that were called to reach that line. Often, this is enough to identify the problem. It is not the limit of `gdb`, though.

`gdb` also provides an environment for debugging programs interactively. Invoking `gdb` with a program enables you to set breakpoints, examine variable values, and monitor variables. If you suspect a problem near a line of code, you can set a breakpoint at that line and run the program. When the line is reached, execution is interrupted. You can check variable values, examine the stack trace, and observe the program's environment. You can single-step through the program, checking values. You can resume execution at any point. By using breakpoints, you can discover many of the bugs in your code that you've missed.

There is an X Window version of `gdb` called `xxgdb`.

`cpp` is another tool that can be used to debug programs. It performs macro replacements, includes headers, and parses the code. The output is the actual module to be compiled. Normally, though, `cpp` is never executed by the programmer directly. Instead it is invoked through `gcc` with either an `-E` or `-P` option. `-E` sends the output directly to the terminal; `-P` makes a file with an `.i` suffix.

Introduction to C++

If C is the language most associated with UNIX, C++ is the language that underlies most graphical user interfaces available today.

C++ was originally developed by Dr. Bjarne Stroustrup at the Computer Science Research Center of AT&T's Bell Laboratories (Murray Hill, NJ), also the source of UNIX itself. Dr. Stroustrup's original goal was an object-oriented simulation language. The availability of C compilers for many hardware architectures convinced him to design the language as an extension of C, allowing a preprocessor to translate C++ programs into C for compilation.

After the C language was standardized by a joint committee of the American National Standards Institute and the International Standards Organization (ISO) in 1989, a new joint committee began the effort to formalize C++ as well. This effort has produced several new features and has significantly refined the interpretation of other language features, but it hasn't yet resulted in a formal language standard.

Programming in C++: Basic Concepts

C++ is an object-oriented extension to C. Because C++ is a superset of C, C++ compilers will compile C programs correctly, and it is possible to write non–object-oriented code in C++.

The distinction between an object-oriented language and a procedural one can be subtle and hard to grasp, especially with regard to C++, which retains all of C's characteristics and concepts. One way to describe the difference is to say that when programmers code in a procedural language, they specify actions that process the data, whereas when they write object-oriented code, they create data objects that can be requested to perform actions on or with regard to themselves.

Thus a C function receives one or more values as input, transforms or acts on them in some way, and returns a result. If the values that are passed include pointers, the contents of data variables can be modified by the function. As the standard library routines show, it is likely that the code calling a function won't know, or need to know, what steps the function takes when it is invoked. However, such matters as the datatype of the input parameters and the result code are specified when the function is defined and remain invariable throughout program execution.

Functions are associated with C++ objects as well. But as you will see, the actions performed when an object's function is invoked can automatically differ, perhaps substantially, depending on the specific type of the data structure with which it is associated. This is known as *overloading* function names. Overloading is related to a second characteristic of C++—the fact that functions can be defined as belonging to C++ data structures, an aspect of the wider language feature known as *encapsulation*.

In addition to overloading and encapsulation, object-oriented languages allow programmers to define new abstract datatypes (including associated functions) and then derive subsequent datatypes from them. The notion of a new class of data objects, in addition to the built-in classes such as integer, floating-point number, and character, goes beyond the familiar ability to define complex data objects in C. Just as a C data structure that includes, for example, an integer element inherits the properties and functions applicable to integers, so too a C++ class that is derived from another class *inherits* the parent class's functions and properties. When a specific variable or structure (instance) of that class's type is defined, the class (parent or child) is said to be *instantiated*.

In the remainder of this chapter, you will look at some of the basic features of C++ in more detail, along with code listings that provide concrete examples of these concepts. To learn more about the rich capabilities of C++, see the additional resources listed at the end of the chapter in the section "Additional Resources."

File Naming

Most C programs will compile with a C++ compiler if you follow strict ANSI rules. For example, you can compile the `hello.c` program shown in Listing 23.1 with the GNU C++ compiler. Typically, you will name the file something like `hello.cc`, `hello.C`, or `hello.cxx`. The GNU C++ compiler will accept any of these three names.

Differences Between C and C++

C++ differs from C in some details apart from the more obvious object-oriented features. Some of these are fairly superficial, including the following:

- The ability to define variables anywhere within a code block rather than always at the start of the block
- The addition of an `enum` datatype to facilitate conditional logic based on case values
- The ability to designate functions as `inline`, causing the compiler to generate another copy of the function code at that point in the program rather than a call to shared code

Other differences have to do with advanced concepts such as memory management and the scope of reference for variable and function names. Because the latter features especially are used in object-oriented C++ programs, they are worth examining more closely in this short introduction to the language.

Scope of Reference in C and C++

The phrase *scope of reference* is used to discuss how a name in C, C++, or certain other programming languages is interpreted when the language permits more than one instance of a name to occur within a program. Consider the code in Listing 23.10, which defines and then calls two different functions. Each function has an internal variable called `tmp`. The `tmp` that is defined within `printnum` is *local* to the `printnum` function—that is, it can be accessed only by logic within `printnum`. Similarly, the `tmp` that is defined within `printchar` is local to the `printchar` function. The scope of reference for each `tmp` variable is limited to the `printnum` and `printchar` functions, respectively.

Listing 23.10. Scope of reference example 1.

```
#include <stdio.h>                /* I/O function declarations */

void printnum  ( int );           /* function declaration      */
void printchar ( char );          /* function declaration      */

main ()
{
   printnum (5);                  /* print the number 5        */
   printchar ('a');               /* print the letter a        */
}

/* define the functions called above                           */
/* void means the function does not return a value             */

   void printnum (int inputnum)
{
   int tmp;
   tmp = inputnum;
   printf ("%d \n",tmp);
}

void printchar (char inputchar)
{
   char tmp;
   tmp = inputchar;
   printf ("%c \n",tmp);
}
```

When this program is executed after compilation, it creates the following output:

```
5
a
```

Listing 23.11 shows another example of scope of reference. In this listing, there is a `tmp` variable that is *global*—that is, it is known to the entire program because it is defined within the `main` function—in addition to the two `tmp` variables that are local to the `printnum` and `printchar` functions.

Listing 23.11. Scope of reference example 2.

```
#include <stdio.h>

void printnum  ( int );          /* function declaration          */
void printchar ( char );         /* function declaration          */

main ()
{
   double tmp;                   /* define a global variable      */
   tmp = 1.234;
   printf ("%f\n",tmp);          /* print the value of the global tmp */
   printnum (5);                 /* print the number 5            */
   printf ("%f\n",tmp);          /* print the value of the global tmp */
   printchar ('a');              /* print the letter a            */
   printf ("%f\n",tmp);          /* print the value of the global tmp */
}

/* define the functions used above                                */
/* void means the function does not return a value                */

void printnum (int inputnum)
{
   int tmp;
   tmp = inputnum;
   printf ("%d \n",tmp);
}

void printchar (char inputchar)
{
   char tmp;
   tmp = inputchar;
   printf ("%c \n",tmp);
}
```

The global `tmp` is not modified when the local `tmp` variables are used within their respective functions, as shown by the output:

```
1.234
5
1.234
a
1.234
```

C++ provides a means to specify a global variable even when a local variable with the same name is in scope. The operator `::` prefixed to a variable name always resolves that name to the global instance. Thus, the global `tmp` variable defined in `main` in Listing 23.11 could be accessed within the `print` functions by using the label `::tmp`.

Why would a language such as C or C++ allow different scopes of reference for the same variable?

The answer to this is that allowing variable scope of reference also allows functions to be placed into public libraries for other programmers to use. Library functions can be invoked merely by knowing their calling sequences, and no one needs to check to be sure that the programmers didn't use the same local variable names. This in turn means that library functions can be improved, if necessary, without impacting existing code. This is true whether the library contains application code for reuse or is distributed as the runtime library associated with a compiler.

NOTE

A runtime library is a collection of compiled modules that perform common C, C++, and UNIX functions. The code is written carefully, debugged, and highly optimized. For example, the `printf` function requires machine instructions to format the various output fields, send them to the standard output device, and check to see that there were no I/O errors. Because this takes many machine instructions, it would be inefficient to repeat that sequence for every `printf` call in a program. Instead, a single, all-purpose `printf` function is written once and placed in the standard library by the developers of the compiler. When your program is compiled, the compiler generates calls to these prewritten programs rather than re-creating the logic each time a `printf` call occurs in the source code.

Variable scope of reference is the language feature that allows small C and C++ programs to be designed to perform standalone functions, yet also to be combined into larger utilities as needed. This flexibility is characteristic of UNIX, the first operating system to be built on the C language. As you'll see in the rest of the chapter, variable scope of reference also makes object-oriented programming possible in C++.

Overloading Functions and Operators in C++

Overloading is a technique that allows more than one function to have the same name. There are at least two circumstances in which a programmer might want to define a new function with the same name as an existing one:

- When the existing version of the function doesn't perform the exact desired functionality, but it must otherwise be included with the program (as with a function from the standard library).
- When the same function must operate differently depending on the format of the data passed to it.

In C, a function name can be reused as long as the old function name isn't within scope. A function name's scope of reference is determined in the same way as a data name's scope: A function that is defined (not just called) within the definition of another function is local to that other function.

When two similar C functions must coexist within the same scope, however, they cannot bear the same name. Instead, two different names must be assigned, as with the `strcpy` and `strncpy` functions from the standard library, each of which copies strings but does so in a slightly different fashion.

C++ gets around this restriction by allowing overloaded function names. That is, the C++ language allows programmers to reuse function names within the same scope of reference, as long as the parameters for the function differ in number or type.

Listing 23.12 shows an example of overloading functions. This program defines and calls two versions of the `printvar` function, one equivalent to `printnum` in Listing 23.11 and the other to `printchar`.

Listing 23.12. An example of an overloaded function.

```
#include <stdio.h>
void printvar (int tmp)
{
   printf ("%d \n",tmp);
}

void printvar (char tmp)
{
   printf ("a \n",tmp);
}

void main ()
{
   int  numvar;
   char charvar;
   numvar = 5;
   printvar (numvar);
   charvar = 'a';
   printvar (charvar);
}
```


The following is the output of this program when it is executed:

```
5
a
```

Overloading is possible because C++ compilers are able to determine the format of the arguments sent to the `printvar` function each time it is called from within `main`. The compiler substitutes a call to the correct version of the function based on those formats. If the function being overloaded resides in a library or in another module, the associated header file (such as `stdio.h`) must be included in this source code module. This header file contains the prototype for the external function, thereby informing the compiler of the parameters and parameter formats used in the external version of the function.

Standard mathematical, logical, and other operators can also be overloaded. This is an advanced and powerful technique that allows the programmer to customize exactly how a standard language feature will operate on a specific data structure or at certain points in the code. Great care must be exercised when overloading standard operators such as +, `MOD`, and `OR` to ensure that the resulting operation functions correctly, is restricted to the appropriate occurrences in the code, and is well documented.

Functions Within C++ Data Structures

A second feature of C++ that supports object-oriented programming, in addition to overloading, is the ability to associate a function with a particular data structure or format. Such functions can be *public* (able to be invoked by any code), can be *private* (able to be invoked only by other functions within the data structure), or can allow limited access.

Data structures in C++ must be defined using the `struct` keyword and become new datatypes added to the language (within the scope of the structure's definition). Listing 23.13 revisits the structure of Listing 23.3 and adds a display function to print out instances of the license structure. Note the alternative way to designate comments in C++, using a double slash. This tells the compiler to ignore everything that follows on the given line only.

Also notice that Listing 23.13 uses the C++ character output function `cout` rather than the C routine `printf`.

Listing 23.13. Adding functions to data structures.

```
#include <iostream.h>
//              structure = new datatype
struct license {
        char name[128];
        char address[3][128];
        int zipcode;
        int height, weight, month, day, year;
        char license_letter;
        int license_number;

        void display(void)
➥// there will be a function to display license type structures
        };

// now define the display function for this datatype

void license::display()
{
   cout << "Name:     "  << name;
   cout << "Address:  "  << address[0];
   cout << "          "  << address[1];
   cout << "          " << address[2] << " " << zipcode;
   cout << "Height:   " << height << " inches";
   cout << "Weight:   " << weight << " lbs";
   cout << "Date:     " << month << "/" << day  << "/" << year;
   cout << "License:  " <<license_letter <<license_number;
}


main()
{
   struct license newlicensee;      // define a variable of type license
   newlicensee.name = "Joe Smith";  //  and initialize it
   newlicensee.address(0) = "123 Elm Street";
   newlicensee.address(1) = "";
   newlicensee.address(2) = "Smalltown, AnyState";
```

```
    newlicensee.zipcode = "98765";
    newlicensee.height = 70;
    newlicensee.weight = 165;
    license.month = 1;
    newlicensee.day = 23;
    newlicensee.year = 97;
    newlicensee.license_letter = A;
    newlicensee.license_number = 567890;

    newlicensee.display;    // and display this instance of the structure
}
```

Note that there are three references to the same `display` function in Listing 23.13. First, the `display` function is prototyped as an element within the structure definition. Second, the function is defined. Because the function definition is valid for all instances of the datatype `license`, the structure's data elements are referenced by the `display` function without naming any instance of the structure. Finally, when a specific instance of `license` is created, its associated `display` function is invoked by prefixing the function name with that of the structure instance.

Listing 23.14 shows the output of this program.

Listing 23.14. Output of the function defined within a structure.

```
Name:     Joe Smith
Address:  123 Elm Street

          Smalltown, AnyState  98765
Height:   70 inches
Weight:   160 lbs
Date:     1/23/1997
License:  A567890
```

Note that the operator << is the bitwise shift left operator except when it is used with `cout`. With `cout`, << is used to move data to the screen. This is an example of operator overloading because the operator can have a different meaning depending on the context of its use. The >> operator is used for bitwise shift right except when used with `cin`; with `cin`, it is used to move data from the keyboard to the specified variable.

Classes in C++

Overloading and associating functions with data structures lay the groundwork for object-oriented code in C++. Full object orientation is available through the use of the C++ class feature.

A C++ class extends the idea of data structures with associated functions by binding (or encapsulating) data descriptions and manipulation algorithms into new abstract datatypes. When a class is defined, the class type and methods are described in the public interface. The class can also have hidden private functions and data members as well.

Class declaration defines a datatype and format, but does not allocate memory or in any other way create an object of the class's type. The wider program must declare an instance, or object, of this type in order to store values in the data elements or to invoke the public class functions. A class is often placed into libraries for use by many different programs, each of which then declares objects that instantiate that class for use during program execution.

Declaring a Class in C++

Listing 23.15 contains an example of a typical class declaration in C++.

Listing 23.15. Declaring a class in C++.

```
#include <iostream.h>
// declare the Circle class
class Circle   {
private:
   double rad;                        // private data member
public:
   Circle (double);                   // constructor function
   ~Circle ();                        // deconstructor function
   double area (void);                // member function - compute area
};

//  constructor function for objects of this class
Circle::Circle(double radius)
{
   rad = radius;
}

//  deconstructor function for objects of this class
Circle::~Circle()
{
   // does nothing
}

// member function to compute the Circle's area
double Circle::area()
{
    return rad * rad * 3.141592654;
}

//       application program that uses a Circle object
main()
{
    Circle mycircle (2);           // declare a circle of radius = 2
    cout << mycircle.area();       // compute & display its area
}
```

The example in Listing 23.15 begins by declaring the `Circle` class. This class has one private member, a floating-point element. The `Circle` class also has several public members, consisting of three functions—`Circle`, `~Circle`, and `area`.

The *constructor function* of a class is a function called by a program in order to construct or create an object that is an instance of the class. In the case of the `Circle` class, the constructor function (`Circle(double)`) requires a single parameter, namely the radius of the desired circle. If a constructor function is explicitly defined, it has the same name as the class and does not specify a return value, even of type `void`.

NOTE

When a C++ program is compiled, the compiler generates calls to the runtime system, which allocates sufficient memory each time an object of class `Circle` comes into scope. For example, an object that is defined within a function is created (and goes into scope) whenever the function is called. However, the object's data elements are not initialized unless a constructor function has been defined for the class.

The *deconstructor function* of a class is a function called by a program in order to deconstruct an object of the class type. A deconstructor takes no parameters and returns nothing. In this example, the `Circle` class's deconstructor function is `~Circle`.

NOTE

Under normal circumstances, the memory associated with an object of a given class is released for reuse whenever the object goes out of scope. In such a case, the programmer can omit defining the deconstructor function. However, in advanced applications or where class assignments cause potential pointer conflicts, explicit deallocation of free-store memory might be necessary.

In addition to the constructor and deconstructor functions, the `Circle` class contains a public function called `area`. Programs can call this function to compute the area of `Circle` objects.

The main program (the `main` function) in Listing 23.15 shows how an object can be declared. `mycircle` is declared to be of type `Circle` and is given a radius of 2.

The final statement in this program calls the function to compute the area of `mycircle` and passes it to the output function for display. Note that the area computation function is identified by a composite name, just as with other functions that are members of C++ data structures outside of class definitions. This usage underscores the fact that the object `mycircle`, of type `Circle`, is being asked to execute a function that is a member of itself, and with reference to itself. The programmer could define a `Rectangle` class that also contains an `area` function, thereby overloading the `area` function name with the appropriate algorithm for computing the areas of different kinds of geometric entities.

Inheritance and Polymorphism

A final characteristic of object-oriented languages, and of C++, is support for class inheritance and for polymorphism.

New C++ classes (and hence datatypes) can be defined so that they automatically *inherit* the properties and algorithms associated with their parent classes. This is done whenever a new class uses any of the standard C datatypes. The class from which new class definitions are created is called the *base class*. For example, a structure that includes integer members will also inherit all the mathematical functions associated with integers. New classes that are defined in terms of the base classes are called *derived classes*. The `Circle` class in Listing 23.15 is a derived class.

Derived classes can be based upon more than one base class, in which case the derived class inherits multiple datatypes and their associated functions. This is called *multiple inheritance*.

Because functions can be overloaded, it is possible that an object declared as a member of a derived class might act differently than an object of the base class type. For example, the class of positive integers might return an error if the program attempts to assign a negative number to a class object, although such an assignment would be legal with regard to an object of the base integer type.

This ability of different objects within the same class hierarchy to act differently under the same circumstances is referred to as *polymorphism*. Polymorphism is the object-oriented concept that many people have the most difficulty grasping. However, it is also the concept that provides much of the power and elegance of object-oriented design and code. A programmer designing an application using predefined graphical user interface (GUI) classes, for instance, is free to ask various window objects to display themselves appropriately without having to concern herself with how the window color, location, or other display characteristics are handled in each case.

Class inheritance and polymorphism are among the most powerful object-oriented features of C++. Together with the other less dramatic extensions to C, these features have made possible many of the newest applications and systems capabilities of UNIX today, including GUIs for user terminals and many of the most advanced Internet and World Wide Web technologies—some of which will be discussed in the subsequent chapters of this book.

GNU C/C++ Compiler Command-Line Switches

There are many options available for the GNU C/C++ compiler. Many of them match the C and C++ compilers available on other UNIX systems. Table 23.7 shows the important switches; look at the man page for `gcc` or the info file on the CD-ROM for the full list and description.

Table 23.7. GNU C/C++ compiler switches.

Switch	*Description*
`-x language`	Specifies the language (C, C++, and assembler are valid values)
`-c`	Compiles and assembles only (does not link)
`-S`	Compiles (does not assemble or link)

Switch	Description
`-E`	Preprocesses only (does not compile, assemble, or link)
`-o` *`file`*	Specifies the output filename (`a.out` is the default)
`-l` *`library`*	Specifies the libraries to use
`-I` *`directory`*	Searches the specified directory for include files
`-w`	Inhibits warning messages
`-pedantic`	Strict ANSI compliance required
`-Wall`	Prints additional warning messages
`-g`	Produces debugging information (for use with `gdb`)
`-p`	Produces information required by `proff`
`-pg`	Produces information for use by `groff`
`-O`	Optimizes

Additional Resources

If you are interested in learning more about C and C++, you should look into the following books:

- *Teach Yourself C in 21 Days*, by Peter Aitken and Bradley Jones
- *C How to Program* and *C++ How to Program*, by H.M. Deitel and P.J. Deitel
- *The C Programming Language*, by Brian Kernighan and Dennis Ritchie
- *The Annotated C++ Reference Manual*, by Margaret Ellis and Bjarne Stroustrup
- *Programming in ANSI C*, by Stephen G. Kochan

Summary

UNIX was built upon the C language. C is a platform-independent, compiled, procedural language based on functions and the ability to derive new, programmer-defined data structures.

C++ extends the capabilities of C by providing the necessary features for object-oriented design and code. C++ compilers correctly compile ANSI C code. C++ also provides some features, such as the ability to associate functions with data structures, which don't require the use of full class-based, object-oriented techniques. For these reasons, the C++ language allows existing UNIX programs to migrate toward the adoption of object orientation over time.

CHAPTER 24

Perl Programming

by Rich Bowen

IN THIS CHAPTER

Perl (Practical Extraction and Report Language) was developed in 1986 by Larry Wall. It has grown in popularity, and is now one of the favorite scripting languages for UNIX platforms.

Perl is similar in syntax to C, but also contains much of the style of UNIX shell scripting. And, thrown in with that, it contains the best features of every other programming language that you have ever used.

Perl is an interpreted language rather than a compiled one, which is either an advantage or a disadvantage, depending on how you look at it. Perl has been ported to virtually every operating system out there, and most Perl programs will run without modifications on any system that you move them to. That is certainly an advantage. In addition, for the small, almost trivial, applications used in everyday server maintenance, you might not want to go to all the trouble of writing the code in C and compiling it.

Perl is very forgiving about such things as declaring variables, allocating and deallocating memory, and variable types, so you can get down to the actual business of writing code. In fact, those concepts really do not exist in Perl. This results in programs that are short and to the point, while similar programs in C, for example, might spend half the code declaring variables.

A Simple Perl Program

To introduce you to the absolute basics of Perl programming, Listing 24.1 illustrates a trivial Perl program.

Listing 24.1. A trivial Perl program.

```
#!/usr/bin/perl
print "Red Hat Unleashed, 2nd edition\n";
```

That's the whole thing. Type that in, save it to a file called `trivial.pl`, `chmod +x` it, and execute it.

If you are at all familiar with shell scripting languages, this will look very familiar. Perl combines the simplicity of shell scripting with the power of a full-fledged programming language.

The first line of this program indicates to the operating system where to find the Perl interpreter. This is standard procedure with shell scripts, and you have already seen this syntax in Chapter 21, "Shell Programming."

If `/usr/bin/perl` is not the correct location for Perl on your system, you can find out where it is located by typing **`which perl`** at the command line. If you do not have Perl installed, you might want to skip forward to the section titled "For More Information" to find out where you can obtain the Perl interpreter.

The second line does precisely what you would expect it to do—it prints the text enclosed in quotes. The `\n` notation is used for a newline character.

Perl Variables and Data Structures

Although it does not have the concept of datatype (`integer`, `string`, `char`, and so on), Perl has several kinds of variables.

Scalar variables, indicated as `$variable`, are interpreted as numbers or strings, as the context warrants. You can treat a variable as a number one moment and a string the next if the value of the variable makes sense in that context.

There is a large collection of special variables in Perl, such as `$_`, `$$`, and `$<`, which Perl keeps track of, and you can use if you want to. (`$_` is the default input variable, `$$` is the process ID, and `$<` is the user ID.) As you become more familiar with Perl, you will find yourself using these variables, and people will accuse you of writing "read-only" code.

Arrays, indicated as `@array`, contain one or more elements, which can be referred to by index. For example, `$names[12]` gives me the 13th element in the array `@names`. (It's important to remember that numbering starts with 0.)

Associative arrays, indicated by `%assoc_array`, store values that can be referenced by key. For example, `$days{Feb}` will give me the element in the associative array `%days` that corresponds with `Feb`.

The following line of Perl code lists all the elements in an associative array (the `foreach` construct is covered later in this chapter):

```
foreach $key (keys %assoc){
     print "$key = $assoc{$key}\n"};
```

NOTE

`$_` is the "default" variable in Perl. In this example, the loop variable is `$_` because none was specified.

Conditional Statements: `if/else`

The syntax of the Perl `if/else` structure is as follows:

```
if (condition) {
     statement(s)
     }
elsif (condition) {
     statement(s)
     }
else {
     statement(s)
     }
```

condition can be any statement or comparison. If the statement returns any true value, the *statement(s)* will be executed. Here, true is defined as

- Any nonzero number
- Any nonzero string; that is, any string that is not `0` or empty
- Any conditional that returns a true value

For example, the following piece of code uses the `if/else` structure:

```
if ($favorite eq "chocolate") {
      print "I like chocolate too.\n"
     }
elsif ($favorite eq "spinach") {
      print "Oh, I don't like spinach.\n";
     }
else {
     print "Your favorite food is $favorite.\n"
     }
```

Looping

Perl has four looping constructs: `for`, `foreach`, `while`, and `until`.

for

The `for` construct performs a statement (or set of statements) for a set of conditions defined as follows:

```
for (start condition; end condition; increment function) {
     statement(s)
     }
```

At the beginning of the loop, the start condition is set. Each time the loop is executed, the increment function is performed until the end condition is achieved. This looks much like the traditional `for/next` loop. The following code is an example of a `for` loop:

```
for ($i=1; $i<=10; $i++) {
      print "$i\n"
     }
```

foreach

The `foreach` construct performs a statement (or set of statements) for each element in a set, such as a list or array:

```
foreach $name (@names) {
     print "$name\n"
     }
```

while

`while` performs a block of statements while a particular condition is true:

```
while ($x<10) {
     print "$x\n";
     $x++;
     }
```

until

`until` is the exact opposite of the `while` statement. It will perform a block of statements while a particular condition is false—or, rather, until it becomes true:

```
until ($x>10) {
     print "$x\n";
     $x++;
     }
```

Regular Expressions

Perl's greatest strength is in text and file manipulation. This is accomplished by using the regular expression (regex) library. Regexes allow complicated pattern matching and replacement to be done efficiently and easily.

For example, the following one line of code will replace every occurrence of the string `Bob` or the string `Mary` with `Fred` in a line of text:

```
$string =~ s/bob¦mary/fred/gi;
```

Without going into too many of the gory details, Table 24.1 explains what the preceding line says.

Table 24.1. Explanation of `$string =~ s/bob¦mary/fred/gi;`.

Element	*Explanation*
`$string =~`	Performs this pattern match on the text found in the variable called `$string`.
`s`	Substitute.
`/`	Begins the text to be matched.
`bob¦mary`	Matches the text `bob` or `mary`. You should remember that it is looking for the text `mary`, not the word `mary`; that is, it will also match the text `mary` in the word `maryland`.
`/`	Ends text to be matched, begin text to replace it with.
`fred`	Replaces anything that was matched with the text `fred`.

continues

Table 24.1. continued

Element	*Explanation*
`/`	Ends replace text.
`g`	Does this substitution globally; that is, wherever in the string you match the match text (and any number of times), replaces it.
`i`	The search text is case-insensitive. It will match `bob`, `Bob`, or `bOB`.
`;`	Indicates the end of the line of code.

If you are interested in the gory details, I recommend the book *Mastering Regular Expressions* by Jeffrey Friedl, which explains regular expressions from the ground up, going into all the theory behind them and explaining the best ways to use them.

Although replacing one string with another might seem like a rather trivial task, the code required to do the same thing in another language, for example, C, is rather daunting.

Access to the Shell

Perl is useful for administrative functions because, for one thing, it has access to the shell. This means that any process that you might ordinarily do by typing commands to the shell, Perl can do for you. This is done with the `` ` ` `` syntax; for example, the following code will print a directory listing:

```
$curr_dir = `pwd`;
@listing = `ls -la`;
print "Listing for $curr_dir\n";
foreach $file (@listing) {
     print "$file";
     }
```

NOTE

The `` ` ` `` notation uses the backtick found above the Tab key, not the single quote.

Access to the command line is fairly common in shell scripting languages, but is less common in higher level programming languages.

Command-Line Mode

In addition to writing programs, Perl can be used from the command line like any other shell scripting language. This enables you to cobble together Perl utilities on-the-fly, rather than having to create a file and execute it.

For example, running the following command line will run through the file `foo` and replace every occurrence of the string `Joe` with `Harry`, saving a backup copy of the file at `foo.bak`:

```
perl -p -i.bak -e s/Joe/Harry/g foo
```

The `-p` switch causes Perl to perform the command for all files listed (in this case, just one file).

The `-i` switch indicates that the file specified is to be edited in place, and the original backed up with the extension specified. If no extension is supplied, no backup copy is made.

The `-e` switch indicates that what follows is one or more lines of a script.

Automation Using Perl

Perl is great for automating some of the tasks involved in maintaining and administering a UNIX machine. Because of its text manipulation abilities and its access to the shell, Perl can be used to do any of the processes that you might ordinarily do by hand.

The following sections present examples of Perl programs that you might use in the daily maintenance of your machine.

Moving Files

One aspect of my job is administering a secure FTP site. Incoming files are placed in an "incoming" directory. When they have been checked, they are moved to a "private" directory for retrieval. Permissions are set in such a way that the file is not shown in a directory listing, but can be retrieved if the filename is known. The person who placed the file on the server is informed via e-mail that the file is now available for download.

I quickly discovered that people were having difficulty retrieving files because they incorrectly typed the case of filenames. This was solved by making the file available with an all-uppercase name and an all-lowercase name, in addition to the original filename.

I wrote the Perl program in Listing 24.2 to perform all those tasks with a single command. When I have determined that a file is to go onto the FTP site, I simply type `move` *`filename`* *`user`*, where *`filename`* is the name of the file to be moved, and *`user`* is the e-mail address of the person to be notified.

Listing 24.2. Moving files on an FTP site.

```
#!/usr/bin/perl
#
#  Move a file from /incoming to /private
$file = @ARGV[0];
$user = @ARGV[1];

if ($user eq "") {&usage}
else {
```

continues

Listing 24.2. continued

```
 9:      if (-e "/home/ftp/incoming/$file")
10:           {`cp /home/ftp/incoming/$file /home/ftp/private/$file`;
11:           chmod 0644, "/home/ftp/private/$file";
12:           `rm -f /home/ftp/incoming/$file`;
13:           if (uc($file) ne $file)  {
14:                $ucfile = uc($file);
15:                `ln /home/ftp/private/$file /home/ftp/private/$ucfile`;
16:               }
17:           if (lc($file) ne $file)  {
18:                 $lcfile = lc($file);
19:                 `ln /home/ftp/private/$file /home/ftp/private/$lcfile`;
20:                }
21:
22: # Send mail
23: open (MAIL, "| /usr/sbin/sendmail -t  ftpadmin,$user");
24: print MAIL <<EndMail;
25: To: ftpadmin,$user
26: From: ftpadmin
27: Subject: File ($file) moved
28:
29: The file $file has been moved
30: The file is now available as
31: ftp://ftp.databeam.com/private/$file
32:
33: ftpadmin\@databeam.com
34: ================================
35: EndMail
36: close MAIL;
37: }
38:
39:     else {  #  File does not exist
40:          print "File does not exist!\n";
41:          }   #  End else (-e $file)
42:
43: } #  End else ($user eq "")
44:
45: sub usage {
46: print "move <filename> <username>\n";
47: print "where <username> is the user that you are moving this for.\n\n";
48: }
```

Without going through Listing 24.2 line-by-line, the following paragraphs take a look at some of the high points that demonstrate the power and syntax of Perl.

In lines 4–5, the array `@ARGV` contains all command-line arguments. The place where one argument ends and another begins is taken to be every space, unless arguments are given in quotes.

In line 9, the `-e` file test tests for the existence of a file. If the file does not exist, perhaps the user gave me the wrong filename, or one of the other server administrators beat me to it.

Perl enables you to open a pipe to some other process and print data to it. This allows Perl to "use" any other program that has an interactive user interface, such as `sendmail`, or an FTP session. That's the purpose of line 23.

The << syntax allows you to print multiple lines of text until the `EOF` string is encountered. This eliminates the necessity to have multiple `print` commands following one another—for example,

```
24: print MAIL <<EndMail;
...
35: EndMail
```

The subroutine syntax allows modularization of code into functions. Subroutines are declared with the syntax shown in lines 45–48, and called with the `&` notation, as shown in line 7:

```
7: ... {&usage}
...
45: sub usage {
...
48: }
```

Purging Logs

Many programs maintain some variety of logs. Often, much of the information in the logs is redundant or just useless. The program shown in Listing 24.3 removes all lines from a file that contain a particular word or phrase, so lines that you know are not important can be purged.

Listing 24.3. Purging log files.

```
#!/usr/bin/perl
#
#       Be careful using this program!!
#       This will remove all lines that contain a given word
#
#       Usage:  remove <word> <file>
###########
$word=@ARGV[0];
$file=@ARGV[1];

unless ($file)  {
print "Usage:  remove <word> <file>\n"; }

else    {
open (FILE, "$file");
@lines=<FILE>;
close FILE;

# remove the offending lines
@lines = grep (!/$word/, @lines);

#  Write it back
open (NEWFILE, ">$file");
for (@lines)    { print NEWFILE }
close NEWFILE;
        }  #  End else
```

Listing 24.3 is fairly self-explanatory. It reads in the file and then removes the offending lines using Perl's `grep` command, which is similar to the standard UNIX `grep`. If you save this as a file called `remove` and place it in your path, you will have a swift way to purge server logs of unwanted messages.

Posting to Usenet

If some portion of your job requires periodic postings to Usenet—a FAQ listing, for example—the following Perl program can automate the process for you. In the sample code, the text that is posted is read in from a text file, but your input can come from anywhere.

The program shown in Listing 24.4 uses the `Net::NNTP` module, which is a standard part of the Perl distribution.

Listing 24.4. Posting an article to Usenet.

```
#!/usr/bin/perl
open (POST, "post.file");
@post = <POST>;
close POST;
use Net::NNTP;

$NNTPhost = 'news';

$nntp = Net::NNTP->new($NNTPhost)
        or die "Cannot contact $NNTPhost: $!";

# $nntp->debug(1);
$nntp->post()
        or die "Could not post article: $!";
$nntp->datasend("Newsgroups: news.announce\n");
$nntp->datasend("Subject: FAQ - Frequently Asked Questions\n");
$nntp->datasend("From: ADMIN <root\@rcbowen.com>\n");
$nntp->datasend("\n\n");
for (@post)     {
$nntp->datasend($_);
}

$nntp->quit;
```

For More Information

The Perl community is large and growing. Since the advent of the WWW, Perl has become the most popular language for Common Gateway Interface (CGI) programming. There is a wealth of sources of information on Perl. Some of the better ones are listed here. The following books are good resources:

- *Programming Perl*, Second Edition, by Larry Wall, Randall Schwartz, and Tom Christiansen (O'Reilly & Associates)

- *Learning Perl* by Randall Schwartz (O'Reilly & Associates)
- *Mastering Regular Expressions* by Jeffrey Friedl (O'Reilly & Associates)
- *CGI Programming with Perl, Visual Basic, and C* by Rich Bowen, et al. (*Web Publishing & Programming Resource Kit*, Volume 4) (Sams.net Publishing)

On Usenet, check out the following:

- `comp.lang.perl.misc`

  Discusses various aspects of the Perl programming language. Make sure that your questions are Perl-specific, not generic CGI questions, because the regulars tend to flame folks who can't tell the difference.
- `comp.infosystems.www.authoring.cgi`

  Discusses authoring of CGI programs, so much of the discussion is Perl-specific. Make sure that your questions are related to CGI, not just Perl. The regulars are very particular about staying on topic.

Check these sites on the World Wide Web:

- `http://www.perl.com/`

  The Perl Language home page, maintained by Tom Christiansen. This is the place to find all sorts of information about Perl, from its history to culture to helpful tips. This is also the place to download the Perl interpreter for your system.
- `http://www.perl.com/CPAN`

  Yes, this is part of the site just mentioned, but it merits its own mention. CPAN (the Comprehensive Perl Archive Network) is the place for you to find modules and programs in Perl. Also, if you end up writing something in Perl that you think is particularly useful, this would be the place to make it available to the Perl community.
- `http://www.perl.org/`

  The Perl Institute. A nonprofit organization dedicated to the advancement of Perl.

Summary

Perl, in the words of its creator, Larry Wall, "combines the best elements of C, `sed`, `awk`, and `sh`," but is also a great language for folks who have no experience with these languages.

Perl's powerful `regex` library and ease of use have made it one of the preferred scripting languages in use today, particularly in the realm of CGI programming. Many people even think of Perl as exclusively a CGI language, when, in fact, it is capable of so much more.

Although this book is focused on Red Hat Linux, Perl is also available for many other platforms, and scripts that you write in Perl on one platform will run without changes on another.

CHAPTER 25

tcl and tk Programming

by Sriranga R. Veeraraghavan

IN THIS CHAPTER

The tcl (pronounced "tickle") scripting language and the tk toolkit are programming environments for creating graphical user interfaces for X Window System. tcl and tk are easy to learn and use, and with them, you can construct user interfaces much faster than with traditional X Window programming methods.

tcl/tk was written by John K. Ousterhout while he was a professor of electrical engineering and computer science at the University of California, Berkeley. It was originally designed to provide a reusable command language for interactive tools, but it has expanded far beyond that and is used in a wide range of software products.

The true power of tcl/tk is that complex graphical applications can be written almost entirely in the tcl scripting language, thus hiding many of the complexities of interface programming encountered in writing interfaces using the C language.

The official tcl/tk Web site is located at http://www.sunscript.com/.

This Web site offers information on releases, bug fixes, and ports along with HTML versions of the manual pages. The site also has links for downloading and installing the latest versions of tcl/tk. Presently, the newest available version of tcl is 7.6p2, and the newest available version of tk is 4.2.

The programs discussed in this chapter are compatible with most versions of tcl and tk.

tcl Basics

tcl is an interpreted language similar to the UNIX shell, which means that tcl commands are first read and then evaluated. tk is a windowing toolkit that uses the tcl syntax for creating GUI components such as buttons, scrollbars, dialogs, and windows.

In order to run tcl, the tcl shell (tclsh) or the windowing shell (wish) is required. Both tclsh and wish are similar to standard UNIX shells like sh or csh, in that they allow commands to be executed interactively or read in from a file. In practice, these shells are seldom used interactively because their interactive abilities are quite limited.

The main difference between tclsh and wish is that tclsh only understands tcl commands, while wish understands both tcl and tk commands.

Interactive Use of tcl

This section briefly covers the interactive use of the tcl shells to illustrate one of its hazards.

To start using tcl interactively, just type tclsh (or wish) at the UNIX shell's prompt. The following prompt should appear:

```
%
```

In this chapter, interactive commands start with the percent character (%). At the prompt, type

```
% echo "hello world"
```

The words `hello world` should appear followed by a new prompt. Now try

```
% puts "hello world"
```

The same output should appear, but there is a big difference between the two. The first command ran the `echo` binary in order to echo the string `"hello world"`, whereas the second command uses the `puts` (put string) `tcl` command. The `echo` version of `"hello world"` works only when `tclsh` is run interactively, which is one of the hazards of using `tclsh` and `wish` interactively. For example, if you put the command

```
echo "hello world"
```

into the file `helloworld.tcl` and then sourced that file from `tclsh`, as in

```
% source helloworld.tcl
```

you would get the following error:

```
invalid command name "echo"
```

To properly use UNIX commands in `tcl`, use the `tcl` command `exec`:

```
% exec echo "hello world"
```

This executes the command with its arguments in a UNIX shell. This is only one example of things that work differently in the interactive mode of the `tcl` shells.

Noninteractive Use of `tcl`

Commonly, `tclsh` and `wish` are used noninteractively, which means that they are invoked on scripts from the UNIX prompt (`$`) such as

```
$ tclsh myprog.tcl
$ wish myprog.tcl
```

or are called from within a script that has as its first line something like the following:

```
#!/usr/bin/wish
```

Usually this first line must be changed for each installation of the script because `wish` or `tclsh` will be in different places. In order to avoid having someone edit the script for each installation, the man page for `tclsh` recommends that the following three lines be used as the first three lines of all `tcl`/`tk` scripts:

```
#!/bin/sh
# the next line restarts using wish \
exec wish "$0" "$@"
```

This means that users only need to have `wish` in their path to use the script. Individual results with this approach could vary depending on the version of `sh` on the system.

The real advantage of noninteractive use of `tcl` is the same as for noninteractive use of the UNIX shell. Noninteractive use allows for many commands to be grouped together and executed by simply typing the name of the script and allows for faster development/debugging of large programs.

The tcl Language

This section contains an introduction to the `tcl` language syntax and its use in scripts. The code in the following section can be run interactively or from a script. The spacing of the output will vary slightly in interactive mode.

Command Structure

The basic structure of a `tcl` command is

```
commandname arguments
```

where *`commandname`* is the command that `tcl` is to execute, and *`arguments`* is the optional arguments to give to that command. The entire line (*`commandname`* and *`arguments`*) is called the command. Commands are separated by newlines (`\n`) or by a semicolon (`;`). If only one command is given on a line, the semicolon is not required. As an illustration, the two commands

```
set foo 0
set bar 1
```

can be written one per line or on the same line:

```
set foo 0; set bar 1;
```

Comments

Other than commands, the only other type of lines in a `tcl` script are comments. As in UNIX shells and Perl, a comment line is a line that begins with a pound symbol (`#`):

```
# this is a comment
```

but unlike in shell, the following is not a comment

```
set foo 0 # initialize foo
```

and will result in an error. The reason is that the `tcl` parser thinks that a command is terminated either by a newline or semicolon, so to include comments on the same line as a command, the command needs to be terminated by a semicolon:

```
set foo 0;# initialize foo
```

Thus, it is probably a good idea to terminate all commands with a semicolon, although it is not required.

Datatypes

`tcl` doesn't support variable types such as `int`, `float`, `double`, or `char`. This means that a variable can be set to a number, a character, or a string at different times in the same program.

Internally, however, tcl treats all variables as strings. When a variable needs to be manipulated, tcl allows numbers (real and integer) to be given in all the forms that are understood by ANSI C. The following are examples of valid numeric values for variables:

74	Integer
0112	Octal, starts with a 0
0x4a	Hexadecimal, starts with 0x
74.	Real
74.0	Real
7.4e1	Real
7.4e+1	Real

Other values are treated as strings and will generate errors if used in mathematical expressions.

Variables

tcl defines two types of variables, scalars and arrays. To create a scalar variable and assign it a value, use the set command. For example,

```
set banana 1;
```

creates the variable banana and gives it a value of 1. To set the value of banana to something different, simply use set again:

```
set banana "Fresh from Brazil";
```

Now the variable banana has the value "Fresh from Brazil". The double quotes tell tcl that all the characters including the spaces make up the value of the variable. (Quoting and substitution are covered later in this chapter in the section "Quoting and Substitution.")

To print out the value of banana, use the puts command:

```
puts $banana;
```

This prints the value of the variable banana to the standard output (sometimes referred to as STDOUT). Putting $ before the name of the variable tells tcl to access the value assigned to that variable. This convention, known as variable substitution, is similar to conventions used in UNIX shells.

To created a one-dimensional array, enter the following:

```
set fruit(0) banana;
set fruit(1) orange;
```

This creates the array variable fruit and assigns to the two named items, 0 and 1, the values banana and orange. The assignments to array indexes need not be in order. The commands

```
set fruit(100) peach;
set fruit(2) kiwi;
set fruit(87) pear;
```

create only three items in the array `fruit`. This is because arrays in `tcl` are like associative arrays, which associate a "key" with a value. Arrays in `tcl` associate a given string with another string. This makes it possible to have array indexes that are not numbers:

```
set fruit(banana) 100
```

This sets the value of item `banana` in the array `fruit` to `100`. The assigned values need not be numeric:

```
set food(koala) eucalyptus;
set food(chipmunk) acorn;
```

To access the value stored in a one-dimensional array variable, use the `$` convention:

```
puts $food(koala);
```

This prints out the value stored in the array `food` at index `koala`. The array index can also be a variable:

```
set animal chipmunk;
puts $food($animal);
```

These commands will output `acorn`, given the previous assignments.

Multidimensional arrays are a simple extension of one-dimensional arrays. They are set as follows:

```
set myarray(1,1) 0;
```

This sets the value of the item at `1,1` in the array `myarray` to be `0`. By separating the indexes by commas, you can make arrays of three, four, or more dimensions:

```
set array(1,1,1,1,1,1) "foo";
```

In addition to setting array values, `tcl` provides the `array` command for getting information about arrays and the `parray` command for printing out information about arrays. First, take a look at the `parray` command. Given the declarations

```
set food(koala) eucalyptus;
set food(chipmunk) acorn;
set food(panda) bamboo;
```

the command

```
parray food
```

will produce the following output:

```
food(chipmunk) = acorn
food(koala)    = eucalyptus
food(panda)    = bamboo
```

Now look at the `array` command and its arguments, which are used to get information about an array and its elements. The basic syntax for an `array` command is as follows:

```
array option arrayname
```

The supported options are discussed later in this section.

One of the most frequently used pieces of information about an array is its size. Given the declarations

```
set fruit(0) banana;
set fruit(1) peach;
set fruit(2) pear;
set fruit(3) apple;
```

The command

```
array size fruit;
```

will return 4. This number is often useful in loops.

Because arrays can have nonsequential or nonnumeric indexes, the array command provides an option for getting elements from an array. Assuming that the food array has been defined as presented earlier, the first thing you need to do to start getting elements is to use startsearch through the array. This is accomplished by first getting a search ID for the array:

```
set food_sid [array startsearch food];
```

The command

```
array startsearch food
```

returns a string, which is the name of the search (see the section called "Quoting and Substitution"). You will need this for future reference, so set its value to that of a variable, in this case food_sid.

To get the first element (and every subsequent element) of the food array, use the following:

```
array nextelement food $food_sid;
```

When the array search is done, terminate the search for the array using

```
array donesearch food $food_sid;
```

One other option to the array command that is frequently in use while iterating through an array is the anymore option. It returns true (a value of 1) if there are any more items in the search. For example,

```
array anymore food $food_sid;
```

returns 1 the first two times it is used with the food array declared earlier.

To dispose of a variable (scalar or array), use the unset command:

```
unset banana;
```

This unsets the variable banana. If you used unset $banana (assuming that banana was set to the value shown earlier) instead of just banana, you would get an error like:

```
can't unset "0": no such variable
```

This occurs because when `$` precedes a variable's name, the value of the variable is substituted in before the command is executed.

Manipulating String Values

The simplest form of string manipulation is the `append` command, which concatenates multiple strings and variables together. As an illustration, the following commands

```
set str1 "Begin";
append str1 " a String";
set str2 " even more text";
append str1 " with some text" " and add" $str2 " to it.";
puts $str1;
```

output

```
Begin a String with some text and add even more text to it.
```

You can achieve the same results using the following commands:

```
set str1 "Begin";
set str1 "$str1 a String";
set str2 " even more text";
set str1 "$str1 with some text and add$str2 to it.";
```

But this will be slower than using `append` because `append` does not do character copying as `set` does.

For more advanced string manipulation, `tcl` provides the `string` command, which understands a whole host of options. The basic syntax of the `string` command is

```
string option string1 string2
```

where *`string1`* and *`string2`* can either be a literal strings (`"this is a string"`) or variables, and *`option`* is one of the following:

`compare`	Returns `-1`, `0`, or `1` depending on whether or not *`string1`* is lexographically less than, equal to, or greater than *`string2`* (similar to the C library function `strcmp`)
`first`	Returns the index of the first occurrence of *`string1`* in *`string2`*, or `-1` if *`string1`* does not occur in *`string2`*
`last`	Returns the index of the last occurrence of *`string1`* in *`string2`*, or `-1` if *`string1`* does not occur in *`string2`*

The following options to the string command interpret *`string2`* as a list of characters to trim from *`string1`*:

`trim`	Removes any leading and trailing characters present in *`string2`* from *`string1`*
`trimleft`	Removes any leading characters present in *`string2`* from *`string1`*

`trimright`	Removes any trailing characters present in *`string2`* from *`string1`*

The following options to the `string` command only take *`string1`* as an argument:

`length`	Returns the number of characters in *`string1`*
`tolower`	Returns a new string with all of the characters in *`string1`* converted to lowercase
`toupper`	Returns a new string with all of the characters in *`string1`* converted to uppercase

Now let's look at a few examples. First, make a string and get its length:

```
set str " Here Is A Test String ";
string length $str;
```

This gives a length of `23` (the `length` option counts whitespace characters). Now get the location of the first and last occurrences of the string `"st"` in `$str`:

```
string first "st" $str;
string last "st" $str
```

This gives a value of `13` for the first occurrence of `"st"` (corresponding to the occurrence in `Test`) and a value of `13` for the last occurrence of `"st"` (`Test` again). What about the `"st"` in `String`? Well, most of the string comparison functions are case- and whitespace-sensitive, so temporarily convert `$str` to lowercase and try again:

```
string last "st" [string tolower $str];
```

This gives a value of `16`, which corresponds to the `"st"` in `String`. Finally, strip off the leading and trailing spaces and get a length for the string:

```
string length [string trim $str " "];
```

The value `21` is returned, which means that the first and last spaces were stripped off.

Manipulating Numeric Values

`tcl` provides two commands for manipulating numeric variables and constants: `incr` and `expr`.

The `incr` command gives `tcl` an equivalent to the C language operators `+=`, `-=`, `++`, and `--`. The basic syntax is

```
incr variable integer
```

where *`variable`* must be an integer. The `incr` command adds the given *`integer`* to the *`variable`*; thus decrementing is handled by giving negative integers. Let's demonstrate its usage. First, create a variable and do an `incr` on it:

```
set a 81;
incr a;
puts $a;
```

$a has a value of 82. By default, incr is the same as ++; if it is not given an integer argument, it will add one to the named variable. Now decrement $a by 3:

```
incr a -3
puts $a
```

Note that $a has a value of 79. One last point is that the integer can be the value of a variable:

```
set a 6;
set b 9;
incr a $b;
puts $a;
```

$a has a value of 15.

For more complex mathematical operations, tcl provides the expr command, which works with all standard ANSI C operators. Operator precedence is mostly the same as in ANSI C.

When any mathematical operations are required, they must be preceded by the expr command. For example, the commands

```
set a 20;
set b 4;
set c $a/$b;
puts $c;
```

result in the output

```
20/4
```

rather than 5, the desired result. To get the right answer, use the expr command:

```
set c [expr $a / $b];
```

In addition to the standard operators of +, -, *, and /, the expr command can be given several options that enable it to perform mathematical operations. The basic syntax is

```
expr function number
```

Some of the functions that expr understands, along with the values they return, are the following:

abs(x)	Absolute value of x
round(x)	The integer value resulting from rounding x
cos(x)	Cosine of x (x in radians)
cosh(x)	Hyperbolic cosine of x
acos(x)	Arccosine of x (0 to pi)
sin(x)	Sine of x (x in radians)
sinh(x)	Hyperbolic sine of x
asin(x)	Arcsine of x (-pi/2 to pi/2)

`tan(x)`	Tangent of x (x in radians)
`tanh(x)`	Hyperbolic tangent of x
`atan(x)`	Arctangent of x (-pi/2 to pi/2)
`exp(x)`	e raised to the power of x
`log(x)`	Natural log of x
`log10(x)`	Log base 10 of x
`sqrt(x)`	The square root of x

The following math function takes two number arguments:

`pow(x,y)`	x raised to the power of y

This is used as follows:

```
set a 2;
set b [expr pow($a,3)];
puts $b;
```

The output will be `8.0`, the value of 2 raised to the third power.

Quoting and Substitution

Quoting and substitution are both used heavily in relation to variables. You saw the most basic version of quoting (using double quotes to make strings) and substitution earlier in this chapter. `tcl` supports one more type of quoting, brace quoting, and one more type of substitution, command substitution.

To review, the most common use of double quotes is to create strings with embedded whitespace:

```
set kiwi "Fresh from New Zealand";
```

Double quotes can also be used to make multiline strings:

```
set kiwi "Fresh from
New Zealand 3 for a dollar";
```

In addition to making multiline strings, the standard ANSI C language escape sequences can be used in `tcl` strings:

```
set kiwi "Fresh from New Zealand\n\t3 for a dollar."
```

This outputs the following:

```
Fresh from New Zealand
3 for a dollar.
```

In addition to this, the two types of substitution can be applied within double-quoted strings. The first type of substitution, variable substitution, is explained in the "Variables" section, earlier in this chapter. In a double-quoted string, you can access the value of a variable by preceding the variable's name with `$`. Thus the following commands

```
set fruit kiwi;
set place "New Zealand";
set how_many 3;
puts "$fruit, fresh from $place, $how_many for a dollar";
```

output this:

```
kiwi, fresh from New Zealand, 3 for a dollar
```

The other type of substitution is command substitution. A command substitution block begins with a left bracket (`[`) and ends with a right bracket (`]`). For example,

```
set len_in 2;     puts "$len_in inches is [expr $len_in*2.54] cm";
```

outputs

```
2 inches is 5.08 cm
```

The `5.08` is the result of the command

```
expr $len_in*2.54
```

Because this command is in brackets, the value that it returns is substituted in. In this case, the `tcl` command `expr` is used, but any `tcl` command can be placed between brackets. Command substitution can be used in most commands, and is not limited to double-quoted commands. For example, the commands

```
set len_in 2;
set len_cm [expr $len_in*2.54];
puts "$len_in inches is $len_cm cm";
```

produce the same output as

```
set len_in 2;     puts "$len_in inches is [expr $len_in*2.54] cm";
```

The other type of quoting available in `tcl` is brace quoting, which is similar to the quoting using single quotes in UNIX shells. Brace quoting creates a string with the given characters, no substitution (command or variable) takes place, and the C language escape sequences are not interpreted. For example, the command

```
puts "This\nis a\nmulti-line\nstring"
```

produces the following output:

```
This
is a
multi-line
string
```

The command

```
puts {This\nis a\nmulti-line\nstring}
```

produces the following output:

```
This\nis a\nmulti-line\nstring
```

To get tabs, newlines, and other special characters in a brace-quoted string, they must be entered physically:

```
puts {This
is a
multi-line
string}
```

This will produce the desired output. The real use for brace-quoted strings comes when certain characters with special meanings need to be given as values for variables. For example, the commands

```
set price 1.00;
puts "Pears, $$price per pound";
```

output

```
Pears, $1.00 per pound
```

but the `$$price` has the potential to be confusing, so it would be better if the variable `price` had the value `$1.00`. You could use brace quoting to achieve the following:

```
set price {$1.00};
puts "Pears, $price per pound";
```

The other use of brace quoting is to defer evaluation and is used in control structures and procedure definitions. In such cases, the values of variables are substituted in after the entire block is read.

Flow Control—`if` and `switch`

`tcl` provides several commands for flow control and supports all the standard ANSI C comparison operators for both string and numeric data.

This section starts with the `if/elseif/else` commands. The simplest `if` statement is one like the following:

```
if {$x < 0} {
set x 10;
}
```

This example only has one line in the body of the `if` clause, but any number of lines and subblocks can be added. If additional tests need to be performed, each test is given in parentheses as follows:

```
if { ($x == "SJ") || ($x == "LA") } {
puts "You Live in California!";
}
```

Tests can be nested as in the following example:

```
if { ( ($arch == "ppc") || ($arch == "intel") ) && ($os != "Linux") } {
puts "Get Linux!";
}
```

Adding an `else` clause to an `if` statement is done as follows:

```
if {$x <= 0} {
set x 10;
} else {
set x 0;
}
```

You can also add as many `elseif` statements as desired:

```
if {$x == 0} {
set x 10;
} elseif {$x == 10} {
incr x -1;
} elseif {$x == 100} {
set x 50;
} else {
set x 0;
}
```

In many cases, adding extra `elseif` statements becomes cumbersome and difficult to understand. To provide a more compact way of expressing the same logic, `tcl` implements the `switch` command. `switch` works by associating a value (string or number) with a block. The preceding `if` statement, when written as a `switch` statement, becomes

```
switch $x {
0 {set x 10;}
10 {incr x -1;}
100 {set x 50;}
}
```

By default, only the block corresponding to the matched value will be executed, but a `switch` statement can implement "fallthrough" if the block is designated as a single minus sign (-). The `switch` statement

```
switch $x {
0 -
10 -
100 {incr x -1}
}
```

is equivalent to the following `if` statement:

```
if { ($x == 0) || ($x == 10) || ($x == 100) } {
incr x -1;
}
```

Loops

`tcl` provides three loop commands:

- `for`
- `foreach`
- `while`

tcl also provides two loop control commands:

- break
- continue

The while loop executes its body while its test condition is true. The structure can be thought of as

```
while {condition} {block}
```

The following is a simple while loop that counts to ten:

```
set x 0;
while {$x < 10} {
incr x;
puts $x;
}
```

The foreach loop iterates over a set of arguments and executes its body each time. The foreach loop has the following structure:

```
foreach variable {items} {block}
```

variable is the name of the variable to which each item in the set *items* will be assigned in turn. Here is an example:

```
foreach element {o c n p li} {
switch $element {
o -
n {puts gas;}
c -
p -
li {puts solid;}
}
}
```

In this case, the list of items to check is specified, but a variable can be used also:

```
set elements "o c n p li";
foreach element $elements {
switch $element {
o -
n {puts gas;}
c -
p -
li {puts solid;}
}
}
```

If a variable instead of a list of items is given, the braces should not be used because the braces will be treated as braces used for quoting.

The for loop allows for the most control while looping. It can be broken down as

```
for {initialization} {condition} {increment} {body}
```

A simple for loop example that counts to 10 is

```
for {set i 0} {$i <= 10} {incr i} { puts $i; }
```

You have seen simple initialization statements, but the initialization and increment parts of the for loop can be as complicated as required.

Now for a look at the loop control commands, break and continue. The break command breaks out of loop and executes the next line of code after the loop's block, while the continue command skips to the next iteration of the loop.

The continue command is really handy for reading in initialization files where comments lines need to be allowed. If the following statement is included in a loop that reads in a file

```
if { [regexp {^#} [string trim $line] ]} {continue;}
```

all lines that start with a pound sign (#) will be skipped.

File I/O and File Info

tcl provides a simple and effective method for file input and output similar to the methods in the C standard I/O library. The first step in file I/O is to open a file and get a file handle or file ID. As an example, the command

```
set f [ open /etc/passwd r];
```

opens the file /etc/passwd with mode r and returns a file handle that is assigned to the variable f. tcl supports the following file open modes:

r	Open for reading only; the file must exist.
r+	Open for reading and writing; the file must exist.
w	Open for writing; the file will be created if it does not exist; otherwise, it is truncated.
w+	Same as w; expect that the file is opened for reading also.
a	Open the file for appending text; the file will be created if it does not exist.
a+	Same as a, except that the file is opened for reading also.

The open command can also be overloaded to run subprocesses with more control than the exec command provides. To open a process instead of a file, the filename is replaced with a brace-quoted string beginning with a pipe character (¦) and containing the command to run. For example, the following command opens a ps for reading:

```
set f [ open {¦ ps } r ];
```

For processes opened in this manner, the tcl command pid returns the process ID of the file handle associated with a process. For the preceding example,

```
pid $f
```

will return the `pid` associated with `$f`, the file handle for the `ps` command that was opened.

If a file (or process) is opened in a mode that supports reading, then you can read from the file using the `gets` command. To process all the lines of a file, the following `while` command is often used:

```
while { [ gets $f line ] >= 0 }
```

This works because the `gets` command returns `-1` when `EOF` is reached. In this case, the `gets` command reads in a line from the file handle `$f` and assigns the value to the variable `line`. In the body of the loop, `$line` can be accessed and manipulated.

If a file is opened for writing, then the `puts` command can be used to write output to the file. If the file handle `$f` corresponds to a file opened for writing, the command

```
puts $f "This is a line of text";
```

will write the string `"This is a line of text"` to the open file.

The only other file I/O command is the `close` command, which takes as its argument a file handle. To close the file you opened earlier, you would simply use

```
close $f;
```

It is probably a good idea to close any file handles that are open at the end of a program. Also, if the same file handle variable is to be reused several times in a program, it is a good idea to close it before the next `open`.

In addition to reading and writing from files, it is sometimes necessary to obtain information about files. `tcl` provides the `file` command to accomplish this. The `file` command's syntax is

```
file option filename
```

where *`filename`* is the name of the file to run the tests on and *`option`* is one of the following options.

The following options return true (`1`) or false (`0`) information about files:

`executable`	True if the file is executable by the current user
`exists`	True if the file exists
`isdirectory`	True if the file is a directory
`isfile`	True if the file is a regular file
`owned`	True if the current user owns the file
`readable`	True if the file is readable by the current user
`writeable`	True if the file is writable by the current user

The following options return additional information about a file:

`atime`	Returns the time the file was last accessed in seconds since Jan 1, 1970

`mtime`	Returns the time the file was last modified in seconds since Jan 1, 1970
`size`	Returns the size of the file in bytes
`readlink`	Returns the value of a symbolic link if the given file is a symbolic link
`type`	Returns a string giving the type of the file

Procedures

Procedures are `tcl`'s equivalent of functions in the C language. To create a procedure, the `proc` command is used, which has the following syntax:

```
proc procedure_name {arguments} {body}
```

The number of arguments is variable, and an empty argument list is specified by `{}`. *`body`* can contain any valid `tcl` statement and can be as long as required.

A simple procedure that takes no arguments is as follows:

```
proc test_proc {} { puts "procedure test"; }
```

To invoke this procedure, simply give its name:

```
test_proc;
```

You will get the output:

```
procedure test
```

A more realistic example is a file output procedure, which takes in as an argument a filename:

```
proc cat {filename} {
set f [open $filename r];
while { [ gets $f line ] >= 0 } {
puts $line;
}
close $f;
}
```

To invoke this procedure with `/etc/passwd` as its argument, use the following:

```
cat /etc/passwd
```

This prints out the contents of `/etc/passwd`.

Three important commands for use in procedures are `return`, `global`, and `catch`. The `global` command is used to give a procedure access to global variables, and the `return` command is used to return a value from a procedure. The `catch` command is useful for detecting errors and returning a failure value.

You can rewrite the `cat` procedure to be a little more robust by doing the following:

```
proc cat {filename} {
```

```
set ret_code 0;
catch {
set f [open $filename r];
while { [ gets $f line ] >= 0 } {
puts $line;
}
close $f;
set ret_code 1;
}
return $ret_code;
}
```

This code demonstrates the use of both `catch` and `return`. If any parts of the procedure fail, it returns `0` (false), but if the `cat` is successful, it returns `1` (true). This information will be useful if `cat` is called with a process to execute as its argument.

The tk Toolkit

The `tk` toolkit is a toolkit that allows X Window graphical user interfaces (GUIs) to be written using the `tcl` scripting language. The `tk` toolkit adds to the `tcl` language by allowing the creation of GUI components called widgets. This section looks briefly at the available `tk` widgets and shows how to create them.

Introduction to Widgets

The basic method for creating a widget is

```
widget_type path option
```

where *`widget_type`* is one of the widget types given in the following list, *`path`* is a window pathname (usually starting with a dot, which is the name of the root window), and *`option`* is any option that the widget understands.

The `tk` toolkit defines the following widget types:

`canvas`	Allows for drawing objects
`entry`	Allows for the input of single line of text
`frame`	Used to contain other widgets
`listbox`	Displays a set of strings and allows for choosing one or more of them
`menu`	Displays a menu bar and menu items
`text`	Displays multiple lines of text
`label`	Displays a single line of static text
`button`	A widget that displays a clickable button
`checkbutton`	Displays a checkable box
`radiobutton`	Displays several mutually exclusive checkable boxes
`scale`	Similar to a scrollbar that sets a value

To create and manipulate widgets, the windowing shell, `wish`, must be used. To invoke `wish` interactively, type `wish` at the UNIX prompt. The following `wish` prompt will appear:

```
%
```

Along with this, an empty window will pop up on the screen. This window is the `wish` root window (called .) and all the widgets that are created will appear with it.

Creating Widgets

This section shows how to create a widget and manipulate it. First, create a button:

```
button .button;
```

So what did that do?

Well, the widget type is specified as `button`, so `tk` created a button. The path is `.button`, so `tk` created the button in the root window (. is the root `tk` window) and named it `button`.

So where is the button, anyway?

The button isn't displayed right now; `tk` simply created it. In order to display the button, you need to tell `tk` how to display the widget. For this, use the `pack` command and give it the `path` to the widget you want to display:

```
pack .button;
```

Now the button is showing, but it's blank (see Figure 25.1). This is where widget's options come into play.

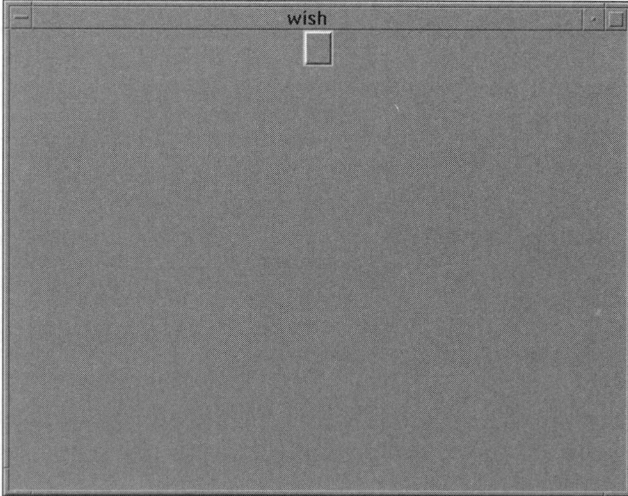

FIGURE 25.1.
A plain button.

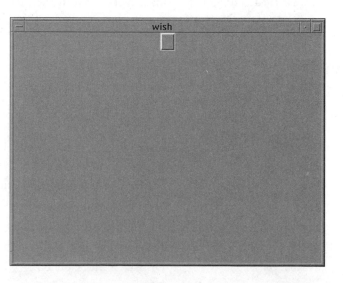

Widget Options

All tk widgets use standard options that control appearance and function. Most widgets understand the following options:

`-background` *color*, `-bg` *color*	The background color of the widget. Valid values are of the form `#RRGGBB`, `#RRRGGGBBB`, or one of the names defined in `/usr/lib/X11/rgb.txt`.
`-foreground` *color*, `-fg` *color*	The foreground color of the widget. Valid values are of the form `#RRGGBB`, `#RRRGGGBBB`, or one of the names defined in `/usr/lib/X11/rgb.txt`.
`-height` *pixels*	The widget's height in pixels.
`-width` *pixels*	The widget's width in pixels.
`-borderwidth` *pixels*, `-db` *pixels*	The width of the widget's border in pixels.
`-padx` *pixels*	Extra space required by the widget in the x direction.
`-pady` *pixels*	Extra space required by the widget in the y direction.
`-relief` *type*	The 3D effect of the widget, where *type* is one of these strings: `flat`, `raised`, `grove`, `ridge`, `sunken`.
`-text` *string*	The string to display in the widget.
`-font` *font*	The font to be used for the text displayed in a widget; valid font definitions are given by the command `xlsfonts`.
`-command` *command*	The `tcl` command to execute when the widget is used; usually this is the name of a procedure or an `exec` statement.

In addition to these options, the `pack` command understands the following options of its own:

`-side` *type*	Controls the order in which widgets are placed. Valid types are `left`, `right`, `top`, or `bottom`. For example, `left` indicates that new widgets should placed to the left of existing widgets.
`-fill` *type*	Controls whether or not widgets are stretched to fill up open space in the window. Valid values are `none`, `x`, `y`, or `both`. For example, `both` indicates that widgets should fill up all open space.
`-expand` *value*	Controls whether or not widgets expand if the window's size increases. *value* is either `0` or `1`, with `1` indicating true.

A tcl/tk Widget Programming Example

Now that you know about the options for widgets and for pack, you can start using them. One of the interesting features of widgets is their reliefs, the widgets' 3D look. To get an idea of how each relief looks, make some labels, using the following:

```
foreach i {raised sunken flat groove ridge} {
label .$i -relief $i -text $i;
pack .$i
}
```

This example iterates through the set of relief types, creating one label for each type, along with setting each label's text to be the relief type. The layout will look similar to Figure 25.2.

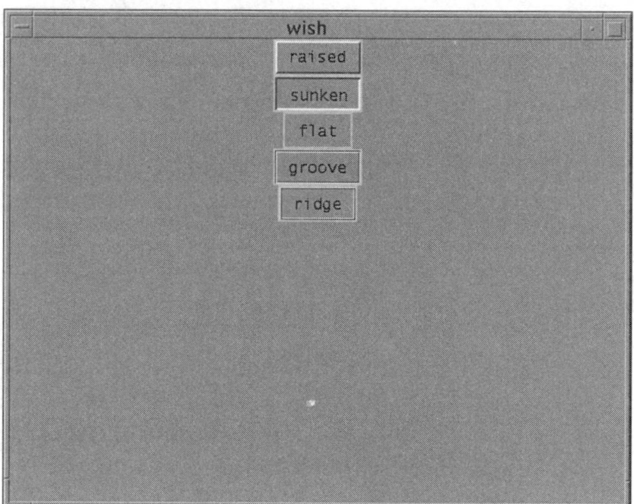

FIGURE 25.2.
Labels of varying reliefs.

There are two things to notice here. First, the labels are not all the same size. Second, the labels are stacked one on top of the other. This is an example of the pack command's default behavior; it determines the size of each widget automatically and then places each widget below the preceding widget that was placed.

Let's make all the labels the same size and pack them next to each other, instead of one on top of the other. There are two ways to do this. The first is to rewrite the loop:

```
foreach i {raised sunken flat groove ridge} {
label .$i -relief $i -text $i -height 10 -width 10;
pack .$i -side left
}
```

The second way is to reconfigure the labels using the configure option, which has the following syntax:

```
widget configure option
```

In this case, you could use the following loop (after the labels are created):

```
foreach i {raised sunken flat groove ridge} {
.$i configure -height 10 -width 10;
pack .$i -side left;
}
```

So why use `configure`?

If `wish` is run interactively, and one version of the loop was given, modifying it and running it again will produce the following error:

```
window name "raised" already exists in parent
```

This is the method in which `wish` tells the programmer that the program has attempted to re-create an existing widget (in this case with the label raised). So, you need to use `configure`. In fact, `configure` is required any time an existing widget needs to be changed.

In this case, the only way to use the new version of the loop is to destroy the existing labels, using the `destroy` command:

```
foreach i {raised sunken flat groove ridge} { destroy .$i }
```

The new result will be similar to Figure 25.3.

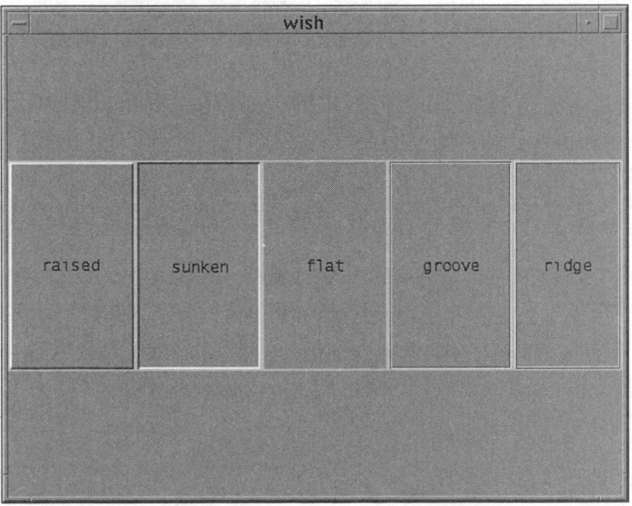

FIGURE 25.3.
Labels of varying `relief`, *packed next to each other.*

Now back to the example. There are two things that look like they should be fixed in Figure 25.3. First, it is difficult to tell the labels apart. Second, most of the window is blank.

You can make the labels easier to distinguish by padding them when they are packed and by increasing their `borderwidths`. To make the labels take up all of the available space, give `pack` the `fill` option for both `x` and `y` and set the `expand` option to true:

```
foreach i {raised sunken flat groove ridge} {
label .$i -relief $i -text $i;
.$i configure -height 5 -width 5 -borderwidth 5;
pack .$i -side left -padx 5 -pady 5 -fill both -expand 1;
}
```

The result will be similar to Figure 25.4.

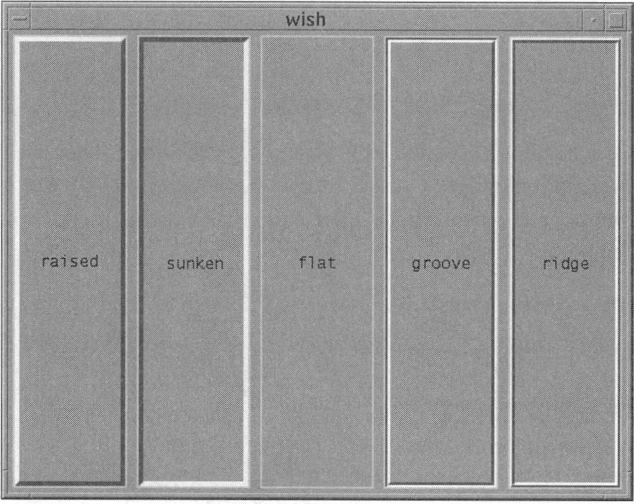

FIGURE 25.4.
Labels of varying `relief`, *version 3.*

This example can be easily changed to use any of the widget types by replacing `label` with a different type of widget.

A `tcl/tk` Interface to `xsetroot`

This section introduces some of the other abilities of the `tk` toolkit by applying them to the development of a GUI front end for the X Window program `xsetroot`.

Most X Window users will be familiar with the X Window program `xsetroot` that can be used to set the background color of the root window, under X11. The actual command is

```
xsetroot -solid color
```

where *`color`* can be given in the form `#RRGGBB`. The front end will allow for colors to be previewed and then applied.

Let's get started. The first thing that you need is a variable that holds the color. Then you need to create two basic frames, one for the main area of the application and another for putting messages in. You will also need a third frame for the controls.

Frames are a handy thing to use because they can be used to pack items of a particular type/function together. Also, they are useful in partitioning up a window into sections that don't change.

Create the frames and the color globally:

```
set color "#000000";
frame .main_frame;
frame .message_frame;
frame .control_frame;
```

Now pack the frames:

```
pack .control_frame -in .main_frame -expand 1 -fill both;
pack .main_frame -anchor c -expand 1;
pack .message_frame -anchor s -padx 2 -pady 2 \
-fill x -expand 1;
```

You also need to create a label to handle messages. I'll do this as a procedure, so it will be easy to modify and execute:

```
proc make_message_label {} {
label .message_label -relief sunken;
pack .message_label -anchor c \
-in .message_frame -padx 2 \
-pady 2 -fill both -expand 1;
}
```

Pack the message label into `.message_frame` so that it is at the bottom of the window at all times.

Now make the scales. You need three scales, one for red, blue, and green, with each one going from 0 to 255. You also need to pack the scales and their corresponding labels in their own frame:

```
proc make_scales {} {
frame .scale_frame;
foreach i {red green blue} {
frame .scale_frame_$i -bg $i;
label .label_$i -text $i -bg $i \
-fg white;
scale .scale_$i -from 0 -to 255 \
-command setColor;
pack .label_$i .scale_$i \
-in .scale_frame_$i;
pack .scale_frame_$i -in .scale_frame \
-side left -padx 2 -pady 2;
}
pack .scale_frame -in .control_frame \
-side left -expand 1;
}
```

This procedure is a good example of using frames. In all, this example creates four frames, one for each slider and label pair and overall frame. Adding the label and the slider to their own frame simplifies the overall layout strategy.

Another example in this procedure is the use of the `-command` option for a widget. Each time the scales change, the command specified by the `-command` option is executed. In this case, the `setColor` command, which sets the global variable `color`, is executed:

```
proc setColor {value} {
global color;
foreach i {red green blue} {
set $i [format %02x [.scale_$i get]];
}
set color "#$red$green$blue";
.preview_label configure -bg $color;
.message_label configure -text "$color";
}
```

You can preview the color change by setting the background color of the widget, `.preview_label`. To create `.preview label`, use the following procedure:

```
proc make_preview {} {
global color;

frame .preview_frame;
label .preview_label -bg $color \
-height 5 -width 5;
pack .preview_label -in .preview_frame \
-padx 2 -pady 2 -fill both \
-anchor c -expand 1;
pack .preview_frame -in .control_frame \
-side bottom -fill both -expand 1 \
-padx 2 -pady 2;
}
```

Now you need to add a few buttons—one to apply the changes, another to quit the program. Use the following procedure:

```
proc make_buttons {} {
frame .button_frame;
button .apply -text "apply" \
-command setRootColor;
button .quit -text "quit" -command exit;
pack .apply .quit -in .button_frame \
-fill both -expand 1 -padx 2 \
-pady 2 -side left;
pack .button_frame -in .main_frame \
-fill both;
}
```

You also need the following procedure, which sets the root color:

```
proc setRootColor {} {
global color;

catch {
exec xsetroot -solid $color;
} msg;

if {$msg != {}} {
set msg "An error occurred";
} else {
set msg "$color";
}

.message_label configure -text $msg;
}
```

Now that you are done with the procedures, invoke them:

```
make_message_label;
make_scales;
make_preview;
make_buttons;
```

You are now ready to test your little `tcl` application. When the application is run, the resulting window should look like Figure 25.5.

FIGURE 25.5.
The `tksetroot` *application.*

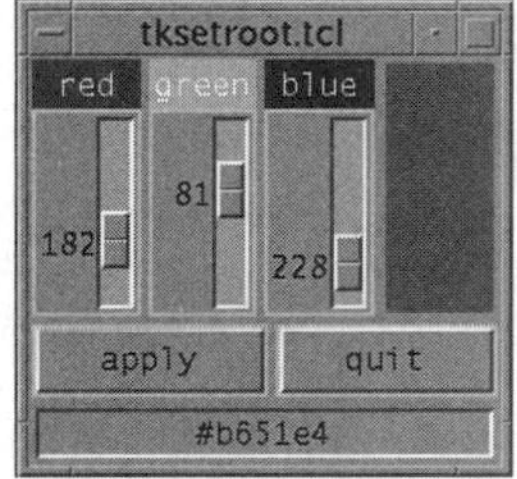

Listing 25.1 contains the complete source code of the `tksetroot` application.

Listing 25.1. tksetroot.

```
set color "#000000";
frame .main_frame;
frame .message_frame;
frame .control_frame;

pack .control_frame -in .main_frame -expand 1 -fill both;
pack .main_frame -anchor c -expand 1;
pack .message_frame -anchor s -padx 2 -pady 2 \
-fill x -expand 1;

proc make_message_label {} {
label .message_label -relief sunken;
pack .message_label -anchor c -in .message_frame \
-padx 2 -pady 2 -fill both -expand 1;
}

proc make_scales {} {
frame .scale_frame;
foreach i {red green blue} {
frame .scale_frame_$i -bg $i;
label .label_$i -text $i -bg $i -fg white;
scale .scale_$i -from 0 -to 255 \
-command setColor;
pack .label_$i .scale_$i -in .scale_frame_$i;
pack .scale_frame_$i -in .scale_frame -side left \
-padx 2 -pady 2;
}
pack .scale_frame -in .control_frame -side left -expand 1;
}
```

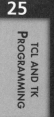

continues

Listing 25.1. continued

```
proc setColor {value} {
global color;
foreach i {red green blue} {
set $i [format %02x [.scale_$i get]];
}
set color "#$red$green$blue";
.preview_label configure -bg $color;
.message_label configure -text "$color";
}

proc make_preview {} {
global color;

frame .preview_frame;
label .preview_label -bg $color \
-height 5 -width 5;
pack .preview_label -in .preview_frame \
-padx 2 -pady 2 -fill both -anchor c \
-expand 1;
pack .preview_frame -in .control_frame \
-side top -fill both -expand 1 \
-padx 2 -pady 2;
}

proc make_buttons {} {
frame .button_frame;
button .apply -text "apply" -command setRootColor;
button .quit -text "quit" -command exit;
pack .apply .quit -in .button_frame -fill both \
-expand 1 -padx 2 -pady 2 -side left;
pack .button_frame -in .main_frame -fill both;
}

proc setRootColor {} {
global color;

catch {
exec xsetroot -solid $color;
} msg;

if {$msg != {}} {
set msg "An error occurred";
} else {
set msg "$color";
}

.message_label configure -text $msg;
}

make_message_label;
make_scales;
make_preview;
make_buttons;
```

Summary

This chapter is an introduction to programming in tcl/tk. The examples demonstrate the power of tcl/tk, which lies in the ability to make user interfaces within a short amount of time and with little code. Although this chapter covers many of the features of tcl/tk, there are many more that are not discussed. I hope that with this chapter as a stepping stone, you will enjoy many years developing tcl/tk applications.

Motif Programming

by Bill Ball

IN THIS CHAPTER

This chapter introduces you to the OSF/Motif programming libraries. You'll learn about the different versions of Motif; how to install Red Hat's Motif 2.0.1 distribution; how Motif programs, or clients, work; how to write and compile a simple Motif client; how to use the programming utilities `imake` and `xmkmf`; and how to possibly save money by using a Motif clone, LessTif.

You'll need to have the GNU `gcc` compiler and associated headers, libraries, and utilities installed on your system. You'll also need to have X and Motif installed on your system if you want to run any Motif clients, including `mwm`. You do not have to run X in order to program with Motif, although it's a lot more fun to compile, run, and see a program in action.

What Is Motif?

First of all, you should understand that unlike the XFree86 distribution of X, Motif is not free. You must pay for a distribution. There are Motif distributions for Linux on the Intel, SPARC, or Alpha platforms. If you want to build Motif clients and distribute them, you'll need to purchase a version for your computer and operating system. And if you want other people to run your clients, you can build the clients in either shared library or static versions, for people who either have or don't have Motif.

If you're on a budget, or object to having to pay for a client license for Motif, don't despair. Later in this chapter in the section "LessTif—An Alternative Motif Clone," you'll learn about LessTif, a cost-free alternative to Motif.

Motif is a toolkit of source headers, libraries, a window manager, `mwm`, demonstration programs, and manual pages. Originally announced in 1988, designed by the Open Software Foundation (OSF) in 1989, and now owned and updated by The Open Group, Motif provides a rich selection of tools to build cross-platform, graphical-interface applications, or clients.

The idea behind Motif is to provide the tools to build consistent, usable, and portable programs for the X Window System. Motif provides functions and system calls to build client interfaces with the following (and almost anything you need to craft graphical interface programs):

- Arrow buttons
- Cascade buttons
- Checkboxes
- Drawn buttons
- File selection dialogs
- List widgets
- Menu bars
- Push buttons

- Radio boxes
- Scrollbars
- Toggle buttons
- Dialogs
- Icons
- Drop-down menus
- Pull-down menus
- Tear-off menus

In fact, there are more than 600 man pages included with each Motif distribution, documenting its clients, function calls, libraries, and window manager. Although you can use X functions to build clients with a Motif look, why not take advantage of all the work put into Motif?

Where Do I Get Motif?

A number of vendors supply Motif for Linux. This book is about Red Hat Linux, so I'll concentrate on the Red Hat distribution. Because the object, or philosophy, of OSF/Motif is to provide cross-platform, source-code level compatibility, you should be able to develop Motif clients on your Intel Linux system that will compile and run on any other computer with a Motif distribution installed.

There are a number of distributors selling Motif for Linux besides Red Hat. Some of these include the following:

- X Inside Corporation (`http://www.xinside.com`)
- Metro Link Incorporated (`http://www.metrolink.com`)
- InfoMagic (`http://www.infomagic.com`)
- Linux Systems Labs (`http://www.lsl.com`)
- Caldera (`http://www.caldera.com`)

What Version of Motif Should I Use?

In order to make an intelligent decision regarding which version of Motif to get, you should know a little about the history and direction of the standard. In 1996, The Open Group acquired the X Window System from the X Consortium, with the aim of integrating X, Motif, and the Common Desktop Environment (CDE). CDE represents the future of Motif, according to The Open Group, and offers graphical interface improvements, support for multiuser applications, and new networking features.

The X Consortium acquired the X Window System from the MIT X Consortium in 1993 and was responsible for the last several releases, the last of which is X11R6.3. Broadway, which is the codename for the next release of the X Window System, is slated to have improvements in network communications to support graphics and audio for use in World Wide Web browsers. The Open Group has pledged to release Broadway under the same terms as the current X Window System.

The current version of Motif is 2.1, although the current version of CDE, which is also 2.1, uses Motif 1.2.5, which was released to support CDE (and which contains fixes made to Motif 1.2 in Motif 2.0). Confused yet? Remember that OSF's aim is to merge X, Motif, and CDE. But what does this mean to the user, and what does this mean to the programmer?

For the user, especially the Red Hat Linux user, the choice is up to you! If you want the Motif 1.2.5 libraries, a drag-and-drop, industry-standard interface, and many other improvements, then CDE is the way to go. You should know that the Motif window manager, `mwm`, goes away in the CDE release, replaced by new terminal managers (based on `dtwm`).

But for the programmer, the choice might not be as clear. According to The Open Group, although Motif 2.0 and CDE may be used together, and Motif 2.0 is binary-compatible with Motif 1.2, "All of the important Motif 2.0 developer features...will be available in CDEnext Motif" (the next version of CDE, to be based on Motif 2.0). This means that The Open Group recommends that programmers use Motif 2.0 now to get the latest programming features, which are not currently in CDE 2.1.

Red Hat Motif Installation

As mentioned before, because this is *Red Hat Linux Unleashed*, this chapter concentrates on the specifics of Red Hat's Motif distribution. Installing Red Hat Motif 2.0.1 is easy. First, make sure that there's enough room on your hard drive. You'll need about 20 megabytes for a full installation. If you just want to run just the Motif window manager, `mwm`, and other Motif clients, you can save about 15 megabytes and just install the Motif libraries and `mwm`.

There are two ways to install Motif from the Red Hat CD-ROM, but both require you to mount the disk to a convenient directory with

```
# mount -t iso9660 /dev/cdrom /mnt/cdrom
```

You can then launch the installation script with

```
# ./install-motif
```

Another way to install the software is to use the `rpm` command. The Red Hat folks have assembled the Motif software into the RPM (Red Hat Package Manager) packages discussed in the following sections.

motif-devel-2.0.1-1.i386.rpm

This package contains the static libraries and `#include` files, or headers, needed to build Motif clients. You'll also find the Motif User Interface Language compiler, `uil`, and the Motif function-call manual pages.

motif-2.0.1-1.i386.rpm

If you just want to run mwm or the Motif Workspace Manager, Wsm, you'll need the shared libraries in this package. More than 800 icons are also installed from this file under the /usr/X11R6/include/X11/icons directory.

motif-mwm-2.0.1-1.i386.rpm

Here's where you'll find not only the window manager, mwm, but also Wsm, which demonstrates just some of the new features of Motif 2.0.1. Also included is panner, pixmap, and a handy bitmap browser, xbmbrowser, which transverses directories and shows what .xpm or .xbm graphics look like a directory at a time.

motif-demosrc-2.0.1-1.i386.rpm

If you're interested in exploring the new features of Motif 2.0.1, need source-code examples to help you learn about Motif programming, or want to read the source to the example clients, install this package. You'll also need to install the development libraries in order to build the examples. Some of the concepts these programs demonstrate are discussed later in this chapter, but here's a list of the examples included:

- airport—Demonstrates Motif drag and drop
- animate—Animates pixel maps in an X window
- drag_and_drop—A thorough demonstration of drag-and-drop features
- draw—A simple graphics application
- earth—The classic rotating earth
- filemanager—A simple, graphical file manager
- fileview—A Motif "more" program
- getsubres—A Motif widget resources viewer
- hellomotif—The classic "Hello, world!"
- hellomotifi18n—A better "Hello, world!" in different languages
- i18ninput—Shows how to handle text input in different languages
- panner—Shows how Motif clients can use virtual screen support
- periodic—Demonstrates displayable Motif widgets
- piano—A simple Motif MIDI application (you'll need MIDI support)
- popups—Shows pop-up menu improvements in Motif 2.0
- sampler2_0—A fairly complete demonstration of Motif 2.0 features
- setdate—Sets the system's date and demos the Motif SpinBox widget
- texteditor—A simple editor with split panes, but no Undo, Print, and so on

- transfer—Demonstrates data transfer between Motif clients
- workspace—Source to Wsm

Along with these programs, there are also 10 other examples in a separate directory.

motif-demos-2.0.1-1.i386.rpm

If you don't want to spend the time building the sample clients from the source code, and just want to try some of the features of Motif, install this package. You'll also need to install the shared libraries in order to run these clients.

A Simple Example of Motif Programming Concepts

This section presents an extremely simple example of a Motif program. You'll learn just enough to get you started. But before getting into the details, let's cover the basic concepts in an overview of programming for Motif.

Although writing programs for the Linux command line in C is fairly simple, if you're familiar with programming for X, you know that there's a lot more involved in writing a windowing program. You have to consider labels, dialogs, windows, scrolling, colors, buttons, and many other features of how a program works besides the internal algorithms that make a program unique. Along with this unique functionality, when you program for X, you should consider consistency and ease of use for the user.

This is where Motif can help you. By providing a rich variety of functions, Motif can help programmers build attractive and easy-to-use programs. In Motif programming, a lot of the program code, especially for smaller programs, is devoted to the graphical interface.

When you write C programs for the Linux command line, you'll generally use the libc libraries. If you write programs for X, you generally will use the Xlib libraries. When you program for Motif, you use X as the window system, and the X Toolkit, or Xt libraries (and others) for the interface.

After you install Motif, you'll find the following libraries under the /usr/X11R6/lib directory:

```
/usr/X11R6/lib/libMrm.a
/usr/X11R6/lib/libUil.a
/usr/X11R6/lib/libXm.a
/usr/X11R6/lib/libXmCxx.a
/usr/X11R6/lib/libMrm.so
/usr/X11R6/lib/libMrm.so.2
/usr/X11R6/lib/libMrm.so.2.0
/usr/X11R6/lib/libXm.so
/usr/X11R6/lib/libXm.so.2
/usr/X11R6/lib/libXm.so.2.0
```

The Motif `#include` files are located under the `/usr/X11R6/include/Mrm`, `/usr/X11R6/include/Xm`, and `/usr/X11R6/include/uil` directories. The location of these libraries and headers is pretty much standard across all computer systems, but if they are located in a different place, this difference will be documented in configuration files and rules files for `imake` and `xmkmf`. (See "Using `imake` and `xmkmf`," later in this chapter, for more on these utilities.)

Widgets and Event-Driven Programming

An important concept to consider when programming for X and Motif is that these programs usually do not just run and quit; these programs are driven by events such as mouse clicks, button pushes, mouse drags, other programs, and keystrokes. Apple Macintosh programmers will feel right at home in programming for Motif. Some of the interface elements that intercept these events are built with Motif routines called widgets, and as you become more proficient, you'll even write some of your own.

If you're just starting off with Motif programming, don't be put off by some of the new terms and concepts about this subject. You'll learn about callbacks, children, classes, composites, coupled resources, gadgets, hierarchies, initiators, instantiation, modality, properties, receivers, and subclasses. Although there isn't enough room in this book to cover all these subjects, Listing 26.1 contains a simple example to get you started.

The Simple Motif Program

Listing 26.1 creates a small window with File, Edit, and Help menus. The application window is resizable, can be minimized or maximized, and in general, responds like any Motif application. This program demonstrates how to create a window, a menu bar, a pull-down menu, buttons, and a pop-up dialog.

It's not a perfect example, as the interface is in the `main()` part of the program, it doesn't use resources, and it really doesn't do anything; I'll leave the internals of how the program might work up to you.

Listing 26.1. `motif_skeleton.c`.

```
/* a simple skeleton Motif program */
#include <Xm/RowColumn.h>
#include <Xm/MainW.h>
#include <Xm/CascadeB.h>
#include <Xm/MessageB.h>
#include <Xm/SeparatoG.h>
#include <Xm/PushBG.h>

Widget skeleton;     /* our application */
/* what happens when user selects Exit */
void skel_exit_action() {
exit(0);
    }
```

continues

Listing 26.1. continued

```
/* destroy a dialog */
void skel_dialog_handler(skel_dialog)
Widget skel_dialog;
{
XtUnmanageChild(skel_dialog);
}

/* create a Help action dialog*/
void skel_help_action()
{
    Arg      args[10];
    Widget   skel_dialog;
XmString skel_string;

    /* store help string */
    skel_string =
XmStringCreateLocalized("This is Skeleton v0.1, a simple Motif client.");

/* build dialog */
skel_dialog = XmCreateMessageDialog (skeleton, "dialog", args, 0);
XtVaSetValues(skel_dialog, XmNmessageString, skel_string, NULL, NULL);

/* call skel_dialog_handler() after OK button is pushed */
XtAddCallback(skel_dialog, XmNokCallback, skel_dialog_handler, NULL);

    /* free storage */
    XmStringFree(skel_string);

    /* display the dialog */
    XtManageChild(skel_dialog);
};

/* main program begins here */
main (argc, argv)
int argc;
char *argv[];
{
    /* declare our widgets, including menu actions */
    Widget    skel_window,            /* main window */
              skel_menubar,           /* main window menu bar */
              skel_filepulldown,      /* File menu */
                  skel_new,
                  skel_open,
                  skel_close,
                  skel_save,
                  skel_exit,
              skel_editpulldown,      /* Edit menu */
                  skel_cut,
                  skel_copy,
                  skel_paste,
              skel_helppulldown,      /* Help menu */
                  skel_version;
    XmString  skel_string;            /* temporary storage */
    XtAppContext skel_app;

XtSetLanguageProc (NULL, NULL, NULL);
```

```
/* give the app a name and initial size */
skeleton = XtVaAppInitialize(&skel_app, "Skeleton", NULL, 0, &argc, argv,
NULL, XmNwidth, 320, XmNheight, 240, NULL);

/* create the main window */
skel_window = XtVaCreateManagedWidget("skel", xmMainWindowWidgetClass, skeleton,
XmNscrollingPolicy, XmAUTOMATIC, NULL);

/* build a menu bar across main window */
skel_menubar = XmCreateMenuBar(skel_window, "skel_menubar", NULL, 0);

/* build the File pull-down menu */
skel_filepulldown = XmCreatePulldownMenu (skel_menubar, "File", NULL, 0);
➥skel_string = XmStringCreateLocalized ("File");

/* create the menu, assign ALT+F as mnemonic key */
XtVaCreateManagedWidget ("File", xmCascadeButtonWidgetClass, skel_menubar,
XmNlabelString, skel_string, XmNmnemonic, 'F', XmNsubMenuId,
➥skel_filepulldown, NULL);

    /* release storage */
    XmStringFree(skel_string);

/* now add File pull-down menu elements */
skel_new = XtVaCreateManagedWidget("New", xmPushButtonGadgetClass,
skel_filepulldown, NULL);
skel_open = XtVaCreateManagedWidget("Open", xmPushButtonGadgetClass,
skel_filepulldown, NULL);
XtVaCreateManagedWidget("separator", xmSeparatorGadgetClass, skel_filepulldown,
        NULL);
skel_close = XtVaCreateManagedWidget("Close", xmPushButtonGadgetClass,
skel_filepulldown, NULL);
skel_save = XtVaCreateManagedWidget("Save", xmPushButtonGadgetClass,
skel_filepulldown, NULL);
XtVaCreateManagedWidget("separator", xmSeparatorGadgetClass, skel_filepulldown,
        NULL);
skel_exit = XtVaCreateManagedWidget("Exit", xmPushButtonGadgetClass,
skel_filepulldown, NULL);

/* add what to do when user selects Exit */
XtAddCallback(skel_exit, XmNactivateCallback, skel_exit_action, NULL);

/* build Edit menu */
skel_editpulldown = XmCreatePulldownMenu(skel_menubar, "Edit", NULL, 0);
skel_string = XmStringCreateLocalized ("Edit");
XtVaCreateManagedWidget ("Edit", xmCascadeButtonWidgetClass, skel_menubar,
XmNlabelString, skel_string, XmNmnemonic, 'E', XmNsubMenuId,
➥skel_editpulldown, NULL);

    /* release storage */
    XmStringFree(skel_string);

/* add Edit pull-down menu elements */
skel_cut = XtVaCreateManagedWidget("Cut", xmPushButtonGadgetClass,
skel_editpulldown, NULL);
skel_copy = XtVaCreateManagedWidget("Copy", xmPushButtonGadgetClass,
skel_editpulldown, NULL);
```

continues

Listing 26.1. continued

```
skel_paste = XtVaCreateManagedWidget("Paste", xmPushButtonGadgetClass,
skel_editpulldown, NULL);

/* build Help menu */
skel_helppulldown = XmCreatePulldownMenu(skel_menubar, "Help", NULL, 0);
➥skel_string = XmStringCreateLocalized ("Help");
XtVaCreateManagedWidget ("Help", xmCascadeButtonWidgetClass, skel_menubar,
XmNlabelString, skel_string, XmNmnemonic, 'H', XmNsubMenuId,
➥skel_helppulldown, NULL);

    /* release storage */
    XmStringFree(skel_string);

/* now move the Help pull-down to right side - thanks, Motif FAQ! */
XtVaSetValues(skel_menubar, XmNmenuHelpWidget, XtNameToWidget(skel_menubar,
"Help"), NULL);

/* now label, create, and assign action to Help menu */
skel_version = XtVaCreateManagedWidget ("Version", xmPushButtonGadgetClass,
skel_helppulldown, NULL);
XtAddCallback(skel_version, XmNactivateCallback, skel_help_action, NULL);

    XtManageChild(skel_menubar);
    XtRealizeWidget(skeleton);
    XtAppMainLoop (skel_app);
    return (0);
}
```

To compile this program, you can use the following command line:

```
# gcc -o skel skeleton.c -L/usr/X11R6/lib -lXm -lXpm -lXt -lXext -lX11
```

This line directs the GNU linker to look in the `/usr/X11/lib` directories for needed libraries. The program is then linked, using the shared `Xm`, `Xpm`, `Xt`, `Xext`, and `X11` libraries. The final size of the program is fewer than 13,000 characters.

How the Program Works

When you program in C to build Linux command-line or X programs, you know that if you use certain routines or functions, you must tell the compiler which `#include` files contain definitions needed by the functions in your program. This program starts out by listing the needed `#include` files for the different functions used in `skeleton.c`.

Next, the declaration of skeleton as a top-level widget makes information about our program available outside `main()`. This is because `skel_help_action()`, which creates a Motif dialog, needs to know whom the dialog belongs to. The next two routines, `skel_exit_action()` and `skel_dialog_handler()`, are what as known as callback routines.

Callback routines make your program work. These routines are called when you push buttons or select menu items and when your program receives information from other programs or the operating system. If you look at `skel_dialog_handler()`, you'll see the following line:

```
XtAddCallback(skel_dialog, XmNokCallback, skel_dialog_handler, NULL);
```

This function tells the program what to do after the dialog appears, and when you either click the OK button, or hit the Enter key—all without a lot of extra code.

`skel_help_action()` is also a callback routine, called in response to the `main()` program line:

```
XtAddCallback(skel_version, XmNactivateCallback, skel_help_action, NULL);
```

In this instance, `skel_help_action()` is run when you pull down the menu item Version from the program's Help menu. The routine `skel_exit_action()` is called when you choose Exit from the program's File menu. After creating room for the text string containing the version information to be displayed, the `skel_help_action()` routine then creates the dialog with

```
skel_dialog = XmCreateMessageDialog (skeleton, "dialog", args, 0);
```

and then fills in required information with the routine

```
XtVaSetValues(skel_dialog, XmNmessageString, skel_string, NULL, NULL);
```

followed by the callback routine designation, and finally, displays the dialog with

```
XtManageChild(skel_dialog);
```

The `main()` routine starts with declarations for different widgets and widget elements. The call to `XtVaAppInitialize()` declares the application name, indicates whether or not the program should read any command-line arguments, and assigns an initial size in pixel width and height.

Sample Program Resources

The initial window size (and many other default actions of all other Motif and many X11 programs) can also be set by using resources. One way to do this is first, open your `.Xdefaults` file in your home directory, then type

```
Skeleton.height: 480
Skeleton.width:  640
```

and save the file. Next, replace the line

```
skeleton = XtVaAppInitialize(&skel_app, "Skeleton", NULL, 0, &argc,
➥argv, NULL, XmNwidth, 320, XmNheight, 240, NULL);
```

with

```
skeleton = XtAppInitialize(&skel_app, "Skeleton",NULL,0, &argc, argv,
        NULL, NULL,0);
```

Rebuild the program and run it. You should see a much larger window than the earlier version. Finally, yet another way to feed resources to this program is to create a file called `Skeleton`, type in the resource strings for width and height mentioned earlier, and save the file into the `/usr/X11R6/lib/X11/app-defaults` directory. This way, the program will start with a default window size for everyone on your system.

Continuing with the example, the client's main window as a managed widget is created next with `XtVaCreateManagedWidget()`; then a menu bar is built across the top of the window with `XmCreateMenubar()`. After that, a pull-down menu is created with `XmCreatePulldownMenu()`, and then a File button is built on the menu, which will respond not only to a mouse click, but also to Alt+F.

Building the rest of the File menu is now easy. Note the callback routine to tell the program what to do when the Exit menu item is selected. After the File menu, the Edit menu is created in the same way, along with the Help menu.

NOTE

Thanks are due to Ken Lee's Motif FAQ for the tip on moving the Help menu string to the end of the main window's menu bar.

Finally, the menu bar is displayed, along with the application, and the program starts waiting for keystrokes, clicks, and other events in `XtAppMainLoop()`.

As you can see, even in a simple Motif program, there's a lot of code devoted to handling the user interface. Using Motif can save you a lot of time and effort because a lot of the code required to build, display, and handle the interface is hidden in the Motif routines. This can free you to concentrate on the internals of what your program does and gives your programs a consistent look and feel.

Shared and Static Libraries

Using shared libraries when you build applications makes sense because program binaries use a lot less space on your hard drive. But what if you want to compile a program for someone else who might not have the Motif libraries installed?

In this case, you might want to build the program using Motif's static libraries. If you do, be prepared to find that a lot of extra code is linked into your program. How much bigger will the program be, and how much of a difference using a static build will this make, you might ask? Let's see! First, you'll build a sample program in two different versions, using the `gcc` compiler option `-static`:

```
# gcc -static -o skel.static skeleton.c -L/usr/X11/lib
➥-lXm -lXpm -lXaw -lXt -lXext -lX11
# gcc -o skel.shared skeleton.c -L/usr/X11/lib
➥-lXm -lXpm -lXaw -lXt -lSM -lICE -lXext -lX11
```

Now let's see the size of the files `skel.static` and `skel.shared`:

```
# ls -l skel.*
-rwxr-xr-x   1 root     root        12708 Sep 12 05:12 skel.shared
-rwxr-xr-x   1 root     root      1978564 Sep 12 05:11 skel.static
```

How about nearly a two-megabyte difference? If you're going to build Motif clients, you'll want to use the shared libraries (usually a default) because, as you can see, you'd quickly run out of room on your hard drive.

The UIL Compiler

Although I don't have enough room to discuss the User Interface Language (UIL), if you want to quickly and easily build your program's interface, you might want to learn this language, and its compiler, `uil`. For details on using the compiler and language, read the `uil` and UIL man pages. A number of the Motif demonstration programs use UIL, so you can read source code examples.

There are also many commercial graphical interface builders that enable you to draw and design your interface, test it, and then, with the click of a button, write out the Motif source code. See the Motif FAQ for more information. (Pointers for the FAQ are at the end of this chapter in the section "For More Information.")

Tutorials and Examples

If you're serious about learning Motif programming, you'll need to have several good books and lots of program examples. If you want a basic introduction, you can also try some on the online tutorials or peruse code examples. Try one of these sites:

- `http://www.cen.com/mw3/code.html`

  Contains a number of useful links to Motif programming code examples, lectures, and tutorials.

- `http://www.iftech.com`

  Contains a Motif programming tutorial you might find helpful when getting started.

- `ftp://ftp.vse.cz`

  Look under `/pub/linux/freeware_for_motif/motif-tutor` for a copy of Jan Borchers' `xmtutor`, an interactive tutorial on Motif programming.

Using `imake` and `xmkmf`

You should be familiar with Todd Brunhoff's `imake` utility and Jim Fulton's `xmkmf` command if you've created or built programs for the X Window System. Like the `make` command, these commands help you save time, prevent errors, and organize your programming tasks by automating the building process.

`imake`, a C preprocessor interface to `make`, uses configuration files found under the `/usr/X11R6/lib/X11/config` directory. These files include `linux.cf`, `lnxLib.rules`, `lnxLib.tmpl`, `lnxdoc.rules`, and `lnxdoc.tmpl`.

The `xmkmf` command, which creates a `Makefile` from an `Imakefile`, is a simple shell script that runs `imake`, telling it where to find the specifics about your system and which command-line parameters need to be passed to your compiler, assembler, linker, and even man-page formatter. Note that you should never run `imake` by itself; always use the `xmkmf` script instead.

Typically, after unpacking the source for an X or Motif program, you use the `xmkmf` command and then the `make` command to build your program. Another of the reasons many programmers use `imake` is to ensure portability. Assuming the `imake` file is written properly, the `xmkmf` command will work on nearly any UNIX system, and that includes Linux.

`imake` works by reading an `Imakefile`. In turn, the `Imakefile` contains directions for the `cpp` compiler preprocessor, whose output is then fed back into `imake`, which in turn, generates the `Makefile` for your program. The magic of `imake` is that it simplifies the job of creating `Makefiles` for every possible computer or operating system your program could be built on or run under.

For example, here's a simple `Imakefile` for our sample program, `skeleton.c`:

```
        INCLUDES = -I.
DEPLIBS = XmClientDepLibs
LOCAL_LIBRARIES = XmClientLibs
SRCS= skeleton.c
OBJS= skeleton.o
PROGRAMS = skel
NormalLibraryObjectRule()
MComplexProgramTarget(skeleton,$(LOCAL_LIBRARIES),$(SYSLIBS))
```

To use this listing, type it in your favorite text editor (such as `nedit`) and save the text as `Imakefile`. Then, use the two commands

```
# xmkmf
# make
```

to build the program. This will also save you a lot of time if you use the edit-compile-run-edit cycle of programming, as you won't have to retype the compiler command line shown earlier in this chapter (`# gcc -o skel skeleton.c -L/usr/X11R6/lib -lXm -lXpm -lXt -lXext -lX11`).

LessTif—An Alternative Motif Clone

Much of the success of Linux is a direct result of the generosity of the thousands of programmers who chose to distribute their software either for free or under the GNU Public License. Motif, as you already know, is not freeware, nor is it distributed under the GPL. As Red Hat Linux users, we're spoiled by the ability to examine program source or make changes as we see fit.

Want the source to Motif for your computer's operating system? It will cost you $17,000 at the time of this writing. If you're interested in building a distribution of Motif for Linux, you can get the price list by browsing to `http://www.opengroup.org/tech/desktop/ordering/motif.price.list.htm`.

For those of us who like source code or want to build Motif-compliant clients without paying for a distribution, there's an alternative: LessTif. This is a Motif clone, designed to be compatible with Motif 1.2. Distributed under the terms of the GNU GPL, LessTif currently builds 26 different Motif clients (probably many more by the time you read this).

You can find a copy of the current LessTif distribution for Linux at `http://www.lesstif.org`.

The current distribution doesn't require that you use `imake` or `xmkmf`, and it comes with shared and static libraries. If you're a real Motif hacker and you're interested in the internals of graphical interface construction and widget programming, you should read the details of how LessTif is constructed. You can get a free copy of Harold Albrecht's book, *Inside LessTif*, at `http://www.igpm.rwth-aachen.de/~albrecht/hungry.html`.

For More Information

If you're interested in finding answers to common questions about Motif, read Ken Lee's Motif FAQ, which is posted regularly to the newsgroup `comp.windows.x.motif`. Without a doubt, this is the best source of information on getting started with Motif, but it won't replace a good book on Motif programming. You can find the FAQ on the newsgroup, or at `ftp://ftp.rahul.net/pub/kenton/faqs/Motif-FAQ`.

An HTML version can be found at `http://www.rahul.net/kenton/faqs/Motif-FAQ.html`.

For information on how to use `imake`, read Paul DuBois' *Software Portability with imake* from O'Reilly & Associates.

For Motif 1.2 programming and reference material, read Dan Heller and Paula M. Ferguson's *Motif Programming Manual* and Paula M. Ferguson and David Brennan's *Motif Reference Manual*, both from O'Reilly & Associates.

For the latest news about Motif or CDE, check The Open Group's site at `http://www.opengroup.org`.

For the latest information, installation, or programming errata about Red Hat's Motif distribution, see `http://www.redhat.com`.

For the latest binaries of LessTif, programming hints, and a list of Motif 1.2-compatible functions and Motif clients that build under the latest LessTif distribution, see `http://www.lesstif.org`.

For official information on Motif 1.2 from OSF, the following titles (from Prentice-Hall) might help:

- *OSF/Motif Programmers Guide*
- *OSF/Motif Programmers Reference Manual*
- *OSF/Motif Style Guide*

For learning about `Xt`, you should look at Adrian Nye and Tim O'Reilly's *X Toolkit Intrinsics Programming Manual, Motif Edition*, and David Flanagan's *X Toolkit Intrinsics Reference Manual*, both from O'Reilly.

Other books about Motif include the following:

- *Motif Programming: The Essentials...and More*, by Marshall Brain, Digital Press
- *The X Toolkit Cookbook*, by Paul E. Kimball, Prentice-Hall, 1995
- *Building OSF/Motif Applications: A Practical Introduction*, by Mark Sebern, Prentice-Hall, 1994

Summary

In this chapter, you've learned about Motif, a commercial software library add-on for Linux that is available from a number of vendors, including Red Hat Software. Although you'll have to decide which version of Motif is best for you, hopefully you'll agree about some of the benefits of using Motif to write programs for the X Window System. By following the example program in Listing 26.1, you've learned a little about how Motif programs work and how to incorporate some of Motif's features into your programs. By using two programming tools included in your Red Hat Linux distribution, `imake` and `xmkmf`, you've also seen how to save time and effort when writing your own programs for Motif or X11. Finally, in this chapter, I've given you some tips on a Motif alternative, LessTif. I hope you'll explore more topics concerning graphical interface programming for X.

gawk Programming

by David B. Horvath, CCP

IN THIS CHAPTER

gawk, or GNU awk, is one of the newer versions of the awk programming language created for UNIX by Alfred V. Aho, Peter J. Weinberger, and Brian W. Kernighan in 1977. The name awk comes from the initials of the creators' last names. Kernighan was also involved with the creation of the C programming language and UNIX; Aho and Weinberger were involved with the development of UNIX. Because of their backgrounds, you will see many similarities between awk and C.

There are several versions of awk: the original awk, nawk, POSIX awk, and of course, gawk. nawk was created in 1985 and is the version described in *The awk Programming Language* (see the complete reference to this book later in the chapter in the section "Summary"). POSIX awk is defined in the *IEEE Standard for Information Technology, Portable Operating System Interface, Part 2: Shell and Utilities Volume 2*, ANSI-approved April 5, 1993 (IEEE is the Institute of Electrical and Electronics Engineers, Inc.). GNU awk is based on POSIX awk.

The awk language (in all of its versions) is a pattern-matching and processing language with a lot of power. It will search a file (or multiple files) searching for records that match a specified pattern. When a match is found, a specified action is performed. As a programmer, you do not have to worry about opening, looping through the file reading each record, handling end-of-file, or closing it when done. These details are handled automatically for you.

It is easy to create short awk programs because of this functionality—many of the details are handled by the language automatically. There are also many functions and built-in features to handle many of the tasks of processing files.

Applications

There are many possible uses for awk, including extracting data from a file, counting occurrences of within a file, and creating reports.

The basic syntax of the awk language matches the C programming language; if you already know C, you know most of awk. In many ways, awk is an easier version of C because of the way it handles strings and arrays (dynamically). If you do not know C yet, learning awk will make learning C a little easier.

awk is also very useful for rapid prototyping or trying out an idea that will be implemented in another language like C. Instead of your having to worry about some of the minute details, the built-in automation takes care of them. You worry about the basic functionality.

TIP

awk works with text files, not binary. Because binary data can contain values that look like record terminators (newline characters)—or not have any at all—awk will get confused. If you need to process binary files, look into Perl or use a traditional programming language like C.

Features

As is the UNIX environment, awk is flexible, contains predefined variables, automates many of the programming tasks, provides the conventional variables, supports the C-formatted output, and is easy to use. awk lets you combine the best of shell scripts and C programming.

There are usually many different ways to perform the same task within awk. Programmers get to decide which method is best suited to their applications. With the built-in variables and functions, many of the normal programming tasks are automatically performed. awk will automatically read each record, split it up into fields, and perform type conversions whenever needed. The way a variable is used determines its type—there is no need (or method) to declare variables of any type.

Of course, the "normal" C programming constructs like if/else, do/while, for, and while are supported. awk doesn't support the switch/case construct. It supports C's printf() for formatted output and also has a print command for simpler output.

awk Fundamentals

Unlike some of the other UNIX tools (shell, grep, and so on), awk requires a program (known as an "awk script"). This program can be as simple as one line or as complex as several thousand lines. (I once developed an awk program that summarizes data at several levels with multiple control breaks; it was just short of 1000 lines.)

The awk program can be entered a number of ways—on the command line or in a program file. awk can accept input from a file, piped in from another program, or even directly from the keyboard. Output normally goes to the standard output device, but that can be redirected to a file or piped into another program. Output can also be sent directly to a file instead of standard output.

Using awk from the Command Line

The simplest way to use awk is to code the program on the command line, accept input from the standard input device (keyboard), and send output to the standard output device (screen). Listing 27.1 shows this in its simplest form; it prints the number of fields in the input record along with that record.

Listing 27.1. Simplest use of awk.

```
$ gawk '{print NF ": " $0}'
Now is the time for all
Good Americans to come to the Aid
of Their Country.
Ask not what you can do for awk, but rather what awk can do for you.
Ctrl+d
```

continues

Listing 27.1. continued

```
6: Now is the time for all
7: Good Americans to come to the Aid
3: of Their Country.
16: Ask not what you can do for awk, but rather what awk can do for you.
$ _
```

NOTE

Ctrl+D is one way of showing that you should press (and hold) the Ctrl (or Control) key and then press the D key. This is the default end-of-file key for UNIX. If this doesn't work on your system, use `stty -a` to determine which key to press. Another way this action or key is shown on the screen is `^d`.

The entire `awk` script is contained within single quotes (`'`) to prevent the shell from interpreting its contents. This is a requirement of the operating system or shell, not the `awk` language.

`NF` is a predefined variable that is set to the number of fields on each record. `$0` is that record. The individual fields can be referenced as `$1`, `$2`, and so on.

You can also store your `awk` script in a file and specify that filename on the command line by using the `-f` flag. If you do that, you don't have to contain the program within single quotes.

NOTE

`gawk` and other versions of `awk` that meet the POSIX standard support the specification of multiple programs through the use of multiple `-f` options. This allows you to execute multiple `awk` programs on the same input. Personally, I tend to avoid this just because it gets a bit confusing.

You can use the normal UNIX shell redirection or just specify the filename on the command line to accept the input from a file instead of the keyboard:

```
gawk '{print NF ": " $0}' < inputs
gawk '{print NF ": " $0}' inputs
```

Multiple files can be specified by just listing them on the command line as shown in the second form above—they will be processed in the order specified. Output can be redirected through the normal UNIX shell facilities to send it to a file or pipe it into another program:

```
gawk '{print NF ": " $0}' > outputs
gawk '{print NF ": " $0}' ¦ more
```

Of course, both input and output can be redirected at the same time.

One of the ways I use awk most commonly is to process the output of another command by piping its output into awk. If I wanted to create a custom listing of files that contained the filename and then the permissions only, I would execute a command like:

```
ls -l ¦ gawk '{print $NF, " ", $1}'
```

$NF is the last field (which is the filename; I am lazy—I didn't want to count the fields to figure out its number). $1 is the first field. The output of ls -l is piped into awk, which processes it for me.

If I put the awk script into a file (named lser.awk) and redirected the output to the printer, I would have a command that looks like:

```
ls -l ¦ gawk -f lser.awk ¦ lp
```

I tend to save my awk scripts with the file type (suffix) of .awk just to make it obvious when I am looking through a directory listing. If the program is longer than about 30 characters, I make a point of saving it because there is no such thing as a "one-time only" program, user request, or personal need.

CAUTION

If you forget the -f option before a program filename, your program will be treated as if it were data.

If you code your awk program on the command line but place it after the name of your data file, it will also be treated as if it were data.

What you will get is odd results.

See the section "Commands On-the-Fly" later in this chapter for more examples of using awk scripts to process piped data.

Patterns and Actions

Each awk statement consists of two parts: the pattern and the action. The pattern decides when the action is executed and, of course, the action is what the programmer wants to occur. Without a pattern, the action is always executed (the pattern can be said to "default to true").

There are two special patterns (also known as blocks): BEGIN and END. The BEGIN code is executed before the first record is read from the file and is used to initialize variables and set up things like control breaks. The END code is executed after end-of-file is reached and is used for any cleanup required (like printing final totals on a report). The other patterns are tested for each record read from the file.

The general program format is to put the `BEGIN` block at the top, any pattern/action pairs, and finally, the `END` block at the end. This is not a language requirement—it is just the way most people do it (mostly for readability reasons).

`BEGIN` and `END` blocks are optional; if you use them, you should have a maximum of one each. Don't code two `BEGIN` blocks, and don't code two `END` blocks.

The action is contained within curly braces (`{ }`) and can consist of one or many statements. If you omit the pattern portion, it defaults to true, which causes the action to be executed for every line in the file. If you omit the action, it defaults to `print $0` (print the entire record).

The pattern is specified before the action. It can be a regular expression (contained within a pair of slashes [`/ /`]) that matches part of the input record or an expression that contains comparison operators. It can also be compound or complex patterns which consists of expressions and regular expressions combined or a range of patterns.

Regular Expression Patterns

The regular expressions used by `awk` are similar to those used by `grep`, `egrep`, and the UNIX editors `ed`, `ex`, and `vi`. They are the notation used to specify and match strings. A regular expression consists of characters (like the letters *A*, *B*, and *c*—that match themselves in the input) and metacharacters. Metacharacters are characters that have special (meta) meaning; they do not match to themselves but perform some special function.

Table 27.1 shows the metacharacters and their behavior.

Table 27.1. Regular expression metacharacters in awk.

Metacharacter	*Meaning*
`\`	Escape sequence (next character has special meaning, `\n` is the newline character and `\t` is the tab). Any escaped metacharacter will match to that character (as if it were not a metacharacter).
`^`	Starts match at beginning of string.
`$`	Matches at end of string.
`.`	Matches any single character.
`[ABC]`	Matches any one of `A`, `B`, or `C`.
`[A-Ca-c]`	Matches any one of `A`, `B`, `C`, `a`, `b`, or `c` (ranges).
`[^ABC]`	Matches any character other than `A`, `B`, and `C`.
`Desk¦Chair`	Matches any one of `Desk` or `Chair`.
`[ABC][DEF]`	Concatenation. Matches any one of `A`, `B`, or `C` that is followed by any one of `D`, `E`, or `F`.
`*`	`[ABC]*`—Matches zero or more occurrences of `A`, `B`, or `C`.

Metacharacter	Meaning
+	[ABC]+—Matches one or more occurrences of A, B, or C.
?	[ABC]?—Matches to an empty string or any one of A, B, or C.
()	Combines regular expressions. For example, (Blue¦Black)berry matches to Blueberry or Blackberry.

All of these can be combined to form complex search strings. Typical search strings can be used to search for specific strings (Report Date), strings in different formats (may, MAY, May), or as groups of characters (any combination of upper- and lowercase characters that spell out the month of May). These look like the following:

```
/Report Date/  { print "do something" }
/(may)¦(MAY)¦(May)/ { print "do something else" }
/[Mm][Aa][Yy]/ { print "do something completely different" }
```


Comparison Operators and Patterns

The comparison operators used by awk are similar to those used by C and the UNIX shells. They are the notation used to specify and compare values (including strings). A regular expression alone will match to any portion of the input record. By combining a comparison with a regular expression, specific fields can be tested.

Table 27.2 shows the comparison operators and their behavior.

Table 27.2. Comparison operators in awk.

Operator	Meaning
==	Is equal to
<	Less than
>	Greater than
<=	Less than or equal to
>=	Greater than or equal to
!=	Not equal to
~	Matched by regular expression
!~	Not matched by regular expression

This enables you to perform specific comparisons on fields instead of the entire record. Remember that you can also perform them on the entire record by using $0 instead of a specific field.

Typical search strings can be used to search for a name in the first field (Bob) and compare specific fields with regular expressions:

```
$1 == "Bob"    { print "Bob stuff" }
$2 ~ /(may)¦(MAY)¦(May)/ { print "May stuff" }
$3 !~ /[Mm][Aa][Yy]/ { print "other May stuff" }
```

Compound Pattern Operators

The compound pattern operators used by awk are similar to those used by C and the UNIX shells. They are the notation used to combine other patterns (expressions or regular expressions) into a complex form of logic.

Table 27.3 shows the compound pattern operators and their behavior.

Table 27.3. Compound pattern operators in awk.

Operator	*Meaning*
&&	Logical AND
¦¦	Logical OR
!	Logical NOT
()	Parentheses—used to group compound statements

If I wanted to execute some action (print a special message, for instance), if the first field contained the value "Bob" and the fourth field contained the value "Street", I could use a compound pattern that looks like:

```
$1 == "Bob" && $4 == "Street" {print"some message"}
```

Range Pattern Operators

The range pattern is slightly more complex than the other types—it is set true when the first pattern is matched and remains true until the second pattern becomes true. The catch is that the file needs to be sorted on the fields that the range pattern matches. Otherwise, it might be set true prematurely or end early.

The individual patterns in a range pattern are separated by a comma (,). If you have twenty-six files in your directory with the names A to Z, you can show a range of the files as shown in Listing 27.2.

Listing 27.2. Range pattern example.

```
$ ls ¦ gawk '{$1 == "B", $1 == "D"}'
B
C
D
```

```
$ ls ¦ gawk '{$1 == "B", $1 <= "D"}'
B
$ ls ¦ gawk '{$1 == "B", $1 > "D"}'
B
C
D
E
$ _
```

The first example is obvious—all the records between `B` and `D` are shown. The other examples are less intuitive, but the key to remember is that the pattern is done when the second condition is true. The second `gawk` command only shows the `B` because `C` is less than or equal to `D` (making the second condition true). The third `gawk` shows `B` through `E` because `E` is the first one that is greater than `D` (making the second condition true).

Handling Input

As each record is read by `awk`, it breaks it down into fields and then searches for matching patterns and the related actions to perform. It assumes that each record occupies a single line (the newline character, by definition, ends a record). Lines that are just blanks or are empty (just the newline) count as records, just with very few fields (usually zero).

You can force `awk` to read the next record in a file (cease searching for pattern matches) by using the `next` statement. `next` is similar to the C `continue` command—control returns to the outermost loop. In `awk`, the outermost loop is the automatic read of the file. If you decide you need to break out of your program completely, you can use the `exit` statement. `exit` will act like the end-of-file was reached and pass control to the `END` block (if one exists). If `exit` is in the `END` block, the program will immediately exit.

By default, fields are separated by spaces. It doesn't matter to `awk` whether there is one or many spaces—the next field begins when the first nonspace character is found. You can change the field separator by setting the variable `FS` to that character. To set your field separator to the colon (:), which is the separator in `/etc/passwd`, code the following:

```
BEGIN { FS = ":" }
```

The general format of the file looks something like the following:

```
david:!:207:1017:David B Horvath,CCP:/u/david:/bin/ksh
```

If you want to list the names of everyone on the system, use the following:

```
gawk --field-separator=: '{ print $5 }' /etc/passwd
```

You will then see a list of everyone's name. In this example, I set the field separator variable (`FS`) from the command line using the `gawk` format command-line options (`--field-separator=:`). I could also use `-F :`, which is supported by all versions of `awk`.

The first field is `$1`, the second is `$2`, and so on. The entire record is contained in `$0`. You can get the last field (if you are lazy like me and don't want to count) by referencing `$NF`. `NF` is the number of fields in a record.

Coding Your Program

The nice thing about awk is that, with a few exceptions, it is free format—like the C language. Blank lines are ignored. Statements can be placed on the same line or split up in any form you like. awk recognizes whitespace, much like C does. The following two lines are essentially the same:

```
$1=="Bob"{print"Bob stuff"}
$1      ==      "Bob"       {      print      "Bob stuff"      }
```

Spaces within quotes are significant because they will appear in the output or are used in a comparison for matching. The other spaces are not. You can also split up the action (but you have to have the opening curly brace on the same line as the pattern):

```
$1      ==      "Bob"       {
                               print     "Bob stuff"
                            }
```

You can have multiple statements within an action. If you place them on the same line, you need to use semicolons (;) to separate them (so awk can tell when one ends and the next begins). Printing multiple lines looks like the following:

```
$1      ==      "Bob"       {
                               print     "Bob stuff"; print     "more stuff";
                            ➥print     "last stuff";
                            }
```

You can also put the statements on separate lines. When you do that, you don't need to code the semicolons, and the code looks like the following:

```
$1      ==      "Bob"       {
                               print     "Bob stuff"
                               print     "more stuff"
                               print     "last stuff"
                            }
```

Personally, I am in the habit of coding the semicolon after each statement because that is the way I have to do it in C. To awk, the following example is just like the previous (but you can see the semicolons):

```
$1      ==      "Bob"       {
                               print     "Bob stuff";
                               print     "more stuff";
                               print     "last stuff";
                            }
```

Another thing you should make use of is comments. Anything on a line after the pound sign or octothorpe (#) is ignored by awk. These are notes designed for the programmer to read and aid in the understanding of the program code. In general, the more comments you place in a program, the easier it is to maintain.

Actions

The actions of your program are the part that tells awk what to do when a pattern is matched. If there is no pattern, it defaults to true. A pattern without an action defaults to {print $0}.

All actions are enclosed within curly braces ({ }). The open brace should appear on the same line as the pattern; other than that, there are no restrictions. An action will consist of one or many actions.

Variables

Except for simple find-and-print types of programs, you are going to need to save data. That is done through the use of variables. Within awk, there are three types of variables: field, predefined, and user-defined. You have already seen examples of the first two—$1 is the field variable that contains the first field in the input record, and FS is the predefined variable that contains the field separator.

User-defined variables are ones that you create. Unlike many other languages, awk doesn't require you to define or declare your variables before using them. In C, you must declare the type of data contained in a variable (such as int—integer, float—floating-point number, char—character data, and so on). In awk, you just use the variable. awk attempts to determine the data in the variable by how it is used. If you put character data in the variable, it is treated as a string; if you put a number in, it is treated as numeric.

awk will also perform conversions between the data types. If you put the string "123" in a variable and later perform a calculation on it, it will be treated as a number. The danger of this is, what happens when you perform a calculation on the string "abc"? awk will attempt to convert the string to a number, get a conversion error, and treat the value as a numeric zero! This type of logic error can be difficult to debug.

TIP

Initialize all your variables in a BEGIN action like this:

```
BEGIN {total = 0.0; loop = 0; first_time = "yes"; }
```

Like the C language, awk requires that variables begin with an alphabetic character or an underscore. The alphabetic character can be upper- or lowercase. The remainder of the variable name can consist of letters, numbers, or underscores. It would be nice (to yourself and anyone else who has to maintain your code once you are gone) to make the variable names meaningful. Make them descriptive.

Although you can make your variable names all uppercase letters, that is a bad practice because the predefined variables (like NF or FS) are in uppercase. It is a common error to type the predefined variables in lowercase (like nf or fs)—you will not get any errors from awk, and this mistake can be difficult to debug. The variables won't behave like the proper, uppercase spelling, and you won't get the results you expect.

Predefined Variables

gawk provides you with a number of predefined (also known as built-in) variables. These are used to provide useful data to your program; they can also be used to change the default behavior of the gawk (by setting them to a specific value).

Table 27.4 summarizes the predefined variables in gawk. Earlier versions of awk don't support all these variables.

Table 27.4. gawk predefined variables.

Variable	*Meaning*	*Default Value (if any)*
ARGC	The number of command-line arguments	
ARGIND	The index within ARGV of the current file being processed	
ARGV	An array of command-line arguments	
CONVFMT	The conversion format for numbers	%.6g
ENVIRON	The UNIX environmental variables	
ERRNO	The UNIX system error message	
FIELDWIDTHS	A whitespace separated string of the width of input fields	
FILENAME	The name of the current input file	
FNR	The current record number	
FS	The input field separator	Space
IGNORECASE	Controls the case sensitivity	0 (case-sensitive)
NF	The number of fields in the current record	
NR	The number of records already read	
OFMT	The output format for numbers	%.6g
OFS	The output field separator	Space
ORS	The output record separator	Newline
RS	Input record separator	Newline
RSTART	Start of string matched by match function	
RLENGTH	Length of string matched by match function	
SUBSEP	Subscript separator	"\034"

The ARGC variable contains the number of command-line arguments passed to your program. ARGV is an array of ARGC elements that contains the command-line arguments themselves. The first one is ARGV[0], and the last one is ARGV[ARGC-1]. ARGV[0] contains the name of the command being executed (gawk). The gawk command-line options won't appear in ARGV—they are interpreted by gawk itself. ARGIND is the index within ARGV of the current file being processed.

The default conversion (input) format for numbers is stored in CONVFMT (conversion format) and defaults to the format string "%.6g". See the section "printf" for more information on the meaning of the format string.

The ENVIRON variable is an array that contains the environmental variables defined to your UNIX session. The subscript is the name of the environmental variable for which you want to get the value.

If you want your program to perform specific code depending on the value in an environmental variable, you can use the following:

```
ENVIRON["TERM"] == "vt100"  {print "Working on a Video Tube!"}
```

If you are using a VT100 terminal, you will get the message Working on a Video Tube!. Note that you only put quotes around the environmental variable if you are using a literal. If you have a variable (named TERM) that contains the string "TERM", you would leave the double quotes off.

The ERRNO variable contains the UNIX system error message if a system error occurs during redirection, read, or close.

The FIELDWIDTHS variable provides a facility for fixed-length fields instead of using field separators. To specify the size of fields, you set FIELDWIDTHS to a string that contains the width of each field separated by a space or tab character. After this variable is set, gawk will split up the input record based on the specified widths. To revert to using a field separator character, you assign a new value to FS.

The variable FILENAME contains the name of the current input file. Because different (or even multiple files) can be specified on the command line, this provides you a means of determining which input file is being processed.

The FNR variable contains the number of the current record within the current input file. It is reset for each file that is specified on the command line. It always contains a value that is less than or equal to the variable NR.

The character that is used to separate fields is stored in the variable FS with a default value of space. You can change this variable with a command-line option or within your program. If you know that your file will have some character other than a space as the field separator (like the /etc/passwd file in earlier examples, which uses the colon), you can specify it in your program with the BEGIN pattern.

You can control the case sensitivity of gawk regular expressions with the IGNORECASE variable. When set to the default, zero, pattern matching checks the case in regular expressions. If you set it to a nonzero value, case is ignored. (The letter A will match to the letter a.)

The variable NF is set after each record is read and contains the number of fields. The fields are determined by the FS or FIELDWIDTHS variables.

The variable NR contains the total number of records read. It is never less than FNR, which is reset to zero for each file.

The default output format for numbers is stored in OFMT and defaults to the format string "%.6g". See the section "printf" for more information on the meaning of the format string.

The output field separator is contained in OFS with a default of space. This is the character or string that is output whenever you use a comma with the print statement, such as the following:

```
{print $1, $2, $3;}
```

This statement print the first three fields of a file separated by spaces. If you want to separate them by colons (like the /etc/passwd file), you simply set OFS to a new value: OFS=":".

You can change the output record separator by setting ORS to a new value. ORS defaults to the newline character (\n).

The length of any string matched by the match() function call is stored in RLENGTH. This is used in conjunction with the RSTART predefined variable to extract the matched string.

You can change the input record separator by setting RS to a new value. RS defaults to the newline character (\n).

The starting position of any string matched by the match() function call is stored in RSTART. This is used in conjunction with the RLENGTH predefined variable to extract the matched string.

The SUBSEP variable contains the value used to separate subscripts for multidimension arrays. The default value is "\034", which is the double quote character (").

NOTE

If you change a field ($1, $2, and so on) or the input record ($0), you will cause other predefined variables to change. If your original input record had two fields and you set $3="third one", then NF would be changed from 2 to 3.

Strings

awk supports two general types of variables: numeric (which can consist of the characters 0 through 9, + or -, and the decimal [.]) and character (which can contain any character). Variables that contain characters are generally referred to as strings. A character string can contain a valid number, text like words, or even a formatted phone number. If the string contains a valid number, awk can automatically convert and use it as if it were a numeric variable; if you attempt to use a string that contains a formatted phone number as a numeric variable, awk will attempt to convert and use it as it were a numeric variable—that contains the value zero.

String Constants

A string constant is always enclosed within the double quotes ("") and can be from zero (an *empty* string) to many characters long. The exact maximum varies by version of UNIX; personally, I have never hit the maximum. The double quotes aren't stored in memory. A typical string constant might look like the following:

```
"UNIX Unleashed, Second Edition"
```

You have already seen string constants used earlier in this chapter—with comparisons and the print statement.

String Operators

There is really only one string operator and that is concatenation. You can combine multiple strings (constants or variables in any combination) by just putting them together. Listing 27.1 does this with the print statement where the string ": " is prepended to the input record ($0).

Listing 27.3 shows a couple ways to concatenate strings.

Listing 27.3. Concatenating strings example.

```
gawk 'BEGIN{x="abc""def"; y="ghi"; z=x y; z2 = "A"x"B"y"C"; print x, y, z, z2}'
abcdef ghi abcdefghi AabcdefBghiC
```

Variable x is set to two concatenated strings; it prints as abcdef. Variable y is set to one string for use with the variable z. Variable z is the concatenation of two string variables printing as abcdefghi. Finally, the variable z2 shows the concatenation of string constants and string variables printing as AabcdefBghiC.

If you leave the comma out of the print statement, all the strings will be concatenated together and will look like the following:

```
abcdefghiabcdefghiAabcdefBghiC
```

Built-in String Functions

In addition to the one string operation (concatenation), gawk provides a number of functions for processing strings.

Table 27.5 summarizes the built-in string functions in gawk. Earlier versions of awk don't support all these functions.

Table 27.5. gawk built-in string functions.

Function	*Purpose*
`gsub(reg, string, target)`	Substitutes `string` in `target` string every time the regular expression `reg` is matched
`index(search, string)`	Returns the position of the `search` string in `string`
`length(string)`	The number of characters in `string`
`match(string, reg)`	Returns the position in `string` that matches the regular expression `reg`
`printf(format, variables)`	Writes formatted data based on `format`; `variables` is the data you want printed
`split(string, store, delim)`	Splits `string` into array elements of `store` based on the delimiter `delim`
`sprintf(format, variables)`	Returns a string containing formatted data based on `format`; `variables` is the data you want placed in the string
`strftime(format, timestamp)`	Returns a formatted date or time string based on `format`; `timestamp` is the time returned by the `systime()` function
`sub(reg, string, target)`	Substitutes `string` in `target` string the first time the regular expression `reg` is matched
`substr(string, position, len)`	Returns a substring beginning at `position` for `len` number of characters
`tolower(string)`	Returns the characters in `string` as their lowercase equivalent
`toupper(string)`	Returns the characters in `string` as their uppercase equivalent

The `gsub(reg, string, target)` function allows you to globally substitute one set of characters for another (defined in the form of the regular expression `reg`) within `string`. The number of substitutions is returned by the function. If `target` is omitted, the input record, `$0`, is the target. This is patterned after the `substitute` command in the `ed` text editor.

The `index(search, string)` function returns the first position (counting from the left) of the `search` string within `string`. If `string` is omitted, `0` is returned.

The `length(string)` function returns a count of the number of characters in `string`. `awk` keeps track of the length of strings internally.

The match(*string*, *reg*) function determines whether *string* contains the set of characters defined by *reg*. If there is a match, the position is returned, and the variables RSTART and RLENGTH are set.

The printf(*format*, *variables*) function writes formatted data converting *variables* based on the *format* string. This function is very similar to the C printf() function. More information about this function and the formatting strings is provided in the section "printf" later in this chapter.

The split(*string*, *store*, *delim*) function splits *string* into elements of the array *store* based on the *delim* string. The number of elements in *store* is returned. If you omit the *delim* string, FS is used. To split a slash (/) delimited date into its component parts, code the following:

```
split("08/12/1962", results, "/");
```

After the function call, results[1] contains 08, results[2] contains 12, and results[3] contains 1962. When used with the split function, the array begins with the element one. This also works with strings that contain text.

The sprintf(format, variables) function behaves like the printf function except that it returns the result string instead of writing output. It produces formatted data converting variables based on the format string. This function is very similar to the C sprintf() function. More information about this function and the formatting strings is provided in the "printf" section of this chapter.

The strftime(*format*, *timestamp*) function returns a formatted date or time based on the *format* string; *timestamp* is the number of seconds since midnight on January 1, 1970. The systime function returns a value in this form. The format is the same as the C strftime() function.

The sub(*reg*, *string*, *target*) function allows you to substitute the one set of characters for the first occurrence of another (defined in the form of the regular expression *reg*) within *string*. The number of substitutions is returned by the function. If *target* is omitted, the input record, $0, is the target. This is patterned after the substitute command in the ed text editor.

The substr(*string*, *position*, *len*) function allows you to extract a substring based on a starting *position* and *length*. If you omit the *len* parameter, the remaining string is returned.

The tolower(*string*) function returns the uppercase alphabetic characters in *string* converted to lowercase. Any other characters are returned without any conversion.

The toupper(*string*) function returns the lowercase alphabetic characters in *string* converted to uppercase. Any other characters are returned without any conversion.

Special String Constants

awk supports special string constants that cannot be entered from the keyboard or have special meaning. If you wanted to have a double quote (") character as a string constant (x = """), how would you prevent awk from thinking the second one (the one you really want) is the end of the string? The answer is by escaping, or telling awk that the next character has special meaning. This is done through the backslash (\) character, as in the rest of UNIX.

Table 27.6 shows most of the constants that gawk supports.

Table 27.6. gawk special string constants.

Expression	*Meaning*
`\\`	The means of including a backslash
`\a`	The alert or bell character
`\b`	Backspace
`\f`	Formfeed
`\n`	Newline
`\r`	Carriage return
`\t`	Tab
`\v`	Vertical tab
`\"`	Double quote
`\x`*NN*	Indicates that *NN* is a hexadecimal number
`\0`*NNN*	Indicates that *NNN* is an octal number

Arrays

When you have more than one related piece of data, you have two choices—you can create multiple variables, or you can use an array. An array enables you to keep a collection of related data together.

You access individual elements within an array by enclosing the subscript within square brackets ([]). In general, you can use an array element any place you can use a regular variable.

Arrays in awk have special capabilities that are lacking in most other languages: They are dynamic, they are sparse, and the subscript is actually a string. You don't have to declare a variable to be an array, and you don't have to define the maximum number of elements—when you use an element for the first time, it is created dynamically. Because of this, a block of memory is not initially allocated; in normal programming practice, if you want to accumulate sales for each month in a year, 12 elements will be allocated, even if you are only processing December at the moment. awk arrays are sparse; if you are working with December, only that element will exist, not the other 11 (empty) months.

In my experience, the last capability is the most useful—the subscript being a string. In most programming languages, if you want to accumulate data based on a string (like totaling sales by state or country), you need to have two arrays—the state or country name (a string) and the numeric sales array. You search the state or country name for a match and then use the same element of the sales array. awk performs this for you. You create an element in the sales array with the state or country name as the subscript and address it directly like the following:

```
total_sales["Pennsylvania"] = 10.15
```

Much less programming and much easier to read (and maintain) than the search one array and change another method. This is known as an associative array.

However, awk does not directly support multidimension arrays.

Array Functions

gawk provides a couple of functions specifically for use with arrays: in and delete. The in function tests for membership in an array. The delete function removes elements from an array.

If you have an array with a subscript of states and want to determine if a specific state is in the list, you would put the following within a conditional test (more about conditional tests in the "Conditional Flow" section):

```
"Delaware" in total_sales
```

You can also use the in function within a loop to step through the elements in an array (especially if the array is sparse or associative). This is a special case of the for loop and is described in the section "The for statement," later in the chapter.

To delete an array element (the state of Delaware, for example), you code the following:

```
delete total_sales["Delaware"]
```

CAUTION

When an array element is deleted, it has been removed from memory. The data is no longer available.

It is always good practice to delete elements in an array, or entire arrays, when you are done with them. Although memory is cheap and large quantities are available (especially with virtual memory), you will eventually run out if you don't clean up.

NOTE

You must loop through all loop elements and delete each one. You cannot delete an entire array directly; the following is not valid:

```
delete total_sales
```

Multidimension Arrays

Although awk doesn't directly support multidimension arrays, it does provide a facility to simulate them. The distinction is fairly trivial to you as a programmer. You can specify multiple dimensions in the subscript (within the square brackets) in a form familiar to C programmers:

```
array[5, 3] = "Mary"
```

This is stored in a single-dimension array with the subscript actually stored in the form 5 SUBSEP 3. The predefined variable SUBSEP contains the value of the separator of the subscript components. It defaults to the double quote (" or \034) because it is unlikely that the double quote will appear in the subscript itself. Remember that the double quotes are used to contain a string; they are not stored as part of the string itself. You can always change SUBSEP if you need to have the double quote character in your multidimension array subscript.

If you want to calculate total sales by city and state (or country), you will use a two-dimension array:

```
total_sales["Philadelphia", "Pennsylvania"] = 10.15
```

You can use the in function within a conditional:

```
("Wilmington", "Delaware") in total_sales
```

You can also use the in function within a loop to step through the various cities.

Built-in Numeric Functions

gawk provides a number of numeric functions to calculate special values.

Table 27.7 summarizes the built-in numeric functions in gawk. Earlier versions of awk don't support all these functions.

Table 27.7. gawk built-in numeric functions.

Function	*Purpose*
atan2(x, y)	Returns the arctangent of y/x in radians
cos(x)	Returns the cosine of x in radians
exp(x)	Returns e raised to the x power
int(x)	Returns the value of x truncated to an integer
log(x)	Returns the natural log of x
rand()	Returns a random number between 0 and 1
sin(x)	Returns the sine of x in radians
sqrt(x)	Returns the square root of x

Function	*Purpose*
`srand(x)`	Initializes (seeds) the random number generator; `systime()` is used if `x` is omitted
`systime()`	Returns the current time in seconds since midnight, January 1, 1970

Arithmetic Operators

`gawk` supports a wide variety of math operations. Table 27.8 summarizes these operators.

Table 27.8. gawk arithmetic operators.

Operator	*Purpose*
`x^y`	Raises `x` to the `y` power
`x**y`	Raises `x` to the `y` power (same as `x^y`)
`x%y`	Calculates the remainder of `x/y`
`x+y`	Adds `x` to `y`
`x-y`	Subtracts `y` from `x`
`x*y`	Multiplies `x` times `y`
`x/y`	Divides `x` by `y`
`-y`	Negates `y` (switches the sign of `y`); also known as the unary minus
`++y`	Increments `y` by 1 and uses value (prefix increment)
`y++`	Uses value of `y` and then increments by 1 (postfix increment)
`--y`	Decrements `y` by 1 and uses value (prefix decrement)
`y--`	Uses value of `y` and then decrements by 1 (postfix decrement)
`x=y`	Assigns value of `y` to `x`. `gawk` also supports operator-assignment operators (`+=`, `-=`, `*=`, `/=`, `%=`, `^=`, and `**=`)

NOTE

All math in `gawk` uses floating point (even if you treat the number as an integer).

Conditional Flow

By its very nature, an action within a `gawk` program is conditional. It is executed if its pattern is true. You can also have conditional programs flow within the action through the use of an `if` statement.

The general flow of an `if` statement is as follows:

```
if (condition)
   statement to execute when true
else
   statement to execute when false
```

`condition` can be any valid combination of patterns shown in Tables 27.2 and 27.3. `else` is optional. If you have more than one statement to execute, you need to enclose the statements within curly braces (`{ }`), just as in the C syntax.

You can also stack `if` and `else` statements as necessary:

```
if ("Pennsylvania" in total_sales)
   print "We have Pennsylvania data"
else if ("Delaware" in total_sales)
   print "We have Delaware data"
else if (current_year < 2010)
   print "Uranus is still a planet"
else
   print "none of the conditions were met."
```

The Null Statement

By definition, `if` requires one (or more) statements to execute; in some cases, the logic might be straightforward when coded so that the code you want executed occurs when the condition is false. I have used this when it would be difficult or ugly to reverse the logic to execute the code when the condition is true.

The solution to this problem is easy: Just use the null statement, the semicolon (;). The null statement satisfies the syntax requirement that `if` requires statements to execute; it just does nothing.

Your code will look something like the following:

```
if (($1 <= 5 && $2 > 3) || ($1 > 7 && $2 < 2))
   ;        # The Null Statement
else
   the code I really want to execute
```

The Conditional Operator

`gawk` has one operator that actually has three parameters: the conditional operator. This operator allows you to apply an if-test anywhere in your code.

The general format of the conditional statement is as follows:

```
condition ? true-result : false-result
```

While this might seem like duplication of the `if` statement, it can make your code easier to read. If you have a data file that consists of an employee name and the number of sick days taken, you can use the following:

```
{ print $1, "has taken", $2, "day" $2 != 1 ? "s" : "", "of sick time" }
```

This prints `day` if the employee only took one day of sick time and prints `days` if the employee took zero or more than one day of sick time. The resulting sentence is more readable. To code the same example using an `if` statement would be more complex and look like the following:

```
if ($2 != 1)
   print $1, "has taken", $2, "days of sick time"
else
   print $1, "has taken", $2, "day of sick time"
```

Looping

By their very nature, `awk` programs are one big loop—reading each record in the input file and processing the appropriate patterns and actions. Within an action, the need for repetition often occurs. `awk` supports loops through the `do`, `for`, and `while` statements that are similar to those found in C.

As with the `if` statement, if you want to execute multiple statements within a loop, you must contain them in curly braces.

TIP

Forgetting the curly braces around multiple statements is a common programming error with conditional and looping statements.

The do Statement

The `do` statement (sometimes referred to as the `do while` statement) provides a looping construct that will be executed at least once. The condition or test occurs after the contents of the loop have been executed.

The `do` statement takes the following form:

```
do
   statement
while (condition)
```

`statement` can be one statement or multiple statements enclosed in curly braces. *`condition`* is any valid test like those used with the `if` statement or the pattern used to trigger actions.

In general, you must change the value of the variable in the condition within the loop. If you don't, you will have a loop forever condition because the test result (*`condition`*) would never change (and become false).

Loop Control

You can exit a loop early if you need to (without assigning some bogus value to the variable in the condition). `awk` provides two facilities to do this: `break` and `continue`.

`break` causes the current (innermost) loop to be exited. It behaves as if the conditional test was performed immediately with a false result. None of the remaining code in the loop (after the `break` statement) executes, and the loop ends. This is useful when you need to handle some error or early end condition.

`continue` causes the current loop to return to the conditional test. None of the remaining code in the loop (after the `continue` statement) is executed, and the test is immediately executed. This is most useful when there is code you want to skip (within the loop) temporarily. The `continue` is different from the `break` because the loop is not forced to end.

The `for` Statement

The `for` statement provides a looping construct that modifies values within the loop. It is good for counting through a specific number of items.

The `for` statement has two general forms—the following

```
for (loop = 0; loop < 10; loop++)
   statement
```

and

```
for (subscript in array)
   statement
```

The first form initializes the variable (`loop = 0`), performs the test (`loop < 10`), and then performs the loop contents (*`statement`*). Then it modifies the variable (`loop++`) and tests again. As long as the test is true, *`statement`* will execute.

In the second form, *`statement`* is executed with `subscript` being set to each of the subscripts in *`array`*. This enables you to loop through an array even if you don't know the values of the subscripts. This works well for multidimension arrays.

`statement` can be one statement or multiple statements enclosed in curly braces. The condition (`loop < 10`) is any valid test like those used with the `if` statement or the pattern used to trigger actions.

In general, you don't want to change the loop control variable (`loop` or `subscript`) within the loop body. Let the `for` statement do that for you, or you might get behavior that is difficult to debug.

For the first form, the modification of the variable can be any valid operation (including calls to functions). In most cases, it is an increment or decrement.

TIP

This example showed the postfix increment. It doesn't matter whether you use the postfix (`loop++`) or prefix (`++loop`) increment—the results will be the same. Just be consistent.

The `for` loop is a good method of looping through data of an unknown size:

```
for (i=1; i<=NF; i++)
     print $i
```

Each field on the current record will be printed on its own line. As a programmer, I don't know how many fields are on a particular record when I write the code. The variable `NF` lets me know as the program runs.

The `while` Statement

The final loop structure is the `while` loop. It is the most general because it executes while the condition is true. The general form is as follows:

```
while(condition)
   statement
```

`statement` can be one statement or multiple statements enclosed in curly braces. *`condition`* is any valid test like those used with the `if` statement or the pattern used to trigger actions.

If the condition is false before the `while` is encountered, the contents of the loop will not be executed. This is different from `do`, which always executes the loop contents at least once.

In general, you must change the value of the variable in the condition within the loop. If you don't, you will have a loop forever condition because the test result (*`condition`*) would never change (and become false).

Advanced Input and Output

In addition to the simple input and output facilities provided by `awk`, there are a number of advanced features you can take advantage of for more complicated processing.

By default, `awk` automatically reads and loops through your program; you can alter this behavior. You can force input to come from a different file, cause the loop to recycle early (read the next record without performing any more actions), or even just read the next record. You can even get data from the output of other commands.

On the output side, you can format the output and send it to a file (other than the standard output device) or as input to another command.

Input

You don't have to program the normal input loop process in `awk`. It reads a record and then searches for pattern matches and the corresponding actions to execute. If there are multiple files specified on the command line, they are processed in order. It is only if you want to change this behavior that you have to do any special programming.

next and exit

The next command causes awk to read the next record and perform the pattern match and corresponding action execution immediately. Normally, it executes all your code in any actions with matching patterns. next causes any additional matching patterns to be ignored for this record.

The exit command in any action except for END behaves as if the end of file was reached. Code execution in all pattern/actions is ceased, and the actions within the END pattern are executed. exit appearing in the END pattern is a special case—it causes the program to end.

getline

The getline statement is used to explicitly read a record. This is especially useful if you have a data record that looks like two physical records. It performs the normal field splitting (setting $0, the field variables, FNR, NF, and NR). It returns the value 1 if the read was successful and zero if it failed (end of file was reached). If you want to explicitly read through a file, you can code something like the following:

```
{ while (getline == 1)
  {
      # process the inputted fields
  }
}
```

You can also have getline store the input data in a field instead of taking advantage of the normal field processing by using the form getline *variable*. When used this way, NF is set to zero, and FNR and NR are incremented.

Input from a file

You can use getline to input data from a specific file instead of the ones listed on the command line. The general form is getline < "*filename*". When coded this way, getline performs the normal field splitting (setting $0, the field variables, and NF). If the file doesn't exist, getline returns -1; it returns 1 on success and 0 on failure.

You can read the data from the specified file into a variable. You can also replace *filename* with stdin or a variable that contains the filename.

> **NOTE**
>
> If you use getline < "filename" to read data into your program, neither FNR nor NR is changed.

Input from a Command

Another way of using the getline statement is to accept input from a UNIX command. If you want to perform some processing for each person signed on the system (send him or her a message, for instance), you can code something like the following:

```
{ while ("who -u" | getline)
  {
      # process each line from the who command
    }
}
```

The `who` command is executed once and each of its output lines is processed by `getline`. You could also use the form `"command" | getline variable`.

Ending Input from a File or Command

Whenever you use `getline` to get input from a specified file or command, you should close it when you are done processing the data. There is a maximum number of open files allowed to `awk` that varies with operating system version or individual account configuration (a command output pipe counts as a file). By closing files when you are done with them, you reduce the chances of hitting the limit.

The syntax to close a file is simply

```
close ("filename")
```

where *`filename`* is the one specified on the `getline` (which could also be `stdin`, a variable that contains the filename, or the exact command used with `getline`).

Output

There are a few advanced features for output: pretty formatting, sending output to files, and piping output as input to other commands. The `printf` command is used for pretty formatting—instead of seeing the output in whatever default format `awk` decides to use (which is often ugly), you can specify how it looks.

printf

The `print` statement produces simple output for you. If you want to be able to format the data (producing fixed columns, for instance), you need to use `printf`. The nice thing about `awk printf` is that it uses syntax that is very similar to the `printf()` function in C.

The general format of the `awk printf` is as follows (the parentheses are only required if a relational expression is included):

```
printf format-specifier, variable1,variable2, variable3,..variablen
printf(format-specifier, variable1,variable2, variable3,..variablen)
```

Personally, I use the second form because I am so used to coding in C.

The variables are optional, but *`format-specifier`* is mandatory. Often you will have `printf` statements that only include *`format-specifier`* (to print messages that contain no variables):

```
printf ("Program Starting\n")
printf ("\f")        # new page in output
```

`format-specifier` can consist of text, escaped characters, or actual print specifiers. A print specifier begins with the percent sign (`%`), followed by an optional numeric value that specifies the

27
GAWK PROGRAMMING

size of the field, then the format type follows (which describes the type of variable or output format). If you want to print a percent sign in your output, you use `%%`.

The field size can consist of two numbers separated by a decimal point (.). For floating-point numbers, the first number is the size of the entire field (including the decimal point); the second number is the number of digits to the right of the decimal. For other types of fields, the first number is the minimum field size and the second number is the maximum field size (number of characters to actually print); if you omit the first number, it takes the value of the maximum field size.

The print specifiers determine how the variable is printed; there are also modifiers that change the behavior of the specifiers. Table 27.9 shows the print format specifiers.

Table 27.9. Format specifiers for awk.

Format	*Meaning*
`%c`	ASCII character
`%d`	An integer (decimal number)
`%i`	An integer, just like `%d`
`%e`	A floating-point number using scientific notation (1.00000E+01)
`%f`	A floating-point number (10.43)
`%g`	`awk` chooses between `%e` or `%f` display format (whichever is shorter) suppressing nonsignificant zeros.
`%o`	An unsigned octal (base 8) number (integer)
`%s`	A string of characters
`%x`	An unsigned hexadecimal (base 16) number (integer)
`%X`	Same as `%x` but using ABCDEF instead of abcdef

NOTE

If you attempt to print a numeric value or variable using `%c`, it will be printed as a character (the ASCII character for that value will print).

The format modifiers change the default behavior of the format specifiers. Listing 27.4 shows the use of various specifiers and modifiers.

Listing 27.4. `printf` format specifiers and modifiers.

```
printf("%d %3.3d %03.3d %.3d %-.3d %3d %-3d\n", 64, 64, 64, 64, 64, 64, 64)
printf("%c %c %2.2c %-2.2c %2c %-2c\n", 64, "abc", "abc", "abc", "abc", "abc")
printf("%s %2s %-2s %2.2s %-2.2s %.2s %-.2s\n",
       "abc", "abc", "abc", "abc", "abc", "abc", "abc")
printf("%f %6.1f %06.1f %.1f %-.1f %6f\n",
       123.456, 123.456, 123.456, 123.456, 123.456, 123.456)

64 064 064 064 064  64 64
@ a  a a   a a
abc abc abc ab ab ab ab
123.456000  123.5 0123.5 123.5 123.5 123.456000
```


When using the integer or decimal (`%d`) specifier, the field size defaults to the size of the value being printed (2 digits for the value `64`). If you specify a field maximum size that is larger than that, you automatically get the field zero filled. All numeric fields are right-justified unless you use the minus sign (`-`) modifier, which causes them to be left-justified. If you specify only the field minimum size and want the rest of the field zero filled, you have to use the zero modifier (before the field minimum size).

When using the character (`%c`) specifier, only one character prints from the input no matter what size you use for the field minimum or maximum sizes and no matter how many characters are in the value being printed. Note that the value `64` printed as a character shows up as `@`.

When using the string (`%s`) specifier, the entire string prints unless you specify the field maximum size. By default, strings are left-justified unless you use the minus sign (`-`) modifier, which causes them to be right-justified.

When using the floating (`%f`) specifier, the field size defaults `.6` (as many digits to the left of the decimal and 6 digits to the right). If you specify a number after the decimal in the format, that many digits will print to the right of the decimal and `awk` will round the number. All numeric fields are right-justified unless you use the minus sign (`-`) modifier, which causes them to be left-justified. If you want the field zero filled, you have to use the zero modifier (before the field minimum size).

The best way to determine printing results is to work with it. Try out the various modifiers and see what makes your output look best.

Output to a File

You can send your output (from `print` or `printf`) to a file. The following creates a new (or empties out an existing) file containing the printed message:

```
printf ("hello world\n") > "datafile"
```

If you execute this statement multiple times or other statements that redirect output to *datafile*, the output will remain in the file. The file creation/emptying out only occurs the first time the file is used in the program.

To append data to an existing file, you use the following:

```
printf ("hello world\n") >> "datafile"
```

Output to a Command

In addition to redirecting your output to a file, you can send the output from your program to act as input for another command. You can code something like the following:

```
printf ("hello world\n") ¦ "sort -t`,`"
```

Any other output statements that pipe data into the same command will specify exactly the same command after the pipe character (¦) because that is how `awk` keeps track of which command is receiving which output from your program.

Closing an Output File or Pipe

Whenever you send output to a file or pipe, you should close it when you are done processing the data. There is a maximum number of open files allowed to `awk` that varies with operating system version or individual account configuration (a pipe counts as a file). By closing files when you are done with them, you reduce the chances of hitting the limit.

The syntax to close a file is simply

```
close ("filename")
```

where *`filename`* is the one specified on the output statement (which can also be `stdout`, a variable that contains the filename, or the exact command used with a pipe).

Functions

In addition to the built-in functions (like `gsub` or `srand`), `gawk` allows you to write your own. User-defined functions are a means of creating a block of code that is accessed in multiple places in your code. They can also be used to build a library of commonly used routines so you do not have to recode the same algorithms repeatedly.

User-defined functions are not a part of the original `awk`—they were added to `nawk` and are supported by `gawk`.

There are two parts to using a function: the definition and the call. The function definition contains the code to be executed (the function itself) and the call temporarily transfers from the main code to the function. There are two ways that command execution is transferred back to the main code: implicit and explicit returns. When `gawk` reaches the end of a function (the close curly brace [}]), it automatically (implicitly) returns control to the calling routine. If you want to leave your function before the bottom, you can explicitly use the return statement to exit early.

Function Definition

The general form of a gawk function definition looks like the following:

```
function functionname(parameter list) {
     the function body
}
```

You code your function just as if it were any other set of action statements and can place it anywhere you would put a pattern/action set. If you think about it, the `function functionname(parameter list)` portion of the definition could be considered a pattern and *the function body* the action.

NOTE

gawk supports another form of function definition where the `function` keyword is abbreviated to `func`. The remaining syntax is the same:

```
func functionname(parameter list) {
     the function body
}
```

Listing 27.5 shows the defining and calling of a function.

Listing 27.5. Defining and calling functions.

```
BEGIN { print_header() }

function print_header( ) {
   printf("This is the header\n");
   printf("this is a second line of the header\n");
}

This is the header
this is a second line of the header
```

The code inside the function is executed only once—when the function is called from within the `BEGIN` action. This function uses the implicit return method.

CAUTION

When working with user-defined functions, you must place the parentheses that contain the parameter list immediately after the function name when calling that function. When you use the built-in functions, this is not a requirement.

Function Parameters

Like C, gawk passes parameters to functions by value. In other words, a copy of the original value is made and that copy is passed to the called function. The original is untouched, even if the function changes the value.

Any parameters are listed in the function definition separated by commas. If you have no parameters, you can leave the parameter list (contained in the parentheses) empty.

Listing 27.6 is an expanded version of Listing 27.5; it shows the pass-by-value nature of gawk function parameters.

Listing 27.6. Passing parameters.

```
BEGIN { pageno = 0;
        print_header(pageno);
        printf("the page number is now %d\n", pageno);
}

function print_header(page ) {
   page++;
   printf("This is the header for page %d\n", page);
   printf("this is a second line of the header\n");
}

This is the header for page 1
this is a second line of the header
the page number is now 0
```

The page number is initialized before the first call to the print_header function and incremented in the function. But when it is printed after the function call, it remains at the original value.

CAUTION

gawk does not perform parameter validation. When you call a function, you can list more or fewer parameters than the function expects. Any extra parameters are ignored, and any missing ones default to zero or empty strings (depending on how they are used).

TIP

You can take advantage of the lack of function parameter validation. It can be used to create local variables within the called function—just list more variables in the function definition than you use in the function call. I strongly suggest that you comment the fact that the extra parameters are really being used as local variables.

There are several ways that a called function can change variables in the calling routines—through explicit return or by using the variables in the calling routine directly. (These variables are normally global anyway.)

The `return` Statement (Explicit Return)

If you want to return a value or leave a function early, you need to code a `return` statement. If you don't code one, the function will end with the close curly brace (`}`). Personally, I prefer to code them at the bottom.

If the calling code expects a returned value from your function, you must code the `return` statement in the following form:

```
return variable
```

Expanding on Listing 27.6 to let the function change the page number, Listing 27.7 shows the use of the `return` statement.

Listing 27.7. Returning values.

```
BEGIN { pageno = 0;
        pageno = print_header(pageno);
        printf("the page number is now %d\n", pageno);
}

function print_header(page ) {
   page++;
   printf("This is the header for page %d\n", page);
   printf("this is a second line of the header\n");
   return page;
}

This is the header for page 1
this is a second line of the header
the page number is now 1
```

The updated page number is returned to the code that called the function.

> **NOTE**
>
> The `return` statement allows you to return only one value back to the calling routine.

Writing Reports

Generating a report in `awk` entails a sequence of steps, with each step producing the input for the next step. Report writing is usually a three-step process: Pick the data, sort the data, and make the output pretty.

Complex Reports

Using awk, it is possible to quickly create complex reports. It is much easier to perform string comparisons, build arrays on-the-fly, and take advantage of associative arrays than to code in another language (like C). Instead of having to search through an array for a match with a text key, that key can be used as the array subscript.

I have produced reports using awk with three levels of control breaks, multiple sections of reports in the same control break, and multiple totaling pages. The totaling pages were for each level of control break plus a final page; if the control break didn't have a particular type of data, then the total page didn't have it either. If there was only one member of a control break, then the total page for that level wasn't created. (This saved a lot of paper when there was really only one level of control break—the highest.)

This report ended up being more than 1,000 lines of awk (nawk to be specific) code. It takes a little longer to run than the equivalent C program, but it took a lot less programmer time to create. Because it was easy to create and modify, it was developed using prototypes. The users briefly described what they wanted, and I produced a report. They decided they needed more control breaks, and I added them; then they realized a lot of paper was wasted on total pages, so the report was modified as described.

Being easy to develop incrementally without knowing the final result made it easier and more fun for me. By my being responsive to user changes, the users were made happy!

Extracting Data

As mentioned early in this chapter, many systems don't produce data in the desired format. When working with data stored in relational databases, there are two main ways to get data out: Use a query tool with SQL or write a program to get the data from the database and output it in the desired form. SQL query tools have limited formatting ability but can provide quick and easy access to the data.

One technique I have found very useful is to extract the data from the database into a file that is then manipulated by an awk script to produce the exact format required. When required, an awk script can even create the SQL statements used to query the database (specifying the key values for the rows to select).

The following example is used when the query tool places a space before a numeric field that must be removed for program that will use the data in another system (mainframe COBOL):

```
{   printf("%s%s%-25.25s\n", $1, $2, $3);    }
```

awk automatically removes the field separator (the space character) when splitting the input record into individual fields, and the formatting %s string format specifiers in printf are contiguous (do not have any spaces between them).

Commands On-the-Fly

The ability to pipe the output of a command into another is very powerful because the output from the first becomes the input that the second can manipulate. A frequent use of one-line awk programs is the creation of commands based on a list.

The find command can be used to produce a list of files that match its conditions, or it can execute a single command that takes a single command-line argument. You can see files in a directory (and subdirectories) that match specific conditions with the following:

```
$ find . -name "*.prn" -print
```

This outputs

```
./exam2.prn
./exam1.prn
./exam3.prn
```

Or you can print the contents of those files with the following:

```
find . -name "*.prn" -exec lp {} \;
```

The find command inserts the individual filenames that it locates in place of the {} and executes the lp command. But if you wanted to execute a command that required two arguments (to copy files to a new name) or execute multiple commands at once, you couldn't do it with find alone. You could create a shell script that would accept the single argument and use it in multiple places, or you could create an awk single-line program:

```
$ find . -name "*.prn" -print ¦ awk '{print "echo bak" $1;
➥print "cp " $1 " " $1".bak";}'
```

This outputs

```
echo bak./exam2.prn
cp ./exam2.prn ./exam2.prn.bak
echo bak./exam1.prn
cp ./exam1.prn ./exam1.prn.bak
echo bak./exam3.prn
cp ./exam3.prn ./exam3.prn.bak
```

To get the commands to actually execute, you need to pipe the commands into one of the shells. The following example uses the Korn shell; you can use the one you prefer:

```
$ find . -name "*.prn" -print ¦
     awk '{print "echo bak" $1; print "cp " $1 " " $1".bak";}' ¦
     ksh
```

This outputs

```
bak./exam2.prn
bak./exam1.prn
bak./exam3.prn
```

Before each copy takes place, the message is shown. This is also handy if you want to search for a string (using the `grep` command) in the files of multiple subdirectories. Many versions of the `grep` command don't show the name of the file searched unless you use wildcards (or specify multiple filenames on the command line). The following uses `find` to search for C source files, `awk` to create `grep` commands to look for an error message, and the shell `echo` command to show the file being searched:

```
$ find . -name "*.c" -print ¦
     awk '{print "echo " $1; print "grep error-message " $1;}' ¦
     ksh
```

The same technique can be used to perform `lint` checks on source code in a series of subdirectories. I execute the following in a shell script periodically to check all C code:

```
$ find . -name "*.c" -print ¦
     awk '{print "lint " $1 " > " $1".lint"}' ¦
     ksh
```

The `lint` version on one system prints the code error as a heading line and then the parts of code in question as a list below. `grep` shows the heading but not the detail lines. The `awk` script prints all lines from the heading until the first blank line (end of the `lint` section).

When in doubt, pipe the output into `more` or `pg` to view the created commands before you pipe them into a shell for execution.

One Last Built-in Function: `system`

There is one more built-in function that doesn't fit in the character or numeric categories: `system`. The `system` function executes the string passed to it as an argument. This allows you to execute commands or scripts on-the-fly when your `awk` code has the need.

You can code a report to automatically print to paper when it is complete. The code looks something like Listing 27.8.

Listing 27.8. Using the `system` function.

```
BEGIN { pageno = 0;
        pageno = print_header(pageno);
        printf("the page number is now %d\n", pageno);
}

# The production of the report would be coded here

END { close ("report.txt");
      system ("lpr -Pmyprinter report.txt");
}

function print_header(page ) {
   page++;
   printf("This is the header for page %d\n", page) > "report.txt";
```

```
   printf("this is a second line of the header\n")  > "report.txt";
}

This is the header for page 1
this is a second line of the header
the page number is now 0
```

The output is the same as that of Listing 27.6 except that the output shows up on the printer instead of the screen. Before printing the file, you have to close it.

Summary

This chapter provides you an introduction to the awk programming language and the GNU awk: gawk. It is a very powerful and useful language that enables you to search for data, extract data from files, create commands on-the-fly, or even create entire programs.

It is very useful as a prototyping language—you can create reports very quickly. After showing them to the user, changes can be made quickly also. Although it is less efficient than the comparable program written in C, it is not so inefficient that you cannot create production programs. If efficiency is a concern with an awk program, it can be converted into C.

For further information, see the following:

> Aho, Alfred V., Brian W. Kernighan and Peter J. Weinberger. *The* awk *Programming Language*. Reading, Mass.: Addison-Wesley, 1988 (copyright AT&T Bell Lab).
>
> See also the man pages for gawk on your system.
>
> GNU awk, gawk, is available on this book's CD-ROM.

Network Programming

by Eric Goebelbecker

IN THIS CHAPTER

"The computer industry has become firmly and irrevocably centered around the network during the past five years or so."

The preceding statement, and several thousand variations on it, has served as the opening for probably tens of thousands magazine articles, editorials, and book chapters since 1995. The subject less frequently used as a topic is this: How are the applications that utilize these networks written? How do computers actually communicate over a network?

Networking and Linux are a natural combination. After all, Linux is a product of the Internet itself because most of the developers collaborated (and still do collaborate) across the world over e-mail, the World Wide Web, and Usenet news. In addition, Linux is based on UNIX, one of the operating systems that many common computer networking technologies were developed on.

Linux is an excellent platform for networking programming because it has mature and full functional networking features. Because Linux provides full support for the sockets interface, most programs developed on other version of UNIX will build and run on Linux with little or no modifications. Textbooks and documentation about UNIX networking are fully applicable to Linux also.

This chapter uses Perl examples to introduce network programming concepts and shows how to create functioning network programs for Linux quickly and easily. Perl was selected because it enables you to focus on network programming concepts instead of application development issues and programming environments. The scripts referred to in the tutorials are also included on the CD-ROM that accompanies this book. Note that when these scripts were developed, the emphasis was on illustrating key network programming concepts, not programming style, robustness, or how to program in Perl. Only basic knowledge of Perl is required to understand the examples, and they are certainly clear enough for C or C++ programmers to follow. For detailed information on the Perl language and how to use it for a wide variety of tasks, see Chapter 24, "Perl Programming."

This chapter is by no means exhaustive because the time and space allotted doesn't allow for coverage of concepts such as protocol layering and routing. This chapter is intended to serve as an introductory tutorial to network programming, with an emphasis on hands-on exercises.

Networking Concepts

This section covers the fundamentals of networking. You will learn what the necessary components of network communication are and how a program uses them to build a connection by following a simple program that retrieves networking information and uses it to connect to another program. By the end of this section, you should have a good understanding of network addresses, sockets, and the differences between TCP (Transmission Control Protocol) and its counterpart UDP (User Datagram Protocol).

Listing 28.1 contains a Perl function that creates a connection to a server using TCP. You can find this function in `network.pl` on the CD-ROM.

Listing 28.1. `makeconn()`—creating a TCP connection.

```
 1: sub makeconn {
 2:
 3:     my ($host, $portname, $server, $port, $proto, $servaddr);
 4:
 5:     $host = $_[0];
 6:     $portname = $_[1];
 7:
 8:      #
 9:      # Server hostname, port and protocol
10:      #
11:     $server = gethostbyname($host) or
12:         die "gethostbyname: cannot locate host: $!";
13:     $port = getservbyname($portname, 'tcp') or
14:         die "getservbyname: cannot get port : $!";
15:     $proto = getprotobyname('tcp') or
16:         die "getprotobyname: cannot get proto : $!";
17:
18:      #
19:      # Build an inet address
20:      #
21:    $servaddr = sockaddr_in($port, $server);
22:
23:
24:      #
25:      # Create the socket and connect it
26:      #
27:    socket(CONNFD, PF_INET, SOCK_STREAM, $proto);
28:    connect(CONNFD, $servaddr) or die "connect : $!";
29:
30:    return CONNFD;
31: }
```


I can summarize this procedure in three essential steps:

1. Build an address.
2. Create a socket.
3. Establish a connection.

The network address is built by retrieving address information in lines 11 and 13, and then assembling it in line 21. In line 27, you create the socket, using protocol information retrieved in line 15. (The protocol information, however, can actually be considered part of the address as you'll see.) In line 28, you finally establish the connection.

Building Network Addresses

The steps involved in building a network address and connecting to it provide a framework for observing how network communication works. I'll spend some time covering each part of this process in order to better prepare you for the hands-on tutorials.

If you've ever configured a PC or workstation for Internet connectivity, you have probably seen an *Internet address* (or *IP address*) similar to `192.9.200.10` or `10.7.8.14`. This is called *dotted-decimal format* and, like many things in computing, is a representation of network addresses that are intended to make things easier for humans to read. The notation that computers, routers, and other internet devices actually use to communicate is a 32-bit number, often called a *canonical address*. When this number is evaluated, it is broken down into four smaller 8-bit (one byte) values, much the way the dotted-decimal format consists of four numbers separated by decimals.

An *internetwork*, or *internet* for short, consists of two or more networks that are connected. In this case, the word *internet* refers to any two networks, not the *Internet*, which has become a proper name for the network that encompasses most of the world. The *Internet Protocol* (IP) was designed with this sort of topography in mind. In order for an internet address to be useful, it has to be capable of identifying not only a specific node (computer), but also which network it resides on. Both bits of information are provided in the 32-bit address. Which portion of the address is related to each component is decided by the *netmask* that is applied to the address. Depending on an organizations needs, a network architect can decide to have more networks or more addresses. For details on *subnetting* networks, see Chapter 13, "TCP/IP Network Management." For the sake of network programming, it's sufficient to know the information stored in an internet address and that individual workstation netmasks have to be correct in order for a message to be successfully delivered.

Dotted-decimal format is easier to read than 32-bit values (especially because many of the possible values can't be printed or would work out to some pretty ponderous numbers), but most people would rather use names than numbers because `gandalf` or `www.yahoo.com` is a lot easier to remember than `12.156.27.4` or `182.250.2.178`. For this reason, the notion of hostnames, domain names, and the domain name system were devised. You can get access to a database of name-to-number mappings through a set of *network library functions*, which provide host (node) information in response to names or numbers. For example, in line 11 of Listing 28.1, you retrieve the address associated with a name with one of these functions, `gethostbyname()`.

Depending on the host configuration, `gethostbyname()` can retrieve the address associated with a name from a file, `/etc/hosts`, from the Domain Name System (DNS) or from the Network Information System (NIS or Yellow Pages). DNS and NIS are network-wide services that administrators use to implify network configuration because adding and updating network address numbers from a central location (and maybe a backup location) is obviously a lot easier than updating files on every workstation in their organization. These systems are also useful for internetworks because the address of a remote host can be determined when it is needed by making a DNS request, rather than needing to exchange configuration files in advance.

One other advantage of using names is that the address that a name is associated with can be changed without affecting applications because the application need only know the name; the address can be discovered at runtime.

To illustrate the use of the `gethostbyname()` function and the difference between dotted-decimal formatted addresses and canonical addresses, try the script in Listing 28.2, called `resolv` on the CD-ROM.

Listing 28.2. resolv.

```
1#!/bin/perl
2 use Socket;
3  $addr = gethostbyname($ARGV[0]);
4  $dotfmt = inet_ntoa($addr);
5  print "$ARGV[0]: numeric: $addr dotted: $dotfmt\n";
```

Line 2 includes the `Socket` module included with Perl 5 distributions. This module is required for all the sample code included in this chapter, including Listing 28.1.

When you run this program, passing it a hostname that you want to see information on, you see something like the following:

```
$ ./resolv www.redhat.com
www.redhat.com: numeric: [unprintable characters] dotted: 199.183.24.253
```

Line 3 passes the name specified on the command line to `gethostbyname()`, which places the canonical address in `$addr`. This address is then passed to `inet_ntoa()`, which returns the same address in dotted-decimal format. (`inet_ntoa` is an abbreviation for internet number to ASCII.) You then print both values out in line 5. As you can see, the 32-bit address looks rather strange when printed.

NOTE

If your Linux workstation is not connected to the Internet, simply specify your own hostname to resolve or another hostname that is in your own `/etc/hosts` file or available to your workstation via DNS or NIS.

If your workstation is on the Internet and you see a different address for `www.redhat.com`, it just means that it has changed—after all, that is one of the reasons that DNS was developed!

Network Services

Being able to locate a computer is a fundamental part of network communication, but it is not the only necessary component in an address. Why do you want to contact a specific host? Do you want to retrieve an HTML document from it? Do you want to log in and check mail? Most workstations, especially those running Linux or any other version of UNIX, provide more than one service to other nodes on a network.

Back in line 13 of Listing 28.1, you called the `getservbyname()` function. This function provides the other value used to form the complete network address. This value, referred to as a *service port number*, is the portion of the address that specifies the service or program that you want to communicate with.

Like host addresses, service ports can be referred to by name instead of number. `getservbyname()` retrieves the number associated with the name specified from the file `/etc/services`. (If NIS is available, the number can also be retrieved from a network database.) Port numbers that are listed in this database are called *well-known ports* because, in theory, any host can connect to one of these services on any other because the numbers at least *ought* to remain consistent. The port numbers that are used by applications don't have to be listed in or retrieved from this database; it's just considered a good idea to list them in `/etc/services` and share them in order to prevent conflicts.

After you have retrieved the two components necessary to build a fully qualified address, you provide them to the `sockaddr_in` function, which builds a `SOCKADDR_IN` structure for us. `SOCKADDR_IN` is the programmatic representation of a network address needed for most socket system calls.

Sockets

Before you can use your addressing information, you need a socket. The `socket()` function in line 27 of Listing 28.1 illustrates how to create one. Some explanation of what sockets are and the types available to a program first will help explain the function.

Sockets are an Application Programming Interface (API) used for network communication. This API was first available with BSD UNIX for the VAX architecture in the early eighties, but has become prevalent in almost all UNIX versions and recently on Windows, along with a variety of other operating systems. System V UNIX has a different interface called the Transport Layer Interface (TLI), but even most system V UNIX versions, such as Solaris 2.*x*, provide socket interfaces. Linux provides a full implementation of the socket interface.

Socket applications treat network connections, or to be more exact, network *endpoints*, the same way most UNIX interfaces are handled—as file handles. The reason for the endpoint qualification is simple: Not all network sessions are connected, and referring to all network streams as connections can be incorrect and misleading. As a matter of fact, after a network endpoint is created and bound and/or connected, it can be written to, read from, and destroyed using the same functions as files. Because of this interface, socket programs tend to be portable between different versions of UNIX and frequently many other operating systems.

Protocols and Socket Types

The socket API is designed to support multiple protocols, called *domains* or *families*. Most UNIX versions support at least two domains: UNIX and Internet. (Two of the other domains are the Xerox Network system and ISO protocol suite.) UNIX domain sockets use the local workstation filesystem to provide communication between programs running on the same workstation only. Internet domain sockets use the Internet Protocol (IP) suite to communicate over the network. As you might guess, you will be concerned with Internet domain sockets.

In the following call to socket(), you specify the scalar variable that you want to have the socket descriptor stored in and three values that describe the type of socket you want to have created—the protocol family, the socket type, and the protocol. I've already covered which protocol family you will use, which is PF_INET, for the Internet.

```
socket(CONNFD, PF_INET, SOCK_STREAM, $proto);
```

The possible socket types are SOCK_STREAM, SOCK_DGRAM, SOCK_RAW, SOCK_RDM, and SOCK_SEQPACKET. The last three are used for low level, advanced operations and are beyond the scope of this chapter.

SOCK_STREAM sockets are connected at both ends, they are reliable, and the messages between them are sequenced. The terms *reliable* and *sequenced* have special meanings in networking. Reliability refers to the fact that the network guarantees delivery: An application can write a packet with the understanding that it will arrive at the other end, unless the connection is suddenly broken by a catastrophic event, such as a host unexpectedly shutting down or the network literally breaking. In the event that the connection is broken, the application will receive timely notification. Sequencing means that all messages are always delivered to the other application in the order that they are sent.

SOCK_DGRAM sockets support connectionless and unreliable datagrams. A *datagram* is typically a fixed-length small message. Applications have no guarantees that datagrams will be delivered, and if they are, in what order. On the surface, it seems that no application would ever want to use SOCK_DGRAM, but as you will see, many applications do for good reasons.

The type of socket is very closely related to the protocol that is used. In the case of the Internet suite, SOCK_STREAM sockets always implement *TCP*, and SOCK_DGRAM sockets implement *UDP*.

The characteristics of the TCP protocol match the characteristics of SOCK_STREAM. TCP packets are guaranteed to be delivered barring a network disaster, such as the workstation on the other end of the connection dropping out, or the network itself suffering a serious, unrecoverable outage. Packets are always delivered in the same order that they are written. Obviously, these properties make the job of a network developer easy because a message can be written and essentially forgotten about, but there is a cost. TCP messages are much more expensive (demanding) than UDP messages in terms of both network and computing resources. The workstations at both ends of a session have to confirm that they have received the correct information, which results in more work for the operating system and more network traffic. The systems also have to track the order in which messages were sent, and quite possibly have to store messages until others arrive, depending on the state of the network "terrain" between the two workstations. (New messages can arrive while others are being retransmitted because of an error.) In addition, the fact that TCP connections are just that, connections, has a price. Every conversation has an endpoint associated with it, so a server that has more than one client has to arbitrate between multiple sockets, which can be very difficult. (See the section "I/O Multiplexing with TCP," later in this chapter, for details.)

UDP, like SOCK_DGRAM, is connectionless and unreliable. Applications have to provide whatever reliability mechanisms are necessary for the job that they are performing. For some applications, that is an advantage because all the mechanisms provided by TCP aren't always needed. For example, DNS, which uses UDP, simply sends a message and waits for a response for a predetermined interval; because DNS is a one-to-one message-to-response protocol, sequencing between client and server is not necessary. UDP is connectionless, so a server can use one socket to communicate with many clients. All clients write to the same address for the server, and the server responds individually by writing to specific client addresses.

UDP messages can also be broadcast to entire networks, which is a blessing to the application that needs to communicate one message to many users, but a curse for the workstations that don't need the message but have to read it in order to figure out that it isn't for them. The ability to broadcast messages over UDP and the fact that the connectionless aspect of UDP makes it difficult to verify the source of messages are two of the reasons why many networking people consider the protocol to be a security risk and dislike even enabling it within their organizations.

Making a Connection

Logically, if you are creating a connection like that of the makeconn() function in Listing 28.1, you need to create a SOCK_STREAM socket with the TCP protocol information retrieved with getprotobyname() in line 15. Take a look at lines 27 and 28 from Listing 28.1, repeated here:

```
27:  socket(CONNFD, PF_INET, SOCK_STREAM, $proto);
28:  connect(CONNFD, $servaddr) or die "connect : $!";
```

After creating the socket in line 27, you then pass it to connect() with the address structure created by sockaddr_in(). The connect() function actually contacts the address specified in the structure and establishes the virtual circuit supported by TCP.

A TCP Client Example

Listing 28.3 puts makeconn() to work in a sample program. client1 can be found on the book's CD-ROM.

Listing 28.3. client1.

```
#!/usr/bin/perl
use Socket;
require "./network.pl";

$NETFD = makeconn($ARGV[0], $ARGV[1]);

#
# Get the message
#
sysread $NETFD, $message, 32768 or die "error getting message : $!";
print "$message \n";
close $NETFD;
```

Run this program with two command-line arguments, the name of a Linux host that is running `sendmail` and the mail port name, `smtp`:

```
$ ./client1 iest smtp
220 iest.home.mxn.com ESMTP Sendmail 8.8.5/8.8.5; Sat, 4 Oct 1997 18:25:08 -0400
```

This program uses `makeconn()` to connect to the `sendmail` program running on the named host and reads the greeting that it sends to a new client when it first connects, using the `sysread()` function.

`sysread()` is one of the functions used for extracting network messages from sockets. It is a wrapper for the UNIX `read()` system call. You cannot use the Perl `read()` function because it is designed for standard I/O, which uses buffering and other high-level features that interfere with network communications. In a real-world application, you would probably read messages with `sysread()` in and out of a buffer of your own and keep careful track of what you had just read because it is possible to be interrupted in a read call by a signal. (You would also install signal handlers.) As this example demonstrates, establishing a client connection and retrieving some data is pretty simple.

> **TIP**
>
> One of the benefits of using Perl for network programming is that it hides the issue of byte ordering between different architectures. Intel x86 chips and Sun SPARC chips, for example, represent values differently. The creators of the Internet introduced a concept of *network byte order*, which programs are supposed to place values in prior to transmission and have to translate back to their network format when they read in messages. Perl does this for us.

A TCP Server Example

Now you'll write your own server for `client1` to connect to. First, you have to place a socket in the listen state. You'll use another function that is defined in `network.pl`, `makelisten()`, which is shown in Listing 28.4.

Listing 28.4. `makelisten()`.

```
sub makelisten {

    my ($portname, $port, $proto, $servaddr);
    $portname = $_[0];

    #
    #  port and protocol
    #
    $port = getservbyname($portname, 'tcp') or
```

continues

Listing 28.4. continued

```
10:     die "getservbyname: cannot get port : $!";
11:     $proto = getprotobyname('tcp') or
12:     die "getprotobyname: cannot get proto : $!";
13:
14:     #
15:     # Bind an inet address
16:     #
17:     socket(LISTFD, PF_INET, SOCK_STREAM, $proto);
18:     bind (LISTFD, sockaddr_in($port, INADDR_ANY)) or die "bind: $!";
19:     listen (LISTFD, SOMAXCONN) or die "listen: $!";
20:     return LISTFD;
21: }
```

The `makelisten()` function creates a TCP socket, binds it to a local address, and then places it in the listen state.

Lines 9 and 11 retrieve the same information that `makeconn()` retrieves in order to create a connection, with the exception of an internet address. `makelisten()` then creates an internet family `SOCK_STREAM` socket, which by definition is a TCP socket, but you specify this explicitly anyway, as in `makeconn()`.

In line 18, the socket is bound to a local address. This tells the system that any messages sent to the specified service port and internet address should be relayed to the specified socket. You use `sockaddr_in()` to build an address from the service port retrieved with `getportbyname()` and with a special address that corresponds to all addresses on the workstation so that connections can be made to all network interfaces and even over any dial-up interfaces on the workstation. This function shows a little laziness in that it passes the `sockaddr_in()` function to `bind()` instead of calling it separately and saving the results.

There are some restrictions on what service ports can be bound. For historical reasons, only the programs executing with superuser access can bind service ports numbered lower than 1024.

After the socket is bound, you can execute `listen()`, which notifies the system that you're ready to accept client connections.

`server1`, the program that uses `makelisten()`, is just as simple as the client and is shown in Listing 28.5. You can find it on the CD-ROM that accompanies this book.

Listing 28.5. `server1`.

```
#!/usr/bin/perl
  use Socket;
  require "./network.pl";

  $hello = "Hello world!";

  $LISTFD = makelisten("test");
```

```
  LOOP: while (1) {
    unless ($paddr = accept(NEWFD, $LISTFD)) {
    next LOOP;
    }
    syswrite(NEWFD, $hello, length($hello));
    close NEWFD;
}
```

In Listing 28.5, you simply place a socket in the listen state using `makelisten()` and then enter a `while` loop that centers on the function `accept()`. The purpose of `accept()` is exactly as it sounds: It accepts client connections. You pass two arguments to `accept()`: a new variable (`NEWFD`) that will contain the socket identifier for the accepted connection and the socket (`$LISTFD`) that has been set up with `listen()`.

Whenever `accept()` returns a connection, you write a string to the new socket and immediately close it.

Before you can test your server, you need to add the entry for the test service that it uses. Add the following three lines to the `/etc/services` file. You will have to be root in order to edit this file.

```
test            8000/tcp
test            8000/udp
test1           8001/udp
```

You have added three entries for your test programs, one for TCP and two others for UDP that you will use later.

Now to test your server, you need to execute the following commands:

```
$ ./server1&
$./client1 iest test
Hello world!
```

`iest` is the hostname of your workstation. The server writes back your greeting and exits. Because the server is executing inside a `while` loop, you can run `./client1` repeatedly. When the test is finished, use `kill` to stop the server:

```
$ ps ax¦ grep server1 ¦ awk '{ print $1 }'
pid
$ kill pid
```

A UDP Example

In order to implement the same test in UDP, you have to set up a `SOCK_DGRAM` socket for both a client and a server. This function, `makeudpcli()`, can also be found in `network.pl` and is shown in Listing 28.6.

Listing 28.6. makeudpcli().

```
sub makeudpcli {

    my ($proto, $servaddr);

    $proto = getprotobyname('udp') or
    die "getprotobyname: cannot get proto : $!";

    #
    # Bind a UDP port
    #
    socket(DGFD, PF_INET, SOCK_DGRAM, $proto);
    bind (DGFD,  sockaddr_in(0, INADDR_ANY)) or die "bind: $!";

    return DGFD;
}
```

In Listing 28.6, you retrieve the protocol information for UDP and then create a `SOCK_DGRAM` socket. You then bind it, but you tell the system to go ahead and bind to any address and any service port; in other words, you want the socket named but don't care what that name is.

The reason for this extra `bind()` is quite straightforward. Because UDP is connectionless, special attention has to be made to addresses when sending and receiving datagrams. When datagram messages are read, the reader also receives the address of the originator so that it knows where to send any replies. If you want to receive replies to your messages, you need to guarantee that they come from a unique address. The call to `bind()` ensures that the system allocates a unique address for you.

Now that you have created a datagram socket, you can communicate with a server, using the program in Listing 28.7, `client2`, which can be found on the CD-ROM.

Listing 28.7. client2.

```
#!/usr/bin/perl

use Socket;
require "./network.pl";

$poke = "yo!";

 $NETFD = makeudpcli();

#
# Work out server address
#
 $addr = gethostbyname($ARGV[0]);
 $port = getservbyname($ARGV[1], 'udp');

 $servaddr = sockaddr_in($port, $addr);

#
# Poke the server
#
```

```
21:  send $NETFD, $poke, 0, $servaddr;
22:
23: #
24: # Recv the reply
25: #
26:  recv $NETFD, $message, 32768, 0 or die "error getting message : $!";
27:  print "$message \n";
28:  close $NETFD;
```

After you create the socket, you still have to resolve the server address, but instead of providing this address to the `connect()` function, you have to provide it to the `send()` function in line 21 so it knows where to, well, send the message. But why are you sending anything to the server at all? After all, in the TCP example in Listing 28.3, the communication is one way.

In the TCP example, the server sends a message as soon as you connect and then closes the session. The act of connecting is in effect a message from the client to the server. Because UDP lacks connections, you have to use a message from the client as a trigger for the conversation.

The server creates a UDP socket in a slightly different manner because it needs to bind a well-known port. It uses `getservbyname()` to retrieve a port number and specifies it as part of the call to `bind()`. Look at `makeudpserv()` in `network.pl` for details.

The server's main loop is actually pretty close to that of the TCP server and is shown in Listing 28.8.

Listing 28.8. server2.

```
#!/usr/bin/perl
#
#
use Socket;
require "./network.pl";

$hello = "Hello world!";

$LISTFD = makeudpserv("test");

while (1) {
    $cliaddr = recv $LISTFD, $message, 32768, 0;
    print "Received $message from client\n";
    send $LISTFD, $hello, 0, $cliaddr;
}
```

Instead of waiting for a client by looping on the `accept()` function, the server loops on the `recv()` function. There is also no new socket to close after the reply is sent to the client.

When these programs are run, you see the following:

```
$ ./server2&
$./client2 iest test
Received yo! from client
Hello world!
```

So you see that from a programmer's standpoint, the differences between UDP and TCP affect not only the socket functions you use and how you use them, but also how you design your programs. Differences such as the lack of a connection and the lack of built-in reliability mechanisms must be seriously considered when you design an application. There is no guarantee, for example, that the server in this section ever receives your poke message. For that reason, a mechanism such as a timer would be employed in a real-world application.

Blocking Versus Nonblocking Descriptors

So far, all the examples in this chapter have relied on blocking I/O. Certain operations, such as reading, writing, and connecting or accepting connections, are set to block when they wait for completion, which brings a program (or thread) to a halt. After `server1` sets up a listen, for example, it enters the `while` loop and calls `accept()`. Until a client connects to the listening socket, the program is halted. It doesn't repeatedly call `accept()`; it calls it once and blocks. This condition is also true for `client2`, which blocks on the `recv()` call until the server replies. If the server is unavailable, the program will block forever. This is especially unwise for an application that uses UDP, but how could a timer be implemented if the call to `recv()` will never return?

Writing can also block on TCP connections when the receiver of the data hasn't read enough data to allow the current write to complete. In order to maintain reliability and proper flow control, the systems on both ends of a connection maintain buffers, usually about 8192 bytes. If these buffers are full in either direction, communications in that direction will cease until some space is freed up. This is yet another concern for servers that are writing large messages to clients that aren't running on very powerful systems or are on remote networks with low bandwidth links. In these scenarios, one client can slow things down for everyone.

Blocking I/O is acceptable for programs that don't have to maintain GUI interfaces and only have to maintain one communications channel. Needless to say, most programs cannot afford to use blocking communications.

I/O is said to be *nonblocking* when an operation returns an error or status code when it cannot be completed. To demonstrate this, run `client2` without running the server. It will start and not return until you halt it by pressing Ctrl+C.

Now run `nonblock`:

```
$ ./nonblock
error getting message : Try again at ./nonblock line 30
```

You receive the `Try again` message from the `recv()` function.

`nonblock`, shown in Listing 28.9, is a modified version of `client2`, which is shown is Listing 28.7. Let's see what changes were made to `client2` to remove blocking.

Listing 28.9. nonblock.

```
1: #!/usr/bin/perl
2: use Socket;
3: use Fcntl;
4: require "./network.pl";
5: $poke = "yo!";
6: $NETFD = makeudpcli();
7: fcntl $NETFD, &F_SETFL, O_NONBLOCK or die "Fcntl failed : $!\n";
8: (rest of file remains the same)
```

A new module, `Fcntl`, is added to the program in line 3, which provides an interface to the `fcntl(2)` system call. It is used to alter file descriptor properties, such as blocking and how it handles certain signals. In line 7, the last line of the modifications to `client2`, you set the `O_NONBLOCK` flag for the UDP socket. The rest of the program is unchanged.

When nonblocking I/O is used, the application designer has to be very careful when handling errors returned from `recv()`, `send()`, and other I/O related functions. When no more data is available for reading or no more data can be written, these functions return error codes. As a result, the application has to be prepared to handle some errors as being routine conditions. This is also true of the C/C++ interfaces.

I/O Multiplexing with UDP

Frequently, applications need to maintain more than one socket or file descriptor. For example, many system services such as Telnet, `rlogin`, and FTP are managed by one process on Linux. In order to do this, the process, `inetd`, listens for requests for these services by opening a socket for each one. Other applications, such as Applix, Netscape, and Xemacs, monitor file descriptors for the keyboard, mouse, and perhaps the network.

Let's set up an example that monitors the keyboard and a network connection. Listing 28.10 is contained in the file `udptalk`, which is included on the CD-ROM.

Listing 28.10. updtalk.

```
#!/usr/bin/perl

use Socket;
require "./network.pl";

 $NETFD = makeudpserv($ARGV[2]);

 $addr = gethostbyname($ARGV[0]);
 $port = getservbyname($ARGV[1], 'udp');

 $servaddr = sockaddr_in($port, $addr);

 $rin = "";
 vec($rin, fileno(STDIN), 1) = 1;
```

continues

Listing 28.10. continued

```
15:  vec($rin, fileno($NETFD), 1) = 1;
16:
17:  while (1) {
18:
19:     select $ready = $rin, undef, undef, undef;
20:
21:     if (vec($ready, fileno(STDIN), 1) == 1) {
22:       sysread STDIN, $mesg, 256;
23:        send $NETFD, $mesg, 0, $servaddr;
24:     }
25:     if (vec($ready, fileno($NETFD), 1) == 1) {
26:         recv $NETFD, $netmsg, 256, 0;
27:        print "$netmsg";
28:        $netmsg = "";
29:     }
30: }
31:   close $NETFD;
```

In order to test this program it must be run in either two windows on the same system or on two different systems. At one command-line session, execute the following command, where `iest` is the host on which the second command will be run:

```
$ ./udptalk iest test test1
```

On the second host, run the following command, where `iest` is the host where the first command was run:

```
$ ./udptalk iest test1 test
```

Each session will wait for keyboard input. Each line that is typed at one program is printed by the other, after you press Enter.

In order to perform the two-way communication required for this exercise, both instances of `udptalk` have to bind a well-known port. To permit this on a single workstation, the program accepts two port names as the second and third command-line arguments. For obvious reasons, two programs cannot register interest in the same port.

In line 6 of Listing 28.10, `udptalk` uses `makeudpserv()` to create a UDP socket and bind it to a well-known port. For the examples here, I used 8000 for one copy and 8001 for the other.

In lines 8–11, you perform the usual procedure for building a network address. This will be the address to which the keyboard input is written.

Lines 13–15 build bit vectors in preparation for the `select()` function. In Perl, a *bit vector* is a scalar variable that is handled as an array of bits; in other words, instead of being evaluated as bytes that add up to characters or numbers, each individual bit is evaluated as a distinct value.

In line 13, you create a variable (`$rin`) and tell the Perl interpreter to clear it. You then use the `vec()` and `fileno()` functions to determine the file number for `STDIN` (the keyboard) and set that bit in `$rin`. Then you do the same for the socket created by `makeudpcli()`. Therefore, if `STDIN` uses file descriptor 1 (which is generally the case), the second bit in `$rin` is set to `1`. (Bit vectors, like other arrays, start numbering indexes at zero.) Fortunately, the `vec()` function can be used to read bit vectors also, so you can treat these data structures as opaque (and sleep a lot better at night for not knowing the details).

`select()` is a key function for systems programmers. Unfortunately, it suffers from an arcane interface that is intimidating in any language. System V UNIX has a replacement, `poll()`, that is a little easier to use, but it is not available on Linux or within Perl. The following is the function description for `select()`:

```
select readfds, writefds, exceptfds, timeout;
```

Like most of the UNIX system interface, this is virtually identical to `select()` in C/C++. `select()` is used for discovering which file descriptors are ready for reading, are ready for writing, or have an exceptional condition. An exceptional condition usually corresponds with the arrival of what is called *out-of-band* or urgent data. This sort of data is most frequently associated with TCP connections. When a message is sent out-of-band, it is tagged as being more important than any previously sent data and is placed at the top of the data queue. A client or server can use this to notify the process on the other end of a connection that it is exiting immediately.

The first three arguments are bit vectors that correspond to the file descriptors that you are interested in reading or writing to or that you are monitoring for exceptional conditions. If you aren't interested in a set of file descriptors, you can pass `undef` instead of a vector. In Listing 28.10, you aren't interested in writing or exceptions, so you pass `undef` for the second and third arguments.

When `select` returns, only the bits that correspond to files with activity are set; if any descriptors aren't ready when `select` returns, their settings are lost in the vector. For that reason, you have `select()` create a new vector and copy it into `$ready`. This is done by passing an assignment to `select()` as the first argument in line 19.

The last parameter is the time-out interval in seconds. `select()` waits for activity for this period. If the period expires with no activity occurring, `select()` will return with everything in the vector cleared. Because `undef` is supplied for *`timeout`* in line 19, `select()` will block until a file is ready.

Inside the `while` loop entered in line 17, you call `select()`, passing it the bit vector built earlier and the new one to be created. When it returns, you check the vector using `vec()` with pretty much the same syntax as you used to set the bits; however because you are using == instead of =, `vec()` returns the value of the bit instead of setting it.

If the bit for `STDIN` is set, you read from the keyboard and send it to the other instance of `udptalk`. If the bit for the socket is set, you read from it and print it to the terminal. This sequence illustrates a very important advantage of the sockets interface. The program is extracting data to and from the network using the same functions as the keyboard and screen.

This process is called *multiplexing* and is the loop at the core of many network-aware applications, although the actual mechanics can be concealed by sophisticated dispatchers or notifiers that trigger events based on which connection is ready to be read from or written to. Something else lacking in Listing 28.10 is the minimum amount of error checking and signal handling that cleans up connections when a quit signal is received.

I/O Multiplexing with TCP

In order to demonstrate TCP multiplexing, it is necessary to create different programs for the client and server. The server, `tcplisten`, is shown in Listing 28.11 and is the one that requires the most scrutiny. The client, `tcptalk`, is on the book's CD-ROM and won't be reprinted here because it resembles the server so closely. I'll explain how the client works as I cover the server.

Listing 28.11. `tcplisten`.

```
#!/usr/bin/perl

use Socket;
require "./network.pl";

 $NETFD = makelisten($ARGV[0]);

 while (1) {

    $paddr = accept(NEWFD, $NETFD);

    ($port, $iaddr) = sockaddr_in($paddr);

    print "Accepted connection from ", inet_ntoa($iaddr),
    " on port number ", $port, "\n";

    $rin = "";
    vec($rin, fileno(STDIN), 1) = 1;
    vec($rin, fileno(NEWFD), 1) = 1;

    while (1)

     select $ready = $rin, undef, undef, undef;

     if (vec($ready, fileno(STDIN), 1) == 1) {
        sysread STDIN, $mesg, 256;
        syswrite NEWFD, $mesg, length($mesg);
     }
     if (vec($ready, fileno(NEWFD), 1) == 1) {
        $bytes = sysread NEWFD, $netmsg, 256;
        if ($bytes == 0) { goto EXIT; }
        print "$netmsg";
        $netmsg = "";
     }
    }
    EXIT: close NEWFD;
    print "Client closed connection\n";
```

```
38:  }
39:
40:  close $NETFD;
```

The server creates a listening socket in line 6 and then immediately enters a `while` loop. At the top of the loop is a call to `accept()`. By placing this in a loop, the server can repeatedly accept client connections, like our other TCP server. The listen socket, `$NETFD`, can accept more than one connection, regardless of the state of any file descriptors cloned from it using `accept()`.

`accept()` returns the address of the connecting client. You use this address in lines 12 and 14 to print out some information about the client. In line 12, you use `sockaddr_in()` to reverse engineer the fully qualified address back into a network address and a service port. Then you use `print` to display it on the terminal. Note the call to `inet_ntoa()` embedded in the `print` command.

Then you set up for a `select()` loop using almost the same code as Listing 28.10. There is, however, a key difference in the way the network connection is handled. You are reading with `sysread()` again, but you are saving the return value.

When a peer closes a TCP connection, the other program receives an end-of-file (EOF) indication. This is signified by marking the socket as ready for reading and returning zero bytes when it is read. By saving the number of bytes returned by `sysread()`, you are able to detect a closed connection and record it and then return to `accept()` at the top of the outer `while` loop.

The following is a server session, followed by the client session that is communicating with it. The client is `tcptalk`, which is included on the CD-ROM, as is a copy of `tcplisten`.

```
$ ./tcplisten test
Accepted connection from 10.8.100.20 on port number 29337
Hello, world.
Goodbye, cruel....
Client closed connection
```

```
$ ./tcptalk iest test
Hello, world.
Goodbye, cruel....
^C
```

Advanced Topics

During the course of this chapter, I've alluded to a few advanced topics. Let's take some time out to touch on a few of them individually.

One of the biggest issues for TCP applications is queueing messages. Depending on the nature of the data being transferred, the network bandwidth available, and the rate at which clients can keep pace with the data being delivered, data can queue up. Experienced application designers generally specify a queueing mechanism and the rules associated with it as part of the initial product description.

UDP applications have to wrestle with data reliability, and some schemes rely on message sequence numbers. All nodes involved in a transaction (or a series of transactions) keep track of a numbering scheme. When a node receives a message out of order, it sends a negative acknowledgment for the message that it missed. This sort of scheme greatly reduces traffic when everything goes well but can become very expensive when things fall out of sequence.

Some applications can use asynchronous I/O in order to service network traffic and other tasks in a single application. This scheme registers interest in a signal that can be delivered whenever a file descriptor has data ready to be read. This method is not recommended, though, because only one signal can be delivered for all file descriptors (so `select()` would still be needed) and because signals are not reliable.

Security is always a big issue, regardless of the protocols being used. UDP is being used less and less over the Internet, essentially because it is very easy to impersonate a host when no connections are required. Even TCP connections, however, can be "spoofed" by someone who has an understanding of the Internet Protocol and WAN technology. For that reason, applications that require a high level of security don't rely on TCP to keep them secure and tend to use encryption and authentication technology.

Summary

This chapter covers a lot of ground in a short time. I introduced essential networking concepts, such as the components of a network address and how an application can form one from symbolic host and service names by looking them up with the resolver functions.

Sockets, the most commonly used network programming interface, are used throughout the chapter. This API enables us to treat network connections and data streams like files, which shortens the network programming learning curve and also makes applications easy to design and maintain.

I also discussed the two most commonly used protocols on the Internet, TCP and UDP. TCP, a connection-oriented protocol, has very robust reliability mechanisms that allow an application to use the network without worrying too much about whether the messages it is sending are reaching the other end. This reliability does carry a price, however, because TCP comes with a certain degree of overhead in terms of speed and bandwidth. TCP also supports only two-way communication, so clients and servers that need to communicate with more than one node have to maintain multiple connections, which can be expensive.

UDP, on the other hand, is a connectionless, datagram-oriented protocol. It comes with virtually no overhead, but applications have to provide their own reliability mechanisms. UDP also supports broadcast, which can be convenient, but also represents a potential problem for some networks.

This chapter introduces some of the fundamental concepts behind network applications. Using these concepts, you will be able to create some simple tools, or you can build on this information by utilizing some of the advanced information available on the Internet and in advanced texts.

The concepts and examples presented here can all be easily applied to C programming because Perl essentially provides "wrappers" to the same system calls that C uses for socket programming. All the functions used here have C equivalents and their own manual pages.

For more information on network programming, see the UNIX socket programming FAQs at `http://www.ibrado.com/sock-faq/`. This page includes a wealth of information, plus pointers to other resources.

IN THIS PART

Appendixes

APPENDIX A

The Linux Documentation Project

IN THIS APPENDIX

This appendix describes the goals and current status of the Linux Documentation Project, including names of projects, volunteers, FTP sites, and so on.

Overview

The Linux Documentation Project (LDP) is working on developing good, reliable docs for the Linux operating system. The overall goal of the LDP is to collaborate in taking care of all of the issues of Linux documentation, ranging from online docs (man pages, `texinfo` docs, and so on) to printed manuals covering topics such as installing, using, and running Linux. The LDP is essentially a loose team of volunteers with no real central organization; anyone who is interested in helping is welcome to join in the effort. We feel that working together and agreeing on the direction and scope of Linux documentation is the best way to go, to reduce problems with conflicting efforts; for example, two people writing two books on the same aspect of Linux wastes someone's time along the way.

The LDP has set out to produce the canonical set of Linux online and printed documentation. Because our docs will be freely available (as per the GNU GPL; see the "Copyright License" section in Appendix C, "The Linux Documentation Project Copyright License") and distributed on the Net, we are able to easily update the documentation to stay on top of the many changes in the Linux world. We're also talking with a few companies about possibly publishing the LDP manuals after more of them become available. (A few smaller companies are printing and distributing LDP manuals even now; more on that later.) If you're interested in publishing any of the LDP works, see the section "Publishing LDP Manuals" in Appendix C.

Getting Involved

To get involved with the LDP, join the `linux-doc` activists mailing list. To do so, send mail to `majordomo@vger.rutgers.edu`. with the line `subscribe linux-doc` in the message body (not the subject). This will add you to the mailing list.

Of course, you'll also need to get in touch with the coordinator of whatever LDP projects you're interested in working on; see the next section.

Current Projects

For a list of current projects, see the `http://www.linux.org` Web site. The best way to get involved with one of these projects is to pick up the current version of the manual and send revisions, editions, or suggestions to the coordinator.

Glossary and Global Index

A glossary of terms and an index for the entire set of LDP manuals is planned. I don't remember who's putting this together; please remind me. `:)` This should be comprehensive as well as a reference. FTP sites for LDP works can be found at `sunsite.unc.edu` in the directory `/pub/Linux/docs`. LDP manuals are found in `/pub/Linux/docs/LDP`, HOWTOs, and other documentation found in `/pub/Linux/docs/HOWTO`. Various ALPHA docs can be found at `tsx-11.mit.edu:/pub/linux/ALPHA/LDP`.

Documentation Conventions

This section outlines the conventions that are currently used by LDP manuals. If you are interested in writing another manual using different conventions, please let us know of your plans first. We'd like the LDP manuals to have a common look and feel, and this is implemented with a LaTeX style file.

The set of printed manuals (that is, everything but the man pages) are formatted using LaTeX. The primary objective is to have PRINTED, not online, manuals. The LaTeX tool (currently under development by Olaf Kirch) can be used to generate plain ASCII (and later, `texinfo`) from the LaTeX source.

Please don't mail me saying that I shouldn't be using LaTeX for the LDP manuals; well over 500 pages of material have already been written in LaTeX, and we're not about to convert. Many a flame war has been sparked over this issue, but it's a done deal. New manuals don't necessarily need to be written using LaTeX, but you should use the same conventions and look as we have implemented with the current manuals.

The printed manuals should use Michael K. Johnson's `linuxdoc.sty` style sheet and documentation conventions, found in the file `linuxdoc.tar.z` under the `alpha` directory. We're trying to achieve a unified look in the manuals, for the sake of both consistency and portability (in this way, we can easily change the look and feel of the manuals by changing `linuxdoc.sty`), so that all of the authors/editors are on common ground using the same style sheet.

The LDP license/copyright should be used to copyright all works. It's a liberal copyleft like the GPL, but applies to printed documents and protects the LDP manuals from publication without our permission. The license is printed in Appendix C.

The copyright for each manual should be in the name of the head writer or coordinator for the project. The Linux Documentation Project isn't a formal entity and shouldn't be used to copyright the docs.

APPENDIX B

Top 50 Linux Commands and Utilities

by David Pitts

IN THIS APPENDIX

This appendix is not meant to replace the man pages; it does not go into anything resembling the detail available in the man pages. This appendix is designed to give you a feel for the commands and a brief description as to what they do. In most cases there are more parameters that can be used than are shown here.

Most of the descriptions also have examples with them. If these examples aren't self-evident, an explanation is provided. This is not an exhaustive list—there are many more commands that you could use—but these are the most common, and you will find yourself using them over and over again.

To keep things simple, the commands are listed in alphabetical order. I would have preferred to put them in order of how often I use them, but that would make locating them quite difficult. However, I do want to summarize by listing what are, at least for me, the ten most common commands—also alphabetically. This list of essential commands could be compared to a list of the top ten words spoken by the cavemen when searching for food and a mate:

1. `cat`
2. `cd`
3. `cp`
4. `find`
5. `grep`
6. `ls`
7. `more`
8. `rm`
9. `vi`
10. `who`

General Guidelines

In general, if you want to change something that already exists, the command to do that will begin with `ch`. If you want to do something for the first time, the command to do that will usually begin with `mk`. If you want to undo something completely, the command will usually begin with `rm`. For example, to make a new directory, you use the `mkdir` command. To remove a directory, you use the `rmdir` command.

The List

The commands listed in this appendix are some of the most common commands used in Red Hat Linux. In cases where the command seems ambiguous, an example is provided. With each of these commands, the man pages can provide additional information, as well as more examples.

.

The . command tells the shell to execute all the commands in the file that are passed an argument to the command. This works in the bash or pdksh. The equivalent in the tcsh is the source command. The following example will execute the command adobe:

```
. adobe
```

&

The & after any other command tells the computer to run the command in the background. By placing a job in the background, the user can then continue using that shell to process other commands. If the command is run in the foreground, the user cannot continue using that shell until the process finishes.

adduser

The adduser command is used by root, or someone else who has the authority, to create a new user. The adduser command is followed by the account name to be created—for example,

```
adduser dpitts
```

alias

The alias command is used to make aliases or alternative names for commands. Typically, these aliases are abbreviations of the actual command. In the following example, the user (probably a DOS user) is adding an alias of dir for a directory listing:

```
alias dir=ls
```

Typing alias by itself will give you a list of all your current aliases. Such a list might look like this:

```
svr01:/home/dpitts$ alias
alias d='dir'
alias dir='/bin/ls $LS_OPTIONS --format=vertical'
alias ls='/bin/ls $LS_OPTIONS'
alias v='vdir'
alias vdir='/bin/ls $LS_OPTIONS --format=long'
```

apropos *<parameter>*

The apropos command literally means appropriate or regarding (others). When it is followed by a parameter, it will search the man pages for entries that include the parameter. Basically, this performs a keyword search on all the man pages. This is the equivalent of the man -k *<parameter>* command.

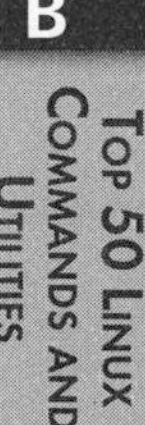

banner

banner prints a large, high-quality banner to standard output. If the message is omitted, it prompts for and reads one line from standard input. For example, enter `$ banner hi` to create the following banner:

```
##                                                           ###
##                                                           ###
################################################################
################################################################
################################################################
################################################################
################################################################
##                            ###
                                 ###
                                 ###
                                 ####
                                 ####
                                 ####
##                            #######
#####################################
#####################################
####################################
################################
#############################
##
##                                 ##
##                                 ##           ####
#####################################         ########
#####################################         ########
#####################################         ########
#####################################          ######
#####################################           ####
##
```

bg

The `bg` command is used to force a suspended process to run in the background. For example, you might have started a command in the foreground (without using `&` after the command), and realized that it was going to take a while, but that you still needed your shell. You could take that process that is currently running and hold down the Ctrl key, and, while it is held down, press the Z key. This places the current process on hold. You can either leave it on hold, just as if you called your telephone company, or you could place that process in the background by typing **`bg`**. This then frees up your shell to allow you to execute other commands.

bind

Used in `pdksh`, the `bind` command enables the user to change the behavior of key combinations for the purpose of command-line editing. Many times people bind the up, down, left, and right arrow keys so that they work the way they would in the Bourne Again Shell (`bsh`). The syntax used for the command is

```
bind <key sequence> <command>
```

The following examples are the `bind` commands to create bindings for scrolling up and down the history list and for moving left and right along the command line:

```
bind `^[[`=prefix-2
bind `^XA`=up-history
bind `^XB`=down-history
bind `^XC`=forward-char
bind `^XD`=backward-char
```

cat

`cat` does not call your favorite feline; instead, it tells the contents of (typically) the file to scroll its contents across the screen. If that file happens to be binary, then the cat gets a hairball and shows it to you on the screen. Typically, this is a noisy process as well. What is actually happening is that the `cat` command is scrolling the characters of the file, and the terminal is doing all it can to interpret and display the data in the file. This interpretation can include the character used to create the bell signal, which is where the noise comes from. As you might have surmised, the `cat` command requires something to display and would have the following format:

```
cat <filename>
```

cd

`cd` stands for change directory. You will find this command extremely useful. There are three typical ways of using this command:

`cd ..`	Moves one directory up the directory tree.
`cd ~`	Moves to your home directory from wherever you currently are. This is the same as issuing `cd` by itself.
`cd` *`directory name`*	Changes to a specific directory. This can be a directory relative to your current location or can be based on the root directory by placing a forward slash (`/`) before the directory name.

These examples can be combined. For example, suppose you were in the directory `/home/dsp1234` and you wanted to go to `tng4321`'s home account. You could perform the following command, which will move you back up the directory one level and then move you down into the `tng4321` directory:

```
cd ../tng4321
```

chgrp

The `chgrp` command is used to change the group associated with the permissions of the file or directory. The owner of the file (and, of course, root) has the authority to change the group associated with the file. The format for the command is simply

```
chgrp <new group> <file>
```

chmod

The `chmod` command is used to change the permissions associated with the object (typically a file or directory). What you are really doing is changing the file mode. There are two ways of specifying the permissions of the object. You can use the numeric coding system or the letter coding system. If you recall, there are three sets of users associated with every object: the owner of the object, the group for the object, and everybody else. Using the letter coding system, they are referred to as `u` for user, `g` for group, `o` for other, and `a` for all. There are three basic types of permissions that you can change: `r` for read, `w` for write, and `x` for execute. These three permissions can be changed using the plus (+) and minus (-) signs. For example, to add read and execute to owner and group of the file `test1`, you would issue the following command:

```
chmod ug+rx test1
```

To remove the read and execute permissions from the user and group of the `test1` file, you would change the plus (+) sign to a minus (-) sign:

```
chmod ug-rx test1
```

This is called making relative changes to the mode of the file.

Using the numeric coding system, you always have to give the absolute value of the permissions, regardless of their previous permissions. The numeric system is based upon three sets of base two numbers. There is one set for each category of user, group, and other. The values are `4`, `2`, and `1`, where `4` equals read, `2` equals write, and `1` equals execute. These values are added together to give the set of permissions for that category. With the numeric coding you always specify all three categories. Therefore, to make the owner of the file `test1` have read, write, and execute permissions, and no one else to have any permissions, you would use the value `700`, like this:

```
chmod 700 test1
```

To make the same file readable and writable by the user, and readable by both the group and others, you would follow the following mathematical logic: For the first set of permissions, the user, the value for readable is `4`, and the value for writable is `2`. The sum of these two is `6`. The next set of permissions, the group, only gets readable, so that is `4`. The settings for others, like the group, are `4`. Therefore, the command would be `chmod 644 test1`.

The format for the command, using either method, is the same. You issue the `chmod` command followed by the permissions, either absolute or relative, followed by the objects for which you want the mode changed:

```
chmod <permissions> <file>
```

chown

This command is used to change the user ID (owner) associated with the permissions of the file or directory. The owner of the file (and, of course, root) has the authority to change the user associated with the file. The format for the command is simply

```
chown <new user id> <file>
```

chroot

The `chroot` command makes the `/` directory (called the root directory) be something other than `/` on the filesystem. For example, when working with an Internet server, you can set the root directory to equal `/usr/ftp`. Then, when someone logs on using FTP (which goes to the root directory by default), he or she will actually go to the directory `/usr/ftp`. This protects the rest of your directory structure from being seen or even changed to by this anonymous guest to your machine. If the person were to enter `cd /etc`, the `ftp` program would try to put him or her in the root directory and then in the `etc` directory off of that. Because the root directory is `/usr/ftp`, the `ftp` program will actually put the user in the `/usr/ftp/etc` directory (assuming there is one).

The syntax for the command is

```
chroot <original filesystem location> <new filesystem location>
```

cp

The `cp` command is an abbreviation for copy; therefore, this command enables you to copy objects. For example, to copy the file `file1` to `file2`, issue the following command:

```
cp file1 file2
```

As the example shows, the syntax is very simple:

```
cp <original object name> <new object name>
```

dd

The `dd` command converts file formats. For example, to copy a boot image to a disk (assuming the device name for the disk is `/dev/fd0`), you would issue the command

```
dd if=<filename> of-/dev/fd0 obs=18k
```

where *`filename`* would be something like `BOOT0001.img`, `of` is the object format (what you are copying to), and `obs` is the output block size.

env

The env command is used to see the exported environment variables. The result of the command is a two-column list where the variable's name is on the left and the value associated with that variable is on the right. The command is issued without any parameters. Hence, typing **env** might get you a list similar to this one:

```
svr01:/home/dpitts$ env
HOSTNAME=svr01.mk.net
LOGNAME=dpitts
MAIL=/var/spool/mail/dpitts
TERM=vt100
HOSTTYPE=i386
PATH=/usr/local/bin:/usr/bin:/bin:.:/usr/local/java/bin
HOME=/home2/dpitts
SHELL=/bin/bash
LS_OPTIONS=--8bit --color=tty -F -b -T 0
PS1=\h:\w\$
PS2=>
MANPATH=/usr/local/man:/usr/man/preformat:/usr/man:/usr/lib/perl5/man
LESS=-MM
OSTYPE=Linux
SHLVL=1
```

fc

The fc command is used to edit the history file. The parameters passed to it, if there are any, can be used to select a range of commands from the history file. This list is then placed in an editing shell. The editor that it uses is based upon the value of the variable FCEDIT. If there is no value for this variable, the command looks at the EDITOR variable. If it is not there, the default is used, which is vi.

fg

Processes can be run in either the background or the foreground. The fg command enables you to take a suspended process and run it in the foreground. This is typically used when you have a process running in the foreground and for some reason, you need to suspend it (thus allowing you to run other commands). The process will continue until you either place it in the background or bring it to the foreground.

file

The file command tests each argument passed to it for one of three things: the filesystem test, the magic number test, or the language test. The first test to succeed causes the file type to be printed. If the file is text (it is an ASCII file), it then attempts to guess which language. The following example identifies the file nquota as a text file that contains Perl commands. A magic number file is a file that has data in particular fixed formats. Here is an example for checking the file nquota to see what kind of file it is:

```
file nquota
nquota: perl commands text
```

find

Did you ever say to yourself, "Self, where did I put that file?" Well now, instead of talking to yourself and having those around you wonder about you, you can ask the computer. You can say, "Computer, where did I put that file?" Okay, it is not that simple, but it is close. All you have to do is ask the computer to find the file.

The `find` command will look in whatever directory you tell it to, as well as all subdirectories under that directory, for the file that you specified. After it has found this list, it will then do with the list as you have asked it to. Typically, you just want to know where it is, so you ask it, nicely, to print out the list. The syntax of the command is the command itself, followed by the directory you want to start searching in, followed by the filename (metacharacters are acceptable), and then what you want done with the list. In the following example, the `find` command searches for files ending with `.pl` in the current directory (and all subdirectories). It then prints the results to standard output.

```
find . -name *.pl -print
./public_html/scripts/gant.pl
./public_html/scripts/edit_gant.pl
./public_html/scripts/httools.pl
./public_html/scripts/chart.no.comments.pl
```

grep

The `grep` (global regular expression parse) command searches the object you specify for the text that you specify. The syntax of the command is `grep` *<text>* *<file>*. In the following example, I am searching for instances of the text `httools` in all files in the current directory:

```
grep httools *
edit_gant.cgi:require 'httools.pl';
edit_gant.pl:require 'httools.pl';
gant.cgi:    require 'httools.pl';  # Library containing reuseable code
gant.cgi:        &date;      # Calls the todays date subroutine from httools.pl
gant.cgi:         &date;   #  Calls the todays date subroutine from httools.pl
gant.cgi:    &header;  # from httools.pl
```

Although this is valuable, the `grep` command can also be used in conjunction with the results of other commands. For example, the following command

```
ps -ef ¦grep -v root
```

calls for the `grep` command to take the output of the `ps` command and take out all instances of the word root (the `-v` means everything but the text that follows). The same command without the `-v` (`ps -ef ¦grep root`) returns all of the instances that contain the word root from the process listing.

groff

`groff` is the front end to the `groff` document formatting program. This program, by default, calls the `troff` program.

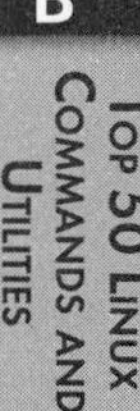

gzip

gzip is GNU's version of the zip compression software. The syntax can be as simple as

```
gzip <filename>
```

but many times also contains some parameters between the command and the filename to be compressed.

halt

The halt command tells the kernel to shut down. This is a superuser-only command (you must "be root").

hostname

hostname is used to either display the current host or domain name of the system or to set the hostname of the system—for example,

```
svr01:/home/dpitts$ hostname
svr01
```

kill

kill sends the specified signal to the specified process. If no signal is specified, the TERM signal is sent. The TERM signal will kill processes that do not process the TERM signal. For processes that do process the TERM signal, it might be necessary to use the KILL signal because this signal cannot be caught. The syntax for the kill command is kill <option> <pid>, and an example is as follows:

```
svr01:/home/dpitts$kill -9 1438
```

less

less is a program similar to more, but which allows backward movement in the file as well as forward movement. less also doesn't have to read the entire input file before starting, so with large input files it starts up faster than text editors such as vi.

login

login is used when signing on to a system. It can also be used to switch from one user to another at any time.

logout

logout is used to sign off a system as the current user. If it is the only user you are logged in as, then you are logged off the system.

lpc

`lpc` is used by the system administrator to control the operation of the line printer system. `lpc` can be used to disable or enable a printer or a printer's spooling queue, to rearrange the order of jobs in a spooling queue, to find out the status of printers, to find out the status of the spooling queues, and to find out the status of the printer daemons. The command can be used for any of the printers configured in `/etc/printcap`.

lpd

`lpd` is the line printer daemon and is normally invoked at boot time from the `rc` file. It makes a single pass through the `/etc/printcap` file to find out about the existing printers and prints any files left after a crash. It then uses the system calls `listen` and `accept` to receive requests to print files in the queue, transfer files to the spooling area, display the queue, or remove jobs from the queue.

lpq

`lpq` examines the spooling area used by `lpd` for printing files on the line printer, and reports the status of the specified jobs or all jobs associated with a user. If the command is invoked without any arguments, the command reports on any jobs currently in the print queue.

lpr

The line printer command uses a spooling daemon to print the named files when facilities become available. If no names appear, the standard input is assumed. The following is an example of the `lpr` command:

```
lpr /etc/hosts
```

ls

The `ls` command lists the contents of a directory. The format of the output is manipulated with options. The `ls` command, with no options, lists all nonhidden files (a file that begins with a dot is a hidden file) in alphabetical order, filling as many columns as will fit in the window. Probably the most common set of options used with this command is the `-la` option. The `a` means list all (including hidden files) files, and the `l` means make the output a long listing. Here is an example of this command:

```
svr01:~$ ls -la
total 35
drwxr-xr-x   7 dpitts   users      1024 Jul 21 00:19 ./
drwxr-xr-x 140 root     root       3072 Jul 23 14:38 ../
-rw-r--r--   1 dpitts   users      4541 Jul 23 23:33 .bash_history
-rw-r--r--   1 dpitts   users        18 Sep 16  1996 .forward
-rw-r--r--   2 dpitts   users       136 May 10 01:46 .htaccess
-rw-r--r--   1 dpitts   users       164 Dec 30  1995 .kermrc
-rw-r--r--   1 dpitts   users        34 Jun  6  1993 .less
-rw-r--r--   1 dpitts   users       114 Nov 23  1993 .lessrc
```

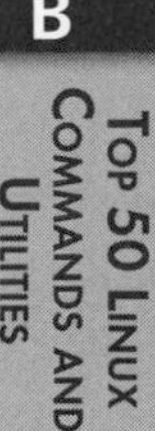

```
-rw-r--r--   1 dpitts   users          10 Jul 20 22:32 .profile
drwxr-xr-x   2 dpitts   users        1024 Dec 20  1995 .term/
drwx------   2 dpitts   users        1024 Jul 16 02:04 Mail/
drwxr-xr-x   2 dpitts   users        1024 Feb  1  1996 cgi-src/
-rw-r--r--   1 dpitts   users        1643 Jul 21 00:23 hi
-rwxr-xr-x   1 dpitts   users         496 Jan  3  1997 nquota*
drwxr-xr-x   2 dpitts   users        1024 Jan  3  1997 passwd/
drwxrwxrwx   5 dpitts   users        1024 May 14 20:29 public_html/
```

make

The purpose of the `make` utility is to automatically determine which pieces of a large program need to be recompiled and then to issue the commands necessary to recompile them.

man

The `man` command is used to format and display the online manual pages. The manual pages are the text that describes, in detail, how to use a specified command. In the following example, I have called the man page that describes the `man` pages:

```
svr01:~$ man man
man(1)                                                        man(1)


NAME
       man - format and display the on-line manual pages
       manpath - determine user's search path for man pages
SYNOPSIS
       man  [-adfhktwW]  [-m system] [-p string] [-C config_file]
       [-M path] [-P pager] [-S section_list] [section] name  ...

DESCRIPTION
       man  formats  and displays the on-line manual pages.  This
       version knows about  the  MANPATH  and  PAGER  environment
       variables, so you can have your own set(s) of personal man
       pages and choose whatever program you like to display  the
       formatted  pages.  If section is specified, man only looks
       in that section of the manual.  You may also  specify  the
       order to search the sections for entries and which prepro-
       cessors to run  on  the  source  files  via  command  line
       options  or  environment  variables.  If name contains a /
       then it is first tried as a filename, so that you  can  do
```

mesg

The `mesg` utility is run by a user to control write access others have to the terminal device associated with the standard error output. If write access is allowed, programs such as `talk` and `write` have permission to display messages on the terminal. Write access is allowed by default.

mkdir

The `mkdir` command is used to make a new directory.

mkefs

The `mkefs` command is used to make an extended filesystem. This command does not format the new filesystem, just makes it available for use.

mkfs

`mkfs` is used to build a Linux filesystem on a device, usually a hard disk partition. The syntax for the command is `mkfs <filesystem>`, where `<filesystem>` is either the device name (such as `/dev/hda1`) or the mount point (for example, `/`, `/usr`, `/home`) for the filesystem.

mkswap

`mkswap` sets up a Linux swap area on a device (usually a disk partition).

The device is usually of the following form:

```
/dev/hda[1-8]
/dev/hdb[1-8]
/dev/sda[1-8]
/dev/sdb[1-8]
```

more

`more` is a filter for paging through text one screen at a time. This command can only page down through the text, as opposed to `less`, which can page both up and down though the text.

mount

`mount` attaches the filesystem specified by `specialfile` (which is often a device name) to the directory specified as the parameter. Only the superuser can `mount` files. If the `mount` command is run without parameters, it lists all the currently mounted filesystems. The following is an example of the `mount` command:

```
svr01:/home/dpitts$ mount
/dev/hda1 on / type ext2 (rw)
/dev/hda2 on /var/spool/mail type ext2 (rw,usrquota)
/dev/hda3 on /logs type ext2 (rw,usrquota)
/dev/hdc1 on /home type ext2 (rw,usrquota)
none on /proc type proc (rw)
```

mv

The `mv` command is used to move an object from one location to another location. If the last argument names an existing directory, the command moves the rest of the list into that directory. If two files are given, the command moves the first into the second. It is an error to have more than two arguments with this command unless the last argument is a directory.

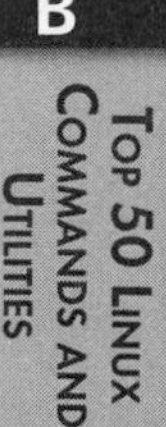

netstat

netstat displays the status of network connections on either TCP, UDP, RAW, or UNIX sockets to the system. The -r option is used to obtain information about the routing table. The following is an example of the netstat command:

```
svr01:/home/dpitts$ netstat
Active Internet connections
Proto Recv-Q Send-Q Local Address          Foreign Address        (State)
User
tcp        0  16501 www.mk.net:www         sdlb12119.sannet.:3148 FIN_WAIT1
root
tcp        0  16501 auth02.mk.net:www      sdlb12119.sannet.:3188 FIN_WAIT1
root
tcp        0      1 www.anglernet.com:www  ts88.cctrap.com:1070   SYN_RECV
root
tcp        0      1 www.anglernet.com:www  ts88.cctrap.com:1071   SYN_RECV
root
udp        0      0 localhost:domain       *:*
udp        0      0 svr01.mk.net:domain    *:*
udp        0      0 poto.mk.net:domain     *:*
udp        0      0 stats.mk.net:domain    *:*
udp        0      0 home.mk.net:domain     *:*
udp        0      0 www.cmf.net:domain     *:*
Active UNIX domain sockets
Proto RefCnt Flags       Type            State           Path
unix  2      [ ]         SOCK_STREAM     UNCONNECTED     1605182
unix  2      [ ]         SOCK_STREAM     UNCONNECTED     1627039
unix  2      [ ]         SOCK_STREAM     CONNECTED       1652605
```

passwd

For the normal user (non-superuser), no arguments are used with the passwd command. The command will ask the user for the old password. Following this, the command will ask for the new password twice, to make sure it was typed correctly. The new password must be at least six characters long and must contain at least one character that is either uppercase or a nonletter. Also, the new password cannot be the same password as the one being replaced, nor can it match the user's ID (account name).

If the command is run by the superuser, it can be followed by either one or two arguments. If the command is followed by a single user's ID, then the superuser can change that user's password. The superuser is not bound by any of the restrictions imposed on the user. If there is an argument after the single user's ID, then that argument becomes that user's new password.

ps

ps gives a snapshot of the current processes. An example is as follows:

```
svr01:/home/dpitts$ ps -ef

PID TTY STAT  TIME COMMAND
10916  p3 S    0:00 -bash TERM=vt100 HOME=/home2/dpitts PATH=/usr/local/bin:/us
10973  p3 R    0:00  \_ ps -ef LESSOPEN=¦lesspipe.sh %s ignoreeof=10 HOSTNAME=s
10974  p3 S    0:00  \_ more LESSOPEN=¦lesspipe.sh %s ignoreeof=10 HOSTNAME=svr
```

pwd

`pwd` prints the current working directory. It tells you what directory you are currently in.

rm

`rm` is used to delete specified files. With the `-r` option (Warning: This can be dangerous!), `rm` will recursively remove files. Therefore if, as root, you type the command `rm -r /`, you had better have a good backup because all your files are now gone. This is a good command to use in conjunction with the `find` command to find files owned by a certain user or in a certain group, and delete them. By default, the `rm` command does not remove directories.

rmdir

`rmdir` removes a given *empty* directory; the word *empty* is the key word. The syntax is simply `rmdir <directory name>`.

set

The `set` command is used to temporarily change an environment variable. In some shells, the `set -o vi` command will allow you to bring back previous commands that you have in your history file. It is common to place the command in your `.profile`. Some environment variables require an equals sign, and some, as in the example `set -o vi`, do not.

shutdown

One time during *Star Trek: The Next Generation*, Data commands the computer to "Shut down the holodeck!" Unfortunately, most systems don't have voice controls, but systems can still be shut down. This command happens to be the one to do just that. Technically, the `shutdown` call

```
int shutdown(int s, int how));
```

causes all or part of a full-duplex connection on a socket associated with `s` to be shut down, but who's being technical? The `shutdown` command can also be used to issue a "Vulcan Neck Pinch" (Ctrl+Alt+Del) and restart the system.

su

`su` enables a user to temporarily become another user. If a user ID is not given, the computer thinks you want to be the superuser, or root. In either case, a shell is spawned that makes you the new user, complete with that user ID, group ID, and any supplemental groups of that new user. If you are not root and the user has a password (and the user should!), `su` prompts for a password. Root can become any user at any time without knowing passwords. Technically, the user just needs to have a user ID of `0` (which makes a user a superuser) to log on as anyone else without a password.

swapoff

No, `swapoff` is not a move from *Karate Kid*. Instead, it is a command that stops swapping to a file or block device.

swapon

Also not from the movie *Karate Kid*, `swapon` sets the swap area to the file or block device by path. `swapoff` stops swapping to the file. This command is normally done during system boot.

tail

`tail` prints to standard output the last 10 lines of a given file. If no file is given, it reads from standard input. If more than one file is given, it prints a header consisting of the file's name enclosed in a left and right arrow (==> <==) before the output of each file. The default value of 10 lines can be changed by placing a `-###` in the command. The syntax for the command is

```
tail [-<# of lines to see>] [<filename(s)>]
```

talk

The `talk` command is used to have a "visual" discussion with someone else over a terminal. The basic idea behind this visual discussion is that your input is copied to the other person's terminal, and the other person's input is copied to your terminal. Thus, both people involved in the discussion see the input for both themselves and the other person.

tar

`tar` is an archiving program designed to store and extract files from an archive file. This tarred file (called a `tar` file), can be archived to any media including a tape drive and a hard drive. The syntax of a `tar` command is `tar <action> <optional functions> <file(s)/directory(ies)>`. If the last parameter is a directory, all subdirectories under the directory are also tarred.

umount

Just as the cavalry unmounts from their horses, filesystems unmount from their locations as well. The `umount` command is used to perform this action. The syntax of the command is

```
umount <filesystem>
```

unalias

`unalias` is the command to undo an alias. In the `alias` command section, earlier in this appendix, I aliased `dir` to be the `ls` command. To unalias this command, you would simply type **`unalias dir`**.

unzip

The unzip command will list, test, or extract files from a zipped archive. The default is to extract files from the archive. The basic syntax is unzip <*filename*>.

wall

wall displays the contents of standard input on all terminals of all currently logged in users. Basically, the command writes to all terminals, hence its name. The contents of files can also be displayed. The superuser, or root, can write to the terminals of those who have chosen to deny messages or are using a program that automatically denies messages.

who

Either the who command calls an owl, which it doesn't, or it prints the login namc, terminal type, login time, and remote hostname of each user currently logged on. The following is an example of the who command:

```
svr01:/home/dpitts$ who
root      ttyp0    Jul 27 11:44 (www01.mk.net)
dpitts    ttyp2    Jul 27 19:32 (d12.dialup.seane)
ehooban   ttyp3    Jul 27 11:47 (205.177.146.78)
dpitts    ttyp4    Jul 27 19:34 (d12.dialup.seane)
```

If two nonoption arguments are passed to the who command, the command prints the entry for the user running it. Typically, this is run with the command who am I, but any two arguments will work; for example, the following gives information on my session:

```
svr01:/home/dpitts$ who who who
svr01!dpitts   ttyp2    Jul 27 19:32 (d12.dialup.seane)
```

The -u option is nice if you want to see how long it has been since that session has been used, such as in the following:

```
svr01:/home/dpitts$ who -u
root      ttyp0    Jul 27 11:44 08:07 (www01.mk.net)
dpitts    ttyp2    Jul 27 19:32   .   (d12.dialup.seane)
ehooban   ttyp3    Jul 27 11:47 00:09 (205.177.146.78)
dpitts    ttyp4    Jul 27 19:34 00:06 (d12.dialup.seane)
```

xhost +

The xhost + command allows xterms to be displayed on a system. Probably the most common reason that a remote terminal cannot be opened is because the xhost + command has not been run. To turn off the capability to allow xterms, the xhost - command is used.

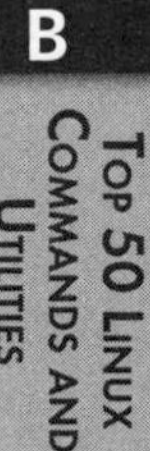

xmkmf

The xmkmf command is used to create the Imakefiles for X sources. It actually runs the imake command with a set of arguments.

xset

The `xset` command sets some of the options in an X Window session. You can use this option to set your bell (`xset b` *<volume> <frequency> <duration in milliseconds>*), your mouse speed (`xset m` *<acceleration> <threshold>*), and many others.

zip

The `zip` command will list, test, or add files to a zipped archive. The default is to add files to an archive.

Summary

If you read this entire appendix, you will have noticed two things. First, I cannot count. There are about seventy commands here, not fifty as the title of the appendix states. Second, you have way too much time on your hands, and need to go out and program some drivers or something!

I hope this appendix has helped you gain an understanding of some of the commands available for your use, whether you are a user, a system administrator, or just someone who wants to learn more about Red Hat Linux. I encourage you to use the man pages to find out the many details left out of this appendix. Most of the commands have arguments that can be passed to them, and, although this appendix attempts to point out a few of them, it would have taken an entire book just to go into the detail that has been provided in the man pages.

APPENDIX C

The Linux Documentation Project Copyright License

IN THIS APPENDIX

Last modified 6 January 1997

The following copyright license applies to all works by the Linux Documentation Project.

Please read the license carefully—it is somewhat like the GNU General Public License, but there are several conditions in it that differ from what you might be used to. If you have any questions, please e-mail the LDP coordinator, `mdw@sunsite.unc.edu`.

Copyright License

The Linux Documentation Project manuals may be reproduced and distributed in whole or in part, subject to the following conditions:

All Linux Documentation Project manuals are copyrighted by their respective authors. THEY ARE NOT IN THE PUBLIC DOMAIN.

- The copyright notice above and this permission notice must be preserved complete on all complete or partial copies.
- Any translation or derivative work of *Linux Installation and Getting Started* must be approved by the author in writing before distribution.
- If you distribute *Linux Installation and Getting Started* in part, instructions for obtaining the complete version of this manual must be included, and a means for obtaining a complete version provided.
- Small portions may be reproduced as illustrations for reviews or quotes in other works without this permission notice if proper citation is given.
- The GNU General Public License referenced below may be reproduced under the conditions given within it.

Exceptions to these rules may be granted for academic purposes: Write to the author and ask. These restrictions are here to protect us as authors, not to restrict you as educators and learners. All source code in *Linux Installation and Getting Started* is placed under the GNU General Public License, available via anonymous FTP from `ftp://prep.ai.mit.edu/pub/gnu/COPYING`.

Publishing LDP Manuals

If you're a publishing company interested in distributing any of the LDP manuals, read on.

By the license given in the previous section, anyone is allowed to publish and distribute verbatim copies of the Linux Documentation Project manuals. You don't need our explicit permission for this. However, if you would like to distribute a translation or derivative work based on any of the LDP manuals, you must obtain permission from the author, in writing, before doing so.

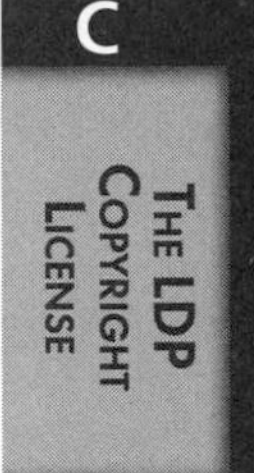

All translations and derivative works of LDP manuals must be placed under the Linux Documentation License given in the preceding section. That is, if you plan to release a translation of one of the manuals, it must be freely distributable by the terms stated in that license.

You may, of course, sell the LDP manuals for profit. We encourage you to do so. Keep in mind, however, that because the LDP manuals are freely distributable, anyone may photocopy or distribute printed copies free of charge, if they wish to do so.

We do not require to be paid royalties for any profit earned from selling LDP manuals. However, we would like to suggest that if you do sell LDP manuals for profit, that you either offer the author royalties, or donate a portion of your earnings to the author, the LDP as a whole, or to the Linux development community. You might also wish to send one or more free copies of the LDP manual that you are distributing to the author. Your show of support for the LDP and the Linux community will be very appreciated.

We would like to be informed of any plans to publish or distribute LDP manuals, just so we know how they're becoming available. If you are publishing or planning to publish any LDP manuals, please send e-mail to Matt Welsh at `mdw@sunsite.unc.edu`.

We encourage Linux software distributors to distribute the LDP manuals (such as the *Installation and Getting Started Guide*) with their software. The LDP manuals are intended to be used as the "official" Linux documentation, and we'd like to see mail-order distributors bundling the LDP manuals with the software. As the LDP manuals mature, we hope they will fulfill this goal more adequately.

Glossary

by David B. Horvath

This is a fairly extensive glossary of terms that are related to the UNIX environment and their definitions. All the authors of this book contributed to this section.

NOTE

The language of the computer field is constantly expanding. If you cannot find a word in this glossary, it is because it is newer than anything the authors knew about or the authors decided is was so obvious that "everyone should already know it."

#—Octothorpe.

$HOME—Environment variable that points to your login directory.

$PATH—Pathname environment variable.

$PATH—The shell environment variable that contains a set of directories to be searched for UNIX commands.

.1—Files with this extension contain manual page entries. The actual extension can be any value between `1` and `9` and can have an alphabetic suffix (`.3x`, `.7`, and so on).

.ag—Applixware graphics file.

.as—Applixware spreadsheet file.

.aw—Applixware word processing file.

.bmp—Bitmap graphics file.

.c—C source file.

.C—C++ source file.

.cc—C++ source file.

.conf—Configuration file.

.cxx—C++ source file.

.db—Database file.

.dvi—Device-independent TeX output.

.gif—GIF graphics file.

.gz—File compressed using the GNU `gzip` utility.

.h—C header file.

.html—HTML document.

`.jpg`—JPEG graphics file.

`.m`—Objective C source file.

`.o`—Compiled object file.

`.p`—Pascal language source file.

`.pbm`—Portable bitmap graphics file.

`.pdf`—Adobe Acrobat file.

`.ps`—PostScript file

`.s`—Assembler language file.

`.tar`—`tar` file.

`.tgz`—Gzipped `tar` file.

`.tif`—TIFF graphics file.

`.txt`—Text document.

`.Z`—File compressed using the `compress` command.

`/`—Root directory.

`/dev`—Device directory.

`/dev/null` file—The place to send output that you are not interested in seeing; also the place to get input from when you have none (but the program or command requires something). This is also known as the *bit bucket* (where old bits go to die).

`/dev/printer`—Socket for local print requests.

`/etc/cshrc` file—The file containing shell environment characteristics common to all users that use the C Shell.

`/etc/group` file—This file contains information about groups, the users they contain, and passwords required for access by other users. The password might actually be in another file, the shadow group file, to protect it from attacks.

`/etc/inittab` file—The file that contains a list of active terminal ports for which UNIX will issue the login prompt. This also contains a list of background processes for UNIX to initialize. Some versions of UNIX use other files, such as `/etc/tty`.

`/etc/motd` file—Message of the day file; usually contains information the system administrator feels is important for you to know. This file is displayed when the user signs on the system.

`/etc/passwd` file—Contains user information and password. The password might actually be in another file, the shadow password file, to protect it from attacks.

/etc/profile—The file containing shell environment characteristics common to all users of the Bourne and Korn shells.

/usr/local—Locally developed public executables directory.

/var/spool—Various spool directories.

[]—Brackets.

{}—Braces.

ANSI—American National Standards Institute.

API—Application Program Interface. The specific method prescribed by a computer operating system, application, or third-party tool by which a programmer writing an application program can make requests of the operating system. Also known as Application Programmer's Interface.

ar—Archive utility.

arguments—See *parameters.*

ARPA—See *DARPA.*

ASCII—American Standard Code for Information Interchange. Used to represent characters in memory for most computers.

AT&T UNIX—Original version of UNIX developed at AT&T Bell Labs, later known as UNIX Systems Laboratories. Many current versions of UNIX are descendants; even BSD UNIX was derived from early AT&T UNIX.

attribute—The means of describing objects. The attributes for a ball might be rubber, red, 3 cm in diameter. The behavior of the ball might be how high it bounces when thrown. Attribute is another name for the data contained within an object (class).

awk—Programming language developed by A.V. Aho, P.J. Weinberger, and Brian W. Kernighan. The language is built on C syntax, includes the regular expression search facilities of grep, and adds in the advanced string and array handling features that are missing from the C language. nawk, gawk, and POSIX awk are versions of this language.

background—Processes usually running at a lower priority and with their input disconnected from the interactive session. Any input and output are usually directed to a file or other process.

background process—An autonomous process that runs under UNIX without requiring user interaction.

backup—The process of storing the UNIX system, applications, and data files on removable media for future retrieval.

`bash`—Stands for GNU Bourne Again Shell and is based on the Bourne shell, `sh`, the original command interpreter.

`biff`—Background mail notification utility.

`bison`—GNU parser generator (`yacc` replacement).

block-special—A device file that is used to communicate with a block-oriented I/O device. Disk and tape drives are examples of block devices. The block-special file refers to the entire device. You should not use this file unless you want to ignore the directory structure of the device (that is, if you are coding a device driver).

boot or boot up—The process of starting the operating system (UNIX).

Bourne shell—The original standard user interface to UNIX that supported limited programming capability.

BSD—Berkeley Software Distribution.

BSD UNIX—Version of UNIX developed by Berkeley Software Distribution and written at University of California, Berkeley.

bug—An undocumented program feature.

C—Programming language developed by Brian W. Kernighan and Dennis M. Ritchie. The C language is highly portable and available on many platforms including mainframes, PCs, and, of course, UNIX systems.

C shell—A user interface for UNIX written by Bill Joy at Berkeley. It features C programming-like syntax.

CAD—Computer-aided design.

cast—Programming construct to force type conversion.

`cat`—Concatenate files command.

CD-ROM—Compact Disk-Read Only Memory. Computer-readable data stored on the same physical form as a musical CD. Large capacity, inexpensive, slower than a hard disk, and limited to reading. There are versions that are writable (CD-R, CD Recordable) and other formats that can be written to once or many times.

CGI—Common Gateway Interface. A means of transmitting data between Web pages and programs or scripts executing on the server. Those programs can then process the data and send the results back to the user's browser through dynamically creating HTML.

character special—A device file that is used to communicate with character-oriented I/O devices like terminals, printers, or network communications lines. All I/O access is treated as a series of bytes (characters).

characters, alphabetic—The letters A through Z and a through z.

characters, alphanumeric—The letters A through Z and a through z, and the numbers 0 through 9.

characters, control—Any nonprintable characters. The characters are used to control devices, separate records, and eject pages on printers.

characters, numeric—The numbers 0 through 9.

characters, special—Any of the punctuation characters or printable characters that are not alphanumeric. Include the space, comma, period, and many others.

child process—See *subprocess*.

child shell—See *subshell*.

class—A model of objects that have attributes (data) and behavior (code or functions). It is also viewed as a collection of objects in their abstracted form.

command-line editing—UNIX shells support the ability to recall a previously entered command, modify it, and then execute the new version. The command history can remain between sessions (the commands you did yesterday can be available for you when you log in today). Some shells support a command-line editing mode that uses a subset of the `vi`, `emacs`, or `gmacs` editor commands for command recall and modification.

command-line history—See *command-line editing*.

command-line parameters—Used to specify parameters to pass to the execute program or procedure. Also known as *command-line arguments*.

configuration files—Collections of information used to initialize and set up the environment for specific commands and programs. Shell configuration files set up the user's environment.

configuration files, shell—For Bourne shell: `/etc/profile` and `$HOME/.profile`.

For Korn and `pdksh` shells: `/etc/profile`, `$HOME/.profile`, and `ENV= file`.

For C and `tcsh` shells: `/etc/.login`, `/etc/cshrc`, `$HOME/.login`, `$HOME/.cshrc`, and `$HOME/.logout`. Older versions might not support the first two files listed.

For `bash`: `/etc/profile/`, `$HOME/.bash_profile`, `$HOME/.bash_login`, `$HOME/.profile`, `$HOME/.bashrc`, and `~/.bash_logout`.

CPU—Central Processing Unit. The primary "brain" of the computer—the calculation engine and logic controller.

daemon—A system-related background process that often runs with the permissions of root and services requests from other processes.

DARPA—(U.S. Department of) Defense Advanced Research Projects Agency. Funded development of TCP/IP and ARPAnet (predecessor of the Internet).

database server—See *server, database*.

device file—File used to implement access to a physical device. This provides a consistent approach to access of storage media under UNIX; data files and devices (like tapes and communication facilities) are implemented as files. To the programmer, there is no real difference.

directory—A means of organizing and collecting files together. The directory itself is a file that consists of a list of files contained within it. The root (`/`) directory is the top level and every other directory is contained in it (directly or indirectly). A directory might contain other directories, known as *subdirectories*.

directory navigation—The process of moving through directories is known as navigation. Your current directory is known as the current working directory. Your login directory is known as the default or home directory. Using the `cd` command, you can move up and down through the tree structure of directories.

DNS—Domain Name Server. Used to convert between the name of a machine on the Internet (`name.domain.com`) to the numeric address (`123.45.111.123`).

DOS—Disk Operating System. Operating system that is based on the use of disks for the storage of commands. It is also a generic name for MS-DOS and PC-DOS on the personal computer. MS-DOS is the version Microsoft sells; PC-DOS is the version IBM sells. Both are based on Microsoft code.

`double`—Double-precision floating point.

dpi—Dots per inch.

EBCDIC—Extended Binary Coded Decimal Interchange Code. The code used to represent characters in memory for mainframe computers.

`ed`—A common tool used for line-oriented text editing.

`elm`—Interactive mail program.

`emacs`—A freely available editor now part of the GNU software distribution. Originally written by Richard M. Stallman at MIT in the late 1970s, it is available for many platforms. It is extremely extensible and has its own programming language; the name stands for editing with macros.

e-mail—Messages sent through an electronic medium instead of through the local postal service. There are many proprietary e-mail systems that are designed to handle mail within a LAN environment; most of these are also able to send over the Internet. Most Internet (open) e-mail systems make use of MIME to handle attached data (which can be binary).

encapsulation—The process of combining data (attributes) and functions (behavior in the form of code) into an object. The data and functions are closely coupled within an object. Instead of all programmers being able to access the data in a structure their own way, they have to use the code connected with that data. This promotes code reuse and standardized methods of working with the data.

environment variables—See *variables, environmental.*

Ethernet—A networking method where the systems are connected to a single shared bus and all traffic is available to every machine. The data packets contain an identifier of the recipient, and that is the only machine that should process that packet.

expression—A constant, variable, or operands and operators combined. Used to set a value, perform a calculation, or set the pattern for a comparison (regular expressions).

FIFO—First In, First Out. See *pipe, named.*

file—Collection of bytes stored on a device (typically a disk or tape). Can be source code, executable binaries or scripts, or data.

file compression—The process of applying mathematical formulas to data, typically resulting in a form of the data that occupies less space. A compressed file can be uncompressed, resulting in the original file. When the compress/uncompress process results in exactly the same file as was originally compressed, it is known as lossless. If information about the original file is lost, the compression method is known as lossy. Data and programs need lossless compression; images and sounds can stand lossy compression.

file, indexed—A file based on a file structure where data can be retrieved based on specific keys (name, employee number, and so on) or sequentially. The keys are stored in an index. This is not directly supported by the UNIX operating system; usually implemented by the programmer or by using tools from an ISV. A typical form is known as *ISAM.*

file, line sequential—See *file, text.*

file, sequential—This phrase can mean either a file that can only be accessed sequentially (not randomly), or a file without record separators (typically fixed length, but UNIX does not know what that length is and does not care).

file, text—A file with record separators. Can be fixed or variable length; UNIX tools can handle these files because the tools can tell when the record ends (by the separator).

filename—The name used to identify a collection of data (a file). Without a pathname, it is assumed to be in the current directory.

filename generation—The process of the shell interpreting metacharacters (wildcards) to produce a list of matching files. This is referred to as filename expansion or globbing.

filename, fully qualified—The name used to identify a collection of data (a file) and its location. It includes both the path and name of the file; typically, the pathname is fully specified (absolute). See also *pathname* and *pathname, absolute.*

filesystem—A collection of disk storage that is connected (mounted) to the directory structure at some point (sometimes at the root). Filesystems are stored in a disk partition and are sometimes referred to as being the disk partition.

`finger`—User information lookup program.

firewall—A system used to provide a controlled entry point to the internal network from the outside (usually the Internet). This is used to prevent outside or unauthorized systems from accessing systems on your internal network. The capability depends on the individual software package, but the features typically include filter packets and filter datagrams, system (name or IP address) aliasing, and rejecting packets from certain IP addresses. In theory, it provides protection from malicious programs or people on the outside. It can also prevent internal systems from accessing the Internet on the outside. The name comes from the physical barrier between connected buildings or within a single building that is supposed to prevent fire from spreading from one to another.

flags—See *options.*

`float`—Single-precision floating point.

foreground—Programs running while connected to the interactive session.

`fseek`—Internal function used by UNIX to locate data inside a file or filesystem. ANSI standard `fseek` accepts a parameter that can hold a value of +2 to -2 billion. This function, used by the operating system, system tools, and application programs, is the cause of the 2GB file and filesystem size limitation on most systems. With 64-bit operating systems, this limit is going away.

FSF—Free Software Foundation.

FTP—File Transfer Protocol or File Transfer Program. A system-independent means of transferring files between systems connected via TCP/IP. Ensures that the file is transferred correctly, even if there are errors during transmission. Can usually handle character set conversions (ASCII/EBCDIC) and record terminator resolution (linefeed for UNIX, carriage return and linefeed for MS/PC-DOS).

gateway—A combination of hardware, software, and network connections that provides a link between one architecture and another. Typically, a gateway is used to connect a LAN or UNIX server with a mainframe (that uses SNA for networking, resulting in the name SNA gateway). A gateway can also be the connection between the internal and external network (often referred to as a firewall). See also *firewall.*

GID—Group ID number.

globbing—See *filename generation.*

GNU—GNU stands for GNU's Not UNIX, and is the name of free useful software packages commonly found in UNIX environments that are being distributed by the GNU project at MIT, largely through the efforts of Richard Stallman. The circular acronym name ("GNU" containing the acronym GNU as one of the words it stands for) is a joke on Richard Stallman's part. One of the textbooks on operating system design is titled *XINU: XINU Is Not UNIX*, and GNU follows in that path.

GPL—GNU General Public License.

`grep`—A common tool used to search a file for a pattern. `egrep` and `fgrep` are newer versions. `egrep` allows the use of extended (hence the *e* prefix) regular expressions; `fgrep` uses limited expressions for faster (hence the *f* prefix) searches.

GUI—Graphical user interface.

here document—The `<<` redirection operator, known as *here document*, allows keyboard input (`stdin`) for the program to be included in the script.

HTML—Hypertext Markup Language. Describes World Wide Web pages. It is the document language that is used to define the pages available on the Internet through the use of tags. A browser interprets the HTML to display the desired information.

i-node—Used to describe a file and its storage. The directory contains a cross-reference between the i-node and pathname/filename combination. Also known as *inode*. A file's entry in disk data structure (`ls -i`).

I-Phone—Internet Phone. This is a method of transmitting speech long distances over the Internet in near real-time. Participants avoid paying long distance telephone charges. They still pay for the call to their ISP and the ISP's service charges.

ICCCM—Inter-Client Communications Conventions Manual.

ICMP—Internet Control Message Protocol. Part of TCP/IP that provides network layer management and control.

`imake`—C preprocessor interface to `make` utility.

inheritance—A method of object-oriented software reuse in which new classes are developed based on existing ones by using the existing attributes and behavior and adding on to them. If the base object is automobiles (with attributes of engine and four wheels and tires; behavior of acceleration, turning, deceleration), a sports car would modify the attributes: engine might be larger or have more horsepower than the default, the four wheels might include alloy wheels and high-speed–rated tires; the behavior would also be modified: faster acceleration, tighter turning radius, faster deceleration.

inode—See *i-node*.

`int`—Integer.

Internet—A collection of different networks that provide the ability to move data between them. It is built on the TCP/IP communications protocol. Originally developed by DARPA, it was taken over by NSF, and has now been released from governmental control.

Internet Service Provider—The people that connect you to the Internet.

IRC—Internet relay chat. A server-based application that allows groups of people to communicate simultaneously through text-based conversations. IRC is similar to Citizen Band radio or the chat rooms on some bulletin boards. Some chats can be private (between invited people only) or public (where anyone can join in). IRC now also supports sound files as well as text; it can also be useful for file exchange.

ISAM—Indexed Sequential Access Method. On UNIX and other systems, ISAM refers to a method for accessing data in a keyed or sequential way. The UNIX operating system does not directly support ISAM files; they are typically add-on products.

ISO—International Standards Organization.

ISP—See *Internet Service Provider.*

ISV—Independent Software Vendor. Generic name for software vendors other than your hardware vendor.

K&R—Kernighan and Ritchie.

kernel—The core of the operating system that handles tasks like memory allocation, device input and output, process allocation, security, and user access. UNIX tends to have a small kernel when compared to other operating systems.

keys, control—These are keys that cause some function to be performed instead of displaying a character. These functions have names: The end-of-file key tells UNIX that there is no more input; it is usually Ctrl+D.

keys, special—See *keys, control.*

Korn shell—A user interface for UNIX with extensive scripting (programming) support. Written by David G. Korn. The shell features command-line editing and will also accept scripts written for the Bourne shell.

LAN—Local Area Network. A collection of networking hardware, software, desktop computers, servers, and hosts all connected together within a defined local area. A LAN could be an entire college campus.

limits—See *quota.*

link file—File used to implement a symbolic link producing an alias on one filesystem for a file on another. The file contains only the fully qualified filename of the original (linked-to) file.

link, hard—Directory entry that provides an alias to another file within the same filesystem. Multiple entries appear in the directory (or other directories) for one physical file without replication of the contents.

link, soft—See *link, symbolic.*

link, symbolic—Directory entry that provides an alias to another file that can be in another filesystem. Multiple entries appear in the directory for one physical file without replication of the contents. Implemented through link files; see also *link file.*

LISP—List Processing Language.

login—The process with which a user gains access to a UNIX system. This can also refer to the user ID that is typed at the login prompt.

lp—Line printer.

`lpc`—Line printer control program.

`lpd`—Line printer daemon.

`lpq`—Printer spool queue examination program.

`lprm`—Printer spool queue job removal program.

`ls`—List directory(s) command.

man page—Online reference tool under UNIX that contains the documentation for the system—the actual pages from the printed manuals. It is stored in a searchable form for improved ability to locate information.

manual page—See *man page.*

memory, real—The amount of storage that is being used within the system (silicon; it used to be magnetic cores).

memory, virtual—Memory that exists but you cannot see. Secondary storage (disk) is used to allow the operating system to enable programs to use more memory than is physically available.

Part of a disk is used as a paging file and portions of programs and their data are moved between it and real memory. To the program, it is in real memory. The hardware and operating system performs translation between the memory address the program thinks it is using and where it is actually stored.

metacharacter—A printing character that has special meaning to the shell or another command. It is converted into something else by the shell or command; the asterisk (*) is converted by the shell to a list of all files in the current directory.

MIME—Multipurpose Internet Mail Extensions. A set of protocols or methods of attaching binary data (executable programs, images, sound files, and so on) or additional text to e-mail messages.

`motd`—Message of the day.

MPTN—MultiProtocol Transport Network. IBM networking protocol to connect mainframe to TCP/IP network.

Mrm—Motif resource manager.

mtu—Maximum transmission unit.

`mwm`—Motif window manager.

Netnews—This is a loosely controlled collection of discussion groups. A message (similar to an e-mail) is posted in a specific area, and then people can comment on it, publicly replying to the same place (posting a response) for others to see. A collection of messages along the same theme is referred to as a thread. Some of the groups are moderated, which means that nothing is posted without the approval of the owner. Most are not, and the title of the group is no guarantee that the discussion will be related. The official term for this is Usenet news.

NFS—Network File System. Means of connecting disks that are mounted to a remote system to the local system as if they were physically connected.

NIS—Network Information Service. A service that provides information necessary to all machines on a network, such as NFS support for hosts and clients, password verification, and so on.

NNTP—Netnews Transport Protocol. Used to transmit Netnews or Usenet messages over top of TCP/IP. See *Netnews* for more information on the messages transmitted.

Null Statement—A program step that performs no operation but to hold space and fulfill syntactical requirements of the programming language. Also known as a *NO-OP* for no-operation performed.

object—An object in the truest sense of the word is something that has physical properties, like automobiles, rubber balls, and clouds. These things have attributes and behavior. They can be abstracted into data (attribute) and code (behavior). Instead of just writing functions to work on data, they are encapsulated into a package that is known as an object.

operator—Metacharacter that performs a function on values or variables. The plus sign (+) is an operator that adds two integers.

options—Program- or command-specific indicators that control behavior of that program. Sometimes called *flags*. The `-a` option to the `ls` command shows the files that begin with . (such as `.profile`, `.kshrc`, and so on). Without it, these files would not be shown, no matter what wildcards were used. These are used on the command line. See also *parameters*.

OSF—Open Software Foundation.

parameters—Data passed to a command or program through the command line. These can be options (see *options*) that control the command or arguments that the command works on. Some have special meaning based on their position on the command line.

parent process—Process that controls another often referred to as the child process or subprocess. See also *process*.

parent process identifier—Shown in the heading of the `ps` command as PPID. The process identifier of the parent process. See also *parent process*.

parent shell—Shell (typically the login shell) that controls another, often referred to as the child shell or subshell. See also *shell.*

password—The secure code that is used in combination with a user ID to gain access to a UNIX system.

pathname—The means used to represent the location of a file in the directory structure. If you do not specify a pathname, it defaults to the current directory.

pathname, absolute—The means used to represent the location of a file in a directory by specifying the exact location, including all directories in the chain including the root.

pathname, relative—The means used to represent the location of a file in a directory other than the current by navigating up and down through other directories using the current directory as a base.

PDP—Personal Data Processor. Computers manufactured by Digital Equipment Corporation. UNIX was originally written for a PDP-7 and gained popularity on the PDP-11. The entire series were inexpensive minicomputers popular with educational institutions and small businesses.

Perl—Programming language developed by Larry Wall. (Perl stands for "Practical Extraction and Report Language" or "Pathologically Eclectic Rubbish Language"; both are equally valid.) The language provides all of the capabilities of `awk` and `sed`, plus many of the features of the shells and C.

permissions—When applied to files, they are the attributes that control access to a file. There are three levels of access: Owner (the file creator), Group (people belonging to a related group as determined by the system administrator), and Other (everyone else). The permissions are usually `r` for read, `w` for write, and `x` for execute. The execute permissions flag is also used to control who may search a directory.

PGP—Pretty Good Privacy encryption system.

`pine`—Interactive mail program.

pipe—A method of sending the output of one program (redirecting) to become the input of another. The pipe character (`¦`) tells the shell to perform the redirection.

pipe file—See *pipe, named.*

pipe, named—An expanded function of a regular pipe (redirecting the output of one program to become the input of another). Instead of connecting `stdout` to `stdin`, the output of one program is sent to the named pipe and another program reads data from the same file. This is implemented through a special file known as a pipe file or FIFO. The operating system ensures the proper sequencing of the data. Little or no data is actually stored in the pipe file; it just acts as a connection between the two.

polymorphism—Allows code to be written in a general fashion to handle existing and future related classes. Properly developed, the same behavior can act differently depending on the derived object it acts on. With an automobile, the acceleration behavior might be different for a station wagon and a dragster, which are subclasses of the superclass automobile. The function would still be `accelerate()`, but the version would vary (this might sound confusing, but the compiler keeps track and figures it all out).

POSIX—Portable Operating System Interface, UNIX. POSIX is the name for a family of open system standards based on UNIX. The name has been credited to Richard Stallman. The POSIX Shell and Utilities standard developed by IEEE Working Group 1003.2 (POSIX.2) concentrates on the command interpreter interface and utility programs.

PostScript—Adobe Systems, Inc. printer language.

PPP—Point-to-Point Protocol. Internet protocol over serial link (modem).

`pppd`—Point-to-Point-Protocol daemon.

`printcap`—Printer capability database.

process—A discrete running program under UNIX. The user's interactive session is a process. A process can invoke (run) and control another program that is then referred to as a subprocess. Ultimately, everything a user does is a subprocess of the operating system.

process identifier—Shown in the heading of the `ps` command as `PID`. The unique number assigned to every process running in the system.

`pwd`—Print working directory command.

quota—General description of a system-imposed limitation on a user or process. It can apply to disk space, memory usage, CPU usage, maximum number of open files, and many other resources.

quoting—The use of single and double quotes to negate the normal command interpretation and concatenate all words and whitespace within the quotes as a single piece of text.

RCS—Revision Control System.

redirection—The process of directing a data flow from the default. Input can be redirected to get data from a file or the output of another program. Normal output can be sent to another program or a file. Errors can be sent to another program or a file.

regular expression—A way of specifying and matching strings for shells (filename wildcarding), `grep` (file searches), `sed`, and `awk`.

reserved word—A set of characters that are recognized by UNIX and related to a specific program, function, or command.

RFC—Request For Comment. Document used for creation of Internet- and TCP/IP-related standards.

`rlogin`—Remote Login. Gives the same functionality as `telnet`, with the added functionality of not requiring a password from trusted clients, which can also create security concerns (see also *`telnet`*).

root—The user that owns the operating system and controls the computer. The processes of the operating system run as though a user, root, signed on and started them. Root users are all-powerful and can do anything they want. For this reason, they are often referred to as superusers. Root is also the very top of the directory tree structure.

routing—The process of moving network traffic between two different physical networks; also decides which path to take when there are multiple connections between the two machines. It might also send traffic around transmission interruptions.

RPC—Remote Procedural Call. Provides the ability to call functions or subroutines that run on a remote system from the local one.

RPM—Red Hat Package Manager.

script—A program written for a UNIX utility including shells, `awk`, Perl, `sed`, and others. See also *shell scripts*.

SCSI—Small Computer System Interface.

`sed`—A common tool used for stream text editing, having `ed`-like syntax.

server, database—A system designated to run database software (typically a relational database like Oracle, SQL Server, Sybase, or others). Other systems connect to this one to get the data (client applications).

SGID—Set group ID.

shell—The part of UNIX that handles user input and invokes other programs to run commands. Includes a programming language. See also Bourne shell, C shell, Korn shell, `tcsh`, and `bash`.

shell environment—The shell program (Bourne, Korn, C, `tcsh`, or `bash`), invocation options and preset variables that define the characteristics, features, and functionality of the UNIX command-line and program execution interface.

shell or command prompt—The single character or set of characters that the UNIX shell displays for which a user can enter a command or set of commands.

shell scripts—A program written using a shell programming language like those supported by Bourne, Korn, or C shells.

signal—A special flag or interrupt that is used to communicate special events to programs by the operating system and other programs.

SLIP—Serial Line Internet Protocol. Internet over a serial line (modem). The protocol frames and controls the transmission of TCP/IP packets of the line.

SNA—System Network Architecture. IBM networking architecture.

stderr—The normal error output for a program that is sent to the screen by default. Can be redirected to a file.

stdin—The normal input for a program, taken from the keyboard by default. Can be redirected to get input from a file or the output of another program.

stdout—The normal output for a program that is sent to the screen by default. Can be redirected to a file or to the input of another program.

sticky bit—One of the status flags on a file that tells UNIX to load a copy of the file into the page file the first time it is executed. This is done for programs that are commonly used so the bytes are available quickly. When the sticky bit is used on frequently used directories, it is cached in memory.

stream—A sequential collection of data. All files are streams to the UNIX operating system. To it, there is no structure to a file; that is something imposed by application programs or special tools (ISAM packages or relational databases).

subdirectory—See *directory*.

subnet—A portion of a network that shares a common IP address component. Used for security and performance reasons.

subprocess—Process running under the control of another, often referred to as the parent process. See also *process*.

subshell—Shell running under the control of another, often referred to as the parent shell (typically the login shell). See also *shell*.

SUID—Set user ID.

superuser—Usually the root operator.

sysadmin—Burnt-out root operator (system administrator).

system administrator—The person who takes care of the operating system and user administrative issues on UNIX systems. Also called a *system manager*, although that term is much more common in DEC VAX installations.

system manager—See *system administrator*.

system programmer—See *system administrator*.

tar—Tape archiving utility.

TCP—Transmission Control Protocol.

TCP/IP—Transport Control Protocol/Internet Protocol. The pair of protocols and also generic name for suite of tools and protocols that forms the basis for the Internet. Originally developed to connect systems to the ARPAnet.

`tcsh`—A C shell-like user interface featuring command-line editing.

`telnet`—Remote login program.

Telnet—Protocol for interactive (character user interface) terminal access to remote systems. The terminal emulator that uses the Telnet protocol is often known as `telnet` or `tnvt100`.

`termcap`—Terminal capability database.

terminal—A hardware device, normally containing a cathode ray tube (screen) and keyboard for human interaction with a computer system.

text processing languages—A way of developing documents in text editors with embedded commands that handle formatting. The file is fed through a processor that executes the embedded commands, producing a formatted document. These include `roff`, `nroff`, `troff`, `RUNOFF`, TeX, LaTeX, and even the mainframe `SCRIPT`.

TFTP—Trivial File Transfer Protocol or Trivial File Transfer Program. A system-independent means of transferring files between systems connected via TCP/IP. It is different from FTP in that it does not ensure that the file is transferred correctly, does not authenticate users, and is missing a lot of functionality (like the `ls` command).

`tin`—Interactive news reader.

`top`—A common tool used to display information about the top processes on the system.

UDP—User Datagram Protocol. Part of TCP/IP used for control messages and data transmission where the delivery acknowledgment is not needed. The application program must ensure data transmission in this case.

UID—User ID number.

UIL—Motif User Interface Language.

URL—Uniform Resource Locator. The method of specifying the protocol, format, login (usually omitted), and location of materials on the Internet.

Usenet—See *Netnews*.

UUCP—UNIX-to-UNIX copy program. Used to build an early, informal network for the transmission of files, e-mail, and Netnews.

variables, attributes—The modifiers that set the variable type. A variable can be string or integer, left- or right-justified, read-only or changeable, and other attributes.

variables, environmental—A place to store data and values (strings and integers) in the area controlled by the shell so they are available to the current and subprocesses. They can just be local to the current shell or available to a subshell (exported).

variables, substitution—The process of interpreting an environmental variable to get its value.

WAN—Wide Area Network.

Web—See *World Wide Web.*

whitespace—Blanks, spaces, and tabs that are normally interpreted to delineate commands and filenames unless quoted.

wildcard—Means of specifying filename(s) whereby the operating system determines some of the characters. Multiple files might match and will be available to the tool.

World Wide Web—A collection of servers and services on the Internet that run software and communicate using a common protocol (HTTP). Instead of the users' having to remember the location of these resources, links are provided from one Web page to another through the use of URLs.

WWW—See *World Wide Web.*

WYSIWYG—What You See Is What You Get.

X—See *X Window System.*

X Window System—A windowing and graphics system developed by MIT, to be used in client/server environments.

X11—See *X Window System.*

X-windows—The wrong term for the X Window System. See *X Window System.*

yacc—Yet another compiler compiler.

What's on the CD-ROM

IN THIS APPENDIX

On the *Red Hat Linux Unleashed, Second Edition* CD-ROM, you will find sample files that have been presented in this book along with a wealth of other applications and utilities.

NOTE

Refer to the `readme.txt` file on the CD-ROM for the latest listing of software.

The following is included on the CD-ROM:

- Red Hat Linux version 4.2 including various kernels
- Security applications
- TCP/IP and UUCP support utilities
- GNU archives
- Programming languages and development tools
- A toy box full of games
- A variety of add-on tools and utilities for customization
- A suite of Internet applications

About the Software

Read all documentation associated with third-party products (usually contained with files named `readme.txt` or `license.txt`) and follow all guidelines.

I

INDEX

Symbols

A

B

C

D

E

F

G

H

I

J-K

L

O

P

Q-R

S

U

V

Maximum RPM

—Edward C. Bailey

The complete reference for the Red Hat Package Manager (RPM) software package that is the heart of the Red Hat Linux distribution. Designed for both novice and advanced users, *Maximum RPM* enables anyone to take full advantage of the benefits of building software packages with the Red Hat Package Manager tools to ensure that they install simply and accurately each and every time.

The RPM is the most requested topic for a book from Linux users, according to Red Hat Software's research. The RPM enables administrators to effectively manage the roll-out of consistent software and upgrades to users.

Maximum RPM was written by the creators of the software for all levels of users (software developers, computer science students, and Linux system administrators).

Price: $39.99 USA/$56.95 CAN *Accomplished–Expert*

ISBN: 0-672-31105-4 *480 pages*

Linux Complete Command Reference

—Red Hat Software

Linux Complete Command Reference contains a number of cross references and jump tables to help the reader locate the Linux function, is the only comprehensive Linux reference available, and is written in a style that Linux and UNIX users are comfortable with. It includes the added bonus of extra examples.

The CD-ROM contains more than 2,000 pages of reference material covering every command, program, and system call available to Linux users.

Price: $49.99 USA/$84.95 CAN *Accomplished–Expert*

ISBN: 0-672-31104-6 *1,200 pages*

UNIX Unleashed, System Administrator's Edition

—Robin Burk and David Horvath, et al.

UNIX Unleashed, System Administrator's Edition and *UNIX Unleashed, Internet Edition* together are an in-depth examination of the UNIX operating system. Written by experts, they include real-world examples, definitions, tips, and tricks. Between them, these two editions cover the specifics of the most popular UNIX variants and the use of UNIX as a full-fledged Internet server platform.

Complete and comprehensive; no other book has this much breadth, depth, and real-world examples. These books cover and compare SVR4, HP-UX, Solaris, AIX, BSD, IRIX, SunOS, and Linux administration. They help you decide which shell works best for you: Bourne, Bourne Again, Korn, or C.

Price: $59.99 USA/$84.95 CAN *Intermediate–Advanced*

ISBN: 0-672-30952-1 *1,400 pages*

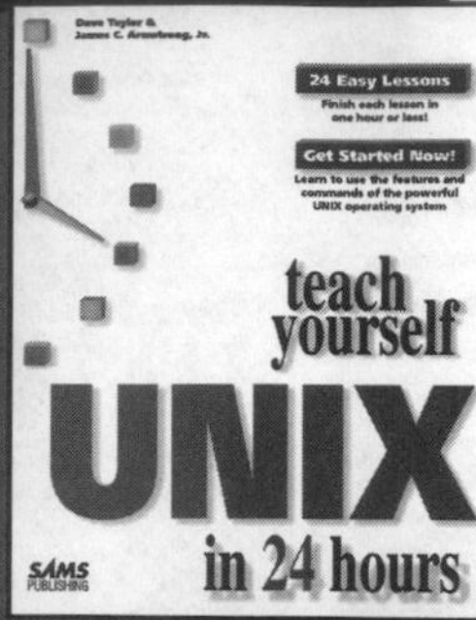

Teach Yourself UNIX in 24 Hours

—Dave Taylor and James Armstrong

UNIX is one of the major operating systems in use today. For people who need to get up and running quickly, this easy-to-follow guide is just the resource. Using detailed explanations and real-world examples, you will have the hands-on experience you need to build a solid understanding of this robust operating system. The proven, successful format of the *Teach Yourself* series guarantees UNIX success in 24 one-hour lessons.

Teach Yourself UNIX in 24 Hours covers all major versions of UNIX. It shows how to create UNIX space, look inside files, edit files, explore the environment, and effectively use power UNIX tools.

Price: $19.99 USA/$28.95 CAN *Casual–Accomplished*

ISBN: 0-672-31107-0 592 pages

Add to Your Sams Library Today with the Best Books for Programming, Operating Systems, and New Technologies

Book ISBN 0-672-31173-9

Technical Support:

If you need assistance with the information in this book or with a CD/Disk accompanying the book, please access the Knowledge Base on our Web site at **http://www.superlibrary.com/general/support**. Our most Frequently Asked Questions are answered there. If you do not find the answer to your questions on our Web site, you may contact Macmillan Technical Support **(317) 581-3833** or e-mail us at **support@mcp.com**.

Installation Instructions

1. Insert the CD-ROM into your CD-ROM drive.
2. View the contents of the CD-ROM by opening File Manager or Windows Explorer and selecting your CD-ROM drive (usually `D:\`).
3. Double-click the `readme.txt` file containing detailed installation instructions.